Macromedia®
ColdFusion®

Shashi Kaparthi
Rakhee Kaparthi

COURSE
TECHNOLOGY
™
THOMSON LEARNING

Australia • Canada • Mexico • Singapore • Spain • United Kingdom • United States

COURSE TECHNOLOGY
™
THOMSON LEARNING

Macromedia® ColdFusion®
by Shashi Kaparthi and Rakhee Kaparthi

Senior Editor:
Jennifer Muroff

Managing Editor:
Jennifer Locke

Development Editor:
Lisa Ruffolo, The Software Resource

Editorial Assistant:
Janet Aras

Production Editor:
Danielle Power

Cover Designer:
Peter Karpick, Aaron Schneider,
Black Fish Design

Compositor:
GEX Publishing Services

Manufacturing Coordinator:
Alexander Schall

BRIEF
Contents

PREFACE   xi

CHAPTER ONE
Introduction to ColdFusion   1

CHAPTER TWO
URL Parameters, Strings, and Other Data Types   55

CHAPTER THREE
Flow Control in ColdFusion   113

CHAPTER FOUR
Form Handling   171

CHAPTER FIVE
Databases and SQL   237

CHAPTER SIX
Data Retrieval Using ColdFusion   281

CHAPTER SEVEN
Data Maintenance with ColdFusion   337

CHAPTER EIGHT
Data Validation   383

CHAPTER NINE
The ColdFusion Application Framework   439

CHAPTER TEN
Interaction with Other Services   499

CHAPTER ELEVEN
Reusing Code and Building a Complete Web Application   565

INDEX   639

TABLE OF
Contents

PREFACE   xi

CHAPTER ONE
Introduction to ColdFusion   1
    Reviewing Hypertext Markup Language   2
    CGI and API   4
    Server-Side Scripting Languages   5
    What Is ColdFusion?   6
    ColdFusion Components   9
        Using ColdFusion Studio   9
        Using ColdFusion Server   10
        Using the ColdFusion Administrator   12
    Exploring the ColdFusion Studio Workspace   13
        Creating and Previewing a New Web Page   15
        Using the Resource Tabs   16
        Using Help   17
        Saving a ColdFusion Template   18
        Expanding the Editor Window   20
    Understanding ColdFusion and the Web   20
    ColdFusion Markup Language   29
        Variables and the CFSET Tag   29
        Understanding Rules for Naming Variables   30
        Creating Comments   30
        Processing Numbers   31
        Using Arithmetic Expressions   31
        Using the CFOUTPUT Tag and Pound (#) Signs   33
        Understanding Operator Precedence   36
        Using Functions to Format Numbers   40
    Browsing a ColdFusion Template Using the Internal Browser   42
    Chapter Summary   45
    Review Questions   46
    Hands-on Projects   47
    Case Projects   54

CHAPTER TWO
URL Parameters, Strings, and Other Data Types   55
    URL Parameter Processing   56
        Using URLs with Parameters in Anchor Tags   60
    Using String Variables   66
        Using String URL Parameters   70
        Encoding URL Special Characters   74
    Using String Expressions   80
        Concatenating Strings Using Pound Signs   83

String Functions   85
    Using String Functions   87
Date-Time Values and Variables   90
    Date-Time Operations   95
Using Boolean Values to Evaluate Expressions   102
    Typeless Expression Evaluation   103
Chapter Summary   105
Review Questions   106
Hands-on Projects   106
Case Projects   112

CHAPTER THREE
Flow Control in ColdFusion   **113**
Using Selection to Control Program Flow   114
    Using CFIF Tags   114
    Working with Relational Operators   118
    Conditional Formatting Using CFIF   124
    Nesting CFIF Tags   127
    Using Logical Operators   134
    Using the CFSWITCH Statement   137
Using Repetition to Perform Repetitive Tasks   140
    FOR Loops   141
    LIST Loops   152
    WHILE loops   157
    Redirection   161
Chapter Summary   163
Review Questions   164
Hands-on Projects   165
Case Projects   169

CHAPTER FOUR
Form Handling   **171**
Understanding HTML Forms   172
Using HTML Form and Control Tags   175
    Understanding the Form Object   175
    Understanding Text Box Controls   176
    Understanding Password Text Box Controls   176
    Understanding Button Controls   176
Handling Form Data   177
Creating a Form   180
Creating a Form Handler   189
Designing and Handling Radio Buttons   192
Designing and Handling Check Boxes   196
    Handling a Single Check Box   197
    Handling Multiple Check Boxes   200
Designing and Handling Select Boxes   206
Designing and Handling Scrolling Text Boxes   209
Designing and Handling Hidden Fields   212
Sending a Form's Results via E-Mail   214

Designing and Handling Image Buttons   220
Chapter Summary   228
Review Questions   229
Hands-on Projects   230
Case Projects   236

CHAPTER FIVE
Databases and SQL   **237**
Organizing Data in Databases   238
   Working with Attributes   238
   Defining Field Data Types and Table Structures   240
Opening a Microsoft Access Database   243
Creating a Table   246
   Creating a Table in Design View   247
   Creating a Table Using SQL   249
Inserting Data   251
   Inserting Data in Datasheet View   251
   Inserting a Record Using SQL   253
Updating Data   255
   Updating Data Using Datasheet View   255
   Updating a Record Using SQL   256
Deleting Records   257
   Deleting a Record Using Datasheet View   257
   Deleting a Record Using SQL   257
Using the SQL SELECT Statement to Extract Data   258
   Extracting Specific Columns from a Table   259
   Extracting Specific Rows from a Table   260
   Extracting Rows Using Conditions   261
   Extracting Rows Using Arithmetic Expressions   262
   Extracting Rows Using the BETWEEN Operator   263
   Extracting Rows Using the IN and NOT IN Operators   264
   Extracting Rows Using the LIKE Operator   265
Using a SELECT Statement to Sort Data   266
Extracting Data from Multiple Tables Using One SELECT Statement   268
   Using the DISTINCT Keyword in SELECT Statements   269
Summarizing Data by Using Functions   270
   Grouping Data and Using Functions   272
Chapter Summary   273
Review Questions   273
Hands-on Projects   274
Case Projects   278

CHAPTER SIX
Data Retrieval Using ColdFusion   **281**
Open Database Connectivity   282
Database Connectivity with ColdFusion   286
   CFQUERY Tag   287
   QUERY Loops   287
   Using a CFLOOP to Process a Subset of Records   291
Columnar Report Generation   294

Displaying Specific Records   299
Creating Navigation Options   302
Tabular Report Generation   309
Group Totals Report Generation   319
Interactive Data Extraction   322
Chapter Summary   327
Review Questions   328
Hands-on Projects   329
Case Projects   335

CHAPTER SEVEN
Data Maintenance with ColdFusion   337

Inserting Data   338
Inserting Data with CFINSERT   338
    Inserting Data with CFQUERY and SQL INSERT   344
Updating Data   349
    Updating Data with CFUPDATE   349
    Updating Data with CFQUERY and SQL UPDATE   353
Deleting Data   357
    Deleting Data with CFQUERY and SQL UPDATE   357
Creating Tables Using ColdFusion   360
Transaction Processing   362
Chapter Summary   371
Review Questions   371
Hands-on Projects   372
Case Projects   382

CHAPTER EIGHT
Data Validation   383

Performing Server-side and Client-side Data Validation   384
    Using JavaScript to Validate Data   384
Designing Forms with ColdFusion   385
    Creating ColdFusion Forms   385
    Text Box Controls   388
Checking for Data Completeness   390
    Generating Customized Error Messages   393
    ColdFusion Radio Buttons and Data Completeness Checks   401
    CF Check Boxes and Data Completeness Checks   406
    Cold Fusion Select Boxes and Data Completeness Checks   409
Data Type Validation Checks   412
Using Range and Limit Checks   418
Using Picture Checks   419
Using Self-Checking Digits or Algorithmic Checks   423
    Dynamically Populating Select Boxes with the CFSELECT Tag   425
Chapter Summary   428
Review Questions   429
Hands-on Projects   430
Case Projects   437

CHAPTER NINE
The ColdFusion Application Framework   **439**

HTTP State Management and Cookies   440
    Default Values for Cookie Variables   449
    Cookie-Based Logon Security   450
Application Framework and Application.cfm   458
    Providing Application-Wide Logon Security   460
Client State Management and Client Variables   463
    Creating Client Variables   465
Sessions and Session Variables   472
    Creating Session Variables   473
    Locking Session Variables and Shared Resources   473
Application Variables   485
Chapter Summary   489
Review Questions   490
Hands-on Projects   491
Case Projects   498

CHAPTER TEN
Interaction with Other Services   **499**

Using E-Mail   500
    Using the CFMAIL Tag   504
Interacting with the Server's File System   514
    Uploading Files with ColdFusion   514
    Listing Files with the CFDIRECTORY Tag   523
    Copying, Renaming, and Deleting Files with the CFFILE Tag   525
    Reading and Writing Text Files   529
    Serving Application Files by Using CFCONTENT   537
    Interacting with Other Web Servers   544
Chapter Summary   553
Review Questions   553
Hands-on Projects   554
Case Projects   564

CHAPER ELEVEN
Reusing Code and Building a Complete Web Application   **565**

Nothebys Auction Company   566
Designing the User Interface   566
    Reusing Code   567
    Reusing Code for Nothebys.com   567
Designing the Database and the Folders   571
    Planning the Folder Structure   573
    Making an ODBC Connection to the Database   574
Browsing Products Requirement   574
    Creating a List Products Template   581
Browsing Auctions Requirement   587
Searching Products Requirement   591

Building the Administration Tool   595
    Guidelines for Implementing the User Interface   596
    Adding the Auctions Administration Requirement   596
    Adding the Categories Administration Requirement   604
    Adding the Products Administration Requirement   611
    Specifying Default Documents   627
Chapter Summary   629
Hands–on Projects   630
Case Projects   638

INDEX   **639**

Preface

Macromedia ColdFusion introduces you to the concepts of creating dynamic Web sites by using the ColdFusion Markup Language (CFML). Macromedia ColdFusion is a popular, reliable, high-performance, proven middleware technology that is easier to use than Active Server Pages or Java Server Pages for building database-driven Web sites. On a database-driven Web site, you can extract information from databases to provide current information about products and services to the visitors of your site. You also can add and change database records based on user selections and keep your information up to date.

This book uses a hands-on approach, where you practice skills and ideas by building a Web site with ColdFusion. You will learn how to create Web pages using CFML, and learn about the ColdFusion Web application server. You will design and deploy Web-based applications, and create dynamic Web sites that interact with databases and other servers by using ColdFusion Studio. In the process, you will work with supporting technologies such as HTML, SQL, and relational database systems.

THE INTENDED AUDIENCE

Macromedia ColdFusion is intended for students who want to create dynamic Web sites that interact with databases by using ColdFusion and CFML. This book provides an introduction to Web programming and server-side programming using the ColdFusion Server. This book assumes that you have a working knowledge of the Internet, HTML, Microsoft Access 2000, Netscape Navigator or Internet Explorer, and relational database concepts. If you are a student in a two-year college or technical school, this book helps you develop Web-based skills. If you are a Management Information Systems, Computer Information Systems, or Computer Science student in a four-year college, this book adds to your programming knowledge. You can use this book in introductory information systems classes as an illustration of programming and HTML. As an introductory Web programming text, you also can use it in a second course in Information Systems for business majors in fields such as Accounting, Finance, and Marketing.

THE APPROACH

Macromedia ColdFusion lets you learn by doing. To facilitate the learning process, the chapters in this book describe important concepts, provide syntax for statements, and include visual aids such as flowcharts, figures, and tables. Examples and solutions are provided for you to examine, study, and practice. Step-by-step exercises help you conceptualize and build ColdFusion templates for creating dynamic database-driven Web sites. Each chapter introduces a separate topic, and also provides a sample case for which you create templates and Web pages. The chapters and the cases build on one another, allowing you to combine concepts to create more sophisticated Web pages. Partially completed templates are provided on the Data Disk so that you can focus on the topic being studied. Each chapter includes Chapter Objectives, a Chapter Summary, Review Questions, Hands-on Projects, and Case Projects that highlight the major concepts that were presented and allow you to apply your knowledge. The Hands-on Projects are guided activities that let you practice and reinforce the techniques and skills you learn within the chapter, and build on the techniques and skills you learned in previous chapters. These Hands-on Projects enhance your learning experience by providing additional ways to apply your knowledge in new situations. At the end of each chapter, several Case Projects direct you to use the skills that you learned in the chapter to create professional-quality real-world Web applications with ColdFusion Server.

OVERVIEW OF THIS BOOK

The examples, steps, projects, and cases in this book will help you achieve the following objectives:

- Learn the ColdFusion Markup Language
- Understand how the Web works
- Learn about several types of interactions between clients and servers
- Create Web pages using HTML and CFML
- Learn about programming in the context of the Web
- Learn about data types and flow control
- Become familiar with SQL
- Reinforce relational database systems concepts
- Create dynamic Web pages that extract information from databases
- Create Web pages that upload and update information in databases
- Develop Web pages that interact with e-mail servers, file systems, and other Web servers
- Create information systems that work on Internet technologies

The hands-on approach of this book is highlighted in the first chapter. **Chapter 1** introduces you to the ColdFusion Server and ColdFusion Studio, the editor you use to create CFML. You will use ColdFusion numeric variables and manipulate them. **Chapter 2** explains URL parameters, strings, date-time values, and Boolean data types. You learn about functions and create interactive Web pages that process URL parameters. In **Chapter 3** you will learn about flow-control in ColdFusion. You are introduced to structured programming concepts such as sequence, selection, and repetition. You also learn about HTTP redirection. **Chapter 4** covers creating forms and handling user-entered data in forms with CFML. **Chapter 5** provides a review of SQL and relational database concepts with Microsoft Access 2000. In **Chapter 6** you build ColdFusion templates to extract data from databases and publish it as Web pages. You use a report design model to organize data extraction concepts. In **Chapter 7** you maintain databases by using ColdFusion. You build systems for inserting, updating, and deleting data from databases with ColdFusion. You also create tables and process database transactions. In **Chapter 8** you learn about data validation to maintain data integrity. You implement data completeness checks, data type checks, range and limit checks, picture checks, and algorithmic checks using CFML. **Chapter 9** introduces you to the ColdFusion application framework. You will learn about the concepts of statelessness and state, cookies, client variables, session variables, and application variables. In **Chapter 10** you learn about the capabilities of ColdFusion for interacting with other services such as e-mail servers, file systems, and Web servers. You send e-mail messages based on form input and database query output. You also upload, copy, rename, delete, and list files on the Web server, and serve application files programmatically. In **Chapter 11**, you build a complete Web application and learn about reusing code to increase productivity.

Each chapter in *Macromedia ColdFusion* includes the following elements to enhance your learning experience:

- **Chapter Objectives**: Each chapter in this book begins with a list of the important concepts to be mastered within the chapter. This list is a quick reference to the contents of the chapter and is a useful study aid.

- **Step-By-Step Methodology**: As new concepts are presented in each chapter, step-by-step instructions allow you to actively apply the concepts you are learning.

- **Tips**: Chapters contain Tips designed to provide you with practical advice and proven strategies related to the concept being discussed. Tips also provide suggestions for resolving problems you might encounter while proceeding through the chapters.

- **Chapter Summaries**: Each chapter's text is followed by a summary of chapter concepts. These summaries recap and revisit the ideas covered in each chapter.

- **Review Questions**: End-of-chapter assessment begins with a set of approximately 15 review questions that reinforce the main ideas introduced in each chapter. These questions ensure that you have mastered the concepts and understand the information presented to you.

Hands-on Projects: Along with conceptual explanations and step-by-step tutorials, each chapter includes Hands-on Projects related to each major topic, and aimed at providing you with practical experience. Some Hands-on Projects provide detailed instructions, while as the book progresses, others require that you apply the materials presented in the current chapter with less guidance. As a result, the Hands-on Projects provide you with practice implementing ColdFusion-based systems in real-world situations.

 Case Projects: Several cases are presented at the end of each chapter. These cases are designed to help you apply what you have learned in the chapter to real-world situations. They give you the opportunity to independently synthesize and evaluate information, examine potential solutions, and make recommendations, much as you would in an actual business situation.

TEACHING TOOLS

The following supplemental materials are available when this book is used in a classroom setting. All of the teaching tools available with this book are provided to the instructor on a single CD-ROM.

Electronic Instructor's Manual. The Instructor's Manual that accompanies this textbook includes:

- Additional instructional material to assist in class preparation, including suggestions for lecture topics.
- Solutions to all end-of-chapter materials, including the Review Questions and Hands-on Projects.

ExamView®. This textbook is accompanied by ExamView, a powerful testing software package that allows instructors to create and administer printed, computer (LAN-based), and Internet exams. ExamView includes hundreds of questions that correspond to the topics covered in this text, enabling students to generate detailed study guides that include page references for further review. The computer-based and Internet testing components allow students to take exams at their computers, and also save the instructor time by grading each exam automatically.

PowerPoint Presentations. This book comes with Microsoft PowerPoint slides for each chapter. These are included as a teaching aid for classroom presentation, can be made available to students on the network for chapter review, or can be printed for classroom distribution. Instructors can add their own slides for additional topics they introduce to the class.

Data Files. Data Files, containing all of the data necessary for steps within the chapters and the Hands-On Projects, are provided through the Course Technology Web site at *www.course.com*, and are also available on the Teaching Tools CD-ROM.

Solution Files. Solutions to the exercises, end-of chapter review questions, and Hands-On Projects are provided on the Teaching Tools CD-ROM and may also be found on the Course Technology Web site at *www.course.com*. The solutions are password protected.

ACKNOWLEDGMENTS

We dedicate this book to our daughter. We love you dearly. You have changed our lives for the better. Thanks to our parents for their support, especially during the past two years. This book would not have been possible without your help. Thanks to all the organizations with which we worked on ColdFusion projects. Helping you helped us.

Thanks also to the reviewers who helped to ensure that this book is accurate and up to date: Gwen Taunton, Southern Union State Community College; Shelly Zimmerman, New Jersey Institute of Technology; Kevin Wishart; and Ana Malitzke-Goes, Northern Virginia Community College, Alexandria.

Read This Before You Begin

TO THE USER

Data Files

To complete the steps and projects in this book, you will need data files that have been created for this book. Your instructor will provide the data files to you. You also can obtain the files electronically from the Course Technology Web site by connecting to *www.course.com*, and then searching for this book title.

Each chapter in this book has its own set of data files that typically include ColdFusion templates and HTML files. The files for each chapter are stored in a separate chapter folder. For example, the files for Chapter 2 are stored in the Chapter02 folder. In addition to these files, the data files include Microsoft Access databases and GIF images. You use the Access databases in the exercises in many chapters; these are stored in the Databases folder. Similarly, because you use images in many chapters, they are stored in the Images folder. Throughout this book, you will be instructed to open files from or save files to these folders.

As you work through the chapters, Hands-on Projects, and Case Projects in this book, you will use the ColdFusion Studio software to edit your documents and then publish these documents on a Web server that has a ColdFusion Server installed. You may use your computer both as a client for editing the Web pages, and as a server for publishing the edited Web pages. This is the primary configuration used in the book. Alternately, your instructor may provide you with a remote Web server that has ColdFusion Server installed. In this case, you can use your computer for editing the ColdFusion pages with ColdFusion Studio and then transfer them using FTP to the remote Web server for publishing the pages.

Using Your Own Computer for Editing and Publishing

To use your own computer to complete the chapters, Hands-on Projects, and Case Projects in this book, you will need the following:

- Windows 2000 Professional operating system
- Internet Information Services 5.0 (IIS)
- ColdFusion Server 4.5 or 5.0
- ColdFusion Studio 4.5
- Microsoft Access 2000
- Latest versions of Internet Explorer or Netscape Navigator
- Data Disk containing the databases and the ColdFusion documents

Installing IIS

The core of the Windows 2000 Web and Application services is the built-in Web server named Internet Information Service (IIS) 5.0. It is included in Windows 2000 Professional and advanced versions. You can install IIS by following the procedure outlined below.

To install IIS on Windows 2000 Professional:

1. Click **Start** on the taskbar, point to **Settings**, and then click **Control Panel**.
2. Double-click the **Add/Remove Programs** icon.
3. In the Add/Remove Programs window, click **Add/Remove Windows Components**.
4. In the Windows Components Wizard dialog box, click the **Internet Information Services (IIS)** box to insert a check mark and then click **Next**. If prompted, insert the Windows 2000 CD.
5. Click **Finish** to complete the installation.
6. Close the Add/Remove Programs window and the Control Panel.

Installing ColdFusion

ColdFusion provides a set of tools that allows you to quickly create and deliver dynamic, interactive, data-driven, Web-based applications. ColdFusion Studio is software that allows developers to design and edit ColdFusion and HTML documents. ColdFusion Server is a Web application server that works with IIS. It processes and delivers the documents created by using ColdFusion Studio. Developers can build electronic commerce and other Web-based applications using these tools. ColdFusion Administrator is a Web-based application for configuring the ColdFusion Server. You must first install ColdFusion Server and then install ColdFusion Studio.

Installing ColdFusion Server 5.0

To install the ColdFusion Server:

1. Navigate to the proper folder on the CD containing the ColdFusion Server software, and then double-click **setup.exe** or the file that you downloaded for evaluation purposes.
2. If you are prompted for a location to save the files, click the **Next** button to select the default location.
3. On the Welcome to the Install Wizard for ColdFusion 5 window, click the **Next** button.
4. Click the **Yes** button to accept the license agreement.
5. In the Customer Information dialog box, enter your name, company, and the serial number of the software, and then click the **Next** button.

6. In the Web Server Selection dialog box, accept Microsoft IIS as the Web server by clicking **Next**.

7. In the Choose Destination Path dialog box, accept the default destinations by clicking **Next**.

8. In the Select Components dialog box, in addition to the default selections, click to check the **Documentation** and **Examples** check boxes, and then click **Next**.

9. In the Assign Passwords dialog box, type an Administrator password twice. This password is useful for administering the ColdFusion Server using the ColdFusion Administrator component after the installation. Type a ColdFusion Studio password twice, or click and select the check box to use the same password, and then click the **Next** button.

10. Review your selections in the Confirm Selections dialog box, and then click the **Next** button.

11. In the ColdFusion 5 Install Wizard Complete dialog box, click **Finish** to restart the computer.

Testing ColdFusion Server Installation

Once you have installed the ColdFusion Server you should check that it works correctly.

To test the installation:

1. If the Welcome to ColdFusion 5 window does not appear on your screen, click **Start** on the taskbar, point to **Programs**, point to **Macromedia ColdFusion Server 5**, and then click **Welcome to ColdFusion**. If your computer is not connected to the Internet, you will see a dialog box asking whether you want to work offline or try again. Click **Try again**.

2. In the Welcome to ColdFusion 5 window, click the **Validate** that the installation was successful link.

3. In the Installation Test page, click the **Test Installation** button.

4. If you see a "Success: Test Query Complete" message, the installation was successful, and ColdFusion Server is working correctly.

If you see an error message, you need to troubleshoot your installation. Visit the Macromedia Web site for troubleshooting help.

Installing ColdFusion Studio

The next step is to install the ColdFusion Studio software.

To install ColdFusion Studio:

1. Navigate to the proper folder on the CD containing the ColdFusion Studio software, and then double-click **setup.exe** or the file that you downloaded for evaluation purposes.

2. On the Welcome window, click the **Next** button.

3. Read the license agreement and click the **Yes** button.

4. In the User Information dialog box, enter your name, company, and the serial number for the software, and then click the **Next** button. Accept the default serial number if you are installing the trial version.

5. In the Choose Destination Location dialog box, accept the default location by clicking **Next**.

6. If the Confirm New Folder dialog box opens, click the **Yes** button to confirm where you will install ColdFusion Studio.

7. In the Choose TopStyle Lite Destination Location, accept the default location by clicking **Next**.

8. In the Select Components dialog box, make sure that both the boxes are checked, and then click **Next**.

9. In the Select Program Folder dialog box, accept ColdFusion Studio 4.5 as the Program Folder by clicking **Next**.

10. In the Start Copying Files dialog box, review the current settings, and then click **Next**.

11. After the installation is completed, click **Finish** to restart the computer.

12. To test the installation, click **Start** on the taskbar, point to **Programs**, point to **ColdFusion Studio 4.5**, and then click **ColdFusion Studio 4.5**. You see the ColdFusion Studio main window.

Copying Files from the Data Disk

After you install the software, you must copy the files from the Data Disk.

To copy the files from the Data Disk:

1. Use Windows Explorer or My Computer to navigate to C:\InetPub\wwwroot. (Instead of C:, you may need to navigate to another drive—the one you are using for ColdFusion.)

2. Create a folder and name it using your last name or your instructor-assigned username. Use this folder name in place of your_username for all the exercises and the projects in the book. For example, name the folder **sTapper**.

3. In Windows Explorer or My Computer, navigate to the Data Disk and select all the folders from **Chapter01** to **Chapter11**, **Databases**, and **Images**. Click **Edit** on the menu bar, and then click **Copy**.

4. Navigate to C:\InetPub\wwwroot*your_username*. This is the folder that you created in Step 2.

5. Click **Edit** on the menu bar, and then click **Paste** to copy all the files from the Data Disk to your hard disk.

6. This book refers to this folder as your folder on the Data Disk. The URL to browse a file named aFile.cfm in this folder with your Web browser is: *http://localhost/your_username/aFile.cfm*. Your computer is both a server and a client.

Using Your Computer for Editing and a Remote Computer for Publishing

To use your own computer to complete the chapters, Hands-on Projects, and Case Projects in this book and publish them on a remote Web server with ColdFusion installed, you will need the following:

- Windows 2000 Professional or a similar operating system
- ColdFusion Studio 4.5
- FTP software
- Microsoft Access 2000
- Latest versions of Internet Explorer or Netscape Navigator
- Data Disk containing the databases and the ColdFusion documents
- Username and password on a remote computer with ColdFusion Server software and an FTP Server installed

Installing ColdFusion Studio

Install the ColdFusion Studio software following the instructions in the previous section.

Installing FTP Software

You can obtain and install a freeware or shareware version of FTP Software. Popular locations on the Web for downloading such software are *www.shareware.com* and *www.tucows.com*.

Copying Files from the Data Disk

After you install the software, you must copy the files from the Data Disk.

To copy the files from the Data Disk:

1. Use Windows Explorer or My Computer to navigate to your desktop or other designated folder.
2. Create a folder and name it using your last name or your instructor-assigned username. Use this folder name in place of your_username for all the exercises and projects in the book. For example, name the folder **sTapper**.
3. In Windows Explorer or My Computer, navigate to the Data Disk and select all the folders from **Chapter01** to **Chapter11**, **Databases**, and **Images**. Click **Edit** on the menu bar, and then click **Copy**.
4. Navigate to *your_username* folder. This is the folder that you created earlier in Step 2.
5. Click **Edit** on the menu bar, and then click **Paste** to copy all the files from the Data Disk to your hard disk.
6. Make a connection to remote server with your FTP software and transfer all the files and the folders to the appropriate folder on the server. Your instructor will give you the details about this process.

7. This book refers to this folder as your folder on the Data Disk. The URL to browse a file named aFile.cfm in this folder with your Web browser is: *http://your_server_domain_name/your_username/aFile.cfm*. Whenever you are instructed to save a file in the exercises, you have to save the file on the local machine, and then FTP it over to the remote server. You also can set up a direct FTP connection in the ColdFusion Studio software. If necessary, refer to the online Help after you work through Chapter 1.

For More Information

You have installed all the software needed for the exercises and the projects in the book. If you have any questions or comments, please visit the authors' Web site for this book at *http://kaparthi.cba.uni.edu/ColdFusion*, contact the authors by e-mail at *kaparthi@uni.edu*, or visit the Course Technology Web site at *www.course.com*.

Visit Our World Wide Web Site

Additional materials designed especially for you might be available for your course on the World Wide Web. Go to *www.course.com*. Periodically search this site for more details.

TO THE INSTRUCTOR

To complete the chapters in this book, your users must use a set of data files. These files are included in the Instructor's Resource Kit. They also may be obtained electronically through the Course Technology Web site at *www.course.com*. Follow the instructions in the Help file to copy the data files to your server or standalone computer. You can view the Help file using a text editor such as WordPad or Notepad. Additionally, you may visit the authors' Web site at *http://kaparthi.cba.uni.edu/ColdFusion* for other information and tips.

Once the files are copied, you should instruct your users how to copy the files to their own computers or workstations. This Read This Before You Begin section also includes instructions for copying the data files. See "Copying Files from the Data Disk" for more information.

The chapters and projects in this book were tested using Windows 2000 Professional with IIS 5.0 as the Web server, ColdFusion Server 5.0, and ColdFusion Studio 4.5.2. The screen shots in the book are from the Internet Explorer 5.5, but all the exercises and the projects should work the same on the Netscape browser.

Course Technology Data Files

You are granted a license to copy the data files to any computer or computer network used by individuals who have purchased this book.

CHAPTER

1

INTRODUCTION TO
COLDFUSION

In this chapter, you will:

- Review the basics of HTML, CGI, API, and server-side scripting
- Learn about ColdFusion Studio and ColdFusion Server
- Use ColdFusion Studio for editing and saving files
- Use ColdFusion Markup Language (CFML)
- Use ColdFusion variables and manipulate them with CFSET tags
- Use expressions and understand operator precedence
- Use ColdFusion functions to format data and solve problems

The rapid growth of the Internet and the increasing popularity of the World Wide Web (WWW) have created dramatic changes in daily life. People use the Internet and World Wide Web for business, entertainment, and information; for example, they shop, make airline and hotel reservations, trade stocks, find jobs, listen to music, get news, and find out about weather and driving conditions. The Web can influence every aspect of people's lives in one form or another.

The Web has grown and increased in popularity for many reasons. One reason is that users don't need a particular kind of computer system to access the Web—they can use a Windows personal computer, Macintosh, or UNIX system. Most of the software needed to use the Web is available for free on the Internet itself. Search engines and navigation tools make finding and browsing Web sites fairly simple. Graphics, animation, and sound make Web pages appealing, interesting, and informative, while also providing links for moving from one Web document to another and to other Web sites.

The Web is easy to access because of its underlying technology. The Web connects two types of computers: servers and clients. Servers are typically large network computers that run administrative software and provide resources to other computers. Clients are typically less powerful computers that access shared network resources provided by the server. Tasks performed on the server computer are called **server-side activities**; tasks performed on the client computer are called **client-side activities**. Typical server-side activities include listening for client requests, retrieving documents, and sending documents to clients. Typical client-side activities include requesting documents from servers and receiving and displaying these documents.

To permit different kinds of computer systems to display these documents, the documents are stored on servers as simple ASCII text files. Developers use **Hypertext Markup Language** (**HTML**) to create and format the documents. Client-side software, known as **Web browsers**, receive these documents and display them by formatting the text and downloading and displaying images and other files based on embedded HTML tags.

If you are a Web developer, you can use ColdFusion to design and deliver electronic commerce and other Web-based applications. ColdFusion is a Web application server that provides a set of tools that you can use to quickly create and deliver dynamic, interactive, data-driven Web-based applications—without learning to program in difficult and time-consuming programming languages. ColdFusion allows you to create dynamic Web sites by using a tag-based, embedded language that is very similar to H TML.

REVIEWING HYPERTEXT MARKUP LANGUAGE

In the early 1990s, the Internet was very disorganized. It was difficult to use the software and tools necessary to find and process its information. To make things simple, physicists at the European Laboratory for Particle Physics (CERN) designed the HTML authoring system for distributing information. Using HTML, authors could publish and organize documents using a simple markup language. HTML allows authors to specify document-formatting information, include pictures and sounds, and reference and link other documents by using hyperlinks.

HTML is an **embedded language**; that is, you insert codes or tags along with the content into a single document. When a Web browser processes an HTML document, it examines the HTML tags and formats the content according to the instructions provided by the tags. For example, the following code includes two tags and content text:

```
<B>Ford</B>
```

This code indicates that the browser should display the word "Ford" in bold text. All HTML documents are stored as simple ASCII text files, including the tags. However, you distinguish tags from content text by enclosing them within angle brackets < and >. The text immediately following the opening angle bracket (<) is the name of the tag. In addition, you can specify optional text, called an **attribute** or an **attribute-value**

pair, within a tag to provide additional formatting instructions. An attribute=value pair contains the attribute name, an equal sign, and the instructions for formatting the tag, as in the following example:

```
anAttribute = "aValue"
```

Most HTML tags appear in pairs. The opening tag turns on a feature and the closing tag turns off the feature. The HTML code <B>Ford</B> has the opening tag <B> and the closing tag </B>. Notice that the closing tag contains the forward slash character. Closing tags do not contain attributes or attribute-value pairs. You can see the contents of a sample HTML document in Figure 1-1. Figure 1-2 displays the same document when seen using a Web browser.

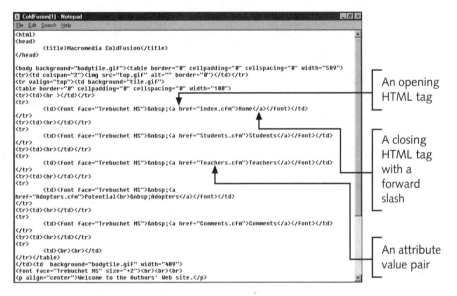

Figure 1-1   An HTML document

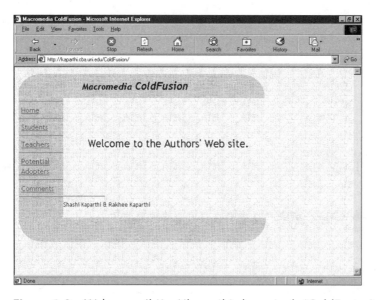

Figure 1-2   Web page (*http://kaparthi.cba.uni.edu/ColdFusion*) displayed by a
Web browser

By using HTML tags, you can define the structure and appearance of a document. You
can specify the appearance of text, embed pictures and graphics, and create hyperlinks
to other documents in your Web site or in other Web sites. You can also create tables and
organize a document as a set of frames. In addition, you can design forms for users to
enter data and send results via their e-mail addresses.

CGI AND API

Because HTML documents can be seen on any kind of computer system and Web
browsers are easy to install and use, using HTML has become a popular method for
developing Web pages and has contributed to the widespread acceptance and usage of
the Web. However, users, developers, and designers have realized the limitations of the
Web. Until recently, standards and technology allowed the transfer of documents from
servers to clients, but this same technology didn't easily allow data transfer back from
clients to servers. New standards needed to be developed that allowed the transfer of
information from clients to servers and to build interactivity into the Web. People also
asked for technologies that would allow them to connect their existing computer-based
information systems to the Web.

To address these concerns, the **Common Gateway Interface** (**CGI**) specification was
released. CGI is a standard for external applications or programs to communicate with
Web servers. An HTML document that a Web server retrieves is **static**, which means it
is a text file that doesn't change until a developer modifies it using some kind of editor.

1

A **CGI program**, on the other hand, is executed in real-time so that it can output information dynamically as needed. The main purpose of a CGI program is to handle client requests for information that is not in HTML format. A CGI program is a separate program that a Web server executes each time a client requests it. You might use a programming language like C/C++ or Visual Basic to write a CGI-executable program.

One of the biggest limitations of CGI is that its programs are run as separate executables, which means that each time a program is executed, much of the computer's resources are consumed. This need for resources limits the number of requests a Web server can handle. To overcome these limitations, Web server vendors have released more efficient replacements for CGI, including Internet Server Application Programming Interface (ISAPI) and Netscape Server Application Programming Interface (NSAPI). Unlike CGI programs, these application programming interface (API) extensions are loaded in the same memory space as the Web server. Using API extensions offers many advantages, including faster page generation, reduced load on the server, increased capability for handling requests, and enhanced security features. Software vendors started selling products based on API extensions to make Web development easier.

At the same time these technical developments were taking place, businesses realized the value of the Web. New businesses were being created at a very fast pace, giving rise to a new way of conducting business called **electronic commerce**, or **e-commerce**. *Amazon.com* started selling books online, E-trade allowed people to trade stocks online, and eBay opened a virtual marketplace where people could buy and sell items in an auction format. During the 1990s, many e-commerce companies went public, causing traditional businesses to revise their strategies and keep up with the competition by "going online." The 1990s also saw a new wave of mergers and acquisitions to combine existing retail businesses with e-commerce sites. Businesses took advantage of technical developments for the Web, but also demanded more flexibility. In particular, businesses wanted to provide customized information based on user requests or selections. This encouraged the development of scripting languages.

SERVER-SIDE SCRIPTING LANGUAGES

Initially, Web sites were used primarily to provide information about a particular company or service. For example, instead of visiting your local Ford dealer to learn basic information about a new car, you could have used Ford's Web site to research information about the exact model that you were considering for purchase. You might have used the Web site to learn about the colors, engine sizes, and body styles that were available for that particular model. You also might have found cost information, such as the sticker price and the price of some basic options. You could have retrieved all of this information by viewing a few Web pages that Ford prepared to answer these basic questions. Ford created these types of Web pages using HTML.

What if you wanted to find out whether a car with some specific features and a certain body style and color was available at your local dealer? What if you wanted to know the exact cost of that car? To accomplish this kind of processing, the Ford Web server should provide dynamic output. The pages that you request aren't static—they are dynamic and based entirely on your input. For this type of interaction to occur, the Web server must be able to process information instead of simply retrieving pages and must generate output as required by your request.

To address the need for dynamic interaction without using sophisticated programming languages such as C, C++, or Visual Basic, vendors designed embedded scripting languages that function on Web server API standards. Two well-known embedded scripting languages are Microsoft's Active Server Pages (ASP), which includes VBScript and JScript, and Macromedia ColdFusion, which processes embedded **ColdFusion Markup Language** (CFML). Both of these embedded scripting languages allow you to build interactive Web sites and provide dynamic output. The focus of this book is ColdFusion.

WHAT IS COLDFUSION?

ColdFusion is a Web application server that lets developers design and deliver e-commerce and other Web-based applications. ColdFusion provides a set of tools that allows you to quickly create and deliver dynamic, interactive, data-driven Web-based applications. You no longer have to program in difficult and time-consuming programming languages to create dynamic Web sites. ColdFusion allows you to create dynamic Web sites by using a tag-based, embedded language that is very similar to HTML. The advantages of using ColdFusion are included in the following list:

- You develop applications using a tag-based language that is embedded in documents in a manner similar to HTML. The ability to embed code allows for rapid creation of documents.

- You do not need to compile, link, or perform other labor-intensive activities associated with developing applications in traditional programming languages. ColdFusion applications are easy to build and test.

- ColdFusion supports more than 70 server-side tags, 200 functions, and 800 third-party components, providing you with most, if not all, of the server-side processing needed to build sophisticated Web applications.

- Applications built using ColdFusion are easy to maintain because the scripts are embedded inside the documents.

- ColdFusion integrates with databases, e-mail servers, file systems, directories, and other enterprise systems, which allows you to develop enterprise-level, complex Web applications quickly and easily.

- ColdFusion uses Web server API and runs as a service, making it very efficient for handling a large number of transactions.

1

- ColdFusion is a scalable architecture that lets you combine many Web servers to handle heavy traffic that involves a large number of customer requests.

- ColdFusion is a cross-platform Web application server that works on servers running on several different operating systems, including Windows 95/98, Windows NT, Windows 2000, Linux, Solaris, and HP-UX.

Given all of these advantages, thousands of companies around the world, including several Fortune 500 companies, use ColdFusion for building and maintaining their online businesses. Two popular Web sites that use ColdFusion to manage their data and applications are *Autobytel.com* and *Crayola.com*. You can understand what ColdFusion can do for you by examining how these sites operate.

Founded in 1995, *Autobytel.com* was the first company to sell cars online. In 1999, *Autobytel.com* generated sales of over $13 billion. *Autobytel.com* uses ColdFusion for its Web site, which offers customers an interactive way of finding information about cars, such as vehicle specifications, vehicle reviews, manufacturer's incentives, and dealer invoice prices. As shown in Figure 1-3, customers can submit purchase requests online to accredited dealers or ask that a car be delivered to a virtual car lot. Customers can also use the Web site to apply for insurance and obtain financing and leasing information. Certified pre-owned vehicles are available for purchase as well. Customers can also register with the service section for personalized assistance with a variety of service and maintenance issues, including service reminders sent by e-mail, appointment scheduling for vehicle maintenance, and recall information. People can sell their used cars through the classifieds section. Given its success in the United States, *Autobytel.com* has started operations in Canada, the United Kingdom, Sweden, and Japan.

Figure 1-3 *Autobytel.com* home page

Binney & Smith, the leading producer of children's art materials and the maker of Crayola products, selected ColdFusion to power *Crayola.com*. As shown in Figure 1-4, *Crayola.com* is a dynamic Web site that offers engaging and interactive arts-and-crafts solutions for parents, educators, and children. Users can find interesting arts-and-crafts projects online. Parents can find information about party ideas, travel tips, book reviews, and other related items by using simple drop-down menus. You can create electronic greeting cards with personalized messages and send them for any occasion. Customers can purchase gifts by receiving gift suggestions based on price, the recipient's age, and product category selections.

Figure 1-4   *Crayola.com* home page

The design requirements of these sites and other Web sites that use ColdFusion can be broken down into a set of basic tasks performed by ColdFusion. In particular, by using ColdFusion you can implement server-side processing to accomplish the following tasks:

- Manipulate numbers, strings, dates, and times and display them in several formats

- Use conditional processing

- Perform a task repeatedly

- Handle data that users enter in HTML forms

- Store and retrieve data in several different database systems that might be stored locally on the Web server or on any other database server

- Extract data from databases and create reports

- Maintain data and process transactions

- Validate data entered by users to ensure the integrity of the information
- Manage cookies and keep track of a series of client interactions with a Web site
- Interact with other services, such as e-mail and file systems
- Upload user-supplied files

To develop and deploy Web applications, ColdFusion provides a set of tools that include the ColdFusion Studio, ColdFusion Server, and ColdFusion Administrator.

COLDFUSION COMPONENTS

ColdFusion consists of three tools. The first component, **ColdFusion Studio**, lets you create Web pages using HTML and CFML. The second component, **ColdFusion Server**, runs the applications that you create in conjunction with a Web server. The third component, **ColdFusion Administrator**, is a Web-based application that allows you to set up and maintain the ColdFusion Server and its interfaces with other services, such as database and mail servers.

In this book, you will build information system applications using ColdFusion Studio. These applications will run on Microsoft Internet Information Services or another server that has ColdFusion installed on it, as specified by your instructor.

Using ColdFusion Studio

Although you could use a program such as Notepad to write the code for ColdFusion documents, most developers find that it is easier to use ColdFusion Studio, which is the tool that contains the editing commands and functions that you need to create, debug, edit, and save ColdFusion documents. ColdFusion Studio is a text editor, and like Notepad or other text-editing programs, it allows you to edit simple ASCII text files. However, ColdFusion Studio offers advantages over other text editors for developing ColdFusion applications. For example, ColdFusion Studio color-codes documents to help you easily identify regular text, HTML tags, HTML attributes, CFML tags, and other scripts. Color-coding also helps you quickly locate errors in your documents. In addition, ColdFusion Studio offers many productivity-enhancing features. Using ColdFusion Studio, you can perform the following tasks:

- Edit multiple documents and switch between them
- Preview documents using the built-in browser or an external browser
- Find and edit documents by using lists of drives, folders, and files through an interface similar to Windows Explorer
- Use tools that automate inserting common HTML and CFML tags

- Browse databases and use drag and drop to create queries that you can save and use in your documents

- Access ColdFusion Studio's extensive online documentation to get help while you are working

Additional features, such as ScreenTips, automatic tag completion, and site views, have made ColdFusion Studio a popular development environment for ColdFusion applications.

Using ColdFusion Server

To understand the role that a ColdFusion Server plays in enhancing the functionality of a Web server, you need to understand and examine the interaction between client computers and servers. First, when you request an HTML document from a Web server, you might type the page's Uniform Resource Locator (URL) in your browser's address field or you might click a hyperlink in an existing document. As mentioned earlier, a Web server listens for requests from client computers, which are called Hypertext Transfer Protocol (HTTP) requests because they are usually formatted according to HTTP specifications. When a Web server receives an HTTP request for an HTML document from a client computer, the request includes information such as the name of the requested document, the path to the document, the Internet Protocol (IP) address of the client computer making the request, the time the request was made, the kind of browser the client is using, and a few other details. Typically, the Web server logs some of these details in a log file or database, retrieves the document, and sends it back to the client computer based on its IP address. If the document is not found, an error message is sent back to the client. When the client receives the HTML document, it uses the HTML tags to format the document according to the instructions contained in the tags. The client may make additional requests to the same server or to other servers if there are any embedded graphics, background images, sound files, style sheets, JavaScript include files, Java applets, or other files required to complete the document. After all of the files needed to complete the document are received, the browser displays the entire formatted document. A web browser may start the process of displaying the document before receiving all the files. It then updates the page as it receives image files and other information. This process is illustrated in Figure 1-5.

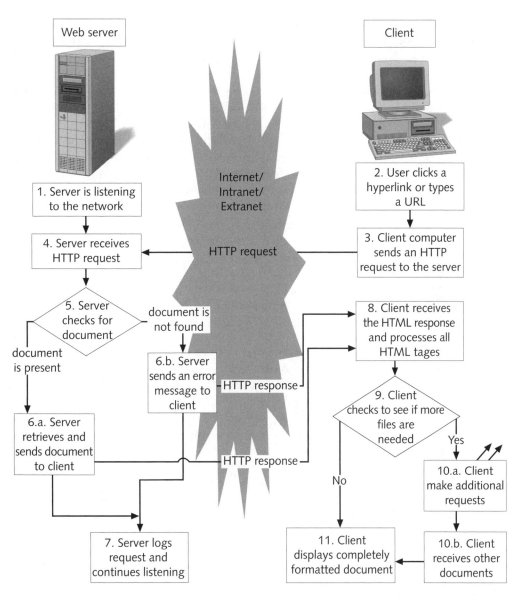

Figure 1-5 Client–server interaction for processing an HTML document request

Now examine what happens when you request a ColdFusion document from a Web server that has a ColdFusion Server installed. You make requests for ColdFusion documents in the same manner that you request other resources on the Web—for example, by typing a URL or by clicking a hyperlink. When you request a ColdFusion document, the client computer sends an HTTP request to the Web server. This HTTP request is formatted like a request for an HTML document, except that now the document name has an extension of .cfm and it is called a **ColdFusion template**. The Web server receives the HTTP request and processes it as a request for a ColdFusion template. The Web server calls the ColdFusion Server and passes all the information that it received in the HTTP request to the ColdFusion Server using Web server API. The ColdFusion Server takes over and retrieves the document from the disk and uses the CFML tags to process the template according to the instructions contained in the tags. After the ColdFusion Server processes the template, the output contains only HTML and other text. The processing performed by the ColdFusion Server could include getting or sending information from or to other services such as database servers, e-mail servers, directory servers, file systems, and other Web servers. The ColdFusion Server sends this information to the Web server, which in turn sends it to the client as an HTTP response. Both the ColdFusion Server and the Web server log these activities. The client computer receives the Web page, which now contains only HTML. It processes the HTML and sends other requests as needed. After the client receives all of the files, the browser formats and displays the complete Web page. This process is shown in Figure 1-6.

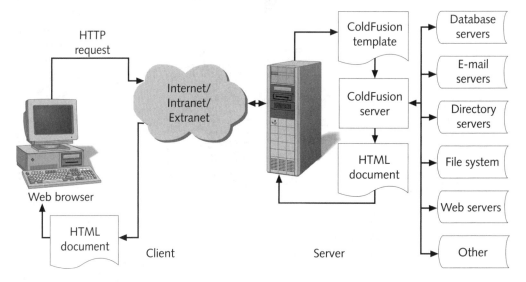

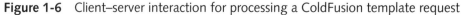

Figure 1-6   Client–server interaction for processing a ColdFusion template request

Using the ColdFusion Administrator

The **ColdFusion Administrator** is a secure, password-protected, Web-based application that allows you to manage the ColdFusion Server. You use the ColdFusion Administrator to configure the ColdFusion Server and control its performance. For example, you can set up the ColdFusion Server to display a contact e-mail address when it encounters an error, or you can configure data sources for interacting with databases. You can turn on several levels of debugging information to assist you with your development. For example, you can specify the mail server that ColdFusion will use for sending e-mail messages.

You can tell ColdFusion what files to use for logging and what information you want logged. You can specify required passwords to allow remote development using ColdFusion Studio and restrict the execution of certain CFML tags that could harm your system when you allow remote development. The ColdFusion Administrator is entirely Web based and also provides a simple, intuitive interface for monitoring the server.

Depending on your server's configuration, you may not be able to access the ColdFusion Administrator.

EXPLORING THE COLDFUSION STUDIO WORKSPACE

You start ColdFusion Studio just like any other application—for example, you can open the start menu, point to Programs, point to ColdFusion Studio 4.5, and then click ColdFusion Studio 4.5. The ColdFusion Studio workspace appears, as in Figure 1-7.

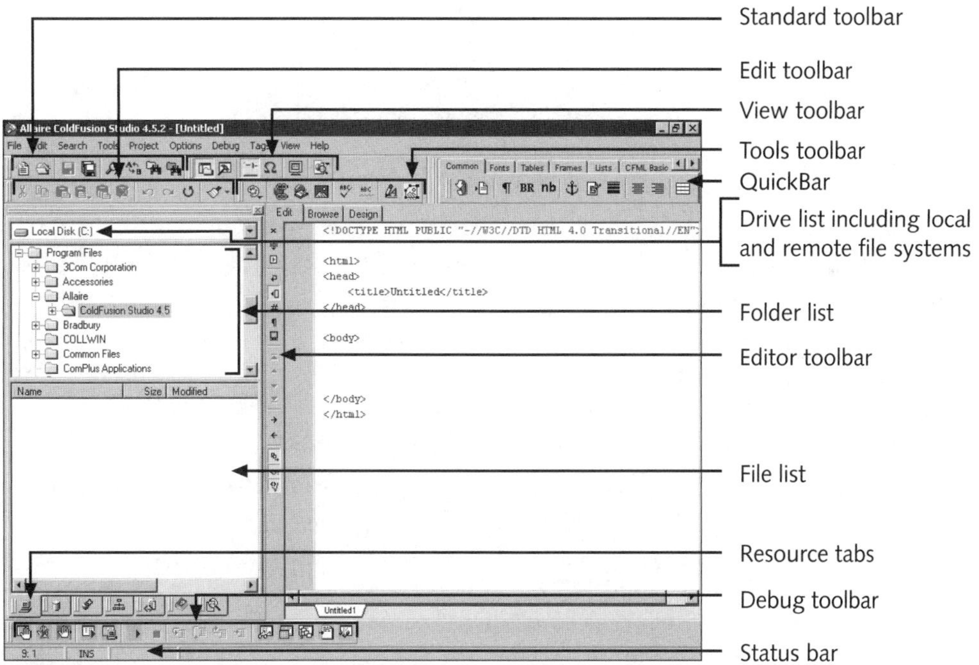

Standard toolbar

Edit toolbar

View toolbar

Tools toolbar

QuickBar

Drive list including local and remote file systems

Folder list

Editor toolbar

File list

Resource tabs

Debug toolbar

Status bar

Figure 1-7   Exploring the ColdFusion Studio workspace

Similar to other Microsoft Windows programs, the ColdFusion Studio program window contains a title bar, a menu bar, and several toolbars. A status bar appears at the bottom of the window.

This book uses ColdFusion Studio 4.5.2. If you are using a different version of ColdFusion Studio, you will see a different version number in the title bar. Also, because the ColdFusion Studio program window can be customized in many ways, your program window might look different. In this book, Internet Explorer is used as the web browser. However, all the examples, exercises, and projects work in Netscape Navigator as well.

The workspace includes the Standard toolbar and View toolbar on the first row below the menu bar on the left, the Edit toolbar and Tools toolbar on the second row below the menu bar on the left, and the QuickBar below the menu bar on the right. These toolbars contain shortcuts for commonly used commands.

Three windows are open in the workspace shown in Figure 1-7. The Resource Tab window appears on the left and currently displays the Drive List and Folder List windows, which include the open drive and folder structure on that drive. Clicking the Drive List list arrow opens the drives and folders on your system. The File List window shows the ColdFusion files on the currently selected drive and in the currently selected folder. The Editor window appears on the right with the Editor Tab at the bottom of the Editor window. The Editor toolbar is a vertical toolbar on the left side of the Editor window.

 Your drive list may not show "C:" because ColdFusion Studio shows the drive that was used the last time the program was closed.

The Resource Tab window has tabs at the bottom to move between the different resources available in ColdFusion Studio. The Debug toolbar appears above the status bar.

You edit new and existing documents in the Editor window. When you are editing multiple documents, the document names appear on the document tabs; click a document tab to switch between documents. You can use the Drive List window and Folder List window to locate and open files quickly. You can even drag and drop image files from the File List window to quickly embed pictures in documents.

You manage your documents by using the Standard toolbar. The Standard toolbar contains buttons for creating a new document, opening an existing document, saving the current document, saving all open documents, and finding and replacing words. The View toolbar lets you hide and display other windows in the workspace, including the Resource Tab window, the Results window, the QuickBar, the Special Characters window, and the external browser. The Edit toolbar includes buttons for editing operations such as cut, copy, and paste. The Tools toolbar has a palette for selecting colors, verifying links, validating documents, viewing thumbnails (small preview pictures) of enclosed images, checking spelling, and creating style sheets and image maps.

When you use the mouse to point to a toolbar button, a ScreenTip displays the button's name.

You use the QuickBar for inserting HTML and CFML tags. This bar is categorized in groups of buttons for inserting commonly used HTML tags; inserting HTML tags for fonts, tables, frames, lists; and for inserting basic and advanced CFML tags.

Similar to other Windows programs, right-clicking an object on the screen opens a shortcut menu.

The Resource Tab window allows you to switch among the different Resource windows: Files, Database, Projects, Site View, Snippets, Help, and Tag Inspector.

Creating and Previewing a New Web Page

In the following exercise, you will create a new Web page using ColdFusion Studio.

To start ColdFusion Studio and create a Web page:

1. Click the **Start** button on the taskbar, point to **Programs**, point to **ColdFusion Studio 4.5**, and then click **ColdFusion Studio 4.5**. Figure 1-7 shows the default program window for ColdFusion Studio. A new document opens in the Editor window. Notice that the new document contains the basic document-structuring HTML tags required for all Web pages and that the insertion point is blinking in the body of the new page.

If your ColdFusion Studio program window looks different from the one shown in Figure 1-7, do the following: right-click any toolbar to open the shortcut menu, click Customize, click the Toolbars tab in the Customize window, click the Reset to Defaults button, and then click the Close button. If necessary, click the Resource Tab button on the View toolbar if the Resource Tab window is not open.

2. If necessary, click the first line below the opening BODY tag in the Editor window, and then type **Hello World Wide Web!**

The text that you typed appears in the body of the Web page, as indicated by the BODY tags. See Figure 1-8.

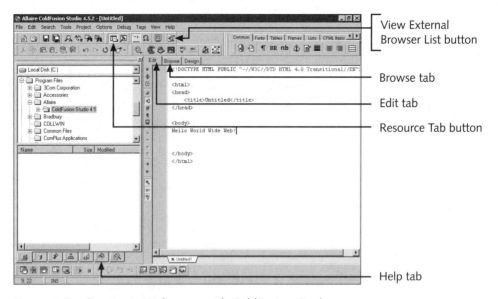

Figure 1-8   Creating a Web page with ColdFusion Studio

3. Click the **Browse tab** on the Editor window. The Browse tab shows how your Web page will appear in a browser. Notice that the tab at the bottom of the Editor window is "X Untitled1." The "X" indicates that the page has not been saved. Because you have not saved this page, the default filename is "Untitled1."

4. Click the **View External Browser List** button on the View toolbar. If necessary, select a browser from the list of all browsers that are installed on your computer. The Untitled Web page opens in the browser that you selected or in the default browser for your computer.

5. Switch to ColdFusion Studio, and click the **Edit tab**.

Using the Resource Tabs

The tabs that appear on the Resource Tab window on the left side of the program window let you view different parts of your application. Table 1-1 describes the different resources.

Table 1-1   Resource Tab Windows and Their Descriptions

Resource Tab	Description
Files	Shows the File List and Folder List windows, which you can use to open a directory list and a file list to locate and open files on local and remote drives
Database	Shows the databases that are attached to your computer and other remote computers; use this window to examine the tables, queries, and data in these databases
Projects	Shows all ColdFusion projects and allows you to manage them
Site View	Shows the interrelationship between all the documents in your site
Snippets	Allows you to manage snippets of code for increased productivity
Help	Displays the Help window for browsing and searching the extensive online documents for using ColdFusion, HTML, and CFML
Tag Inspector	Allows you to examine all of the tags in your document, you can specify values for tag attributes

Using Help

The Help window gives you access to the ColdFusion Studio Help system.

To use Help references:

1. Click the **Help tab** on the Resource Tab window. The Help window opens and displays the contents of the Help system. Notice that the Help categories are divided into logical parts, with categories for administering ColdFusion Server, HTML References, Tag Definitions, Using ColdFusion Studio, and others.

2. Double-click the **Using ColdFusion Studio** category to open it. Twelve topics appear in this category. You can use these topics when you need help performing a task in ColdFusion Studio.

3. Double-click **Chapter 3 Configuring Web Browser**, and then double-click **Configuring Web Browsers**. The Configuring Browsers topic opens in the right pane, as shown in Figure 1-9. Read the information in this page to learn how to change the browser that you will use to view CFML application pages.

4. When you are finished reading, click the **Edit tab** on the Editor window, and then click the **Files tab** on the Resource Tab window.

You can use the Help tab whenever you need Help while working in ColdFusion Studio. The Help system is very comprehensive and contains all of the information provided in the manuals that are shipped with the ColdFusion Studio software.

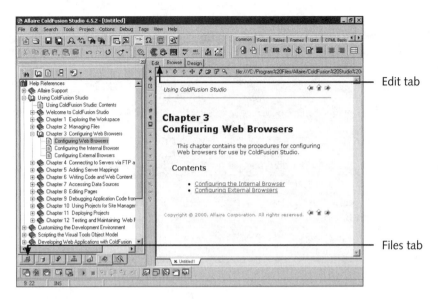

Edit tab

Files tab

Figure 1-9   Using Help in ColdFusion Studio

Saving a ColdFusion Template

When you save a ColdFusion template, you have the option of saving the file on your local computer system or on a remote Web site that has an FTP server or ColdFusion installed.

 The steps in this book ask you to save your ColdFusion templates in the default path to the Microsoft Internet Information Services 5.0 for Windows 2000. Your instructor will provide you with alternate instructions if you are using a different configuration to process ColdFusion templates.

To save a ColdFusion template:

1. Click the **Save** button on the Standard toolbar. The Save As dialog box opens, as shown in Figure 1-10. The default folder in which to save ColdFusion Studio appears in the Look in list box.

2. Click the **Look in** list arrow to navigate to and open the **Chapter01** folder on your Data Disk.

3. In the File name text box, type **Hello**, and then click the **Save** button.

   ColdFusion Studio saves your Web page as Hello.cfm in the Chapter01 folder on your Data Disk. Notice that the tab at the bottom of the Editor window now displays the filename "Hello.cfm." The path in the title bar displays the full path to your document, as shown in Figure 1-11. The filename extension .cfm indicates that this is a ColdFusion template.

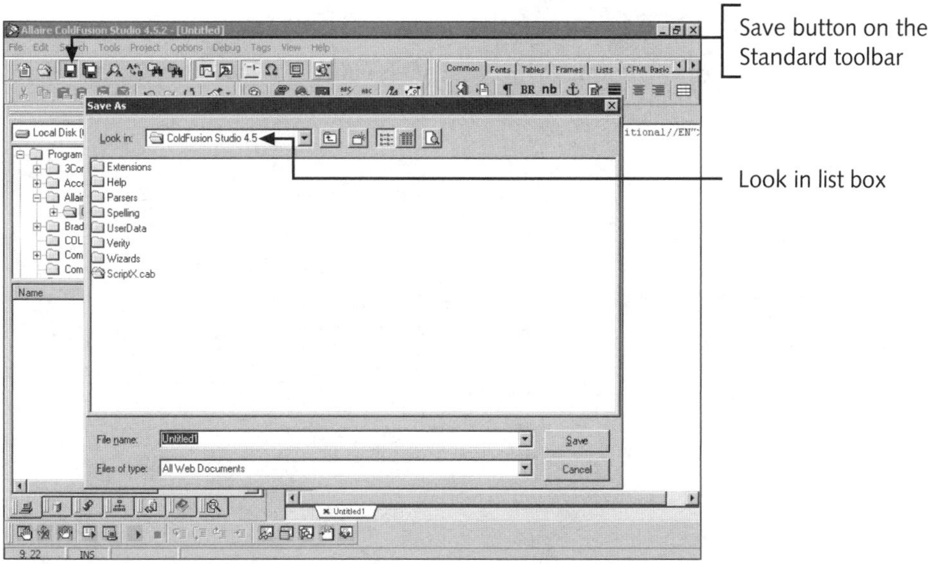

Figure 1-10   Save As dialog box

As you are working through the chapters in this book, you will save your files on a Data Disk. The Data Disk might be a disk in drive A, a zip drive, a hard drive, or a network server. Your instructor will provide you with a location to which to save your Web pages. The default location shown in this book is to store Data Files in the path C:\Inetpub\wwwroot\your_username\Chapter## and to display Web pages from the local Web server, localhost.

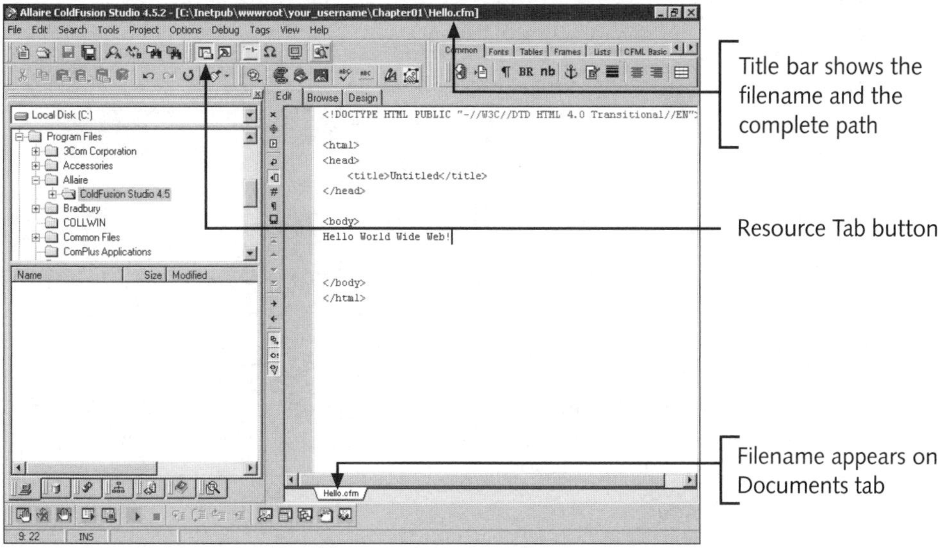

Figure 1-11   Saving a template

Expanding the Editor Window

While you are creating and revising your Web pages, you might want to enlarge the program window to display more of your document.

To expand the Editor window:

1. Click the **Resource Tab** button on the View toolbar. The Editor window is resized to fill the program window, as shown in Figure 1-12.

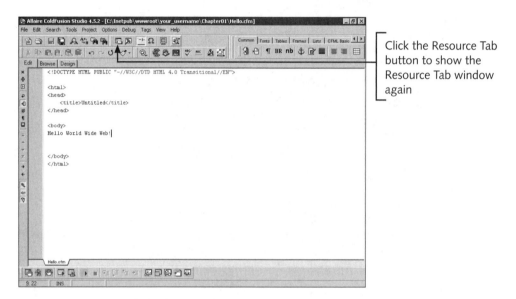

Click the Resource Tab button to show the Resource Tab window again

Figure 1-12   Expanded Editor window

In this book, you will work with the expanded Editor window most of the time so that you can see more of your document's contents. If you need to see the Resource Tab window again, click the Resource Tab button.

UNDERSTANDING COLDFUSION AND THE WEB

The real power of ColdFusion is its capability to enhance static HTML documents into Web pages that can process tasks. You may already be familiar with some methods that you can use to embed small programs, such as Java applets, JavaScript, and VBScript, in a Web page. These programs give you a way to make static Web pages do more. Consider the following example: an online hardware store wants to display detailed pricing information about products on its Web site. Figure 1-13 shows a static HTML document that displays information about a specific kitchen sink.

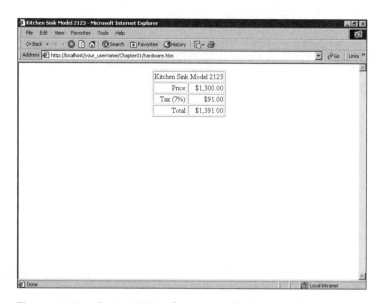

Figure 1-13 Static HTML document displaying information about a kitchen sink

You can use ColdFusion Studio to create the HTML code for the simple Web page shown in Figure 1-13.

To create a new Web page:

1. Click the **New** button on the Standard toolbar. A new document opens in the Editor window. Notice that the new document contains the required structural HTML codes for a Web page: HTML, HEAD, TITLE, and BODY and the HTML version information at the top.

2. Select the word **Untitled**, which appears between the TITLE tags, and then type **Kitchen Sink Model 2123**. Notice that the content that you added to the TITLE tags, "Kitchen Sink Model 2123," appears as black text. ColdFusion changes the color of text in a template to indicate whether it is an HTML tag, a user-entered value in a tag, or content that appears in the template. This line of code changes the title of the Web page from "Untitled" to "Kitchen Sink Model 2123." This text will appear in the browser's title bar when a browser displays the template.

3. Click the insertion point on the blank line below the opening BODY tag. See Figure 1-14. Notice that the status bar displays the text 9: 1, which indicates the current position of the insertion point. The first number, 9, indicates that the insertion point appears on line 9. The second number, 1, indicates that the insertion point is positioned in the first column.

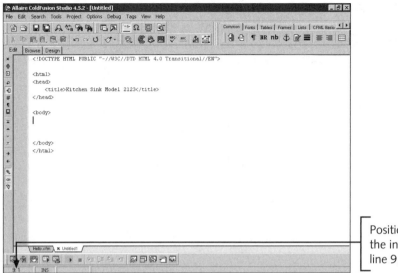

Position 9:1 indicates that the insertion point is on line 9, first character

Figure 1-14   Status bar shows the position of the insertion point

HTML tags are not case sensitive; you can type your HTML tags in uppercase, lowercase, or mixed-case letters. The HTML tags used in the programs in this book will appear in lowercase letters. When a tag is used in the text's narrative, it will appear in all uppercase letters so that you can easily distinguish tags.

4. Click the insertion point to position it on line 8, column 6 (between the word "body" and the closing bracket in the BODY tag), press the **spacebar**, wait for a few seconds, and then type **bgcolor="white"**. Notice that a pop-up window opens when you are typing. For now, just ignore this **tag insight** window. In addition, the HTML code <body bgcolor= and the closing bracket (>) appear as dark blue text. ColdFusion changes HTML tags to dark blue to make them easier to locate in a template. The user-entered value "white" appears in blue type, indicating that this is a user-entered value for an attribute. This line of code sets the background color of the Web page to white.

5. Press the **Down Arrow** key to move to line 9, and then type **<table align="center" border="1">**. Notice that ColdFusion adds the closing TABLE tag for you. This feature is known as **Tag completion**, and is useful when you are creating a template. However, if you have a typing error in your code, the tag completion feature will not add the correct closing tags. Make sure that you type the closing tags in case you change opening tags to correct typing errors. In later chapters you will turn this feature off by using the Tag Completion button on the Editor toolbar. Also, notice that the TABLE tags and the ALIGN and BORDER properties appear in green text. The user-entered values "center" and "1" are blue.

You can use the Tags menu and the QuickBar to insert common HTML tags in a document. When you select a tag, ColdFusion Studio will insert the opening and closing tags for the item that you selected, saving you some typing.

6. Press the **Enter** key, and then type **<tr>**. This is the opening tag for one row in a table. Notice that the tag is green in color and that ColdFusion adds the closing TR tag for you.

7. Type **<td align="center" colspan="2">Kitchen Sink Model 2123**.

ColdFusion adds the closing TD tag for you. This completes the first row in the table.

8. Move the insertion point so that it is to the right of the closing bracket for the TR tag, press the **Enter** key, and then type **<tr><td align="right">Price:**.

ColdFusion Studio adds the closing TD and TR tags for you, so you can move the insertion point to the correct position and continue typing.

9. Move the insertion point so that it is to the right of the closing bracket for the /TD tag, and then type **<td align="right">$1,300.00**.

ColdFusion Studio adds the closing TD and TR tags for you. See Figure 1-15.

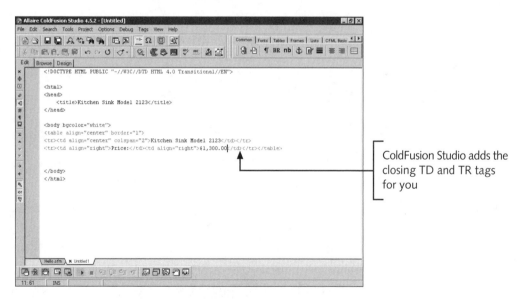

ColdFusion Studio adds the closing TD and TR tags for you

Figure 1-15   Editing a ColdFusion template

10. Move the insertion point to the right of the closing bracket for the closing TR tag on line 11, press the **Enter** key, and then type the following two lines

of text, being careful not to duplicate closing tags that are added by ColdFusion Studio:

\<tr>\<td align="right">Tax (7%):\</td>\<td align="right">$91.00\</td>\</tr>

\<tr>\<td align="right">Total:\</td>\<td align="right">$1,391.00\</td>\</tr>

11. Move the insertion point to the right of the closing bracket for the TR tag on line 13, and then press the **Enter** key. The closing TABLE and BODY tags appear on lines 14 and 17. See Figure 1-16.

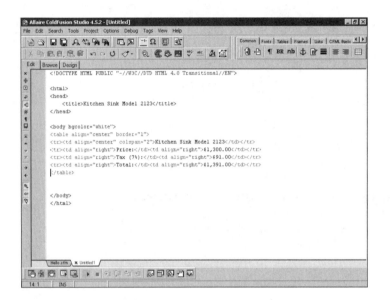

Figure 1-16   Completed ColdFusion template

You finished entering the HTML code that created the Web page shown in Figure 1-13. Now you can save your work and use the Browse tab to preview it.

To save your file and preview it:

1. Click the **Save** button on the Standard toolbar. The Save As dialog box opens.

2. Click the **Look in** list arrow to find and open the **Chapter01** folder on your Data Disk.

3. Type **hardware.htm** in the File name text box, and then click the **Save** button. The Web page is saved on your Data Disk.

4. Click the **Browse** tab on the Editor window. The Web page contains a table, as shown in Figure 1-17.

Allaire ColdFusion Studio 4.5.2 - [C:\Inetpub\wwwroot\your_username\Chapter01\hardware.htm]

File   Edit   Search   Tools   Project   Options   Debug   Tags   View   Help

Common | Fonts | Tables | Frames | Lists | CFML Basic

Edit   Browse   Design

file:///C:/Inetpub/wwwroot/your_username/Chapter01/cf~hardware.htm ──── Browse tab

Kitchen Sink Model 2123	
Price:	$1,300.00
Tax (7%):	$91.00
Total:	$1,391.00

Documents tab indicates
that multiple documents
are open

Hello.cfm hardware.htm

14:1   INS   Done

Figure 1-17   Preview of the document using the Browse tab

Tip

If your table does not look like the one shown in Figure 1-17, click the Edit tab and then check your HTML code for errors. Make any necessary changes, save the file by clicking the Save button on the Standard toolbar, and then click the Browse tab.

This Web page displays a product's title, price, sales tax amount, and total cost. This information is neatly formatted in an HTML table. A table header displays the product title, and the HTML code right-aligns the labels and values in the table's cells.

A customer will access this information by using an Internet browser, such as Netscape Navigator or Microsoft Internet Explorer, and by typing the document's URL in the browser's address field. Although you use easy-to-remember domain names in URLs, computers on the Web actually connect using equivalent numeric IP addresses. For example, the equivalent IP address for the University of Northern Iowa's Web server (*www.uni.edu*) is 134.161.1.13. Certain IP addresses are reserved for special purposes. If you send a request from a Web browser to a Web server at the loopback address 127.0.0.1, the request is sent back to the Web server on the same computer, the one using the Web browser that originated the request. The domain name localhost is synonymous with 127.0.0.1. You can test all your Web pages and applications by using http://localhost/ as the protocol and domain name in the URLs. You are essentially using the same computer as a client and as a server.

If you are developing and saving files to your local computer, you can access this document by using the URL *http://localhost/your_username/Chapter01/hardware.htm*, as shown in Figure 1-13. If this document were published on a Web server, its URL would be *http://server_domain_name/your_username/Chapter01/hardware.htm*. When a customer types this URL in a browser's address field, the customer's browser sends an HTTP request to the Web server on which the page is stored (server_domain_name). The Web server retrieves the requested document (hardware.htm) from the correct folder (Chapter01) and sends it to the customer's computer. The browser interprets the HTML code and displays an appropriately formatted page.

Manually coding Web pages for every product at the hardware store might work if the store only sells a few products and every customer pays the same tax rate. However, depending on its size, a hardware store typically sells hundreds or thousands of products. If the hardware store's Web site uses HTML files like the one you just created, you would need hundreds and even thousands of HTML files—one for each product—to represent your store's inventory. Any change in the product prices or tax rate would require you to change the code in every Web page in the site, creating a nightmare for the Web administrator. If you can only make the Web server perform calculations, you could solve at least a part of the maintenance problem!

A ColdFusion Server enhances the capabilities of a Web server to perform simple to complex calculations, solving the problem of needing to manually code HTML documents. Figure 1-18 shows the processing of a ColdFusion template in a Web site that has a ColdFusion Server installed.

You can use CFML to enhance the capability of the hardware.htm page to make the Web page calculate the sales tax and total amounts, thereby alleviating the administrator of having to manually program this information. Figure 1-19 shows the modified code for the CFM template. In the following sections, you will learn about the CFML that creates this template.

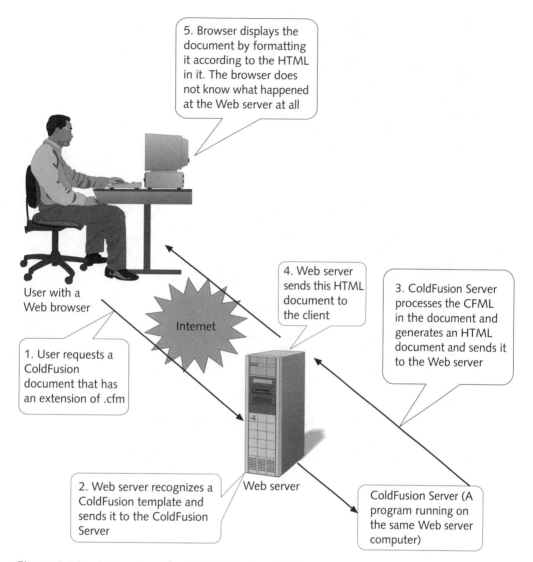

Figure 1-18   Processing of a ColdFusion template

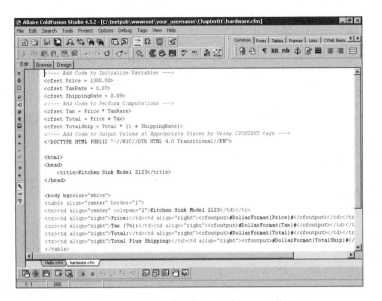

Figure 1-19 CFML for the kitchen sink example

The code shown in Figure 1-19 creates the Web page shown in Figure 1-20 when viewed in a browser. Now the Web page itself calculates the tax and total amounts. If you change the tax rate or the price of an item, ColdFusion will update these amounts automatically.

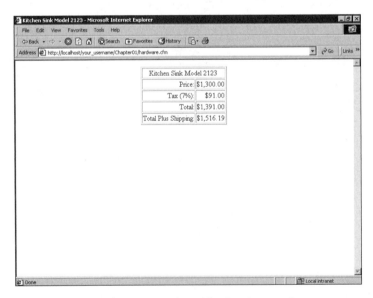

Figure 1-20 Web page produced by hardware.cfm

COLDFUSION MARKUP LANGUAGE

If you closely examine the hardware.cfm file shown in Figure 1-19, you will notice two new tags that are not found in HTML documents: <cfset> and <cfoutput>. These tags are CFML tags. **CFML** is a server-side markup language that is used in combination with HTML to enable server-side processing by manipulating data, displaying output, and interacting with databases. As shown in Figure 1-18, when a user requests a document that has an extension of .cfm, the Web server recognizes that it is a **ColdFusion template** (also known as **document** or **page**) and sends it to the ColdFusion Server for processing. The ColdFusion Server processes the template by interpreting the CFML and performing the indicated actions. (The ColdFusion Server does not process the HTML code in the document.) The CFML in the document might instruct the ColdFusion Server to manipulate data, perform calculations, access data from databases, work with files and folders, retrieve e-mail messages, or output data. After the ColdFusion Server processes the CFML, it returns a document to the Web server that contains only the HTML code needed to display the Web page. In other words, the ColdFusion Server creates a new page that only contains HTML. The HTML document is returned to the Web server, which then sends it to the user's computer, where the browser interprets and displays the HTML code as an appropriately formatted Web page.

Adding the ColdFusion Server to the process of sending requests from a client to a Web server provides the capability to do some processing and then to send the results to the client. Most processing and data manipulation in computer programs is done by assigning values to variables. Similarly, variables and variable manipulation are fundamental building blocks for building ColdFusion templates.

Variables and the CFSET Tag

Variables are fundamental to most programming systems. A **variable** is a named location in the computer's memory. Using appropriate programming statements, programmers can store values in (or assign values to) variables so they can manipulate them. Most processing in computer systems occurs in this fashion. In ColdFusion, the **CFSET tag** is used for defining and assigning values to ColdFusion variables. CFML statements are generally known as tags because CFML statements are combined with HTML tags. The syntax, or programming rules, for writing these tags is similar to that for writing HTML tags. Most statements have an opening and closing tag that is very similar to HTML.

Consider the following statement (tag) from hardware.cfm:

```
<cfset Price = 1300.00>
```

When the ColdFusion Server is processing hardware.cfm and encounters this statement, the ColdFusion Server recognizes that this tag is part of CFML and executes it. A storage place in the computer's memory is given the name "Price," and a value of 1300.00 is stored in it. After the value is stored in the computer's memory, the ColdFusion Server executes the next statement. Statements are executed sequentially until the entire file has been processed. Any code that is not part of CFML is left as is.

Consider the next statement from hardware.cfm:

```
<cfset TaxRate = 0.07>
```

When the ColdFusion Server executes this statement, a variable named TaxRate is created, and a value of 0.07 is assigned to it. You can see that it is very easy to create variables and assign values to them by using the CFSET tag.

Understanding Rules for Naming Variables

You probably noticed the use of the lowercase and uppercase letters in naming variables. Variables in ColdFusion are not case sensitive; in other words, variables named using different cases are still the same. For example, TaxRate and taxrate are the same variable. However, it is always a good practice to use case consistently. Typically, you should use title case for variables, which means you should capitalize the first letter of every word. You cannot use spaces in variable names. As a general rule, ColdFusion variable names must begin with a letter and can consist of letters, numbers, or the underscore character (_). For example, Price, TaxRate, and Number_1 are valid variable names, but First Name, 2b_or_not2b, and divisible/2 are invalid. The use of a period in variable names carries a special significance and is discussed in later chapters.

By now, you might be wondering about the following code that appears in the hardware.cfm file:

```
<!--- Add Code to Initialize Variables ---> and <!--- Add
Code to Perform Computations --->
```

This code creates a comment, as described in the next section.

Creating Comments

Just like in other programming languages, you can use CFML tags to enclose comments. Similar to HTML comments, ColdFusion comment opening tags start with an opening bracket (<) and an exclamation point (!) and are followed by three dashes instead of just two. The tag to close a ColdFusion comment is three dashes followed by a closing angle bracket (--->). When the ColdFusion Server encounters the <!--- and ---> tags, it ignores all of the text between the tags. Comments are very useful for documenting templates, such as describing a template's function, author, last modification date, and the template's logic and design. As is the case in most programming languages, it is a good idea to use comments to document your templates to provide essential information about them to other people who use them.

Processing Numbers

Originally, computers were designed to process numbers and to use those numbers to perform computations. Even now, much of computer processing uses numbers. As demonstrated in the hardware.cfm example, ColdFusion lets you work with numbers, such as 1300.00 and 0.07. ColdFusion can process **integers** (numbers without decimal or fractional parts) and **real numbers** (numbers with decimal parts). Developers can use both kinds of numbers as needed in a single template. ColdFusion supports the range of numbers from -10^{300} to 10^{300}, and most results are accurate to 12 decimal places. When using real numbers in a template, you need to type a leading zero in numbers that are less than 1.0 and greater than −1.0. For example, 0.07 is a valid real number, but .07 is not. ColdFusion displays very small and very large numbers by using a scientific notation. In **scientific notation**, you can express any value by using a number between 1 and 10 and the appropriate power of 10, which multiplies the number by the power of 10. For example, the value 16,000,000 (1.6×10^{7}) in scientific notation is 1.6E7, and the value 0.00426 (4.26×10^{-3}) in scientific notation is 4.26E-3.

Using Arithmetic Expressions

You have already seen how to use a CFSET tag to assign values to variables. You can also use the CFSET tag to perform computations and to assign the results to variables. Consider the following statement:

```
<cfset TaxRate = 0.07>
```

In this statement, the entry to the right of the equal sign is a value (0.07). You can also enter an expression on the right of the equal sign. A ColdFusion **expression** is similar to a mathematical expression; it can contain values, variables, and mathematical or arithmetic operators. For example, in the hardware.cfm file, the ColdFusion server processes and evaluates the statement <cfset Tax = Price * TaxRate> by using the value of 1300.00 stored in the Price variable and the value of 0.07 stored in the TaxRate variable, and then it uses the multiplication operator (*) to multiply the variables. The ColdFusion Server multiplies 1300.00 by 0.07, gets a result of 91.00, and then assigns the result to a new variable named Tax. Similarly <cfset Total = Price + Tax> adds the variables Price and Tax (1300.00 + 91.00), gets a result of 1391.00, and assigns the result to a variable named Total. In each of these statements, the current values assigned to the variables are used to perform a calculation, the result of which is stored to the left of the equal sign.

These types of expressions are called arithmetic expressions. **Arithmetic expressions** are formed by combining values and/or variables and arithmetic operators in a logical manner. Table 1-2 lists ColdFusion arithmetic operators, their descriptions, and a few examples of their usage.

Table 1-2   ColdFusion Arithmetic Operators

Operator	Description	Restrictions	Examples
+	Addition	None	Price + TaxRate
-	Subtraction	None	CarCost - DownPayment
*	Multiplication	None	Price * TaxRate
/	Division	The right operand cannot be zero	InterestRate / 12
^	Exponentiation	The left operand cannot be zero	Principle * (1 + InterestRate / 12) ^ 4
MOD	Gives the remainder (modulus) after a number is divided by a divisor; the result has the same sign as the divisor	The right operand cannot be zero	14/3 = (4 with a remainder of 2), therefore 14 MOD 3 = 2; or Row Number MOD 2
\	Divides two integer values to result in an integer	The right operand cannot be zero	9 \ 4 = 2, or Number _of_Cols \ 7

You can change the hardware.htm file to use CFML, as you will see next, so that your page will process expressions that use variables and arithmetic operators.

To create variables using the CFSET tag:

1. Switch to ColdFusion Studio, if necessary, and click the **Edit** tab on the Editor window. The HTML code for the hardware.htm file appears.

2. Click **File** on the menu bar, and then click **Save As**.

3. Make sure that the **Chapter01** folder on your Data Disk appears in the Look in list box, and then change the text in the File name text box to **hardware.cfm**.

4. Click the **Save** button. You saved a copy of your HTML file with the ColdFusion file extension, .cfm. The tab at the bottom of the Editor window now shows the filename hardware.cfm. This filename and its path appear in the title bar, as well.

5. Click at the beginning of line 1 in the document, press the **Enter** key, press the **Up** arrow key to move to the new line, click the **CFML Basic** tab on the QuickBar, and then click the **ColdFusion Comment** button. Note that on an 800 × 600 resolution monitor, only half of the Comment button is visible. The opening and closing comment tags (<!--- and--->) are added to the first line, and the insertion point appears within the comment tags. You can type your comment at the location of the insertion point.

6. Type **Add Code to Initialize Variables**, press the **End** key to move to the end of the current line, and then press the **Enter** key.

7. Type **<cfset Price = 1300.00>**, and then press the **Enter** key. When this statement is executed after a user requests this document, the ColdFusion Server creates a variable named Price and assigns the value 1300.00 to it.

ColdFusion Studio has a debugging feature known as **tag validation**. As soon as a tag is completed in the editor, the tag is validated. Notice that a message appears on the status bar indicating that this tag has been validated. You may also see other informative messages about tag validation in the status bar. Depending on your computer's processor speed, this might take a second or two.

8. Type **<cfset TaxRate = 0.07>**, and then press the **Enter** key. You created a variable named TaxRate and assigned the value 0.07 to it.

9. Click the **ColdFusion Comment** button, and then type **Add Code to Perform Computations**.

10. Press the **End** key, press the **Enter** key, and then type the following code, pressing the **Enter** key after the first line:

```
<cfset Tax = Price * TaxRate>
<cfset Total = Price + Tax>
```

11. Click the **Save** button on the Standard toolbar to save the file.

Now your page includes statements to create the variables named Price and TaxRate and the expressions to calculate the tax and the total amounts. The next items that you need to add to your page are statements to add the results of these expressions to the page.

Using the CFOUTPUT Tag and Pound (#) Signs

When the ColdFusion server is processing a ColdFusion template, the ColdFusion Server sends HTML code to the Web server "as is" and executes actions specified by CFSET tags by assigning values to variables. When ColdFusion performs computations, it needs a mechanism to communicate the results with the browser. A **CFOUTPUT tag** displays the results generated by a CFSET statement. When ColdFusion encounters the <cfoutput> tag, it starts processing text by looking for variables enclosed in pound (#) signs, such as #Price#. If the ColdFusion Server encounters any HTML, it is sent as is to the server without any changes. When ColdFusion encounters a variable enclosed in pound signs, it sends the variable's value to the server. This processing stops when ColdFusion encounters a closing </cfoutput> tag. A developer can perform calculations and assign values to variables by using CFSET statements and then output the results by using CFOUTPUT tags as neatly formatted in HTML. In general, you cannot use other CFML tags inside CFOUTPUT tags.

To produce output in the hardware.cfm file, you will need to add the following three CFOUTPUT statements:

```
<cfoutput>#Price#</cfoutput>
<cfoutput>#Tax#</cfoutput>
<cfoutput>#Total#</cfoutput>
```

When the ColdFusion Server encounters the <cfoutput> in <cfoutput>#Price#</cfoutput>, it starts processing the text and looks for variables enclosed in pound signs. When #Price# is processed, the value 1300.00 is substituted for the variable named Price. Similarly, the values 91.00 and 1391.00 are substituted for #Tax# and #Total#. You will add these statements to your file next.

To add CFOUTPUT statements to the hardware.cfm file:

1. Press the **Enter** key, click the **Coldfusion Comment** button on the Quickbar to create the opening and closing comment tags, and then type **Add Code to Output Values at Appropriate Places by Using CFOUTPUT Tags**.

2. Select **$1300.00** in line 18 (the HTML code that creates the second row of the table), and then type **<cfoutput>#Price#**.

   Notice that after you type the opening CFOUTPUT tag, ColdFusion Studio automatically adds the closing CFOUTPUT tag for you.

 CFML tags are not case sensitive; the tags </CFOUTPUT> and </cfoutput> are the same. If you want to convert your tags to all uppercase or to all lowercase letters, click Edit on the menu bar, and then click Convert Tag Case. Then you can select the option to convert all tags to the desired case. The code in this book will use lowercase tags.

3. On the next line, select **$91.00**, and then type **<cfoutput>#Tax#**.

   Again, ColdFusion Studio enters the closing tag for you.

4. On the next line, select $1,391.00, and then type **<cfoutput>#Total#**.

   See Figure 1-21.

5. Click the **Save** button on the Standard toolbar to save the file.

6. Click the **program button** on the Windows taskbar at the bottom of your screen for your browser, select the text in the address field, type **http://localhost/your_username/Chapter01/hardware.cfm**, and then press the **Enter** key. If your file is located on a remote server, type the domain name for your Web server instead of localhost. Now the values 1300.00, 91, and 1391 are created by the variables. See Figure 1-22.

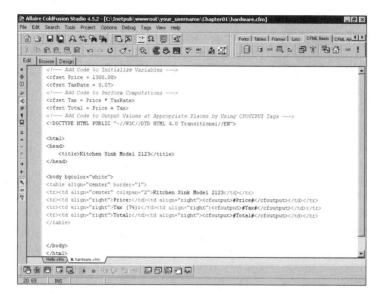

Figure 1-21   CFOUTPUT tags added to file

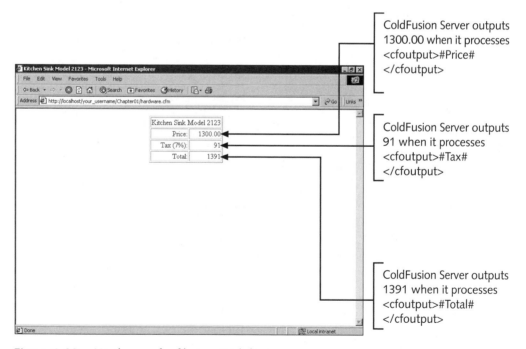

Figure 1-22   Hardware.cfm file in a Web browser

Because a browser interprets HTML, you might be wondering what happens to the CFML code when a browser displays the page. You can see the HTML code that is generated by the ColdFusion Server by opening hardware.cfm in a Web browser and examining the page's source code.

To view the HTML code for a ColdFusion template:

1. Click **View** on the menu bar of the Web browser, and then click **Source**. Figure 1-23 shows the source code in Internet Explorer. Notice that the page doesn't contain any CFML tags because the ColdFusion Server converted the entire page into HTML so a browser can interpret and display it. In addition, the CFOUTPUT statements show the values assigned to the variables but not the CFOUTPUT statements themselves.

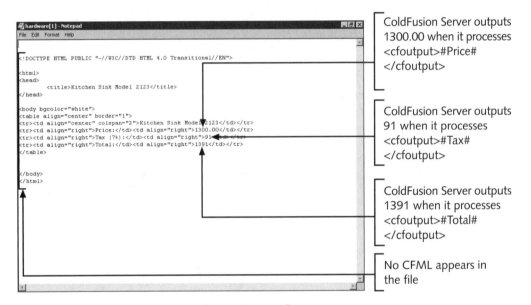

ColdFusion Server outputs 1300.00 when it processes <cfoutput>#Price# </cfoutput>

ColdFusion Server outputs 91 when it processes <cfoutput>#Tax# </cfoutput>

ColdFusion Server outputs 1391 when it processes <cfoutput>#Total# </cfoutput>

No CFML appears in the file

Figure 1-23   HTML source code for hardware.cfm

If you are using Netscape Navigator, click View on the menu bar, and then click Page Source. Your source code will look the same.

2. Click the **Close** button to close the window that contains the source code.

Understanding Operator Precedence

When evaluating expressions containing more than one operator, ColdFusion uses a system of operator precedence. For example, when ColdFusion evaluates the expression 6 - 3 * 2, the multiplication operation is performed first, so 6 - (3 * 2) would be evaluated as 6 - 6, for a result of 0. If a system with no operator precedence were to evaluate this expression, it would have resulted in $(6 - 3) * 2 = 3 * 2 = 6$. Table 1-3 shows arithmetic operators in order of their precedence. The second column identifies the precedence when similar operators exist in the same expression (such as $6 * 5 / 5 * 6$).

Table 1-3   Arithmetic Operator Precedence (Highest to Lowest)

Operator	Multiple Similar Operators	Precedence
( )	Inner to outer, left to right	First
^	Right to left	Second
* and /	Left to right	Third
\	Left to right	Fourth
MOD	Left to right	Fifth
+ and -	Left to right	Sixth

You can also use parentheses in an expression to make the ColdFusion Server process the expressions contained in parentheses before processing and evaluating any other expression. Suppose you need to add a row to your table that identifies the total cost to ship an item to a customer. The shipping price is calculated by adding 9% (ShippingRate) of the item's total to the total [that is, Total + Total * ShippingRate or Total * (1 + ShippingRate)].

To add the shipping row to the table:

1. Switch to ColdFusion Studio.

2. Navigate to the end of line 20 (the line that outputs the Total), press the **Enter** key, and then type **<tr><td align="right">Total Plus Shipping:**.

3. Move the insertion point to the right of the closing bracket of the </td> tag, and then type **<td align="right"><cfoutput>#TotalShip#**.

   See Figure 1-24.

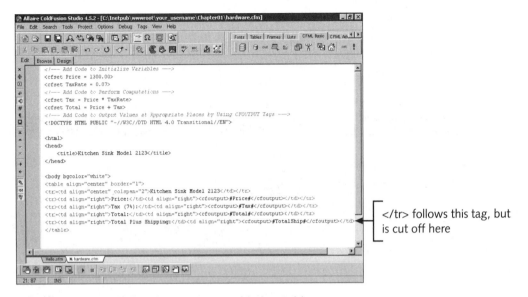

Figure 1-24   Total Plus Shipping now added to table

 You can also copy and paste code when adding code that is the same as or similar to existing code. For example, you can select line 20, click the Copy button, create a new line below line 20, click the Paste button, and then make your changes to the pasted line.

Now, you need to initialize a variable named ShippingRate that stores the value 0.09.

To initialize a variable:

1. Create a new line below line 3 (the CFSET statement that initializes the TaxRate variable), and then type **<cfset ShippingRate = 0.09>**.

   You initialized a variable named ShippingRate. Next, add the code to calculate the total plus shipping.

2. Create a new line below line 7 (the CFSET statement that computes the Total), and then type **<cfset TotalShip = Total * (1 + ShippingRate)>**. See Figure 1-25.

3. Click the **Save** button on the Standard toolbar, click the **program button** on the Windows taskbar for your browser, and then click **Refresh**. See Figure 1-26.

 Netscape users should click the Reload button instead of the Refresh button.

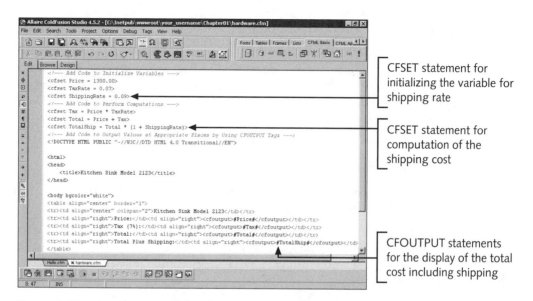

Figure 1-25   Initialization of the shipping rate and computation of the total plus shipping

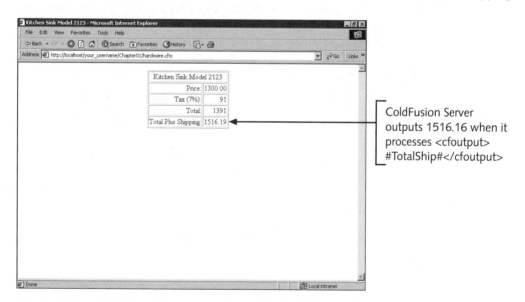

Figure 1-26   Total Plus Shipping row added to the table

You might have noticed that the values produced by the CFOUTPUT tags don't display the values as currency. In ColdFusion, you format output by using functions.

Using Functions to Format Numbers

A ColdFusion **function** is similar to a mathematical function—it processes one or more input values and returns a single output value. You can use functions to perform complex mathematical calculations, generate random numbers, control the way data is displayed, and so on. Next you will modify the hardware.cfm template and use the DollarFormat function to display output as currency.

To format output using the DollarFormat function:

1. Switch to ColdFusion Studio.

2. On line 20, which creates the second row in the table for Price, select **#Price#**, and then type **#DollarFormat(Price)#**.

    This code changes the Price variable to format it with a dollar sign and two decimal places. Remember that the ColdFusion Server will process everything between the pound signs, including the DollarFormat function that you just added.

 You may have noticed that a pop-up window with the word "number" in it opened when you typed the DollarFormat function. This feature is called the function insight feature and helps you design functions by telling you what the function is expecting as input.

3. On the next line, change #Tax# to **#DollarFormat(Tax)#**.

4. On the next line, change #Total# to **#DollarFormat(Total)#**.

5. On the next line, change #TotalShip# to **#DollarFormat(TotalShip)#**.

6. Click the **Save** button on the Standard toolbar to save your changes, switch to the browser, and then reload the page. Your output now is formatted as currency, as shown in Figure 1-27.

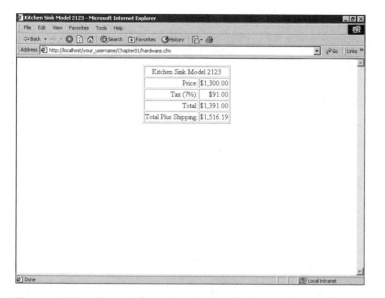

Figure 1-27   Output formatted using the DollarFormat function

The DollarFormat function has the syntax DollarFormat(an_expression). The DollarFormat function processes a value, a variable, or an expression that forms its input (also known as an **argument**) and returns the value formatted with a dollar sign and two decimal places. When you want to format numbers with two decimal places and without dollar signs, you can use the DecimalFormat function. The DecimalFormat function has the syntax DecimalFormat(an_expression). When you want to format numbers to more than two decimal places, use the NumberFormat function. The NumberFormat function has the syntax NumberFormat(an_expression, "a_mask"). The NumberFormat function formats a value, a variable, or an expression according to the rules specified by the mask. A **mask** is a series of special characters with a certain formatting significance. A mask can contain characters such as 9 and/or a period to specify the required formatting. A mask digit of 9 is used for a digit and the period shows the location of the decimal point in the output. If you want to format the result of an expression to three decimal places you could use the function NumberFormat(an_expression, "99999.999"). You can also use a comma in the mask to format numbers using commas to separate thousands. For example, NumberFormat(101100,",99999999.99") generates an output of 101,100.00. Notice that there is a comma before the first 9 inside the quotation marks, indicating that commas should be used to separate thousands. The online Help system provides a description of all the numeric and other functions available in ColdFusion. Some of the useful functions for manipulating numbers are summarized in Table 1-4.

Table 1-4   Useful Arithmetic Functions

Function Name	Description	Example
Abs	Returns the absolute value of a number	Abs(Error)
Ceiling	Returns the closest integer greater than a given number	Ceiling(NumberOfCartons)
DecrementValue	Returns integer part of number decremented by one	DecrementValue(Counter)
Exp	Returns *e* raised to the power of number; the constant *e* equals 2.71828182845904, the base of the natural logarithm	Exp(Log(6))
Fix	Returns the closest integer less than *number* if *number* is greater than or equal to 0; returns the closest integer greater than *number* if *number* is less than 0	Fix(NumberOfProducts)
IncrementValue	Returns integer part of *number* incremented by one	IncrementValue(Counter)
Int	Returns the closest integer smaller than a number	Int(Days/7)
Log	Returns the natural logarithm of a number; natural logarithms are based on the constant *e*	Log(Exp(3))
Log10	Returns the logarithm of number to base 10	Log10(1000)
Max	Returns the higher of two values; this function has two arguments	Max(Number1,Number2)
Min	Returns the lower of two values	Min(10,2)
Rand	Returns a random decimal number in the range 0 to 1	Rand()
Randomize	Seeds the random number generator in ColdFusion with the integer part of a number; returns a value between 0 and 1 that should be discarded	Randomize(1234)
RandRange	Returns a random integer between two specified numbers	RandRange(1,10)
Round	Rounds a number to the closest integer	Round(Number_of_Rows)
Sqr	Returns a positive square root of a number	Sqr(number)

BROWSING A COLDFUSION TEMPLATE USING THE INTERNAL BROWSER

To browse a ColdFusion template using the ColdFusion Studio internal browser, you have to first set up a development mapping. A **development mapping** tells ColdFusion Studio what URL to use for browsing a particular file that you are editing. After you set up a development mapping, you can use the Browse tab on the Editor window to browse ColdFusion templates.

To set up development mapping:

1. Switch to ColdFusion Studio, click **Options** on the menu bar, and then click **Settings**. The Settings dialog box opens, as shown in Figure 1-28. This dialog box has two panes. You can select a feature in the left pane and modify the settings in the right pane.

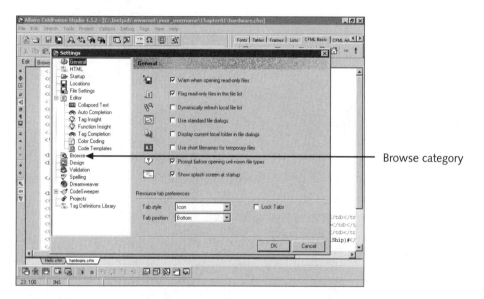

Figure 1-28   Settings dialog box

2. Select **Browse** in the left pane, and click the **Development Mappings** button in the right pane. The Remote Development Settings dialog box opens, as shown in Figure 1-29.

3. Click the **Select Folder** button for specifying the studio path. The Select Directory dialog box opens and displays the drives and folders on your computer.

4. Navigate to and select the **your_username** folder in **C:\Inetpub\wwwroot**.

The configuration you are using may be different. Your instructor will provide you with the information necessary for completing this section.

5. Click the **OK** button. The Remote Development Settings dialog box now shows the Studio Path as C:\Inetpub\wwwroot\your_username. The CF Server path is C:\Inetpub\wwwroot\your_username, and the Browser Path is http://127.0.0.1/.

6. Change the browser path to **http://localhost/your_username**, and then click the **Add** button. The mapping appears in the Mappings list. See Figure 1-30.

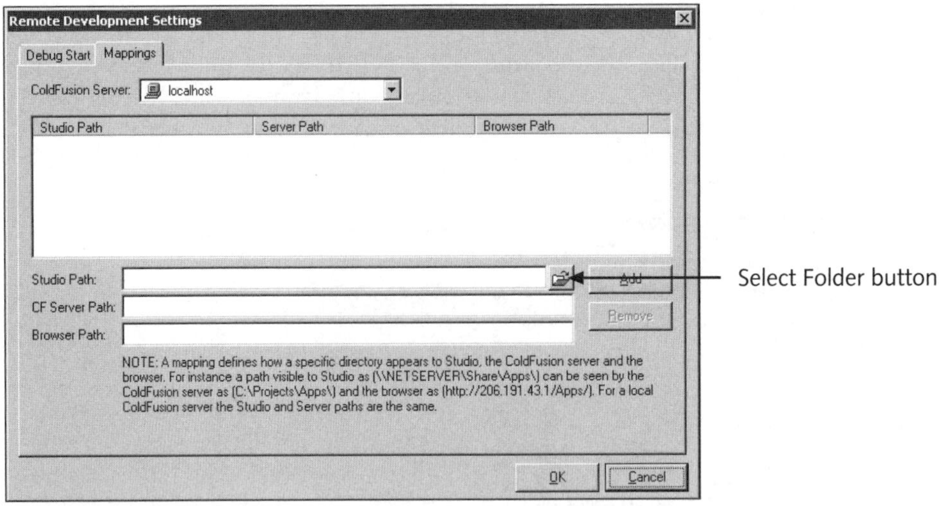

Figure 1-29   Remote Development Settings dialog box

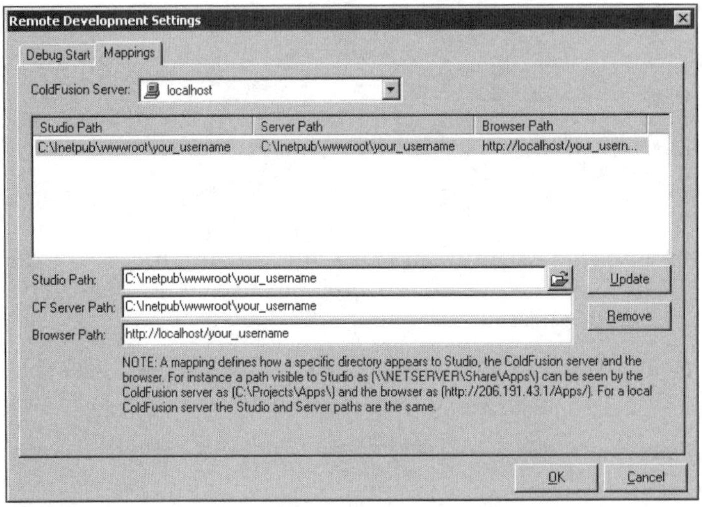

Figure 1-30   Remote Development Settings with the new mapping

7. Click the **OK** button to close the Remote Development Settings dialog box, and then click the **OK** button to close the Settings dialog box.

Once a mapping is set up you can easily browse ColdFusion templates.

To browse a ColdFusion template in ColdFusion Studio:

1. Click the **Browse tab** on the Editor window. The internal browser displays the page as it would appear if viewed in a Web browser. See Figure 1-31.

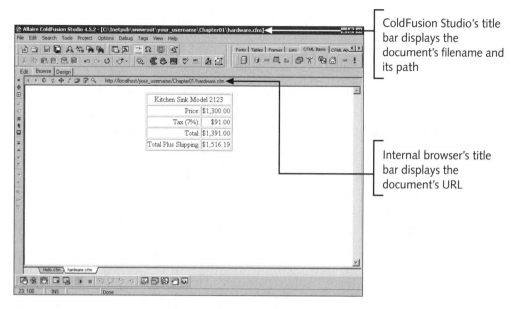

ColdFusion Studio's title bar displays the document's filename and its path

Internal browser's title bar displays the document's URL

Figure 1-31   Viewing a ColdFusion template using the internal browser

2. Click the **Close** button on the ColdFusion Studio title bar to close ColdFusion, and then click the **Close** button to close your browser.

CHAPTER SUMMARY

◻ The World Wide Web connects two types of computers: servers and clients. Servers have a Web server software installed that continuously listens to the network for client requests, and clients have a Web browser installed that can request documents from the Web server.

◻ Documents on Web servers are simple ASCII text files with HTML tags. HTML is an embedded language for formatting and displaying content in Web pages. HTML tags are enclosed in brackets and typically include an opening and closing tag. You can include optional attributes or attribute-value pairs in an opening tag to further modify a tag's function.

◻ CGI and API standards enhance the capability of a Web server to perform server-side processing. Server-side scripting languages are embedded languages that use these capabilities.

◻ ColdFusion is a complete Web application server for designing and delivering electronic commerce and other Web-based applications. It is a set of tools that allows you to rapidly create and deliver dynamic, interactive, data-driven, Web-based applications.

❏ ColdFusion has three components. First, ColdFusion Studio is a program for creating and editing HTML documents and CFML templates. Second, ColdFusion Server is a service running on the server that communicates with the Web server and processes ColdFusion templates. Third, the ColdFusion Administrator is a Web-based application that you use for setting parameters associated with the ColdFusion Server.

❏ ColdFusion Markup Language (CFML) is a server-side markup language that is used in combination with HTML to enable server-side processing by manipulating data, displaying output, and interacting with databases.

❏ In ColdFusion, the CFSET tag is used for creating and assigning values to ColdFusion variables.

❏ ColdFusion comment opening tags start with an opening bracket (<) and an exclamation point (!) and are followed by three dashes. The tag to close a ColdFusion comment is three dashes followed by a closing bracket (--->).

❏ ColdFusion allows you to work with integers as well as real numbers.

❏ You can use a CFSET tag to perform computations and assign results to variables.

❏ Arithmetic expressions are formed by combining values and/or variables and arithmetic operators in a logical manner.

❏ A CFOUTPUT tag displays values of variables enclosed in pound (#) signs.

❏ ColdFusion implements a system of operator precedence.

❏ You can use ColdFusion functions to format data for display as well as to perform complex computations.

REVIEW QUESTIONS

1. What is a ColdFusion Server? How does it enhance the capabilities of a Web server?

2. What happens when a Web server with a ColdFusion Server receives a request for a file that has a filename extension of .cfm?

3. What are variables? How do you assign values to variables?

4. What is the function of a CFSET tag?

5. What is CFML?

6. How do you include comments in a ColdFusion template?

7. What kinds of numbers can you use in a ColdFusion template? For each number type, give a brief example of its use.

8. What arithmetic operators can you use in a ColdFusion template?

9. What is operator precedence? Which operator has the highest precedence? Which operator has the lowest precedence?

10. What is the significance of using pound signs in a CFOUTPUT tag?

11. What function would you use to format a number with three decimal places?

HANDS-ON PROJECTS

Project 1: Create a Web Page to Compute Dollars and Cents

Use ColdFusion Studio to create the Web page shown in Figure 1-32. This page displays the total value of coins in cents and dollars in an HTML table. First, design the HTML document with the table and the labels. Then use CFSET tags at the beginning of the document to initialize the following variables with the following values: Pennies: 23; Nickels: 8; Dimes: 34, and Quarters: 12. Use two CFSET statements to initialize a Total_In_Cents variable and a Total variable. The Total_In_Cents variable computes Pennies * 1 plus Nickels * 5 plus Dimes * 10 plus Quarters * 25. The Total variable divides the results of the Total_In_Cents variable by 100. Enter the CFOUTPUT statements to display the resulting values in the second column. Format the Total output as currency. When you are finished, save the file as Ch1Pr1.cfm in the Chapter01 folder on the server, and then preview the output using the Browse tab.

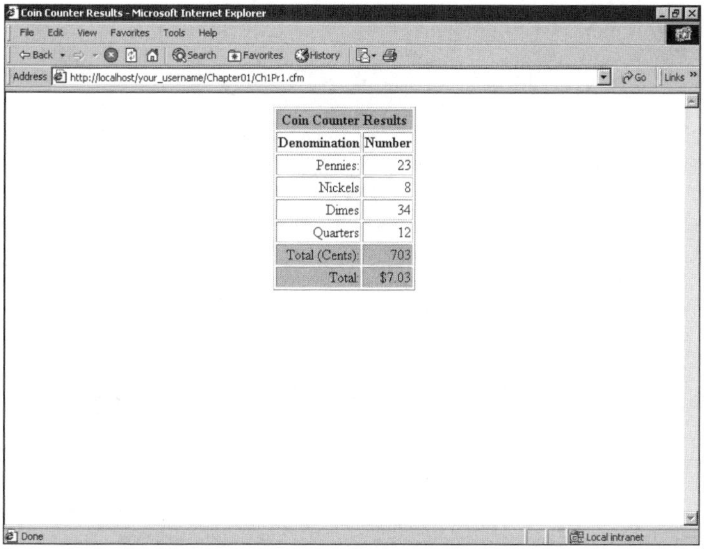

Coin Counter Results	
Denomination	Number
Pennies:	23
Nickels	8
Dimes	34
Quarters	12
Total (Cents):	703
Total	$7.03

Figure 1-32

Project 2: Create a Web Page to Add Products to a Shopping Cart

Use ColdFusion Studio to create the Web page shown in Figure 1-33. A user adds three products to a shopping cart at an e-commerce site selling software products. The company is currently offering a promotional discount of 15% and shipping is free. Design a ColdFusion template that shows the amount the user owes in an HTML table. Use CFSET tags to initialize the following variables with the following values: Price1 = 34.00, Price2 = 45.00, and Price3 = 56.00. Then create the following CFSET statements to calculate the discounted amounts: Net1 = Price1 * (1-15/100), Net2 = Price2 * (1 - 15/100), and Net3 = Price3 * (1 - 15/100). The Total variable is calculated using a CFSET statement with the expression Total = Net1 + Net2 + Net3. Use CFOUTPUT statements to format dollar values as currency. When you are finished, save the file as Ch1Pr2.cfm in the Chapter01 folder on the server, and then preview the output using the Browse tab.

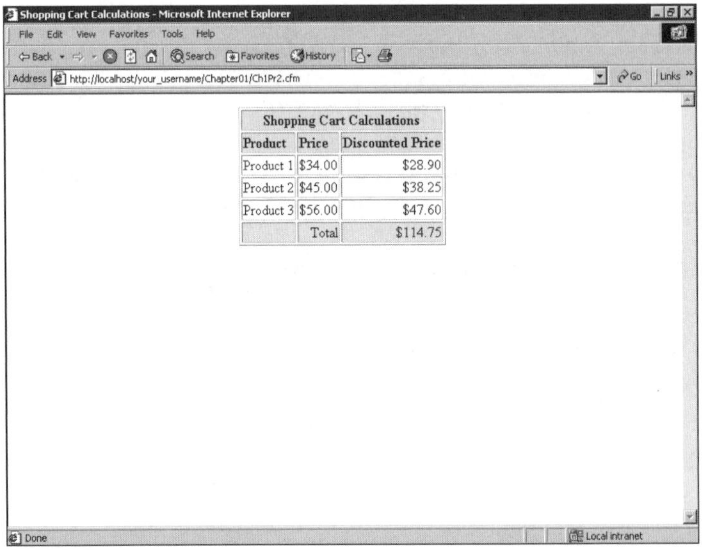

Figure 1-33

Project 3: Create a Web Page to Show Product Information

A department store is having a red tag sale. Red-tagged items are marked down 75%. As part of its promotional efforts, the department store wants you to set up a page on its Web site as shown in Figure 1-34. Design a ColdFusion template to show a product's price, discount, discounted price, sales tax, and total price. Use CFSET tags to assign 5.0 to variable Price, 0.75 to variable DiscountRate, and 0.07 to variable TaxRate. Compute Discount as Price * DiscountRate, DiscountedPrice as Price - Discount, Tax as DiscountedPrice * TaxRate, and TotalPrice as DiscountedPrice + Tax. The template's output should be formatted as an HTML table. Format dollar amounts as currency. When you are finished, save the file as Ch1Pr3.cfm in the Chapter01 folder on the server, and then view the output in your Web browser.

1

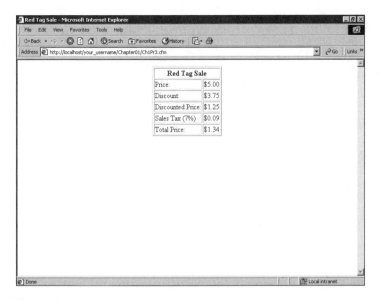

Figure 1-34

Project 4: Create a Web Page to Analyze Certificates of Deposit

A regional bank provides customer decision support tools on its Web site. They want you to provide a tool that would help customers with analysis of CDs (Certificates of Deposit). When a customer invests a particular amount in a CD (Principal), each year the customer earns interest at a particular interest rate (InterestRate). During the first year the interest is on the principal, and in the second year it is on the sum of the principal and the interest earned in the first year and so on. So if the term of the CD is TermYears, then the amount when the CD matures is Principal * (1 + InterestRate) ^ TermYears. Develop a ColdFusion template that uses variables for principal, interest rate, and term in years and computes and displays interest earned and amount at maturity. Assume that interest is compounded annually as in the formula given above. Compute the interest earned as Amount at maturity - Initial Investment. Format dollar amounts as currency and output the results in an HTML table, as shown in Figure 1-35. Use an amount of 1000 at a rate of 6% (0.06) for a term of 4 years to test your program. When you are finished, save the file as Ch1Pr4.cfm in the Chapter01 folder on the server, and then view the output using your Web browser.

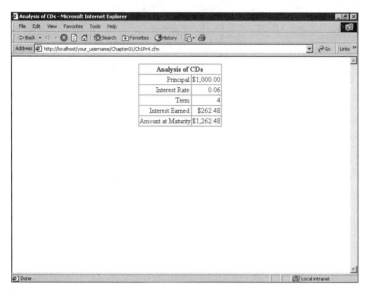

Figure 1-35

Project 5: Create a Web Page to Compute Commissions and Mileage Reimbursements

Sales persons in a networking services company earn a commission of 15% on every sale they make. They are also reimbursed for driving at a rate of $0.325 per mile. Employees can use a Web page on the company's intranet to compute their commissions and mileage reimbursements. Develop a ColdFusion template to perform computations and display commissions, mileage reimbursements, and total amount to be paid to the salespersons, as shown in Figure 1-36. Use CFSET tags and initialize variables SaleAmount and MilesDriven. Use values of $3,500.00 and 64 miles as test data. Compute and display initial values and computations neatly formatted using HTML tables. Display dollar amounts as currency. When you are finished, save the file as Ch1Pr5.cfm in the Chapter01 folder on the server, and then preview the output using your Web browser. Start by initializing variables CommissionRate, MileageRate, SaleAmount, and MilesDriven. Compute Commission as SaleAmount * CommissionRate and MileageReimbursement as MilesDriven * MileageRate. Compute the total amount paid to the sales person as the sum of Commission and MileageReimbursement.

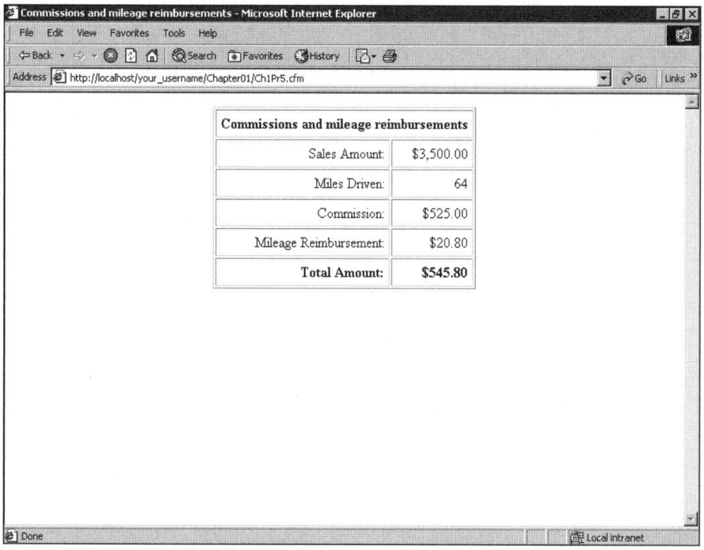

Figure 1-36

Project 6: Create a Web Page to Calculate Retirement Information

An online discount stock brokerage provides tools for assisting customers in planning for their retirement. When a customer invests $5000.00 each year in bonds and $10,000.00 each year in stocks, how much would the customer have in 20 years? Use a ColdFusion template to calculate and display appropriately formatted amounts, as shown in Figure 1-37. Assume that bonds yield 6% per year and stocks yield 12% per year. If an amount 'a' is invested each year in an investment that yields 'r%' rate of return, then amount accumulated over 'n' number of years is given by the expression:

$$\frac{a(1-(1+\frac{r}{100})^{n})}{(1-(1+\frac{r}{100}))}$$

When you are finished, save the file as Ch1Pr6.chm in the Chapter01 folder on the server, and then view the output using a Web browser.

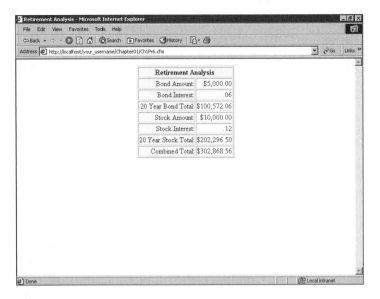

Figure 1-37

Project 7: Create a Web Page to Create Financial Statements

A credit card company displays customer monthly statements online on the Web. The starting balance for a customer for the month of May is $345.00. During the month, a customer made a few purchases that total $134.00 and made a payment of $250.00. Develop a ColdFusion template to show the customer's statement summary, as shown in Figure 1–38. Display dollar amounts as currency. When you are finished, save the file as Ch1Pr7.cfm in the Chapter01 folder on the server, and then view your output using a Web browser.

Project 8: Create a Web Page to Calculate the Price of Silver

Silver costs U.S. $5.08 per ounce. A North American precious metals dealer wants to post the cost of silver in both dollars per ounce and dollars per gram on his Web site. One ounce equals 28 grams. Develop a ColdFusion template to compute and display the cost of silver in both units in an HTML table, as shown in Figure 1–39. The template should also display the cost per ounce and per gram in Canadian dollars. Assume that one U.S. dollar is worth 1.4743 Canadian dollars. Display dollar amounts as currency. When you are finished, save the file as Ch1Pr8.cfm in the Chapter01 folder on the server, and then view the output using your Web browser. Because one ounce equals 28 grams, the cost of 28 grams is $5.08. One gram would cost 5.08 / 28. Because one U.S. dollar is worth 1.4743 Canadian dollars, 1 ounce of silver would cost 5.08 * 1.4743 Canadian dollars. Use a variable named ExchangeRate, and assign it a value of 1.4743. Use a variable named CostOfSilver, and assign it a value of 5.08. Use variables named CANSilverOunce, CANSilverGram, and USSilverGram for the price of an ounce of silver in Canadian dollars, the price of a gram of silver in Canadian dollars, and the price of a gram of silver in U.S. dollars, respectively.

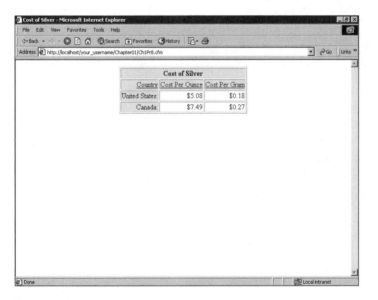

Figure 1-38

Figure 1-39

CASE PROJECTS

1. Identify some of the basic tasks performed by ColdFusion on the system used by OneTravel.com located at *www.onetravel.com*.

2. Research the case studies available at *www.macromedia.com*, and write a one-page report on how companies are using ColdFusion.

3. Investigate *www.w3.org*, and write one-page summary on the recent developments in the HTTP specification.

CHAPTER

2

URL PARAMETERS, STRINGS, AND OTHER DATA TYPES

In this chapter, you will:

♦ Learn about URL parameters
♦ Create interactive Web pages that process URL parameters
♦ Learn about strings, date-time values, and Boolean data types
♦ Use ColdFusion string variables, expressions, and functions
♦ Create and use ColdFusion date-time variables
♦ Format date-time values
♦ Learn about Boolean functions
♦ Learn about typeless expression evaluation

In Chapter 1, you used ColdFusion Studio for editing, saving, and browsing HTML documents and ColdFusion templates. You also used CFML and saw how it relates to programming languages. You used variables and constants and manipulated them with the CFSET tag by using arithmetic expressions and mathematical functions. Most of what you did in Chapter 1 involved initializing, processing, and outputting numbers. In this chapter, you will first learn about passing data to ColdFusion templates by using URL parameters and then learn about other types of data including strings, dates and times, and Boolean values, that you can process using ColdFusion.

URL PARAMETER PROCESSING

In Chapter 1, you learned how to initialize variables, perform computations, and display results while working with Cold Fusion templates. Although the templates process information, they are not truly dynamic. You must use ColdFusion Studio to modify the values assigned to variables in the CFSET tags. For example, suppose the sales tax rate used in the Kitchen Sink template changes from 7% to 5%; you must use the editor and change the value assigned to the TaxRate variable from 0.07 to 0.05.

To update Web documents, the HTTP specification allows you to pass data to a ColdFusion document by appending name-value pairs to its URL. You must create the name-value pairs using specific characters that define the **URL parameters**. For example, you can pass data to the hardware.cfm ColdFusion template by appending a name-value pair to its URL as follows:

```
http://localhost/your_username/Chapter01/hardware.cfm?
TaxRate=0.05
```

Note that a questionmark (?) follows the name of the document and an equal sign (=) comes between the parameter name and its value. These URL parameters indicate that the TaxRate variable in the hardware.cfm document should change to 0.05.

You can append multiple parameters to URLs by using an ampersand (&) between name-value pairs as follows:

```
http://localhost/your_username/Chapter01/hardware.cfm?
TaxRate=0.05&ShippingRate=0.06
```

In this example, the parameters in the URL indicate that the TaxRate variable in hardware.cfm should change to 0.05 and the ShippingRate variable should change to 0.06.

When the Web server receives a URL with parameters, it uses Web server API to send the data to the ColdFusion Server. The ColdFusion Server creates special variables using the URL data it receives from the Web server and then executes the ColdFusion template. You access the data in the URL parameters by using variables of the form URL.parameter_name. In hardware.cfm, for example, you access the data in the URL parameters by using variables in the following form:

```
URL.TaxRate and URL.ShippingRate
```

Note the period in each variable name. These variables are said to be in the URL **scope**.

In the following example, you will modify the hardware.cfm template and make it a truly interactive template that can receive and process a parameter in its URL.

To create and view a template that processes a URL parameter:

1. Start ColdFusion Studio.

2. If the Editor window occupies the entire screen and the Resource Tab window is not visible, click the **Resource Tab** button to display the Resource Tab window.

3. If necessary, click the **Files** tab at the bottom of the window. In the Files Window, navigate to the Chapter02 subfolder in your Data Disk folder.

4. Double-click **hardware.cfm** to open it for editing. This is a copy of the hardware.cfm template you created at the end of the exercises in Chapter 1.

5. Click the **Resource Tab** button to close the Resource Tab window. See Figure 2-1.

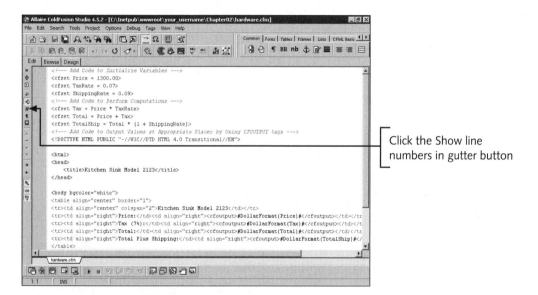

Click the Show line numbers in gutter button

Figure 2-1   The initial hardware.cfm document

6. Click the **Show line numbers in gutter** button on the Editor toolbar. Line numbers appear in the gutter, as shown in Figure 2-2. The insertion point appears in line 1, column 1.

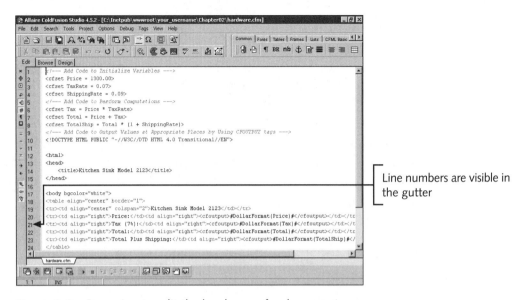

Line numbers are visible in the gutter

Figure 2-2 Preparing to edit the hardware.cfm document

7. Select **0.07** in line 3, and type **URL.TaxRate** to modify the CFSET tag to <cfset TaxRate = URL.TaxRate>. See Figure 2-3.

As mentioned earlier, when the ColdFusion Server executes this document and finds the URL parameter, it creates a variable named URL.TaxRate. You are assigning the value of this variable to the original variable named TaxRate. The value of the parameter that the user passes to the document is now assigned to the variable named TaxRate. ColdFusion performs computations and produces results as usual. Note that TaxRate and URL.TaxRate are two different variables. ColdFusion creates URL.TaxRate when it receives the URL parameter and it creates TaxRate when it processes the CFSET tag. You can use different names for the parameter and the variable if you wish.

8. Select **7%** on line 21, and type **<cfoutput>#TaxRate#**. Note that the closing </cfoutput> is inserted by ColdFusion Studio. See Figure 2-3.

9. Click the **Save** button on the Standard toolbar to save the document.

10. Start your Web browser.

11. Select the text in the address Field and type **http://localhost/ your_username/Chapter02/hardware.cfm?TaxRate=0.05**, and press **Enter**. See Figure 2-4. The ColdFusion Server executes the hardware.cfm template and uses a value of 0.05 as the TaxRate.

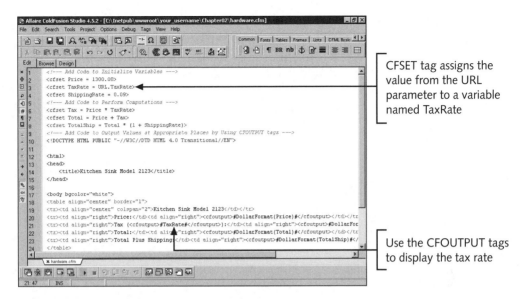

CFSET tag assigns the value from the URL parameter to a variable named TaxRate

Use the CFOUTPUT tags to display the tax rate

Figure 2-3   The modified hardware.cfm document

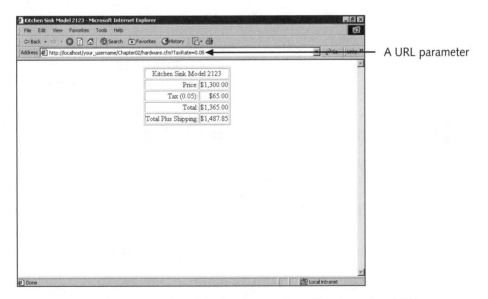

A URL parameter

Figure 2-4   Web page produced by hardware.cfm with a tax rate of 5%

12. Change the tax rate value passed to the hardware.cfm template by modifying its URL to **http://localhost/your_username/Chapter02/ hardware.cfm?TaxRate=0.09** and pressing **Enter**. See Figure 2-5.

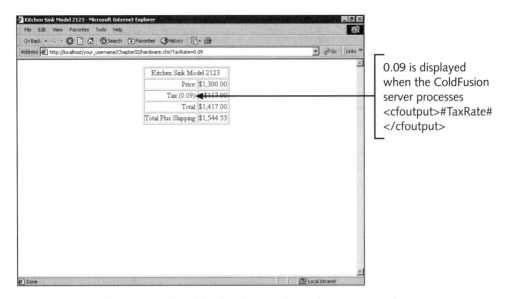

Figure 2-5   Web page produced by hardware.cfm with a tax rate of 9%

The costs of the kitchen sink are computed with a new value for the tax rate.

You will receive an unsolved parameter error if you invoke the document without any URL parameters by using http://localhost/your_username/Chapter02/ hardware.cfm. In a later chapter, you will learn about assigning default values for URL parameters to prevent this kind of error.

Using URLs with Parameters in Anchor Tags

Obviously, you can't expect users to type URLs along with name-value pairs in address fields of Web browsers. A useful way of passing parameters to ColdFusion documents is to create hyperlinks in other documents by using HTML anchor tags. To create a hyperlink that contains name-value pairs as URL parameters, use the following syntax:

```
<a href="relative orabsolute URL?
a_parameter=a_value&another_parameter=another_value...">
hyperlink text</a>
```

For example, the following HTML code creates a hyperlink that invokes the ColdFusion document for displaying the results using a tax rate of 6.5%:

```
<a href="hardware.cfm?TaxRate=0.065">Minnesota</a>
```

The kitchen supply company you worked with in Chapter 1 must charge sales tax in Illinois, Iowa, and Minnesota because it has retail operations in those states. They do not need to charge for sales tax in other states. You have been asked to design a Web page that would provide cost information depending on where the product is being shipped. Use a sales tax rate of 8.00% for Illinois shipments, 7.00% for Iowa shipments, 6.25% for Minnesota shipments, and 0.00% for shipments to all other states. An HTML document named states.htm is available on your data disk. It contains a list of all states. You must create hyperlinks to the hardware.cfm template with relevant parameters in it.

To create hyperlinks to ColdFusion templates that process URL parameters:

1. Switch to ColdFusion Studio.

2. Click **File** on the menu bar, and then click **Open**. ColdFusion Studio displays a file Open dialog box. See Figure 2-6.

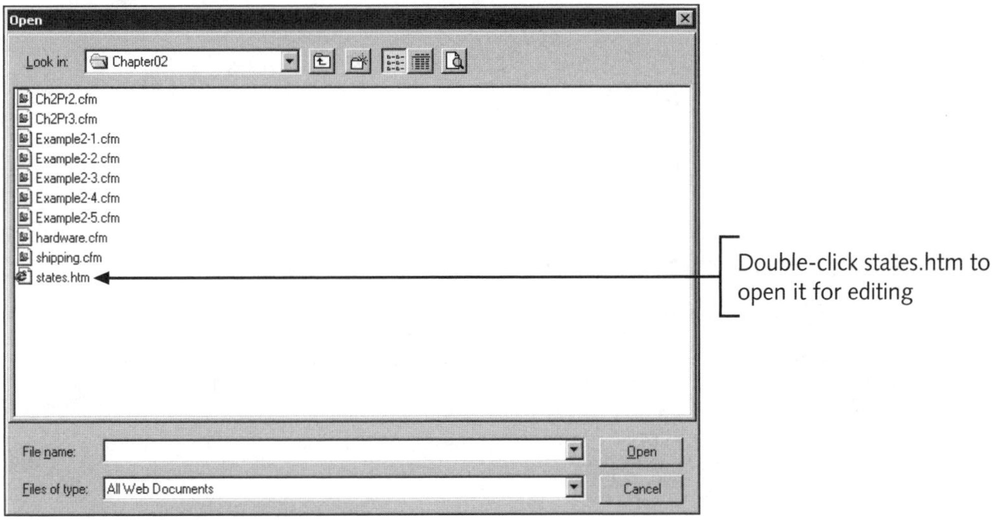

Double-click states.htm to open it for editing

Figure 2-6 File Open dialog box

3. Double-click **states.htm** to open it for editing. See Figure 2-7.

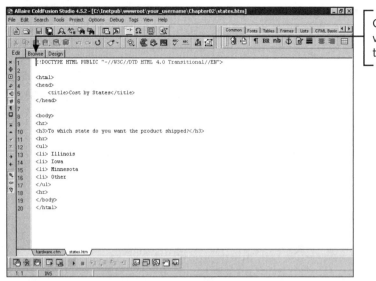

Click the Browse tab to view the document using the internal browser

Figure 2-7 Editing the states.htm document

4. Click the **Browse** tab to see what the document looks like in the internal Web browser. See Figure 2-8.

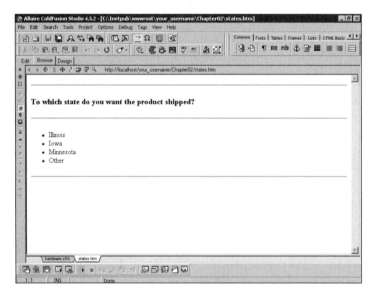

Figure 2-8 Web page displayed by states.htm in the internal browser

Your task is to create hyperlinks by inserting anchor tags around each of the items in the list. When the user clicks any of the hyperlinks, the cost of the kitchen sink should appear using the appropriate sales tax rate for that state. For example, when the user clicks Illinois, the kitchen sink total cost information should include a sales tax rate of 8.00%.

5. Click the **Edit** tab to switch back to the editor.

6. Select **Illinois** in line 13. See Figure 2-9. Click the **Anchor** button in the Common QuickBar. The Tag Editor – A dialog box opens.

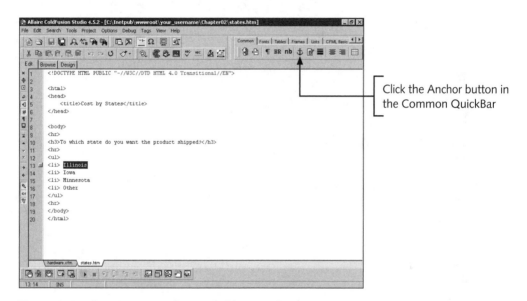

Click the Anchor button in the Common QuickBar

Figure 2-9   Creating an anchor in ColdFusion Studio

7. Type **hardware.cfm?TaxRate=0.08** in the HREF text box. See Figure 2-10.

8. Click the **OK** button. ColdFusion Studio inserts a set of anchor tags around Illinois. See Figure 2-11.

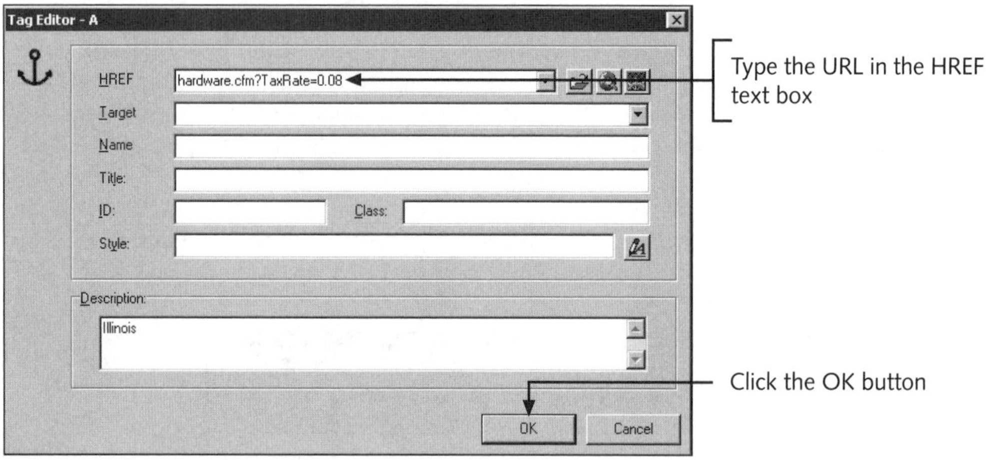

Figure 2-10   The Tag Editor – A dialog box

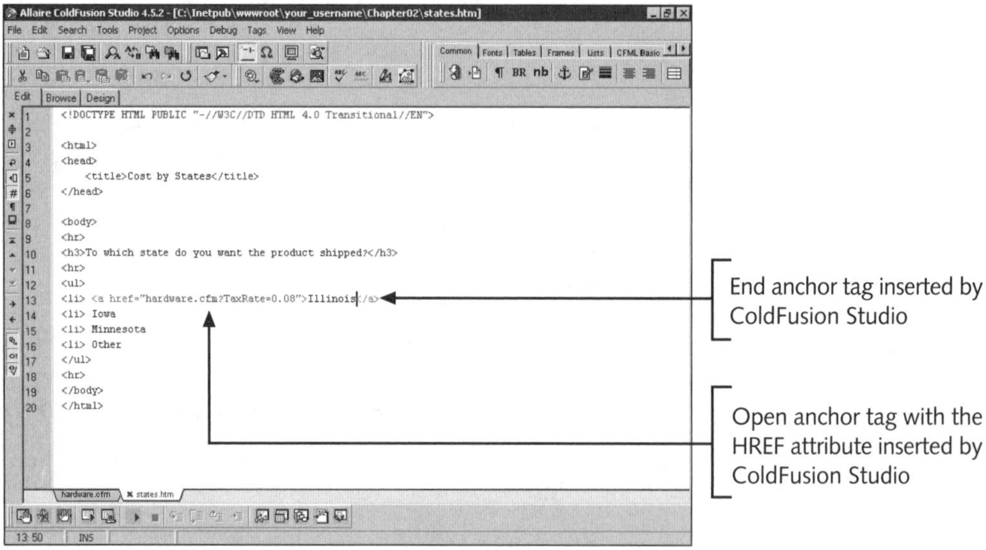

Figure 2-11   States.htm document with an anchor tag

9. Insert another anchor tag for Iowa with an HREF attribute set to **hardware.cfm?TaxRate=0.07**.

10. Insert an anchor tag for Minnesota with an HREF attribute set to **hardware.cfm?TaxRate=0.0625**.

11. Finally, insert an anchor tag for Other with an HREF attribute set to **hardware.cfm?TaxRate=0.00**. See Figure 2-12.

2

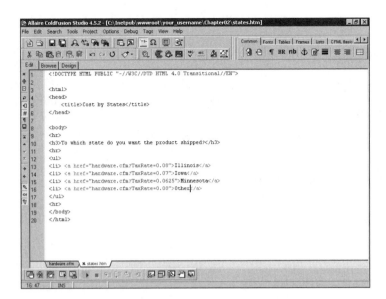

Figure 2-12   States.htm document with four hyperlinks

12. Click the **Save** button on the Standard toolbar to save the file.

13. Switch to your Web browser and open **http://localhost/your_username/ Chapter02/states.htm**. See Figure 2-13.

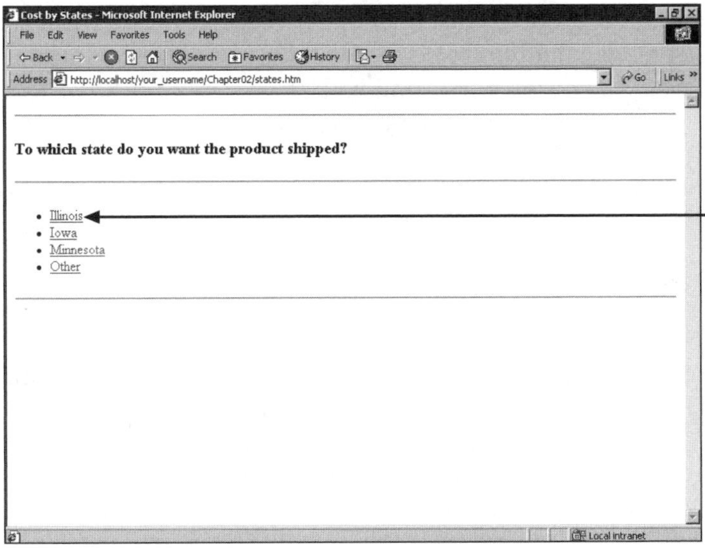

Click the Illinois hyperlink

Figure 2-13   Web page produced by states.htm in the Web browser

14. Click **Illinois**.

The page sends a request to the Web server for hardware.cfm along with a URL parameter and a value. The Web server invokes the ColdFusion Server and passes it the data on the URL. The ColdFusion Server creates a variable named URL.TaxRate and starts executing the hardware.cfm template. Variables are initialized to appropriate values, variable TaxRate is assigned the value of 0.08, computations are performed, and the results are incorporated into an HTML document. The HTML document is sent to the Web server, which in turn sends it to the client. The Web browser receives the HTML document and displays it as shown in Figure 2-14.

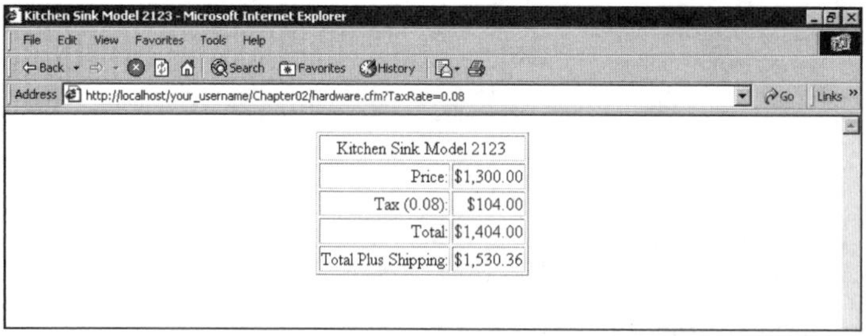

Figure 2-14   Web page displayed by the browser after you click Illinois

15. Click the **Back** button on your browser toolbar and click another hyperlink. Then close all open windows.

The Web page the browser displays after you click Illinois (see Figure 2-14) doesn't clearly show that the tax rate is for the state of Illinois. What if the user had accidentally clicked Iowa instead of clicking Illinois? How would the user know? It would be very helpful to display the name of the state along with the tax rate in the cost table. To do that, you need to pass URL parameters with text data, such as state names, instead of numbers, such as tax rates. You will learn how to use URL parameters for passing text data like state names and processing them in ColdFusion templates in the next section.

USING STRING VARIABLES

Traditionally, computer processing has involved working with numbers. Today, developers more often use computer systems to work with text rather than numbers. Word processing, electronic mail, and Web browsers are all popular computer applications that process text. They require mechanisms for storing and manipulating text that are similar to the methods they have for storing and manipulating numbers. ColdFusion, similar to other programming or scripting languages, allows you to store text in variables and then to manipulate these variables.

String variables are similar to numeric variables—they are named locations in the computer's memory that store values. With string variables, however, the values are text

2

rather than numbers. The rules for naming variables that store text are similar to those for storing numeric data [that is, string variable names must begin with a letter and can consist of letters, numbers, or the underscore character (_)].

You can assign text to string variables by using a CFSET tag. Text that should be treated as a string is enclosed in quotation marks so the ColdFusion Server can distinguish it as text and not as another variable. For example, "Waterloo" is text data and Waterloo is a variable; therefore, a valid CFSET statement that assigns the text data Waterloo to a variable named City is <cfset City = "Waterloo"> and *not* <cfset City = Waterloo>. Using traditional programming language terminology, text data such as "Waterloo" is also called a **string literal**.

Using CFSET tags, developers can assign values (text data or string literals) to variables and then output them by using CFOUTPUT tags. String variables in <cfoutput></cfoutput> tags that are enclosed in pound (#) signs are processed like their numerical counterparts— text stored inside variables enclosed in pound signs is output when the ColdFusion Server encounters it.

In commercial Web sites, Web pages such as hardware.cfm would be much larger—they would include menus, advertisements, navigation bars, graphics, and other elements. If the hardware store creates a template that it can use for many different products, it should use variables, not only for prices and tax rates, but also for product names. You can initialize these variables at the top of the page and then use CFOUTPUT statements in the appropriate places to display them. When information changes, such as when prices increase or tax rates change, you only have to change the values of these variables, and the ColdFusion Server does the processing and output for you.

Next, you will change the product name to a variable that stores text data. To create variables that store text:

1. Start ColdFusion Studio.

2. Click **File**, click **Open**, and navigate to the Chapter02 subfolder in your Data Disk folder.

3. Double-click **hardware.cfm** to open it for editing.

4. With the insertion point on line 1, column 1, press the **Enter** key, and then press the **Up Arrow** key to move to the new line.

5. Click the **CFML Basic** tab in the QuickBar, click the **ColdFusion Comment** button to insert the opening and closing comment tags, type **Add Code to Initialize String Variable ProductName**, and then press the **End** key.

6. Press **Enter**, and then type **<cfset ProductName = "Kitchen Sink Model 2123">**.

This code will create a variable named ProductName and store the text value "Kitchen Sink Model 2123" in it. The product's name also appears in the browser's title bar and in the first table row when the page is displayed in a browser. You can change these items and display the product name using the string stored in the variable, or you can create another string variable named docTitle and assign the value stored in the ProductName variable. In the next step, you use the variable named docTitle. In a later exercise, you will modify this variable by adding the name of the state for which the cost is displayed.

7. Press **Enter** and type **<cfset docTitle = ProductName>**. When the ColdFusion Server processes this statement, the value of the variable ProductName (Kitchen Sink Model 2123) will be assigned to variable docTitle. Note that there are no quotation marks around ProductName because it is a variable.

8. Click at the end of line 11, which creates the TotalShip variable, press **Enter**, and then create the following comment: **Add Code to Output Product Name in Title Bar (docTitle) as well as in Table Header (ProductName).**

9. Select the text **Kitchen Sink Model 2123** in the TITLE tags, and then type **<cfoutput>#docTitle#** (ColdFusion Studio will add the closing CFOUTPUT tag for you).

10. On line 23 (which creates the first row in the table), select the text **Kitchen Sink Model 2123**, and then type **<cfoutput>#ProductName#**. ColdFusion Studio will add the closing CFOUTPUT tag for you. See Figure 2-15.

11. Click the **Save** button on the Standard toolbar to save the program.

12. Start your Web browser, and open the document **states.htm** from your Chapter02 subfolder on your Data Disk (http://localhost/your_username/Chapter02/states.htm).

13. Click **Illinois**. Your Web browser displays the hardware.cfm document with a URL parameter TaxRate set to a value of 0.08. See Figure 2-16. Note that this is the hardware.cfm document with string variables.

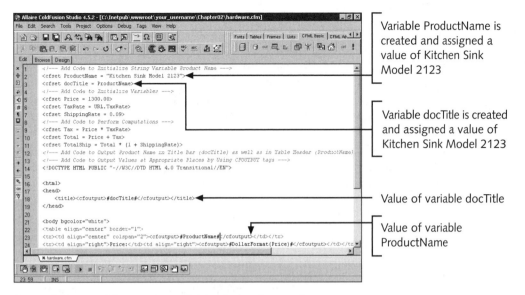

Figure 2-15   Adding string variables to hardware.cfm

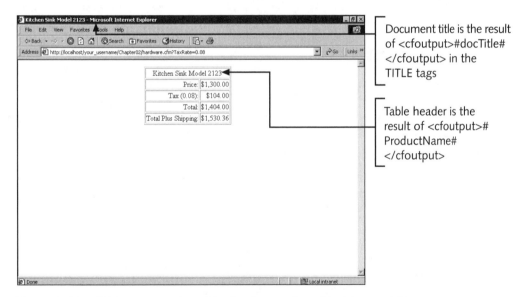

Figure 2-16   Web page produced by hardware.cfm with string variables

Notice that the quotation marks in the CFSET tag do not appear in the output. The quotation marks are delimiters for the string literals; they are not actually part of the text data.

When the ColdFusion Server encounters the tag <cfset ProductName = "Kitchen Sink Model 2123">, a variable named ProductName is created and assigned a text value of "Kitchen Sink Model 2123." When ColdFusion Server processes the tag <cfset docTitle = ProductName>, a variable named docTitle is created and assigned the same value of "Kitchen Sink Model 2123." When the ColdFusion Server encounters the tag <title><cfoutput>#docTitle#</cfoutput></title>, the TITLE tags are transmitted as HTML, and the CFOUTPUT tags make the ColdFusion Server look for variables enclosed in pound signs and substitute the value stored in the variable named docTitle for #docTitle#. CFOUTPUT processing is turned off by the closing tag (</cfoutput>), and the document's title is transmitted as HTML (<title>Kitchen Sink Model 2123</title>). In other words, you set the document's title by using a variable's output.

The first row of the table, where you entered <cfoutput>#ProductName#</cfoutput>, is processed in the same manner. The surrounding HTML tags are not changed, but the CFOUTPUT tag changes the enclosed variable to its stored value, which is Kitchen Sink Model 2123.

 Because quotation marks are used as delimiters for string literals, you must type two quotation marks together to produce a quotation mark in the output. For example, a browser would display the variable stored as <cfset Name = "William ""Buck"" Rogers"> as William "Buck" Rogers in the output.

Using String URL Parameters

Similar to how you created interactive Web pages by using numeric URL parameters in the previous exercises, you can create interactive Web pages that process string URL parameters with text data. The format for string URL parameters is similar to numeric URL parameters. For example, you can pass text data to the hardware.cfm ColdFusion template by appending a name-value pair to its URL as follows:

```
http://localhost/your_username/Chapter01/hardware.cfm?
State=Iowa
```

You can append multiple parameters to URLs by using the & sign between name-value pairs. These parameters can be of the same type or different types. For example, the following URL is a valid URL with parameters:

```
http://localhost/your_username/Chapter01/hardware.cfm?TaxR
ate=0.08&State=Illinois
```

When the Web server receives such a URL with parameters, it uses Web server API to send the data to the ColdFusion Server. The ColdFusion Server creates two variables named URL.TaxRate and URL.State. It also assigns values 0.08 and "Illinois" to the variables.

As mentioned previously, you can make the hardware Web page easier to interpret and use by displaying the name of the state along with the tax rate. In the following exercise, you will modify the hardware.cfm template so that it can receive and process a string parameter in its URL. First you will edit states.htm to pass in the additional parameter, and then you will edit the hardware.cfm file to receive and process the additional parameter.

To create a template for processing string URL parameters:

1. Switch to ColdFusion Studio.

2. Click **File**, click **Open**, navigate to the Chapter02 folder if necessary, and double-click **states.htm** to open it for editing.

3. Insert the cursor on line 13, position 40, between 0.08 and " in the anchor tag for the state of Illinois, and type **&State=Illinois** to modify the anchor tag to **<a href="hardware.cfm?TaxRate=0.08&State=Illinois">**. See Figure 2-17.

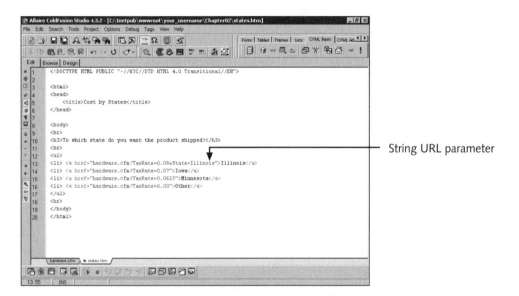

String URL parameter

Figure 2-17   Editing states.htm document to pass string URL parameters

4. Modify the anchor tag for Iowa to:

   <a href="hardware.cfm?TaxRate=0.07&State=Iowa">

5. Modify the anchor tag for Minnesota to:

   <a href="hardware.cfm?TaxRate=0.0625&State=Minnesota">

6. Modify the anchor tag for other states to:

   <a href="hardware.cfm?TaxRate=0.00&State=Other">

7. Click the **Save** button on the Standard toolbar to save the document.

8. Click the **hardware.cfm** tab in the document list tab at the bottom to edit the document. Your next task is to modify the hardware.cfm template to receive and process the State URL parameter.

9. Insert the cursor at the end of line 6 where you are initializing the variable TaxRate using the URL.TaxRate variable created by ColdFusion Server, and press the **Enter** key.

10. Type **<cfset State = URL.State>** to initialize a variable named State to the value of the URL parameter named State.

11. Modify line 26 and change the output of the tax rate from:

   <cfoutput>#TaxRate#</cfoutput> to
   <cfoutput>#TaxRate# - #State#</cfoutput>

   See Figure 2-18.

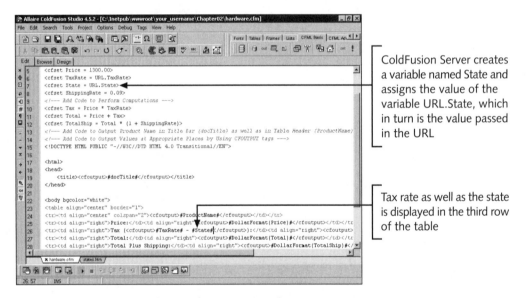

ColdFusion Server creates a variable named State and assigns the value of the variable URL.State, which in turn is the value passed in the URL

Tax rate as well as the state is displayed in the third row of the table

Figure 2-18   Editing hardware.cfm to process the State URL parameter

12. Save the document.

13. Switch to your Web browser and open **http://localhost/your_username/ Chapter02/states.htm**.

14. Click the **Refresh** (or **Reload**) button on the toolbar of your Web browser to make sure that the document is the most recent version of the states.htm document.

15. Move the pointer over **Illinois**, and examine the status bar to see that the URL consists of two URL parameters, TaxRate and State. See Figure 2-19.

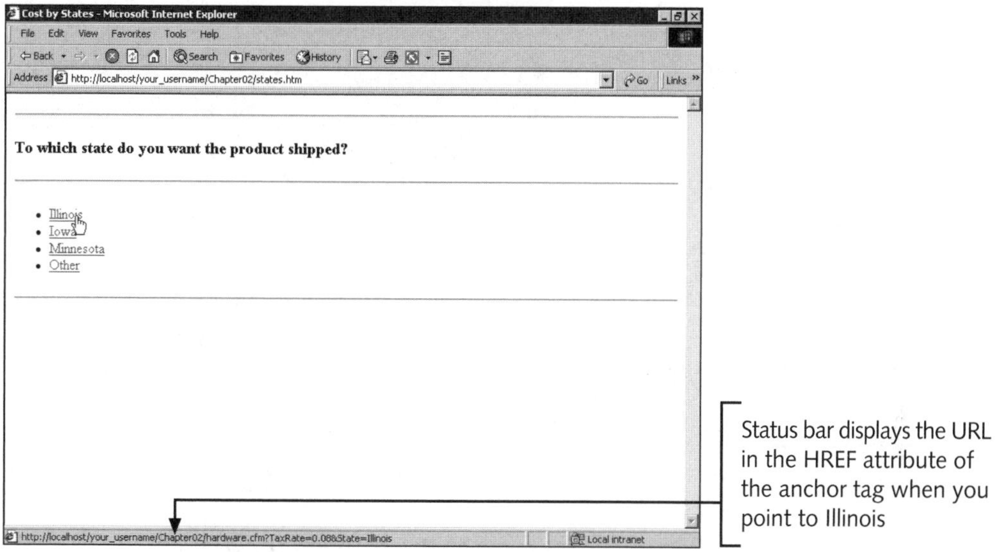

Status bar displays the URL in the HREF attribute of the anchor tag when you point to Illinois

Figure 2-19   Web page displayed by the newly modified states.htm document

16. Click **Iowa**.

A request is sent to the Web server for hardware.cfm along with two URL parameters and their values. The Web server invokes the ColdFusion Server and passes it the data on the URL. The ColdFusion Server creates variables named URL.TaxRate and URL.State and starts executing the hardware.cfm template. Variables are initialized to appropriate values, numeric variable TaxRate is assigned the value of 0.08, string variable State is assigned the value of "Iowa", computations are performed, and the results are incorporated into the HTML document generated. The tax rate is displayed along with the name of the state in the third row of the table when the ColdFusion Server processes <cfoutput>#TaxRate - #State#</cfoutput>. The HTML document is sent to the Web server, which in turn sends it to the client. The Web browser receives the HTML document and displays it, as shown in Figure 2-20.

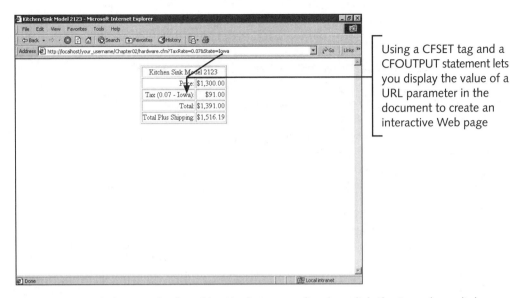

Using a CFSET tag and a CFOUTPUT statement lets you display the value of a URL parameter in the document to create an interactive Web page

Figure 2-20   Web page displayed by the browser after you click the Iowa hyperlink

17. Click the **Back** button on the toolbar of your Web browser, and experiment by clicking the other hyperlinks.

You have successfully created a template for processing string URL parameters and created hyperlinks to it in another document.

You may have noticed in the previous exercise that the output makes sense when you click Illinois, Iowa, and Minnesota, but it doesn't make sense when you click Other. The caption in the table Tax (0.00 – Other) is not informative when viewed by itself. What does Other mean? It means that the state is not Illinois, Iowa, or Minnesota; specifically, it is a mail-order sale that does not require sales tax. A caption such as Tax (0.00 – Mail Order) is more informative than Tax (0.00 – Other). However, you cannot use a value of Mail Order for the State URL parameter instead of Other because "Mail Order" contains a space. To use special characters such as spaces, you must encode them in the URL.

Encoding URL Special Characters

Certain characters such as /, :, ?, =, and & have a special meaning in URLs. If you want to use these characters as values for your URL parameters, you must encode them to prevent errors. Suppose you have a URL of a ColdFusion document to which you want to pass a string literal containing multiple words and spaces, such as "Mail Order." The use of spaces in URLs will confuse some browsers. You must encode spaces in URLs by using the code %20. You encode characters by using a three-character code: a percent sign and two hexadecimal digits indicating the position of the character in the ASCII table. Typically, any character other than a letter, number, or any of the characters $, -, _, +, !, *, ', and (), should be encoded.

To encode URL special characters and view a ColdFusion document:

1. Select the text in the address Field of your Web browser.

2. Type **http://localhost/your_username/Chapter02/hardware.cfm? TaxRate=0.00&State=Mail%20Order**, and press the **Enter** key.

The %20 is translated into a space character by the Web server and passed to the ColdFusion Server along with the rest of the data in the URL parameters. The ColdFusion Server processes these values by creating URL-scoped variables similar to the previous exercises to produce the Web page shown in Figure 2-21.

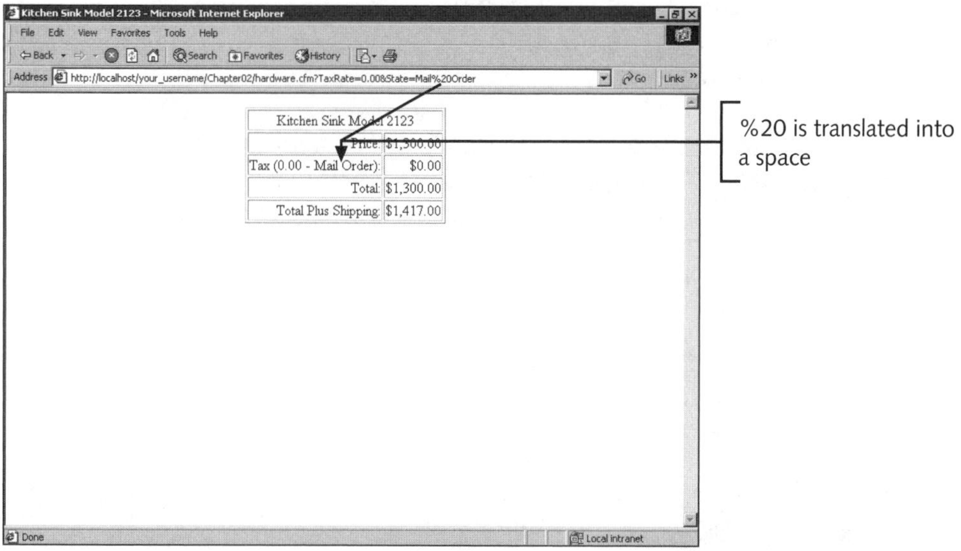

%20 is translated into a space

Figure 2-21   Web page with encoded characters produced by hardware.cfm

Tip

The HTTP specification allows you to use the plus sign (+) character to represent a space in URLs because it is a common character and saves some typing. In the previous exercise, typing
http://localhost/your_username/Chapter02/
hardware.cfm?TaxRate=0.00&State=Mail+Order
would produce the same result as typing
http://localhost/your_username/Chapter02/
hardware.cfm?TaxRate=0.00&State=Mail%20Order.

Obviously, you can't expect users to encode characters and type them in URLs. As you did before, you have to provide links in other documents to such templates. Even when providing hyperlinks in other documents, it is difficult for developers to remember codes for all special characters. ColdFusion makes such a task easy for you by providing a string function that encodes URL special characters.

URLEncodedFormat Function

CFML offers you a function to encode characters and strings to make it easy for you to program ColdFusion documents with URL parameters. The URLEncodedFormat function takes as an argument a string and returns the value encoded using the encoded scheme. Use this function whenever you encode parameters passed on URLs in anchor tags.

Your Data Disk contains an example (Example2-1.cfm) that illustrates the use of the URLEncodedFormat function to generate a table of special characters and their encoding.

To explore the URLEncodedFormat function:

1. Switch to ColdFusion Studio.

2. Click **File**, click **Open**, and double-click **Example2-1.cfm** to open it for viewing. See Figure 2-22.

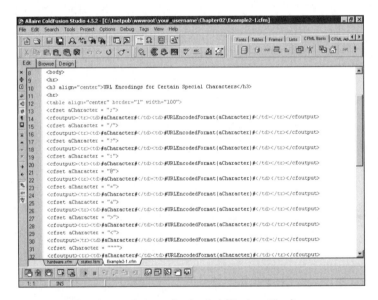

Figure 2-22   Example2-1.cfm in ColdFusion Studio

3. Study the example. Note that after it displays the header for the Web page, it creates an HTML table. Then it initializes a variable named aCharacter to the text data ";". In the table row, it displays the value of the variable aCharacter and then the value generated by the URLEncodedFormat function using aCharacter as its argument. In other words, it displays a special character in the first column and then its URL encoding in the second column. This process is repeated for other special characters. Then comes the table end tag and the rest of the document structuring end tags.

4. Switch to your Web browser.

5. Type **http://localhost/your_username/Chapter02/Example2-1.cfm** in the address field, and press **Enter** to open the example. See Figure 2-23.

2

```
URLEncodedFormat - Function - Microsoft Internet Explorer                     _ 8 X
File   Edit   View   Favorites   Tools   Help                                      
Back  -           Search   Favorites   History                          
Address   http://localhost/your_username/Chapter02/Example2-1.cfm          Go   Links »
```

URL Encodings for Certain Special Characters

;	%3B
/	%2F
?	%3F
:	%3A
@	%40
=	%3D
&	%26
>	%3E
<	%3C
"	%22
#	%23
%	%25
{	%7B
}	%7D
|	%7C

```
Done                                                          Local intranet
```

Figure 2-23   Web page produced by Example2-1.cfm

 Tip Notice that Example2-1 (see Figure 2-22) uses a pair of quotation marks for one quote character, as mentioned in the earlier section about string delimiters. In a later section, you will learn that pound signs (#) in string literals carry a special significance in ColdFusion; Example2-1 also uses a pair of pound signs (##) for one pound sign (#).

6. Close all open programs.

To create hyperlinks using the URLEncodedFormat function:

1. Start ColdFusion Studio, and open the **states.htm** HTML document from the Chapter02 subfolder on your Data Disk.

2. Click **File**, click **Save As**, and type **states.cfm** in the File name text box. You want to save the HTML document as a ColdFusion template. If a document includes CFML, save it as a ColdFusion template with an extension of .cfm. See Figure 2-24.

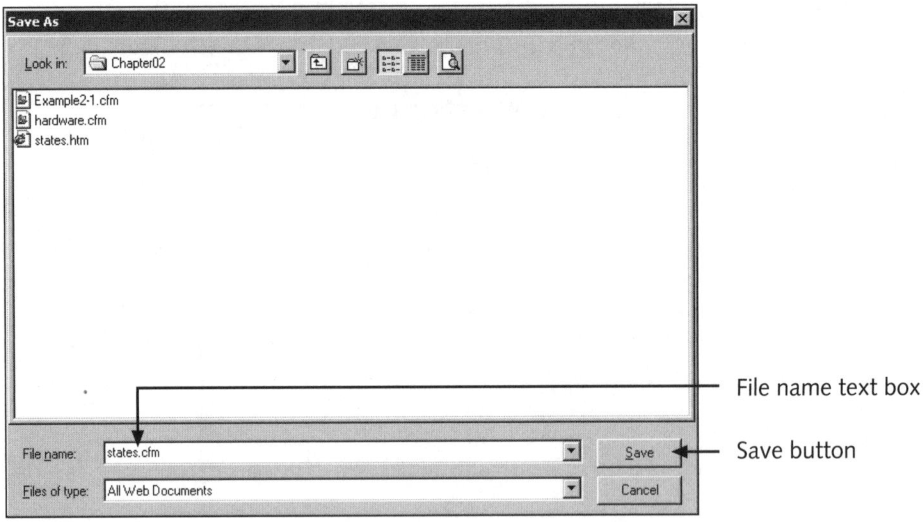

Figure 2-24   Save As dialog box in ColdFusion Studio

3. Click the **Save** button to save a copy of the HTML document as a ColdFusion template.

4. Select **State=Other** in line 16, and type **State=<cfoutput> #URLEncodedFormat("Mail Order / No Sales Tax") #**. Notice that ColdFusion Studio types the closing </cfoutput> tag for you.

5. If you cannot see the entire line of code, click the **Word wrap** button on the vertical Editor toolbar that appears on the left side of the window. ColdFusion Studio wraps the line as shown in Figure 2-25.

6. Save the file with the same name and location.

7. Start your Web browser, and open the **http://localhost/your_username/ Chapter02/states.cfm** template.

8. Click **View**, and then click **Source**. The Web browser displays the HTML source code for the document in another window, as shown in Figure 2-26. Notice that the spaces have been encoded to %20 and the / character has been encoded to %2F.

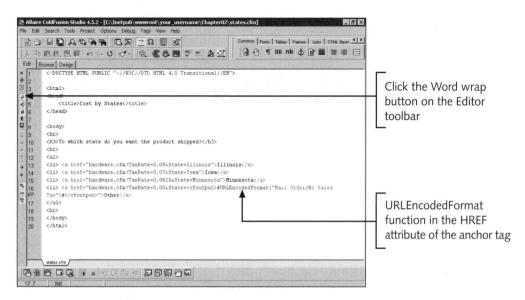

Figure 2-25   States.cfm file with the URLEncodedFormat function

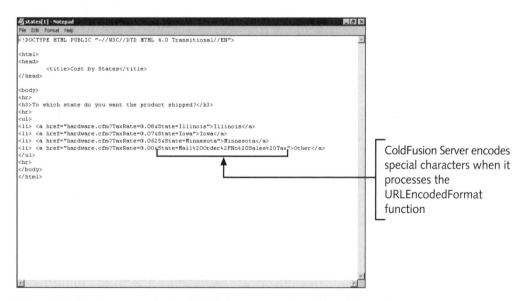

Figure 2-26   Source code for the Web page produced by states.cfm

9. Close the Source code window.

10. Click **Other**. See Figure 2-27. Notice that the table caption contains meaningful text.

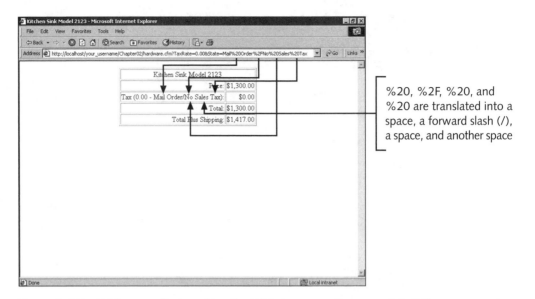

Figure 2-27   Web page displayed by the Web browser after you click Other

11. Close all open programs. You have successfully used the URLEncodedFormat function to pass text data that includes special characters.

USING STRING EXPRESSIONS

Similar to the concept of arithmetic expressions that you form by using numerical variables and arithmetic operators, ColdFusion allows you to form string expressions by using string variables and a string operator. For example, suppose you are working with a database that includes a FIRST field to store first names and a LAST field to store last names. When you want to display or print the full name, you **concatenate**, or connect, one field after another. If you want to display the first name followed by the last name, you include a space between field names, as in FIRST LAST. If you want to display the last name followed by the first name, you include a comma and a space, as in LAST, FIRST.

In the same way, you can concatenate strings in ColdFusion by using the concatenation operator (&). The concatenation operator connects, or links, two strings (operands) to produce a larger string containing both string operands. For example, to connect a person's first and last names, you need to connect the First string and the Last string with the concatenation operator, as in First & Last. To insert the space, you include quotation marks around a space, as in First & " " & Last. The following example (Example2-2.cfm) illustrates strings and the concatenation operator.

```
<cfset FirstName = "Rakhee">
<cfset LastName = "Kaparthi">
<cfset FullName = FirstName & " " & LastName>
<cfoutput>
```

```
<table align="center" border="1">
<tr><td align="right">First name:</td><td>#FirstName#</
td></tr>
<tr><td align="right">Last name:</td><td>#LastName#</td></
tr>
<tr><td align="right">Full name:</td><td>#FullName#</td></
tr>
</table>
</cfoutput>
```

When the ColdFusion Server executes Example 2-2, it first processes the CFSET tag and creates a string variable named FirstName and assigns it a value "Rakhee." Then it creates another variable named LastName and assigns it text data "Kaparthi." When it processes the third CFSET statement, it creates a variable named FullName, evaluates the string expression FirstName & " " & LastName to concatenate "Rakhee" & " " & "Kaparthi" to get "Rakhee Kaparthi," and assigns it to variable FullName. Finally, it processes the CFOUTPUT tags. All HTML is output as is. Variables within pound signs are processed, and the respective values are substituted in the appropriate locations. See Figure 2-28.

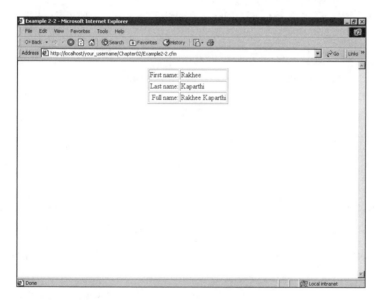

Figure 2-28 Web page displayed by Example2-2.cfm

Also, notice that the example uses only one set of CFOUTPUT tags. In Chapter 1, you used multiple sets of CFOUTPUT tags in the same program. Even though you can use one set of CFOUTPUT tags for a large block of text, you cannot use other CFML tags inside CFOUTPUT tags in general. In later chapters, you will use more CFML tags, so you will have to use more CFOUTPUT tags. Depending on the situation, you may want to enclose each variable to be output in CFOUTPUT tags or an entire block of text in a pair of CFOUTPUT tags.

To experiment with Example2-2.cfm:

1. Start your Web browser, and open **http://localhost/your_username/ Chapter02/Example2-2.cfm**. (See Figure 2-28.)

2. Start ColdFusion Studio, and open **Example2-2.cfm** for editing.

3. Change the value assigned to variable FirstName to your first name.

4. Change the value assigned to variable LastName to your last name.

5. Save the file using the same name and location.

6. Switch to your Web browser, and reload the document. Notice that the Web page displays your first name, last name, and full name.

Your client, the owner of the kitchen supply store, wants you to modify the hardware.cfm document. He wants to display the state as well as the product name in the title of the Web browser when someone views the hardware Web page. Your task is to implement this requirement. You can do so using the string concatenation operator to form an expression that will be assigned to the docTitle variable. You decide to concatenate the ProductName and the State URL parameter to retrieve the expression for the document's title.

To concatenate strings in the hardware.cfm template:

1. Switch to ColdFusion Studio, and open **hardware.cfm** from the Chapter02 subfolder on your data disk.

2. Click to the left of the closing bracket (>) on line 3, position 30.

3. Type a space followed by **& "-" & URL.State** to modify the CFSET tag as follows:

   <cfset docTitle = ProductName & "-" & URL.State>

4. Save the file using the same name and location.

5. Switch to your Web browser, and open the **states.cfm** template.

6. Click **Minnesota**.

7. Examine the output and see that the state name now appears on the title bar of the Web browser, as shown in Figure 2-29. The state name from the URL has been concatenated with the ProductName to form the docTitle variable. This variable is output in the title tags to obtain the desired effect. The Web browser displays all the text in the TITLE tags in its title bar.

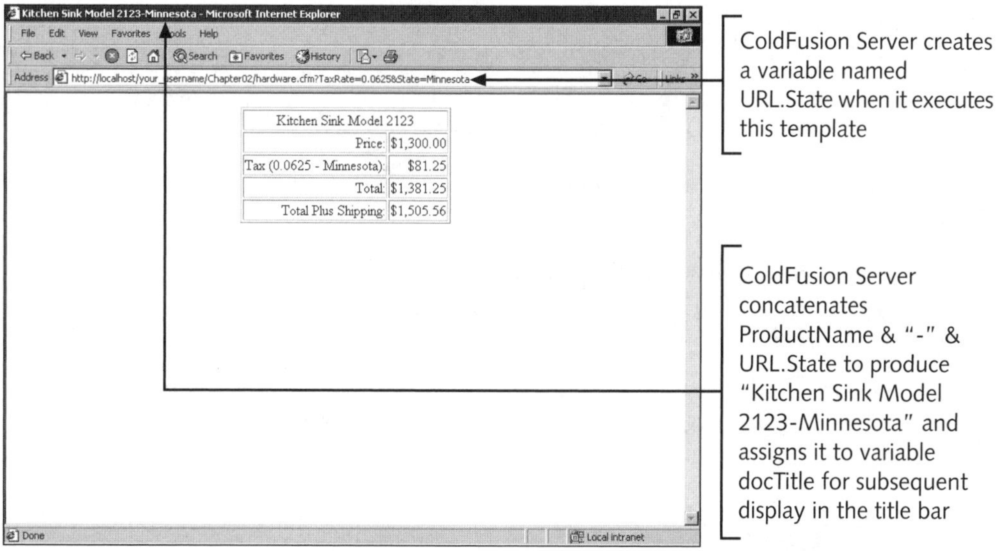
Kitchen Sink Model 2123-Minnesota - Microsoft Internet Explorer
http://localhost/your_username/Chapter02/hardware.cfm?TaxRate=0.0625&State=Minnesota
Kitchen Sink Model 2123
Price: $1,300.00
Tax (0.0625 - Minnesota): $81.25
Total: $1,381.25
Total Plus Shipping: $1,505.56
ColdFusion Server creates a variable named URL.State when it executes this template
ColdFusion Server concatenates ProductName & "-" & URL.State to produce "Kitchen Sink Model 2123-Minnesota" and assigns it to variable docTitle for subsequent display in the title bar

Figure 2-29 Web page displayed by hardware.cfm with string concatenation operators

8. Close all open programs.

Tip Unlike other programming languages, ColdFusion allows you to construct string literals that span multiple lines. For example, the following string literal is valid:

```
"
a
b
c
d
e
f
".
```

This string literal is actually stored as "↲a↲b↲c↲d↲e↲f↲", where ↲ is a carriage return character. Storing strings over multiple lines allows you to create very long string literals. In a later chapter, you will learn how to construct e-mail messages that span multiple lines without any complicated operators or expressions.

Concatenating Strings Using Pound Signs

You are already familiar with using pound signs around variables and functions in CFOUTPUT statements. ColdFusion substitutes values of variables and functions enclosed in pound signs in CFOUTPUT statements. A similar effect is produced when ColdFusion processes variables and functions enclosed in pound signs that make up string literals in CFSET tags. Values of variables and values returned by functions are substituted, and the string literal is assigned to the variable. If the value of a variable named Price is 1300.00, the following statement:

```
<cfset PricePhrase = "The price of the product is
#DollarFormat(Price) #.">
```

would assign the following string literal to the variable named PricePhrase:

```
The price of the product is $1,300.00.
```

This code is essentially the same as using <cfset PricePhrase = "The price of the product is " & DollarFormat(Price) & ".">. You can avoid using many concatenation operations by using this technique.

You can also use pound signs around numeric variables in string literals. The following example (Example2-3.cfm) illustrates the use of pound signs around numeric variables for dynamically creating a statement in another computer language:

```
<cfset pPrice = 100.00>
<cfset pInventory = 50>
<cfset SQL = "SELECT * FROM PRODUCTS WHERE Price <
#pPrice# AND Inventory > #pInventory#">
<cfoutput>#SQL#</cfoutput>
```

When the ColdFusion Server executes Example2-3.cfm, it creates the variables pPrice and pInventory, and assigns the values 100.00 and 50 to them, respectively. When the ColdFusion Server executes the highlighted third CFSET tag, it substitutes the values of the variables pPrice and pInventory for #pPrice# and #pInventory# in the string literal and assigns the result to the variable SQL. The CFOUTPUT tags display this value, as shown in Figure 2-30.

Example 2-3 - Microsoft Internet Explorer
File   Edit   View   Favorites   Tools   Help
⇦ Back ▾ ⇨ ▾ ⊗ 🔁 🏠	⊗ Search 🔲 Favorites 🕘 History	🔳 ▾ 🖨
Address 🔲 http://localhost/your_username/Chapter02/Example2-3.cfm   ▼ 🔗 Go Links »
SELECT * FROM PRODUCTS WHERE Price < 100.00 AND Inventory > 50

Figure 2-30   Web page displayed by Example2-3.cfm

All the examples used in this book are available on the Data Disk in the respective chapter folders. You can study the code and experiment with the examples as needed.

This technique is very useful; you will use it in later chapters for extracting data from databases. You will query databases to create Web pages that respond to user input. You can make ColdFusion search through databases to find items of interest.

STRING FUNCTIONS

You have already seen the use of the URLEncodedFormat function, which is an example of a string function. Similar to numeric functions, string functions process one or more arguments and return a single value. In this section, you will learn about some functions that process string arguments. Table 2-1 shows some useful string functions and their purpose.

Table 2-1   String Functions

Function	Purpose	Syntax
Find	Returns the first index of an occurrence of a substring in a string from a specified starting position; returns 0 if substring is not in string; the search is case sensitive	Find(substring, string [, start])
FindNoCase	Returns the first index of an occurrence of a substring in a string from a specified starting position; returns 0 if substring is not in string; the search is case insensitive	FindNoCase(substring, string [, start])
LCase	Returns string converted to lowercase	LCase(string)
Left	Returns the count number of characters from the beginning of a string argument	Left(string, count)
Len	Returns the length of a string	Len(string)
Mid	Returns count number of characters from string beginning at start position	Mid(string, start, count)
Replace	Returns string with occurrences of substring1 being replaced with substring2 in the specified scope	Replace(string, substring1, substring2 [, scope]) Scope: "ONE" -- Replace only the first occurrence (default) "ALL" -- Replace all occurrences
ReplaceNoCase	Returns string with occurrences of substring1 being replaced regardless of case matching with substring2 in the specified scope	ReplaceNoCase(string, substring1, substring2 [, scope]) Scope: "ONE" -- Replace only the first occurrence (default) "ALL" -- Replace all occurrences
Reverse	Returns string with reversed order of characters	Reverse(string)
Right	Returns the rightmost count number of characters of a string	Right(string, count)
Trim	Returns string with both leading and trailing spaces removed	Trim(string)
UCase	Returns string converted to uppercase	UCase(string)

For example, the length function represented as Len(aString) returns an integer that counts the number of characters in a string. For example, Len("Is this a long question?") returns a value of 24: the argument has 19 letters, 4 spaces, and the ? character. The following function returns a value of 12 because it counts all the 6 carriage return characters as well as 6 regular characters:

Function Len("a
b
c
d
e
f
")

ColdFusion Studio provides comprehensive online help that provides reference information and examples. In the following exercise, you will use the help feature to learn about a string function.

To learn about the UCase function using ColdFusion Studio:

1. Start ColdFusion Studio.

2. Click the **Resource Tab** button on the View toolbar to display the Resource Tab window if it is not visible.

3. Click the **Help Resource Tab**.

4. Click the **+** sign for CFML Language Reference to expand its list of topics. See Figure 2-31.

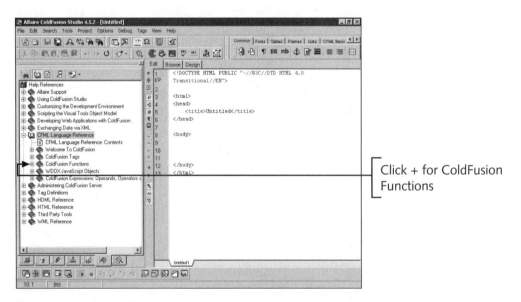

Figure 2-31   CFML language reference help in ColdFusion Studio

5. Click the + sign for ColdFusion Functions.

6. Double-click **String Functions**. The internal browser displays all the CFML string functions available.

7. If necessary, scroll down the right pane and click the **UCase** hyperlink. A description of the function is displayed along with its syntax and an example. See Figure 2-32.

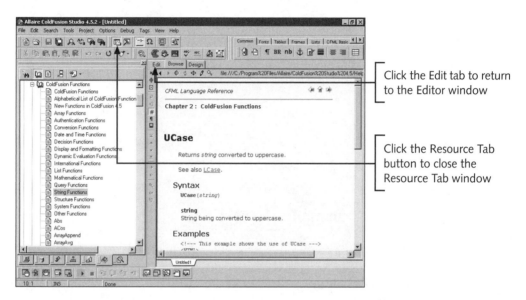

Figure 2-32   Description of the UCase string function in ColdFusion Studio

8. Click the **Resource Tab** button to close the Resource Tab window.

9. Click the **Edit** tab to return to the Editor window.

Using String Functions

You use string functions when you have to manipulate string variables in ColdFusion templates. To create dynamic and interactive Web sites, you have to provide for a variety of conditions. For example, you may want to use the length function to figure out how long a sentence is and then use that value for setting the width of a table or the font size. You may want to use to the Find or FindNoCase function to search for text containing key words that users are interested in. You may want to convert all the text data entered by users to uppercase or lowercase before populating a database to maintain consistent data in a database.

One of your clients, a Fun with Words Web site, asks you to design a ColdFusion template that takes a string URL parameter phrase and displays a Web page that identifies whether the word is a palindrome. A palindrome is a word, phrase, verse, or sentence that reads the same backward or forward. For example, the sentence "Dee saw a seed" is a palindrome.

To design a template that determines whether a phrase is a palindrome:

1. If necessary, switch to ColdFusion Studio. Your task is to create a template that helps users identify palindromes. See Figure 2-33.

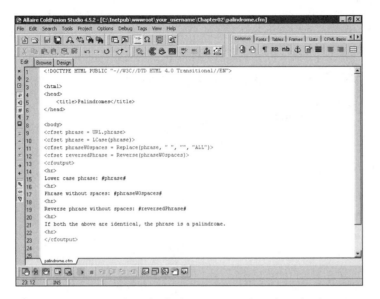

Figure 2-33   Template for helping users identify palindromes

2. Click **File**, and then click **New Document** to open a new document for editing. The insertion point appears on line 9, position 1.

3. Type **<cfset phrase = URL.phrase>**, and press **Enter**.

   When the ColdFusion Server executes this statement, it creates a new variable named phrase. It assigns it the value of the URL parameter named phrase. You are assuming that the user will type a URL parameter named phrase when requesting this document. If so, ColdFusion would create a variable named URL.phrase before the execution of this template and assign it the value of the URL parameter similar to what you saw in earlier exercises.

4. Type **<cfset phrase = LCase(phrase)>**, and press **Enter**.

   When the ColdFusion Server executes this statement, it first evaluates the expression on the right side of the equal sign. The function LCase is evaluated. All characters in the text contained in the variable phrase are converted to lowercase, and the resultant string is assigned to the same variable phrase. Essentially, the Server overwrites the phrase variable with a string consisting of entirely lowercase characters.

2

5. Type **<cfset phraseWOspaces = Replace(phrase,"","","ALL") >**, and press **Enter**.

Note that there is a space in the first set of quotation marks and nothing in the second set. Also note that the scope argument is specified as "All" indicating that all occurrences of the target substring should be replaced. See Table 2-1 for a complete description of the Replace function. When the ColdFusion Server executes this statement, it first processes the Replace function. All occurrences of spaces are replaced with an empty string to essentially remove all spaces from the phrase. The value returned by the Replace function that is the phrase without spaces is assigned to a new variable named phraseWOspaces.

6. Type **<cfset reversedPhrase = Reverse(phraseWOspaces) >**, and press **Enter**. When the ColdFusion Server executes this statement, it reverses all the characters in the phrase without spaces and assigns this newly formed string to a variable named reversedPhrase.

7. Type the following code for output of the results.

```
<cfoutput>
<hr>
Lower case phrase: #phrase#
<hr>
Phrase without spaces: #phraseWOspaces#
<hr>
Reversed phrase without spaces: #reversedPhrase#
<hr>
If both the above are identical, the phrase is a
palindrome.
<hr>
</cfoutput>
```

8. Select **Untitled** on line 5, and type **Palindromes**.

9. Click the **Save** button. Save the template in the C:\InetPub\wwwroot\ your_username\Chapter02 folder as **palindrome.cfm**.

10. Open your Web browser, if necessary.

11. Select the text in the address Field, type **http://localhost/your_username/ Chapter02/palindrome.cfm?phrase=Star+comedy+by+Democrats**, and then press **Enter**.

When the ColdFusion Server executes this template, it first processes the CFSET tag, creates a variable named phrase, and assigns it a value of "Star comedy by Democrats." Remember that a plus sign (+) in the value of a URL parameter is translated into a space. The second CFSET tag converts this phrase to lowercase letters and then assigns it back to the same variable. The third CFSET tag uses the Replace function to remove all spaces from phrase. (A more complete program would also include functions to remove all other punctuation marks, such as commas and exclamation points.) The fourth CFSET tag creates a new variable and assigns it a value obtained by reversing all characters in phrase.

The remaining statements output the information obtained by processing the string data and determine whether the phrase is a palindrome. Your Web browser should display a Web page as shown in Figure 2-34. Notice that both the phrase without spaces and the reversed phrase are identical. Therefore, the phrase "Star comedy by Democrats" is a palindrome.

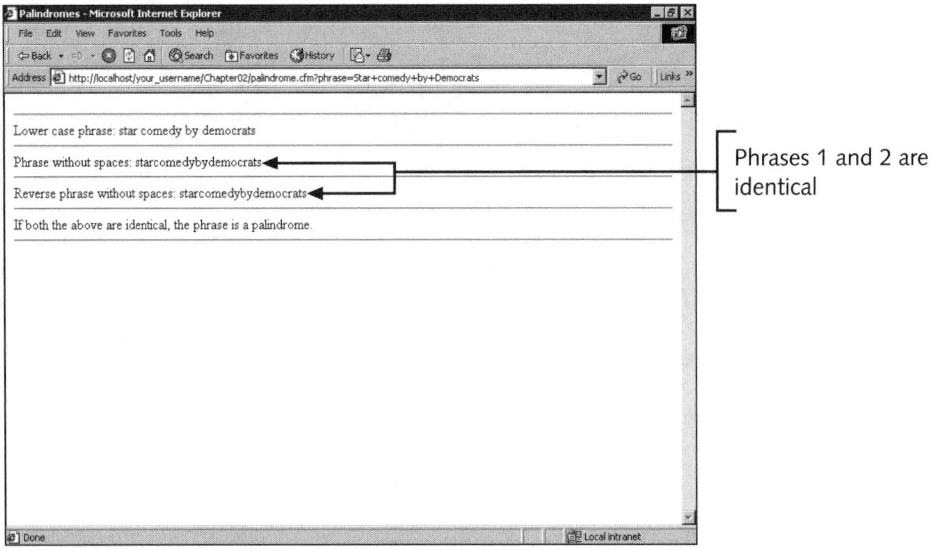

Figure 2-34   Web page displayed by palindrome.cfm with a URL parameter

12. Close all open programs.

In this section, you learned about strings. In the next section, you will learn about another useful data type for storing dates and times.

DATE-TIME VALUES AND VARIABLES

In addition to storing numbers and strings, you can also store and manipulate date-time values and variables containing dates and times. In ColdFusion, you can specify date and time values starting from 100 A.D. and ending with 9999 A.D. You create dates and times by using appropriate functions. The CreateDateTime function has the following syntax:

```
CreateDateTime(year, month, day, hour, minute, second)
```

where year, month, day, hour, minute, and second are all numbers. The valid ranges for date-time values are as follows:

- month: 1 to 12
- day: 1 to 31
- hour: 0 to 23

2

- minute: 0 to 59

- second: 0 to 59

Two-digit years less than or equal to 29 are interpreted as 21st century years (2000 to 2029), and other two-digit years are interpreted as 20th century years (1930, 1999). To avoid confusion, you can use four-digit years. The CreateDateTime function returns a valid date-time object that you can assign to a date-time variable. The variable-naming conventions are similar to numeric and string variables. You use the CreateDate function to create a date object. It takes the numeric arguments year, month, and day. You create a time object by using the CreateTime function. It takes the numeric arguments hour, minute, and second.

Your client has requested you to time-stamp the hardware.cfm template so that users know that the information is current. To simplify the task of maintaining the template, you will initialize a date-time variable at the top and display the time stamp at the bottom in a footnote.

To create a date-time variable and display its value:

1. Start ColdFusion Studio.

2. Open the **hardware.cfm** template in the Chapter02 subfolder on your Data Disk. Notice that the insertion point is in line 1 at position 1 after ColdFusion Studio opens the document.

3. Press the **Enter** key to insert a new line, and press the **Up Arrow** key to move back up to the newly inserted line.

4. Insert a ColdFusion comment, and type **Add Code to Initialize Date-Time Variable lastUpdated**.

5. Press the **End** key to move to the end of the line.

6. Press **Enter** to insert another line, and type **<cfset lastUpdated = CreateDateTime(2003, 5, 19, 14, 15, 50) >**.

7. Scroll down and click at the end of the </table> tag on line 31. Press **Enter** and type **

** to insert five line breaks. You can also click the **BR** button on the Common QuickBar five times to insert five line breaks.

8. Press **Enter** and type **<hr align="left" width="100">** to insert an horizontal rule 100 pixels wide that is aligned to the left.

9. Press **Enter** and type **last updated on: <cfoutput>#lastUpdated#**. Notice that ColdFusion Studio types the closing </cfoutput> tag.

10. Save the document with the same name and location.

11. Start your Web browser, and open **states.cfm** in the Chapter02 folder.

12. Click the **Minnesota** hyperlink to display the hardware.cfm document with the time stamp. See Figure 2-35.

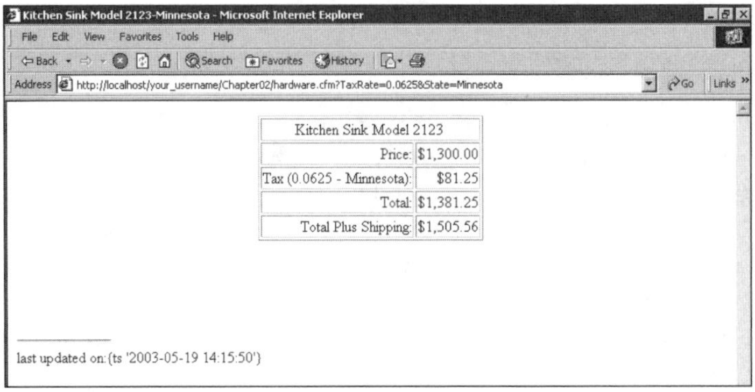

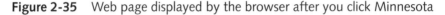

Figure 2-35 Web page displayed by the browser after you click Minnesota

13. Notice that the last updated information is displayed on the Web page as {ts '2003-05-19 14:15:50'}. You will modify the date and time format in the next exercise.

To display the date-time value in a format that is easy to understand, you have to use the DateFormat function. The DateFormat function allows you to display dates formatted in several different ways, as specified by using a mask. Similar to the concept of a mask for specifying number formats, date masks contain letters that signify different kinds of formatting. Table 2-2 summarizes date format masks.

Table 2-2 Date Format Masks

Mask	Description
d	Day of the month as an integer with no leading zero for single-digit days (1, 2, 3, 13, 14, 15, etc.)
dd	Day of the month as an integer with a leading zero for single-digit days (01, 02, 03, etc.)
ddd	Day of the week as a three-letter abbreviation (Mon, Tue, Wed, etc.)
dddd	Day of the week as its full name (Monday, Tuesday, Wednesday, etc.)
m	Month as an integer with no leading zero for single-digit months (1 = January, 2 = February, etc.)
mm	Month as an integer with a leading zero for single-digit months (01 = January, 02 = February, etc.)
mmm	Month as a three-letter abbreviation (Jan, Feb, Mar, etc.)
mmmm	Month as its full name (January, February, March, etc.)
y	Year as last two digits with no leading zero for years less than 10 (1 = 2001, 2 = 2002, etc.)
yy	Year as last two digits with a leading zero for years less than 10 (01 = 2001, 02 = 2002, etc.)
yyyy	Year represented by four digits (2001, 2002, etc.)

Similarly, the TimeFormat function uses a mask with letters to specify different kinds of formatting. Table 2-3 summarizes time formatting masks.

Table 2-3   Time Formatting Masks

Mask	Description
h	12-hour clock hours with no leading zero for single-digit hours (2:15, 3:15, etc.)
hh	12-hour clock hours with a leading zero for single-digit hours (02:15, 03:15, etc.)
H	24-hour clock hours with no leading zero for single-digit hours (2:15, 14:15, etc.)
HH	24-hour clock hours with a leading zero for single-digit hours (02:15, 14:15, etc.)
m	Minutes with no leading zero for single-digit minutes
mm	Minutes with a leading zero for single-digit minutes
s	Seconds with no leading zero for single-digit seconds
ss	Seconds with a leading zero for single-digit seconds
t	Single character time marker (A or P)
tt	Multiple character time marker string (AM or PM)

The following example (Example 2-4.cfm) illustrates the use and output of date-time values:

```
<cfset showTime = createDateTime(2003, 8, 23, 15, 40, 0)>
Movies show times in different formats:
<cfoutput>
<ul>
<li>#DateFormat(showTime, "mmm-dd-yyyy") # ----
#TimeFormat(showTime, "hh:mm:ss") #
<li>#DateFormat(showTime, "mmmm d, yyyy") # ----
#TimeFormat(showTime, "hh:mm:sstt") #
<li>#DateFormat(showTime, "mm/dd/yyyy") # ----
#TimeFormat(showTime, "HH:mm:ss") #
</ul>
</cfoutput>
```

The Web page displayed by Example2-4.cfm is shown in Figure 2-36.

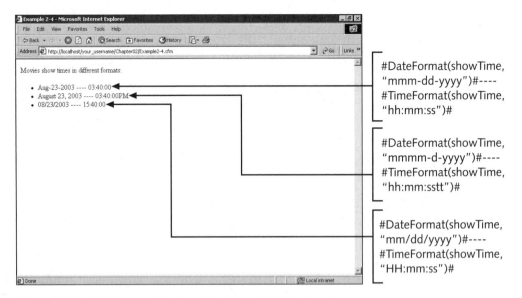

Figure 2-36 Web page displayed by Example2-4.cfm

To modify hardware.cfm to display a properly formatted last updated time stamp:

1. Switch to ColdFusion Studio, and open **hardware.cfm** if necessary.

2. Modify line 34 to **last updated on: <cfoutput>#DateFormat(lastUpdated, "mmmm d, yyyy")# – #TimeFormat(lastUpdated, "hh:mm:sstt")# </cfoutput>**.

3. Save the document with the same name and location.

4. Switch to your Web browser, and open **states.cfm**.

5. Click **Minnesota**. See Figure 2-37.

Figure 2-37 Web page with a properly formatted date-time value

6. Close all open programs.

2

Similar to using functions for manipulating numbers and strings, ColdFusion has several functions for manipulating date-time values and variables. Table 2-4 lists a few date-time functions and their purposes. The CFML language reference in ColdFusion Studio gives you a complete list of all the date and time functions and describes their usage and syntax.

Table 2-4   Date-Time Functions

Function	Purpose	Syntax
CreateDate	Returns a valid date-time object	CreateDate(year, month, day)
CreateDateTime	Returns a valid date-time object	CreateDateTime(year, month, day, hour, minute, second)
CreateTime	Returns a valid time variable in ColdFusion	CreateTime(hour, minute, second)
CreateTimeSpan	Creates a date-time object for adding and subtracting other date-time objects	CreateTimeSpan(days, hours, minutes, seconds)
DateAdd	Returns a date to which a specified time interval has been added	DateAdd(datepart, number, date)
DateDiff	Returns the number of intervals in whole units of type Datepart by which Date1 is less than Date2	DateDiff(datepart, date1, date2)
DateFormat	Returns a formatted date-time value; if no mask is specified, DateFormat function returns date value using the dd-mmm-yy format	DateFormat(date [, mask])
Now	Returns the current date and time as a valid date-time object	Now()

Date-Time Operations

You process date-time values and variables by using functions. You create values using appropriate functions and assign them to variables using the CFSET tag, as seen in the previous exercise. You also use functions to output these values in desired formats. To perform operations such as addition and subtraction, you have to use a function. You use the DateAdd function for performing addition and subtraction. The syntax for the DateAdd function is given below:

DateAdd(datepart, *a_number*, date)

The DateAdd functions returns a date-time value that is the result of adding a_number of years, quarters, months, weeks, days, hours, minutes, or seconds (datepart) to date. You use a code to specify the datepart to use. You use "yyyy" if you want to add years, "q" for quarters, "m" for months, "d" for days, "ww" for weeks, "h" for hours, "n" for minutes, and "s" for seconds. You have to use a negative value for a_number if you want to subtract from the date to get a value in the past. The following example (Example2-5.cfm) illustrates the use of the DateAdd function:

```
<cfset dateOfManufacture = CreateDate(2003,  5,  21)>
<cfset dateOfExpiration = DateAdd("m",  3,
dateOfManufacture) >
<cfoutput>
<table align="center" border="">
<tr>
    <th colspan="2">Canned Vegetables - Batch 786</th>
</tr>
<tr>
    <td align="right">Date of Manufacture:</td>
    <td>#DateFormat(dateOfManufacture, "mmm-dd-
    yyyy")#</td>
</tr>
<tr>
    <td align="right">Date of Expiration:</td>
    <td>#DateFormat(dateOfExpiration, "mmm-dd-
    yyyy")#</td>
</tr>
</table>
</cfoutput>
```

When you open this example in your Web browser, the Web page shown in Figure 2-38 is displayed. Suppose a manufacturer wants to set the expiration date of canned vegetables three months after the date of manufacture. You use the DateAdd function to add three months to the date of manufacture to figure out the expiration date. You then display the results formatted in an HTML table.

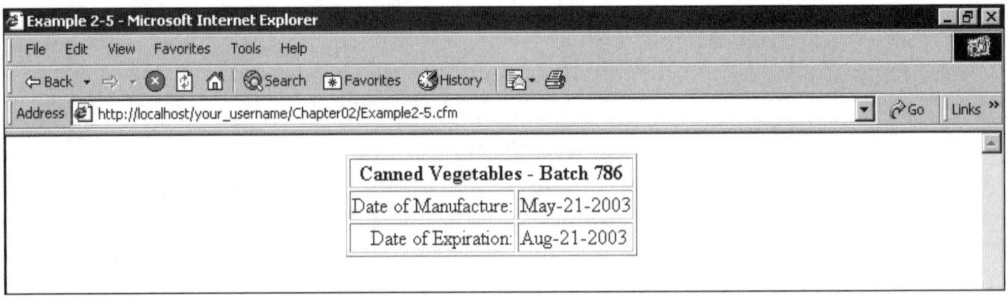

Figure 2-38   Web page displayed by Example2-5.cfm

Your project manager asks you to modify the kitchen sink Web pages. He has learned that your client ships its products in one of two ways. Customers can receive their product in two days if they use priority shipping and in five days if they use standard shipping. Priority shipping costs 15% and standard shipping costs 9% of the total. The sales tax requirement is still the same. After examining the requirements, you decide to use the DateAdd function to compute the expected date of delivery by adding 2 or 5 days to today's date. You can obtain today's date by using the Now() function.

To add the two shipping methods to the kitchen sink system:

1. Start your Web browser, and open **shipping.cfm** in your Chapter02 sub-folder. See Figure 2-39. The shipping.cfm template lists the two kinds of shipping customers can use. You have to design anchor tags for both shipping methods. The words Standard and Priority should link to states.cfm so that users can select their state next. These hyperlinks to states.cfm should have two parameters, one for the shipping rate and the other for the date of delivery. You can compute the date of delivery by using the DateAdd function.

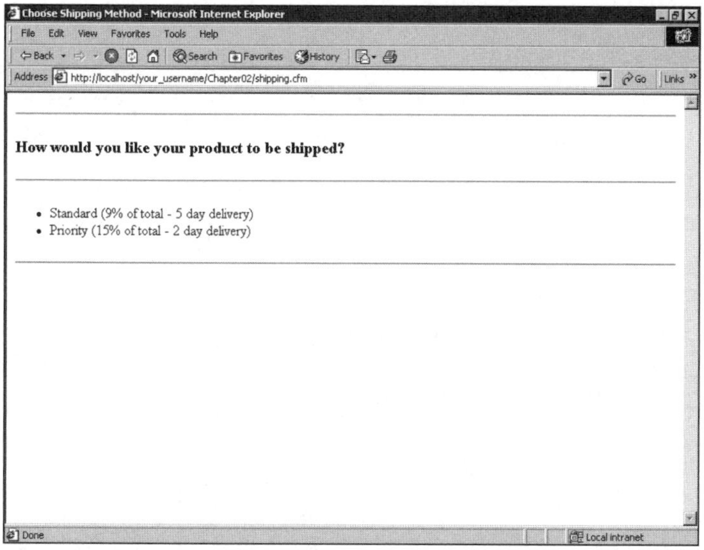

Figure 2-39   Web page displayed by shipping.cfm

2. Start ColdFusion Studio.

3. Open **shipping.cfm** in the Chapter02 subfolder on the data disk. ColdFusion Studio opens the document with the insertion point at the beginning of line 1.

4. Type **<cfset standardDate = DateAdd("d",5,Now()) >**, and press **Enter**. You are adding 5 to today's date to get the date of delivery for standard shipping. The Now() function returns today's date.

5. Type **<cfset priorityDate = DateAdd("d",2,Now()) >**, and press **Enter**. You are adding 2 to today's date to get the date of delivery for priority shipping.

6. Select **Standard** in line 15.

7. Click the **Common** tab on the QuickBar, if necessary.

8. Click the **Anchor** button on the Common QuickBar.

9. Type the following in the HREF textbox:

states.cfm?ShippingRate=0.09&DeliveryDate=<cfoutput>
#URLEncodedFormat(DateFormat(standardDate, "mmm-dd-yyyy")
) #</cfoutput>

When the user clicks this hyperlink, a request is sent for the states.cfm document with two URL parameters, the ShippingRate and the DeliveryDate. Note that the delivery date is formatted as a date and encoded by using the URLFormatFunction. It is enclosed in CFOUTPUT tags.

10. Click the **OK** button, and ColdFusion Studio inserts the anchor tag for you.

11. Select **Priority** on line 16, and click the **Anchor** button on the Common QuickBar.

12. Type the following in the HREF textbox:

states.cfm?ShippingRate=0.15&DeliveryDate=<cfoutput>
#URLEncodedFormat(DateFormat(priorityDate, "mmm-dd-yyyy")
) #</cfoutput>

Click **OK**. Note that the shipping rate is 0.15 and the date in the DateFormat function is priorityDate. See Figure 2-40.

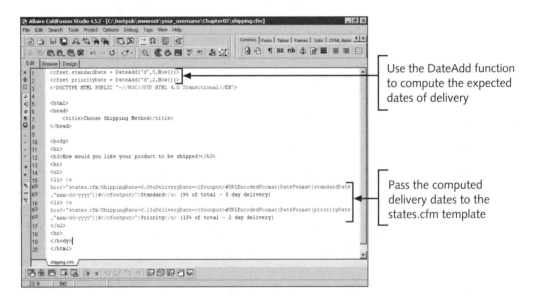

Figure 2-40   Editing the shipping.cfm template in ColdFusion Studio

13. Click the **Save** button to save the template with the same name and location.

Your next task is to modify the states.cfm template so that the shipping preferences are passed onto the hardware.cfm template. Essentially, the URL parameters received by states.cfm have to be duplicated in the HREF for the different states listed.

To modify states.cfm to include shipping information:

1. In ColdFusion Studio, open **states.cfm** in the Chapter02 subfolder.

2. Click in line 13, position 55 (that is, inside the HREF attribute), after State=Illinois before the quotation mark.

 This book always refers to line numbers in the gutter. Status bar line numbers vary depending on the resolution of the monitor and the status of the Word Wrap feature.

3. Type the following: **<cfoutput>&ShippingRate= #URL.ShippingRate#&DeliveryDate=#URL.DeliveryDate#**

Note that </cfoutput> is inserted by ColdFusion Studio. The URL parameters received by this template are being passed onto the hardware.cfm template as its URL parameters.

4. Select the text that you typed in Step 3 and the </cfoutput> tag. Copy the selection to the Clipboard.

5. Paste the selection in line 15 in the HREF attribute to the right of the name-value pair State=Iowa.

6. Copy and paste the information for Minnesota and Other, as shown in Figure 2-41.

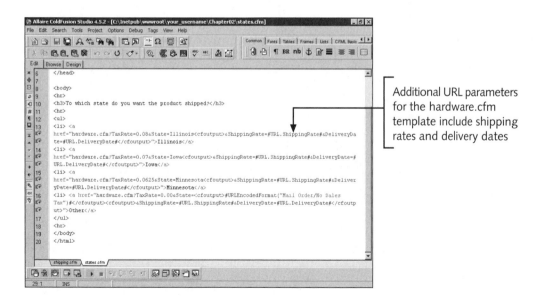

Additional URL parameters for the hardware.cfm template include shipping rates and delivery dates

Figure 2-41   Editing states.cfm in ColdFusion Studio

7. Save your work.

The last task in this sequence of steps is to modify the hardware.cfm to use the shipping rate information and display the expected delivery date.

To modify the hardware.cfm template to incorporate two shipping methods:

1. In ColdFusion Studio, open **hardware.cfm**.

2. Select **0.09** in line 10, and replace it by typing **URL.ShippingRate**. You are using the shipping rate from the URL parameter.

3. Scroll down and copy to the Clipboard the HTML code for the entire table row for displaying the total cost plus shipping (line 30).

4. Paste the selection at the beginning of line 31, to the left of the </table> tag.

5. Select **Total Plus Shipping** in the newly inserted row 31, and then replace it by typing **Expected delivery date**.

6. Select **DollarFormat(TotalShip)** in the same line, and then replace it by typing **URL.DeliveryDate**. See Figure 2-42.

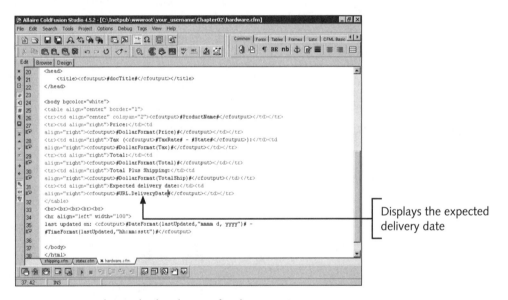

Displays the expected delivery date

Figure 2-42   Editing the hardware.cfm document

7. Save your work.

8. Switch to your Web browser, and refresh **shipping.cfm**. See Figure 2-43. Note that each of the shipping methods is now a hyperlink. The expected delivery dates are computed and are part of the HREF attributes.

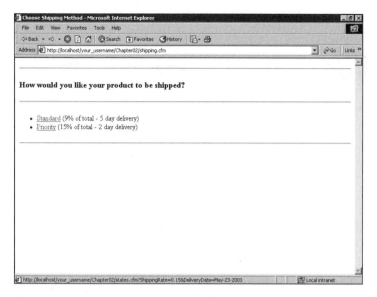

Figure 2-43   Web page displayed by shipping.cfm after the modifications

9. Click the **Priority** hyperlink.

10. The states.cfm template is displayed in your Web browser. See Figure 2-44. Notice that each of these hyperlinks are now passing the URL information to the hardware.cfm template.

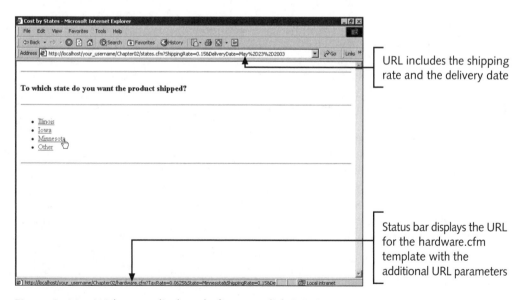

Figure 2-44   Web page displayed after you click Priority

11. Click the **Minnesota** hyperlink. You Web browser displays hardware.cfm, as shown in Figure 2-45. The expected date of delivery is May 23, 2003.

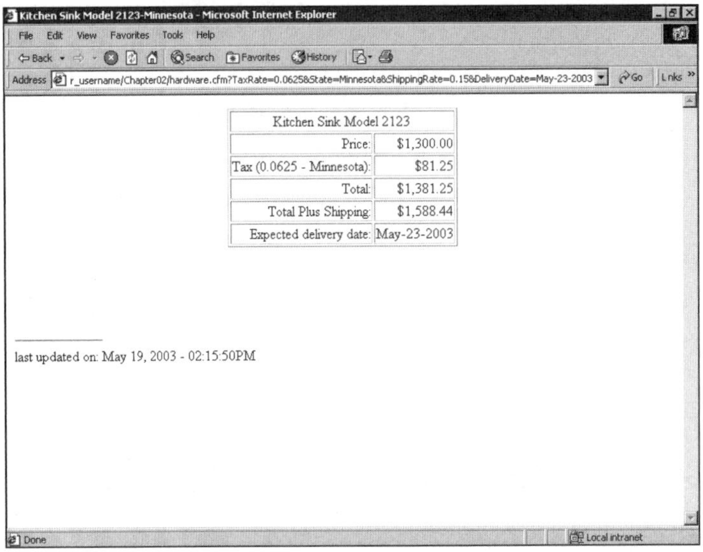

Figure 2-45   Web page displayed by the final hardware.cfm after you click Minnesota

12. Experiment by clicking other combinations of shipping methods and states. Close all your programs.

You have successfully processed date and time variables and used them in a sequence of Web pages. In the next section, you will learn about another type of variable—Boolean variables and the values they store.

Using Boolean Values to Evaluate Expressions

A **Boolean variable** stores the Boolean values TRUE and FALSE. For example, if you want to present a user with a first-time welcome screen on his or her first arrival at your Web site and a different welcome screen on subsequent visits, you may want to use a Boolean variable named FirstVisit. FirstVisit would store a value of TRUE (meaning that a user is visiting for the first time) or FALSE (meaning that the user has previously visited the Web site) for each user. You can use Boolean variables in situations where a program must take action. The server must evaluate statements to test whether they are true or false, and take a predefined a course of action based on the results. You will learn more about Boolean values in another chapter. Important functions that return Boolean values are listed in Table 2-5.

Table 2-5   Boolean Functions

Function	Purpose	Syntax
IsDate	Returns TRUE if string can be converted to a date-time value; otherwise returns FALSE; note that ColdFusion converts the Boolean return value to its string equivalents, "Yes" and "No"	IsDate(string)
IsDefined	Evaluates a string value to determine if the variable named in the string value exists; IsDefined returns TRUE if the specified variable is found or FALSE if it is not found	IsDefined("variable_name")
IsLeapYear	Returns TRUE if the year is a leap year; otherwise, returns FALSE	IsLeapYear(year)
IsNumeric	Returns TRUE if string can be converted to a number; otherwise, returns FALSE	IsNumeric(string)

Typeless Expression Evaluation

Unlike traditional programming languages, ColdFusion evaluates an expression even if it contains data and operators of different types. To do so, ColdFusion converts the data, or operands, into types that the operators require. This ability is called **typeless expression evaluation**. If you are using functions and the arguments are different from required types, the arguments are converted into required data types, as long as the data you are using is reasonable. If ColdFusion cannot convert the data, it generates an error. Table 2-6 describes conversions performed by typeless expression evaluations.

Table 2-6   Conversions Performed by Typeless Expression Evaluation

FROM/TO	Numeric	String	Date-Time	Boolean
Numeric	No need	Number is converted using the default format Example: "--" & 12000 & "--" is --12000--	According to ColdFusion internal representation	TRUE if Number is not 0, FALSE if it is 0
String	If a string can be converted it is, otherwise generates an error Example: 2 * "123" is 246	No need	Conversion into appropriate date-time values if specification is in a valid format, otherwise results in an error Example: "June 18, 2002 02:34:12", "June 18, 2002 2:34a", "June 18, 2002 2:34am", "June 18, 2002 02:34am", and "June 18, 2002 2am" are all valid and will be converted	"Yes" to TRUE, "No" to FALSE, if string can be converted to a number, TRUE if number is not 0, FALSE if it is 0
Date-Time	To internal Cold-Fusion format, a real number where integer part corresponds to date and decimal part corresponds to time; difference between two consecutive days is 1	ODBC time-stamp format Example: CreateDateTime (2002,6,28,16,30,0) is {ts '2002-06-28 16:30:00'}	No need	Error
Boolean	TRUE is converted to 1 and FALSE is converted to 0	TRUE is converted to "Yes" and FALSE is converted to "No"	Error	No need

CHAPTER SUMMARY

❐ URL parameters are name-value pairs appended to URLs in a specific format. You create dynamic Web pages by using URL parameters. Format URLs with URL parameters by using a question mark (?) after the name of the document. Use an equal sign (=) between the parameter and its value. Multiple parameters are separated by using an ampersand (&).

❐ The ColdFusion Server creates special variables of the form URL.parameter_name when it receives a request for a template with URL parameters. The value of the URL parameter is assigned to this variable. You can use this variable in the template for subsequent processing and output. These variables are in URL scope. If multiple parameters are present, it creates multiple variables.

❐ Users may type URLs with URL parameters in address fields of Web browsers. Developers may use URLs with URL parameters in HREF attributes of anchor tags.

❐ In addition to numeric variables, ColdFusion allows you to use string variables, date-time variables, and Boolean variables.

❐ String variables allow you to store text data. The rules for naming variables that store text are similar to those for storing numeric data; that is, string variable names must begin with a letter and can consist of letters, numbers, or the underscore character (_). Text that should be treated as a string is enclosed in quotation marks so the ColdFusion Server can distinguish it as text and not as another variable.

❐ Encode reserved characters in URLs to prevent unintended consequences. You encode characters by using a three-character code: a percent sign and two hexadecimal digits indicating the position of the character in the ASCII table.

❐ The URLEncodedFormat function takes a string as its argument and returns a value that is encoded using the scheme necessary for encoding characters in URLs.

❐ You can concatenate multiple strings by using a concatenation operator represented by the ampersand symbol (&). The concatenation operator connects, or links, two strings (operands) to produce a larger string containing both string operands.

❐ ColdFusion substitutes values of variables and functions enclosed in pound signs in string literals, effectively allowing you to concatenate strings without using the & operator.

❐ ColdFusion provides several useful string, date-time, and Boolean functions in addition to numeric functions.

❐ You use date-time variables and values for manipulating dates and times in ColdFusion templates. You use Boolean variables for storing values TRUE and FALSE.

❐ ColdFusion implements a system of typeless expression evaluation. If you are using functions and the arguments are different from required types, the arguments are converted into required data types, as long as the data you are using is reasonable.

REVIEW QUESTIONS

1. What are URL parameters? How do you format URLs with URL parameters?

2. How do you access URL parameters in ColdFusion templates?

3. What is the URLEncodedFormat function, and why do you have to use it?

4. What are string variables and literals?

5. How do you concatenate strings in ColdFusion?

6. List three string functions, and explain their usage.

7. What are date-time variables?

8. How do you use the DateAdd function?

9. What are Boolean values?

10. What is typeless expression evaluation?

11. Explain how strings would be converted in the various other data types.

HANDS-ON PROJECTS

Project 1: Design a Customized Welcome Page

A local Jeep dealer is improving its Web site to remain competitive with other Jeep dealers in the area. One goal for the new site is to provide returning customers with personalized service. The dealer's Web site currently uses a ColdFusion Server. The information systems manager, Jay Iona, wants you to design the Web page shown in Figure 2-46, which includes a welcome message that appears after customers identify the manufacturer and model of their cars. For example, if a user owns a 1995 Jeep Grand Cherokee, the welcome message would be "Dear Valued 1995 Jeep Grand Cherokee Owner:"

Use a string variable to store information about the car a customer owns, and output this variable's value in designated locations in the welcome message to provide customized messages. When you are finished, save the file as **Ch2Pr1.cfm** in the Chapter02 folder on the server, and then preview the output using your Web browser. Notice that the car's manufacturer and model appear in the title of the Web browser too.

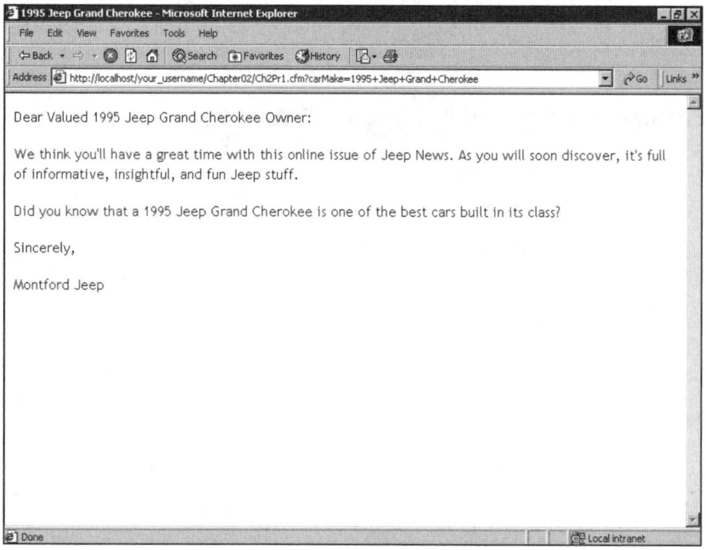

Figure 2-46

Modify the template so that it uses a URL parameter named carMake. Run your program with a URL parameter and a value as follows: http://localhost/your_username/Chapter02/Ch2Pr1.cfm?carMake=2003+Jeep+Grand+Cherokee.

Project 2: Work with String Variables and String Literals

Start ColdFusion Studio. Open Ch2Pr2.cfm in the Chapter02 subfolder on your Data Disk. It contains the following code:

```
<cfset quotation1 = "___type text here___">
<cfset quotation2 = "___type text here___">
<cfset quotation3 = "___type text here___">

<html>
<head>
     <title>Quotes to quote</title>
</head>

<body>
Quotes to quote:
<ul>
<cfoutput>
<li> #quotation1#
<li> #quotation2#
<li> #quotation3#
</cfoutput>
</ul>
</body>
</html>
```

Modify the template by typing text in the highlighted lines so that the Web browser displays the page shown in Figure 2-47. Note that there are two lines in each quotation.

Figure 2-47

Project 3: Format Date-Time Variables

A large university operates a shuttle service between its two campuses. The buses start operating at the North campus at 7:30 AM and depart every 30 minutes for the South campus. Modify the Ch2Pr3.cfm template that now displays before-noon shuttle schedules departing from the North campus in a neatly formatted table, as shown in Figure 2-48. A partial template named Ch2Pr3.cfm is available on the Data Disk for your use. It contains the following code:

```
<cfset time1 = createtime(7, 30, 0) >
<cfset time2 = createtime(8, 0, 0) >
<cfset time3 = createtime(8, 30, 0) >
<cfset time4 = createtime(9, 0, 0) >
<cfset time5 = createtime(9, 30, 0) >
<cfset time6 = createtime(10, 0, 0) >
<cfset time7 = createtime(10, 30, 0) >
<cfset time8 = createtime(11, 0, 0) >
<cfset time9 = createtime(11, 30, 0) >
<cfset time10 = createtime(12, 0, 0) >

<html>
<head>
    <title>Bus Schedule</title>
</head>
```

```
<body>

YOUR TABLE HERE

</body>
</html>
```

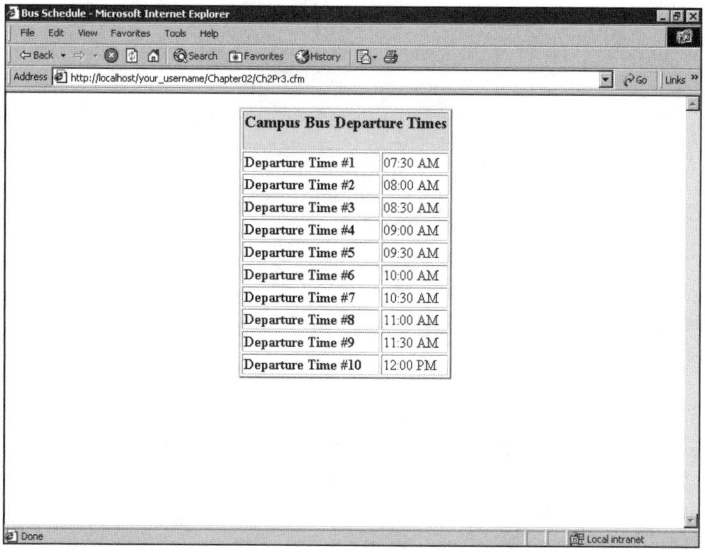

2

Figure 2-48

Project 4: Design a Template that Removes Lowercase Vowels

A university designs titles for courses on student transcripts by removing all the lower-case vowels (a, e, i, o, u) from the actual titles. Design a ColdFusion template that accepts a URL parameter (title) and displays the title as it appears on the transcript. Save this file as **Ch2Pr4.cfm** in your Chapter02 folder. Figure 2-49 shows a Web page that you should use as a guideline for this project. Run your template and try it out on the titles for all the courses that you are taking this semester.

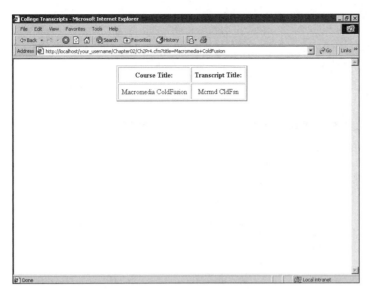

Figure 2-49

Project 5: Design a Template that Converts Word Case

Design a ColdFusion template that takes a parameter named Word. This document displays this word in sentence case (first letter in uppercase and the rest in lowercase). Save your file as **Ch2Pr5.cfm**. Test your program with the following data: great, tiGGer, and SPELLBOUnd. See Figure 2-50. Use a variable named Word and assign the value from the URL parameter to it. Use the LCase function, and create a variable named lcWord. Use the UCase function, and create a variable named ucWord. Concatenate the first character of ucWord using the Left function and the other characters by using the Right function to get scWord. Use the Len function to get the length of the word, and subtract 1 from it to determine the value to use in the Right function. Display the scWord and the original word in a table, as shown in Figure 2-50.

Figure 2-50

Project 6: Design a Template to Specify Color Preferences

An Internet portal allows users to specify their color preferences for viewing documents. They permit users to specify the page background color and text color by using URL parameters named bgColor and textColor by using named colors or RGB color specifications. You can specify your first name by using a parameter named firstName. Use string variables for storing user preferences, and display a sample document by using these variables as shown in Figure 2-51. (*Hint*: Remember that a BODY tag in HTML can have attributes for specifying these colors like BGCOLOR, TEXT.) When you are finished, save the file as **Ch2Pr6.cfm** in the Chapter02 folder on the server, and then preview the output in your Web browser. Test your program by using http://localhost/your_username/Chapter02/Ch2Pr6.cfm?firstName=Shashi&bgColor=lightyellow&textColor=blue.

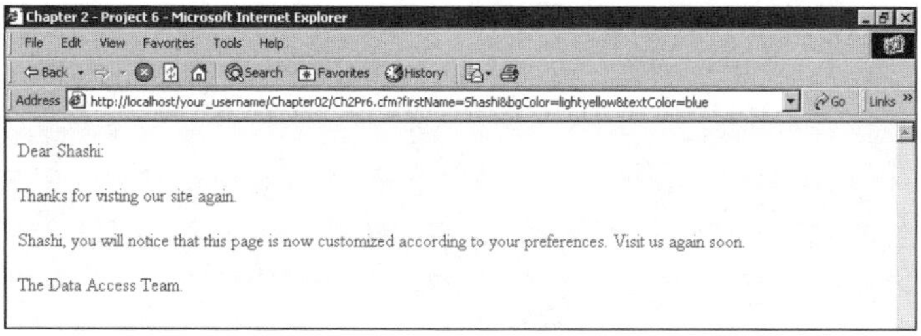

Figure 2-51

Project 7: Design a Template that Computes Age

Design a ColdFusion template that accepts a person's date of birth as a URL parameter and computes his/her age today and displays it. The URL parameter should be named dob, and it should be in the format mm/dd/yyyy. Display the output using a caption, as shown in Figure 2-52. Save the file as **Ch2Pr7.cfm**. (*Hint*: Because ColdFusion allows typeless expression evaluation, you can directly use the variable created by ColdFusion (URL.dob) in the DateDiff function to compute the difference between the date today (Now()) and the person's date of birth.)

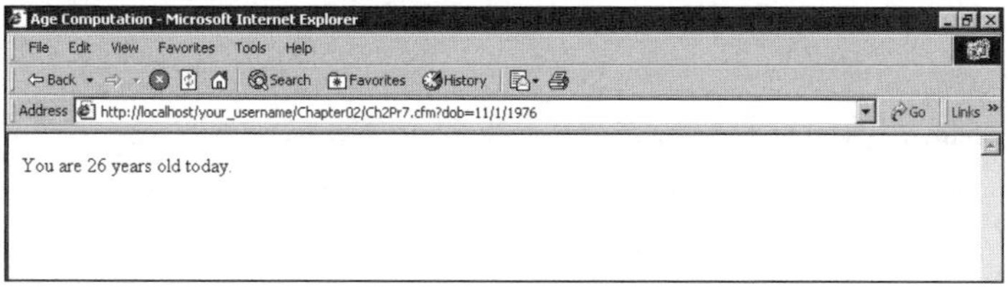

Figure 2-52

Project 8: Design a Template that Shows Salary Increases

A company has set a policy that ties salary increases to years of service of employees. For each year an employee has worked with the company, he or she receives a 0.6% increase in salary. The company posts this information on its intranet. Design a ColdFusion template that uses a date URL parameter (startDate) for specifying the starting date of an employee and a numeric URL parameter (salary) to capture the current salary. The template should compute and display the salary increase the employee receives. When you are finished, save the file as **Ch2Pr8.cfm** in the Chapter02 folder on the server, and then view the output using your Web browser with the URL http://localhost/your_username/Chapter02/Ch2Pr8.cfm?startDate=8/1/1992&salary=56000. See Figure 2-53. Note that your solution may differ from the one shown in Figure 2-53.

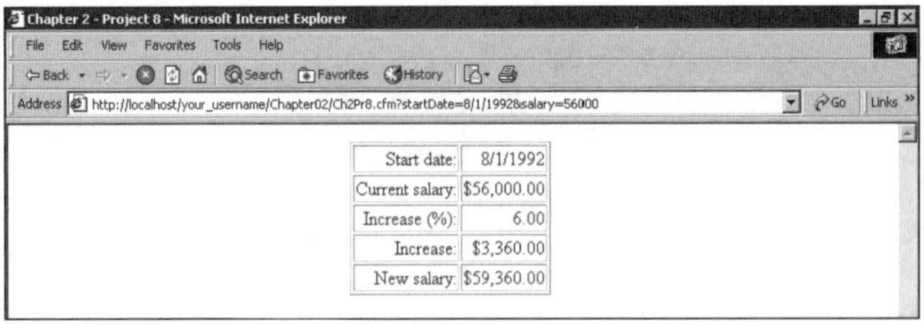

Figure 2-53

CASE PROJECTS

Case Project 1

Open *www.onetravel.com* in your Web browser. What URL parameters is the home page processing? Try to identify the purpose of each of the parameters.

Case Project 2

A fun with Math Web site has requested you to design Web pages for teaching children multiplication. Design a template that lists the numbers 0 to 9, where each number is a hyperlink. When the user clicks any of the numbers, a second page is displayed containing a list of the numbers 0 to 9. When the user clicks any of these numbers, a third Web page multiplies the numbers chosen and displays them along with the result.

Case Project 3

Open *www.google.com*, and search the Web for RFC 1738. What is it? Write a paragraph explaining RFC 1738.

3

FLOW CONTROL IN COLDFUSION

In this chapter, you will:

♦ Learn about program flow control in ColdFusion
♦ Use three structured programming flow-control constructs: sequence, selection, and repetition
♦ Understand and use conditions, relational operators, and logical operators
♦ Use ColdFusion CFIF and CFSWITCH statements for implementing selection
♦ Use ColdFusion CFLOOP statements to create FOR loops, LIST loops, and WHILE loops
♦ Use the ColdFusion CFLOCATION statement to redirect a Web page to a new URL

In Chapters 1 and 2, you learned that a computer program contains a series of statements that are executed sequentially from beginning to end. A ColdFusion Server processes ColdFusion statements enclosed in HTML tags in a similar fashion. HTML in a template is output as is; ColdFusion statements are processed sequentially from beginning to end. When the ColdFusion Server encounters an output statement, it produces HTML and generated text in the appropriate places.

When a program's statements are executed one after another in a step-by-step fashion, the program has a **sequence flow-control structure**. Sometimes, however, you have to deviate from sequentially processing statements. For example, you might need to execute sets of statements repeatedly, or you may need to stop processing at a certain statement. When you must change the order in which statements are executed or when you need to choose statements that should be executed, use flow-control statements.

USING SELECTION TO CONTROL PROGRAM FLOW

In computer programming, you often need to select a course of action depending on circumstances. **Selection** is a flow-control construct where you instruct the computer to examine two or more alternatives and then choose a course of action to solve a problem. For example, recall the shipping rates example you worked on in Chapter 2. The shipping rates a company charges depend upon whether a customer wants priority shipping or standard shipping. To model situations like these that require selection, you use conditions. A **condition** is a comparison of two quantities. At a particular time a condition is either true or false. You use relational operators to compare quantities in conditions. For example, you can determine whether a person is an adult by comparing the person's age to 21. If the person's age is greater than or equal to 21, that person is an adult. In the previous statement, "greater than or equal to" is a **relational operator**. This relational operator is represented as **GE** in ColdFusion. If the person's age is assigned to a variable named personsAge, the condition in ColdFusion to determine if the person is an adult is personsAge GE 21. Depending on the value stored in the variable named personsAge, the condition personsAge GE 21 is evaluated as either true or false. If the value of the variable personsAge is 30, the condition is true and the person is an adult. If value of the variable is 15, the condition is false and the person is not an adult.

Using CFIF Tags

When you need to select an action to perform based on the result of a condition, you can use a CFIF tag. A **CFIF tag** is a flow-control tag that you use to set up a selection construct in ColdFusion. A CFIF tag has the following syntax:

```
<CFIF condition>
     True action
<CFELSE>
     False action
</CFIF>
```

This syntax introduces three new tags: CFIF, CFELSE, and /CFIF. To set up a selection construct in ColdFusion, you start with the CFIF tag followed by some code, then you have the CFELSE tag followed by some more code, and finally you have the closing /CFIF tag. You must always use these three tags in the CFIF-CFELSE-/CFIF sequence. When a ColdFusion Server executes a CFIF tag, it evaluates the condition specified in it (**CFIF condition**). If this CFIF condition evaluates to true, the ColdFusion Server performs the true action, which includes all of the CFML and HTML between the CFIF and CFELSE statements. If the true action is executed, the ColdFusion Server skips the false action and continues executing the statement below the closing CFIF tag. If the CFIF condition evaluates to false, the ColdFusion Server skips the true action and performs the false action. The false action includes all of the statements between the CFELSE tag and the closing CFIF tag. After executing the false action, the ColdFusion Server executes the statements below the closing CFIF tag. As you can see, a CFIF tag allows you to perform an action when a condition is true and to perform a different action when a condition is false. A flowchart for this situation is shown in Figure 3-1.

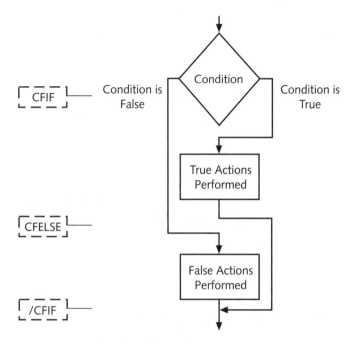

Figure 3-1   Flowchart for a CFIF tag

You can modify a CFIF tag by excluding the CFELSE tag. Essentially, the CFELSE part of a CFIF statement is optional. If you exclude the CFELSE tag, the CFIF tag executes an action if a condition is true; otherwise it skips the action. The syntax for such a CFIF tag is as follows:

```
<CFIF condition>
      True action
</CFIF>
```

If the CFIF condition evaluates to true, the true action is performed. If the CFIF condition evaluates to false, it doesn't perform the true action.

NikRealty, located in Hudson, IA, was started in the early 1990s by Nikitha Little and has grown steadily. It services the northeast Iowa area including Waterloo, Cedar Falls, Hudson, Cedar Rapids, and other nearby communities. It employs about ten people and specializes in residential real estate sales. Nikitha is technologically savvy and realizes that the growth in the Internet and the Web can either be an opportunity or a threat to her business, depending on her technology strategy. She has hired you as a consultant to help her business. Throughout this book, you will be working on exercises and projects related to this business organization. Nikitha believes that her Web site should not only provide information about the properties that they have for sale but also assist customers with their decisions. One of her agents, Kelly Kernan, has requested you to design a template that helps customers to decide whether they should rent or buy a house. She says that a simple rule of thumb for deciding whether to buy or rent is to consider how long you are going to occupy a house. If you expect to live for five or more years in the house, buying is better than renting; otherwise it's not. She has asked you to design a Web page that takes this logic into consideration. You have decided to use a URL parameter named occupationYears for providing the input to the template.

You will create a ColdFusion template to study the workings of a CFIF statement.

To create a ColdFusion template with a CFIF statement:

1. Start ColdFusion Studio. A new ColdFusion template opens. If necessary, expand the Editor window and click the **Show line numbers in gutter** button on the vertical Editor toolbar to display the line numbers in the Editor window.

2. If necessary, click at the beginning of line 9, below the <body> tag and type **<cfset occupationYears = URL.occupationYears>** and press the **Enter** key. You are creating a new variable named occupationYears and assigning the value of the URL parameter to it.

3. On line 5, change the title of the document from untitled to **Rent Vs Buy**. Enter the code for the CFIF tag shown in Figure 3-2.

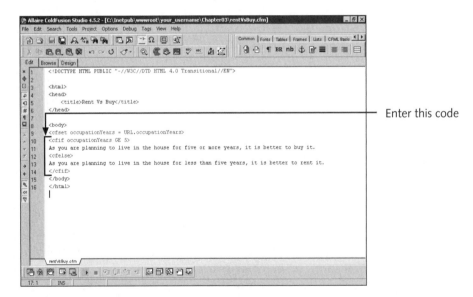

Enter this code

Figure 3-2   Template for rent vs. buy decision

4. Click the **Save** button on the Standard toolbar, and then navigate to the Chapter03 subfolder on your Data Disk.

5. Type **rentVsBuy.cfm** in the File name text box, and then click the **Save** button. The template is saved in the Chapter03 folder on the server.

Even though you can directly use the URL.occupationYears variable in the CFIF tag, it is a good practice to create a regular variable and assign it the value from the URL parameter. You should always try to implement a three-part program logic that includes an initialization/input part, a processing part, and an output part.

6. Start your Web browser, and open **http://localhost/your_username/ Chapter03/rentVsBuy.cfm?occupationYears=7**. See Figure 3-3.

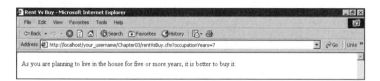

Figure 3-3   Web page displayed by rentVsBuy.cfm?occupationYears=7

When the ColdFusion Server executes this program, the variable occupationYears is assigned the value of the URL parameter occupationYears, which is 7 in this case. When the server processes the CFIF tag, it evaluates the condition `occupationYears GE 5`. Because the variable occupationYears has a value of 7 and 7 is greater than or equal to 5, the condition evaluates to true and the ColdFusion Server performs the true action and displays the text "As you are planning to live in the house for five or more years, it is better to buy it." A flowchart for this example is shown in Figure 3-4.

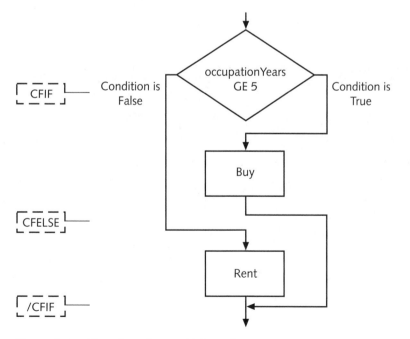

Figure 3-4   Flowchart for rentVsBuy.cfm

Now see what happens when you change the value of the URL parameter occupationYears.

To change the parameter to display the false action:

1. In your Web browser, click at the end of the text in the Address text box, press **Backspace** to delete **7**, and then type **3** to replace 7.

2. Press the **Enter** key to open the template with the new value for the URL parameter. Because the occupationYears variable now stores a value that is not greater than or equal to 5, the false action of the CFIF statement is executed to produce the output "As you are planning to live in the house for less than five years, it is better to rent it." See Figure 3-5.

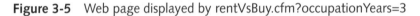

Figure 3-5   Web page displayed by rentVsBuy.cfm?occupationYears=3

Working with Relational Operators

You used a relational operator in the rentVsBuy.cfm template to perform the comparison "greater than or equal to". You can use all six standard relational operators in ColdFusion. Table 3-1 describes these standard relational operators along with the operator symbols.

Table 3-1   Standard Relational Operators in ColdFusion

Operator	Description
GE	Greater than or equal to
GT	Greater than
LE	Less than or equal to
LT	Less than
EQ	Equal to
NEQ	Not equal to

In ColdFusion, IS and IS NOT are alternate symbols for EQ and NEQ. ColdFusion also supports some nonstandard relational operators. **Contains** is a useful operator that checks to see if the string on the right of the operator is contained in the string on the left and returns true if it is. An opposite effect is produced by the **does not contain** operator.

In the previous exercise, you saw how to use a single CFIF tag for the rent vs. buy decision. ColdFusion templates may contain as many CFIF tags as needed. The following example (Example3-1.cfm) illustrates the use of all six standard relational operators by using multiple CFIF tags.

```
<cfset X = URL.X>
<cfset Y = URL.Y>
<table border=1 align=center>
<tr><th>Use of six standard relational operators</th></tr>
<tr><td>
<cfoutput>1. Is #X# GE #Y#? </cfoutput> -
<cfif X GE Y>
TRUE
<cfelse>
FALSE
</cfif>
</td></tr><tr><td>
<cfoutput>2. Is #X# GT #Y#? </cfoutput> -
<cfif X GT Y>
TRUE
<cfelse>
FALSE
</cfif>
</td></tr><tr><td>
<cfoutput>3. Is #X# LE #Y#? </cfoutput> -
<cfif X LE Y>
TRUE
<cfelse>
FALSE
</cfif>
</td></tr><tr><td>
<cfoutput>4. Is #X# LT #Y#? </cfoutput> -
<cfif X LT Y>
TRUE
<cfelse>
FALSE
</cfif>
</td></tr><tr><td>
<cfoutput>5. Is #X# EQ #Y#? </cfoutput> -
<cfif X EQ Y>
TRUE
<cfelse>
FALSE
</cfif>
</td></tr><tr><td>
<cfoutput>6. Is #X# NEQ #Y#? </cfoutput> -
<cfif X NEQ Y>
TRUE
<cfelse>
FALSE
</cfif>
</td></tr>
</table>
```

This program takes two URL parameters, assigns them to two variables (X, Y), and tests a different relational operator in each row of the table. Notice that the second row in the table is highlighted. Each of the other rows is identical to this row except for its relational operator. Also note that the values of variables are displayed in the form of a question, and a CFIF tag shows whether a condition is true or false in each row.

To use relational operators with CFIF tags:

1. If necessary, switch to your Web browser.

2. Type **http://localhost/your_username/Chapter03/Example3-1.cfm? X=20&Y=10** or an equivalent URL in the Address text box of your Web browser. Then press the **Enter** key. The ColdFusion Server executes the example and displays a Web page, as shown in Figure 3-6.

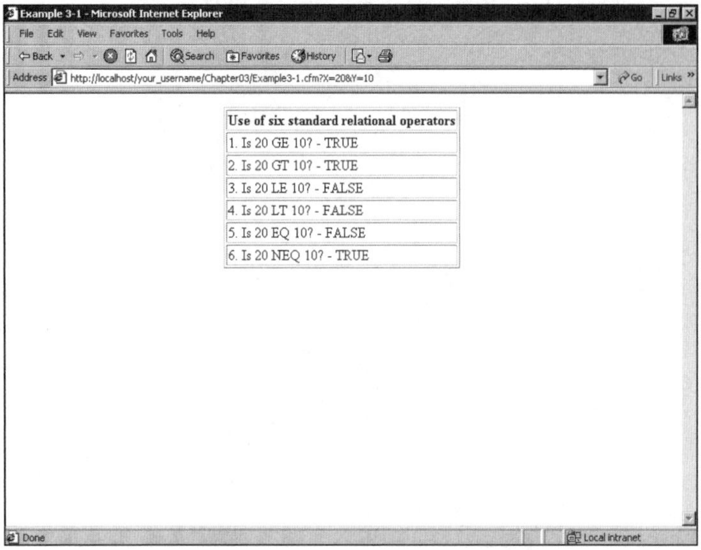

Figure 3-6   Web page displayed by Example3-1cfm?X=20&Y=10

When the ColdFusion Server executes the template, variable X is assigned the value 20, and variable Y is assigned the value 10. When it executes the second table row that is highlighted, it processes the CFOUTPUT tags and outputs values of variables X and Y as 2. Is 20 GT 10? - . Then it executes the CFIF tag and evaluates the CFIF condition 20 GT 10. Because 20 is greater than 10, the condition is true and the true action is performed.

The true action just contains the text TRUE and this text is output, and the false action consisting of the text FALSE is skipped. Further, examine the output and verify that conditions with GE, GT, and NEQ are true and conditions with LE, LT, and EQ are false.

3. Replace **X=20** with **X=10** in the Address text box to modify the URL to http://localhost/your_username/Chapter03/Example3-1.cfm?X=10&Y=10, and then press **Enter**. See Figure 3-7. Notice that now the conditions with GE, LE, and EQ evaluate to true and the others evaluate to false.

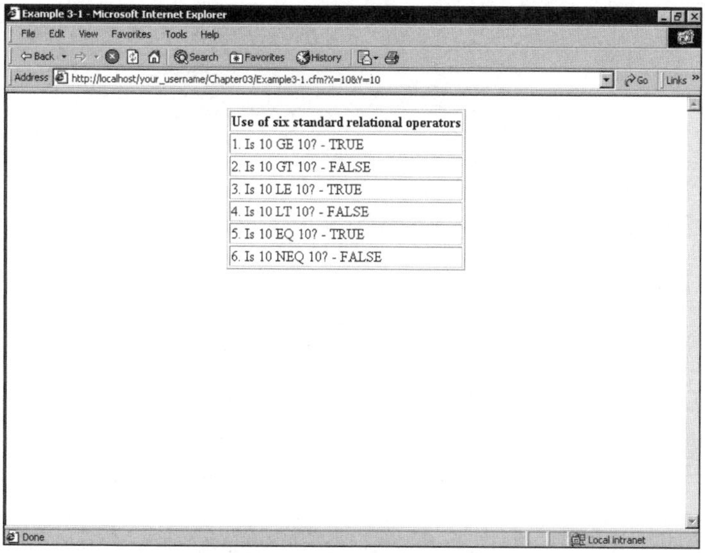

Figure 3-7   Web page displayed by Example3-1.cfm?X=10&Y=10

4. In the Address text box of your browser, type **http://localhost/ your_username/Chapter03/Example3-1.cfm?X=a&Y=b**, and then press **Enter**. The ColdFusion Server executes the template without any errors and displays a Web page, as shown in Figure 3-8.

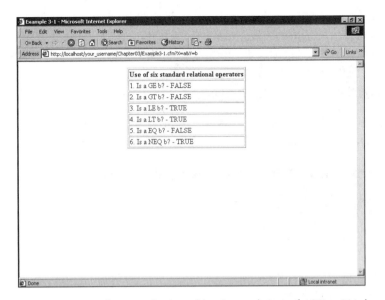

Figure 3-8   Web page displayed by Example3-1.cfm?X=a&Y=b

Conditions and CFIF tags work with strings too. In the output, note that conditions with LE, LT, and NEQ evaluate to true and the others to false. What does a string being less than another string mean? A string or a string literal that would appear earlier in a dictionary (alphabetical order) is less than a string that would appear later.

5. In the Address text box of your browser, type **http://localhost/your_username/Chapter03/Example3-1.cfm?X=a&Y=A**, and then press **Enter**. See Figure 3-9. ColdFusion performs a case-insensitive comparison while evaluating conditions with string variables and literals (that is, a and A are treated the same).

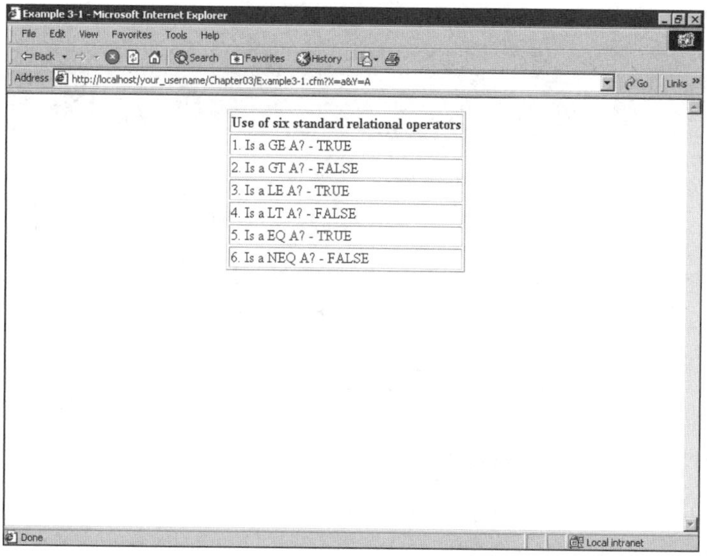

Figure 3-9   Web page displayed by Example3-1.cfm?X=a&Y=A

As you now know, CFIF conditions work with numbers as well as strings. In fact, you can form conditions by using all the different data types that you learned about in the previous two chapters. Table 3-2 summarizes the interpretations of relational operators when used with different data types.

Table 3-2   Relational Operators and Basic Data Types

Relational Operator in ColdFusion	Result When Using Numbers	Result When Using Strings	Result When Using Date-Time Values
X GE Y	Number X is greater than or equal to number Y	String X follows string Y alphabetically or is the same while treating lowercase and uppercase letters the same	X occurs later than or at the same time as Y
X GT Y	Number X is greater than number Y	String X follows string Y alphabetically while treating lowercase and uppercase letters the same	X occurs later than Y
X LE Y	Number X is less than or equal to number Y	String X precedes string Y alphabetically or is the same while treating lowercase and uppercase letters the same	X occurs earlier than or at the same time as Y
X LT Y	Number X is less than number Y	String X precedes string Y alphabetically while treating lowercase and uppercase letters the same	X occurs earlier than Y

Table 3-2   Relational Operators and Basic Data Types (continued)

Relational Operator in ColdFusion	Result When Using Numbers	Result When Using Strings	Result When Using Date-Time Values
X EQ Y	Number X is equal to number Y	String X is the same as string Y while treating lowercase and uppercase letters the same	X occurs at the same time and date as Y
X NEQ Y	Number X is not equal to number Y	String X is different from string Y while treating lowercase and uppercase letters the same	X and Y occur at different times and/or dates

Conditional Formatting Using CFIF

A very useful application of CFIF tags is to highlight situations that deserve special attention. For example, you can use CFIF tags to format table cells or use font colors to highlight important data. Suppose you want to develop a Web page for NikRealty that includes house prices and highlights the good deals. You could include a table on the page that shows house prices in the cells of the table; prices less than $100,000 have a red background color. To set this up in a ColdFusion template, consider the HTML code you need to change the background color of a table cell—you set the BGCOLOR attribute of the TD tag to the required color using its name or its RGB color code. The code <td bgcolor = "red"> would color the particular cell red. When the price of a house listed in the table is lower than $100,000, you output this code; if the price is not lower than $100,000, you output a TD tag without any attributes. As you have two possible actions from which to choose, you need to use a CFIF tag. In the following exercise, you create this table and use a CFIF tag to assign conditional formatting.

To use a CFIF tag for conditional formatting:

1. Switch to ColdFusion Studio, and open **displayPrice.cfm** in the Chapter03 subfolder on your Data Disk. See Figure 3-10.

   Examine the code in the template. It assigns the value of a URL parameter named housePrice to a variable named housePrice. It also displays a table with one row and two columns. The label "List price of the house:" is displayed in the first cell, and the value of the variable housePrice is formatted as currency and displayed in the second cell. Remember that your task is to highlight good deals by changing the background color of the second cell to red when house prices are less than $100,000.

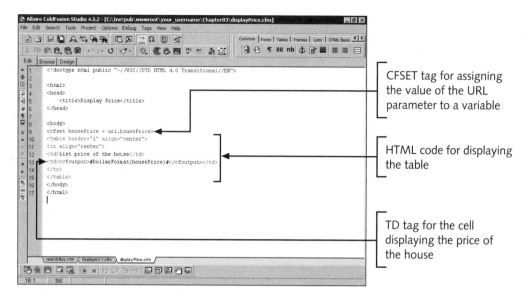

CFSET tag for assigning the value of the URL parameter to a variable

HTML code for displaying the table

TD tag for the cell displaying the price of the house

Figure 3-10   Initial displayPrice.cfm in ColdFusion Studio

2. Select **<td>** at the beginning of line 13, and type **<cfif housePrice LT 100000>** to replace it. Then press the **Enter** key. Notice that ColdFusion Studio inserts the closing /CFIF tag.

3. Type **<td bgcolor = "red">**, and press **Enter**.

4. Press the **Del** key five times to delete the </td> text that ColdFusion Studio has inserted because of its tag completion feature.

5. Type **<cfelse>**, and press **Enter**.

6. Type **<td>**, and press **Enter**.

7. Press **Del** five times to delete the </td> text that ColdFusion Studio has inserted. See Figure 3-11.

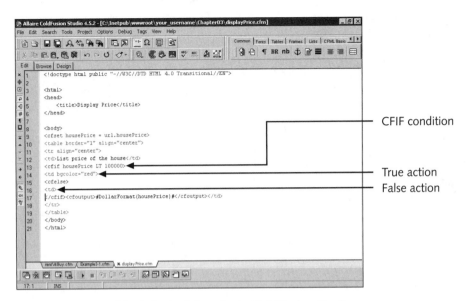

Figure 3-11 Modified displayPrice.cfm in ColdFusion Studio

8. Click the **Save** button on the Standard toolbar to save the file.

9. Switch to your Web browser and type **http://localhost/your_username/ Chapter03/displayPrice.cfm?housePrice=95000**. Press **Enter**. See Figure 3-12. Note that the statements between the CFIF and CFELSE tags have been executed because the price of the house is less than $100,000, making the background color of the cell red.

Figure 3-12 Web page displayed by displayPrice.cfm?housePrice=95000

10. In the Address text box of your Web browser, change the value of the URL parameter to **125000**. See Figure 3-13.

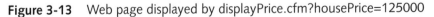

Figure 3-13 Web page displayed by displayPrice.cfm?housePrice=125000

Now the statements between the CFIF and CFELSE tags are skipped, and the statements between the CFELSE and /CFIF tags are executed, resulting in the output of <td> and a cell without a red background.

Nesting CFIF Tags

Sometimes you need to make complex decisions in programs by testing a series of conditions instead of only one condition. In these cases, you can enclose CFIF tags within other CFIF tags. When CFIF tags are enclosed in other CFIF tags, you have **nested CFIF tags**. Figure 3-14 shows a flowchart for a nested CFIF statement. The first CFIF condition is called the **outer condition**; the second CFIF condition is called the **inner condition**.

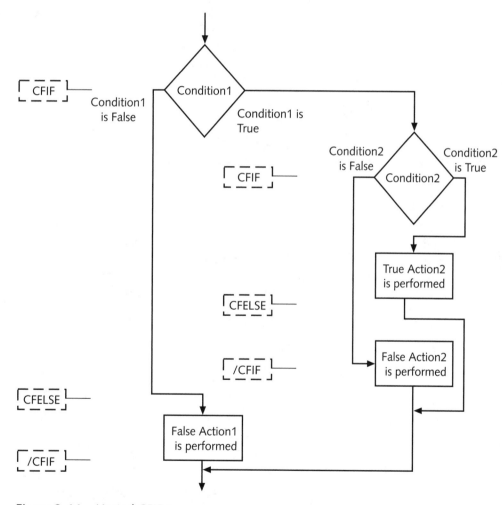

Figure 3-14   Nested CFIF tags

For example, you could nest CFIF tags to test whether a person is female and an adult. First you could test to see if the person is an adult by asking for his or her age. If the age is greater than or equal to 21, the person is an adult. So Condition1 would be "is person GE 21?". If that condition is true, processing continues to Condition2. Now you could ask the person for his or her gender. You could assign a value of "M" for male and "F" for female. Condition2 could be "is gender EQ "F"?". If that condition is true, a specified action is performed.

Proper care should be taken when nesting statements. If an inner CFIF statement is part of the action to be taken when the outer condition is true, you should make sure that the entire inner CFIF statement (the CFIF, CFELSE and /CFIF tags) is included between the outer CFIF and CFELSE tags. If the inner CFIF statement is part of the action to be taken when the outer condition is false, you should make sure that the entire inner CFIF statement is included between the outer CFELSE and /CFIF tags. It is easier to examine your nested CFIF statements if you indent the inner statements, as shown in the following syntax.

```
<CFIF Condition1>
      <CFIF Condition2>
            True action 2
      <CFELSE>
            False action 2
      </CFIF>
<CFELSE>
      False action 1
</CFIF>
```

When the ColdFusion Server executes the outer CFIF statement, it evaluates Condition1. If Condition1 evaluates to false, then the server performs False action 1, skips all statements in the inner CFIF statement, and continues executing the program below the outer CFIF statement. If Condition1 evaluates to true, then the server performs True action 1, which includes testing Condition2 and executing True action 2 or False action 2. Depending on the result of Condition2, the execution continues with the statement below the outer CFIF statement. The following example (Example3-2.cfm) illustrates nested CFIF statements.

```
<cfset housePrice = URL.housePrice>
<cfset numBedrooms = URL.numBedrooms>
<table border="1" align="center">
<tr align="center">
<td>List price of the house</td>
<cfif housePrice LT 100000>
      <cfif numBedrooms LE 2>
      <td bgcolor="red"><font color="Black">
      <cfelse>
      <td bgcolor = "green"><font color="White">
      </cfif>
<cfelse>
<td><font color="Black">
```

```
</cfif><cfoutput>#DollarFormat(housePrice)#</cfoutput>
</font></td>
</tr>
</table>
```

Using this code, you can modify the table for NikRealty. The two conditions are a house price less than $100,000 having less than or equal to two bedrooms. When a house price is less than $100,000 and has two or fewer bedrooms, the price appears as black text on a red background. If the house price is less than $100,000 but has more than two bedrooms, the price appears as white text on a green background. If neither of the conditions is true, the price appears in the default format, black text on a white background.

To use nested CFIF tags with Example3-2.cfm:

1. Use your Web browser to open **Example3-2.cfm?housePrice= 75000&numBedrooms=3** in the Chapter03 folder. See Figure 3-15.

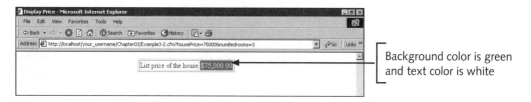

Background color is green and text color is white

Figure 3-15   Web page displayed by Example3-2.cfm?housePrice=75000&numBedrooms=3

When the ColdFusion Server executes Example3-2.cfm, it creates two variables—housePrice & numBedrooms and assigns them 75000 and 3, respectively. The code for the table is output next. The outer CFIF condition is evaluated as true because the house price of $75,000 is less than $100,000. The ColdFusion Server takes the true action, which consists of a second CFIF statement. The ColdFusion Server evaluates the second CFIF condition to false because the number of bedrooms (3) is not less than or equal to 2. The true action 2 is skipped and the false action 2 is executed, resulting in the code for setting the background color of the cell to green and the font color of the text to white.

2. Change the URL to **Example3-2.cfm?housePrice= 75000&numBedrooms=2** in the Address text box of your Web browser, and press the **Enter** key to view it. See Figure 3-16.

Background color is red and text color is black

Figure 3-16   Web page displayed by Example3-2.cfm?housePrice=75000&numBedrooms=2

This time, the outer condition is true and the inner condition is also true, resulting in a red background color for the cell.

3. Finally, change the URL to **Example3-2.cfm?housePrice= 125000&numBedrooms=2** in the Address text box of your Web browser, and press **Enter** to view it. See Figure 3-17.

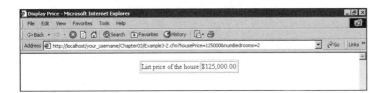

Figure 3-17   Web page displayed by Example3-2.cfm?housePrice=125000&num Bedrooms=2

This time, the outer condition is false so the inner condition is not evaluated. This results in a cell with the default background color.

You can combine a CFELSE and a CFIF tag by using a CFELSEIF tag. By using CFELSEIF tags, you create a more general form of the CFIF statement that tests a series of conditions until a true condition is encountered. Then the ColdFusion Server executes the action for the true condition. The syntax for a CFIF statement containing CFELSEIF clauses is as follows:

```
<CFIF Condition1>
    Action 1
<CFELSEIF Condition2>
    Action 2
<CFELSEIF Condition3>
    Action 3
<CFELSE>
    Action 4
</CFIF>
```

A flowchart for the CFIF statement with CFELSEIF clauses is shown in Figure 3-18.

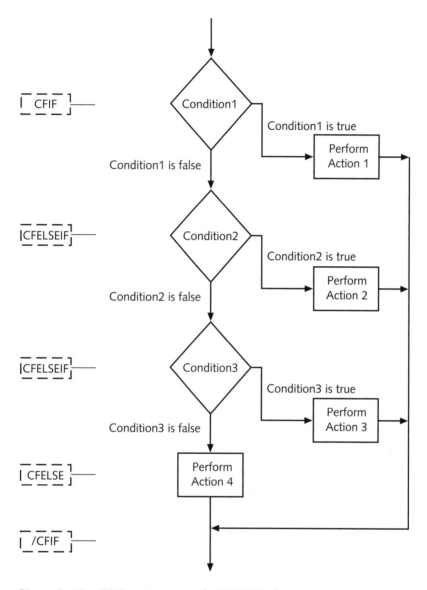

Figure 3-18   CFIF statement with CFELSEIF clauses

A CFIF statement with CFELSEIF clauses is useful to model situations where you must test multiple conditions to determine the actions to be performed. Typically, the conditions are mutually exclusive. Considering the previous CFIF statement and those in the flowchart, if Condition1 is true, action 1 is performed and everything else is skipped; then the statements below the closing CFIF tag are executed. If Conditon1 is false, Condition2 is tested. Action 2 is performed if Condition2 is true and everything else is skipped. Condition3 is tested if Condition2 is false. If Condition3 is true, Action 3 is performed, and if it is false, Action 4 is performed.

Nikitha has implemented a rating scheme to motivate her agents. Agents with sales totaling a million dollars or more receive four stars. Agents with sales less than a million but over $500,000 receive three stars, and others receive two stars. One of your project members has designed a template named rateAgents.cfm that takes a URL parameter named sales and outputs the agent's rating. This template uses a CFIF tag with CFELSEIF clauses. Your project manager has asked you to test this template.

To test a CFIF tag with CFELSEIF clauses:

1. Switch to ColdFusion Studio, and close all open documents.

2. Open **rateAgents.cfm** in the Chapter03 folder on your Data Disk. See Figure 3-19.

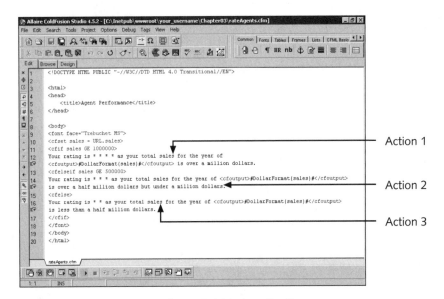

Figure 3-19   rateAgents.cfm in ColdFusion Studio

Notice that the template has a CFIF tag with a CFELSEIF clause. The condition in the CFIF tag is sales GE 1000000, and the condition in the CFELSEIF is sales GE 500000.

3. Switch to your Web browser, and type the URL: **http://localhost/your_username/Chapter03/rateAgents.cfm?sales=1234567**. Press **Enter**. See Figure 3-20.

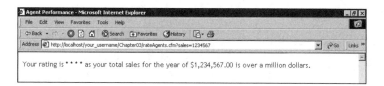

Figure 3-20   Web page displayed by rateAgents.cfm?sales=1234567

When the ColdFusion Server executes this template, variable sales is assigned a value of 1,234,567. Because this value is greater than 1,000,000, the CFIF condition is true and a four star rating is shown, as in Figure 3-20. The other parts of the CFIF tag are skipped.

4. Modify the URL in the Address text box by selecting **1234567** and replacing it with **555000**, and then press the **Enter** key. See Figure 3-21.

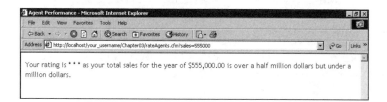

Figure 3-21   Web page displayed by rateAgents.cfm?sales=555000

When the ColdFusion Server executes rateAgents.cfm this time, the value of the variable sales is 555,000. The CFIF condition is false, so the CFELSEIF condition is evaluated. This condition is true, so the corresponding action is performed. The template shows a three star rating, as shown in Figure 3-21.

5. Finally, modify the URL in the Address text box by selecting **555000** and replacing it with **125000**, and then press **Enter**. See Figure 3-22.

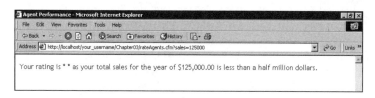

Figure 3-22   Web page displayed by rateAgents.cfm?sales=125000

When the ColdFusion Server executes rateAgents.cfm this time, the value of the variable sales is 125,000. The CFIF condition is false, as is the CFELSEIF condition. Because both conditions are false, the action in the CFELSE clause is performed. The template shows a two star rating, as shown in Figure 3-22.

Using Logical Operators

Sometimes you will encounter situations that are complex and difficult to model with nested CFIF statements. For example, to use a tax table to compute the income tax on a person's income, you must compare the person's income with two quantities. In this situation, you would need one CFIF statement for every amount in the tax table, resulting in hundreds of CFIF statements. An easier way to compute the tax is to use a logical operator. A **logical operator** lets you combine simple conditions to form complex conditions. For example, the simple conditions "is person GE 21" and "is person female" could be combined into one statement using the AND logical operator ("is person GE 21 AND is person female"). Other logical operators allowed in ColdFusion are OR and NOT. If Condition1 and Condition2 are simple conditions, "Condition1 AND Condition2" is a complex condition that is true when both the simple conditions are true; otherwise it is false. "Condition1 OR Condition2" is true when either of the two simple conditions is true or if both conditions are true; it is false when both conditions are false. The NOT operator works on only one condition and reverses its true value. "NOT Condition1" is true when Condition1 is false, and "NOT Condition1" is false when Condition1 is true.

As part of the decision support tools on the NikRealty Web site, you have been asked to design a template that implements the logic shown in Table 3-3 for rating properties based on their location and price evaluations.

Table 3-3   Location–Price Decision Support Tool

Location\Price	Low	High
Excellent	Must see	Serious consideration
Fair	Serious consideration	Waste of time

One of your project members has designed a template named rateProperty.cfm using CFIF tags with the AND logical operator, and you are examining this template.

To use the AND logical operator with rateProperty.cfm:

1. Switch to ColdFusion Studio, and close any open documents.

2. Open **rateProperty.cfm** in the Chapter03 folder on your Data Disk. See Figure 3-23.

   Note that there are four CFIF tags, one for each of the four possible property ratings in Table 3-3. All the CFIF conditions are complex conditions using the AND logical operator. They combine two simple conditions, one for testing the location and the other for testing the price. If both the simple conditions are true, the complex condition is true.

3. Switch to your Web browser and type **http://localhost/your_username/ Chapter03/rateProperty.cfm?location=fair&price=low** in the Address text box, and then press the **Enter** key. Your Web browser displays the page shown in Figure 3-24.

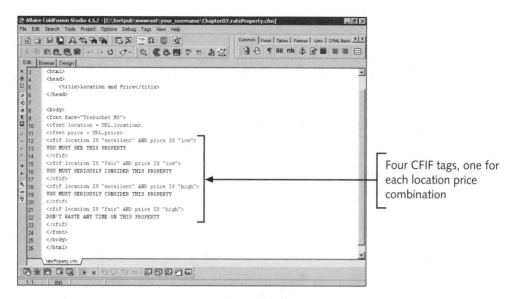

Four CFIF tags, one for each location price combination

Figure 3-23   rateProperty.cfm in ColdFusion Studio

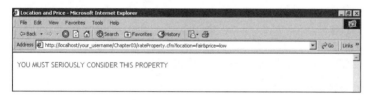

Figure 3-24   Web page displayed by rateProperty.cfm?location=fair&price=low

Given these values for variables location and price, condition location IS "excellent" is false, condition price IS "high" is false, condition location IS "fair" is true, and condition price IS "low" is true. Only the complex condition in the second CFIF tag is true, and the complex conditions in other CFIF tags are false. This produces the message YOU MUST SERIOUSLY CONSIDER THIS PROPERTY, as shown in Figure 3-24.

4. Modify the URL in the Address text box of your Web browser to **rateProperty.cfm?location=excellent&price=low**, and then press **Enter**. See Figure 3-25.

Figure 3-25   Web page displayed by rateProperty.cfm?location=excellent&price=low

This time, both the simple conditions in the first CFIF tag are true, producing the message YOU MUST SEE THIS PROPERTY.

5. Modify the URL in the Address text box of your Web browser to **rateProperty.cfm?location=excellent&price=hig**, and then press **Enter**. See Figure 3-26.

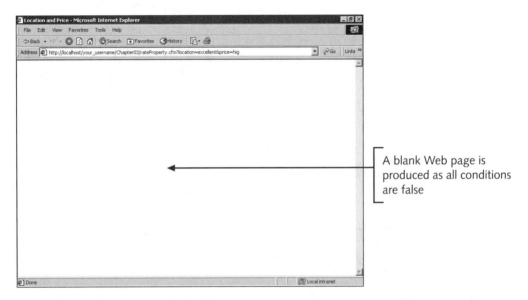

Figure 3-26   Web page displayed by rateProperty.cfm?location=excellent&price=hig

Notice that the value of the price parameter has been intentionally misspelled. This time, none of the complex conditions are true because price is neither low nor high. None of the CFIF actions are performed, resulting in an empty Web page.

In the previous exercise, you used relational operators and logical operators in one long condition. When you use multiple relational operators and logical operators, similar to the concept of operator precedence in arithmetic expressions, ColdFusion implements operator precedence, as shown in Table 3-4.

Table 3-4   Operator Precedence for Relational and Logical Operators

Operator Precedence (Highest to Lowest)
( )
EQ, NEQ, LT, LE, GT, GE
NOT
AND
OR

As shown in Table 3-4, conditions in parentheses are evaluated first, relational operators are evaluated second, followed by evaluation of a NOT operator, then an AND operator, and finally an OR operator. To prevent any confusion, it is always a good practice to use parentheses to clarify the order of evaluation for operators.

Using the CFSWITCH Statement

A **CFSWITCH statement** allows you to select an action to be performed from several different actions, based on the value of a particular expression. Each action is associated with a value-list. A **value-list** is a set of values separated by commas. If the value of the expression is in an actions value-list, then the action is executed. The general form of the CFSWITCH statement is as follows:

```
<CFSWITCH EXPRESSION="expression">
<CFCASE VALUE="value-list1"> Action1 </CFCASE>
<CFCASE VALUE="value-list2"> Action2 </CFCASE>
<CFCASE VALUE="value-list3"> Action3 </CFCASE>
<CFDEFAULTCASE>Action4</CFDEFAULTCASE>
</CFSWITCH>
```

The CFSWITCH tag has an attribute named EXPRESSION. You can set this attribute to any valid expression. This expression is termed the **selector expression** because its result is the basis for the selection of the action to be performed. The value of the selector expression is the **selector value**. The /CFSWITCH tag ends the CFSWITCH tag. Each possible action is coded in a set of CFCASE /CFCASE tags. The CFCASE tag has an attribute VALUE that you set to the value-list for that action. The default action to be performed if there is no match is coded in a set of CFDEFAULTCASE /CFDEFAULTCASE tags. The flowchart for the CFSWITCH statement is shown in Figure 3-27.

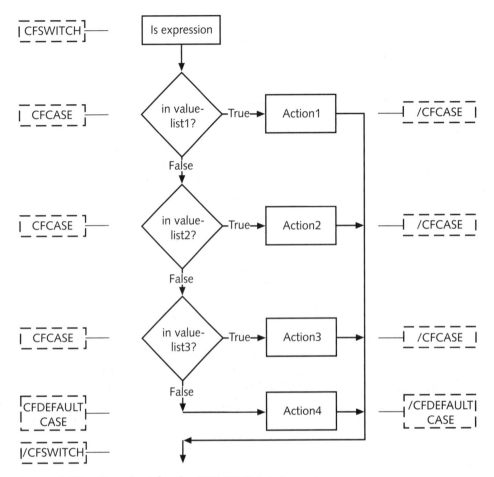

Figure 3-27   Flowchart for the CFSWITCH statement

When the ColdFusion Server executes a CFSWITCH statement, it evaluates the selector expression and compares the resulting selector value with the values in value-list1. If the value exists in value-list1, the Server performs Action1, skips all of the other case clauses, and continues executing the program by processing the statements below the closing CFSWITCH tag. If the selector value is not in value-list1, then the Server evaluates the second CFCASE tag and checks to see if it is in value-list2. If it is in value-list2, the Server performs Action2, and so on. If there is no match for any of the case clauses, the Server performs the action in the CFDEFAULTCASE tags.

The following example (Example3-3.cfm) illustrates the use of a CFSWITCH statement:

```
<cfset topping = URL.topping>
<hr>
<cfoutput>Price of #topping# topping is</cfoutput>
<cfswitch expression="#topping#">
<cfcase value="GreenPeppers,Mushrooms"> $0.50</cfcase>
```

```
<cfcase value="Jalapenos,Pepperoni"> $1.00</cfcase>
<cfdefaultcase>$0.25</cfdefaultcase>
</cfswitch>
<hr>
```

 Note that there are no spaces in the value-list "GreenPeppers,Mushrooms". If you type spaces in a value-list, such as "GreenPeppers, Mushrooms", the ColdFusion Server interprets the values in the list as "GreenPeppers", and, "_Mushrooms" where the underscore (_) indicates a space.

To use the CFSWITCH tag with Example3-3.cfm:

1. In the Address text box of your Web browser, type **http://localhost/ your_username/Chapter03/Example3-3.cfm?topping=Mushrooms**, and press the **Enter** key. See Figure 3-28.

Figure 3-28   Web page displayed by Example3-3.cfm?topping=Mushrooms

When the ColdFusion Server processes this request, it assigns the value Mushrooms to variable topping. It outputs this value in the text enclosed in the CFOUTPUT tags. Then it processes the CFSWITCH tag and evaluates the expression #topping# to Mushrooms. It compares the selector-value (Mushrooms) to each value in the first CFCASE tag's value-list and finds a match. Because there is a match, it executes the action in the first set of CFCASE /CFCASE tags and displays the text $0.50, resulting in an output of "Price of Mushrooms toppings is $0.50," as shown in Figure 3-28. Because there is a match, the rest of the cases are not evaluated, and the statements below the /CFSWITCH are executed.

2. In the Address text box of your Web browser, type **http://localhost/ your_username/Chapter03/Example3-3.cfm?topping=Jalapenos**, and press **Enter**. See Figure 3-29.

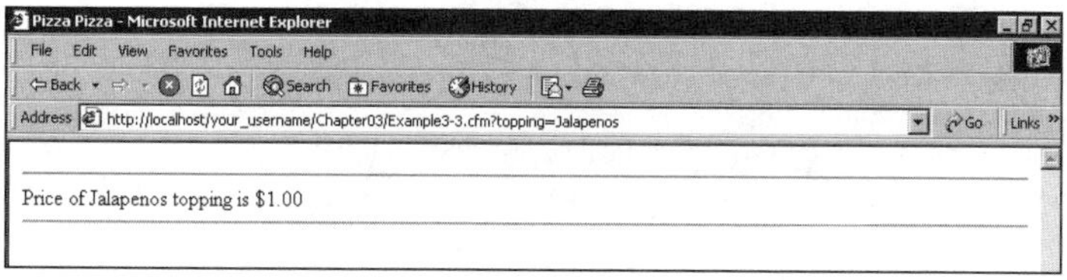

Figure 3-29   Web page displayed by Example3-3.cfm?topping=Jalapenos

When the ColdFusion Server processes this request, it assigns the value Jalapenos to the variable topping. It outputs this value in the text enclosed in the CFOUTPUT tags. Then it processes the CFSWITCH tag and evaluates the expression #topping# to Jalapenos. It compares the selector-value (Jalapenos) to each value in the first CFCASE tag's value-list and does not find a match. Because there are no matches, it compares the selector-value to each value in the second CFCASE tag's value-list. Because it finds a match here, it executes the corresponding action and displays the text $1.00, resulting in an output of "Price of Jalapenos toppings is $1.00," as shown in Figure 3-29. The default case is skipped, and the statement below the /CFSWITCH tag is executed next.

3. In the Address text box of your Web browser, type **http://localhost/ your_username/Chapter03/Example3-3.cfm?topping=Onions**, and press **Enter**. See Figure 3-30.

Figure 3-30   Web page displayed by Example3-3.cfm?topping=Onions

When the ColdFusion Server processes this request, it assigns the value Onions to variable topping. It outputs this value in the text enclosed in the CFOUTPUT tags. Then it processes the CFSWITCH tag and evaluates the expression #topping# to Onions. It compares the selector-value (Onions) to each value in the first CFCASE tag's value-list and it does not find a match. Because there are no matches, it compares the selector-value to each value in the second CFCASE tag's value-list and does not find a match here either. Because it doesn't find a match in any of the value-lists, the Server executes the action enclosed in the CFDEFAULTCASE /CFDEFAULTCASE tags and displays the text $0.25, resulting in an output of "Price of Onions toppings is $0.25," as shown in Figure 3-30. The statement below the /CFSWITCH tag is executed next.

USING REPETITION TO PERFORM REPETITIVE TASKS

Sometimes your programs need to perform the same task more than once, such as when you need to process payroll for every employee in an organization. When you need to execute a set of statements in a program many times, you can use repetition flow-control statements. To create repetition flow-control statements in ColdFusion, you use a CFLOOP tag. Using the CFLOOP tag, you can implement FOR loops, LIST loops,

WHILE loops, and QUERY loops. When you know exactly how many times a set of statements must be executed, you use FOR loops. You use a WHILE loop for executing a set of statements repeatedly as long as a certain condition is true. A LIST loop allows you to execute a set of statements repeatedly. For each execution, a variable takes a different value from a value-list. The following sections describe FOR loops, LIST loops, and WHILE loops. You will learn about the QUERY loops in subsequent chapters.

FOR Loops

As mentioned previously, a **FOR loop** allows you to execute a set of statements for a predefined number of times. A FOR loop in ColdFusion has four attributes—INDEX, FROM, TO, and STEP—and its syntax is shown below:

```
<CFLOOP INDEX= "for_variable"
FROM= "start_value" TO= "end_value"
STEP= "increment_value">
Statements containing HTML and CFML that are to be
executed in the loop
</CFLOOP>
```

You must set the **INDEX attribute** to the name of a variable that controls the execution of the loop (**control variable**). You set the **FROM attribute** to a value or an expression that provides the start value to be assigned to this control variable. The **TO attribute** stores an end value for the control variable. When the ColdFusion Server executes a FOR loop like the one in the preceding syntax, the control variable (for_variable) is first assigned start_value, and all statements between the CFLOOP tags are executed. Then increment_value is added to for_variable, and the statements between the CFLOOP tags are executed again. This process is repeated as long as the value of the for_variable is not more than the value in end_value. When the value in for_variable exceeds the value in end_value, repetition is terminated, and processing continues by executing the statement below the closing CFLOOP tag. The flowchart for a ColdFusion FOR loop is shown in Figure 3-31.

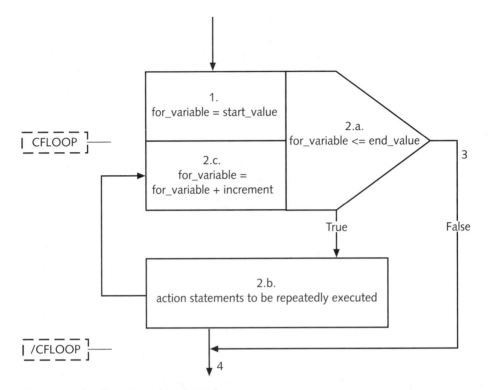

Figure 3-31   Flowchart for a FOR loop

In real estate, location is considered to be very important. If you ask any realtor what are the three important factors for choosing a property, the cliché is that they would say "Location, location, location." In the following exercise, you will create a simple FOR loop for displaying this list of the three most important real estate decision factors.

To create a FOR loop:

1. Switch to ColdFusion Studio, and close all open documents.

2. Click the **New** button on the Standard toolbar to create a new template.

3. Select the text **Untitled** that appears within the TITLE tags, and then type **FOR loop example**.

4. Enter the following code between the BODY tags:

```
<ul>
<cfloop index="i" from="1" to="3">
<li><b>Location</b></li>
</cfloop>
</ul>
```

5. Save the document as **factors.cfm** in the Chapter03 folder on the server, and then view the results in a browser. See Figure 3-32.

Figure 3-32   Web page displayed by factors.cfm

6. In your Web browser, click **View** on the menu bar, and then click **Source**. The source code for the FOR loop example page appears in a Notepad window, as shown in Figure 3-33.

Netscape users should click **View** on the menu bar, and then click **Page Source** to view the source code for a Web page.

```
<!DOCTYPE HTML PUBLIC "-//W3C//DTD HTML 4.0 Transitional//EN">

<html>
<head>
        <title>FOR loop example</title>
</head>

<body>
<ul>

<li><b>Location</b></li>

<li><b>Location</b></li>

<li><b>Location</b></li>

</ul>
</body>
</html>
```

Figure 3-33   HTML source code for the Web page displayed by factors.cfm

When the ColdFusion Server encounters HTML from the <html> to the <ul> tag in the template, the HTML is sent as is to the browser. When the ColdFusion Server executes the statement <cfloop index="i" from="1" to="3">, it assigns a value of 1 to variable i, and executes the statements between the CFLOOP tags. The statements between the CFLOOP tags are just HTML code (<li>Location</li>); this code is sent as is to the browser. After the first line is displayed, the FOR loop uses the default STEP value (1) to increment the variable i from 1 (the FROM value) to 2. Because the value 2 is still in the range of the FOR loop (from="1" to="3"), the loop continues and transmits the HTML code (<li>Location</li>)

again to the browser. The loop is repeated until the value of the variable i is 4, which ends the loop, and the HTML code below the closing CFLOOP tags is transmitted as is. This FOR loop displays the same output three times as a bulleted list.

7. Close Notepad.

The tag-completion feature in ColdFusion Studio is very useful when creating a template. When you are modifying an existing template, it is easier if you turn it off.

To turn off the tag-completion feature in ColdFusion Studio:

1. Switch to ColdFusion Studio.

2. Click the **Tag completion** button on the Editor toolbar to deselect it, as shown in Figure 3-34.

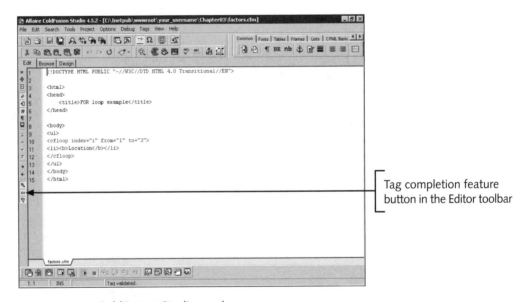

Tag completion feature button in the Editor toolbar

Figure 3-34   ColdFusion Studio workspace

In the next exercise, you will modify this template and output the factors in an HTML table instead of as a bulleted list, as shown in Figure 3-35.

Figure 3-35   Important real estate factors in an HTML table

As mentioned in Chapter 1, most dynamic Web sites extract data from database tables to create Web pages. Very often, the data that is extracted from database tables is presented in the form of HTML tables. In later chapters, you will learn about QUERY loops that extract data from database tables. In this exercise, you will use loops to present data in HTML tables.

To create a dynamic table for important real estate factors:

1. Click **File** on the menu bar of ColdFusion Studio, click **Save As**, and then save the factors.cfm file as **factorsTable.cfm** in the Chapter03 folder on the server.

2. Change the document title to **Tables on the fly**.

3. On line 2, type the following code to initialize a variable named numOfRows: **<cfset numOfRows = URL.Rows>**

4. Replace the <ul> tag with **<table align="center" border="1" width="75%">**.

5. In the CFLOOP tag, replace to="3" with **to="#numOfRows#"**.

6. Replace the </ul> tag with **</table>**.

7. Replace the line <li>Location</li> with the following text: **<tr><td> </td><td>Location</td></tr>**

 Some Web browsers do not display the border for cells that contain nothing or for cells that contain only spaces. To ensure that these Web browsers display a border, you have to use a non-breaking space character ( ) in empty cells.

Your code should look like the code shown in Figure 3-36. If necessary, make any changes before continuing.

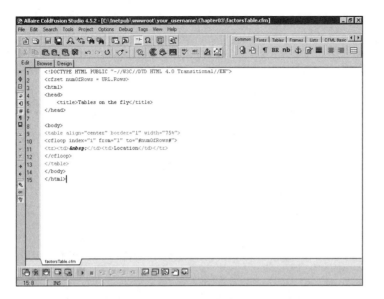

Figure 3-36   factorsTable.cfm in ColdFusion Studio

8. Click the **Save** button on the Standard toolbar.

9. Switch to your Web browser, and type the following URL: **http://localhost/ your_username/Chapter03/factorsTable.cfm?Rows=3** Press **Enter**. The output produced by this template is shown in Figure 3-35.

10. Click **View** on the menu bar, and then click **Source**. Notice that the HTML code contains three rows in the table. These rows were created by the loop.

11. Close Notepad. You can change the value of the Rows URL parameter to any other number to create a table with that number of rows. For example, change the value to 10, and the ColdFusion Server will execute the loop 10 times, creating a table with 10 rows, as shown in Figure 3-37.

12. You have successfully displayed data in an HTML table by using a FOR loop.

You can also use a loop to print the control variable's current value. In the next exercise, you will output the value of the control variable i in the cells in the first column.

To add a statement to print the value of the control variable:

1. Return to ColdFusion Studio, and then select **nbsp;** on line 11.

2. Type **<cfoutput>#i#</cfoutput>** to replace the selection.

3. Save the template with the same name and location.

4. Switch to your Web browser, and click the **Refresh** (or **Reload**) button. See Figure 3-38.

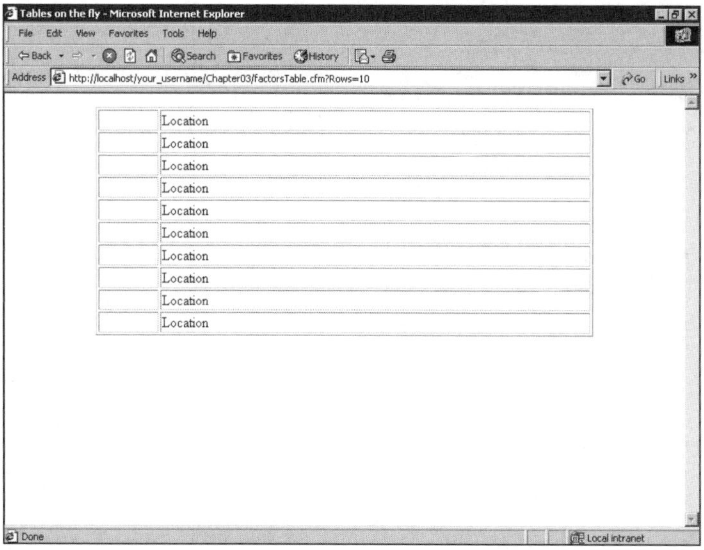

Figure 3-37   Table with ten rows

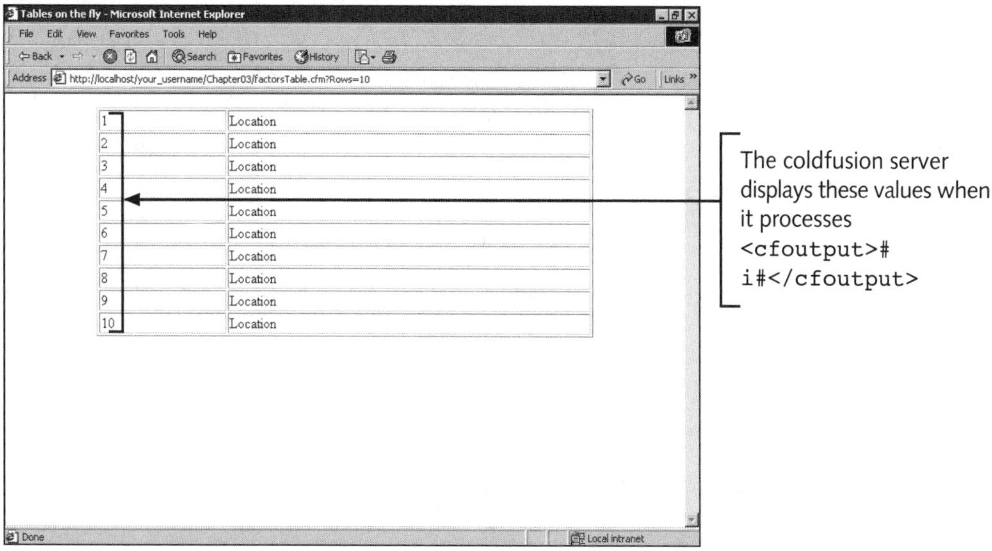

Figure 3-38   Table with row numbers

5. Click **View** on the menu bar, and then click **Source**. The source code for this Web page opens in Notepad. If necessary, maximize Notepad. See Figure 3-39.

```
factorsTable[1] - Notepad
File Edit Format Help
<!DOCTYPE HTML PUBLIC "-//W3C//DTD HTML 4.0 Transitional//EN">

<html>
<head>
        <title>Tables on the fly</title>
</head>

<body>
<table align="center" border="1" width="75%">

<tr><td>1</td><td>Location</td></tr>

<tr><td>2</td><td>Location</td></tr>

<tr><td>3</td><td>Location</td></tr>

<tr><td>4</td><td>Location</td></tr>

<tr><td>5</td><td>Location</td></tr>

<tr><td>6</td><td>Location</td></tr>

<tr><td>7</td><td>Location</td></tr>

<tr><td>8</td><td>Location</td></tr>

<tr><td>9</td><td>Location</td></tr>

<tr><td>10</td><td>Location</td></tr>

</table>
</body>
</html>
```

Figure 3-39   HTML code for the Web page displayed by factorsTable.cfm?Rows=10

The ColdFusion Server initializes the variable numOfRows to 10 and outputs ten rows in the table. It outputs the value of the control variable i in the first cell in each row. The loop keeps generating table rows until the value of i is 11. After that the loop ends, the ColdFusion Server executes the statements below the closing CFLOOP tag. You can check the ending value of variable i by using a CFOUTPUT statement.

To check the control variable's value after the loop has terminated:

1. Close the Notepad program window, and then return to ColdFusion Studio.

2. If the line numbers are not visible in the gutter, click the **Show line numbers in gutter** button in the Vertical Editor toolbar. After line 13, insert a new line that reads: **<cfoutput>#i#</cfoutput>**.

3. Save the template, click the program button for your browser on the taskbar, and then click the **Refresh** (or **Reload**) button to reload the page. See Figure 3-40.

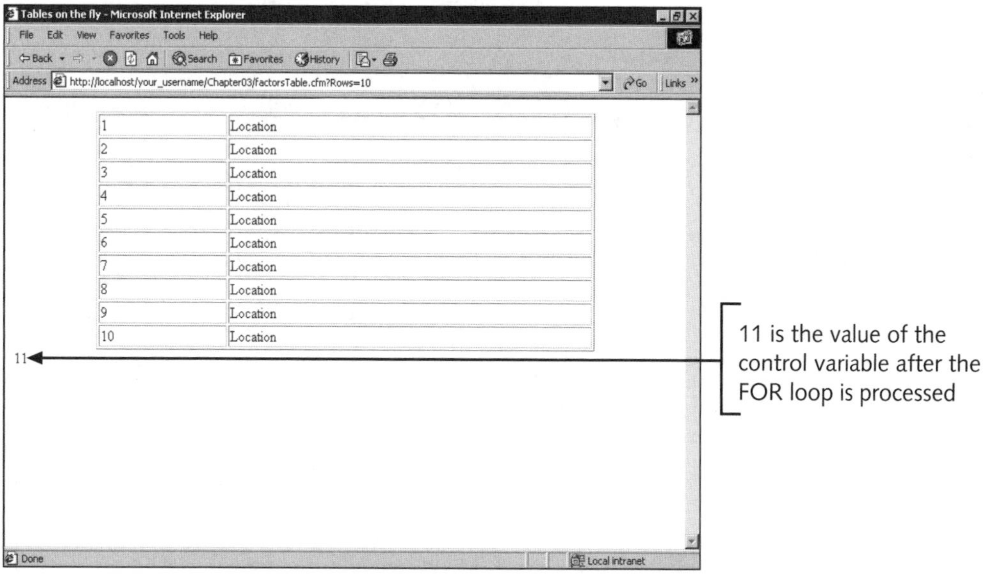

Figure 3-40   Web page with the control variable's value at the end of the FOR loop

Finally, it is easier to show data in tables if you use two different colors for adjacent rows. Modify the previous example so that even numbered rows have a light green background. You can determine if a number is even by dividing it by 2 and examining the remainder. If the remainder is zero, the number is even; otherwise it is odd. Remember from Chapter 1 that the MOD operator computes the remainder when you divide two numbers. The flowchart for this program is shown in Figure 3-41.

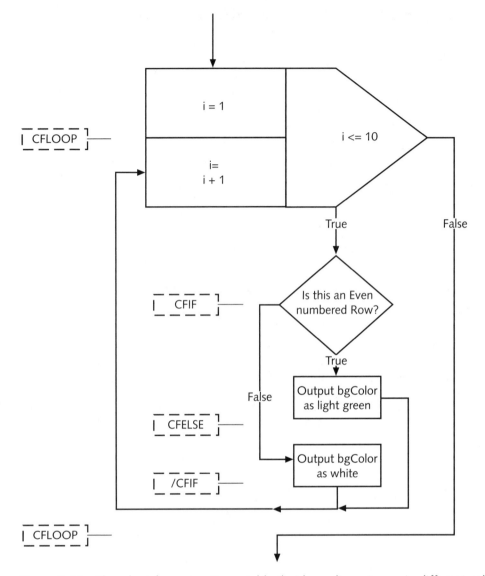

Figure 3-41 Flowchart for generating a table that has adjacent rows in different colors

To color adjacent rows with two different colors:

1. Switch to ColdFusion Studio.

2. Select <tr> on line 1, and type the following code over the selection, as shown in Figure 3-42:

```
<tr
<!--- Notice that this CFIF tag is inside the TR tag --->
<cfif i MOD 2 EQ 0>
bgcolor="lightgreen"
<cfelse>
```

```
bgcolor = "white"
</cfif>
>
```

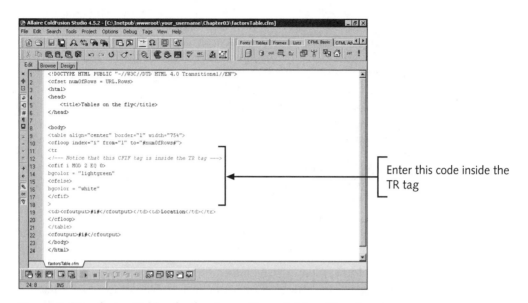

Enter this code inside the
TR tag

Figure 3-42   factorsTable.cfm for generating a table with colored rows

3. Save the template, and then view the output in a browser. If necessary, refresh the page to see the output. See Figure 3-43.

Even-numbered rows use
a light green background
color

Figure 3-43   Web page displayed by factorsTable.cfm?Rows=10

When the ColdFusion Server executes the code, it initializes the variable numOfRows to 10, outputs the HTML TABLE tag as is, and then continues executing with CFLOOP. The variable i is assigned a value of 1, and statements inside the loop are executed. The Server evaluates the condition in the CFIF statement. Expression 1 MOD 2 is evaluated and results in 1, which is not equal to 0, and therefore the condition is false. Because the condition is false, the statements between the CFIF and CFELSE tags are skipped, and the statements between the CFELSE and closing /CFIF tags are executed, which outputs bgcolor="white" to the Web browser. The rest of the HTML table row is output as is, and the value of variable i (1) is output, followed by other HTML table cells. Execution reaches the closing CFLOOP tag, the variable i is incremented by 1 to 2, and statements inside the loop are executed again. Another row is output with 2 in the first cell of the first column. The CFIF condition now evaluates to (2 MOD 2) EQ 0, which is 0 EQ 0, which is true. Statements between the CFIF and CFELSE tags are executed, and text bgColor = "lightgreen" is transmitted to the browser. Execution of the CFIF statement is repeated again and again. When the value of i is 11, it is greater than the specified end value of 10, and execution of statements inside the loop terminates and statements below the loop are executed next.

Attributes of FOR loops should be numeric or data types such as dates that you can convert to numeric values because the control variable is incremented after each repetition—you can't increment a control variable by "a," but you can increment it by 1. Even though FOR loops are very powerful, they have some limitations. For example, values taken by control variables must be in a mathematical series that starts with a particular value and increments by a constant amount. You have more flexibility in specifying values that should be assigned to control variables by using LIST loops.

LIST Loops

ColdFusion LIST loops allow you to implement a repetition construct in ColdFusion templates. Similar to FOR loops, LIST loops have a control variable. LIST loops allow you to list the values for the control variable, instead of mathematically computing them as in FOR loops. LIST loops have two attributes. The first attribute, INDEX, must be set to the name of the control variable. The second attribute, LIST, must be set to a value-list (values separated by commas similar to the one you used in the CFSWITCH tag). The syntax for a LIST loop is as follows:

```
<CFLOOP INDEX= "list_variable" LIST= "value_list">
Statements containing HTML and CFML that are to be
executed repeatedly
</CFLOOP>
```

A flowchart for a LIST loop is shown in Figure 3-44.

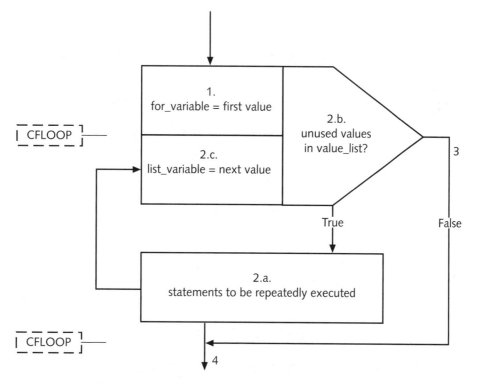

Figure 3-44   Flowchart for a LIST loop

When the ColdFusion Server executes a LIST loop, the list_variable is assigned the first value in the value_list, and it executes all statements between the CFLOOP tags. Then the second value in the value_list is assigned to list_variable, and statements between the CFLOOP tags are executed again. This process is repeated for every value in value_list. After the last value from value_list is assigned, statements are executed once, and then repetition is terminated and processing continues by executing the statement below the closing CFLOOP tag.

The following example (Example3-4.cfm) uses a LIST loop to create links to some computer companies:

```
Links to some computer companies:
<ul>
<cfloop index="company" list="Cisco,Compaq,Dell,Gateway,
HP,IBM,Intel,Microsoft,Oracle,Sun">
<cfoutput>
<li><a href="http://www.#company#.com">#company#</a></li>
</cfoutput>
</cfloop>
</ul>
```

To use LIST loops:

1. Switch to your Web browser, and type the URL: **http://localhost/your_username/Chapter03/Example3-4.cfm**. Press **Enter**. See Figure 3-45.

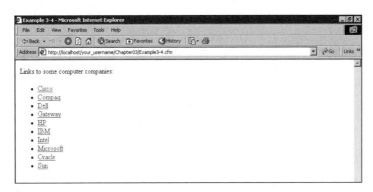

Figure 3-45   Web page displayed by Example3-4.cfm

2. Click **View** on the menu bar, and then click **Source**. The Notepad program opens with the HTML source code for the document, as shown in Figure 3-46.

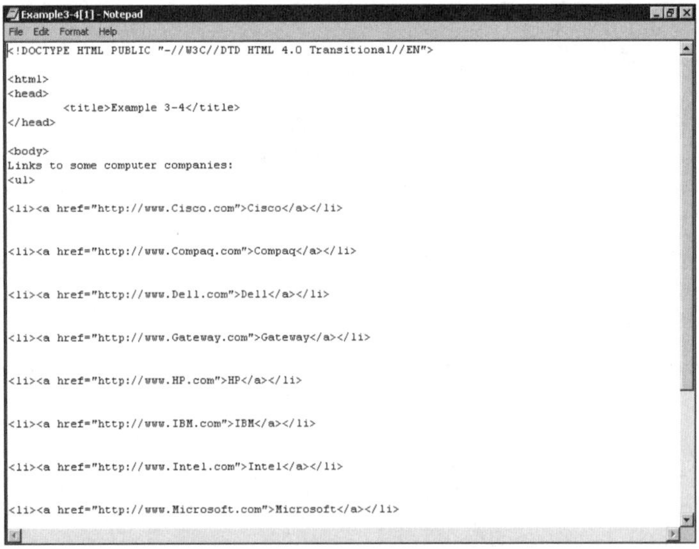

Figure 3-46   HTML source code for Example3-4.cfm

When the ColdFusion Server executes Example3-4.cfm, all the HTML code before the CFLOOP tag is sent as is to the Web browser. Then it processes the CFLOOP tag. It creates a variable named company, assigns it Cisco, and starts executing the statements inside the CFLOOP tags. It processes the CFOUTPUT tags next and substitutes Cisco for #company# in the HREF attribute, as well as in the anchor tags, to produce the code for a list item with a hyperlink, as shown in Figure 3-46. The Web browser interprets this code and displays a hyperlink, as shown in Figure 3-45. When the server encounters the /CFLOOP tag, it assigns the next value in the value-list (Compaq) to variable company. It executes the statements inside the loop again to produce another hyperlink. This process is repeated until the values in the value-list are all used. Then the Server outputs the code below the /CFLOOP tag.

3. Close Notepad.

4. Click any of the hyperlinks in your Web browser.

You have been asked to design a ColdFusion document (listFeatures.cfm) that accepts a URL parameter named features. URL parameter features can be set to a value-list that describes important features of properties listed for sale by NikRealty. Your template should display these features neatly formatted in an HTML table.

To design a template for displaying property features in an HTML table:

1. Switch to ColdFusion Studio.

2. Click **File** on the menu bar, and then click **Close All** to close all open documents.

3. Click **File** on the menu bar, and then click **New Document**. ColdFusion Studio starts a new document with the HTML document structuring tags.

4. Change the title of the document to **Property features**. The completed document is shown in Figure 3-47.

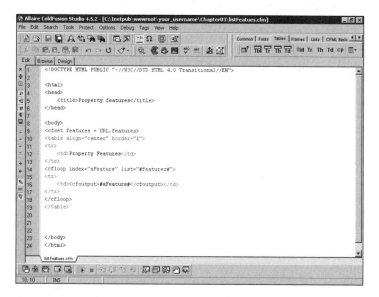

Figure 3-47   listFeatures.cfm in ColdFusion Studio

5. Insert the cursor below the BODY tag, type **<cfset features = URL.features>**, and press the **Enter** key. When the ColdFusion Server executes this statement, it creates a new variable named features and assigns it the value of the URL parameter features.

6. Click the **Tables** tab on the QuickBar.

7. Click the **Table Sizer (QuickTable)** button.

8. Click the first cell in the second row to generate the code for a 1 by 2 table.

9. Type **Property Features** between the TD tags in the first row of the table.

10. Select **<table>** on line 10, and type **<table align="center" border="1">** to replace it.

11. Type **<cfoutput>#aFeature#</cfoutput>** in the TD tags for the second row on line 15. See Figure 3-48.

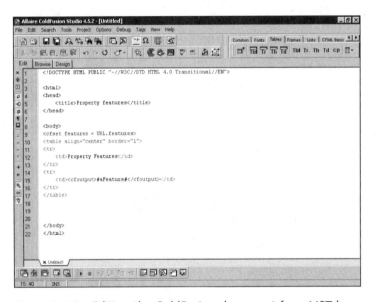

Figure 3-48 Editing the ColdFusion document for a LIST loop

12. Insert the cursor at the end of </tr> on line 13, and press **Enter** to insert a new line. Then type **<cfloop index="aFeature" list="#features#">**.

13. Insert a new line after line 17, and type **</cfloop>** to code the end loop tag.

14. Click the **Save** button on the Standard toolbar, navigate to the Chapter03 folder, type **listFeatures.cfm** as the name for the template, and then click the **Save** button.

Your next task is to test the template.

To test listFeatures.cfm:

1. Switch to your Web browser, and type the URL:
   http://localhost/your_username/Chapter03/listFeatures.cfm?
   features=Master+Bedroom,Workshop,Skylights,3-Car+Garage,
   Cathedral+Ceilings. Press **Enter**. See Figure 3-49.

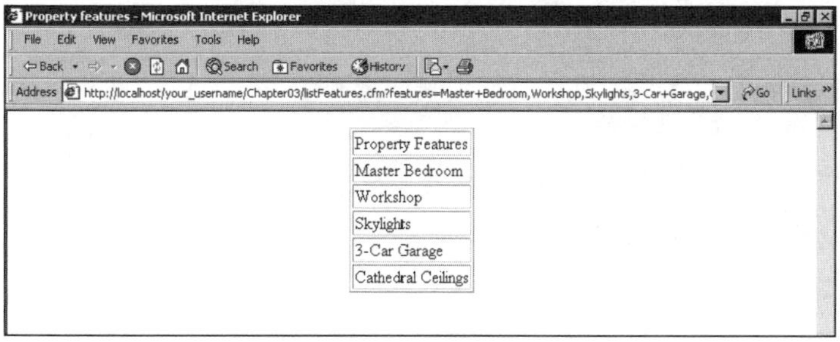

Figure 3-49   Web page displayed for listFeatures.cfm

When the ColdFusion Server executes listFeatures.cfm, it creates a
URL scoped variable named URL.features and assigns it Master
Bedroom,Workshop,Skylights,3-Car Garage,Cathedral Ceilings by
interpreting + as a space. You learned about this in the section on URL
encoding in Chapter 2. All the HTML code before the CFSET statement is
sent to the Web browser. It assigns the value in URL.features to a regular
variable named features when it processes the CFSET statement. It sends the
code for the table before the CFLOOP tag. The ColdFusion Server substitutes the value for #features# and sets the value of the LIST attribute to
"Master Bedroom,Workshop,Skylights,3-Car Garage,Cathedral Ceilings,"
creates a variable named aFeature, and assigns it Master Bedroom. It outputs
a table row with this value. Variable aFeatures is assigned Workshop next, and
so on. Finally, the HTML text at the bottom of the document is sent. When
the Web browser receives the complete document, it displays the Web page
shown in Figure 3-49.

2. Experiment with other value-lists in the URL.

3. Close all programs.

WHILE loops

FOR loops and LIST loops execute a set of statements repeatedly a certain number of
times. The number of times a set of statements is executed with a WHILE loop depends

upon the situation. A WHILE loop in ColdFusion has only one attribute, which is known as a while-condition. The syntax for a ColdFusion WHILE loop is as follows:

```
<CFLOOP CONDITION= "while-condition">
Statements containing HTML and CFML that are to be
executed repeatedly
</CFLOOP>
```

A flowchart for a ColdFusion WHILE loop is shown in Figure 3-50.

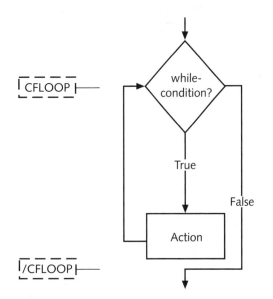

Figure 3-50   Flowchart for a WHILE loop

When a ColdFusion Server executes a WHILE loop, the while-condition is tested; if it is true, the Server executes all statements between the CFLOOP tags. The Server tests the while-condition again. If the while-condition is true, the statements between the CFLOOP tags are executed again; otherwise, repetition ends and the Server continues by executing the statement below the closing CFLOOP tag. Make sure that values of expressions being compared in a while-condition change due to actions performed by inside statements so that normal termination of the loop can occur.

A client is interested in listing a property for sale with NikRealty. A comparative study of recently sold properties suggests an expected price of $125,000 for the client's property. The client wants to list the property at $160,000. He wants to reduce the price by 5% each month until it is sold. If it is sold when the price is just below $125,000, he wants to know how long the property has been listed for sale. One of your project members has designed a ColdFusion template (timeTillSale.cfm) that accepts three URL parameters, listPrice (160000), expectedPrice (125000), and priceReduction (0.05), and displays the time the property is expected to be on the market for sale. Your task is to experiment with the template to learn from it.

To use WHILE loops:

1. Start ColdFusion Studio.

2. Open **timeTillSale.cfm** in your Chapter03 folder on the Data Disk. See Figure 3-51.

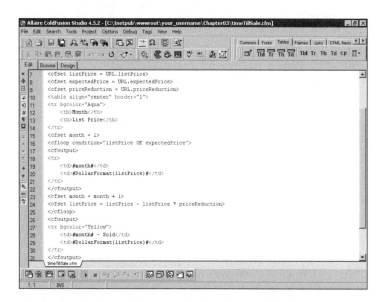

Figure 3-51   timeTillSale.cfm in ColdFusion Studio

3. Start your Web browser.

4. In the Address text box, type **http://localhost/your_username/ Chapter03/timeTillSale.cfm?listPrice=160000&expectedPrice=125000 &priceReduction=0.05**, and press the **Enter** key. Your Web browser displays the page shown in Figure 3-52.

Month	List Price
1	$160,000.00
2	$152,000.00
3	$144,400.00
4	$137,180.00
5	$130,321.00
6 - Sold	$123,804.95

Figure 3-52   Web page displayed to calculate time until sale

5. Click **View** on the menu bar, and then click **Source**. The Notepad program opens with the HTML source code for the document, as shown in Figure 3-53.

```
timeTillSale[1] - Notepad
File  Edit  Format  Help
<!DOCTYPE HTML PUBLIC "-//W3C//DTD HTML 4.0 Transitional//EN">
<html>
<head>
        <title>Expected Time Till Sale</title>
</head>
<body>

<table align="center" border="1">
<tr bgcolor="Aqua">
        <th>Month</th>
        <th>List Price</th>
</tr>

<tr>
        <td>1</td>
        <td>$160,000.00</td>
</tr>

<tr>
        <td>2</td>
        <td>$152,000.00</td>
</tr>

<tr>
        <td>3</td>
        <td>$144,400.00</td>
</tr>

<tr>
        <td>4</td>
```

Figure 3-53   HTML code created by timeTillSale.cfm in Notepad

6. Compare Figures 3-51 and 3-53. When the ColdFusion Server executes timeTillSale.cfm variables listPrice, expectedPrice and priceReduction are created and assigned the appropriate values from the URL query string. The Server sends the HTML for the table header to the Web browser. It creates a variable named month and assigns it a value 1. It evaluates the condition in the CFLOOP tag. The list price of $160,000 is greater than the expected price of $125,000, and the condition is true. Statements inside the loop are executed. It displays the month and the list price formatted as currency in a table row. You are assuming that the property does not sell at this price. Variable month is incremented by 1 to 2. A new list price is computed by applying the proper reduction. The condition in the CFLOOP tag is evaluated with the new list price. It is still true. Statements inside the loop are executed, and a table row is displayed. Month is incremented to 3, and a newer list price is computed. Processing occurs in this fashion until the condition is false. The condition is false when the list price is not greater than the expected price. When the condition is false, the processing of the statements inside the loop is terminated, and the statements below the loop are executed. A final row of the table is output with the caption Sold. The rest of the code completes the code for the document.

7. Close Notepad.

8. Change the list price to **180000** in the Address text box of your Web browser, and press **Enter**. See Figure 3-54. It now takes nine months to sell the property.

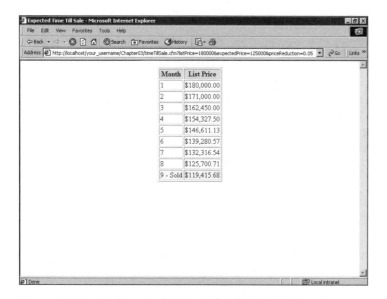

Figure 3-54   Web page displayed for $180,000 list price

> 9. Close all programs.

Redirection

Just as you can use flow control within a template, you can also use flow control within a Web site. For example, within any Web site, hyperlinks let users connect to other Web pages. Usually a user must click a hyperlink to open the hyperlink's target. Web site designers sometimes need a way to load a new page in the browser without requiring any interaction from the user. For example, when a user clicks a button to send the data entered into a form to a ColdFusion Server, the Server might process the data and then send a redirection instruction back to an application's home page with a URL parameter with a confirmation message. In such a case, you might see a "data processed successfully" message at the top with the home page below it. This redirection is usually transparent to the user. **Redirection** is part of the HTTP protocol that allows designers to send an "object has moved message" to a Web browser with information for its new location. You can redirect users to other pages in ColdFusion by using the CFLOCATION tag. Its syntax is as follows:

```
<CFLOCATION URL="aURL">
```

When the ColdFusion Server processes this statement, all execution stops and the Server sends a redirection instruction to the browser by sending an HTTP "object has moved" message back to the browser along with a specified URL. The browser is tricked into thinking that this page is now at a new location and sends an appropriate Web server request. You can specify the parameter "aURL" as a **relative location** that does not include a complete path or as an **absolute location** that includes a complete path. A relative location is translated into an absolute location by appending the path of the current page to it. When you use an absolute location, you can even redirect a user to another Web site.

 You should use relative locations as much as possible. It is much easier to maintain a Web site with relative links, especially when you need to move content and reorganize the site's folder structure, because the links are relative to the location of the files.

To create a template to redirect a user to another location:

1. Start ColdFusion Studio.

2. Click the **New** button on the Standard toolbar to create a new template.

3. Insert a new line at the top of the template (a new line 1). Type **<cflocation** and then press the **Spacebar**. After a few seconds, the tag insight menu opens, as shown in Figure 3-55.

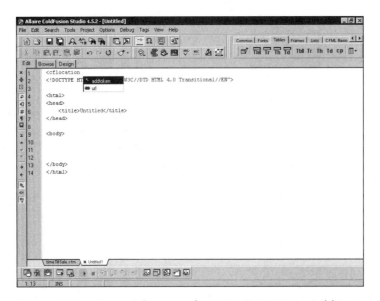

Figure 3-55   Tag insight menu for CFLOCATION in ColdFusion Studio

4. Double-click **url** in the tag insight menu to insert its code on line 1. A new tag insight menu opens with options for inserting the URL for the redirection. Your choices are FTP (File Transfer Protocol), HTTP, or HTTPS (a secured HTML page).

 If the tag insight menu is hidden, press the Backspace key a couple of times and retype the letters.

3

5. Double-click **http://** to insert it into the code, and then type **kaparthi.cba.uni.edu/ColdFusion**.

6. Press the **End** key and type **>**.

7. Save the file as **goToAuthors.cfm** in the Chapter03 folder on the server.

8. Switch to your Web browser, and open **http://localhost/your_username/Chapter03/goToAuthors.cfm**.

   The ColdFusion Server executes the CFLOCATION tag and sends an "object has moved" HTTP response to the Web browser with the new location of the object. Your Web browser sends another request out to this new location and automatically opens the authors' home page for this book. Unless you knew about the redirection, you wouldn't have known that the redirection took place.

 You must have an Internet connection to open the authors' Web site.

9. Close your browser, and then close ColdFusion Studio.

CHAPTER SUMMARY

❑ In this chapter, you learned about three structured programming flow-control constructs and how to implement them in ColdFusion. According to sequence construct, statements in a program are executed one after another from beginning to end. You use a selection construct to model situations where statements to be executed are chosen based on circumstances. When you want statements to be executed repeatedly, you use the repetition construct.

❑ You implement the selection construct by using the CFIF tag and the CFSWITCH tag.

❑ You learned about conditions, relational and logical operators, and their use in selection statements.

❑ ColdFusion supports the six standard relational operators represented as GT, LT, GE, LE, EQ, and NEQ. ColdFusion also supports the logical operators AND, OR, and NOT.

❑ ColdFusion implements a system of relational and logical operator precedence.

❑ For implementing repetition, you use FOR loops, LIST loops, and WHILE loops. You saw their implementation in ColdFusion through the use of the CFLOOP tag and its attributes.

❐ A FOR loop in ColdFusion has four attributes. You set the first attribute, INDEX, to the name of the control variable. The second is the FROM attribute, and the third is the TO attribute. Finally, the fourth attribute STEP, is optional. The control variable is assigned values in a mathematical series starting with the value in the FROM attribute and increments by the value in the STEP attribute or 1. When the value of the control variable is more than the value of the TO attribute, the Server stops executing the statements within the loop.

❐ ColdFusion LIST loops have two attributes. The first is named INDEX and the second is named LIST. The control variable in the INDEX attribute is assigned each value in the LIST attributes value-list, and the statements inside the loop are executed.

❐ A WHILE loop in ColdFusion has only one attribute associated with it. This attribute is called the while-condition. As long as this condition is true, the ColdFusion Server executes the statements inside the CFLOOP tags.

❐ The CFLOCATION tag is used to implement an HTTP request redirection.

REVIEW QUESTIONS

1. What is flow control in ColdFusion?
2. Which ColdFusion statements allow you to implement a selection flow-control construct?
3. What are the six standard relational operators in ColdFusion?
4. What is the meaning of EQ when comparing numbers?
5. What is the meaning of GE when comparing strings?
6. What is the meaning of LT when comparing dates?
7. What are logical operators? Do all logical operators require two conditions?
8. Which ColdFusion statements allow you to implement a repetition flow-control construct?
9. What CFLOOP attributes are used in a FOR loop and how do you use them?
10. What CFLOOP attributes are used in a LIST loop and how do you use them?
11. What CFLOOP attributes are used in a WHILE loop and how do you use them?
12. Give the statements needed to simulate the following FOR loop by using a WHILE loop: <cfloop index="x" from="1" to="10">...</cfloop>.
13. If a FOR loop with an index running from 1 to 10 is enclosed in a LIST loop with 15 elements, how many times does the Server execute the statements inside the inner loop?
14. What is redirection? What ColdFusion tag allows you to implement a redirection?

HANDS-ON PROJECTS

Project 3-1: Use CFIF Statements to Display Customer Status

A regional bank decides to offer a preferred status to its checking account customers if they have more than $5,000.00 on deposit in their account. Customers with other accounts or with deposits less than $5,000.00 in checking accounts are given a regular status.

Given the type of account a customer has as a URL parameter named accType and the amount on deposit as a URL parameter named balance, design a ColdFusion template to classify the customer into one of two categories: Preferred Status or Regular Status. Use an outer CFIF statement to select an action based on whether a customer has a checking account or some other account with the bank. Design an inner CFIF statement to check the account balance and to assign the proper status to the account. Use a string variable named status, and assign it a literal "Preferred" or "Regular."

Use Figure 3-56 to design your template and its output. When you are finished, save the template as **Ch3Pr1.cfm** in the Chapter03 folder on the server. Test your template by opening:

Ch3Pr1.cfm?accType=Checking&balance=6000

Ch3Pr1.cfm?accType=Checking&balance=4000

and

Ch3Pr1.cfm?accType=Savings&balance=6000.

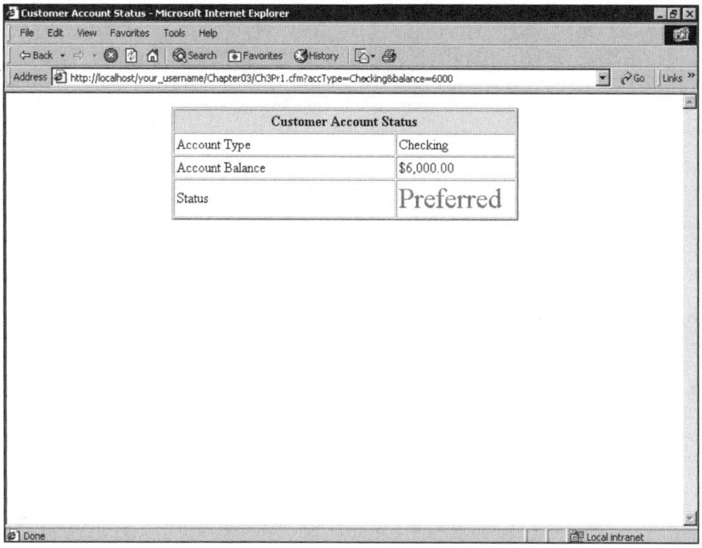

Figure 3-56

Project 3-2: Use a Series of CFIF Statements to Determine Student Grades

An instructor assigns grades to students based on their scores according to the following scheme: Students receive an A for a score of 90 or better, a grade of B for scores of 80 to 89, a grade of C for scores of 70 to 79, a grade of D for scores of 60 to 69, and a grade of F for scores below 60. Design a template that calculates and displays a grade for a student based on his or her score available as a URL parameter named score. See Figure 3-57. (*Hint*: Use a series of CFIF statements—one for every grade a student can earn.) When you are finished, save your template as **Ch3Pr2.cfm** in the Chapter03 folder on the server. Test your template by trying out Ch3Pr2.cfm?score=78, Ch3Pr2.cfm?score=86, Ch3Pr2.cfm?score=99, Ch3Pr2.cfm?score=63, and Ch3Pr2.cfm?score=28.

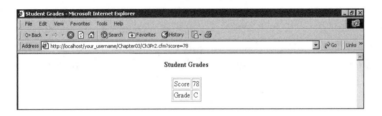

Figure 3-57

Project 3-3: Use a CFSWITCH Statement to Design a Word Game

An educational software company provides sample programs on its Web site as part of a promotional campaign. It has hired you to create a ColdFusion template that identifies a letter of the alphabet as a vowel (A, E, I, O, or U) or consonant (all letters that are not vowels). This letter is available as a URL parameter named letter. See Figure 3-58. (*Hint*: Use a CFSWITCH statement with a value-list containing vowels.) If a letter is not a vowel, it is a consonant (default case). When you are finished, save your template as **Ch3Pr3.cfm** in the Chapter03 folder on the server. Test your template by opening Ch3Pr3.cfm?letter=U, Ch3Pr3.cfm?letter=a, and Ch3Pr3.cfm?letter=z.

Figure 3-58

Project 3-4: Use LIST Loops to Generate Web Site Passwords

Randomly generated passwords are easy to forget and pose a security threat because users often write them down. A leading Internet portal assigns passwords to users by combining two words and a number so that they are easy to remember and hard to guess. Design a ColdFusion template that combines all words in the list "cold, fusion, static, dynamic" with all words in the list "cat, dog, rat" to produce a bulleted list of valid passwords. This template should process two URL parameters named list1 and list2. For simplicity, you are not required to add a number. See Figure 3-59. (*Hint*: Use two LIST loops nested within each other to produce all possible combinations of words.) When you are finished, save your template as **Ch3Pr4.cfm** in the Chapter03 folder on the server. Test your template by opening
Ch3Pr4.cfm?list1=cold,fusion,static,dynamic&list2=cat,dog,rat.

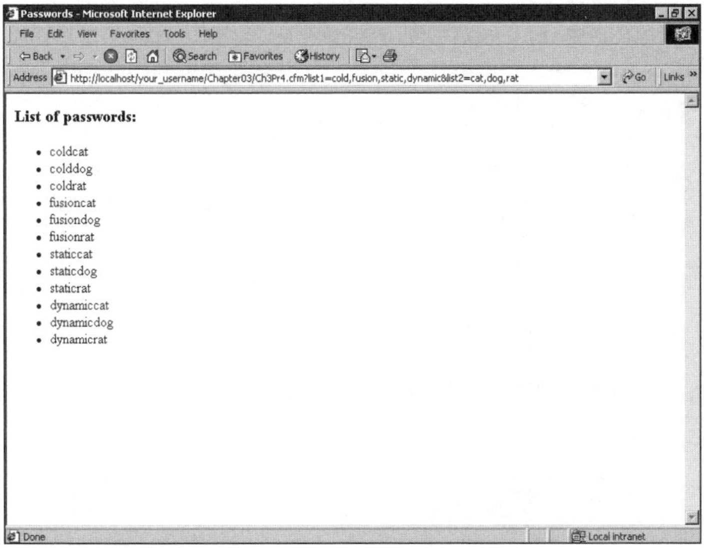

Figure 3-59

Project 3-5: Use Loops to Calculate the Price of a Pizza and its Toppings

An online pizza delivery company charges $6.00 for a medium cheese pizza, $1.00 for hot peppers, and $0.50 each for additional toppings. If a customer orders a medium pizza with mushrooms, onions, hot peppers, and black olives, compute and display a bill showing the number of toppings and the total price. See Figure 3-60. Use a URL parameter named toppings to capture the customer's topping preferences. When you are finished, save your template as **Ch3Pr5.cfm** in the Chapter03 folder on the server. Test your template with URL Ch3Pr5.cfm?toppings=mushrooms,onions,hot+peppers,black+olives.

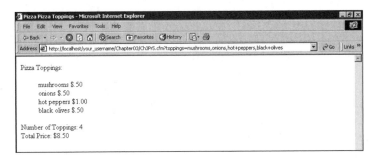

Figure 3-60

Project 3-6: Use Nested LIST Loops to Generate RGB Colors

Recollect from your HTML that you represent colors by using a six-digit code consisting of three two-digit RGB color codes. For example 22FF88 is a color. A good rule for ensuring that Web page colors are displayed properly on different kinds of monitors is known as the divisible-by-three rule. According to this rule, colors made from RGB colors with color codes 00, 33, 66, 99, CC, and FF are displayed the best. Generate a table that displays Internet-safe colors. See Figure 3-61. (*Hint*: Use three nested LIST loops—one for red, one for green, and the other for blue. For example, the CFLOOP tag for red would be <cfloop index="red" list="00,33,66,99,CC,FF">.) Loop over the allowable values for these colors and display an appropriately formatted table row. When you are finished, save your template as **Ch3Pr6.cfm** in the Chapter03 folder on the server. Test your program, and debug if there are any errors.

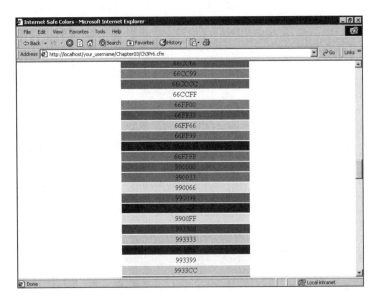

Figure 3-61

Project 3-7: Use a WHILE Loop to Compute CD Maturity Amounts

A bank wants to provide useful decision tools on its Web site as a service to its customers. Design a ColdFusion calculator that uses a given interest rate (URL parameter named interestRate) to determine how many years it would take a particular deposit amount (URL parameter named amount) to grow to $100,000.00. (*Hint:* Initialize a variable named years to 0. Use a WHILE loop with the condition "amount LE 100000." Increment variable year by one each time the loop is executed and compute the total amount after a year within the loop.) Display the output as shown in Figure 3-62 when the amount reaches $100,000.00. When you are finished, save your template as **Ch3Pr7.cfm** in the Chapter03 folder on the server. Test your template with URLs Ch3Pr7.cfm?amount=5000&interestRate=0.07 and Ch3Pr7.cfm?amount=10000&interestRate=0.12.

Figure 3-62

Project 3-8: Use a CFSWITCH Statement to Display a Random Web Page

Design a ColdFusion template to display any one of the following pages randomly: *www.apple.com, www.compaq.com, www.dell.com, www.e4me.com, www.gateway.com, www.hp.com,* and *www.microsoft.com.* (*Hint:* Use the ColdFusion function RandRange(1, 7) to select a random integer between 1 and 7.) Select the URL for the redirection based on the random integer generated using a CFSWITCH statement. Use an appropriate tag for redirecting the user to that URL. When you are finished, save your template as **Ch3Pr8.cfm** in the Chapter03 folder on the server. Test your program.

CASE PROJECTS

Case Project 1

An online store wants to display information about an upcoming red tag sale on its Web site. Given URL parameters for the product's name, its price, and its discount as a percentage, design a ColdFusion template to output information (product name, discount, price, discounted price) in a neatly formatted table. Table cells with discounts greater than 75% should be colored red, and those with discounts between 50% and 75% should be colored yellow; cells with other discounts should be colored green.

Case Project 2

A large organization wants to give a year-end bonus to employees. The Human Resources department wants to display information about bonuses on the company's intranet. Bonuses depend on years an employee has worked for the company and are to be paid according to a scheme shown in the table below. Given the date the employee joined the company in the format "MM/DD/YYYY," design a ColdFusion template to present bonus information in a neatly formatted fashion.

Years of Service	Bonus (% of Annual Salary)
≥ 30	50%
≥ 20, < 30	40%
≥ 10, < 20	30%
≥ 5, < 10	20%
< 5	10%

Case Project 3

A midwestern company wants to analyze their customer data. They want to identify the state a customer belongs to based on their telephone area code according to the following table:

Area Code	State
319, 515, 712	Iowa
218, 320, 507	Minnesota
414, 608, 715, 920	Wisconsin
308, 402	Nebraska
314, 417, 636, 660, 816	Missouri
Other	Other

Design a ColdFusion template that uses a URL parameter named customersAreaCode and outputs the state the customer belongs to. Experiment with different values for parameter customersAreaCode.

4

FORM HANDLING

> **In this chapter, you will:**
>
> ♦ Learn about the interaction between a Web browser and a Web server for handling forms
> ♦ Design HTML forms
> ♦ Use text boxes, password boxes, command buttons, radio buttons, checkboxes, select boxes, text areas, image controls, and hidden fields to control data entry in a form
> ♦ Design ColdFusion form handlers for handling forms and accessing data entered in different types of controls
> ♦ Build a complete form application

In previous chapters, you saw two kinds of interaction between Web clients and servers. First, when a client requests an HTML document from a Web server, the Web server retrieves the document and sends it to the client. The browser formats and displays the document according to its embedded HTML tags. Second, when a client requests a ColdFusion template from the Web server, the Web server transfers control to the ColdFusion Server, the ColdFusion Server executes the embedded CFML tags in the document, and then it sends the HTML document to the Web server that subsequently sends it to the client computer. The browser formats the document according to its HTML tags and displays it. In this chapter, you will learn about another kind of interaction between Web clients and servers, where the client requests an HTML document or ColdFusion template that contains a form.

UNDERSTANDING HTML FORMS

When a client requests an HTML document or a ColdFusion template that contains a form, the Web server retrieves the document and sends it to the client. The browser processes the embedded HTML tags and displays the document along with the form. The user enters data in the form and submits it. The Web server receives this data along with the name of the ColdFusion template that should process it. The ColdFusion template that processes a form is called the form handler. A **form handler** contains CFML code to process the data received by the ColdFusion Server. The Web server passes control to the ColdFusion Server along with the data the user entered. The ColdFusion Server uses the form handler to process the data and then outputs an HTML document. The ColdFusion Server sends the HTML document to the Web server, which subsequently sends it to the client. Typically, the document the client receives is a confirmation page to let users know that the data was processed successfully. The browser then displays the document. This process is shown in Figure 4-1.

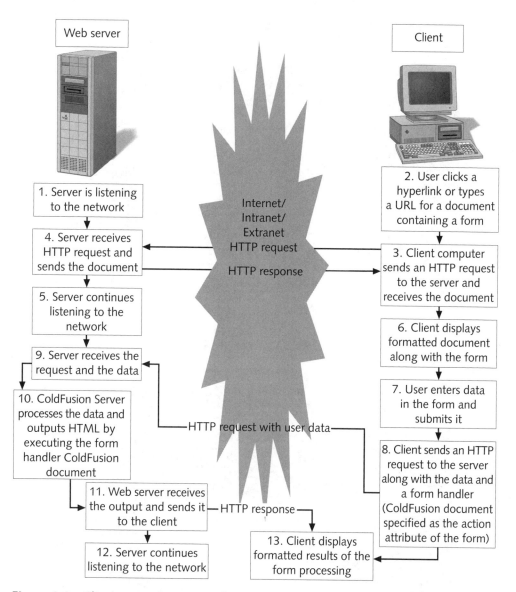

Figure 4-1   Client–server interaction for processing a form

You find this kind of processing in most Web sites. For example, consider the *Crayola.com* Web site. When you click the Where to Buy? button on the home page, the target of the hyperlink is a Web page that contains a form, as shown in Figure 4-2. This form contains a text box for entering a zip code, a list box with a list of product categories, and a Submit button. If you enter your zip code in the text box and use the list box to select a product category, you can click the Find Stores button to open a new Web page with a list of nearby stores that sell products in the product category that you selected.

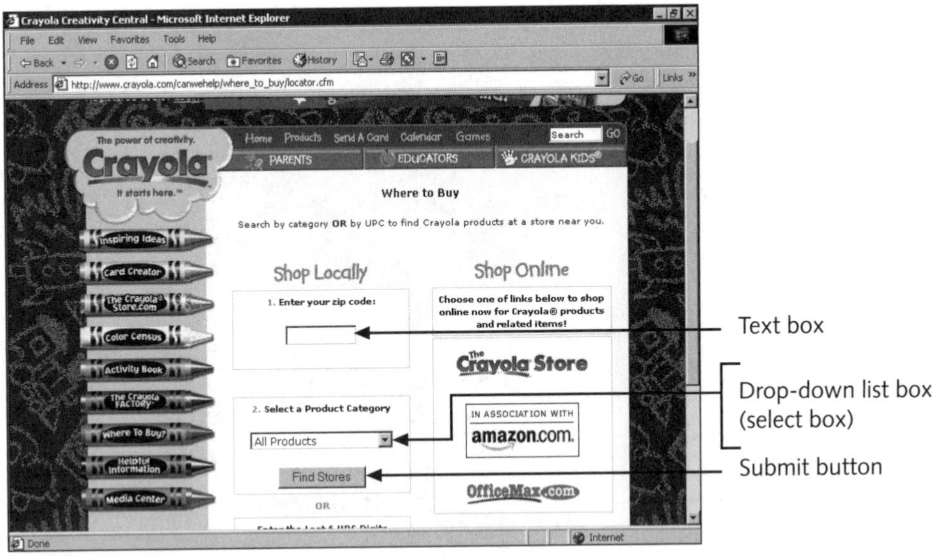

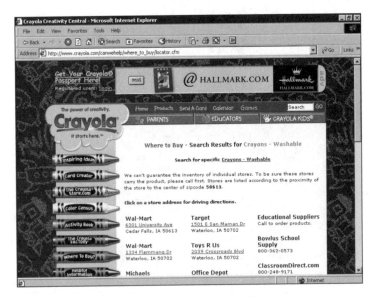

Figure 4-2   An HTML form

If you enter 50613 in the text box, for example, select Crayons – Washable as the product category, and then click the Find Stores button, the Web page shown in Figure 4-3 opens.

Figure 4-3   Web page with the form handler results

As you can see, using a form allows you to build interactivity into your Web site. You can design Web sites that ask users for input and then respond to their requests. If you

4

surf the Web, you have probably encountered many Web sites that use forms and form processing to respond to your choices. Search engines such as Google allow you to enter search phrases to find hyperlinks to Web pages that are closely related to the search phrases you entered. Web sites such as *SmartMoney.com* allow you to enter a stock symbol and click a button to display that stock's current performance information. Electronic commerce sites such as *Amazon.com* allow you to search for books that relate to a specific topic and then buy those books by entering your shipping address, credit card number, and other necessary information. You can even use a form to send and receive e-mail messages by using services such as *Hotmail.com*. Without its ability to process forms, the Web wouldn't be as interactive—and as useful—as it is today.

In your study of HTML, you may have learned that there are two stages for designing HTML forms. First, you create the form and the necessary controls to collect the data that you need. Second, you need to design or specify a form handler to process the data collected by the form on the server. Designing and processing forms in ColdFusion works the same way. First, you design the form using HTML or CFML controls, and then you create a ColdFusion form handler to process the data entered in the form. So you really need two files when creating forms: one for the form and another for the form handler.

Depending on your needs and your expertise with designing forms, in addition to using an HTML document and a ColdFusion form handler, you might also be able to use a ColdFusion template and a ColdFusion form handler, or a ColdFusion template that works both as a form and a form handler to collect and process form data.

USING HTML FORM AND CONTROL TAGS

A **form** is an object in an HTML document. An HTML document can contain one or more forms. The HTML FORM tag encloses the entire form. Forms can contain text, other HTML tags, graphics, and one or more controls. A **control** is an object in a form, such as a text box or a radio button, that you use to collect data,. You use the HTML INPUT tag to create controls where users can enter data in a form. The INPUT tag has an attribute named TYPE for specifying what kind of control to create in the form. Most INPUT controls use the NAME attribute to assign unique names to each control or set of controls. For example, the code <input type="text" name="first"> creates a one-line text box named first. Assigning proper names is an important task because it will make it easier to identify the form data when it is processed on the server. You can specify other information with these controls, such as a size for text boxes or a default value for checkboxes or radio buttons.

Understanding the Form Object

A FORM tag has two important attributes: ACTION and METHOD. The value for the ACTION attribute is the URL of the ColdFusion form handler that will process the form. When a user submits the form, the Web server passes the user-entered data to the ColdFusion Server along with the name of the ColdFusion form handler specified in the ACTION attribute. The ColdFusion Server makes this data available to the form handler specified in the ACTION attribute and then executes it.

How the ColdFusion form handler accesses data depends on the value in the form's METHOD attribute. The **METHOD attribute** can have one of two values: GET or POST. The more common way to send form data to a server is to use the POST method. When you use the **POST method**, the Web browser sends the user-entered data as a file attachment to the Web server. The POST method has three main advantages: there is no size limit on the amount of data that the Web browser can transfer to the server, the data is not easily visible on the URL, and there is more security for the Web application. You will use the POST method in the examples in this chapter. The following syntax example shows how to create a form using the POST method.

```
<form action="form handler filename" method="post">
form contents here
</form>
```

Understanding Text Box Controls

You use a **text box** control to collect data, such as a person's name or address. You create text boxes in a form by using the INPUT tag with a value of "text" for the TYPE attribute. The NAME attribute is required to uniquely identify the control and its data. Other useful attributes include SIZE, which lets you specify the text box width in characters, and the optional VALUE attribute, which lets you specify a default value in the text box when the form is created. The following syntax creates a text box control:

```
<input type="text" name="text box name" size="size" value=
"initial value">
```

Understanding Password Text Box Controls

Password text boxes are special text boxes that display asterisks when users type data in them. You create password text boxes in a form by using the INPUT tag with a value of "password" for the TYPE attribute. Similar to standard text boxes, you use the NAME attribute to uniquely identify the control and its data. You can use the SIZE attribute to specify the width of the text box in characters. The following syntax creates a password text box control:

```
<input type="password" name="text box name" size="size">
```

Understanding Button Controls

Most forms have at least one button that users click to submit the form and its contents to the server for processing. After submitting a form to the server, the server usually sends a form confirmation page back to the client so the user can verify that the server received the form. Sometimes the form confirmation page shows the data the user entered into the form and asks the user to confirm its accuracy. You create a Submit button by assigning the value "submit" to the TYPE attribute of the INPUT tag. The NAME attribute for a Submit button is optional. The value of the VALUE attribute is displayed as a caption on the button by the Web browser when the form is loaded. The following syntax creates a Submit button in a form.

```
<input type="submit" value="button caption" name="button
name">
```

You can also create a Reset button in a form, which users click to clear the form fields. The following syntax creates a Reset button in a form:

```
<input type="reset" value="button caption">
```

HANDLING FORM DATA

The Web page shown in Figure 4-4 contains a form with text box controls and a Submit button that lets users enter their username and password and then click the Login button to submit the form to the server.

At NikRealty, some customers choose to use the NikRealty Web site to view the status of an offer on a home for sale. In these cases, Nikitha provides them with a username and password so they can access pages that contain personal information in the Web site.

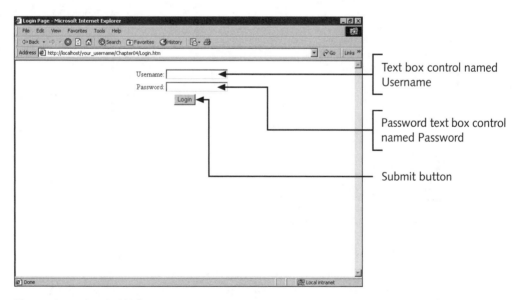

Figure 4-4   Login Web page

After the users enter their username and password and click the Login button, the Web browser uses the POST value of the METHOD attribute to send the form data as an attachment to the Web server. Using Web server API, the data is passed from the file to the ColdFusion Server, which then executes the ColdFusion form handler specified in the ACTION attribute. The ColdFusion Server creates variables in the FORM scope for the data it receives, similar to the way it creates variables in the URL scope for processing URL parameters. The ColdFusion Server creates variables with the word "form" plus a period and the control name. For example, if you want to access the data entered in the text box with a NAME attribute value of "username," you use the variable form.username. The ColdFusion Server creates variables for every control and then assigns to these variables the data passed to the Web server by the Web browser. You'll open this page in ColdFusion to examine its coding.

To view a ColdFusion form and form handler:

1. Start ColdFusion Studio.

2. Click the **Open** button on the Standard toolbar, browse to your Chapter04 folder on the server, and then double-click **Login.htm** to open that file in ColdFusion Studio. See Figure 4-5.

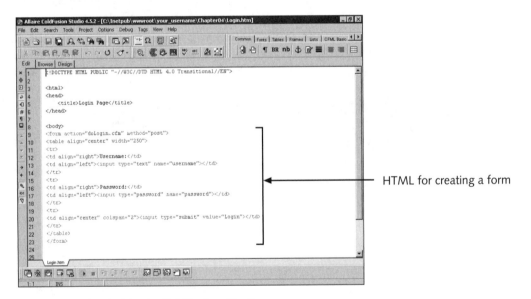

HTML for creating a form

Figure 4-5   Login.htm in ColdFusion Studio

3. Start your Web browser.

4. In the Address text box of your Web browser, type **http://localhost/your_username/Chapter04/Login.htm**, and then press the **Enter** key to open Login.htm in your Web browser.

5. Click in the **Username** text box, type **nikitha**, press the **Tab** key to move to the Password text box, type **goodWeather**, and then click the **Login** button. If a dialog box opens with an option to remember your password, click **No**. The ColdFusion form handler for this Web page, doLogin.cfm, processes the data, and then the CFOUTPUT tags display it on the screen. See Figure 4-6. Notice that the path to the file shows the name of the form handler instead of the Web page that you started with.

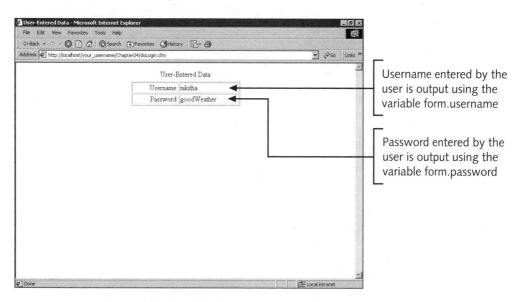

Username entered by the user is output using the variable form.username

Password entered by the user is output using the variable form.password

Figure 4-6   Web page displayed by form handler doLogin.cfm

6. Switch to ColdFusion Studio, click the **Open** button on the Standard toolbar, and then open the file **doLogin.cfm** from the Chapter04 folder on the server. See Figure 4-7. Notice that the form handler uses a table enclosed in CFOUTPUT tags to echo the username and password that you entered. The variables prefixed by "form." are enclosed in pound signs to output the values the ColdFusion Server stored there. These values are the same ones that you entered and that were transferred to the Web server by the client.

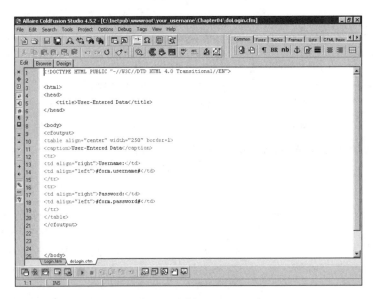

Figure 4-7   doLogin.cfm in ColdFusion Studio

 If necessary, click the Show line numbers in gutter button on the vertical Editor toolbar to show line numbers in the Editor window. In addition, make sure that the Tag insight button is selected and that the Tag completion feature is not selected.

Once you enter the data and click the Submit button, the client sends a request to the Web server with your data. Then the Web server transfers the data to the ColdFusion Server. Once the form handler processes the data and outputs it as HTML, the HTML is transferred from the ColdFusion Server to the Web server, which transfers the HTML to the client. The Web browser then displays the data as a Web page.

Once the user data is accessible in ColdFusion templates, you can perform many tasks with it. You can use complex flow control structures, store the data in databases, interact with other services such as mail servers, generate e-mail messages, and so on. You can even create sophisticated e-commerce sites enriched with true interactivity.

CREATING A FORM

Recall that to create a form, you create an HTML document and use the HTML FORM tag to enclose the entire form. Then you include text, other HTML tags, and graphics in the document. You also can use the INPUT tag to include one or more controls, such as text boxes and radio buttons.

Nikitha knows that many home buyers—especially those moving to Hudson, Iowa, from another town—use the Web to identify homes to visit on future house-hunting trips. She wants to design a form on the NikRealty Web site that prospective buyers can use to schedule private showings of properties with NikRealty agents. Figure 4-8 contains the design specification for the form. You will use ColdFusion Studio to create the form and its form handler as you complete this chapter. To make sure that this form has a professional appearance, you will create a two-column table that can store the form's contents. The first table column will store the control labels, and the second table column will store the controls.

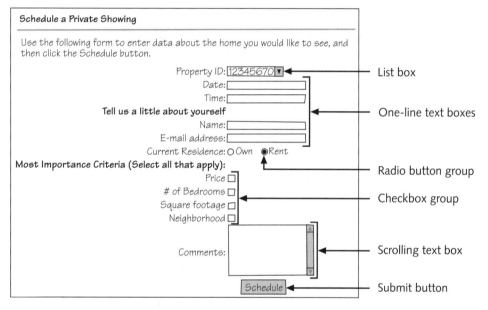

Figure 4-8   Sketch of form to create

To create an HTML document with a form in ColdFusion Studio:

1. Click **File** on the menu bar, and then click **Close All** to close the Login form and its form handler.

2. Click the **New** button on the Standard toolbar to create a new document. The insertion point should be on line 9 of the new document.

3. Type **<hr>** on line 9 to create a horizontal line, and then press the **Enter** key.

The QuickBar contains tabs and buttons for inserting common HTML tags into your documents. In this book, you usually type the HTML tags, but you can locate the buttons on the QuickBar and use them instead of typing the tags directly. You can use the ScreenTips to identify buttons by their name or function.

4. Type **\<h3\>Schedule a Private Showing\</h3\>** on line 10, and then press **Enter**.

5. On line 11, type **\<hr\>** to create a horizontal line.

6. On line 5, select the text **Untitled**, and then type **Schedule a Private Showing**.

7. Click line 12, and then type **Use the following form to enter data about the home you would like to see, and then click the Schedule button.** You have added the page title, two horizontal lines, a heading, and some text to the page. See Figure 4-9.

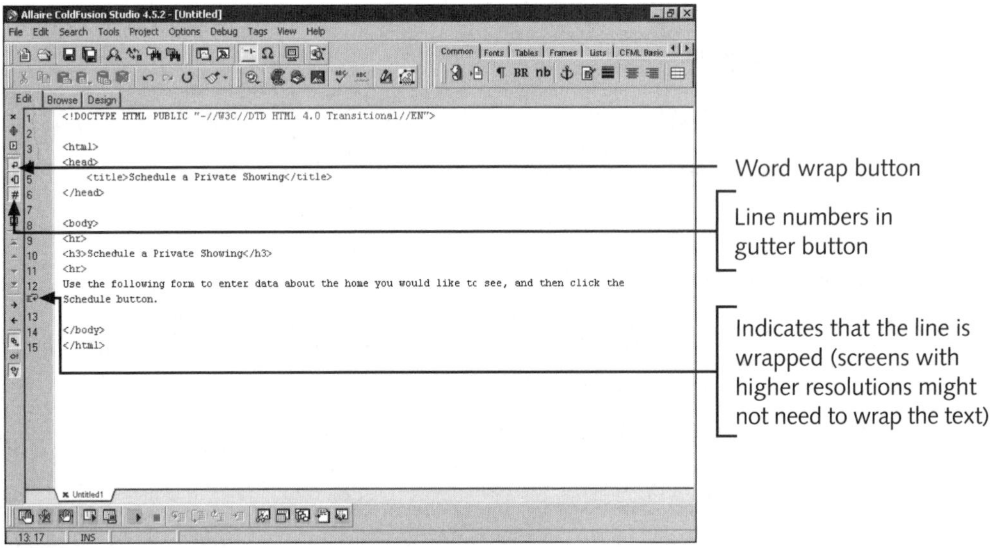

Figure 4-9 Editing the new document in ColdFusion Studio

If the document scrolls to the right as you type the code, click the Word wrap button on the vertical Editor toolbar to keep all code in the window.

8. Click the **Save** button on the Standard toolbar, browse to the Chapter04 folder on the server, and then save the file as **scheduleShowing.htm**.

Now you can create the form and the table that will hold the control labels and the controls.

To create the form:

1. On line 13, type **\<form**, and then press the **Spacebar**. After a few seconds, the Tag insight menu opens and highlights the first item (action). Press the **Enter** key to select the ACTION attribute. ColdFusion Studio enters the

ACTION attribute, an equal sign, and a pair of double quotation marks. The insertion point appears within the double quotation marks, where you will add the name of the form handler.

If your screen resolution is set to 800 × 600 and the word wrap feature is enabled, the status bar shows 14:7 as the position of the cursor. Position 14:7 is actually on line 13 because line 12 wraps to the next line. Use the line numbers in the gutter to position the insertion point correctly. Click the Show line numbers in gutter button if necessary. The position indicated in the status bar changes according to your screen resolution and the setting of the Word wrap feature. Line numbers in this book always refer to the line numbers in the gutter. Use the line numbers in the gutter to position your insertion point in the exercises.

2. Type **processSchedule.cfm**, press the **End** key, and then press the **Spacebar**. The Tag insight menu opens again. This time you need to select the METHOD tag.

3. Double-click **method** in the Tag insight menu list. ColdFusion adds the METHOD tag, the equal sign, and a pair of double quotation marks, and positions the insertion point between the quotation marks. You will use the POST method to send the forms results to the Web server. You can select the POST method from the Tag insight menu that opened.

4. Double-click **post** in the Tag insight menu list.

5. Type **>**, press **Enter** twice, and then type **</form>** to enter the closing FORM tag to finish creating the form. See Figure 4-10.

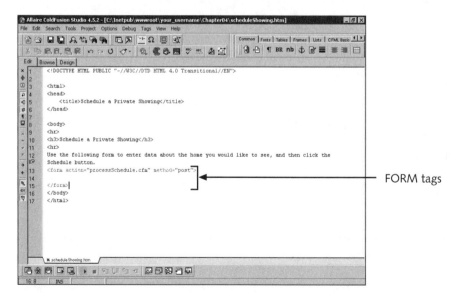

FORM tags

Figure 4-10   scheduleShowing.htm in ColdFusion Studio

ColdFusion Studio might display a warning about the CFFORM tag on the status bar after you type the closing bracket for the opening FORM tag. You can ignore this warning for now; the warning will close when you start another action.

6. Click the **Save** button on the Standard toolbar to save the page.

Now your Web page contains a form object. Recall that you need to create the controls and their labels in a table, so you can control the appearance of the form's contents when displayed by a browser. Using a table to design a form gives you more control over the form's appearance.

To add a table to the form:

1. Press the **Up** arrow key to move the insertion point to line 14, and then click the **Tables** tab on the QuickBar. The Tables tab contains buttons that you can use to quickly create a table.

To turn on the QuickBar, click View on the menu bar, and then click QuickBar.

2. Click the **Table Sizer (QuickTable)** button on the Tables tab. See Figure 4-11. You can use this menu to select the number of rows and columns for the new table.

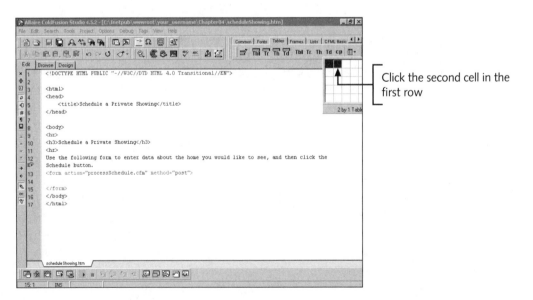

Figure 4-11   Table Sizer (QuickTable) in ColdFusion Studio

Use ScreenTips to make it easier to identify buttons on the toolbars. Rest the mouse on a button for a few seconds, and the ScreenTips feature displays the name of the button.

3. Point to the **second box** in the first row. Notice that the menu shows that you have selected a 2 by 1 table, that is, a table with two columns and one row.

4. Click the **second box** in the first row. The menu closes and ColdFusion inserts the HTML code to create a table with two columns and one row. You will center align the table on the Web page.

Remember that you can use the ALIGN attribute in several ways in tables. You use the ALIGN attribute of the TABLE tag to align the entire table on the Web page. You use the ALIGN attribute of the TD tag to align the content of an individual cell. You use the ALIGN attribute of the TR tag to align the content of all the cells in the row.

5. Click line 14, column 7 (between e and the > in the opening TABLE tag), press the **Spacebar**, wait for the Tag insight menu to appear, press the **Enter** key to select the ALIGN attribute, and then press **Enter** to select the CENTER value. ColdFusion Studio enters the code to center align the table on the Web page. Nikitha's sketch indicates that text in the first column of the table will be right aligned, so you will set the ALIGN attribute for the TD tag, which creates the first cell in the table, to right.

6. Click line 16, column 8 (between the d and the > in the first opening <td> tag), press the **Spacebar**, press **Enter** to select the ALIGN attribute, and then double-click **right** in the Tag insight menu. This code creates a right-aligned cell in the first column of the table. Nikitha's plan shows that the table will contain 14 rows total. Instead of creating each row individually, you can copy the code on lines 16–19 to the Clipboard and then paste it 14 times to create the next 13 rows.

7. Use the mouse to select all of lines 15–18 (the code that creates one row in the table) and the first position on line 19. Make sure that the selection starts and ends as shown in figure 4-12. Any discrepancies will make it difficult for you to complete the rest of the steps.

8. Click the **Copy** button on the Edit toolbar to copy the selection to the Clipboard, and then click the **Paste** button on the Edit toolbar 14 times to create a table with two columns and 14 rows, where all text in the first column is right aligned. Note that the first time you click Paste, you paste the text over the selection.

9. Press **Ctrl + Home** to scroll to the top of the document.

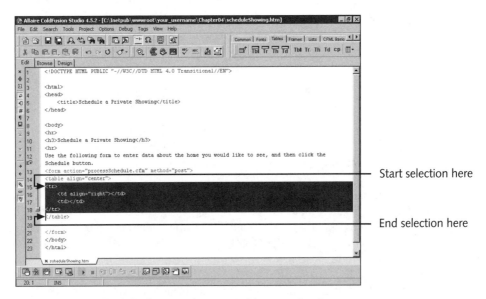

Figure 4-12   scheduleShowing.htm in ColdFusion Studio

You created the table to hold the controls and their labels. Now you can add the labels to the cells in the first column.

To add labels to the cells in the first column:

1. Click line 16, column 23, and then type **Property ID:** to create the first label.

2. Click line 20, column 23, and then type **Date:** to create the second label.

3. Use Figure 4-13 to create the labels in the remaining cells in the first column.

4. Click the **Save** button on the Standard toolbar to save the document, and then click the **Browse** tab on the Editor window to view your work so far. See Figure 4-14.

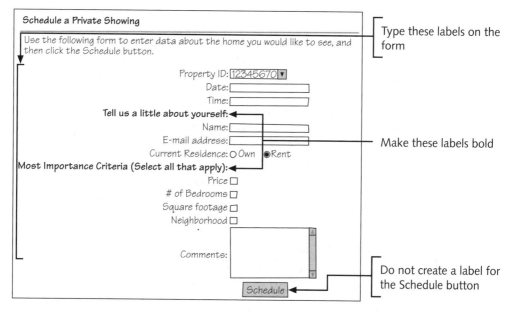

Type these labels on the form

Make these labels bold

Do not create a label for the Schedule button

Figure 4-13   Sketch of form to create

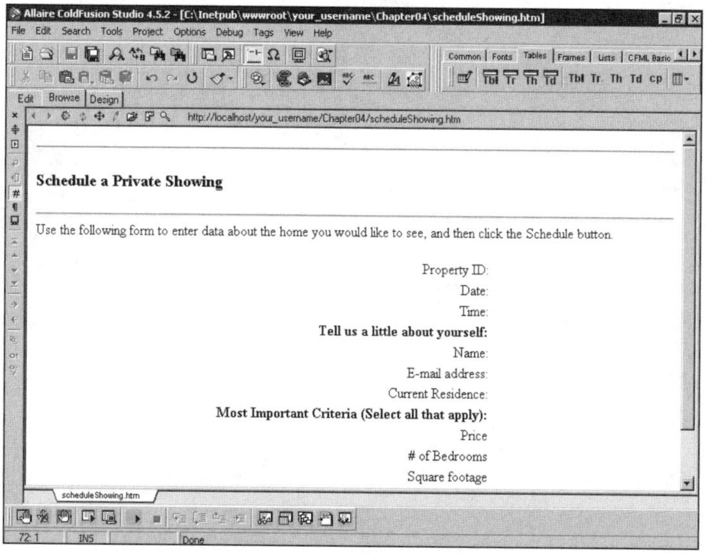

Figure 4-14   Preview of scheduleShowing.htm in the internal browser

The control labels in the first column of the table are completed. Now you can add the text box controls in the second column to collect the data. As you are working, refer back to Figure 4-8 to review Nikitha's sketch of the page.

To add the text box controls to the form:

1. Click the **Edit** tab on the Editor window, scroll up the document, and then click line 21, column 9. This is the cell to the right of the one containing the Date: label. You will create a text box control in this cell.

2. Type **<input**, and then press the **Spacebar** to open the Tag insight menu. Scroll down the list in the Tag insight menu and double-click **type**, and then scroll down the next Tag insight menu and double-click **Text**.

3. Press the **Spacebar**, scroll down the Tag insight menu and double-click the **name** attribute, type **scheduleDate**, press the **Right** arrow key, press the **Spacebar**, scroll down the Tag insight menu and double-click the **size** attribute, type **30**, press the **Right** arrow key, and then type **>**. You created a text box control named scheduleDate that is 30 characters wide. See Figure 4-15.

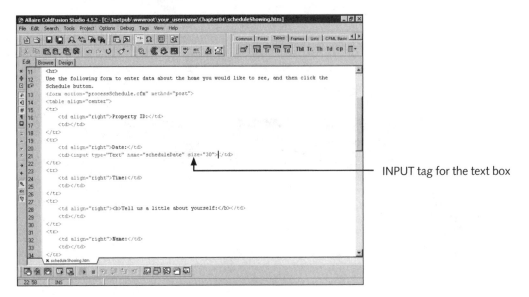

 INPUT tag for the text box

Figure 4-15   Partially completed scheduleShowing.htm with a text box

4. Repeat Steps 1–4, modifying as necessary to create a text box control named **scheduleTime** with 30 characters, starting on line 25, column 9.

> Instead of using the Tag insight menus to create your HTML code, you can type the code directly (for example, for Step 4 you could type <input type="Text" name="scheduleTime" size="30">). Entering HTML code is a matter of personal preference. Use whichever method you prefer.

5. In the column next to the Name caption, create a text box named **clientName** with 30 characters.

6. In the column next to the E-mail address caption, create a text box named **clientEmail** with 30 characters.

7. Save the document, and then click the **Browse** tab on the Editor window to preview your work. Refresh the window. See Figure 4-16.

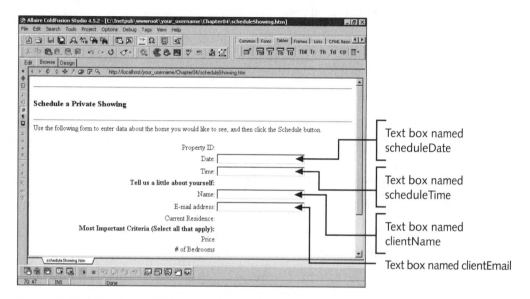

Figure 4-16   Preview of the Web page with text boxes

Next, you will add the Submit button to the form. The button will include the caption "Schedule."

To add the Submit button to the form:

1. Click the **Edit** tab on the Editor window, and then click line 69, column 9. You will add the Submit button in the second column of the last row in the table.

2. Use the Tag insight menus to add a Submit button with the value Schedule, or simply type **<input type="Submit" value="Schedule">**.

3. Save the document, and then preview it using the **Browse** tab. Refresh the window.

CREATING A FORM HANDLER

Your form is taking shape. However, you still need to add the checkboxes and radio buttons. You also need to create the form handler (processSchedule.cfm) to process the data gathered by the form. You can create the form handler at any time during the design process. Sometimes it is a good idea to create the form and its form handler at the same time, so you can preview the results as you go. Right now, Nikitha's design requires a form handler that simply outputs the data the user enters. Eventually, Nikitha wants the form handler to send an e-mail message to the agent in charge of the property.

To create the form handler:

1. Click the **Edit** tab on the Editor window, and then click the **New** button on the Standard toolbar.

2. With the insertion point on line 9, type **\<hr>**, and then press the **Enter** key.

3. On line 10, type **\<h3>Please verify the information that you entered:\</h3>**, and then press **Enter**.

4. Type **\<hr>**, and then press **Enter**.

5. If necessary, click the **Tables** tab on the QuickBar, and use the **Table Sizer (QuickTable)** button to create a table with two columns and four rows (a 2 by 4 table).

6. On line 14, column 9, type **Date:**.

7. On line 18, column 9, type **Time:**.

8. On line 22, column 9, type **Name:**.

9. On line 26, column 9, type **E-mail address:**.

10. Save the document as **processSchedule.cfm** in the Chapter04 folder on the server.

Now enter the CFOUTPUT tags to display the user data in the form handler. The data the user entered will be displayed in the cells in the second column of the table.

To display user data in the form handler:

1. Click line 15, column 9, and then type **\<cfoutput>#form.scheduleDate#\</cfoutput>**. Remember that the user data is stored using the word "form" plus a period, followed by the control's name. This control's name is scheduleDate, so the CFOUTPUT tag uses the name form.scheduleDate.

2. Click line 19, column 9, and then type **\<cfoutput>#form.scheduleTime#\</cfoutput>**.

3. Click line 23, column 9, and then type **\<cfoutput>#form.clientName#\</cfoutput>**.

4. Click line 27, column 9, and then type **\<cfoutput>#form.clientEmail#\</cfoutput>**.

5. Click line 30, and then type **\<hr>** to draw a horizontal line below the table. See Figure 4-17.

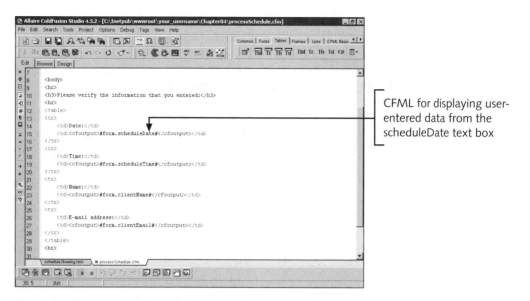

CFML for displaying user-entered data from the scheduleDate text box

4

Figure 4-17   processSchedule.cfm in ColdFusion Studio

6. Save the file.

7. Switch to your Web browser, and open **http://localhost/your_username/Chapter04/scheduleShowing.htm**.

8. Enter tomorrow's date (in the format MM/DD/YYYY) in the Date text box, type **4:30 PM** in the Time text box, and then type your name and e-mail address in the appropriate text boxes. See Figure 4-18.

Figure 4-18   Form with user-entered data

9. Click the **Schedule** button. If a dialog box opens with an option to enable Auto Complete, click **No**. The data that you entered is processed on the ColdFusion Server and then displayed by the form handler. See Figure 4-19.

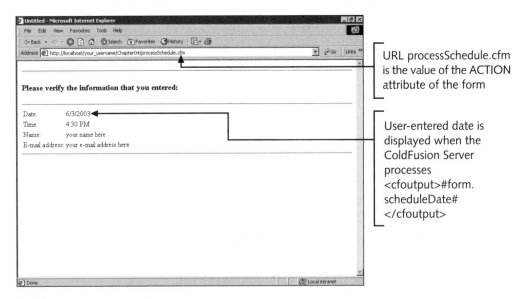

Figure 4-19   Web page displayed by the form handler with user-entered data

So far, you have created a form with text boxes and a Submit button and designed a form handler for it. Now you need to return to the scheduleShowing.htm document and create the radio buttons that store information about the prospective buyer's home status—rent or own.

DESIGNING AND HANDLING RADIO BUTTONS

Use radio buttons when you need to allow users to select one option from a group of mutually exclusive options. For example, if you want users to select a price range for a house, you could create a set of radio buttons, such as one with a "Less than $100,000" label, another with a "$101,000 – $145,000" label, and so on. The user can select only one price range, or one radio button.

The syntax to create a radio button is <input type="radio" name="*common name*" value="*radio button value*">. The VALUE attribute stores the value of the radio button. For example, in Nikitha's plan there are two radio buttons to indicate whether the user owns or rents his or her current residence. Both radio buttons should have the same name. The NAME attribute stores the HTML name of the radio button. Radio buttons that are part of the same group—which means they relate to the same category—must have the same value for the NAME attribute. If you click the Own radio button, the VALUE attribute for the Own radio button sends the value "Own" to the server; if you click the Rent radio button, the VALUE attribute for the Rent radio button sends the value "Rent" to the server. You use the optional CHECKED attribute to specify the default radio button that the browser should select when the form is displayed. However, in a single radio button group, a user can select only one radio button.

 It is always a good practice to specify a default selected radio button. If you do not specify a default selected radio button, a user might submit a form without selecting any radio button, in which case you may get unpredictable results.

To gain a better understanding of her clients' needs, Nikitha wants the Schedule a Private Showing page to collect data about each client's situation and preferences. When helping her clients to purchase a home, Nikitha needs to know whether they own or rent their current residence. If buyers have a property to sell, they might be able to purchase a home of greater value using the equity in their current home. If buyers are renting their current home, they might need to investigate different loan programs or undergo a credit check. Asking clients if they own or rent is an ideal situation to model using radio buttons because the answer can be only one of these two possibilities. You will add the radio button group to the form next.

To enhance a form using radio buttons:

1. Switch to ColdFusion Studio.

2. Click the **scheduleShowing.htm** document tab at the bottom of the window.

3. Scroll the document as necessary, and then click line 41, column 9 . This is where you will insert the radio button controls. The first radio button will have the name "currentResidence" (the common name) and the value "Own".

4. Use the Tag insight menus to enter the following code or type the following code directly:

    \<input type="radio" name="currentResidence" value="Own"\>.

    The INPUT tag doesn't store the label for the radio button, so you must type it outside of the INPUT tag that creates the control.

5. Type **Own**, and then press the **Spacebar**. Now you can create the second radio button, which also has the name "currentResidence." The value is "Rent."

6. Use the Tag insight menus to enter the following code or type the following code directly:

    \<input type="radio" name="currentResidence" value="Rent" checked\>

    This code creates the second radio button control. Notice the CHECKED attribute, which specifies that this radio button will be selected when the form opens in the browser.

7. Type **Rent** to create the label for the radio button control. See Figure 4-20.

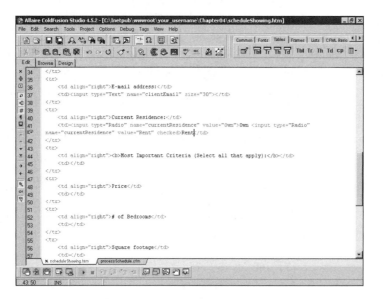

Figure 4-20   scheduleShowing.htm with the HTML for radio buttons

8. Save the file.

9. Switch to your Web browser, and open **scheduleShowing.htm**.

10. Refresh the document if the radio buttons are not displayed. The Rent radio button is automatically selected. See Figure 4-21.

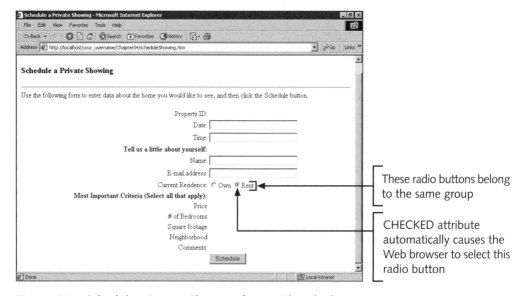

These radio buttons belong to the same group

CHECKED attribute automatically causes the Web browser to select this radio button

Figure 4-21 Schedule a Private Showing form with radio buttons

Next you will need to create the code in the form handler to process the radio buttons.

To add code to the form handler to process the radio buttons:

1. Switch to ColdFusion Studio.

2. Click the **processSchedule.cfm** tab at the bottom of the Editor window to view the code for the form handler. You can copy the last row in the table to the Clipboard, paste it as a new table row, and then edit the code to output the values stored by the radio buttons.

3. Select the entire last row in the table (all of lines 25–28), and then click the **Copy** button on the Edit toolbar to copy the code to the Clipboard.

4. Click line 29, column 1 (the line with the closing TABLE tag), click the **Paste** button on the Edit toolbar, and then press the **Enter** key. A new row is added to the table.

5. On line 30, select **E-mail address** (between the TD tags), and then type **Current Residence**.

6. On line 31, select **clientEmail** (between the CFOUTPUT tags), and then type **currentResidence**. See Figure 4-22.

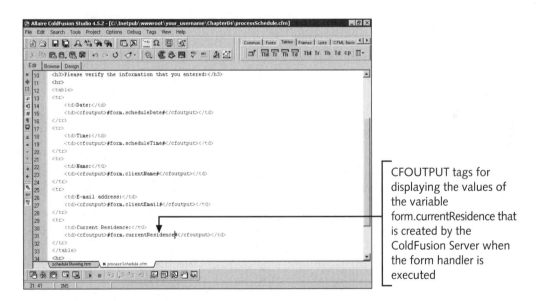

CFOUTPUT tags for displaying the values of the variable form.currentResidence that is created by the ColdFusion Server when the form handler is executed

Figure 4-22   processSchedule.cfm with CFML for handling a radio button

7. Save the processSchedule.cfm template.

8. Switch to your Web browser.

9. Click the **Own** radio button, and then click the **Schedule** button. The form handler processes the Own radio button and displays its value. See Figure 4-23.

Notice that the Rent radio button is unchecked by the browser when you check the Own radio button. The Rent radio button is unchecked because it has the same name as the Own radio button. As mentioned previously, only one radio button out of all radio buttons that have a common name can be checked at any time.

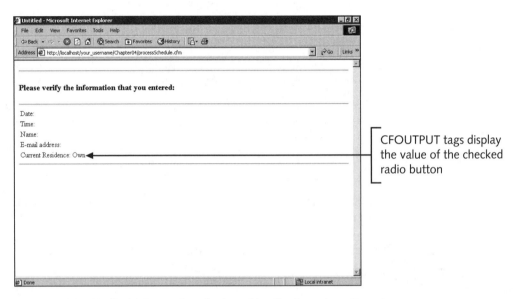

CFOUTPUT tags display the value of the checked radio button

Figure 4-23   Radio button value displayed by the form handler

DESIGNING AND HANDLING CHECKBOXES

When you need to allow users to select one or more options from a group of related choices, you can use a checkbox group. Checkboxes do not have to be mutually exclusive. For example, if you want users to select one or more options from a list, you can use checkboxes.

The syntax to create a checkbox is <input type="checkbox" name="*common name*" value="*checkbox value*">. The VALUE attribute stores the value of the checkbox that is sent to the server. The NAME attribute identifies the group to which the checkbox belongs. Just like radio buttons, checkboxes in a group usually relate to one category or topic. When a user selects a checkbox and then submits the form to the server for processing, the Web browser sets the value of the variable to the value specified by the VALUE attribute. You can use the optional CHECKED attribute to indicate that a checkbox should be selected when the browser opens the form.

You can use one or more checkboxes in a form. A checkbox group might also contain multiple checkboxes, as shown in Nikitha's form design (see Figure 4-8), where clients can indicate which housing options are important to them. You create checkboxes for these different situations in the same way. However, processing checkboxes is done differently, depending on the situation.

Handling a Single Checkbox

When you use only one checkbox with a particular name (for example, when the checkbox group consists of only one checkbox) and the user selects it, the server processes the checkbox in the same way as other form controls. If the checkbox group name is chkBox, the ColdFusion Server creates a variable named form.chkBox in which to output the value stored in the checkbox. If no value is specified, the variable is assigned the value "on." According to the HTML/HTTP specification, a Web browser in its interaction with the Web server treats a checkbox that is not selected as if it does not exist in the form; if the user does not select the checkbox, then no variable with the name of that checkbox is passed to the Web server. If the variable name for a checkbox is chkBox and chkBox is not selected, the ColdFusion Server will generate an undefined parameter error message and terminate execution of the page.

You must use the CFPARAM tag to process unselected checkboxes. The CFPARAM tag has two attributes: NAME and DEFAULT. The tag allows you to test for the existence of an optional variable specified by its NAME attribute. If the variable exists, processing continues and the value is not changed. If the variable does not exist, it is created and set to the value of the DEFAULT attribute. You must define the value for a checkbox in a form that is not selected by using a CFPARAM tag at the beginning of the form handler. Usually the value of a checkbox that is not selected is "off." For example, if the user does not select the checkbox, there is no variable named form.chkBox passed to the form handler. When the ColdFusion Server executes the CFPARAM tag, a new variable named form.chkBox is created and assigned a value "off." A CFPARAM tag for handling this situation is <cfparam name="form.chkBox" default="off">. If the form.chkBox variable already exists (in other words, the user selected the checkbox), then the Server ignores the default value in the CFPARAM tag and continues processing other statements.

The following example (Example4-1.htm) illustrates an HTML form with one checkbox:

```
<form action="processApp.cfm" method="post">
Check this box if you currently own your house:
<input type="checkbox" name="own" value="yes"><br><br><br>
<input type="submit" value="Apply">
</form>
```

The following form handler (processApp.cfm) uses a CFPARAM tag to handle the situation when the user does not check the checkbox:

```
<cfparam name="form.own" default="no">
<html>
<head>
<title>Application Form-Handler</title>
</head>
<body>
<cfif form.own is "yes">
```

```
You have indicated that you OWN your current home.
<cfelse>
You have indicated that you DO NOT OWN your current home.
</cfif>
</body>
</html>
```

Figure 4-24 shows the Web page displayed by Example4-1.htm. It is a form with one checkbox named own with a value yes and a Submit button with a caption Apply.

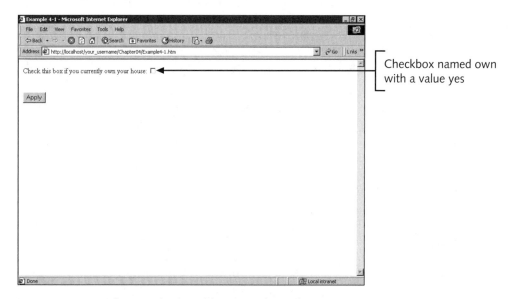

Checkbox named own with a value yes

Figure 4-24   Web page displayed by Example4-1.htm

Figure 4-25 shows the Web page displayed by the form handler when the user clicks the button after checking the checkbox. When the user submits the form, the user-entered data is sent to the Web server. The Web server transfers controls to the ColdFusion Server and makes the data the user entered available to it. The ColdFusion Server creates a variable named form.own and assigns it the value yes. It then executes the statements in processApp.cfm. First it processes the CFPARAM tag. Because a variable named form.own already exists, it ignores the default value and continues by processing the other statements. It evaluates the CFIF condition to true and outputs "You have indicated that you OWN your current home."

Figure 4-26 shows the Web page displayed by the form handler when the user clicks Apply without checking the checkbox. When this request is sent to the Web server, as mentioned previously, the Web browser does not send any checkbox data to the Web server. The Web server transfers control to the ColdFusion Server, and it starts executing processApp.cfm. There is no form data and it does not create any form variables. It executes the CFPARAM tag. It tests for the existence of a variable named form.own. The Server creates the form.own variable as the existence test fails and assigns it the value no. It evaluates the CFIF condition to false and outputs "You have indicated that you DO NOT OWN your current home."

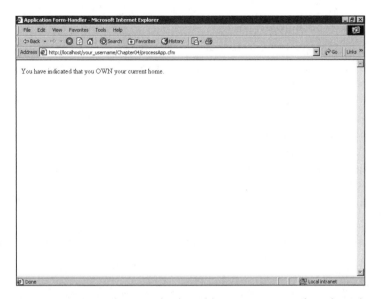

Figure 4-25 Web page displayed by processApp.cfm when the checkbox is checked

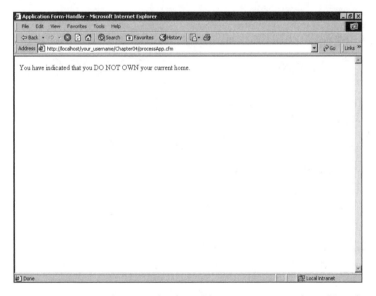

Figure 4-26 Web page displayed by processApp.cfm when the checkbox is not checked

In this example, you learned how to handle a single checkbox. In the next section you will learn about handling situations that require multiple checkboxes in a group.

Handling Multiple Checkboxes

A checkbox group can contain more than one checkbox. In this case, each checkbox in the group has the same name and a different value associated with it. In any checkbox group, a user may select all, some, or none of the checkboxes. If a user doesn't select any checkbox in a checkbox group, then no variable for the checkbox group is sent to the ColdFusion Server for processing. In this case, you must add a CFPARAM tag to the form handler to process the default situation. If the user selects one checkbox, a variable for the checkbox group is created and the value in that checkbox is assigned to that variable. When a user selects more than one checkbox in a checkbox group, the values stored in those checkboxes are sent to the ColdFusion Server as a comma-delimited value-list. To process multiple selected checkboxes, you use a LIST loop flow-control structure in the form handler.

Based on her experience, Nikitha has identified a home's price, number of bedrooms, total square feet (square footage), and neighborhood as some important criteria for home buyers. Nikitha's form design lets users select none or one or more of these options using checkboxes. You'll add this checkbox group to the form next.

To add checkboxes to a form:

1. Switch to ColdFusion Studio.

2. Click the **scheduleShowing.htm** tab at the bottom of the window, if necessary.

3. Click in line 49, column 9 between the TD tags. You will add the Price checkbox here.

4. Use the Tag insight menus to enter the following code or type the following code directly:

   <input type="checkbox" name="criteria" value="Price">

   You can copy, paste, and edit this INPUT tag to create the code for the other checkboxes.

5. Use the mouse to select the entire INPUT tag on line 49, and then click the **Copy** button on the Edit toolbar.

6. Click line 53, column 9, click the **Paste** button on the Edit toolbar, select the text **Price** in the VALUE attribute on line 55, and then type **Bedrooms**.

7. Click line 57, column 9, click the **Paste** button on the Edit toolbar, select the text **Price** in the VALUE attribute on line 59, and then type **Square Footage**.

8. Click line 61, column 9, and repeat Step 5 to change the text Price to **Neighborhood**. See Figure 4-27.

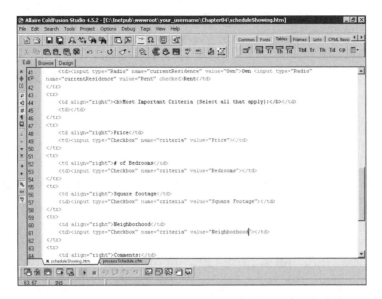

Figure 4-27   scheduleShowing.htm with CFML for checkboxes

9. Save the file.

10. Switch to your Web browser, and type **http://localhost/your_username/ Chapter04/scheduleShowing.htm** to open **scheduleShowing.htm**. Refresh the browser if necessary. Scroll down the document to see the checkboxes that you just created. See Figure 4-28.

Figure 4-28   Schedule a Private Showing page with checkboxes

The next step in the design process is to modify the form handler to process data entered in the checkboxes. A user does not have to select any of the checkboxes, so you need to use a CFPARAM tag to specify a default value. A default value of "Not answered" is appropriate for this situation.

To modify the form handler to process checkboxes:

1. Switch to ColdFusion Studio.

2. Click the **processSchedule.cfm** tab on the bottom of the Editor window to open it.

3. Click line 1, column 1, press the **Enter** key, and then press the **Up** arrow key to move the insertion point to the new line.

4. Use the Tag insight menus to enter the following code or type the following code directly:

   <cfparam name="form.criteria" default="Not answered">

   This CFPARAM tag indicates that the default value of the criteria variable is "Not answered" if no checkboxes from the criteria group are selected. Next, you will add a new row to the table to display the values selected from the checkbox group by the user.

5. Select lines 30–33, click the **Copy** button on the Edit toolbar, click line 34, column 1, click the **Paste** button on the Edit toolbar, and then press **Enter**.

6. On line 35, select **Current Residence**, and then type **Important Criteria**.

7. On line 36, select **currentResidence**, and then type **criteria**. See Figure 4-29. Make sure that your code matches the code shown in Figure 4-29, including the line numbers. Modify your document if necessary.

8. Save the file.

9. Switch to your Web browser.

10. Click the **Price** and **Square footage** checkboxes, and then click the **Schedule** button. The form handler displays the important criteria that you selected. See Figure 4-30.

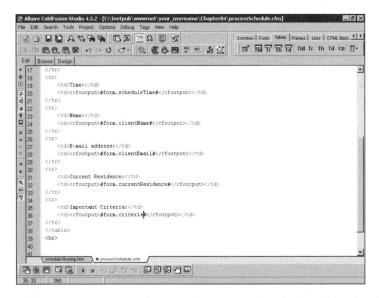

Figure 4-29   processSchedule.cfm with CFML for handling checkboxes

Figure 4-30   Confirmation page displaying selected important criteria

11. Click the **Back** button, make sure that no checkboxes are selected, and then click the **Schedule** button. The CFPARAM tag in the form handler assigns the default value to variable form.criteria and displays it in the form as "Not answered." See Figure 4-31.

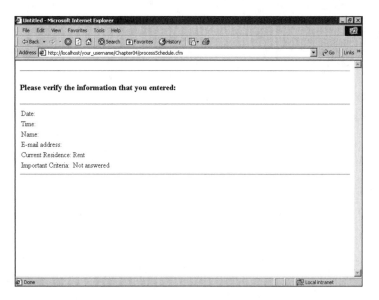

Figure 4-31   Confirmation page displayed when none of the checkboxes are selected

When you check more than one checkbox, you generate a list of comma-separated values. You can process this value-list using a LIST loop. Once you use a LIST loop, you can access the values of each checked box and then display them in neatly formatted lists or tables. You also can perform additional processing, such as inserting values into database tables or sending e-mail.

To display values of selected checkboxes in a bulleted list:

1. Switch to ColdFusion Studio. If necessary, click the **processSchedule.cfm** document tab at the bottom.

2. Select **<cfoutput>#form.criteria#</cfoutput>** in line 36.

3. Replace the selection with the following code, also shown in Figure 4-32:

```
<ul>
<cfloop index="c" list="#form.criteria#">
<li><cfoutput>#c#</cfoutput></li>
</cfloop>
</ul>
```

4. Save your work.

5. Switch to your Web browser, and open **scheduleShowing.cfm**.

6. Check the **Price**, **Square footage**, and **Neighborhood** checkboxes, and then click the **Schedule** button. See Figure 4-33.

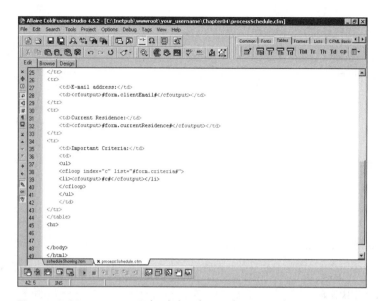

Figure 4-32   processSchedule.cfm with CFML for processing checkboxes with LIST loops

Figure 4-33   Confirmation page displaying selected important criteria as a bulleted list with a LIST loop

Although checkboxes and radio buttons are useful controls, they are difficult to use when you want to present many options. For example, if your form design requires the user to select a U.S. state, you need at least 50 radio buttons. Fifty radio buttons would probably fill the entire page, making it unattractive and uninviting. In such situations, you can use list boxes or select boxes instead of checkboxes or radio buttons.

DESIGNING AND HANDLING SELECT BOXES

When you need to present users with many related options, you can use a select box in a form. A **select box**, also known as a list box or a drop-down menu, hides the list of choices until the user clicks the list arrow on the control. The syntax for a select box is as follows:

```
<select name="select box name">
 <option value="option value">first option name
 <option value="option value">second option name
 .
 .
 .
</select>
```

The NAME attribute of the SELECT tag identifies the name of the variable to the ColdFusion Server. The VALUE attribute of the OPTION tag specifies the value of that choice in the list; when selected, this value is sent to the Server for processing. The text following the OPTION tag is the description displayed in the select box. You can use the optional SELECTED attribute in the OPTION tag to indicate the default selection when the form first opens. If you omit this attribute, then the first option in the list is displayed by default. If you do not specify a value in the optional SIZE attribute, the select box displays only one choice in the list when the form is opened. You can set the value in the SIZE attribute to specify the number of lines to display when the form is opened. The default value for the SIZE attribute is 1.

If you need to let users select more than one option in a select box, you can include the optional MULTIPLE attribute in the SELECT tag. Users can select multiple options by selecting the first choice, pressing and holding down the Ctrl key (or the Command key on a Macintosh), and then selecting the other options. When users select more than one option in a select box, the form handler receives a variable with a list of comma-delimited values similar to the case when users select multiple checkboxes. You have to use a LIST loop to handle this user-entered data.

If a user doesn't select any option in a select box with a size larger than 1, you must use a CFPARAM tag in the form handler to process the default case, similar to how you process a checkbox group with no selected checkboxes.

Because property numbers are randomly generated and difficult to remember, Nikitha decides to use a select box so users can select the properties from a list. Using a list reduces the possibility of typing errors. The select box will display one line of options. In addition, the select box will show the first value in the list as the default selection.

To add a select box to the form:

1. Switch to ColdFusion Studio.

2. Click the **scheduleShowing.htm** tab at the bottom.

3. Click line 17, column 9 to position the insertion point in the cell to the right of the Property ID: label. Press the **Enter** key to insert a new line.

4. Use the Tag insight menus to enter the following code or type the following code directly:

<select name="propertyID">

5. Press the **Enter** key, and then use the Tag insight menus to enter the following code or type the following code directly:

<option value="1234570">1234570

This code creates the first option in the list. You did not include the SELECTED tag, so this option will be selected by default when the form is first opened. Notice that the HTML name and its label in the form are the same.

6. Press **Enter**, and then enter the other three options in the select box, as shown in Figure 4-34.

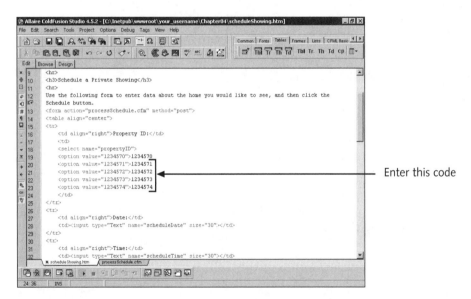

Figure 4-34   scheduleShowing.htm with HTML for a select box

7. Click at the end of line 23 and press **Enter**. Type **</select>** to complete the select box.

8. Save your work.

The next step is to revise the form handler to process the select box.

To modify the form handler to process a select box:

1. Click the **processSchedule.cfm** tab at the bottom of the Editor window, select lines 14–17, and then click the **Copy** button on the Edit toolbar. You'll paste this code as a new first row in the table, where you will output the property ID selections made in the select box.

2. Click line 14, column 1, click the **Paste** button on the Edit toolbar.

3. Select the text **Date** on line 15, and then type **Property ID**.

4. Select the text **form.scheduleDate** on line 16, and then type **form.propertyID**. See Figure 4-35. Make sure that your code matches the code shown in Figure 4-35, including line numbers. Modify your document if necessary.

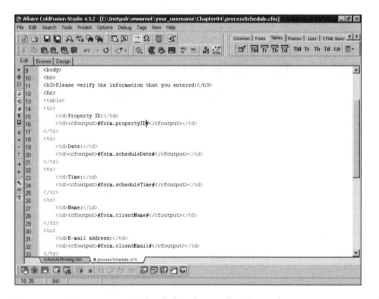

Figure 4-35   processSchedule.cfm with CFML for processing a select box

5. Save your work.

6. Switch to your Web browser, and open **scheduleShowing.htm**. Refresh the page, if necessary, to see the select box.

7. Click the **Property ID list arrow**, click **1234572** in the list, scroll down the form, if necessary, and then click the **Schedule** button. The form handler processes the option that you selected and displays it in the page. See Figure 4-36.

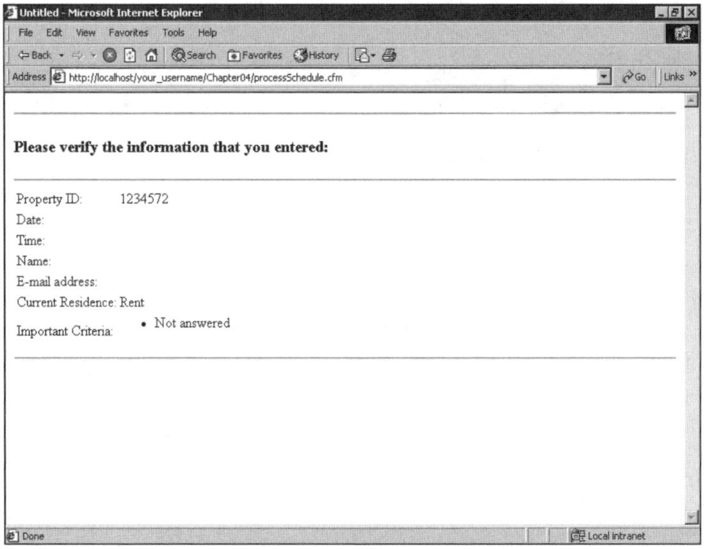

Figure 4-36   Confirmation page displaying selected property ID

DESIGNING AND HANDLING SCROLLING TEXT BOXES

When you need to collect open-ended data longer than a short phrase or sentence, you can use a scrolling text box. A **scrolling text box** displays a specified amount of space and accepts text. The syntax for a scrolling text box is as follows:

```
<textarea name="scrolling text box name" cols="number of
columns" rows="number of rows" wrap="wrap value"> Default
text </textarea>
```

The NAME attribute of the TEXTAREA tag is the HTML name of the scrolling text box control. You access data entered in a scrolling text box by using the form.name convention that you used for other controls in form handlers. The ROWS and COLS attributes allow you to size the text area. The ROWS attribute controls the number of lines displayed in the scrolling text box, and the COLS attribute controls the number of characters visible in a single line. Another useful attribute is WRAP, which you can set to "soft" to have text entered by the user wrap to the next line in the control. Even when the WRAP attribute is set to "soft," the text is sent to the server as one long line for processing. You handle scrolling text boxes in the form handler in ways similar to how you handle text boxes and other controls. The text between the TEXTAREA tags appears in the text box when the form is first displayed. Users can edit this text and type their own text in the text box.

Nikitha wants users to be able to enter comments as necessary to elaborate on their home-buying needs. She uses a scrolling text box to collect this optional data.

To create a scrolling text box in the form:

1. Switch to ColdFusion Studio.

2. Click the **scheduleShowing.htm** tab at the bottom of the window.

3. Scroll down the file, and then click line 73, column 9.

 The status bar position varies depending on the status of the word wrap feature and the size of your screen. Use the line numbers in the gutter to position the insertion point correctly.

4. Use the Tag insight menus to enter the following code or type the following code directly:

   <textarea name="comments" cols="25" rows="5" wrap="soft"> </textarea>

   This code creates a scrolling text box named "comments" with 5 lines and 25 characters visible in the control. When users enter data into this control, the WRAP attribute will wrap text to the next line. If you see a warning message, you can ignore it.

5. Save your work.

The next step is to modify the form handler to process data entered into the scrolling text box control.

To modify the form handler to process input from a scrolling text box:

1. Click the **processSchedule.cfm** tab at the bottom of the Editor window, click line 47, column 6, and then press the **Enter** key to move the closing TABLE tag to the next line.

2. Select rows 34–37, click the **Copy** button on the Edit toolbar, click line 48, column 1, click the **Paste** button on the Edit toolbar.

3. On line 49, select the text **Current Residence**, and then type **Comments**.

4. On line 50, select the text **form.currentResidence**, and then type **form.comments**. See Figure 4-37.

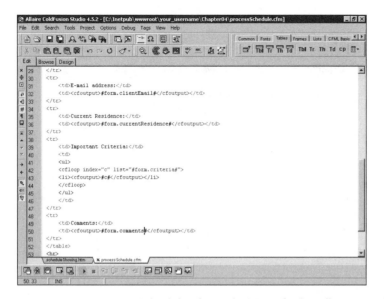

Figure 4-37   processSchedule.cfm with CFML for handling a scrolling text box

5. Save your work.

6. Switch to your Web browser, and open **scheduleShowing.htm**.

7. Scroll down the page, click in the **Comments** text box, and then type **This is the only time that we will be able to look at properties while we are in town so we are hoping that you will be available.** See Figure 4-38.

COLS="25"

ROWS="5"

Scroll bar appears when the number of typed lines exceeds the values in the ROWS attribute

Figure 4-38   Text entered in scrolling text box

8. Click the **Schedule** button. The form handler processes the data that you entered in the scrolling text box. See Figure 4–39.

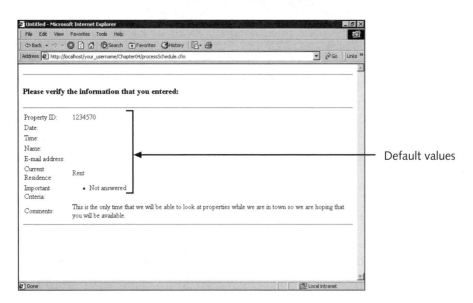

Figure 4-39   Result of data entered in scrolling text box

DESIGNING AND HANDLING HIDDEN FIELDS

In certain situations, you may need to create form controls with values that are not visible to users. In these situations, you can create hidden fields. Hidden fields allow you to pass data from one Web page to another. To create a hidden field, you use the tag <input type="hidden" name="*hidden field name*" value="*value*">. To access a value stored in a hidden field in the form handler, you use the form.name convention. You use the VALUE attribute to specify the value of this variable. Because the Web browser does not display a hidden field, users cannot change its value. The hidden field is hidden when the page is viewed using a browser; however, a sophisticated user could examine the HTML source code for the document and determine that hidden fields are being used to pass values and variables from one document to another.

The following example (Example4-2.htm) illustrates the use of hidden fields:

```
<hr>
<h3>Real Estate Trivia</h3>
<hr>
<form action="processQuiz.cfm" method="post">
What was the median sales price for houses sold in the
U.S. during the year 1999?<hr>
<input type="radio" name="answer" value="a">A. $ 70,000<br>
<input type="radio" name="answer" value="b">B. $100,000<br>
```

```
<input type="radio" name="answer" value="c">C. $130,000<br>
<input type="radio" name="answer" value="d">D. $150,000<br>
<input type="radio" name="answer" value="e" checked>E.
None of the above.<br><br>
<input type="hidden" name="correctAnswer" value="c">
<input type="Submit" value="Submit">
</form>
<hr>
```

4

In this code example, the highlighted line uses a hidden field to store the correct quiz answer as a hidden field named correctAnswer. This answer would be available to the ColdFusion form handler in the variable named form.correctAnswer. Figure 4-40 shows the Web page created by this code. Notice that the hidden field doesn't appear in the page.

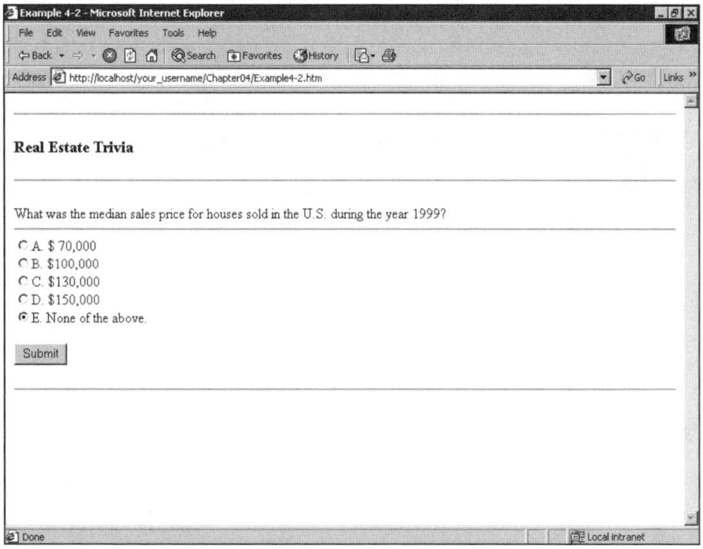

Figure 4-40   Web page with a hidden field

The user can select one of five radio buttons to answer the trivia question. When the user clicks the Submit button, the form is sent to the ColdFusion Server. The code for the form handler (processQuiz.cfm) that processes this page is as follows:

```
<html>
<head>
<title>Quiz Results</title>
</head>
<body>
<hr>
<h3>Real Estate Trivia Results</h3>
<hr>
```

```
<cfif form.answer eq form.correctAnswer>
You are correct. You have a good knowledge of real estate
trivia.
<cfelse>
You are incorrect. The correct answer is $130,000.
</cfif>
<hr>
</body>
</html>
```

If the user selects the radio button that stores a value that is equal to the value stored in the variable form.correctAnswer, the CFIF condition evaluates to true. The ColdFusion Server outputs the phrase indicating that the user answered the question correctly. If the user selects a radio button whose value does not equal the value stored in the variable form.correctAnswer, the CFELSE statement outputs a statement indicating that the user did not answer the question correctly. Figure 4-41 shows the form handler's output when the question is answered correctly.

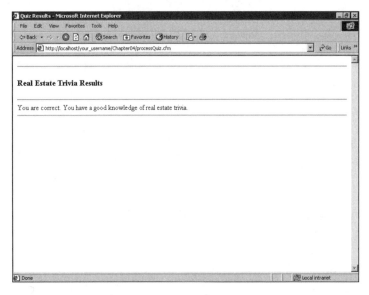

Figure 4-41   Real estate trivia results

In the next section, you will use a hidden field to complete the NikRealty form.

SENDING A FORM'S RESULTS VIA E-MAIL

When you use a form to collect data, give the user a chance to confirm the results. For example, you can echo the user input or add information to the data.

The form handler for NikRealty's scheduleShowing.htm page echoes the user's input. Before this information is sent to someone at NikRealty, Nikitha wants users to examine the data and then click a button with the caption "Above information is correct – schedule the showing," which causes the Web browser to send the form data to NikRealty via e-mail.

 For this exercise to work, your computer should be configured to send e-mail. In a later chapter, you will learn about sending e-mail using ColdFusion that does not require any special configuration on client computers.

To send a form's results via e-mail, you specify the recipient's e-mail address in the ACTION attribute of the FORM tag. When the client clicks the button to submit the form, the form results will be sent via e-mail to NikRealty. As you are giving the user a chance to examine the data prior to it being e-mailed, you need another form on the confirmation page with a Submit button and data to be e-mailed. You can use a hidden field for the text of the e-mail message. The hidden field allows you to put the user-entered data into another form contained in the form handler, without the user's knowledge. Within that hidden field, you can include a CFOUTPUT tag to send the form results as a semicolon-delimited list of user-entered values.

To modify a form handler by including a form in it to send data via e-mail:

1. Switch to ColdFusion Studio.

2. Make sure that you are editing the **processSchedule.cfm** file, and then click at the end of </table> on line 52, and press the **Enter** key.

3. Use the Tag insight menus to enter the following code or type the following code directly:

   <form action="mailto:your_e-mail_address?subject=Request for a showing"

   This code creates the form and sends the form results via e-mail to the address specified by your_e-mail_address. The subject line of the e-mail message will be "Request for a showing," so that people at NikRealty will know that the content of the e-mail message is from the Web page and that the user is requesting a showing. See Figure 4-42.

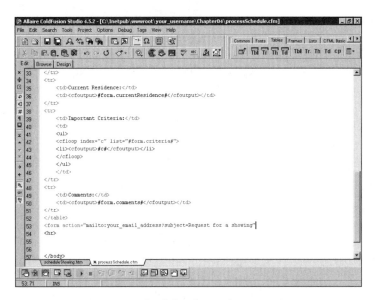

Figure 4-42   processSchedule.cfm with a partial FORM tag

When entering your e-mail address as a mailto, be sure to include your user-name and your domain name, as in student@university.edu.

Next, you need to complete the form and include the METHOD attribute. When you send e-mail messages from a client by using forms, you need to specify the encryption type as text so that the messages can be read in plain text. Other encryption types are useful for data being sent to Web servers. You will learn about these in later chapters.

4. Press the **Spacebar**, and then use the Tag insight menus to enter the following code or type the following code directly:

method="post" enctype="text/plain">

You will use a hidden field to store the form results as a comma-delimited list. The field is hidden so that users cannot see it in the form handler. The name of this field will be client-data.

5. Press **Enter**, and then use the Tag insight menus to enter the following code or type the following code directly:

<input type="Hidden" name="client-data"

Next, include the VALUE attribute, along with the list of values to include.

6. Press the **Spacebar**, and then type
value="<cfoutput>#form.propertyID#;#form.scheduleDate#;#form
.scheduleTime#;#form.clientName#;#form.clientEmail#;#form.
currentResidence#;#form.criteria#;#form.comments#
</cfoutput>">. See Figure 4-43.

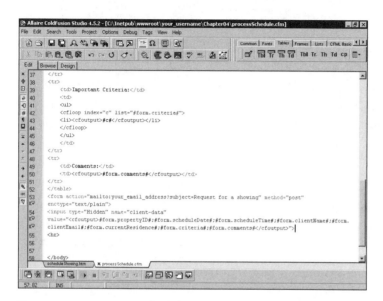

Figure 4-43   processSchedule.cfm with a hidden field

Now, complete the form handler by adding the code for the Submit button.

7. Press **Enter**, and then use the Tag insight menus to enter the following code or type the following code directly:

<input type="Submit" value="Above information is correct –
schedule the showing ">

8. Press **Enter**, and type **</form>** to close the form.

9. Save your work.

10. Switch to your Web browser, and open **scheduleShowing.htm**.

11. Use the form to enter data of your choice, and then click the **Schedule** button. The data that you entered appears in the form handler, along with the new Submit button that you created. Figure 4-44 shows the data for one user.

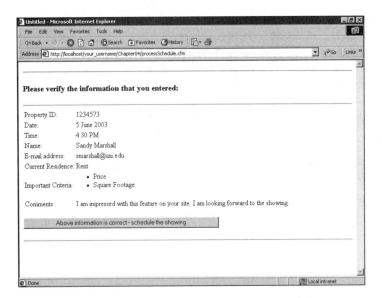

Figure 4-44   Confirmation page with user-entered data

12. Click the **Above information is correct – schedule the showing** button. Depending on the type of browser that you have, a dialog box might open. If necessary, click **OK**. Figure 4–45 shows the dialog box that opens if you are using Microsoft Internet Explorer.

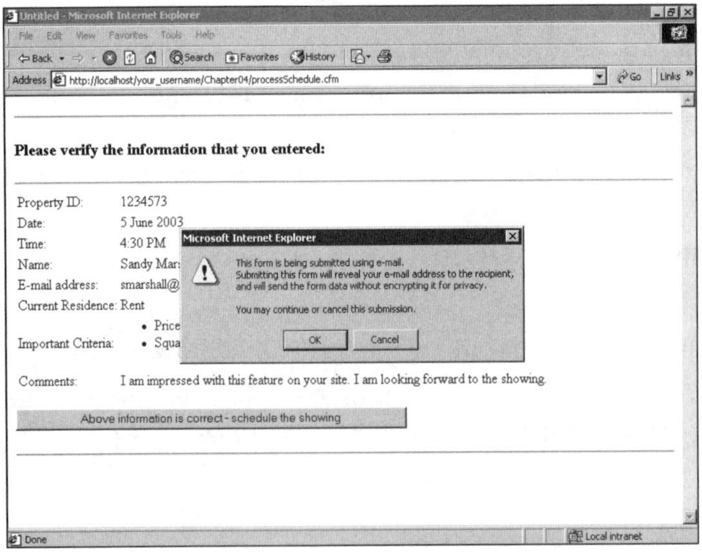

Figure 4-45   Dialog box that opens before sending e-mail

If a dialog box opens and tells you that this feature is not installed, insert the requested CD into the correct drive, and then click the OK button. If you do not have the requested CD, click the Cancel button. Your Web browser must be configured to send e-mail for this application to work. If you are working on a computer that is not connected to the Internet, this application will not work. In a later chapter, you will learn how to send e-mail directly from the server.

13. If necessary, start your default e-mail program, and connect to your server. Click the **Send/Receive** button (or whichever button downloads your mail messages), and then you should see the message sent from the form. See Figure 4–46.

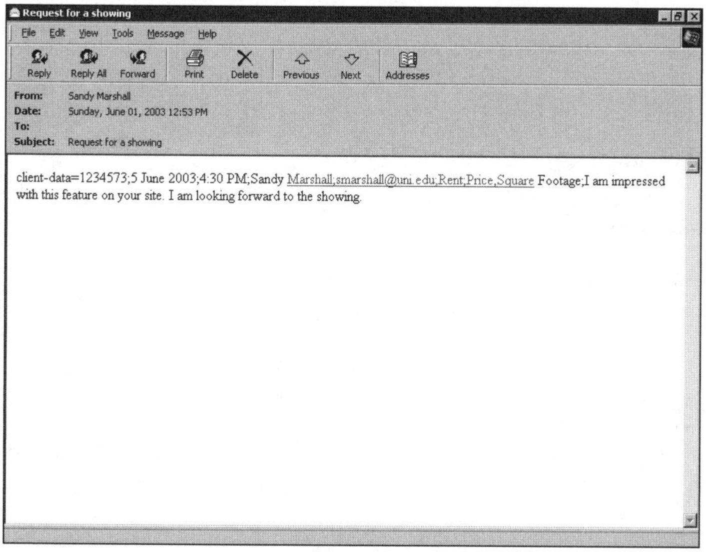

4

![E-mail message window titled "Request for a showing" with toolbar buttons Reply, Reply All, Forward, Print, Delete, Previous, Next, Addresses. From: Sandy Marshall. Date: Sunday, June 01, 2003 12:53 PM. To: Subject: Request for a showing. Message body: client-data=1234573;5 June 2003;4:30 PM;Sandy Marshall,smarshall@uni.edu;Rent;Price;Square Footage;I am impressed with this feature on your site. I am looking forward to the showing.]

Figure 4-46   E-mail message with form results

Using e-mail to submit form data is often unreliable because the methods used by different browsers for sending e-mail messages vary. In addition, some older browser versions cannot display and use these types of forms. You are also assuming that clients have a properly configured browser and an e-mail account from which to send e-mail messages. Typically, computers used in public facilities may not be configured for sending e-mail. As mentioned earlier, you will learn about using the ColdFusion Server to send e-mail directly in a later chapter to overcome these problems.

DESIGNING AND HANDLING IMAGE BUTTONS

Depending on the graphical design of your Web site, you may want to use images or icons, instead of buttons, with simple captions to submit forms. You can use an INPUT tag with the TYPE attribute set to "image" to create an image that submits the form when the user clicks it. The graphic file containing the image must be located on the Web server, and its URL should be the value of the SRC (source) attribute of the INPUT tag. When the user clicks the image, the Web browser submits the data entered in all the form controls along with two additional variables, x and y. The variables x and y are available in the ColdFusion form handler specified by the ACTION attribute of the form as form.x and form.y. These variables are the coordinates of the pixel where the user clicked the image. The origin for the coordinate system is the upper-left corner of the image. Variable x is the number of pixels the mouse click is to the right of the left edge of the image, and variable y is the number of pixels the mouse click is from the top of the image. You can use variables x and y for simulating image maps, where larger images include multiple commands for actions depending on what part of the image the user clicks.

In the NikRealty example, if you change the INPUT tag for submitting the form to use a graphic, you would replace the following code:

```
<input type="submit" value="Above information is
correct — schedule the showing">
```

with the following code:

```
<input type="image" src="submit.gif">
```

With this change made, the user will click the submit.gif image (see Figure 4-47) to submit the form. You can use any image to submit a form. This image contains descriptive text so the user can identify its function.

When the user submits the form, two additional values are included in the e-mail message: the x coordinate and the y coordinate, indicating the exact location where the user clicked the image. If the image contains only one command, as shown in this example, then the x and y coordinates aren't significant in the results.

Nikitha is pleased with the form that you created. However, she is concerned about clients using a select box to select the property ID number. The select box currently contains five options representing five properties—in the future, the select box might contain hundreds of options to represent the many properties for sale in the area. Each property has a page that provides a description of the property, and sometimes this description includes a picture of the property. Nikitha asks you to provide a link in each property's description page that clients can click to request a showing. This change means that you can use the same form as the current one, except that the property select box will preselect the property using its property ID number when the client clicks the hyperlink. You learned about passing parameters on URLs that are part of anchors in earlier chapters and are excited to implement this requirement.

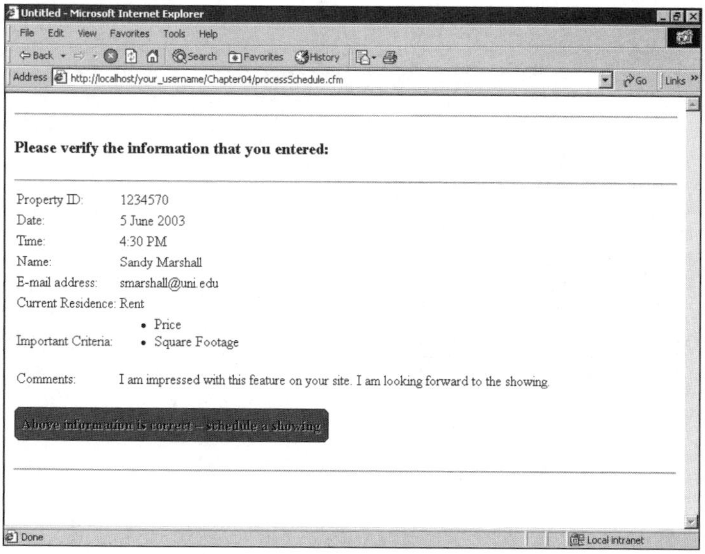

Figure 4-47   Form with an image submit button

To add a hyperlink to a form for preselecting data:

1. Switch to your Web browser, if necessary.

2. In the Address text box of your browser, type:

   http://localhost/your_username/Chapter04/1234573.htm,

   and then press the **Enter** key to open the HTML document. See Figure 4-48. This page provides a description of one of the properties available for sale, along with its picture.

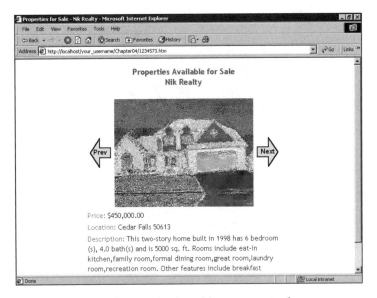

Figure 4-48 Web page displayed by 1234573.cfm

3. Switch to ColdFusion Studio.

4. Click the **Open** button on the Standard toolbar, and then open the **1234573.htm** file in the Chapter04 folder on your Data Disk. See Figure 4-49. Note that the images are located in a subfolder of your_username folder named Images. These images are located in a separate subfolder because you will use them again in subsequent chapters.

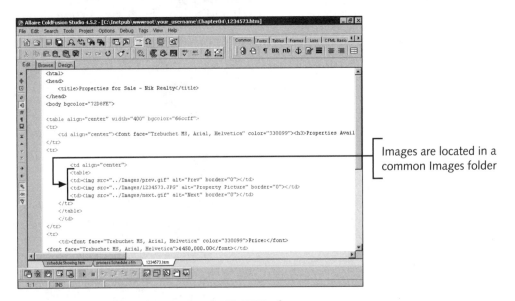

Images are located in a common Images folder

Figure 4-49 HTML source code of 1234573.cfm

5. Click line 35, column 80, between the FONT tags, and then type **I like this property, please schedule a private showing.**

6. Click the **Resource Tab** button on the View toolbar to turn on the display of the Resource Tab window, and then click the **Files** tab at the bottom of the Resource Tab window, if necessary.

7. In the top window, navigate to the Chapter04 folder on the server, and then open it to display its file listing in the lower window. See Figure 4-50.

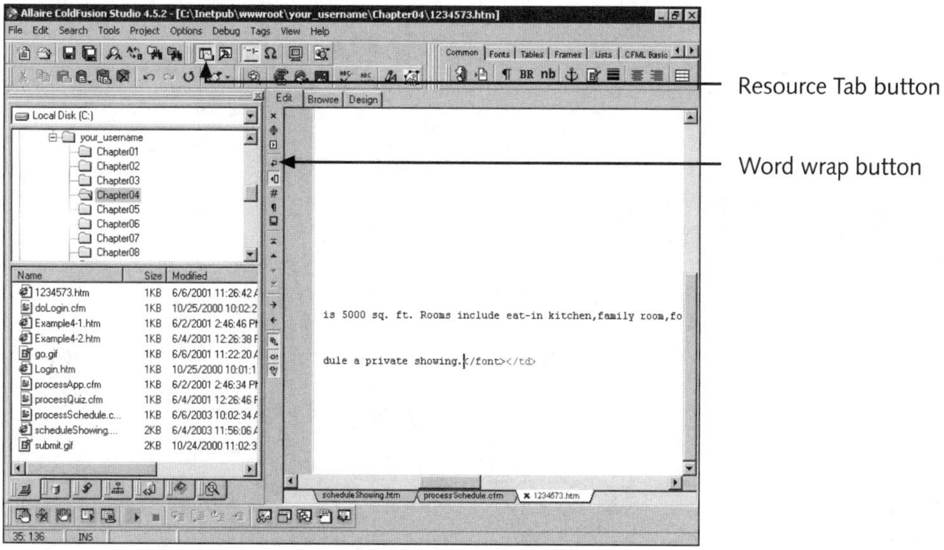

Resource Tab button

Word wrap button

Figure 4-50   Editing 1234573.htm in ColdFusion Studio

8. If necessary, click the **Word wrap** button on the vertical Editor toolbar. ColdFusion Studio wraps the lines and displays all the code in the window. See Figure 4-51.

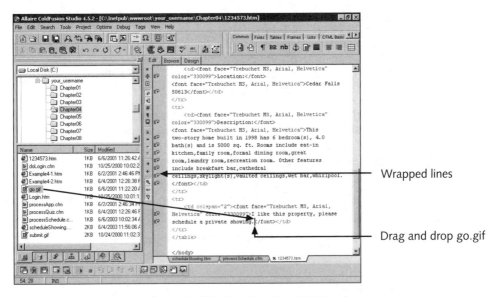

Figure 4-51 1234573.htm in ColdFusion Studio with Word wrap on

9. Drag the **go.gif** file from the lower Resource Tab window to the right of the sentence you just typed in the Editor window to insert an image tag that displays the go.gif image. See Figure 4-52.

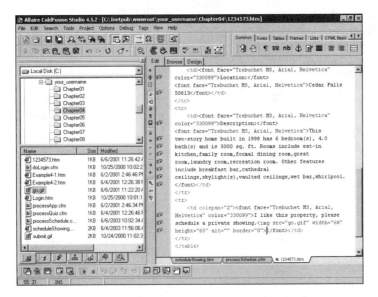

Figure 4-52 1234573.htm with the HTML for displaying an image

10. Click the **Resource Tab** button on the View toolbar to close the Resource Tab windows.

With the image added to the page, you can use the QuickBar to add the URL to it.

To add a URL to the image tag:

1. Use the mouse to select the image tag that you just inserted (<img src="go.gif" width="68" height="65" alt="" border="0">), and then click the **Common** tab on the QuickBar, if necessary.

> To turn on the QuickBar, click View on the menu bar, and then click QuickBar.

2. Click the **Anchor** button on the Common tab. The Anchor dialog box opens.

3. In the HREF text box, type **scheduleShowing.cfm?PropertyID=1234573**. See Figure 4-53.

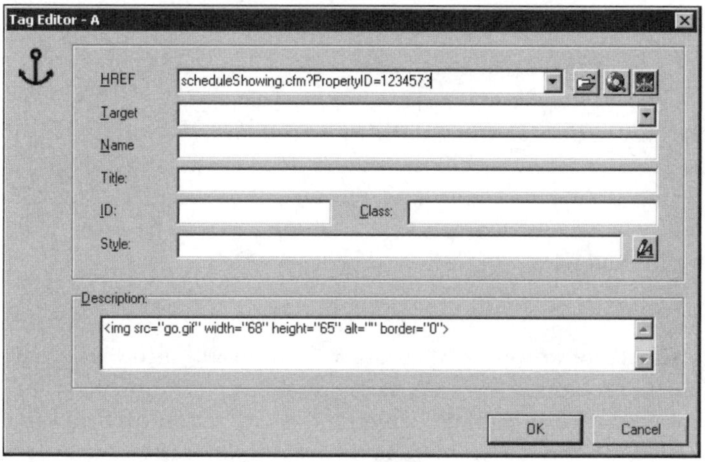

Figure 4-53   Tag Editor – A dialog box

4. Click the **OK** button. You added code to make the go.gif image a hyperlink to scheduleShowing.cfm with a URL parameter named PropertyID and a value 1234573.

5. Save your work.

6. Switch to your Web browser, and refresh the document. Scroll down to the end of the document, and notice that the Web browser displays the Go image and that it is a hyperlink. See Figure 4-54.

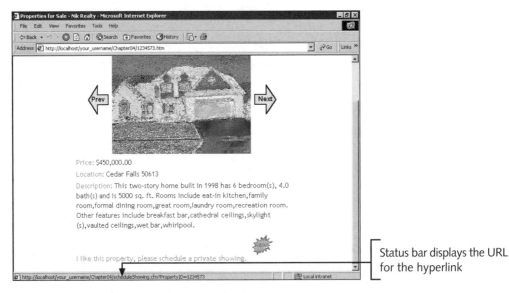

Status bar displays the URL
for the hyperlink

Figure 4-54   Web page with hyperlinked image

Notice that the URL for the Go button containing the parameter appears on the status bar. The URL specifies a file named scheduleShowing.cfm; the current file is scheduleShowing.htm. You'll need to change the filename for the Go button to work correctly. You are changing the filename to make it a ColdFusion template for processing URL parameters.

7. Switch to ColdFusion Studio.

8. Click the **scheduleShowing.htm** tab at the bottom of the Editor window, click **File**, and then click **Save As**. A dialog box opens showing a list of folders. Change the filename in the File name text box to **scheduleShowing.cfm**, and then click the **Save** button. ColdFusion Studio creates a copy of the file with an extension of .cfm. When this file is requested, the ColdFusion Server will execute it.

9. Click line 20, column 28, to the right of value="1234570," press the **Spacebar** (you can ignore the Tag insight menu that opens), and then type **<cfif URL.PropertyID EQ 1234570>Selected</cfif>**. If the CFIF condition is true, then the word "Selected" is output, and the browser will preselect this option.

10. Enter the CFIF statements for the other options in the select box, as shown in Figure 4-55, and then save the file. Use Copy and Paste to speed up your editing.

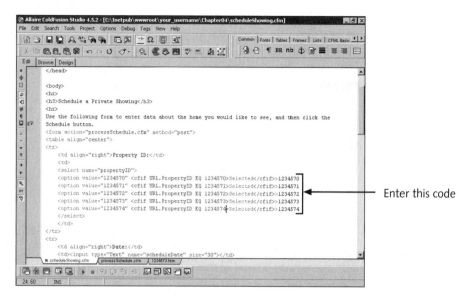

Figure 4-55   Select box with CFIF statements for preselecting options

11. Save your work.

12. Switch to your Web browser, and then click the **Go** button. The Property ID select box shows the correct value for the selected property. See Figure 4-56.

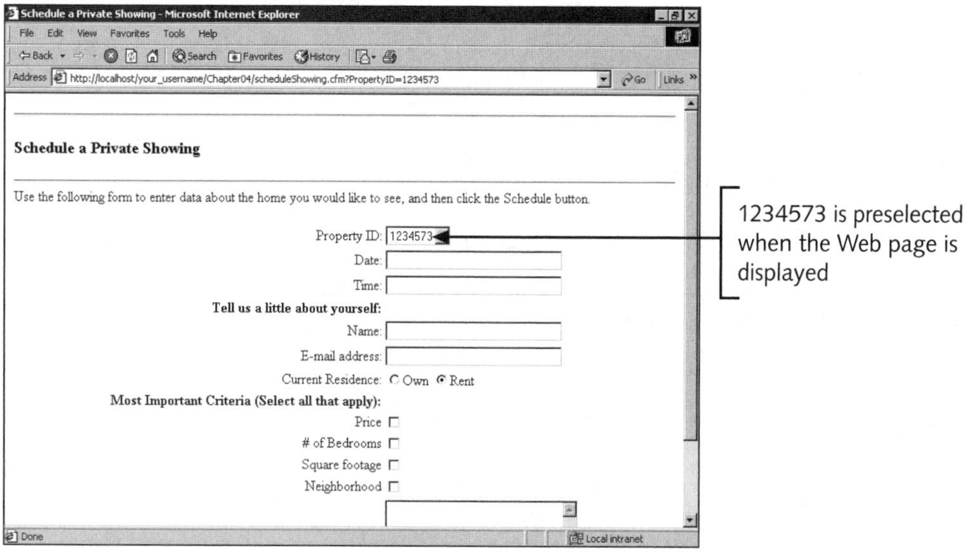

Figure 4-56   Form with a preselected option

13. Use the menu command for your browser to display the source code for the page. Notice that the fourth option in the select box shows the value "Selected." See Figure 4-57.

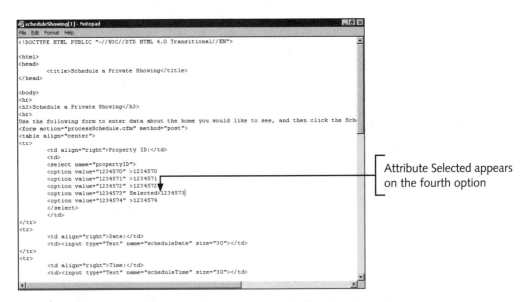

Figure 4-57   Notepad with the HTML source code for the selected option

14. Close Notepad, your browser, and ColdFusion Studio.

In this chapter, you learned about forms and form handling. In later chapters, you will apply these concepts to design interactive Web sites.

CHAPTER SUMMARY

- Forms are objects in HTML documents that are useful for collecting data from users.

- Forms contain data-entry controls. Some of the data-entry controls include text boxes, password boxes, Submit buttons, radio buttons, checkboxes, select boxes, text areas, image buttons, and hidden fields.

- You use the INPUT tag to create text boxes, password boxes, Submit buttons, and hidden fields.

- Use the SELECT tag to create select boxes. Use the OPTION tag inside SELECT tags for specifying the options available in the select box.

- Adding forms to a Web site is usually a two-step process. First, you have to design the form, and then you have to design a form handler for processing the data entered in the form.

❑ You specify the filename of the form handler in the ACTION attribute of a form. When the form is submitted, the ColdFusion Server executes the ColdFusion form handler.

❑ User-entered values are accessible in a ColdFusion form handler by using the form. notation. Form.control_name gives you access to the value entered by the user when the method for the form submission is specified as POST.

❑ The CFPARAM tag allows you to specify default values for form-submitted variables to prevent errors in case users don't select any checkboxes or do not select any items from select boxes.

4

REVIEW QUESTIONS

1. What are the three kinds of interactions between Web browsers and Web servers?

2. What are forms?

3. How do you design a form in HTML?

4. Describe the attributes for a FORM tag.

5. List any three types of controls that you can use in forms.

6. How do you use an INPUT tag to design a password text box?

7. What is the syntax for a select box and its options?

8. What is a ColdFusion form handler?

9. How do you access user-entered values in ColdFusion form handlers?

10. If a form contains many radio buttons, how does the browser know which button to uncheck when another is checked?

11. What is a CFPARAM tag? How do you use it to handle checkboxes?

12. What kind of a loop is most suitable for processing multiple checkboxes?

13. Which attribute tells the browser to preselect a particular option in a select box?

14. How do you specify a default value for a scrolling text box?

15. How do you design an image button for submitting a form? What additional data is sent to the Web server when a user clicks an image button?

HANDS-ON PROJECTS

Project 4-1: Design an HTML Form and a ColdFusion Form Handler for Counting Coins

Design an HTML form, as shown in Figure 4-58. This form contains data-entry controls (text boxes and a Submit button) that let a bank teller enter the number of pennies, nickels, dimes, and quarters in a customer's deposit. Use a two-column table with right-aligned labels and left-aligned controls. Save this file as **Ch4Pr1.htm** in the Chapter04 folder.

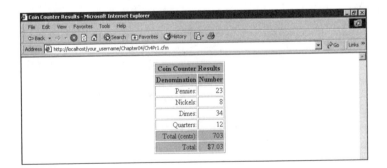

Figure 4-58

Create a form handler for this form, which should display the total value of coins in cents and in dollars as an HTML table. Use two CFSET statements to initialize a Total_In_Cents variable and a Total variable. The Total_In_Cents variable computes Pennies * 1 plus Nickels * 5 plus Dimes * 10 plus Quarters * 25. The Total variable divides the results of the Total_In_Cents variable by 100. Enter the CFOUTPUT statements to display the resulting values in the second column. Format the Total output as currency. When you are finished, save the form handler as **Ch4Pr1.cfm** in the Chapter04 folder on the server, and then open the form (Ch4Pr1.htm) in your Web browser. Use the following values: Pennies: 23, Nickels: 8, Dimes: 34, and Quarters: 12, and submit the form to test your program. It should look like Figure 4-59.

Figure 4-59

Project 4-2: Design a Form and a Form Handler for Computing Discounts

A department store is having a red tag sale. Red-tagged items are marked down 75%. As part of its promotional efforts, the department store wants you to set up a form on its Web site as shown in Figure 4-60.

Figure 4-60

Design a Web page named Ch4Pr2.htm that contains a form with a text box for entering the price of a product and an image Submit button with a caption Go. Use Go.gif from the Data Disk. Design a ColdFusion form handler to show this product's price, discount, discounted price, sales tax, and total price. Use CFSET tags to assign the user-entered value to variable price, 0.75 to variable DiscountRate, and 0.07 to variable TaxRate. Compute Discount as Price * DiscountRate, DiscountedPrice as Price − Discount, Tax as DiscountedPrice * TaxRate, and TotalPrice as DiscountedPrice + Tax. The template's output should be formatted as an HTML table. Format dollar amounts as currency. When you are finished, save the file as **Ch4Pr2.cfm** in the Chapter04 folder on the server, and then view the form in your Web browser. Test your program by entering a price of $50.00 and $100.00. See Figure 4-61.

Figure 4-61

Project 4-3: Design a Form and a Form Handler for Student Transcript Course Titles

A university designs titles for courses on student transcripts by removing all the lower-case vowels (a, e, i, o, u) from the actual titles. Design a form with a text box and a Submit button in an HTML document with the filename **Ch4Pr3.htm**. Use a caption for the Submit button as "Display Transcript Title." See Figure 4-62.

Figure 4-62

Design a ColdFusion form handler that processes the data entered in the text box (title) and displays the title as it appears on the transcript. Save this file as **Ch4Pr3.cfm** in your Chapter04 folder. Open your form and try it out on the titles for all the courses that you are taking this semester. See Figure 4-63.

Figure 4-63

Project 4-4: Design Web Pages for Computing a Person's Age

Design an HTML form containing four controls for entering a date of birth: a select box for selecting the month, a text box for entering the day, a text box for entering the year, and a Submit button with a caption Display Age. See Figure 4-64.

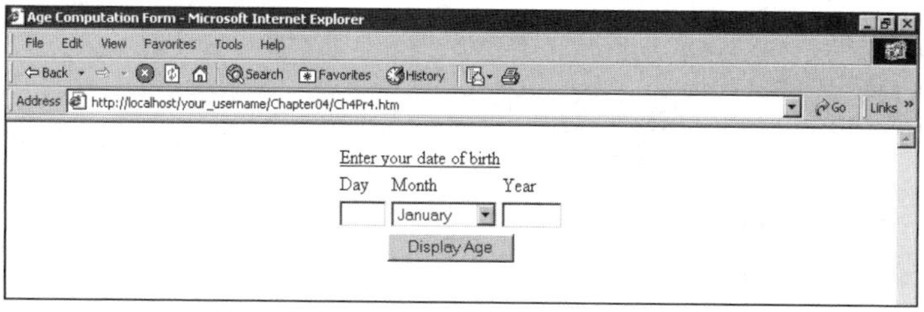

Figure 4-64

The select box should contain options with descriptions for all 12 months and values 1–12. Save the form as **Ch4Pr4.htm** in the Chapter04 folder on your Data Disk. Design a ColdFusion form handler named **Ch4Pr4.cfm** for this form that computes the user's age today and displays it. Use a CFSET tag to create a variable named dob, and assign a date-value to it using the CreateDate() function. You can use the form variables directly in the function as CreateDate(FORM.year, FORM.month, FORM.day). Display the age as shown in Figure 4-65. Use the DateDiff function to compute the difference between the date today—(Now())—and the person's date of birth. Test your program with 1 November, 1982. See Figure 4-65.

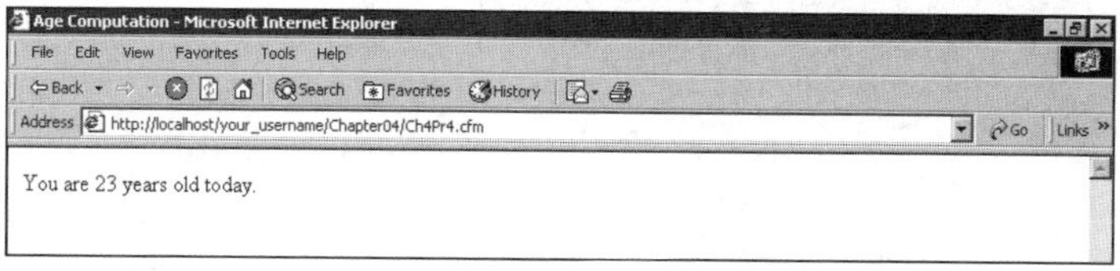

Figure 4-65

Project 4-5: Send Confirmation to a Form User

Design an HTML form that lets a customer order a sub online, as shown in Figure 4-66. Save the file as **Ch4Pr5.htm**. Design a ColdFusion form handler to process the data entered in the form. The form handler should echo the data entered by the user in a neatly formatted table and present a button to confirm the order, as shown in Figure 4-67. Note that the confirmation page is summarizing the order and computing its total. The prices are given in Figure 4-66. Use a LIST loop to list all the toppings. Use a variable Total to keep track of the total cost. You can use CFIF statements or the CFSWITCH statement to process the radio buttons. When the user clicks the Confirm Order button, the data should be sent to your e-mail address. Save the form handler as **Ch4Pr5.cfm** in the Chapter04 folder. Test your program by selecting Wheat bread, Chicken Sub, and Lettuce, Green Peppers, Pickles, and Mayo as the toppings. For these values, the confirmation page should contain a hidden field (<input type="Hidden" name="client-data" value="Bread:Wheat;Type:Chicken;Toppings:Lettuce,Green Peppers,Pickles,Mayo">) that would be e-mailed to you when the customer clicks the Confirm Order button.

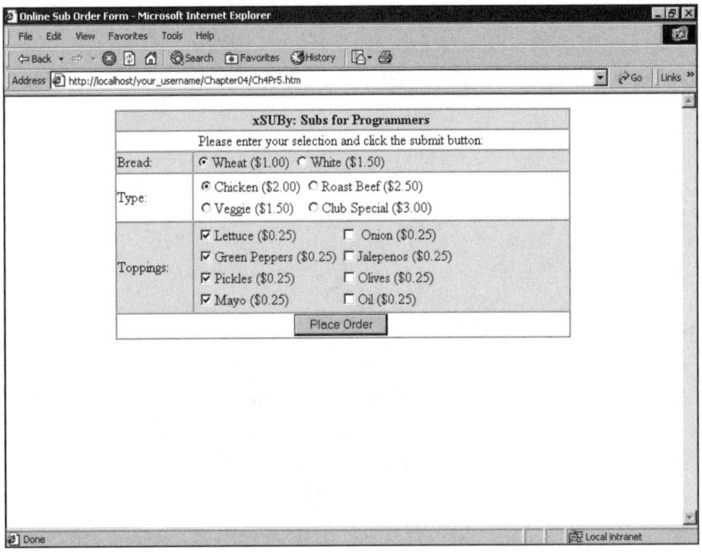

Figure 4-66

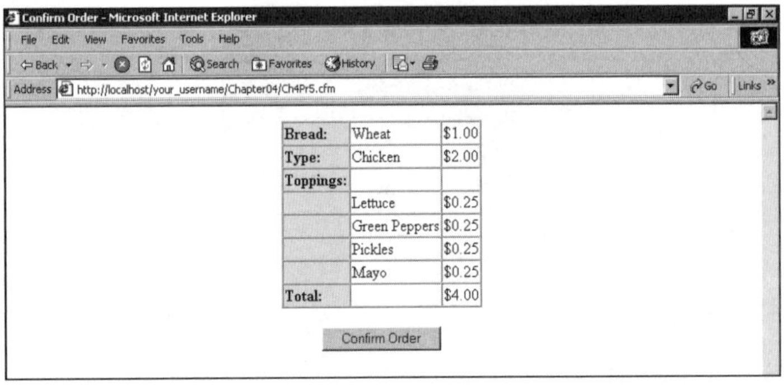

Figure 4-67

Project 4-6: Perform a Calculation on Data Entered in a Form

Design a form (**Ch4Pr6.htm**) containing a text box with the label "Enter the temperature in Fahrenheit" and a Submit button with the caption "Convert to Celsius," as shown in Figure 4-68.

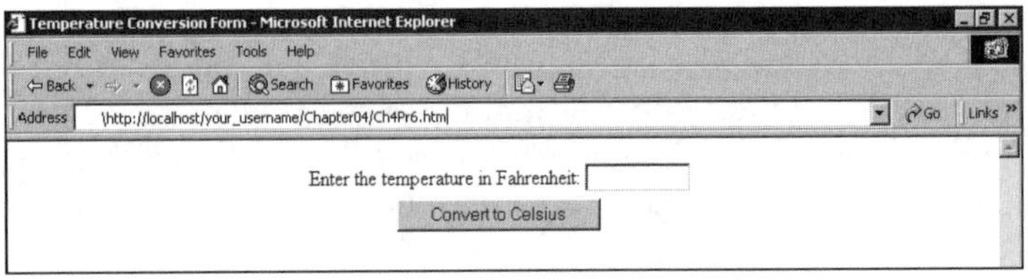

Figure 4-68

When the user enters a temperature and clicks the Submit button, the form handler should compute the equivalent temperature in Celsius and display it, as shown in Figure 4-69. The formula for the conversion is: C = (5/9) * (F-32). Note that the temperature in Celsius is formatted to two decimal places using the DecimalFormat function. Save the form handler as **Ch4Pr6.cfm**. Test your program on several different values. At what value is the temperature in Fahrenheit the same as the temperature in Celsius?

A temperature of 72 °F is equivalent to 22.22 °C.

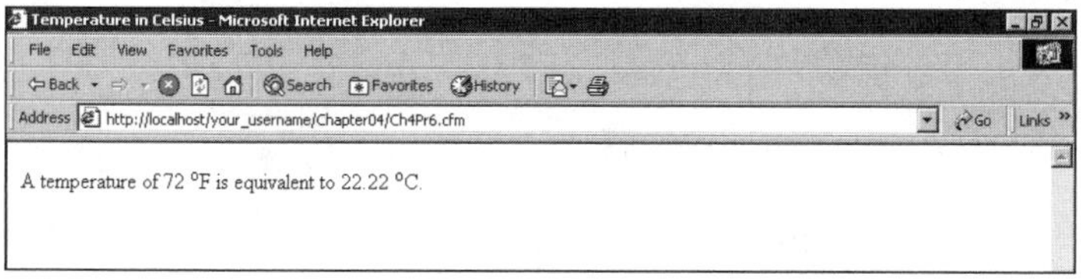

Figure 4-69

Project 4-7: Conditionally Format a Table

Design a form with three text boxes to specify RGB values as two-digit hexadecimal values and a Submit button. Save this file as **Ch4Pr7.htm**. Design a form handler to display a one-cell table with a width of 100 and a border set at 1 and a 5 line breaks tags (<br>) in it. The background color of the table cell should change according to the values entered in the textboxes for R, G, and B (Red, Green, and Blue in hexidecimal notation). Save this file as **Ch4Pr7.cfm**. Assign values "FF," "66," and "CC" to test the program. See Figures 4-70 and 4-71 for the form and its form handler.

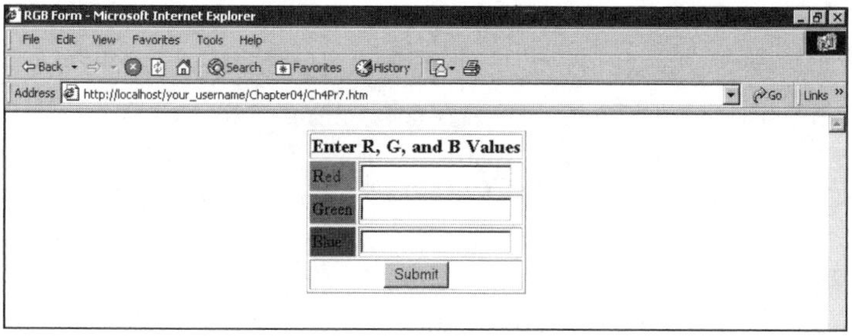

Enter R, G, and B Values
Red
Green
Blue
Submit

Figure 4-70

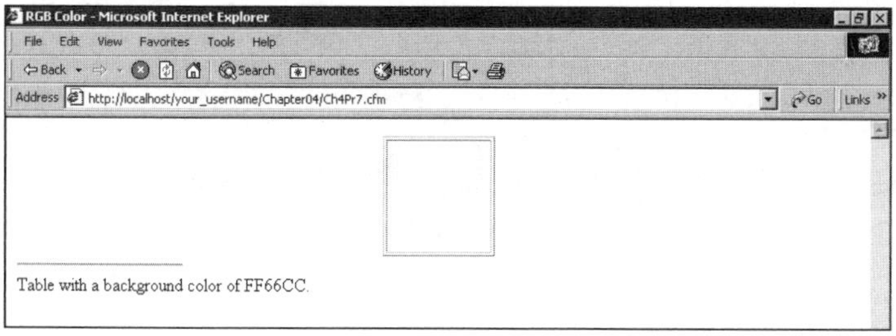

Table with a background color of FF66CC.

Figure 4-71

Project 4-8: Add Select Boxes to a Form

Modify the form you created for NikRealty by using select boxes instead of a text box for users to enter dates. Use three select boxes: one for the month (Jan–Dec), one for the day (1–31), and one for the year (2002–2010). Modify the form handler to create a date object and display it in the form of 09/25/2002. When you are finished, save the HTML document as **Ch4Pr8.htm** and the form handler as **Ch4Pr8.cfm**.

CASE PROJECTS

Case Project 1

Design a "tell us more about yourself so that we can serve you better" form for NikRealty. Collect information about client preferences for houses. Think about all the different characteristics that may be of importance. Try to use as many different kinds of controls as possible. The form handler should echo this data neatly.

Case Project 2

Design a check-out form for an e-commerce site. It should contain the following fields: Name, Address, City, State, Zip, Phone, E-mail address, ProductID, Quantity, and a Submit button with a caption Next. When the user clicks the Submit button, all the user-entered data should be displayed along with a button with the caption "Above information is correct – place the order." When the user clicks this button, e-mail should be sent to you with the order data.

Case Project 3

There is a form handler on your Data Disk named debug_a_form.cfm. It displays all the form data it receives along with the variable names. Change the form handler for scheduleShowing.htm to debug_a_form.cfm, and try it out. Experiment with several other forms and answer the following questions:

a. Can a form contain multiple Submit buttons? If a form can contain multiple Submit buttons, what happens when a user clicks one of these buttons? Use the NAME attribute and name these Submit buttons. What happens when users click these buttons now?

b. What variables are sent to the Web server when an image Submit button is clicked? How can you tell if a user has clicked the left side of an image or the right side of an image? How can you tell if a user has clicked the top half of an image or the bottom half of an image?

c. Can a Web page contain multiple forms? Do you need a Submit button for each form? Can you use a different form handler for each form? Can multiple forms share the same controls?

5

DATABASES AND SQL

In this chapter, you will:

♦ Learn about organizing data in a database

♦ Learn about tables, records, fields, and data hierarchy

♦ Learn about data types and table structures

♦ Use Access and Structured Query Language (SQL) to create, update, and maintain a database

♦ Insert, update, and delete records using Access and SQL

♦ Extract data from databases using SQL SELECT statements

Even if you didn't realize it, you probably have visited many Web sites that interact with databases to provide output in the form of dynamic Web pages. In this chapter, you will learn how to store and maintain data in a database. You will also use Structured Query Language (SQL) to extract data from databases. You will insert data into a database, update data in a database, and delete data from a database. You will learn about databases and SQL using a popular relational database management system, Microsoft Access 2000. Once you are comfortable using SQL to accomplish these tasks, in later chapters you will use databases with ColdFusion templates to create interactive, dynamic Web sites.

ORGANIZING DATA IN DATABASES

Data is important for any organization to function. A university has to keep track of data about students, faculty, staff, courses, grades, tuition, salaries, facilities, and so on. A bank has to keep track of customers, checking accounts, savings accounts, loans, deposits, withdrawals, employees, salaries, and so on. Obviously, if an organization does not keep track of data accurately and efficiently, it will not survive for long. Because data management is vital to the success of any organization, most organizations use computer-based database management systems.

To store existing data in a computer-based database management system, you must first analyze any existing systems and then plan to organize the data into a new structure. An **entity** is any object about which data is stored, such as people, things, or places. For example, when a university needs to store data about students and faculty members, students and faculty are examples of entities in database terminology. The university also stores the name, address, phone number, and other descriptive information about each student enrolled at the university. Characteristics of an entity are called **attributes**. When you are planning to store data in a database, you have to analyze each object for which you are storing data (the entities) and the characteristics of each object (the entity's attributes).

Working with Attributes

In Chapter 4, you created a Web page that lets visitors to the NikRealty Web site request a private showing of certain listed properties. You used a static Web page that described a particular property. Now Nikitha wants every listed property of NikRealty to be available through this Web site. To add this functionality to the Web site, you must integrate the site with a database. The database must include information about the properties available for sale, as well as the listing agent. The properties (houses for sale, for example) and agents will become the database entities. Your team has decided to use Microsoft Access 2000 to store the data about properties and agents.

The first entity—Properties—has multiple attributes that describe each property for sale. These attributes include a unique identification number and the following details about the house: number of stories, year built, number of bedrooms, number of bathrooms, total square footage, different kinds of rooms available, other special features, price, location, zip code, the filename of the house's picture, and the listing agent's identification number. After identifying the attributes of the Properties entity, you need to name the attributes according to the rules of the database management system that you will use to store them. In Access, the following rules apply to naming attributes and entities:

- A name can contain up to 64 characters.

- A name can contain letters, numbers, and spaces, but it cannot contain a period, square brackets ([and]), or an exclamation point.

- A name cannot begin with a space character.

- Each attribute name must be unique for a particular entity. You can, however, use identical attribute names for different entities.

Based on these rules, you will create the attributes of the Properties entity shown in Figure 5-1. Notice that the attributes all follow a consistent style. The attribute names do not include spaces, and each new word begins with a capital letter. The attribute names are also short, and it is easy to infer the kind of data that each attribute will store.

PropertyID	Rooms
TypeOfHouse	OtherFeatures
YearBuilt	Price
NumBedrooms	Location
NumBathrooms	ZipCode
Area	ImageFilename
	AgentID

Figure 5-1   Attributes of the Properties entity

In database terminology, attributes are also known as **fields**; the names that you decided for each attribute are known as **field names**. The collection of fields for each property listed for sale makes up one **record**. The entire set of records for an entity is known as a **database table**, or simply a **table**. You can visualize this data as a collection of objects. You can think of the organization of data in a database in terms of a hierarchy, as shown in Figure 5-2.

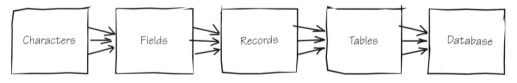

Figure 5-2   Data hierarchy

One record completely describes a property, or in more general terms, one record completely describes an entity. For example, the first property that will become part of the Properties table contains the data shown in Table 5-1. The data creates one record, or row, in the Properties table.

Table 5-1   One Record in the Properties Table

Field Name	Data
PropertyID	NIK4568
TypeOfHouse	two-story home
YearBuilt	1990
NumBedrooms	3
NumBathrooms	1.5
Area	2000
Rooms	great room,laundry room,master bedroom
OtherFeatures	hardwood floors,skylight(s),whirlpool
Price	243543
Location	Cedar Rapids
ZipCode	52401
ImageFilename	MVC-867E.JPG
AgentID	JPP

Defining Field Data Types and Table Structures

Examine the record shown in Table 5-1, and note that some of the fields contain numbers and others contain text. Similar to the concept of data types in ColdFusion, database fields can store different kinds of data. After you identify entities and attributes, the next step in organizing and structuring data is to identify what kind of data will be stored in each field. A related step is determining how many characters will be stored in each field. The number of characters that a field will store is known as its **field size**. If you know that a field will never store more than six characters, then you can determine that its field size will be 6. Ensuring that the field sizes are similar to the amount of data the field will eventually store conserves resources and controls the size of the database itself.

In addition to determining the field size for each field in a table, you must also consider the type of data that each field will store and assign it an appropriate data type. The **data type** determines what values the field can store and other field properties, such as how much space is required to store the values. You select a data type based on the data to be stored in the field. Access supports the data types shown in Table 5-2.

Table 5-2   Access Data Types

Data Type	Description	Field Size
Text	The default data type for all fields; stores text and/or numbers; used to store text values and numbers that don't require calculations, such as names and phone numbers	Up to 255 characters; the default field size is 50
Memo	Used to store lengthy text or combinations of text and numbers	Up to 64,000 characters
Number	Used to store numeric data used in mathematical calculations, except for currency values	1, 2, 4, or 8 bytes
Date/Time	Used to store date and time values for the years 100 through 9999 in a variety of date formats	8 bytes
Currency	Used to store currency values and numeric data used in mathematical calculations involving data with one to four decimal places; accurate to 15 digits on the left side of the decimal separator and to 4 digits on the right side	8 bytes
AutoNumber	Used to store a unique sequential (incremented by 1) number or random number assigned by Access when a new record is added to a table; AutoNumber fields cannot be updated	4 bytes
Yes/No	Used to store values in fields that contain only one of two values (Yes/No, True/False, or On/Off)	1 bit
OLE Object	Used to store objects created in other programs (such as Word documents or Excel workbooks) that can be linked or embedded in an Access table	Up to 1 gigabyte
Hyperlink	Used to store hyperlinks that connect your field to files located on a network	Up to 64,000 characters
Lookup Wizard	Used to create a field that lets you look up a value from another table or from a list of values	Usually 4 bytes, depending on the size of the lookup field

5

When you assign the Number data type to a field, you need to specify the field size according to what types of values the field will contain. Be sure to select a data type that is appropriate for the data that you will store in the field so you can conserve database resources. A good rule of thumb is to use the smallest data type that will store the largest value in the field. In other words, if the field will store only whole numbers with values of 1 to 100, the Byte field size is the best choice. There are six field sizes for the Number data type:

- *Byte*: Stores whole numbers only from 0 to 255 (no fractions or decimals)

- *Decimal*: Stores very large and very small positive and negative numbers with up to 28 decimal places

- *Integer*: Stores whole numbers only from –32,768 to 32,767
- *Long Integer*: Stores whole numbers only from –2,147,483,648 to 2,147,486,647
- *Single*: Stores very large and very small numbers with up to 7 decimal places
- *Double*: Stores very large and very small numbers with up to 15 decimal places

Based on the information contained in Table 5-2, your team reviewed her data and then selected data types and field sizes for the fields in the Properties table. Table 5-3 shows the table's structure. Notice that the Text data type is used to describe fields that will contain text data and numeric data that will not be used in calculations, and that the Price field uses the Currency data type. This table structure will ensure that each field uses the minimum amount of memory required to store the data it contains.

Table 5-3   Properties Table Structure

Field Name	Data Type	Size	Examples of Data
PropertyID	Text	7	NIK4568
TypeOfHouse	Text	50	two-story home
YearBuilt	Number	Integer	1990
NumBedrooms	Number	Integer	4
NumBathrooms	Number	Single	3, 3.5
Area	Number	Integer	3909
Rooms	Text	150	laundry room,master bathroom,master bedroom,workshop
OtherFeatures	Text	150	cathedral ceilings,hardwood floors,pantry,walk-in closet(s)
Price	Currency		$243,543.00
Location	Text	50	Cedar Rapids
ZipCode	Text	10	52401
ImageFilename	Text	50	MVC-867E.JPG
AgentID	Text	3	JPP

Table 5-4 shows the structure of the Agents table, which stores information about the agents working for NikRealty.

Table 5-4   Agents Table Structure

Field Name	Data Type	Size	Examples of Data
AgentID	Text	3	RTH
FirstName	Text	50	Richard
MiddleInitial	Text	1	T
LastName	Text	50	Hadik
EmailAddress	Text	50	rhadik@nikrealty.com
Address	Text	255	873 Main Street
City	Text	50	Cedar Rapids
State	Text	2	IA
ZipCode	Text	10	52402
WorkPhone	Text	30	(319) 555-2873

OPENING A MICROSOFT ACCESS DATABASE

After planning the table structure and determining the appropriate data types and field sizes for each field, one of your team members created the tables using Access and entered records into them. The Realtor database is stored on your Data Disk in the Databases folder. You will examine the Properties and Agents tables next.

To open and examine an Access database:

1. Click the **Start** button on the taskbar, point to **Programs**, and then click **Microsoft Access**. Access starts and opens the Startup dialog box. You can use this dialog box to open a blank database, to use a wizard to create a new database, or to open an existing database, which is the default selection. You will open the database saved on your Data Disk.

2. With the **Open an existing file** option button and the **More Files** option selected, click the **OK** button. The Open dialog box opens.

3. Use the **Look in** list arrow to open the Databases folder on your Data Disk, and then double-click **Realtor.mdb** in the list box. The Realtor database opens in the Database window. See Figure 5-3.

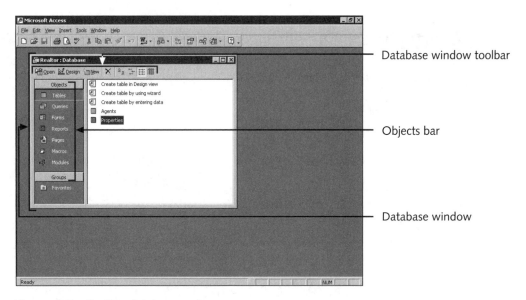

Figure 5-3 Realtor database

The Database window is the main window in Microsoft Access. When you open a database, the Database window lists all of the objects in the database, including tables, forms, reports, and queries. The **Objects bar** on the left side of the Database window lets you navigate among the different objects in a database. When you first open the Realtor database, make sure Tables is selected in the Objects bar. The Realtor database contains two tables—Agents and Properties. The Agents table stores information about agents, and the Properties table stores information about properties listed for sale. In addition to storing tables, you can also use Access to create other objects, including queries, forms, reports, and data access pages. **Queries** allow you to extract data from tables that matches criteria you specify. **Forms** allow you to look at data in a format that matches how you might view the data using a paper form. **Reports** allow you to extract data in a form suitable for printing. When you use Access with ColdFusion, you work with tables and queries most often.

To examine an Access table:

1. If necessary, click the **Agents** table in the Database window to select it, and then click the **Design** button on the Database window toolbar. The Design view window opens and shows you the design of the Agents table. Notice that each field in the table occupies one line of the Design view grid. In addition, when you select a field name in the list, the Field Properties pane shows the field size and properties for the selected field. You can also see the data type for each field, as well as any optional descriptions. See Figure 5-4.

2. Press the **Down Arrow** key. Notice that the FirstName field is selected and its properties appear in the Field Properties pane.

3. Continue pressing the **Down Arrow** key until you have viewed the field properties for each field in the Agents table.

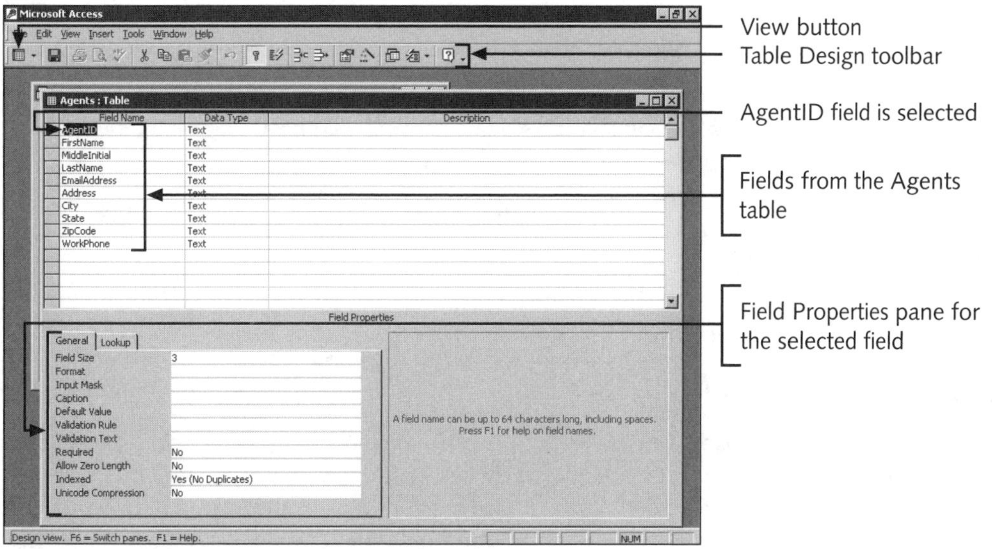

Figure 5-4   Design view for the Agents table

4. Click the **View** button on the Table Design toolbar to change to Datasheet view, and then examine the data in the Agents table. You can use the horizontal scroll bar at the bottom of the Datasheet view window to view the data for each record. See Figure 5-5.

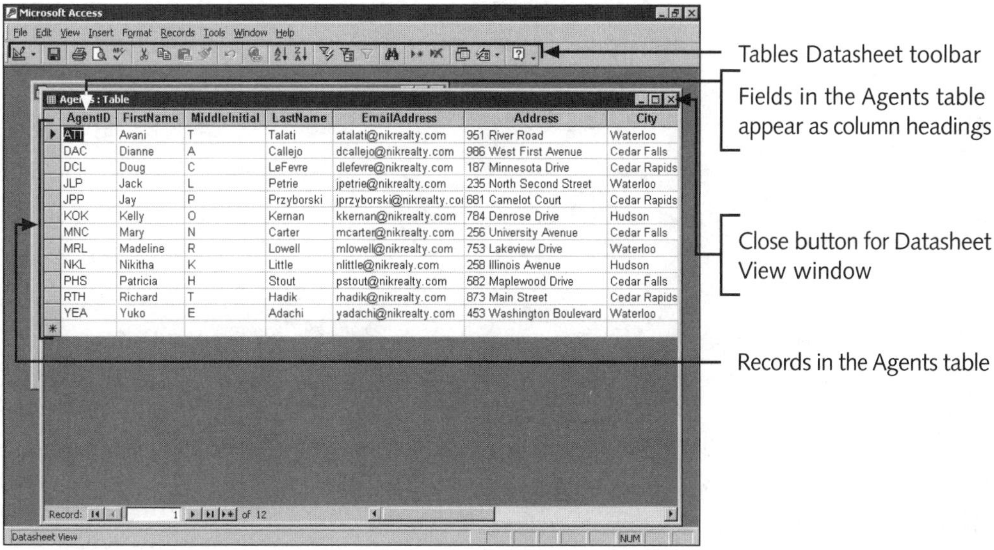

Figure 5-5   Datasheet view of the Agents table

5. Click the **Close** button on the Datasheet view window to close it. You return to the Database window.

6. Click the **Properties** table in the Database window, and then click the **Design** button on the Database toolbar. The Properties table opens in Design view. View the field properties for each field.

7. Click the **View** button on the Table Design toolbar to view the data in the Properties table.

8. Close the Datasheet view window.

CREATING A TABLE

One of the capabilities that you want to eventually build in the Web site for NikRealty is to capture data that customers enter when they request private showings of properties listed in the database. The Web page that you created in Chapter 4 appears in Figure 5-6. You will need to create tables in the database to collect the information entered into this Web page.

Figure 5-6 scheduleShowing.htm Web page

To capture this data, you have decided to create two more tables: one that captures customer information and another that captures their requests for showings. As mentioned earlier, the steps necessary for creating a table are as follows:

- Determine the entities

- Determine the field names

- Assign appropriate data types and field sizes

In consultation with Nikitha, you have decided to structure the new tables as shown in Tables 5-5 and 5-6.

Table 5-5   Customers Table Structure

Field Name	Data Type	Size	Examples of Data
CustomerID	AutoNumber	Long Integer	1, 2, 3
ClientName	Text	50	John Q. Doe
ClientEmail	Text	50	JohnDoe@Qmail.com
CurrentResidence	Text	4	Own, Rent
Criteria	Text	100	Price,Bedrooms,Square Footage,Neighborhood
Comments	Text	255	I am looking forward to working with you.

Table 5-6   Requests Table Structure

Field Name	Data Type	Size	Examples of Data
RequestID	AutoNumber	Long Integer	1, 2, 3
CustomerID	Number	Long Integer	1, 2, 3
ScheduleDateTime	Date/Time	General Date	6/19/2003 5:43:00 PM
PropertyID	Text	7	NIK4567, 1234582

Creating a Table in Design View

Now that you have determined the table's structure, the next step is to create the table using Access. You can create tables by using the Design view window in Access or by using commands from SQL. SQL is useful for working with the database when you are using ColdFusion.

You will create the Requests table using Design view.

To create a table using Design view:

1. Double-click **Create table in Design view** in the Database window. The Design view window opens, as shown in Figure 5-7.

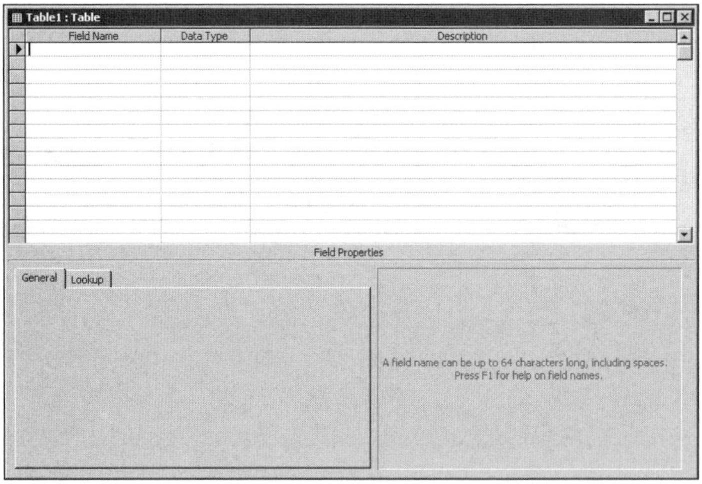

Figure 5-7   New table created in Design view

2. Type **RequestID** as the first field name, and then press the **Tab** key to move to the Data Type column.

3. Type **A** to select the AutoNumber data type.

> When selecting a data type in Design view, you can type the first letter (or letters) of the data type that you want to assign to the field, or you can click the list arrow that appears in the field's row to select the desired data type from a list.

4. Click the **Primary Key** button on the Table Design toolbar to set this field as the primary key for this table. Notice that a key icon appears to the left of the RequestID field name to indicate that this field is the table's primary key. A **primary key** is one or more fields whose value or values uniquely identify each record in a table. In a relationship, a primary key is used to refer to specific records in one table from another table. A primary key is called a **foreign key** when another table refers to it. You can have only one primary key in a table. An Employees table, for example, could use the employee's Social Security Number as the primary key, because this number will uniquely identify each employee's record in the table.

5. Click the **Field Name column** in the second row, type **CustomerID** as the field name for the second field, press the **Tab** key, and then type **n** to select the Number data type.

6. Press the **F6** key to move to the Field Properties window, if necessary change the Field Size to Long Integer, and then click the **Field Name** column in the third row.

7. Use Table 5-6 to enter the remaining rows in the Requests table design. When you are finished, click the **Save** button on the Table Design toolbar, type **Requests** in the Table Name text box of the Save As dialog box, and then click the **OK** button. Access saves the table design in the Realtor database.

8. Close the Design view window. Notice that the Requests table now appears in the Database window. You can open the table in Datasheet view to begin entering data into it.

Creating a Table Using SQL

You can also use SQL to create a new table. The syntax for creating a table using SQL is as follows:

CREATE TABLE *tablename (fieldname1 datatype1* [*(size1)*] [PRIMARY KEY], *fieldname2 datatype2* [*(size2)*] …)

When you execute the CREATE TABLE command in a database system that supports SQL, it will create the table named *tablename. Fieldname1, fieldname2*, and so on are the names of the fields in the table, and *datatype1, datatype2*, and so on are the data types of the fields. The sizes for text fields are specified in parentheses. Optional items appear in square brackets. Typing the keywords PRIMARY KEY after the primary key field indicates the table's primary key. Although the allowable data types vary between SQL implementations, certain data types are allowed by most systems. Access supports common data types, such as COUNTER for AutoNumber fields, CHAR(*size*) for text fields with the field size indicated by the integer *size*, INTEGER for numbers without fractions, REAL for real numbers with fractional parts, TIMESTAMP for date/time data types, and MONEY for currency data types.

The following example shows the SQL command to create the Requests table that you just created in Design view.

Code Example 5.1

```
CREATE TABLE Requests (
  RequestID COUNTER PRIMARY KEY,
  CustomerID INTEGER,
  ScheduleDateTime TIMESTAMP,
  PropertyID CHAR(7) )
```

If you executed the SQL command shown in Code Example 5.1, Access would create the Requests table that you created in Design view. You'll create the Customers table using SQL next.

To create the Customers table using SQL:

1. Click the **Queries** object in the Database window.

2. Double-click **Create query in Design view**. The Show Table dialog box opens.

3. Click the **Close** button in the Show Table dialog box to close it without adding any tables to the query. The Select Query window opens.

4. Click the **View** button on the Query Design toolbar. The Select Query window shown in Figure 5-8 opens. The only statement (SELECT;) is selected.

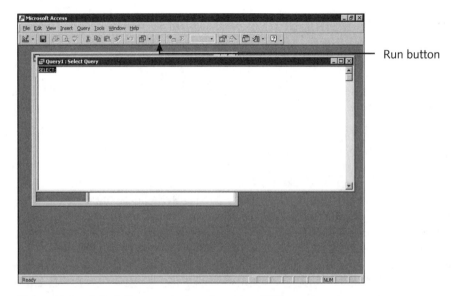

Figure 5-8 Select Query window for using SQL

5. With the SELECT statement selected, type the following SQL command:

```
CREATE TABLE Customers (
 CustomerID COUNTER PRIMARY KEY,
 ClientName CHAR(50),
 ClientEmail CHAR(50),
 CurrentResidence CHAR(4),
 Criteria CHAR(100),
 Comments CHAR(255) )
```

6. Click the **Run** button on the Query Design toolbar to execute the query. The query will create the Customers table, and the Select Query window will remain open.

7. Close the Select Query window, and then click the **No** button to close it without saving it.

You can save the query that creates a table if you think that you might need to run it again. However, usually you only create a table once.

8. Click the **Tables** object in the Database window. There is a new table named Customers that was created when you executed the SQL CREATE TABLE command.

9. Select the **Customers** table in the Database window, and then click the **Design** button on the Database window toolbar. Examine the table's design to verify that it matches the SQL statement that you executed. Notice the primary key field and sizes for the fields. See Figure 5-9.

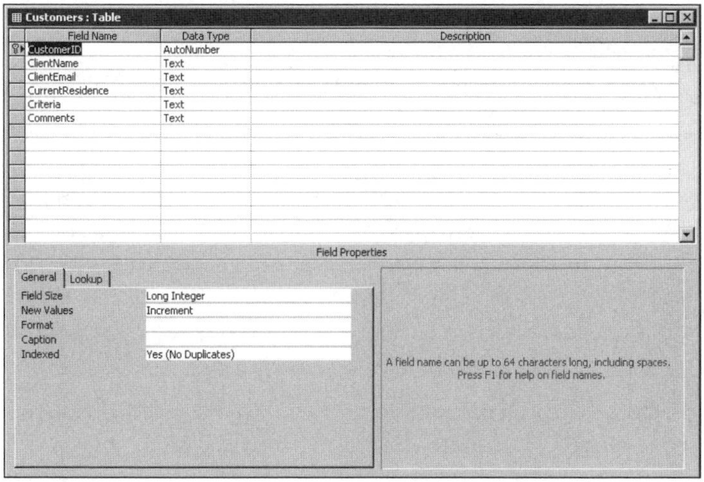

Figure 5-9 Customers table in Design view

10. Close the Design view window.

Now that you have created the Customers and Requests tables, you can start inserting data into them.

INSERTING DATA

In the following sections, you will insert data into the Customers and Requests tables using Datasheet view and SQL.

Inserting Data in Datasheet View

Consider the data shown in Table 5-7 that one user entered into the Schedule a Private Showing Web page (see Figure 5-6).

Table 5-7 Data Entered in the Web Page

Form Item	Data
PropertyID	NIK4573
ScheduleDate	6/5/2003
ScheduleTime	4:30 PM
ClientName	Sandy Marshall
ClientEmail	smarshall@uni.edu
CurrentResidence	Rent
Criteria	Rent,Price,Square Footage
Comments	I am impressed with this feature on your site. I am looking forward to the showing.

Your task is to now insert this information into the Customers and Requests tables. You have two tables for storing this data because of the possibility that a particular customer may make multiple requests. When a customer makes multiple requests, the second request is stored in the Requests table with the proper CustomerID. It is not necessary to store the customer data again. This is proper normalized database design, and it minimizes redundant data.

Based on a comparison of the form data shown in Table 5-7 with the structure of the Customers and Requests table, you have decided to insert data as shown in Tables 5-8 and 5-9.

Table 5-8 Record to Insert into the Customers Table

Field Name	Data
ClientName	Sandy Marshall
ClientEmail	smarshall@uni.edu
CurrentResidence	Rent
Criteria	Rent,Price,Square Footage
Comments	I am impressed with this feature on your site. I am looking forward to the showing.

Table 5-9 Record to Insert into the Requests Table

Field Name	Data
CustomerID	1
ScheduleDateTime	6/5/2003 4:30:00 PM
PropertyID	NIK4573

You'll insert a record into the Customers table using Datasheet view.

To insert a record in Datasheet view:

1. Double-click the **Customers** table in the Database window. The Customers table opens in Datasheet view. See Figure 5-10.

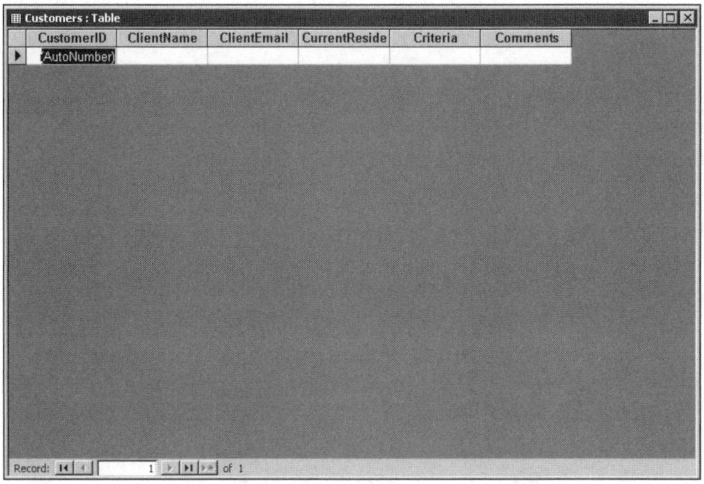

Figure 5-10   Customers table in Datasheet view

2. Press the **Tab** key to move to the ClientName field.

3. Type **Sandy Marshall** in the ClientName field, and then press the **Tab** key.

4. Type **smarshall@uni.edu** in the ClientEmail field, and then press the **Tab** key.

5. Type **Rent** in the CurrentResidence field, and then press the **Tab** key.

6. Type **Price,Square Footage** in the Criteria field, and then press the **Tab** key.

7. Type **I am impressed with this feature on your site. I am looking forward to the showing.** in the Comments field, and then press the **Tab** key. Notice that the insertion point moves to the CustomerID field of the next record.

8. Close the Datasheet view.

Inserting a Record Using SQL

The syntax for inserting a record into a table using SQL is as follows:

INSERT INTO *tablename* (*fieldname1, fieldname2...*) VALUES (*value1, value2...*)

When you execute the INSERT INTO command in a database that supports SQL, the database will insert a record into the table named *tablename*. *Value1* would be inserted into the field named *fieldname1*; *value2* would be inserted into the field named *fieldname2*, and so on. You must enter the values *value1*, *value2...* based on the their data types. In Access, strings must be enclosed in single quotation marks and dates must be enclosed in pound signs. Numbers are typed directly without any delimiters.

When executing SQL from ColdFusion, remember that pound signs have a special significance in ColdFusion. To avoid errors, use two pound signs instead of one as delimiters for dates in INSERT statements.

The same record that you just added would be inserted using the INSERT statement shown in Code Example 5.2.

Code Example 5.2

```
INSERT INTO Customers (ClientName, ClientEmail, CurrentRes
idence, Criteria, Comments)
VALUES ('Sandy Marshall', 'smarshall@uni.edu', 'Rent',
'Price,Square Footage', 'I am impressed with this
feature on your site. I am looking forward to the
showing.')
```

When you execute this SQL statement, it would insert a record just like the one you inserted using Datasheet view. Next, you'll insert a record into the Requests table using SQL.

To insert a record into the Requests table using SQL:

1. Click the **Queries** object in the Database window.

2. Double-click **Create query in Design view**.

3. Click the **Close** button in the Show Table dialog box to close it without adding any queries to the query.

4. Click the **View** button on the Query Design toolbar. The SELECT statement is already selected. When you type the SQL command, you will delete it.

5. Type the following SQL command:

   INSERT INTO Requests (CustomerID, ScheduleDateTime, PropertyID)
   VALUES (1, #6/5/2003 4:30:00 PM#, 'NIK4573')

   Note that the numbers are entered without any delimiters, the date is delimited by pound signs, and the PropertyID is a text field that is delimited with single quotation marks.

6. Click the **Run** button on the Query Design toolbar to execute this query. A dialog box opens and asks if you want to append 1 row(s) to the table.

7. Click the **Yes** button to add the row to the table, click the **Close** button to close the Select Query window, and then click the **No** button.

8. Click the **Tables** object in the Database window, and then double-click the **Requests** table. A new record was added to the table.

9. Close the Datasheet view window.

To insert additional records:

1. Using whichever method you prefer (Datasheet view or SQL), insert the following records into the Requests table:

```
CustomerID: 1
RequestTime: 6/6/2003 4:30:00 PM
PropertyID: NIK4574

CustomerID: 1
RequestTime: 6/6/2003 6:30:00 PM
PropertyID: NIK4570
```

> If you use Design view to enter the records, make sure that you press the Tab key after entering the PropertyID for the third request, or you will not save the record in the table.

2. Close the window that you used to enter the data. Do not save any changes if you created a query.

The Requests table now contains three records.

UPDATING DATA

When you insert data into a table, you are adding new records into it. When you need to change data in an existing record, you need to update the data. You can update data in Datasheet view or by using the SQL UPDATE command.

Updating Data Using Datasheet View

To update data in Datasheet view, you open the table in Datasheet view, navigate to the record to update, and use the mouse and keyboard to edit the data as necessary.

To update the PropertyID in an existing record in the Requests table:

1. Double-click the **Requests** table to open it in Datasheet view.

2. Use the mouse to select the PropertyID **NIK4573**, and then type **9999999** to replace it.

3. Press the **Tab** key. You updated the first record, and the insertion point moves to the first field in the next record. The RequestID for the first record is 1.

4. Close the Datasheet view window.

Updating a Record Using SQL

To update a record using SQL, you use the UPDATE command. The syntax for the UPDATE command is as follows:

```
UPDATE tablename
    SET fieldname1 = value1, fieldname2 = value2 …
    [WHERE condition]
```

When you execute the UPDATE command in a database system that supports SQL, it will update one or more records in the table named *tablename* where the *condition* is true. For these records, *value1* would be the new value of the field named *fieldname1*; *value2* would be the new value of the field named *fieldname2*, and so on. Just as when using the INSERT command, you must delimit the values *value1, value2…* correctly based on their data types. Conditions in UPDATE statements are similar to conditions in ColdFusion. Conditions are comparisons of fields and values constructed by using the six relational operators (=, >, <, >=, <=, and < >). You will learn more about conditions later in this chapter.

The following example illustrates an UPDATE statement:

Code Example 5.3

```
UPDATE Customers
    SET Criteria = 'Not Answered'
    WHERE CustomerID = 1
```

When you execute this SQL statement, it will update the record for the customer with CustomerID 1 and change the Criteria field to "Not Answered."

 Be sure the WHERE condition is correct before you execute UPDATE statements. If you omit the WHERE condition part of the UPDATE statement, every record in the table will be updated. Data that is changed once cannot be recovered.

To update a record in the Requests table using SQL:

1. Click the **Queries** object in the Database window.

2. Double-click **Create query in Design view**, click the **Close** button to close the Show Table dialog box, and then click the **View** button on the Query Design toolbar.

3. Type the following SQL command:

```
UPDATE Requests
    SET PropertyID = 'NIK4573'
    WHERE RequestID = 1
```

4. Click the **Run** button on the Query Design toolbar to execute the query, and click the **Yes** button to update the row.

5. Close the Select Query window, and then click the **No** button.

6. Click the **Tables** object in the Database window, and then double-click the **Requests** table. The PropertyID field for the first record is now NIK4573.

7. Close the Datasheet view window.

 Notice that you used the Select Query window for creating tables, inserting records, and updating records. Actually, you can use the Select Query window to execute any valid SQL command supported by Access.

DELETING RECORDS

When you no longer need a row in a table, you can use Datasheet view or SQL to delete it.

Deleting a Record Using Datasheet View

To delete a record in Access, you select the entire row in Datasheet view, and then press the Delete key. Access will ask you to confirm the deletion before permanently removing the selected row from the table.

To delete a record in Datasheet view:

1. Double-click the **Requests** table to open it in Datasheet view.

2. Click in any field where the RequestID is **2**.

3. Click the **Delete Record** button on the Table Datasheet toolbar, and then click the **Yes** button to delete the record. The record is permanently deleted from the Requests table, which now has two records.

4. Close the Datasheet view window.

Deleting a Record Using SQL

The syntax for the DELETE SQL statement is as follows:

```
DELETE FROM tablename
    [WHERE condition]
```

When you execute the DELETE statement, you will delete one or more records in the table named *tablename* when the *condition* is true. Conditions in SQL DELETE statements are similar to conditions in SQL UPDATE statements. The following example illustrates a DELETE statement:

Code Example 5.4

```
DELETE FROM Customers
     WHERE CustomerID = 2
```

When you execute this SQL statement, it will delete every record in the table that has the CustomerID 2. If no records match this condition, the DELETE statement will not delete any records.

 As with UPDATE statements, be sure the WHERE condition is accurate before you execute DELETE statements. You could potentially delete all the data in a table. Deleted records cannot be recovered.

To delete a record in the Requests table using SQL:

1. Use the Select Query window and SQL to execute the following SQL DELETE statement:

   DELETE FROM Requests
   WHERE RequestID = 3

2. Use Datasheet view for the Requests table to verify that it now contains only one row (RequestID 1).

3. Close the Datasheet view window for the Requests table.

USING THE SQL SELECT STATEMENT TO EXTRACT DATA

So far, you have used SQL commands to create tables, insert and delete records, and update table data. In this section, you will learn about another important use of SQL statements. When you have a database system that stores data, your most important and frequent task is to retrieve the data. You retrieve data from databases by using SQL SELECT statements. SELECT statements are used to answer questions about the data in a database, and so they are also known as queries. Queries are statements or objects that answer your questions by extracting data from database tables. Because the complete syntax for a SQL SELECT statement is very complex, this section introduces you to the SELECT statement in incremental phases.

Extracting Specific Columns from a Table

A simple but useful syntax for the SELECT statement is as follows:

```
SELECT fieldname1, fieldname2… FROM tablename
```

When you execute a SELECT statement, it outputs an object that is similar to a table. The output of the SELECT statement includes rows from the table named *tablename*. It contains only those columns that are specified in the SELECT statement (*fieldname1*, *fieldname2*…) from the table. All the rows from *tablename* are included. Only the columns specified in the SELECT statement are output for each row in the output.

You execute SQL SELECT statements in Access using the same general procedure outlined in the previous section that you used to run other types of SQL statements.

To execute a SELECT statement in Access:

1. Use the Select Query window and SQL to enter the following SQL SELECT statement:

   SELECT PropertyID, TypeOfHouse, Area FROM Properties

2. Click the **Run** button on the Query Design toolbar to execute the SELECT statement. See Figure 5-11. Only the columns (fields) PropertyID, TypeOfHouse, and Area are included in the output. Also notice that there are 310 records in the output; this number is the same as the number of properties listed in the Properties table.

Only the specified fields in the SELECT statements are included in the output

310 records are selected

Figure 5-11   Output of SQL SELECT statement to extract columns

3. Close the Select Query window without saving changes.

Extracting Specific Rows from a Table

You can include a WHERE clause in a SELECT statement to select only those rows that meet one or more criteria. The syntax for a SELECT statement that includes a WHERE clause is as follows:

```
SELECT fieldname1, fieldname2... FROM tablename
   WHERE condition
```

The output of this SELECT statement selects rows from the table named *tablename* and only those columns that are specified in the SELECT statement. Only the rows from *tablename* for which the *condition* is true are included in the output.

To create a SELECT statement that includes a condition:

1. Use the Select Query window and SQL to enter the following SQL SELECT statement:

   **SELECT PropertyID, Price, Location FROM Properties
   WHERE Price < 150000**

2. Click the **Run** button on the Query Design toolbar to execute the SELECT statement. The output appears in Figure 5-12. Notice that only those rows where the price is less than $150,000 are included in the output. The output also includes only those fields that you specified in the SELECT statement: PropertyID, Price, and Location.

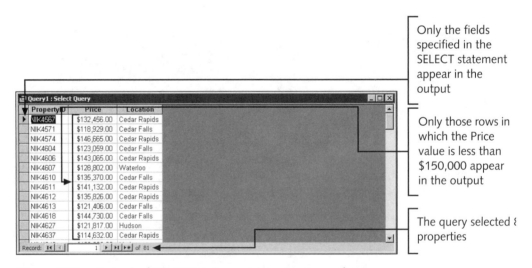

Only the fields specified in the SELECT statement appear in the output

Only those rows in which the Price value is less than $150,000 appear in the output

The query selected 8 properties

Figure 5-12   Output of SELECT statement to extract specific rows

3. Close the Select Query window without saving changes.

When you specify a condition in a SELECT statement, it acts like a filter. The condition is evaluated for every record in the table. If the Price of the property is less than $150,000, then the condition is true and the record is included in the output. If the condition is false, then that record is not included in the output.

Extracting Rows Using Conditions

Similar to conditions in ColdFusion, you design conditions in SQL statements by comparing two quantities with one of the six standard relational operators or other operators. The two quantities that are compared include fieldnames and/or values. The data types for the two quantities that you are comparing must be the same. The six standard relational operators are >, <, >=, <=, =, and < >. Other useful operators include the BETWEEN, IN, NOT IN, LIKE, and NOT LIKE operators, which you will learn about later in this chapter.

Similar to the concept of logical operators in ColdFusion, you can use the SQL AND and OR operators to construct complex conditions from simple conditions.

The following example illustrates a SQL statement for extracting specific rows and columns using the equals relational operator with a text field:

To create a SELECT statement that includes a comparison:

1. Use the Select Query window and SQL to enter the following SQL SELECT statement:

```
SELECT PropertyID, Price, Location FROM Properties
  WHERE Location = 'Hudson'
```

2. Click the **Run** button on the Query Design toolbar to execute the SELECT statement. The output appears in Figure 5-13.

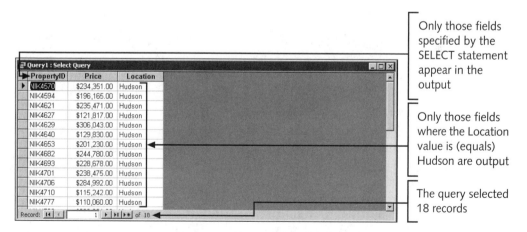

Only those fields specified by the SELECT statement appear in the output

Only those fields where the Location value is (equals) Hudson are output

The query selected 18 records

Figure 5-13   Output of SELECT statement that includes a condition

3. Close the Select Query window without saving changes.

Notice that the output now includes 18 rows, all of which include the value Hudson in the Location field. The output includes the PropertyID, Price, and Location fields for each row selected by the query. The ability to select rows based on comparisons provides you with the opportunity to answer the following types of questions about the data: Which of the properties listed for sale are located in Hudson? How many properties are listed for sale in Hudson? What are the prices of listed properties located in Hudson?

Extracting Rows Using Arithmetic Expressions

In addition to being able to compare values with operators, you can also use the WHERE clause to select rows based on arithmetic expressions. You can construct arithmetic expressions by using field names, values, and arithmetic operators (+, -, *, /, ^).

 If you want to select all fields in a table, you can use the asterisk (*) wildcard instead of listing them in the SELECT statement. However, you should use this technique only if you are planning to use all these fields. Selecting only the fields you plan to use gives you the best performance.

To create a SELECT statement that includes an arithmetic expression:

1. Use the Select Query window and SQL to enter the following SQL SELECT statement:

```
SELECT * FROM Properties
 WHERE Price / Area <= 60
```

2. Click the **Run** button on the Query Design toolbar to execute the SELECT statement. The output appears in Figure 5-14.

3. Close the Select Query window without saving changes.

The SQL statement uses an asterisk (*) in the list of fields to indicate that you want to include all of the table's fields in the output. The WHERE condition includes an arithmetic expression constructed by using the division (/) operator. The expression Price / Area <= 60 selects only those rows in the table with a price per square foot that is less than or equal to $60. Notice that 14 such properties are listed for sale.

If you want the price per square foot displayed, you can create an alias for the expression so you can treat it as a field. To do so, you use the AS keyword in the SELECT statement. SELECT Price / Area AS PricePerSFoot FROM Properties is a valid SQL SELECT statement. It displays the ratio of price to area for every record under the column heading PricePerSFoot. In addition to arithmetic expressions, you can string expressions and the concatenation operator (&) in SQL statements too. SELECT FirstName & ' ' & MiddleInitial & ' ' & LastName AS AgentName FROM Agents is a valid SQL SELECT statement that outputs all the agents' full names under the column heading AgentName.

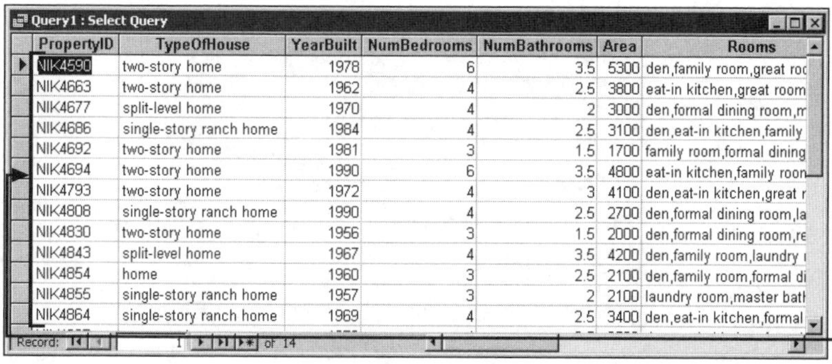

Query1 : Select Query

PropertyID	TypeOfHouse	YearBuilt	NumBedrooms	NumBathrooms	Area	Rooms
NIK4590	two-story home	1978	6	3.5	5300	den,family room,great roc
NIK4663	two-story home	1962	4	2.5	3800	eat-in kitchen,great room
NIK4677	split-level home	1970	4	2	3000	den,formal dining room,m
NIK4686	single-story ranch home	1984	4	2.5	3100	den,eat-in kitchen,family
NIK4692	two-story home	1981	3	1.5	1700	family room,formal dining
NIK4694	two-story home	1990	6	3.5	4800	eat-in kitchen,family roon
NIK4793	two-story home	1972	4	3	4100	den,eat-in kitchen,great r
NIK4808	single-story ranch home	1990	4	2.5	2700	den,formal dining room,la
NIK4830	two-story home	1956	3	1.5	2000	den,formal dining room,re
NIK4843	split-level home	1967	4	3.5	4200	den,family room,laundry
NIK4854	home	1960	3	2.5	2100	den,family room,formal di
NIK4855	single-story ranch home	1957	3	2	2100	laundry room,master batl
NIK4864	single-story ranch home	1969	4	2.5	3400	den,eat-in kitchen,formal

Record: 1 of 14

Only those records where the price per square foot is less than or equal to $60 are selected

Figure 5-14 Output of SELECT statement with arithmetic expression

Extracting Rows Using the BETWEEN Operator

Sometimes you might need to find rows where a field value falls within a particular range. For example, you might need to select only those properties that are priced between $130,000 and $180,000 for a buyer who is looking to purchase a home in that price range. In this situation, you can construct the WHERE clause in two ways. The first way is to use the AND operator to combine two conditions that will produce the desired output: Price >= 130000 AND Price <= 180000. The second way is to use the BETWEEN operator to indicate the range of values to include in the output: Price BETWEEN 130000 AND 180000. Both queries will select the same rows, so it is really a matter of personal preference as to which method you use. The BETWEEN operator is very useful for working with date and time values.

To create a SELECT statement that includes a BETWEEN operator:

1. Use the Select Query window and SQL to enter the following SQL SELECT statement:

```
SELECT PropertyID, Price, Location FROM Properties
 WHERE Price BETWEEN 130000 AND 180000
```

2. Click the **Run** button on the Query Design toolbar to execute the SELECT statement. The output appears in Figure 5-15.

Prices for selected
properties are
between $130,000
and $180,000

Figure 5-15   Output of SELECT statement with BETWEEN operator

3. Close the Select Query window without saving changes.

The query output shows that there are 75 properties listed for sale and priced between $130,000 and $180,000.

Extracting Rows Using the IN and NOT IN Operators

You can use the IN and NOT IN operators to specify a group of rows to select based on a value that appears in a list. For example, if you are interested in listing properties that are located in either Cedar Falls or Hudson, you can create a query to select those records in one of two ways. The first way is to construct a WHERE condition that uses the OR operator **Location = 'Cedar Falls' OR Location = 'Hudson'**; the second way is to construct a WHERE condition that uses the IN operator **Location IN ('Cedar Falls', 'Hudson')**. These two WHERE clauses will produce the same output.

To create a SELECT statement that uses the IN operator:

1. Use the Select Query window and SQL to enter the following SQL SELECT statement:

```
SELECT PropertyID, Price, Location FROM Properties
   WHERE Location IN ('Cedar Falls', 'Hudson')
```

2. Click the **Run** button on the Query Design toolbar to execute the SELECT statement. The output appears in Figure 5-16.

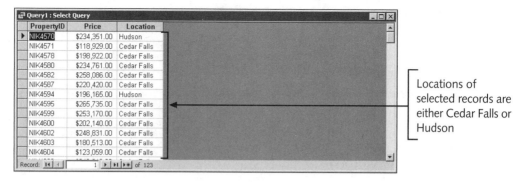

Locations of selected records are either Cedar Falls or Hudson

Figure 5-16   Output of SELECT statement with IN operator

3. Close the Select Query window without saving changes.

The query output shows that 123 properties are listed for sale in Cedar Falls and Hudson.

The NOT IN operator has the opposite effect of the IN operator. The clause WHERE Location IN ('Cedar Falls', 'Hudson') selects only those rows where the value in the Location field is Cedar Falls or Hudson. You could obtain the same results by listing the cities that you do not want in the output. There are only four cities represented in the database, so the WHERE clause WHERE Location NOT IN ('Cedar Rapids', 'Waterloo') would select rows where the value in the Location field is not Cedar Rapids or Waterloo and produce the same output.

Extracting Rows Using the LIKE Operator

The LIKE operator is very useful for searching text data for a partial match. To identify partial matches, you have to use wildcard characters in SQL. The asterisk (*) wildcard character represents any number of any characters, and the question mark (?) wildcard character represents any single character. If a customer is interested in houses that have a laundry room, you construct the WHERE clause as WHERE Rooms LIKE '*laundry*'.

To create a SELECT statement that includes the LIKE operator:

1. Use the Select Query window and SQL to enter the following SQL SELECT statement:

   SELECT PropertyID, Price, Rooms FROM Properties
   WHERE Rooms LIKE '*laundry*' AND Location = 'Waterloo'

2. Click the **Run** button on the Query Design toolbar to execute the SELECT statement. The output appears in Figure 5-17.

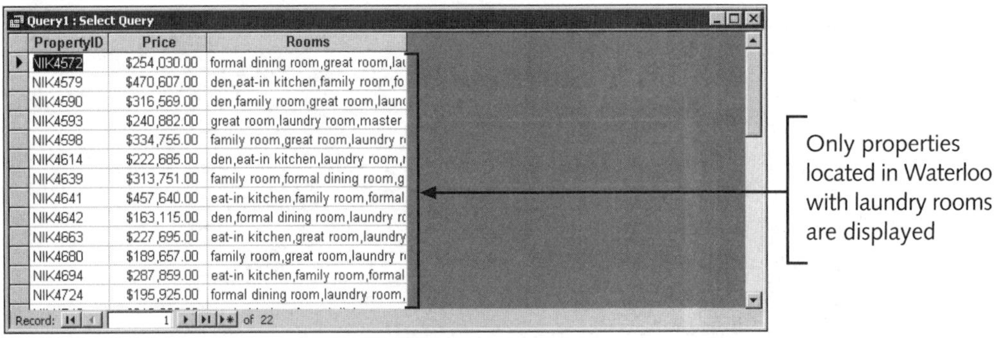

Figure 5-17   Output of SELECT statement with LIKE operator

3. Close the Select Query window without saving changes.

The query output shows that 22 properties are located in Waterloo that include the word "laundry" anywhere in the Rooms field. A case-insensitive comparison is performed when you use the LIKE operator.

USING A SELECT STATEMENT TO SORT DATA

You can use an ORDER BY clause in a SELECT statement to sort data based on criteria that you specify. The syntax for the ORDER BY clause is as follows:

```
SELECT fieldname1, fieldname2… FROM tablename
     WHERE condition
     ORDER BY sort_fieldname1 [DESC] [, sort_fieldname2]
     [DESC]...]
```

When you execute this SELECT statement, the output will list records from the table named *tablename* for the indicated columns. Only those rows from *tablename* for which the *condition* is true are included. In addition, the rows in the output are listed in ascending order based on the values in the field named *sort_fieldname1*. If the keyword DESC is used, then the rows in the output are listed in descending order based on the values in the field named *sort_fieldname1*. You can use the ORDER BY clause to sort numeric, text, and date-time values. Numeric data is arranged by numeric value, text data is arranged alphabetically, and date-time values are arranged in chronological order. If multiple fields are included, then the data is sorted on the first field; if the contents of the first field are the same, then the second field is used, and so on.

To create a SELECT statement that includes an ORDER BY clause:

1. Use the Select Query window and SQL to enter the following SQL SELECT statement:

```
SELECT PropertyID, Price, Location FROM Properties
WHERE Price > 400000
ORDER BY Location, Price
```

2. Click the **Run** button on the Query Design toolbar to execute the SELECT statement. The output appears in Figure 5-18.

5

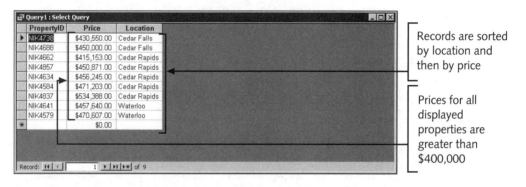

Figure 5-18   Output of SELECT statement by ORDER BY clause

3. Close the Select Query window without saving changes.

This SELECT statement displays the property IDs, prices, and locations of properties that are priced at more than $400,000 and sorts the results first by location and then within location by price.

EXTRACTING DATA FROM MULTIPLE TABLES USING ONE SELECT STATEMENT

Once a buyer is interested in a property, he or she may want to contact the listing agent with an e-mail message to ask questions about the property or to inquire about the property's status (for sale, under contract, sold, etc.). In this case, the buyer needs a way to determine the e-mail address of the listing agent for the desired property by using its PropertyID number. Because the Properties table stores the PropertyID and the AgentID, and the Agents table stores the agent's e-mail address, you must **join** the Properties and Agents tables to obtain the agent's e-mail address. To join two tables, both tables must contain at least one field that is common in both tables. Typically, this common field is a primary key in one of the tables. The AgentID field appears in the Properties and Agents table, so that is the common field. The AgentID is also the primary key of the Agents table. The syntax for a SELECT statement for extracting data from multiple tables is as follows:

```
SELECT tablename1.fieldnameA, tablename1.fieldnameB…
tablename2.fieldnameX, tablename2.fieldnameY… FROM
tablename1, tablename2
        WHERE tablename1.fieldnameI = tablename2.fieldnameJ
```

When you execute this SELECT statement, it will produce output that contains information from two tables named *tablename1* and *tablename2*. The fields *fieldnameA* and *fieldnameB* are extracted from *tablename1*, and fields *fieldnameX* and *fieldnameY* are extracted from *tablename2*. The rows are joined on the contents of *fieldnameI* from *tablename1* and *fieldnameJ* from *tablename2*. Because both tables contain a common field that is used to join them, you must **qualify** the field names to distinguish which table the requested field is from by writing matching field names as *tablename.fieldname*.

To create a SELECT statement that selects rows from two tables:

1. Use the Select Query window and SQL to enter the following SQL SELECT statement:

```
SELECT Properties.PropertyID, Properties.Price,
    Agents.FirstName & ' ' & Agents.MiddleInitial & ' ' &
    Agents.LastName AS AgentName, Agents.EmailAddress
FROM Properties, Agents
WHERE Properties.AgentID = Agents.AgentID
ORDER BY Properties.PropertyID
```

2. Click the **Run** button on the Query Design toolbar to execute the SELECT statement. The output appears in Figure 5-19.

3. Close the Select Query window without saving changes.

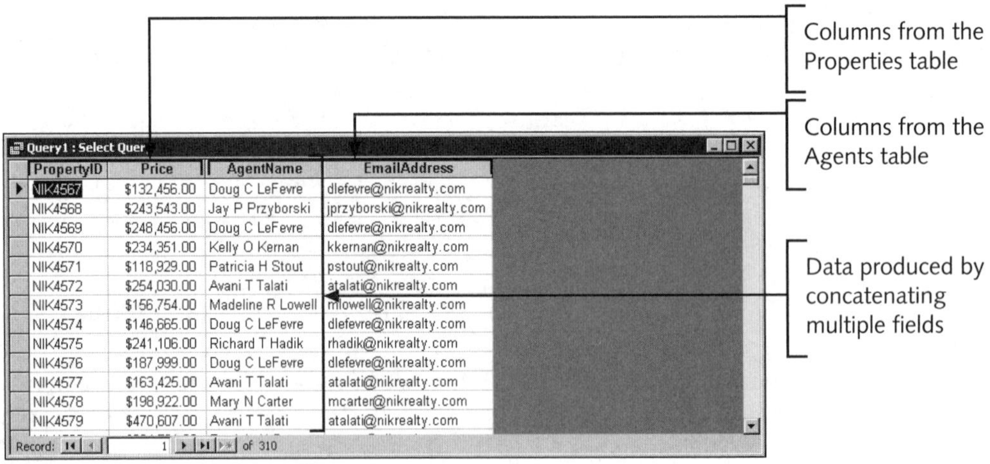

Figure 5-19   Output from a SELECT statement joining two tables

The SELECT statement selects rows from the Properties and Agents tables based on the requested fields in the SELECT clause. For each record in the Properties table, the PropertyID and Price are displayed. The system compares the AgentID for the property with the contents of the AgentID field in the Agents table (WHERE Properties.AgentID = Agents.AgentID) and extracts the name and e-mail address of the agent. When you join tables, they have a relationship to each other. Systems that allow you to create relationships are **relational database systems**. Essentially, you are joining two tables based on the contents of a common field and extracting data from both tables.

Another concept illustrated by the SELECT statement is the use of operators in the field list, computation of expressions, and field aliases. The agent's first name, middle initial, and last name are concatenated with spaces to produce a calculated field with the name AgentName. The AS keyword provides the name of the column that is the result of the expression. The ORDER BY clause is added to sort the data according to the PropertyID field. It can be used on any of the fields that are selected or computed by the SQL SELECT statement.

Using the DISTINCT Keyword in SELECT Statements

When you extract only a few columns from a table, it is possible that the data could contain duplicate rows. When you think that this might happen, you can use the DISTINCT keyword to eliminate all but one occurrence of such rows. For example, you may want to find cities in which properties are listed for sale. If you execute the statement SELECT Location FROM Properties, the output will display 310 records—the Location field from every record in the table. More useful data would be to execute a query that shows you the cities in which properties are located and to eliminate duplicates. You can use the DISTINCT keyword to eliminate redundant data.

To create a SELECT statement that eliminates duplicate rows:

1. Use the Select Query window and SQL to enter the following SQL SELECT statement:

   ```
   SELECT DISTINCT Location FROM Properties
   ```

2. Click the **Run** button on the Query Design toolbar to execute the SELECT statement. The output appears in Figure 5-20.

5

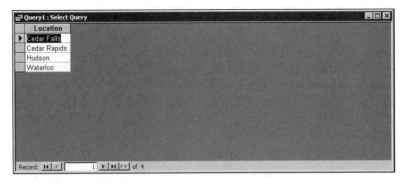

Figure 5-20 Output of SELECT statement that eliminates duplicate rows

Notice that the output contains four rows—one for each city in which NikRealty has properties listed.

3. Close the Select Query window without saving changes.

SUMMARIZING DATA BY USING FUNCTIONS

The COUNT function counts the number of records. The syntax for the COUNT function is as follows:

```
SELECT COUNT(*) AS NumberOfRecords FROM tablename1
    [WHERE condition]
```

When you execute this SELECT statement, it will produce output that contains one column named NumberOfRecords and one row where the value in the NumberOfRecords field is the number of records in *tablename1*. When necessary, you can add a WHERE clause to the SELECT statement to count the number of records that match a particular criterion.

To create a SELECT statement that uses the COUNT function:

1. Use the Select Query window and SQL to enter the following SQL SELECT statement:

```
SELECT COUNT(*) AS NumHighPriced FROM Properties
    WHERE Price >= 400000
```

2. Click the **Run** button on the Query Design toolbar to execute the SELECT statement. The output appears in Figure 5-21. There are nine properties that cost $400,000 or more.

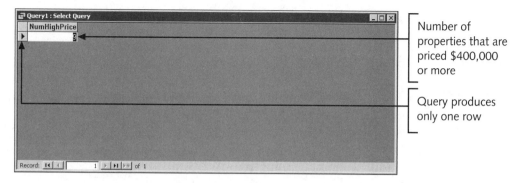

Number of properties that are priced $400,000 or more

Query produces only one row

Figure 5-21   Output of SELECT statement that uses the COUNT function

   3. Close the Select Query window without saving changes.

You can use other functions in SELECT statements as well. The AVG function calculates the average of the values in a specified field. The MAX function calculates the highest value in a particular field. The MIN function calculates the minimum value in a particular field. The SUM function computes the sum of all values in a field.

To create a SELECT statement that uses functions:

   1. Use the Select Query window and SQL to enter the following SQL SELECT statement:

      SELECT AVG(Price) AS Average, MAX(Price) AS Maximum, MIN (Price) AS Minimum, SUM(Price) AS Total FROM Properties

   2. Click the **Run** button on the Query Design toolbar to execute the SELECT statement. If necessary, increase the column widths to see all the data. The output appears in Figure 5-22. The output shows the average price, maximum price, and minimum price of properties listed for sale, as well as the combined total for all listed properties.

Figure 5-22   Output of SELECT statement that uses AVG, MAX, MIN, and SUM functions

   3. Close the Select Query window without saving changes.

Grouping Data and Using Functions

Instead of counting records in the entire table, you may need to count the records that have a particular value in one of the fields. In fact, you may want to use all the functions on rows that have a particular value in one of the fields. For example, you may want to find out how many properties are listed for sale in each city. To answer a question like that, you have to use functions in combination with a GROUP BY clause. The syntax for a SELECT statement with functions and a GROUP BY clause is as follows:

```
SELECT Function AS Result, fieldnameG FROM tablename1
       GROUP BY fieldnameG
```

When you execute this SELECT statement, its output will contain two columns named *Result* and *fieldnameG* with multiple rows, one for each distinct value of *fieldnameG*. The function specified as *Function* is evaluated for each set of records that contain a particular value of *fieldnameG*.

To create a SELECT statement that uses a GROUP BY clause:

1. Use the Select Query window and SQL to enter the following SQL SELECT statement:

```
SELECT Location, COUNT(*) AS NumProperties, AVG(Price)
AS Average, MAX(Price) AS Maximum, MIN(Price) AS Minimum,
SUM(Price) AS Total
    FROM Properties
    GROUP BY Location
```

2. Click the **Run** button on the Query Design toolbar to execute the SELECT statement. The output appears in Figure 5-23. The output shows the desired statistics for each city's listings.

Location	NumProperties	Average	Maximum	Minimum	Total
Cedar Falls	105	$205,549.48	$450,000.00	$92,134.00	$21,582,695.00
Cedar Rapids	119	$215,728.45	$534,388.00	$82,467.00	$25,671,685.00
Hudson	18	$207,351.72	$306,043.00	$110,060.00	$3,732,331.00
Waterloo	68	$202,884.66	$470,607.00	$71,424.00	$13,796,157.00

Each row represents city in the output

Figure 5-23   Output of SELECT statement that uses the GROUP BY clause

3. Close the Select Query window without saving changes.

4. Close Access.

Now that you are familiar with SQL, in the next chapter you will learn about using ColdFusion and SQL to extract data from databases and output it as a Web page.

CHAPTER SUMMARY

❏ When you want to design a database, analyze existing systems in terms of entities and objects.

❏ The data hierarchy describes the organization of data in relational database systems: Databases are collections of tables, tables are collections of records, records are collections of fields, and fields are collections of characters.

❏ Access allows you to design fields using the following data types: Text, Memo, Number, Date/Time, Currency, AutoNumber, Yes/No, OLE Object, Hyperlink, and Lookup Wizard.

❏ You create tables by using Access Design view or the SQL CREATE TABLE statement.

❏ You insert data into tables by using the SQL INSERT statement. You perform other database maintenance operations like deleting and updating data using the SQL DELETE and UPDATE statements, respectively.

❏ The SQL SELECT statement allows you to extract data from one or more tables. Specific columns can be extracted. Rows that match specific criteria are extracted. Data can be sorted using the ORDER BY clause. You can compute statistics by using aggregate functions, and you group data using the GROUP BY clause.

REVIEW QUESTIONS

1. What are entities and attributes?

2. How is data organized in a relational database management system?

3. What is a primary key?

4. What are the different field data types in Access? Briefly describe each data type.

5. What is SQL?

6. What is the syntax for the SQL statement that you use for creating tables? Briefly explain the statement.

7. What are the two ways in which you can delete records in Access?

8. What is the syntax for the SQL UPDATE statement? Why do you need a WHERE clause in this statement?

9. How do you use SQL to extract data from a single table?

10. In order to extract data from two or more tables, what is required of the data in each table?

11. List eight operators that you can use in WHERE clauses in SQL. Briefly describe their functions.

12. What is the purpose of the ORDER BY clause in SQL SELECT statements?

13. What is the significance of the following keywords in SQL SELECT statements: AS and DISTINCT?

14. How do you use aggregate functions in SQL?

15. What is the purpose of using a GROUP BY clause in a SQL SELECT statement?

16. Can you perform computations in SQL SELECT statements? If so, what are some of the operators that you can use?

HANDS-ON PROJECTS

Project 5-1: Use SQL to Insert a New Record

Dianne Callejo has just listed a new property for NikRealty and needs to enter it as a new record in the Realtor database. The property is a two-story home that was built in 1975. It has three bedrooms and two and a half bathrooms. The total square footage is 2100 and the listing price is $121,621. It includes a master bedroom and a laundry room. Its features include hardwood floors and a pantry. The house is located in Cedar Falls and its zip code is 50613. Dianne has not yet taken a picture of the property, so you can use the generic graphic NA.jpg, which is used for properties that do not have pictures available. Before inserting the new record, determine the following:

1. In which table will you add the record?

2. What is the next available PropertyID number?

3. What is the AgentID number?

4. What is the SQL statement to add the new record?

After determining the answers to these questions, use SQL to insert the record into the Realtor database.

Project 5-2: Analyze Data and Add It to the Database

A new customer makes the following three requests using the Schedule a Private Showing Web page.

Determine the following:

1. In which tables will you add the records?

2. How many records would you add in these tables?

3. What is the CustomerID for this customer?

4. What are the SQL statements for inserting these records?

5. Insert the data into the appropriate tables in the Realtor database.

Form Item	First Request	Second Request	Third Request
PropertyID	NIK4570	NIK4572	NIK4573
ScheduleDate	6/12/2003	6/12/2003	6/13/2003
ScheduleTime	4:30 PM	5:30 PM	4:30 PM
ClientName	Ruth Francis	Ruth Francis	Ruth Francis
ClientEmail	FrancisR@myMail.com	FrancisR@myMail.com	FrancisR@myMail.com
CurrentResidence	Own	Own	Own
Criteria	Price	Price	Price
Comments	I start my job here next month. I am in a hurry.		

Project 5-3: Use SQL to Extract Data

Write appropriate SQL SELECT statements to extract data from the Properties table and answer the following questions:

1. How many properties are listed for sale with NikRealty? Select only the PropertyID column.

2. How many of the properties listed for sale are located in Cedar Rapids? Select the PropertyID and Location columns.

3. How many of the properties listed for sale are located in either Cedar Falls or Waterloo? Select the PropertyID and Location columns.

4. How many properties listed for sale cost more than $300,000 and have five or more bedrooms? Select the PropertyID, Price, and NumBedrooms columns.

Project 5-4: Join Tables and Extract Data

Write appropriate SQL SELECT statements to join the Properties and Agents tables to extract data and answer the following questions:

1. How many properties are listed with Jack Petrie as the agent? Select PropertyID and AgentName (alias) columns.

2. How many properties that are listed with Jack Petrie as the agent cost less than $200,000? Select PropertyID, Price, and AgentName (alias) columns.

3. How many Cedar Falls properties are listed with agents who live in Waterloo? Select PropertyID, Location, AgentName (alias), and City columns.

Project 5-5: Join Tables and Use Aggregate Functions

Write appropriate SQL SELECT statements to join the Properties and Agents tables, and use aggregate functions to extract data and answer the following questions:

1. How many properties does each agent list? Display LastName and NumProperties columns as shown in Figure 5-24. Write the SQL for your solution.

Query1 : Select Query

LastName	NumProperties
Adachi	14
Callejo	34
Carter	41
Hadik	36
Kernan	14
LeFevre	34
Little	6
Lowell	18
Petrie	17
Przyborski	46
Stout	30
Talati	21

Record: 1 of 12

Figure 5-24

2. What is the average price of properties listed by each agent? What is the maximum price, minimum price, and the total price of all properties listed by each agent? Display LastName, Average, Maximum, Minimum, and Total columns, as shown in Figure 5-25. Write the SQL for your solution.
3. How many properties in Cedar Rapids does each agent list? Display LastName, NumProperties, and Location, as shown in Figure 5-26. Write the SQL for your solution.

Query1 : Select Query

LastName	Average	Maximum	Minimum	Total
Adachi	$208,874.21	$332,872.00	$117,019.00	$2,924,239.00
Callejo	$205,780.62	$415,153.00	$98,709.00	$6,996,541.00
Carter	$201,178.07	$395,079.00	$92,134.00	$8,248,301.00
Hadik	$224,139.19	$534,388.00	$116,252.00	$8,069,011.00
Kernan	$212,122.71	$306,046.00	$110,060.00	$2,969,718.00
LeFevre	$211,785.29	$450,871.00	$107,355.00	$7,200,700.00
Little	$229,343.17	$315,360.00	$115,242.00	$1,376,059.00
Lowell	$192,724.94	$457,640.00	$79,576.00	$3,469,049.00
Petrie	$194,984.59	$334,755.00	$116,156.00	$3,314,738.00
Przyborski	$209,206.46	$456,245.00	$82,467.00	$9,623,497.00
Stout	$210,353.77	$450,000.00	$93,592.00	$6,310,613.00
Talati	$209,620.14	$470,607.00	$71,424.00	$4,402,023.00

Record: 1 of 12

Figure 5-25

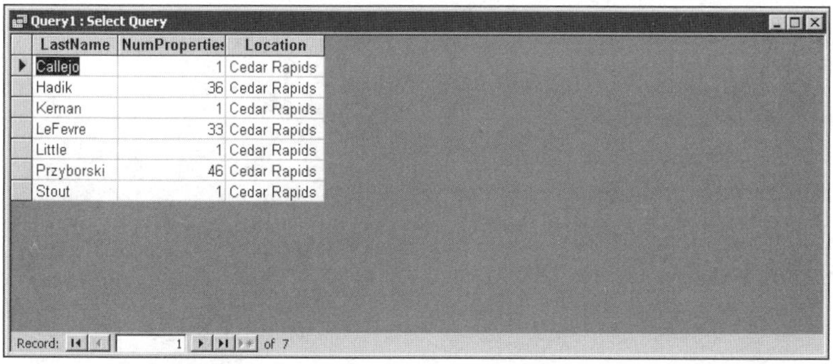

Figure 5-26

Project 5-6: Use SELECT Statements with Arithmetic Expressions

Write appropriate SQL SELECT statements to extract data from the Properties table that use computations to answer the following questions:

1. The company receives a commission of 7% on the sale price of a property. What is the potential commission for the property with PropertyID NIK4589? Select PropertyID and PotCommission columns, as shown in Figure 5-27. Write the SQL for your solution.

Figure 5-27

2. Sixty-five percent of the total commission is paid to the agent. What is the potential commission for the listing agent of PropertyID NIK4589? Select PropertyID, LastName, and AgentCommission columns, as shown in Figure 5-28. Write the SQL for your solution.

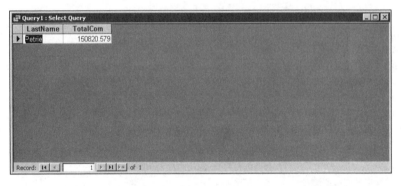

Figure 5-28

3. What is the potential total commission to agent Jack Petrie? Select LastName and TotalCom columns, as shown in Figure 5-29. Write the SQL for your solution.

Figure 5-29

CASE PROJECTS

Case Project 1

Instead of just deleting sold properties, Nikitha wants you to keep track of sold properties so that she can understand her business better. You have decided to keep track of sold properties by storing them in a new table named SoldProperties. Nikitha has decided that the image is no longer necessary, but she wants you to keep track of the price (to be named listPrice), salePrice, dateSold, and all the other fields from the existing properties table.

1. Plan the structure of the SoldProperties table.

2. Write a SQL statement for creating the SoldProperties table. Do not create the table yet.

When a property is sold, all the data from the existing record is extracted, it is inserted into the SoldProperties table, and the original record is deleted from the properties table. Design the following SQL statements that should be executed when a property is sold:

a. Write a SQL statement for extracting data from the Properties table for the sold property with a known PropertyID.

b. Write a SQL statement for inserting data into the SoldProperties table. Use fictitious data for now. Later on you will learn about using variables in SQL statements.

c. Write a SQL statement for deleting the property that has been sold from the Properties table.

Case Project 2

HardwareStore.com has hired you to set up an e-commerce site. Arjun Partha, the Vice President in charge of Marketing, is your primary contact. Arjun wants you to design Web pages that display product information, allow customers to add products to a shopping cart, and then let them check out. Products have a unique ID, a description, and a price and belong to a Product Category. Product categories have a description, and an ID. Analyze this situation with a perspective of building a database to store the data by answering these questions. What are the entities about which you want to store data? What are their attributes? What data should be displayed in the product Web pages? What customer information would you collect on the Web site? What database changes have to be made when customers select products and add them to their shopping cart? What database changes should be made when customers check out? There is a file named HardwareStore.mdb in the databases folder on your data disk. Examine it in Access. How well does this database measure up to your analysis?

Case Project 3

Using *www.google.com* or any search engine of your choice, research the Internet for SQL subqueries. Provide a definition of subqueries. Give an example of a subquery. Using a subquery, write the SQL statement to display the ID, Description, and the price for the Product with the highest price in the HardwareStore.mdb database.

6

DATA RETRIEVAL USING COLDFUSION

In this chapter, you will:

♦ Learn about Open Database Connectivity (ODBC) standards

♦ Set up an ODBC connection using ColdFusion Administrator

♦ Create query objects and record sets

♦ Execute SQL SELECT statements in ColdFusion

♦ Use QUERY loops for extracting data from databases

♦ Generate columnar reports, tabular reports, and group-total reports

♦ Create templates for extracting data interactively

In the previous chapter, you learned about databases, data storage, and data retrieval using SQL. In this chapter, you will apply these concepts and extract data from databases using ColdFusion and then publish that data on a Web server. For ColdFusion to access data stored in Microsoft Access databases or from database servers, you must first set up connections to the databases.

OPEN DATABASE CONNECTIVITY

Open Database Connectivity (**ODBC**) is Microsoft's standard for connecting Windows applications to databases and database servers. ODBC provides an open, vendor-neutral way of accessing data stored in a variety of proprietary personal computer, minicomputer, and mainframe databases. An ODBC driver is systems software that runs on the Web server and provides the functionality for connecting databases to other applications. Figure 6-1 shows how an ODBC driver connects a client computer, a Web server, and a database.

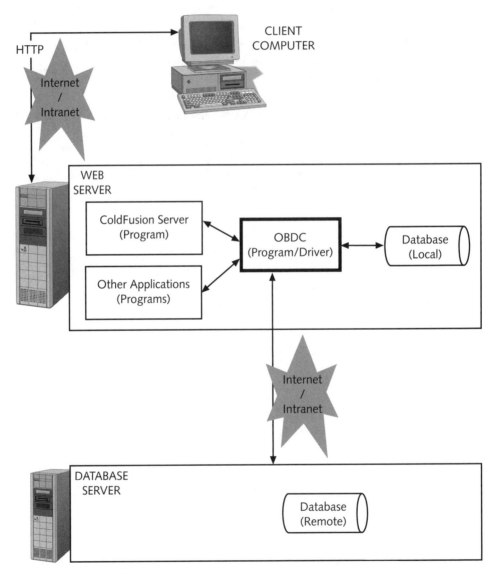

Figure 6-1   Role of the ODBC driver

To access data from a database in ColdFusion, you must first set up an ODBC connection to the database. The ODBC driver interacts with the database, and the ColdFusion Server interacts with the ODBC driver. Every ODBC connection has a **data source name**, which is useful for accessing the data in its database. ODBC is based on the specification of the SQL Access Group, an industry standards group. With ODBC, you can use SQL, which lets you store data, create tables, update data, and complete other database tasks regardless of which database system contains the data. Once you have a ColdFusion application working, you can easily **upsize** the database that contains your data from Microsoft Access to an Oracle Server or a SQL server by changing the ODBC connection. This change does not require any changes to the CFML. You use ColdFusion Administrator to set up or change ODBC connections.

To complete the NikRealty Web site, you will need to set up an ODBC connection to the NikRealty database that is stored on the server.

To set up an ODBC connection:

1. Click the **Start** button on the taskbar, point to **Programs**, point to **Macromedia ColdFusion Server 5**, and then click **ColdFusion Administrator**. The ColdFusion Administrator Login page opens in a browser. See Figure 6-2.

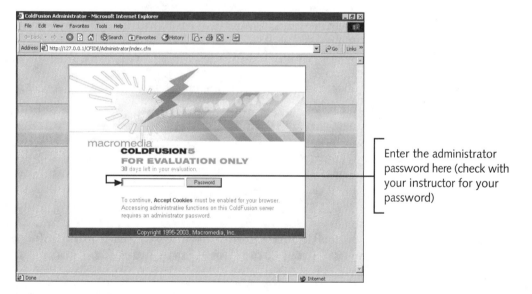

Enter the administrator password here (check with your instructor for your password)

Figure 6-2   ColdFusion Administrator login page

Depending on the configuration of your system, your instructor may have already set up an ODBC connection for you. You must have an administrator's password to complete the following steps. Check with your instructor before completing these steps. If you cannot complete these steps at the computer, read them so you can learn how to set up an ODBC connection.

2. Enter the administrator password for your server, and then click the **Password** button. The ColdFusion Administrator page opens and displays the Web-based console for configuring the ColdFusion Server settings and managing its resources. See Figure 6-3.

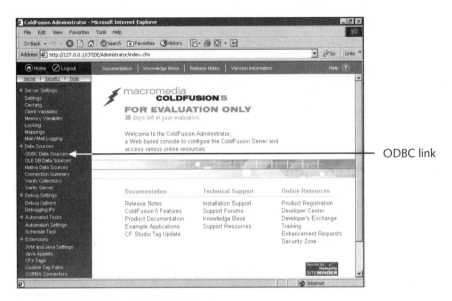

ODBC link

Figure 6-3 ColdFusion Administrator page

3. Click the **ODBC Data Sources** link in the data sources section on the left side of the page. The Web page shown in Figure 6-4 opens. This page lets you select the ODBC driver for the database that contains your data. It might also display a list of data sources available to ColdFusion that have already been configured.

4. Click the **ODBC Driver** list arrow to display a list of database drivers for database systems available on your computer.

5. Click **Microsoft Access Driver (*.mdb)** in the list, if necessary.

6. Click in the **Data Source Name** text box, and then type your username. You will use this data source name (your username) to identify the database connection in ColdFusion.

7. Click the **Add** button. The Create ODBC Data Source page opens.

8. Click the **Browse Server** button to the right of the Database File text box. If you are the first one to use this feature on the computer, a Security Warning dialog box opens. If it opens, click the **Yes** button. The Select File on the Server page opens. Open the Databases folder in the c:\Inetpub\wwwroot\your_username folder the server, click the **Realtor.mdb** file to select it, and then click the **Apply** button. The Create ODBC Data Source page now shows the data source name and the full path to the Realtor.mdb file that you just selected.

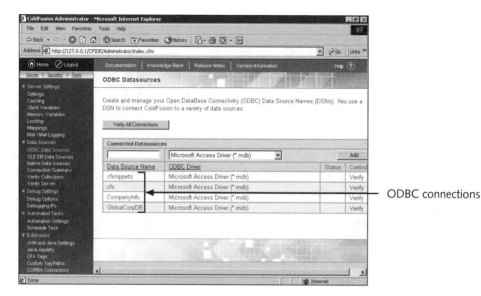

Figure 6-4   ODBC Data Sources page

9. Click the **CF Settings** button to display additional settings for the connection. See Figure 6-5.

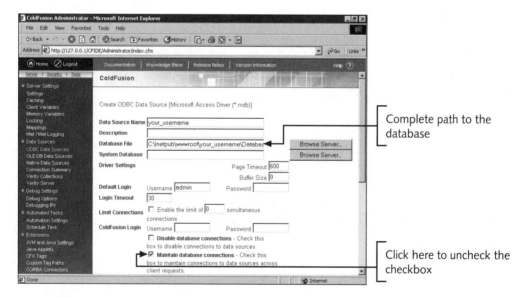

Figure 6-5   Create ODBC Data Source page

10. Click the **Maintain database connections** checkbox to clear it. Even though you may lose some performance when you clear this, doing so allows you to make changes to the database using Access or other programs.

11. Scroll to the bottom of the page, and then click the **Create** button. An ODBC connection to the database is established and ColdFusion tests the database connection. Any error is reported with suggestions for troubleshooting. See Figure 6-6. You have successfully established an ODBC connection named your_username to the Realtor.mdb database.

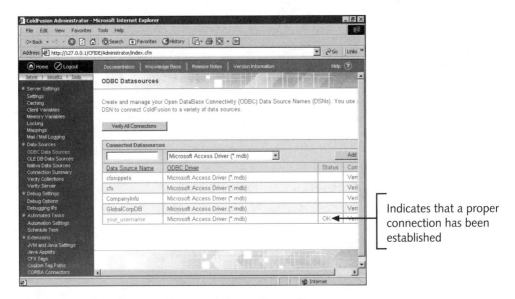

Indicates that a proper connection has been established

Figure 6-6   ODBC connection made to Realtor.mdb

12. Close the browser to exit ColdFusion Administrator.

Now that you have established a connection to the database, you can design ColdFusion templates that extract data from the database and publish them on the server.

DATABASE CONNECTIVITY WITH COLDFUSION

Extracting data and publishing it on the Web with ColdFusion is a two-step process. The first step involves executing a SQL SELECT statement to extract the data from the database into the computer's memory. This data is called a query object (or just a query) or a record set. The second step involves using a repetition flow control structure to loop through the records in the record set and output the data.

CFQUERY Tag

You use the CFQUERY tag to execute a SQL SELECT statement in a ColdFusion template. The syntax for the CFQUERY tag is as follows:

```
<cfquery datasource="datasource_name" name="query_name">
SQL SELECT statement
</cfquery>
```

The CFQUERY tag has two important attributes. The DATASOURCE attribute is the data source name of the ODBC connection. The second attribute is the NAME of the query. The guidelines for query names are the same as those for variable names. When the ColdFusion Server processes a CFQUERY statement, it executes the SQL SELECT statement against the database specified in the ODBC connection named datasource_name. The result of the SQL SELECT statement is stored in the server's memory as a query object. You use a QUERY loop flow-control structure to process the data in the query object.

QUERY Loops

ColdFusion QUERY loops implement a repetition flow-control structure. For each repetition, you have access to the data in a particular record in the database query object. QUERY loops have one important parameter—the name of the query object. The syntax for a QUERY loop is as follows:

```
<cfloop query="query_name">
Statements containing HTML and CFML that are to be exe-
cuted repeatedly with access to data from the query
</cfloop>
```

The flowchart for a QUERY loop appears in Figure 6-7.

To understand how a QUERY loop works, you can visualize the query object in the computer's memory as the table shown in Figure 6-7. When the ColdFusion Server executes the QUERY loop, if the query object contains any records, the first record in the query object is the current record. It is useful to picture an arrow pointing to the current record. The ColdFusion Server creates variables in the computer's memory—one for each field in the query—using the field names. Each variable created in this manner is assigned the value of the field in the current record. Initially, because the first record is the current record, the values in the first record are assigned to these variables. Then the ColdFusion Server executes all statements between the CFLOOP tags. The second row in the query object becomes the current record, all the values in the second row are assigned to the variables that are named after the fields, and the statements between the CFLOOP tags are executed again. This process is repeated for every record in the query object. After the last record is processed, statements are executed once and then repetition is terminated and processing continues by executing the statement below the closing CFLOOP tag. The statements in the CFLOOP tags use the variables that the ColdFusion Server has created based on the fields in the query. You can output these values using CFOUTPUT tags and pound signs, or use these variables in computations or for any other purpose based on your application requirements.

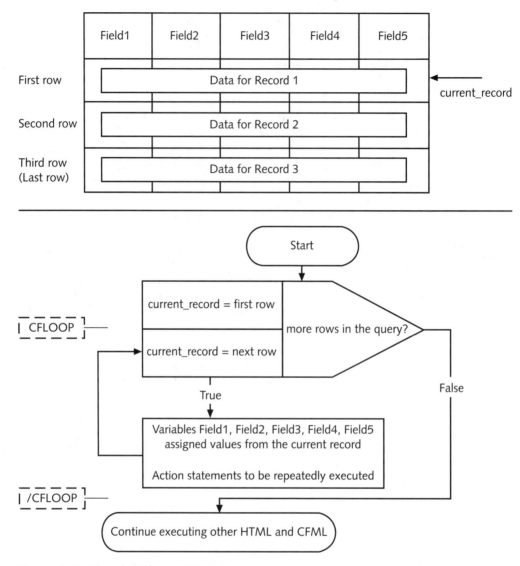

Figure 6-7   Flowchart for a QUERY loop

The following example (Example6-1.cfm) illustrates the data retrieval using the CFQUERY tag that is output using a QUERY loop:

Code Example 6-1

```
<cfquery datasource="your_username" name="getLocations">
SELECT DISTINCT Location, ZipCode FROM Properties
</cfquery>
<html>
<head>
<title>Locations Example</title>
</head>
<body>
<h3> List of Zip Codes and Locations with Properties for
Sale</h3>
<ul>
<cfloop query="getLocations">
<li> <cfoutput>#ZipCode#</cfoutput> -
 <cfoutput>#Location#</cfoutput>
</cfloop>
</ul>
</body>
</html>
```

The code in Code Example 6-1 produces the output shown in Figure 6-8.

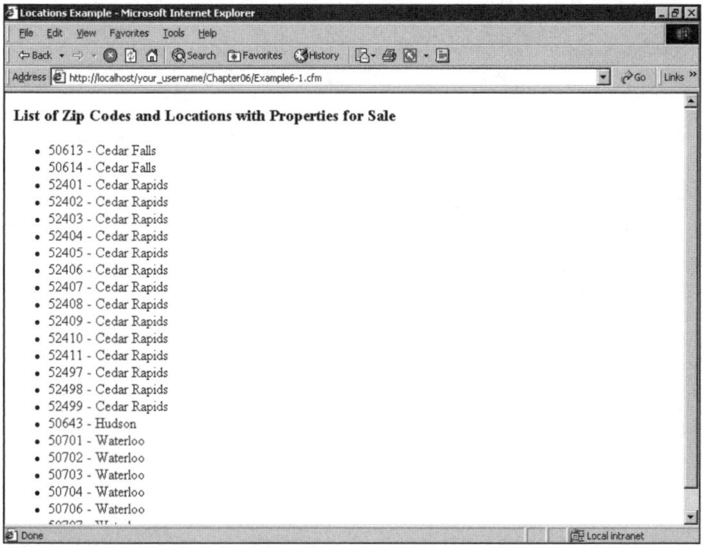

Figure 6-8   Web page displayed by Example6-1.cfm

When the ColdFusion Server executes the template, the SQL SELECT statement is executed against the ODBC data source named your_username. The ODBC data source points to the Realtor.mdb database file. The SQL SELECT statement selects data from the Properties table and the CFOUTPUT tags output it. See Figure 6-9.

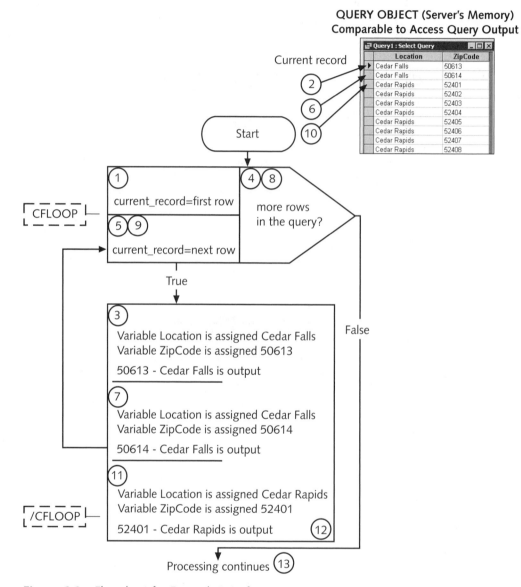

Figure 6-9   Flowchart for Example6-1.cfm

This query object is associated with the name getLocations. Then, the rest of the template code is processed. The HTML is output as is and the CFML is processed. When the ColdFusion Server executes the CFLOOP statement, the query object with the name getLocations (the one previously created) is used to execute the statement. The numbers in the following discussion correspond to the circled numbers in Figure 6-9.

1. Because the query object contains some records, the first row is activated as the current record. You can compare the query object in the Server's memory with the output produced in Microsoft Access by using a similar SQL statement, as shown in Figure 6-9. There is no need for Access to be installed on the server computer. This comparison is only for the purposes of learning about how data retrieval works. Such a comparison is useful for relating the concepts that you learned in the previous chapter and the concepts that you are learning in this chapter.

2. The current record pointer points to the first row of the query object in the server's memory.

3. Variables corresponding to the field names Location and ZipCode are created. The variable Location is assigned the value Cedar Falls and the variable ZipCode is assigned the value 50613. The statements inside the CFLOOP tags are executed next. The CFOUTPUT tags are processed, and the values of the variables Location and ZipCode are output as 50613 - Cedar Falls in the Web page.

4. The ColdFusion Server checks for more records.

5. The next record is activated as the current record.

6. The current record pointer moves to the second record.

7. The variable Location is assigned the value Cedar Falls, the variable ZipCode is assigned the value 50614, and 50614 - Cedar Falls is output in the Web page.

8. The ColdFusion Server checks for more records.

9. The next record is activated as the current record.

10. The current record pointer moves to the third record.

11. The variable Location is assigned the value Cedar Rapids, the variable ZipCode is assigned the value 52401, and 52401 - Cedar Rapids is output.

12. Processing continues in a similar manner until all records are processed. Once all the records are processed, processing continues below the /CFLOOP tag.

13. The rest of the document is output. The results appear in a list because of the embedded HTML tags <ul>, <li>, and </ul>.

Using a CFLOOP to Process a Subset of Records

Optionally, a QUERY loop can have two additional attributes named STARTROW and ENDROW with values startrow_value and endrow_value. All the records in the query object are numbered sequentially starting from 1 at the top. Processing starts with the record numbered startrow_value and continues until the record numbered endrow_value is processed. This allows you to restrict the output to a certain number of records in the record set or the query object. For example, you can use these attributes to display records in multiple pages consisting of ten records each.

The syntax for a QUERY loop with these additional attributes is as follows:

```
<cfloop query="query_name" startrow="startrow_value"
endrow="endrow_value">
Statements containing HTML and CFML that are to be exe-
cuted repeatedly with access to data from the query
</cfloop>
```

The following example (Example6-2.cfm) illustrates processing of a subset of data using a QUERY loop with the STARTROW and ENDROW attributes.

Code Example 6-2

```
<cfquery datasource="your_username" name="getLocations">
SELECT DISTINCT Location, ZipCode FROM Properties
</cfquery>
<html>
<head>
<title>Locations Example 2</title>
</head>
<body>
<h3> List of Zip Codes and Locations with Properties for
Sale</h3>
<ul>
<cfloop query="getLocations" startrow="16" endrow="18">
<li> <cfoutput>#ZipCode#</cfoutput> -
 <cfoutput>#Location#</cfoutput>
</cfloop>
</ul>
</body>
</html>
```

The code in Code Example 6-2 produces the output shown in Figure 6-10.

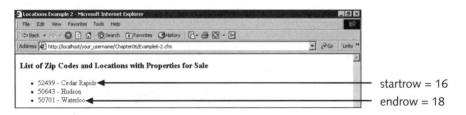

Figure 6-10   Web pages displayed by Example6-2.cfm

The ColdFusion Server creates a query object similar to the previous example. This query object is associated with the name getLocations. Then the rest of the template code is processed. The HTML is output as is and the CFML is processed. When the ColdFusion Server executes the CFLOOP statement, the query object with the name getLocations (the one previously created) is used to execute the statement. The numbers in the discussion below correspond to the circled numbers in Figure 6-11.

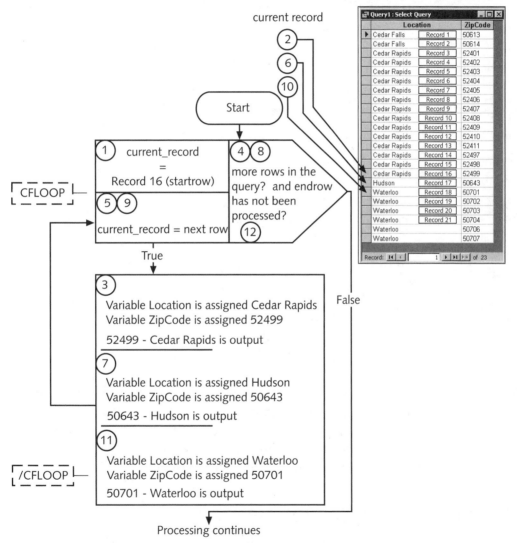

Figure 6-11   Processing a subset of records in a query object

1. The row numbered startrow is activated as the current record. (The 16th row is activated as the current record because the value of the attribute STARTROW is 16.)

2. The current record pointer points to the 16th row of the query object in the server's memory.

3. Variables corresponding to the field names Location and ZipCode are created. The variable Location is assigned the value Cedar Rapids and variable ZipCode is assigned the value 52499. The statements inside the CFLOOP tags are executed next. The CFOUTPUT tags are processed, and the values of variables ZipCode and Location are output as 52499 – Cedar Rapids.

4. The ColdFusion Server checks for more records. It also checks to determine if the endrow (row 18) has been processed.

5. The next record (record 17) is activated as the current record.

6. The current record pointer moves to the 17th record.

7. The variable Location is assigned the value Hudson, the variable ZipCode is assigned the value 50643, and 50643 – Hudson is output.

8. Endrow has not been processed yet, so processing in the loop continues.

9. The next record (record 18) is activated as the current record.

10. The current record pointer moves to the 18th record.

11. The variable Location is assigned the value Waterloo, the variable ZipCode is assigned the value 50701, and 50701 – Waterloo is output.

12. The ColdFusion Server checks for more records. It also checks to determine if endrow (record 18) has been processed. There are more records to process, but the endrow (record 18) has been processed. Therefore, execution of the statements inside the loop is stopped, and control is transferred to the statement below the closing CFLOOP tag.

13. The rest of the document is output. Similar to the Code Example 6-1, the results appear as a list because of the embedded HTML tags <ul>, <li>, and </ul>.

When the STARTROW and ENDROW are the same value, only one record is processed. This technique of setting the STARTROW and the ENDROW value the same is useful for extracting a single record from a query record set and is the basis for the following section on columnar report generation.

COLUMNAR REPORT GENERATION

When you extract data from a database table one row at a time, typically you extract data from all the fields (columns) and generate a report containing information from them. This process of extracting and displaying data is called **columnar report generation**.

Nikitha wants you to design ColdFusion templates that allow potential clients to browse through the properties available for sale one at a time. She wants you to display a picture of the property along with its price and location. Further, she wants you to display the rest of the information as sketched in Figure 6-12.

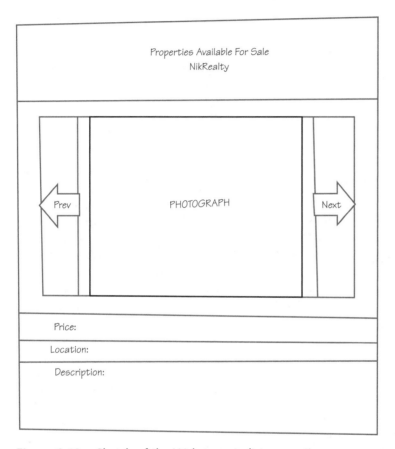

Figure 6-12 Sketch of the Web page to list properties

To extract data from a table and display it one record at a time:

1. Start ColdFusion Studio, and then open the file **detail.cfm** in the Chapter06 folder on your data disk.

2. Click the **Browse** tab on the Editor window to preview the Web page.

3. Click the **Edit** tab on the Editor window, and then examine the code that created this page.

Your first task is to extract data from the Properties table and display the first record in the format shown in Figure 6-12. You will modify this template to display other properties later in the chapter. To display the data, you will use a CFQUERY tag and a SELECT statement.

To prepare to use a CFQUERY tag to retrieve data:

1. With the insertion point on line 1, column 1, press the **Enter** key, press the **Up Arrow** key to move to the new line, type **<cfquery datasource= "your_username" name="getData">**, and then press **Enter**.

2. Type **SELECT * FROM Properties** to extract all the fields and all the records from the Properties table.

3. Press **Enter**, and then type **</cfquery>**. The CFQUERY now contains the SQL statement to select all records from the Properties table. You will add a CFLOOP to select only the first record.

4. Click line 10, column 1, type **<cfloop query="getData" startrow="1" endrow="1">**, and then press **Enter**. See Figure 6-13.

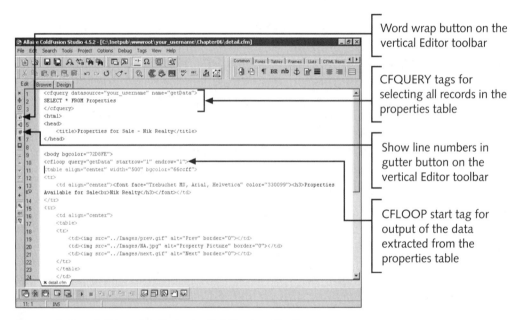

Word wrap button on the vertical Editor toolbar

CFQUERY tags for selecting all records in the properties table

Show line numbers in gutter button on the vertical Editor toolbar

CFLOOP start tag for output of the data extracted from the properties table

Figure 6-13   Editing detail.cfm in ColdFusion Studio

Depending on the status of the Word wrap feature, your line numbers might be different. If necessary, turn on the Word wrap feature by clicking the Word Wrap button on the vertical Editor toolbar, and then, if necessary, turn on the display of line numbers in the gutter by clicking the Show line numbers in gutter button on the vertical Editor toolbar. Use the gutter line numbers instead of the status bar to position the insertion point correctly in the steps.

This statement will design the QUERY loop for extracting data from the query object created by the CFQUERY tag. Notice that the values for the STARTROW and the

ENDROW attributes are both equal to 1, indicating that the loop will process only the first record, or the first property. When the ColdFusion Server executes this statement, it will create variables corresponding to the fields selected in the SELECT statement. Because all the fields in the properties table are selected in the SELECT statement, it will create variables named PropertyID, TypeOfHouse, YearBuilt, NumBedrooms, NumBathrooms, Area, Rooms, OtherFeatures, Price, Location, ZipCode, ImageFilename, and AgentID. Then, it will assign values from the fields in the first record of the Properties table to variables with the same names as the fields. It will assign the value of the PropertyID field in the first record (NIK4567) to variable PropertyID, the value of the TypeOfHouse field (Home) to variable TypeOfHouse, and so on. All the variables that are created and the values assigned to them are shown in Table 6-1.

Table 6-1   Data Extracted from the first Record

Variable	Value
PropertyID	NIK4567
TypeOfHouse	Home
YearBuilt	1953
NumBedrooms	3
NumBathrooms	1
Area	1300
Rooms	eat-in kitchen,great room,laundry room
OtherFeatures	hardwood floors,walk-in closet(s),wet bar
Price	$132,456.00
Location	Cedar Rapids
ZipCode	52498
ImageFilename	MVC-005E.JPG
AgentID	DCL

To use a CFQUERY tag to retrieve data:

1. Click line 39, column 1, type **</cfloop>** to close the QUERY loop, and then press the **Enter** key. Notice that the entire table is enclosed in the QUERY loop. You have to output the values extracted from the database table in the appropriate locations next.

2. On line 20, select **NA.jpg** and replace it with the following text: **<cfoutput> #ImageFilename#</cfoutput>**. This statement will output the property image filename for the property. Notice that you are using the appropriate path to the Images folder that contains these graphics on the data disk. Also, the value of this variable is the data in the field named ImageFilename. This CFOUTPUT statement will output the filename of the picture for the record selected by the query. For example, for the first record, the partial

HTML code generated would be <img src="../Images/MVC-005E.JPG" alt="Property Picture" border="0">. The browser would make an additional request to the Web server to serve the image file when it processes the IMG tag, and then it would display it after it receives the file.

3. On line 28, select _____, and type **<cfoutput>#DollarFormat(Price)# </cfoutput>**. When the ColdFusion Server executes this statement, it will format the value in the variable named Price for the current record as currency and output it. Remember that the first record is the current record because the values of attributes STARTROW and ENDROW are both equal to 1, as mentioned previously.

4. On line 32, select _____, and type **<cfoutput>#Location# - #ZipCode# </cfoutput>**. This statement will output the value in the Location variable, a space, a hyphen, a space, and then the value in the ZipCode variable for the current record.

5. Edit line 36 by outputting the appropriate variables as follows: **<cfoutput>**This **#TypeOfHouse#** was built in **#YearBuilt#** and has **#NumBedrooms#** bedroom(s), **#NumBathrooms#** bath(s), and is **#Area#** square feet. Rooms include: **#Rooms#**. Other features include: **#OtherFeatures#.</cfoutput>**

6. Save the file and then view it in your Web browser by opening **http://localhost/ your_username/Chapter06/detail.cfm**. See Figure 6-14.

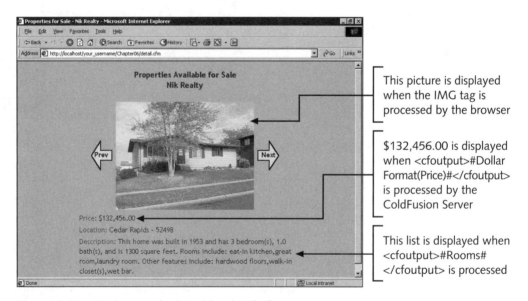

Figure 6-14   Web page displayed by detail.cfm

The template correctly selected the first record from the Properties table and displayed information from it using the CFOUTPUT tags. The Prev and Next arrows will eventually let the user browse other records selected by the query. You will add this capability later in the chapter.

Notice that the Rooms and OtherFeatures fields contain comma-separated value-lists with no spaces after the commas. To make the output correct grammatically, you need spaces after the commas. You can use the REPLACE string function to replace all occurrences of commas in those fields with a comma and a space.

To modify detail.cfm by using the REPLACE function:

1. Switch to ColdFusion Studio.

2. Select **#Rooms#** on line 36, and type **#Replace(Rooms,",",",** and then a space followed by **","ALL")#**. When the ColdFusion Server processes this function, it will replace ALL occurrences of commas in the value of variable Rooms with commas followed by spaces and display it.

3. Similarly select **#OtherFeatures#** on line 36, and type **#Replace(OtherFeatures,",",",** and then a space followed by **","ALL")#**. When the ColdFusion Server processes this function, it will replace ALL occurrences of commas in the value of variable OtherFeatures with commas followed by spaces and display it.

4. Save the file.

5. Switch to your Web browser and refresh the document. Notice that there are now spaces after the commas in the list of rooms and other features.

Now that you have output the first property successfully, you will modify the template to display other specific properties.

DISPLAYING SPECIFIC RECORDS

You can use the STARTROW and ENDROW values to select specific records from a table, as you will see next.

To change the rows selected by the template:

1. Switch to ColdFusion Studio, and then on line 10, change the value for the ENDROW attribute from 1 to **3**.

2. Save the file, and then refresh the document in your Web browser. Scroll down the page. You will see three property listings because the QUERY loop is executed three times and displays records 1, 2, and 3 on this single Web page. Three records are selected because the START ROW is 1 and the END ROW is 3.

3. Switch to ColdFusion Studio, and then on line 10, change the value of the STARTROW attribute from 1 to **3**.

4. Save the file, and then refresh the document in your Web browser. Notice that only the third property in the table is displayed this time and the values of both the STARTROW and the ENDROW attributes are equal to 3.

Essentially, the objective of this exercise is to reinforce the importance of the STARTROW and ENDROW attributes. To summarize, if you use the same value for the STARTROW and ENDROW attributes, only one record is displayed from the Properties table and the position of this record corresponds to the value of these attributes. If you want a simple way to control which property is displayed, you should use a variable (for example, displayRecordNumber) and use this variable to set the value of the STARTROW and ENDROW attributes. Next, you will modify the template to use a variable for controlling the display. To add a variable to control which property is displayed:

1. Switch to ColdFusion Studio, click line 1, column 1, press the **Enter** key, and then press the **Up Arrow** key to move to the new line.

2. Type **<cfset displayRecordNumber = 233>**. When the ColdFusion Server executes this statement, it will create a variable named displayRecordNumber and assign a value of 233 to it. This variable will be used as the value for the STARTROW and ENDROW attributes so that you can control which property is displayed by manipulating the value of this variable.

3. On line 11, select the value **3** for the STARTROW attribute, and then type **#displayRecordNumber#**. When the ColdFusion Server executes this statement, it will use the current value of the displayRecordNumber variable (233) as the value for the STARTROW attribute.

4. On the same line, replace the value 3 for the ENDROW attribute with **#displayRecordNumber#**. Similar to the STARTROW attribute, when the ColdFusion Server executes this statement, it will use the current value of the displayRecordNumber variable (233) as the value for the ENDROW attribute. Because the STARTROW and ENDROW attributes are both set to 233, the Server will display the 233rd record.

5. Save the file and refresh it in your Web browser. You are now displaying the 233rd property in the Properties table. See Figure 6-15.

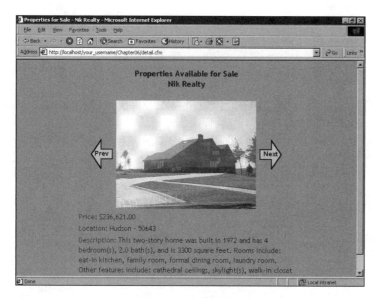

Figure 6-15   Displaying the 233rd property

You can display any property that you want without changing the CFML in the document by using a URL parameter. Therefore, it makes more sense to use a parameter on the URL to control which property is displayed rather than hard-coding the record number of the property to be displayed. In the following exercise, you will modify the detail.cfm template to use a URL parameter.

To add URL parameter processing to the template:

1. Switch to ColdFusion Studio, click line 1, column 1, press the **Enter** key, and then press the **Up Arrow** key to move to the new line.

2. Type **<cfparam name="URL.recNo" default="1">**. When the ColdFusion Server executes this statement, it checks to see whether there is a parameter on the URL named recNo. If there is a parameter with that name, no action is taken. If there is no parameter on the URL with that name, the Server creates a variable and assigns a value of 1 to it.

In Chapter 4, you learned about using the CFPARAM tag for assigning default values to form variables. The CFPARAM tag can be used for assigning default values to URL parameters too. When this document is opened in the browser without any URL parameter, the CFPARAM tag will create a variable named URL.recNo and assign it a value of 1. Essentially, opening this document without a URL parameter is the same as opening the document with ?recNo=1 appended to the document's URL.

3. On line 2, select **233**, and then type **URL.recNo**. When the ColdFusion Server executes this statement, it assigns the value of the URL parameter to the variable named displayRecordNumber. Remember that this variable sets the value of the STARTROW and ENDROW attributes in the QUERY loop to control which property is displayed.

4. Save the file, switch to your browser, select the URL in the Address text box, type **http://localhost/your_username/Chapter06/ detail.cfm?recNo=125**, and then press **Enter**. See Figure 6-16. You are viewing the 125th property in the Properties table. This record was selected by the parameter you added to the URL.

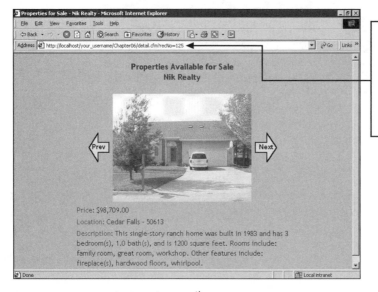

URL parameter recNo is assigned to variable displayRecordNumber and this variable is used as the value for the STARTROW and ENDROW attributes in the QUERY loop

Figure 6-16   Displaying the 125th property using a URL parameter

CREATING NAVIGATION OPTIONS

The detail.cfm template contains two pictures that produce the Prev and Next arrow buttons. When this page is completed, a user will click the Prev button to return to a previous property listing selected by the query. Clicking the Next button will show the next property listing selected by the query. You'll need to activate these buttons to provide them with the functionality to scroll through the records selected by the query. As you are passing the record number of the property to be displayed using the recNo URL parameter, all you need are links to the same document with appropriate record numbers for the next property and the previous property. In general, if you are viewing the displayRecordNumber property, the next property is displayRecordNumber + 1 and the previous property is displayRecordNumber - 1. For example, if you are viewing the 125th property, the next property is record number 126 and the previous property is record number 124.

To activate the navigation buttons:

1. Switch to ColdFusion Studio, if necessary, click at the end of line 2, and the press the **Enter** key to insert a new line.

2. Type **<cfset nextProperty = displayRecordNumber + 1>**, and then press **Enter**.

3. Type **<cfset previousProperty = displayRecordNumber – 1>**.

4. On line 23, select the entire IMG tag (**<img src="prev.gif" alt="Prev" border="0">**), as shown in Figure 6-17.

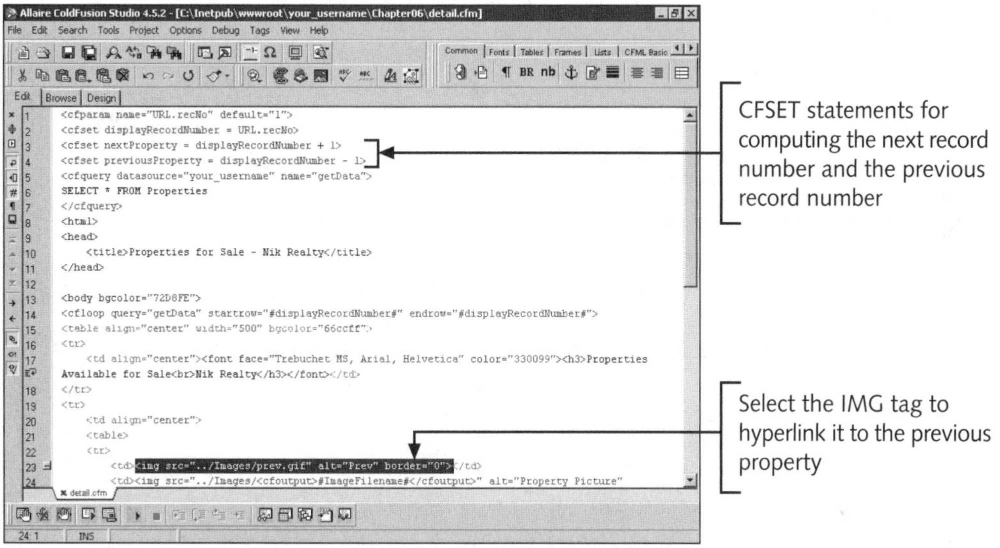

CFSET statements for computing the next record number and the previous record number

Select the IMG tag to hyperlink it to the previous property

Figure 6-17   Adding navigation capabilities to detail.cfm

5. Click the **Anchor** button on the Common tab on the QuickBar. The Anchor dialog box opens.

6. In the HREF text box, type **detail.cfm?recNo=<cfoutput> #previousProperty#</cfoutput>**, and then click the **OK** button. The Anchor dialog box closes. Notice that ColdFusion Studio has inserted anchor tags around the image. See Figure 6-18. You have created a hyperlink to the previous property in the properties table.

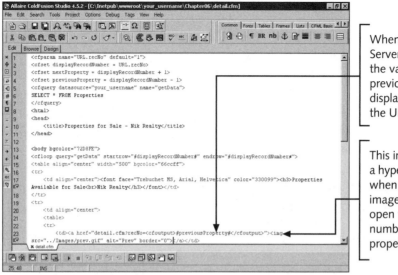

When the ColdFusion Server processes this tag, the value of variable previousProperty is displayed as the value of the URL parameter recNo

This image will appear as a hyperlink in the browser; when the user clicks the image, the template will open with the record number for the previous property

Figure 6-18 Anchor tags inserted around the Prev button image

7. Scroll down, if necessary, and on line 25, select the entire IMG tag, click the **Anchor** button on the QuickBar, type **detail.cfm?recNo=<cfoutput>#nextProperty#</cfoutput>** in the HREF text box, and then click the **OK** button. You have created a hyperlink to the next property in the Properties table.

8. Save the file, switch to your browser, and then click the **Refresh** or **Reload** button to reload the page.

9. Move the pointer over the **Next** button. Notice that the image is now a hyperlink and that the URL in the browser's status bar displays …recNo=126. The hyperlink that you created now uses the next record as its target. See Figure 6-19.

10. Move the pointer over the **Prev** button. It is also a hyperlink and the URL in the browser's status bar displays …recNo=124.

11. Click the **Next** button. The browser displays record number 126, as indicated by the URL in the Address text box. See Figure 6-20.

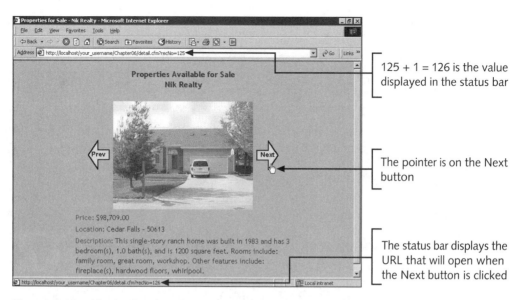

Figure 6-19   Navigation buttons are set up

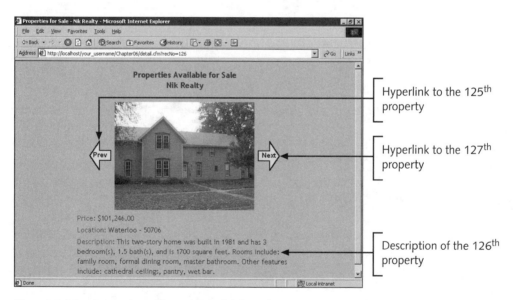

Figure 6-20   Record number 126 is displayed

12. Click the **Prev** button to return to the previous record (125).

13. Navigate through the list of properties and experiment with the template.

Finally, consider what would happen if the first property is displayed and a user clicks the Prev button. If the first property is displayed, the previous property's record number is computed as displayRecordNumber – 1, and the result would be zero. The server would be requesting a document with URL ...display.cfm?recNo=0. The ColdFusion Server would generate an error because the STARTROW attribute of the QUERY loop would be zero, which isn't a valid request. To design the template to prevent this error, you have to use a CFIF statement and display the previous image only when the variable named previousProperty has a value of greater than zero (GT 0).

Similarly, you have to think about what would happen if the last property is currently displayed and a user clicks the Next button. The STARTROW attribute would be greater than the number of records in the query object and the statements in the QUERY loop could not be executed, resulting in the display of a blank page. To fix this potential problem, you have to use a CFIF statement and display the Next button only when the value of the variable named nextProperty is less than the number of records in the query's record set (LE to the number of records in the record set). Obviously, the next question that comes up is how do you determine the number of records in a query object? When the ColdFusion Server executes the CFQUERY tag with the name query_name, it creates a variable named query_name.recordcount and sets its value to the number of records in the query object. You can use this variable in the CFIF statement for the Next button.

To selectively display the navigation buttons:

1. Switch to ColdFusion Studio, and then click line 23, column 13 (between the opening TD and A tags on the line that creates the Prev button).

2. Type **<cfif previousProperty GT 0>**.

3. Click between the closing A and TD tags on the same line, and then type **</cfif>**. See Figure 6-21. When the ColdFusion Server executes this CFIF statement, it displays the Prev button only if the value of the previousProperty variable is greater than zero.

4. Click between the opening TD and A tags on the line that outputs the Next button (line 25), and then type **<cfif nextProperty LE getData.recordcount>**.

5. Click between the closing A and TD tags on the same line, and then type **</cfif>**. See Figure 6-22. When the ColdFusion Server executes this CFIF statement, it displays the Next button only if the value of the nextProperty variable is less than or equal to the number of records in the query record set object.

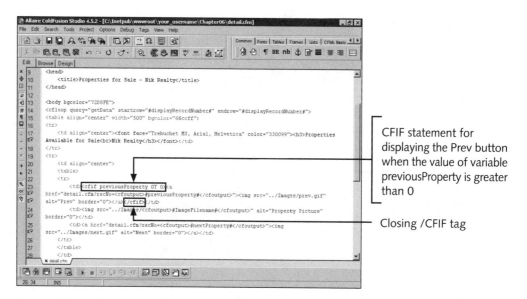

CFIF statement for displaying the Prev button when the value of variable previousProperty is greater than 0

Closing /CFIF tag

Figure 6-21   Controlling the display of the Prev button

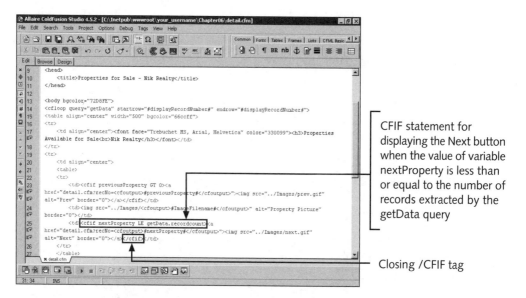

CFIF statement for displaying the Next button when the value of variable nextProperty is less than or equal to the number of records extracted by the getData query

Closing /CFIF tag

Figure 6-22   Controlling the display of the Next button

6. Save the file, switch to your browser, edit the URL in the Address text box to **http://localhost/your_username/Chapter06/detail.cfm?recNo=1**, and then press the **Enter** key. See Figure 6-23. The browser displays the first record. Notice that the Prev button is not displayed.

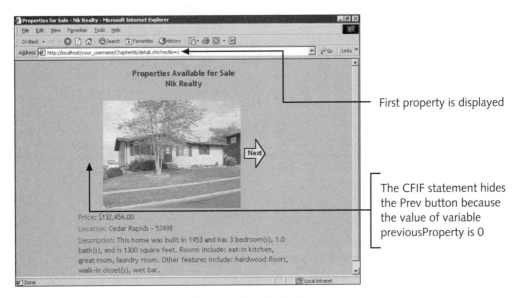

First property is displayed

The CFIF statement hides the Prev button because the value of variable previousProperty is 0

Figure 6-23 Record number 1 displayed in the browser

7. Click the **Next** button. See Figure 6-24. Notice that both buttons are displayed now.

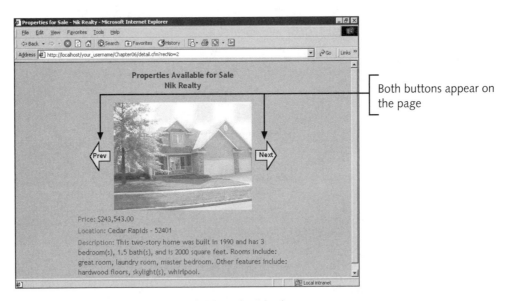

Both buttons appear on the page

Figure 6-24 Record number 2 displayed in the browser

8. Edit the URL in the Address text box so it reads **http://localhost/ your_username/Chapter06/detail.cfm?recNo=311**, and then press **Enter**. See Figure 6-25. Notice that the Next button is not displayed. This is

the last property in the table and the value of variable nextProperty is 312, which is not less than or equal to the value of the variable getData.record-count (311, or the number of records in the table).

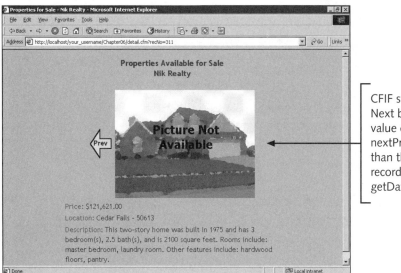

Figure 6-25   Record number 311 displayed in the browser

If your Web browser displays a blank page, it is because the table has only 310 records. Record number 311 should have been inserted as part of the projects in Chapter 5. If your browser displays a blank page, try the following URL: http://localhost/your_username/Chapter06/detail.cfm?recNo=310.

9. Close all programs.

Your template now displays one property at a time (one record at a time). You extracted all the fields from one record and displayed them in an attractive manner, and you also provided buttons to navigate through the record set. In other words, you generated a columnar report; all columns from a particular record are displayed. In the next section, you will learn about tabular report generation.

TABULAR REPORT GENERATION

When multiple rows (records) are extracted from database tables and displayed in the form of a table on one page, you are generating a tabular report. Typically, you have navigation buttons to advance to the next set of records or return to the previous set of records.

Nikitha is pleased with the detail.cfm ColdFusion template that allows potential clients to browse through the properties available for sale one at a time. However, she is concerned about clients having to spend a lot of time viewing all of the properties in the Properties table. She now wants you to design a template that displays four records at a time in the form of a table with just the price, location, and a thumbnail of the property (smaller version of the picture). The template should also allow potential clients to view a page with more property details if they want to. She has sketched her requirements, which appear in Figure 6-26. Your task now is to create this template.

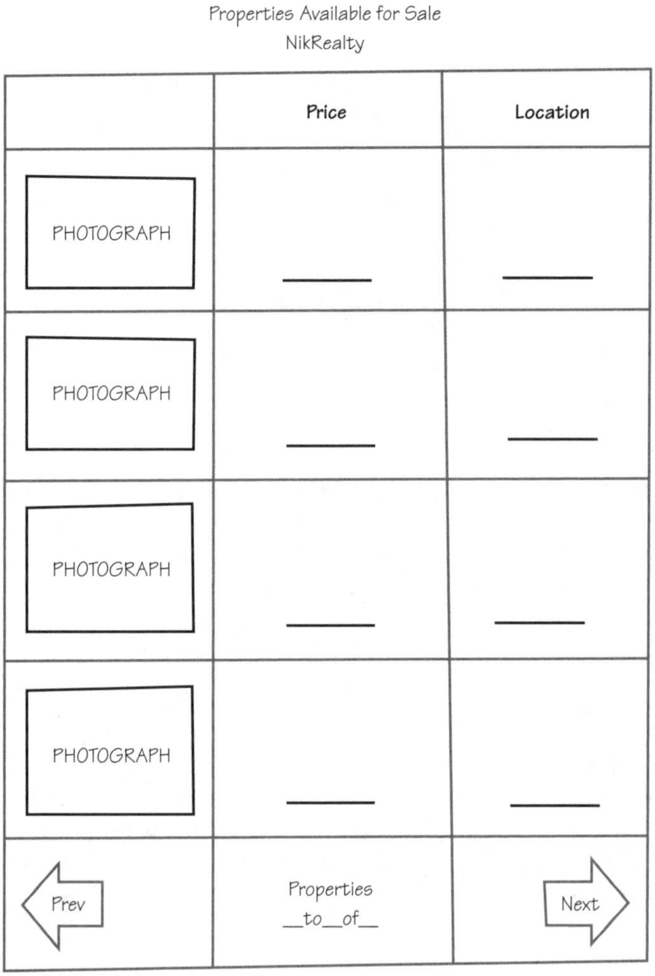

Figure 6-26   Sketch of the tabular report

To extract data from a table and display it as a tabular report:

    1. Start ColdFusion Studio, and then open **tabular.cfm** in the Chapter06 folder on the Data Disk.

2. Study the HTML code, and then view the document in your Web browser by typing **http://localhost/your_username/Chapter06/tabular.cfm** in its Address text box. See Figure 6-27. When you compare this with the requirements sketched in Figure 6-26, you will notice that this table has only one row, instead of four. Your task is to enclose the row of the table inside the QUERY loop that loops four times to display four rows in the table and at the same time to display each property's information in a single row.

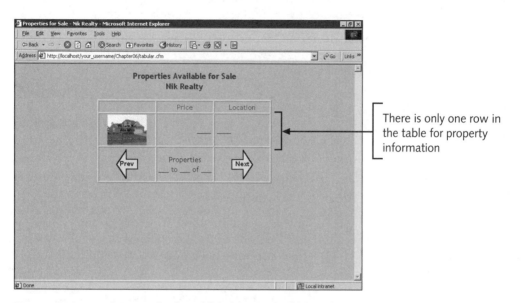

There is only one row in the table for property information

Figure 6-27   Web page displayed by the initial tabular.cfm

3. Switch to ColdFusion Studio, click line 1, column 1, press the **Enter** key, and then press the **Up Arrow** key to move to the new line.

4. Type **<cfparam name="URL.recNo" default="1">**, and then press **Enter**. When the ColdFusion Server executes this statement, it checks to see if there is a parameter named recNo on the URL. If there is one, no action is taken. If there is no parameter on the URL, it creates a variable named URL.recNo and assigns it a value of 1. In other words, if you type in the URL for this template without a parameter, it is the same as typing the URL with the parameter recNo=1.

5. Type **<cfset startrow=URL.recNo>**, and then press **Enter**. The record number that is passed on the URL is the number of the property that will be displayed first. When the ColdFusion Server executes this statement, it assigns the value of the URL parameter recNo to a newly created variable named startrow. You want to display a total of four properties at a time, so the end row will be startrow+3.

6. Type **<cfset endrow=startrow+3>**, and then press **Enter**. When the server executes this statement, it creates a variable named endrow and assigns it a value that is equal to the sum of the value of the startrow and the number 3. Your next task is to compute variables used for navigating from one set of records to another set. If records startrow to endrow are being displayed, the first record in the next set of records will be startrow+4.

7. Type **<cfset nextProperty=startrow+4>**, and then press **Enter**. The first record of the previous set of records will be the startrow-4.

8. Type **<cfset previousProperty=startrow-4>**, and then press **Enter**. Finally, you need to execute the SQL SELECT query to select all the records in the properties table.

9. Type **<cfquery datasource="your_username" name="getData">**, and then press **Enter**.

10. Type **SELECT * FROM Properties**, and then press **Enter**.

11. Type **</cfquery>** to close the QUERY loop.

12. Save the file and refresh it in your Web browser. Notice that the output is still the same. Fix any errors you may get.

You have initialized some variables and executed a CFQUERY tag. The output remains the same because you have not used any output statements. In the next set of steps, you will add the QUERY loop flow-control statement and output the values of fields at the appropriate points.

To output the values extracted using a CFQUERY and display them:

1. Switch to ColdFusion Studio, scroll down if necessary, and click at the beginning of line 23.

2. Hold down the **Shift** key and click at the beginning of line 29 to select lines 23 to 28, as shown in Figure 6-28.

3. If necessary, drag the left border of the QuickBar to the left to display the CFML Flow tab, and then click the **CFML Flow** tab.

4. Click the **CFLOOP** button on the CFML tab. The Tag Editor - CFLOOP dialog box opens.

5. Click the **Query Loop** tab in the CFLOOP dialog box to display the Query Loop options.

6. Type **getData** in the Query Name text box.

7. Type **#startrow#** in the Start Row text box.

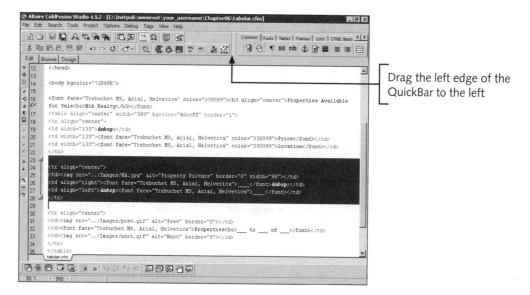

Figure 6-28   Selected text for repeated execution in a QUERY loop

8. Type **#endrow#** in the End Row text box. See Figure 6-29.

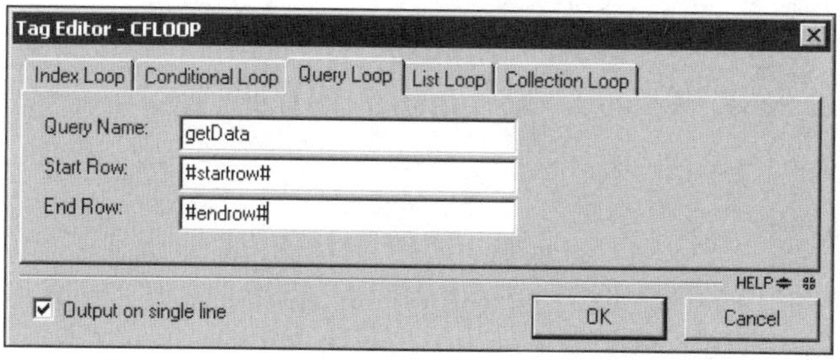

Figure 6-29   Tag Editor - CFLOOP dialog box

9. Make sure that the **Output on single line** check box is selected, and then click the **OK** button. Notice that ColdFusion Studio inserts a CFLOOP tag in your document, as shown in Figure 6-30. When the ColdFusion Server executes this statement, it displays the data from the query object starting with the startrow record and ending with the endrow record. Four rows will be displayed: startrow, startrow+1, startrow+2, and startrow+3. The variable endrow has a value equal to startrow+3.

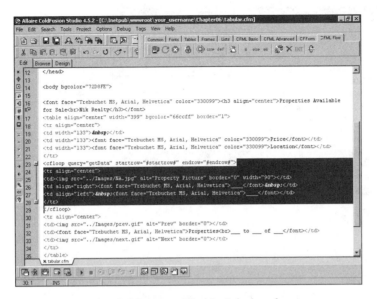

Figure 6-30 CFLOOP tags added to tabular.cfm

10. Click **Options** on the menu bar, click **Customize**, and then click the **Reset to Default**s button. Notice that the toolbars have been reset to the initial default state.

11. Click the **Close** button to close the Customize dialog box.

12. On line 25, select **NA.jpg**, and then type **<cfoutput>#ImageFilename#</cfoutput>**. (The status bar may show a different number depending on your monitor's resolution; as always, the line numbers here refer to the line numbers in the gutter.)

13. On line 26, select _____, and type **<cfoutput>#DollarFormat(Price)#</cfoutput>**.

14. On line 27, select _____, and type **<cfoutput>#Location#</cfoutput>**.

15. Scroll down if necessary, and on line 32, select ___ **to** ___ **of** ___, and then type **<cfoutput>#startrow# to #endrow# of #getData.record count#</cfoutput>**. See Figure 6-31.

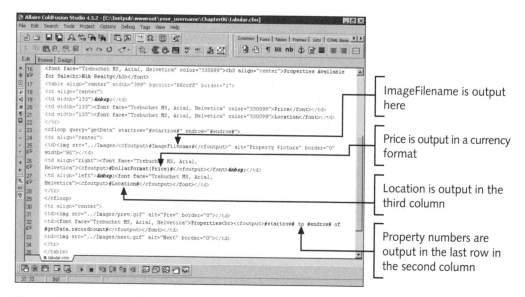

ImageFilename is output here

Price is output in a currency format

Location is output in the third column

Property numbers are output in the last row in the second column

Figure 6-31   tabular.cfm with CFOUTPUT tags

16. Save the document.

17. Switch to your Web browser and refresh http://localhost/your_username/Chapter06/tabular.cfm. See Figure 6-32.

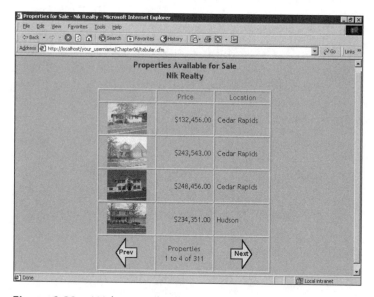

Figure 6-32   Web page displayed by tabular.cfm showing properties 1 to 4

18. Switch to ColdFusion Studio and study the code.

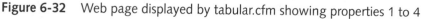

The Web browser sends a request to the Web server for tabular.cfm. The Web server recognizes that it is a ColdFusion document and transfers control to the ColdFusion Server. The ColdFusion Server executes the document. Because there is no parameter on the URL, the ColdFusion Server creates a variable named URL.recNo and assigns it a value of 1 when it processes the CFPARAM tag. Variables startrow, endrow, nextProperty, and previousProperty are created and assigned appropriate values. The CFQUERY is executed, and all the records from the properties table are extracted. Variable getData.recordcount is created and assigned a value equal to the number of records in the query. Then, the Server outputs the HTML code as is. When the QUERY loop is executed, the table row is output four times with the data from the first four records in the query object. Notice that the WIDTH attribute of the IMG tag is 90 pixels. When the Web browser processes this tag, it reduces the width of the property image to 90 pixels. The picture appears as a thumbnail. The price, location, and other variables are output at the appropriate locations to render the Web page as a tabular report. Your next task is to make the navigation buttons operational.

To activate the navigation buttons:

1. On line 31, select the entire IMG tag, click the **Common** tab on the QuickBar if necessary, and then click the **Anchor** button on the Common tab. The Anchor dialog box opens.

2. Type **tabular.cfm?recNo=<cfoutput>#previousProperty#</cfoutput>** in the HREF text box, and click the **OK** button. Notice that ColdFusion Studio inserts an anchor tag in the template. You are hyperlinking the Prev button to the same template with an appropriate starting record number computed on line 5.

3. On line 33, select the entire IMG tag, click the **Anchor** button, type **tabular.cfm?recNo=<cfoutput>#nextProperty#</cfoutput>** in the HREF text box, and then click the **OK** button. You are hyperlinking the Next button to the same template with an appropriate starting record number computed on line 4.

4. Similar to what you did in the columnar report, you have to hide the Prev button at the beginning of the records in the table and the hide the Next button at the end of records in the table. Use Figure 6-33 to add the CFIF statements to control the appearance of the Prev and Next buttons in the template.

5. Save the file, switch to your Web browser, and refresh tabular.cfm.

6. Navigate the record set by clicking the Next and Prev buttons. Notice that the record number in the URL changes in increments of four because you are viewing four records at a time.

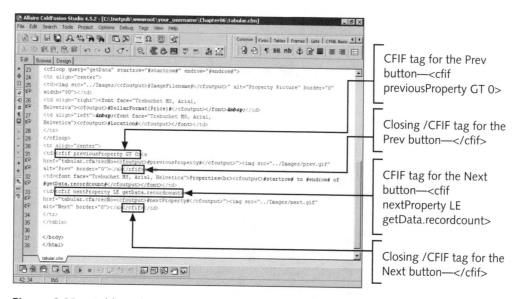

CFIF tag for the Prev button—<cfif previousProperty GT 0>

Closing /CFIF tag for the Prev button—</cfif>

CFIF tag for the Next button—<cfif nextProperty LE getData.recordcount>

Closing /CFIF tag for the Next button—</cfif>

Figure 6-33 Adding the CFIF statements to tabular.cfm

To decrease the download times for the images, typically you need two graphics for each property. One would be a regular picture like those on the Data Disk, and others would be smaller versions of these files or thumbnail graphics. To accommodate this, you would need another field in the properties table named thumbnailFilename.

Finally, your task is to make each of these smaller graphics a hyperlink so that clients can open a page with more details about the selected properties by clicking the picture.

To create picture hyperlinks:

1. Switch to ColdFusion Studio, and then on line 25 select the entire IMG tag for the property picture.

2. Click the **Anchor** button on the Common tab on the QuickBar. Similar to the recordcount property of a query, the currentrow property of query has a value equal to the position of the current record in the query object. You will hyperlink this image to the detail.cfm template with an appropriate value for the URL parameter. Remember that you created detail.cfm earlier in the chapter.

3. In the HREF text box, type **detail.cfm?recNo=<cfoutput>#getData.currentrow#</cfoutput>**, and then click the **OK** button. Notice that ColdFusion Studio inserts an anchor tag for you.

4. Save the file, type **http://localhost/your_username/Chapter06/tabular.cfm** in the Address text box, and then press the **Enter** key. Click the **Refresh** or **Reload** button. Point to the second picture. Notice that the

pointer changes to the hyperlink pointer, indicating that this picture is a hyperlink. See Figure 6-34.

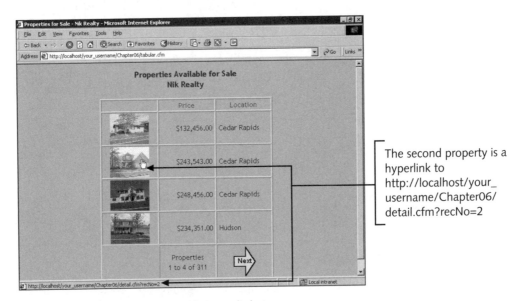

The second property is a hyperlink to http://localhost/your_username/Chapter06/detail.cfm?recNo=2

Figure 6-34 Tabular report with hyperlinks

5. Click the second picture. The detailed Web page for that property opens. See Figure 6-35.

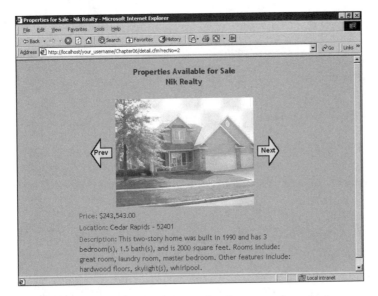

Figure 6-35 Detailed Web page for the second property

You have successfully extracted multiple records from a database table and displayed them in an HTML table. You have provided buttons to navigate from one set of records to another set. Further, each property picture is a hyperlink to a Web page that displays detailed information about that property. Such a capability whereby a user can look up detailed information from a summary is known as a **data drill-down** capability.

GROUP TOTALS REPORT GENERATION

In the previous two sections, you learned how to extract data from database tables and display one record at a time and how to display multiple records in a tabular format. In this section, you will display records in a tabular format and also compute statistics about groups of records to summarize data. This kind of reporting is useful for designing information systems that allow business managers to monitor organizational performance.

Nikitha wants you to design a few templates that will help her to better understand business trends so she can effectively manage her organization. She wants you to design a template that will be posted on the company's intranet—and not on the Internet for public use—that will display the total of all property prices, the average property price, the number of listed properties in a single location, and the properties with the maximum and minimum prices in each location where NikRealty is currently listing properties for sale. To provide Nikitha with this information, you will need to create a group totals report. Earlier, one of your project members created a template to display the required statistics for the properties listed in Hudson. You will need to change the template to dynamically create reports for all locations.

To create a group totals report:

1. Switch to ColdFusion Studio, and close all open files.

2. Open the file **statistics.cfm** in the Chapter06 folder on the Data Disk.

3. Click the **Browse** tab on the Editor window toolbar to preview the page. Notice that the page lists the number of properties currently for sale in Hudson, along with the sum, average, maximum, and minimum price for all properties listed in Hudson.

4. Click the **Edit** tab on the Editor window, and then carefully study the code that created this template. This template extracts data from the Properties table and displays it in an HTML table. The SQL SELECT statement uses a WHERE clause to select only those properties from the city of Hudson. The QUERY loop outputs the information in an HTML table. Notice that you are using only one set of CFOUTPUT tags for enclosing all the variables. Your task now is to display summary information for all the locations. Because locations may be added or deleted from the NikRealty sales area, and subsequently from the Properties table, you will need to query the database for all locations with properties listed.

5. Click line 1, column 1, press the **Enter** key, and then press the **Up Arrow** key to move the insertion point to the new line.

6. Type **<cfquery datasource="your_username" name="getLocations">**, and then press **Enter**.

7. Type **SELECT DISTINCT Location FROM Properties**, and then press **Enter**.

8. Type **</cfquery>** to close the query tag.

9. Click at the end of the BODY tag on line 9, and press **Enter**.

10. Type **<cfloop query="getLocations">**. You are designing a template with nested query loops. The outer loop will loop over all the locations, and the inner loop will display summary information for each location. Note that the inner loop will loop only once for each outer loop because there is only one record in the query object.

11. Click at the end of line 43 (which contains the closing CFLOOP tag for the inner loop), press **Enter**, and then type **</cfloop>** to close the outer query loop.

The next step is to use the variable named Location (in the inner loop), which is created when the ColdFusion Server executes the outer loop.

To output the Location in the outer loop and to use it in the inner query:

1. Select the word **Hudson** on line 12, and then type **<cfoutput>#Location#</cfoutput>**. When the ColdFusion Server executes this statement, it will display the value of the Location field in the current record as a heading for the table.

   Now you have to change the SQL in the inner loop to display summary information from the location in the current record.

2. On line 16, select the word **Hudson** in the WHERE clause, and then type **#Location#**. See Figure 6-36.

3. Save the file, and view http://localhost/your_username/Chapter06/statistics.cfm in your Web browser. See Figure 6-37.

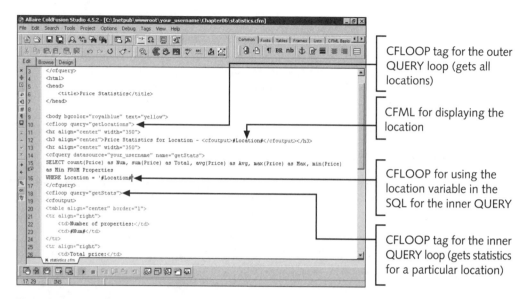

Figure 6-36   Editing statistics.cfm in ColdFusion Studio

CFLOOP tag for the outer QUERY loop (gets all locations)

CFML for displaying the location

CFLOOP for using the location variable in the SQL for the inner QUERY

CFLOOP tag for the inner QUERY loop (gets statistics for a particular location)

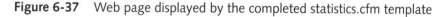

Figure 6-37   Web page displayed by the completed statistics.cfm template

Output generated by the inner loop when the outer loop processes the statements inside it the first time

Output generated by the inner loop when the outer loop processes the statements inside it the second time

The statistics.cfm template contains the following SQL statement:

```
SELECT count(Price) as Num, sum(Price) as Total, avg(Price
) as Avg, max(Price) as Max, min(Price) as Min FROM
Properties
WHERE Location = '#Location#'
```

6

When the ColdFusion Server executes this statement, the Server substitutes the value of the variable Location for #Location# and then it executes the SQL statement. This is a very powerful technique that allows you to create dynamic SQL statements. You are changing the SQL statement that is executed each time the outer QUERY loop is executed. This technique is also useful for building a capability of interactive data extraction into Web design.

INTERACTIVE DATA EXTRACTION

By using variables enclosed in pound signs in CFQUERY tags, you can dynamically change the SQL SELECT statements being executed. This allows you to extract data from databases based on user requests.

Based on the feedback received from some of NikRealty's clients, Nikitha has requested you to design a form that will narrow the number of properties displayed in the detail.cfm template. Clients have indicated that price, location, and number of bedrooms are very important criteria when they search for a new house. You have to design both the form as well as the form handler for this application.

To design the search criteria form by dynamically populating a select box:

1. Switch to ColdFusion Studio, if necessary, and close all open documents.

2. Open **searchForm.cfm** in the Chapter06 folder on the Data Disk.

3. Click the **Browse** tab on the Editor window to preview the page. This page lets a user enter a maximum amount for their home purchase and a minimum number of bedrooms. You'll add the information to collect data about the desired location next.

4. Click the **Edit** tab on the Editor window, and then carefully examine the code that created this template. This template contains a form with the ACTION attribute set to a form handler named processSearch.cfm, which you will create later. There are two text box input controls named maxPrice and minBedrooms, which collect the maximum price and the number of bedrooms desired by the client. The form also contains a submit button with the caption "Find Properties." Because you want to limit the locations to only those available in the Properties table, you will extract data from the database and populate a select box with all possible locations that are stored in the database.

5. Click line 1, column 1, and create a blank line. Move the insertion point to the new line, type **<cfquery datasource="your_username" name="getLocations">**, and then press the **Enter** key.

6. Type **SELECT DISTINCT Location FROM Properties**, and then press **Enter**.

7. Type **</cfquery>**. See Figure 6-38.

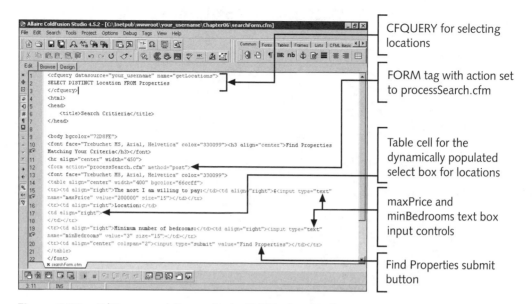

Figure 6-38   Editing searchForm.cfm in ColdFusion Studio

8. Click at the end of line 17, press **Enter**, type **<select name="Location">** **<cfloop query="getLocations"><cfoutput>**, and then press **Enter**.

9. Type **<option value="#Location#">#Location#**, and then press **Enter**.

10. Type **</cfoutput></cfloop></select>**.

11. Save the file and view it in your Web browser.

12. Click the **Location** list arrow. See Figure 6-39. You have extracted data from a database table and populated a select box. The SELECT statement used the DISTINCT operator and the Location field. The QUERY loop outputs options in the select box—one for each record in the query object. You can't submit the form yet, however, because there is no form handler.

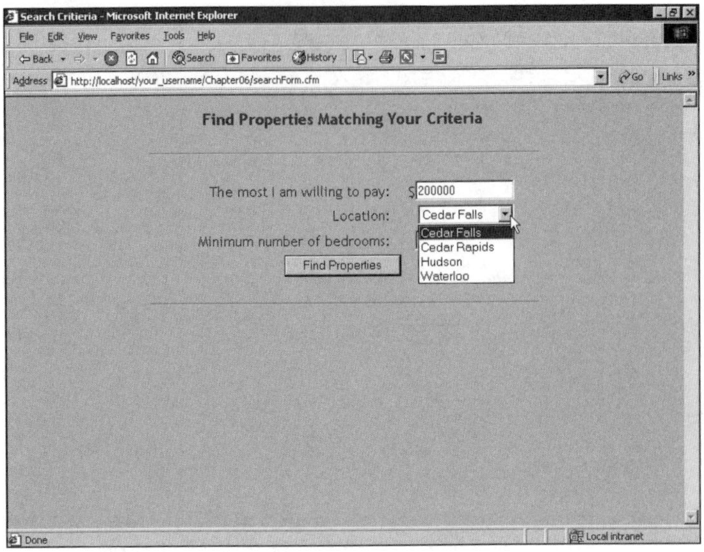

Figure 6-39   Web page displayed by searchForm.cfm

The next task is to design the form handler for this data. The form handler for this form is going to be very similar to the detail.cfm application. You will need to add a WHERE clause to the SQL SELECT statement that utilizes the data the user enters in the form. You need properties with prices lower than the value entered and located in the requested location with the minimum number of bedrooms specified. The WHERE clause for this situation is WHERE Price<=#maxPrice# AND Location="#Location#"AND NumBedrooms>=#minBedrooms#. You also have to keep in mind that there are navigation buttons for looking at the next property and the previous property, and you need to make the template extract data matching these criteria even when those buttons are clicked. You have to design the template to handle data posted by the form as well as be able to process data passed as URL parameters.

To design the form handler for dynamic extraction of data:

1. Switch to ColdFusion Studio, open the file **detail.cfm**, and then save it as **processSearch.cfm** in the Chapter06 folder on the Data Disk.

2. Click at the end of line 6 (which contains the SELECT statement), press the **spacebar**, and then type **WHERE Price<=#maxPrice# AND Location='#Location#' AND NumBedrooms>=#minBedrooms#**. See Figure 6-40. Notice that you did not type the "form." prefix for the form variables. Even though you have been using FORM.control_name as the format for accessing the data entered in form controls, the prefix FORM. is optional. Whenever a variable is used, the ColdFusion Server checks to see if there are any regular variables of that name. If there aren't any, it checks to see if there are any FORM variables or URL parameters of that name and

uses them if found. Similarly, the prefix URL. for accessing URL parameters is also optional. You have to use the prefixes whenever possible to avoid confusion for anybody reading your code. Here you are not using the prefixes because you are going to use form variables once in the SELECT statement and then you want to use URL parameters later on when the user clicks the navigation buttons. When the ColdFusion Server executes this statement, it substitutes the values entered by the user in the WHERE clause, and then the SQL SELECT statement extracts only those properties that match the criteria specified by the user. Ignore any warnings that appear.

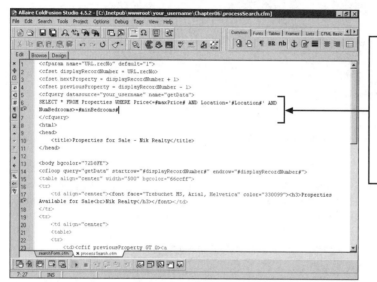

WHERE clause selects properties with prices less than or equal to the maximum requested price, the desired location, and the number of bedrooms greater than or equal to the requested minimum number of bedrooms

Figure 6-40   Revising the SELECT statement

3. Save the processSearch.cfm file.

4. Switch to your Web browser. Do not change the price or the number of bedrooms, select **Hudson** as the location, and then click the **Find Properties** button. See Figure 6-41. Notice that the first property is located in Hudson. Notice that the URL in the Address text box of your Web browser shows the name of the form handler, processSearch.cfm. Move the pointer over the Next button and notice that it is still linked to the detail.cfm file. If you click the Next button, the next property in the Properties table will be selected, instead of the next property located in Hudson. You need to change the links so that they point to the searchForm.cfm template and pass the user-entered criteria as URL parameters.

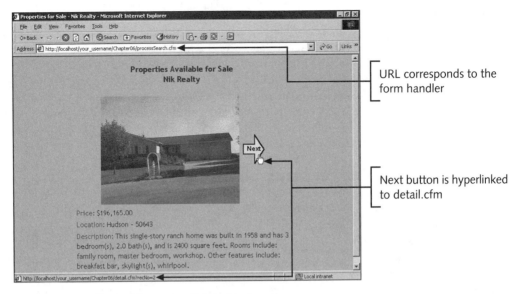

URL corresponds to the form handler

Next button is hyperlinked to detail.cfm

Figure 6-41   Output for properties in Hudson

5. Switch to ColdFusion Studio, and on line 23, change the value of the HREF attribute to **processSearch.cfm?recNo=<cfoutput>#previousProperty #&maxPrice=#maxPrice#&Location=#URLEncodedFormat(Location) #&minBedrooms=#minBedrooms#</cfoutput>**. See Figure 6-42.

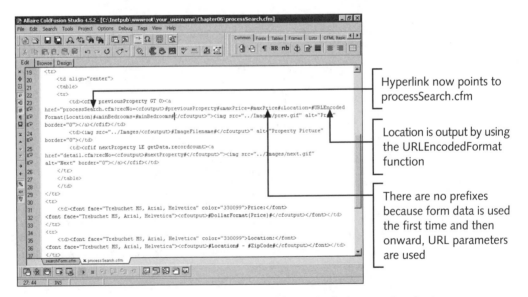

Hyperlink now points to processSearch.cfm

Location is output by using the URLEncodedFormat function

There are no prefixes because form data is used the first time and then onward, URL parameters are used

Figure 6-42   Code to navigate only properties that match the search criteria

This template needs the criteria that the user entered again when the user clicks the Next button. You are passing the values entered as URL parameters. The second time this template is executed, the SQL SELECT statement will process the variables that have been passed as parameters on the URL. This is the reason you did not use URL. prefix or FORM. prefix for these variables. The first time, they are the data the user entered directly in the form, and the second time around, it is the data passed on the URL. Notice that you are using the URLEncodedFormat function for the location variable, which allows for the possibility that there could be spaces in the Location and you need to encode it. It is a good practice to enclose all parameters passed on URLs in this fashion. You can save some typing by not using this function on parameters that are numbers.

6. On line 25, change the value of the HREF attribute to **processSearch.cfm?recNo=<cfoutput>#nextProperty#&maxPrice=#maxPrice#&Location=#URLEncodedFormat(Location)#&minBedrooms=#minBedrooms#</cfoutput>**.

7. Save the **processSearch.cfm** file, and browse the **searchForm.cfm** file again. Select **Hudson** as the location, do not change the price and bedroom default values, and then click the **Find Properties** button. Click the **Next** button until you see all seven properties that match your criteria. Notice the URL when navigating among the properties. You can also experiment by changing the price and number of bedroom values and then clicking the Find Properties button.

8. Close your browser and ColdFusion Studio.

This chapter is important because it ties together all the concepts that you learned in all previous chapters. You extracted data from databases and published it in the form of Web pages. You created columnar reports, tabular reports, and group-total reports. Further, you built interactive Web sites that respond to user requests and extract data.

CHAPTER SUMMARY

- Open Database Connectivity (ODBC) is a Microsoft standard for interfacing applications to databases. You use ColdFusion Administrator to setup ODBC data sources, which you can then access using ColdFusion.

- Extracting data from databases and publishing it on the Web is a two-part process. The CFQUERY tag is used for executing SQL SELECT statements to create query record set objects with data extracted from databases. A QUERY loop created using the CFLOOP tag is used for implementing a repetition flow-control structure to access and display data from all the records in the record set.

❐ When you present complete information (all or most fields) about an entity one record at a time, you are generating a columnar report. This report is useful for presenting all the details about a particular entity. Typically, navigation buttons are provided to navigate from one record to another.

❐ When you present partial information or all information about multiple records in the form of a table, you are generating a tabular report. Typically, navigation buttons are provided to navigate from one set of records to another.

❐ Group total reports are useful for designing management information systems. Tabular reports are presented along with summaries of critical data items.

❐ ColdFusion allows you to use variables enclosed in pound signs in CFQUERY tags with included SQL statements. This feature allows you to build interactive data extraction features in Web sites.

REVIEW QUESTIONS

1. What is ODBC? Describe its importance for building database-driven Web sites with ColdFusion.

2. Describe the two-step process for extracting data from databases and publishing it on a Web site.

3. What tags would you use to extract data from database tables in a ColdFusion template? How do these tags work? Where is the data stored after it is extracted?

4. What CFLOOP attributes are needed to design a QUERY loop? What is the significance of each attribute?

5. How would you display the total number of records in a query object named query_name?

6. What is a columnar report and how do you generate one?

7. How do you design a navigation mechanism for a columnar report?

8. How do you restrict navigation past the end of the records in a table? What is the name of the query variable needed to accomplish this? How do you restrict navigation past the beginning of records in a table?

9. What is a tabular report and how do you generate one?

10. What are the similarities and differences between the navigation design for tabular reports and columnar reports?

11. What is the name of the variable created prior to each execution of the statements inside a QUERY loop that identifies the number of the record being processed?

12. What is a data drill-down capability in information systems design?

13. How do you create a group totals report?

14. How would you build a capability for interactively extracting data from databases using ColdFusion?

15. A query named getBanks extracts columns BankID and BankName from a database table. Give the code for the QUERY loop to dynamically populate a select box named Bank. Use the BankName for the description and the BankID as the value for the options.

HANDS-ON PROJECTS

Project 1: Columnar Report Generation

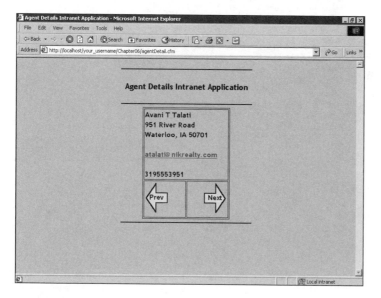

Nikitha has requested that your organization design an intranet application for displaying all details of agents, as shown in Figure 6-43. Your graphics department has designed a document named agentDetail.cfm using data for one of the agents. It is available on the Data Disk. Your task is to convert it into a database-driven Web page by implementing the following:

1. Examine the Agents table in the NikRealty database in Microsoft Access, and then design a CFQUERY tag for extracting information from it in ColdFusion Studio.

2. Design a columnar report, and display information from the database at the appropriate locations in the HTML table.

3. Build a navigation capability by hyperlinking the navigation buttons appropriately.

4. Prevent navigation beyond the data records by using appropriate CFIF statements for controlling the display of the navigation buttons.

5. Save the file using the same name (agentDetail.cfm), and test your application.

Figure 6-43

Project 2: Tabular Report Generation

NikRealty agents are very excited with the Agent Details Intranet Application that you created in Project 1. They find it to be a convenient way for sending e-mail to each other. They requested that your organization simplify the process of finding an agent by designing a Web page that lists all the agents' names, as shown in Figure 6-44. Your task is to design a tabular report by implementing the following:

1. Create a new template named **agentTabular.cfm**, and save it in the Chapter06 folder on the server.

2. Design CFQUERY tags to extract agent names from the Agents table.

3. Design a QUERY loop to output the data, as shown in Figure 6-44.

4. Implement a data drill-down capability. Display the ../Images/drill-down.gif graphic for each agent, and hyperlink it to the detailed information obtained by agentDetail.cfm for the particular agent.

5. Save the file with the above changes, and test your application.

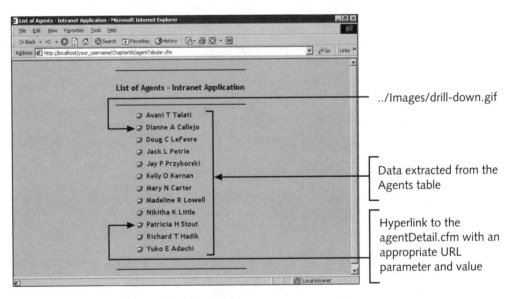

Figure 6-44

Project 3: Create a Group Totals Report

Create a group totals report, as shown in Figure 6-45. Nikitha wants to use this report to monitor the performance of her agents. Notice that the table's title has the full name of each agent in the Agents table of the Realtor database. The data in the table includes summary information like the number of properties listed by each agent, the total dollar amount of all listed properties, and the average, maximum, and minimum price of all listed properties for each agent below the heading that contains their name. When you are finished, save the template as **agentStatistics.cfm** in the Chapter06 folder on the server. Remember that you need two nested QUERY loops to design a group totals report. The outer QUERY loop loops over all the records in the Agents table, and the inner QUERY and its loop displays summary information from the Properties table.

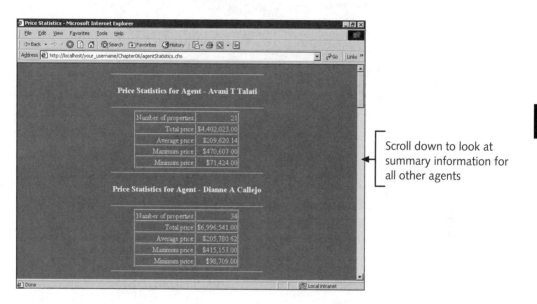

Scroll down to look at summary information for all other agents

Figure 6-45

Project 4: Display the Listing Agents Information with a Property's Information

1. Open **detail.cfm** in ColdFusion Studio, and save it as **Ch6Pr4.cfm**.

2. Click Search and then Replace, and replace all occurrences of detail.cfm in the template with Ch6Pr4.cfm.

3. Add CFML to display the name of the agent along with an appropriate caption at the bottom of the property description, as shown in Figure 6-46. First you need an appropriate query to extract the data, and then you need another QUERY loop to display the data.

4. Hyperlink the name of the agent to Ch6Pr4b.cfm with a URL parameter named AgentID and an appropriate value for it. Open agentDetail.cfm in ColdFusion Studio. Save it as **Ch6Pr4b.cfm**.

5. Modify the template so that the agent's detailed information is displayed to the customer, as shown in Figure 6-47, when they click the agent name hyperlink. (*Hint*: You have to use the value of the URL parameter in the SQL SELECT statement to extract the listing agent's information.)

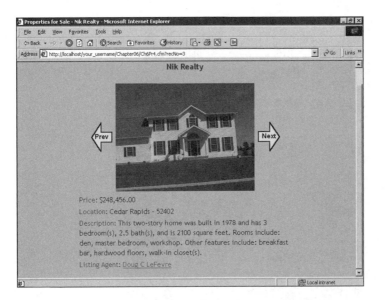

Figure 6-46

Figure 6-47

Project 5: Generate a Tabular Report with Data from Multiple Tables

Design a template named listOfRequests.cfm that displays all the customer requests for showings, as shown in Figure 6-48. The date, time, and property IDs are available in the Requests table. The agent's last name is available in the Agents table, and the client name is available in the Customers table. You need a SQL SELECT statement in a CFQUERY tag to join all the tables in the NikRealty database (Requests, Customers, Properties, and Agents). Further, the records have to be in alphabetical order by the agent's last name and then in reverse chronological order by the date and time for the showings. The QUERY loop should output the data in a neatly formatted HTML table, as shown in Figure 6-48.

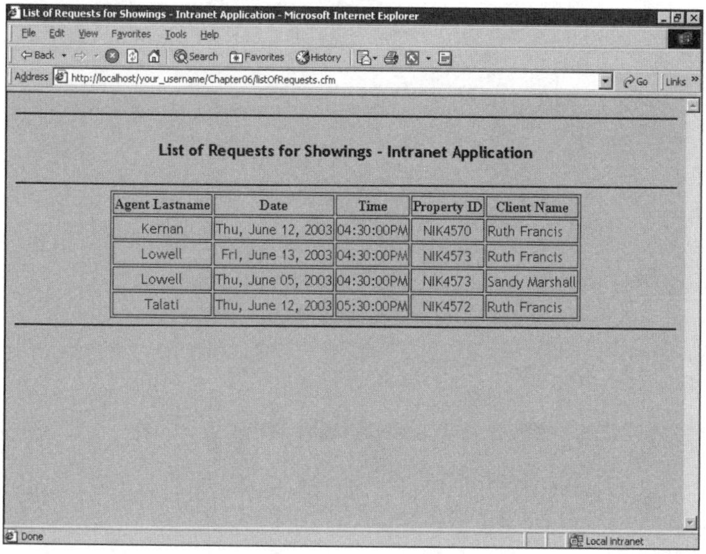
List of Requests for Showings - Intranet Application - Microsoft Internet Explorer
File Edit View Favorites Tools Help
Back Search Favorites History
Address http://localhost/your_username/Chapter06/listOfRequests.cfm
Go Links
List of Requests for Showings - Intranet Application
Agent Lastname | Date | Time | Property ID | Client Name
Kernan | Thu, June 12, 2003 | 04:30:00PM | NIK4570 | Ruth Francis
Lowell | Fri, June 13, 2003 | 04:30:00PM | NIK4573 | Ruth Francis
Lowell | Thu, June 05, 2003 | 04:30:00PM | NIK4573 | Sandy Marshall
Talati | Thu, June 12, 2003 | 05:30:00PM | NIK4572 | Ruth Francis
Done
Local intranet

Figure 6-48

Project 6: Add Additional Search Criteria

1. Open **searchForm.cfm** using ColdFusion Studio. Save it as **searchForm2.cfm**.
2. Change the action attribute of the form to processSearch2.cfm.
3. Open **processSearch.cfm**, and save it as **processSearch2.cfm**.
4. Search and replace all occurrences of processSearch.cfm with processSearch2.cfm.
5. Add other search criteria to the form in searchForm2.cfm: Minimum price (textbox named minPrice) and maximum age (textbox named minYearBuilt) of the house, as shown in Figure 6-49.
6. Modify processSearch2.cfm so that it takes into account these additional criteria and displays the properties found.
7. Modify the hyperlinks in the navigation buttons to incorporate these additional criteria, as shown in Figure 6-50.

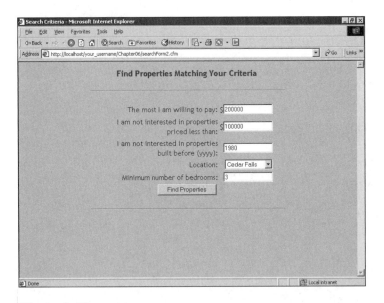

Figure 6-49

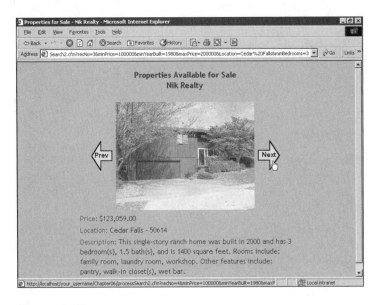

Figure 6-50

CASE PROJECTS

1. Create an ODBC connection to HardwareStore.mdb on your Data Disk named your_username_store. Examine the database in Microsoft Access. Your task is to design a data drill-down storefront application to this database. Design a template named displayCategories.cfm that displays a list of all the product categories from the Categories table as a bulleted list. When the user clicks any category, all the products in that category should be displayed as a bulleted list.

2. Design a columnar report (productDetail.cfm) to display information about all products in the hardware store. Provide navigation buttons. Design a tabular report (productTabular.cfm) displaying 10 products at a time, and provide links to detailed descriptions in the columnar report.

3. Design an intranet application for the hardware store. The management wants you to create a list of all the customer names and the total amount of all their product selections next to the customer names. The amount for each product is its price * the quantity. The total amount is the sum of the amounts for all the products selected by customer.

6

DATA MAINTENANCE WITH COLDFUSION

In this chapter, you will:

♦ Maintain databases using ColdFusion

♦ Use the ColdFusion tags CFINSERT, CFUPDATE, and CFTRANSACTION

♦ Design ColdFusion templates for inserting data using SQL INSERT statements

♦ Update data using SQL UPDATE statements

♦ Design form handlers for inserting, updating, and deleting data

♦ Create tables by using ColdFusion

♦ Learn about and process database transactions

In the previous chapter, you extracted data from databases and built a dynamic Web site. For the NikRealty Web site, the data in the database is the most important part of the site—the Web pages would be useless without it. Because the data in the database is so important, you must have a way to update existing data and add and delete data from the database. In this chapter, you will learn how to maintain data in databases using ColdFusion and HTML forms. In particular, you will use an HTML form to insert user-entered data and update and delete data in databases. You will also learn how to manipulate data in a database and process multiple database operations, or transactions.

Inserting Data

One reason you insert data into databases in dynamic database-driven Web sites is so that users can view current content. Consider the *Autobytel.com* Web site that you saw in Chapter 1. Periodically, the Web developers for Autobytel must insert new data about pre-owned vehicles available for sale. If customers want to use the "My Garage" feature to track service to a particular vehicle, they must sign up for the service. When they sign up, their customer information is inserted into the database. If a Web site allows for personalization, user preferences have to be inserted into a database as well. A financial information site that allows users to maintain their portfolios will have server-side programming that inserts user data into a database. The online store that Crayola manages allows employees to insert new products into the databases.

For tasks such as adding new products, you can design programs in the database system that allow users to enter data. For example, you could have a system designed in Microsoft Access or Visual Basic for entering data into the database. Or, you can design HTML forms and ColdFusion templates to insert data. For some applications, such as those collecting customer preferences via the Web, you can use HTML forms and ColdFusion templates. The primary advantages of using HTML forms and ColdFusion templates for inserting data are similar to the advantages of using Web-based technologies in general—ease of use and accessibility. Many employees can maintain databases by using a Web browser and a computer connected to the Internet. You don't need sophisticated software or complex network environments.

In Chapter 4, you inserted data using the Table Datasheet View in Access and also by using SQL commands. In this section, you will insert data using ColdFusion and CFML. You can insert data into databases using the CFINSERT tag or the CFQUERY tag. Although the CFINSERT tag is easy to use, you cannot use it in all situations. The CFQUERY tag allows you to execute SQL INSERT statements. It is a bit more complicated to use than the CFINSERT tag, but it can handle all situations.

Inserting Data with CFINSERT

Inserting data with CFINSERT usually requires the creation of two pages: a page with an HTML form to collect the data to insert and a form handler with the CFINSERT tag to actually insert the data. When designing the HTML form for use with the form handler containing the CFINSERT tag, you must use form field names that are identical to the field names in the table into which you are inserting data. The CFINSERT tag has the following syntax:

```
<CFINSERT
    DATASOURCE="datasource_name"
    TABLENAME="table_name"
    FORMFIELDS="formfield1, formfield2..."
    >
```

As mentioned previously, the CFINSERT tag usually is part of a form handler routine. When the ColdFusion Server executes the CFINSERT tag, data entered in the HTML form is inserted into the corresponding (and identically named) fields in the table named *table_name* in the database pointed to by the ODBC data source named *datasource_name*. The optional FORMFIELDS parameter is a comma-delimited list of form fields that you want to insert into the table. If the form has more fields than the list has, only the fields in the list are inserted. If you want to insert all the form fields, you can omit the FORMFIELDS parameter. If the form field names and table field names do not match, an error is generated. The same rules apply for inserting data using the CFINSERT tag as for using the SQL INSERT statement. Each new record that you insert must contain a unique primary key value. If you attempt to insert a new record without a primary key field value, or a new record with a duplicate primary key value, the server will return an error and reject the insertion. When the primary key of the table is an autonumber (counter) field, you should not include a form field that corresponds to the primary key in the FORMFIELDS attribute. The database automatically computes the new value of the primary key field for autonumber (counter) field types when new records are inserted.

7

Nikitha is pleased with the database-driven Web site that you created for her. She is excited about its capabilities and the ease of use with which prospective clients can examine the properties available for sale. Her next task is for you to finish creating a site administration tool (called site admin tool for short) that will allow her and other agents to use a Web browser to insert information about new properties available for sale. The site admin tool will also let agents change a property's description, delete a property from the database, and process the sale of a property. All of these functions will ensure that the database is current and accurate.

Before creating the form handler to insert properties, you will examine the existing partial system created by other members on your project.

To examine the partial system for inserting properties:

1. Start your Web browser, type **http://localhost/your_username/ Chapter07/Version1/admin.cfm** in the Address text box of your browser, and then press the **Enter** key to load this page from the server. See Figure 7-1.

   The preliminary Site Admin Tool page contains a simple menu with four items. The first item is a hyperlink that opens a page where agents can insert a new property into the database. The second item is a hyperlink that opens a page where agents can change an existing property's description. The third item is a hyperlink that opens a page where agents can delete a property from the database. The last item is a hyperlink that opens the page for initiating the database changes that are needed to process a property that has been sold. You will learn about changing, deleting, and processing records later in this chapter.

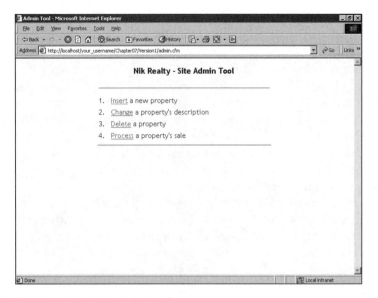

Figure 7-1   Site Admin Tool page

    2. Click **Insert**. The first page in the process for inserting a property opens. See Figure 7-2.

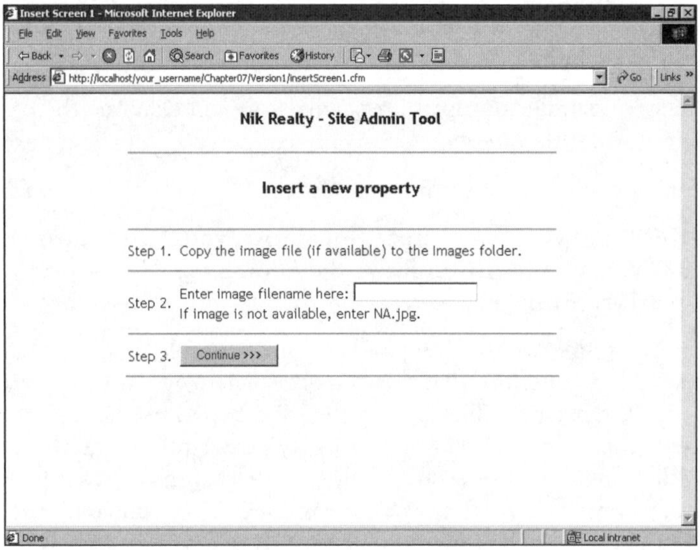

Figure 7-2   Insert Screen 1 page

This page contains an HTML form that provides the necessary steps for inserting a new property. Notice that the name of the document you are currently browsing is insertScreen1.cfm and that it is located in a subfolder named Version1 in the Chapter07 folder. When an agent encounters this page, she will follow the instructions in the page to copy the property's image file to the Images folder on the server. Then the agent will enter the image's filename in the text box and click the Continue button.

3. Start ColdFusion Studio, and open the **insertScreen1.cfm** file in the Version1 folder on the server. Examine the code in the page so you understand how it works. You will notice that the form has the METHOD attribute set to POST and the ACTION parameter set to insertScreen2.cfm, which is the form handler. The name of the text box that an agent uses to enter the property's image file is imageFilename.

4. Using Windows Explorer or FTP software, copy the file **MVC-205E.JPG** from the Chapter07 folder to the Images folder on the server. You are doing what an agent would do to insert a property into the database.

5. Switch to the Web browser, type **MVC-205E.JPG** in the text box for entering the image filename, and then click the **Continue** button. The second screen in the process for inserting a property opens, as shown in Figure 7-3.

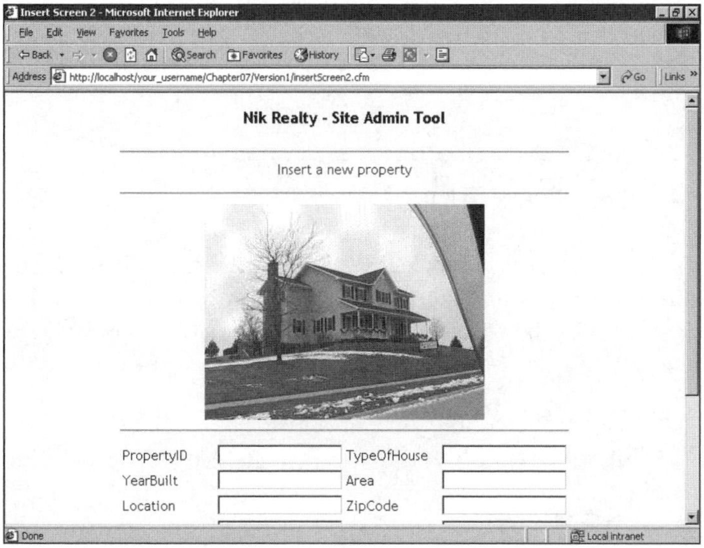

Figure 7-3   Insert Screen 2 page

The name of the document that you are currently browsing is insertScreen2.cfm. This file is the form handler for insertScreen1.cfm. The image filename that you specified in insertScreen1.cfm, MVC-205E.JPG, appears in the page. The next task in the process of inserting a record is to enter the correct values in the text boxes to describe the new property. The captions for these text boxes are identical to the field names in the Properties table in the Realtor database.

6. Switch to ColdFusion Studio, open the **insertScreen2.cfm** file in the Version1 folder, and then carefully examine the code in this form handler. You will notice that this form uses a form handler named insertScreen3.cfm. The image is displayed using the CFOUTPUT tags with the user-entered value in the imageFilename text box in the insertScreen1.cfm page.

7. Switch to the Web browser, and then, if necessary, scroll the page so you can see the ImageFilename text box. Notice that the value you entered in the previous form, MVC-205E.JPG, appears in this text box. An agent would use the text boxes in this form to enter information about the new property and then click the Continue button.

8. Click the **Continue** button without entering any data. The Web browser opens an Object Not Found error page, as shown in Figure 7-4.

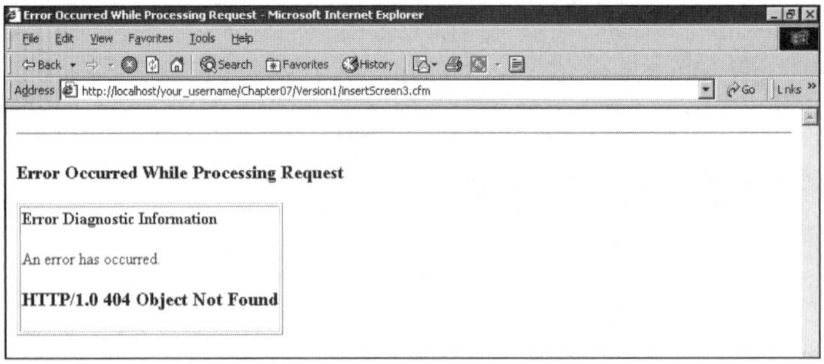

Figure 7-4   Object Not Found page

This error occurs because you have not yet created the form handler named insertScreen3.cfm on the server. Your next task is to create this ColdFusion template, which will insert the data entered in the form into the Properties table and display a confirmation message so the agent will know that the insertion process was completed successfully.

To create the form handler to process the insertion:

1. Switch to ColdFusion Studio, and then click the **New** button on the Standard toolbar.

2. On line 5, change the current title of the document ("Untitled") to **Insert Screen 3**.

3. On line 2, type **<cfinsert**, and then press the **Enter** key.

4. Type **datasource="your_username"** on line 3, and then press **Enter**.

5. Type **tablename="Properties"** on line 4, and then press **Enter**.

6. On line 5, type **formfields="PropertyID, TypeOfHouse, YearBuilt, NumBedrooms, NumBathrooms, Area, Rooms, OtherFeatures, Price, Location, ZipCode, ImageFilename, AgentID"**, and then press **Enter**.

7. Type **>** on line 6.

8. On line 13, type the following confirmation message in the body of the document: **Data inserted successfully. Click <a href="admin.cfm"> here</a> to return to the Site Admin Tool.**

9. Save the file as **insertScreen3.cfm** in the Version1 subfolder of the Chapter07 folder on the Data Disk, and switch to your Web browser.

10. Click the **Back** button on your Web browser, and then enter the following information in the form. Use the Tab key to move between fields.

    Property ID: **NIK4880**
    TypeOfHouse: **two-story home**
    YearBuilt: **1992**
    Area: **3200**
    Location: **Hudson**
    ZipCode: **50643**
    Price: **285000.00**
    NumBedrooms: **4**
    NumBathrooms: **3.5**
    Rooms: **den,family room,laundry room,master bathroom,master bedroom,workshop**
    OtherFeatures: **central vacuum system,fireplace(s),hardwood floors**
    ImageFilename: **MVC-205E.JPG** (this value will already be entered)
    AgentID: **MRL**

11. Click the **Continue** button. All the data entered in the form is posted to the Web server. The ColdFusion form handler gets the data from the Web server. The ColdFusion Server executes the CFINSERT statement. All the data in the form is processed, and the data in the form fields specified in the FORMFIELDS parameter of the CFINSERT tag is inserted as a new record into the Properties table. A confirmation message is displayed, as shown in Figure 7-5. You have successfully designed a ColdFusion form handler with a CFINSERT tag that inserts user-entered data from an HTML form into an Access database.

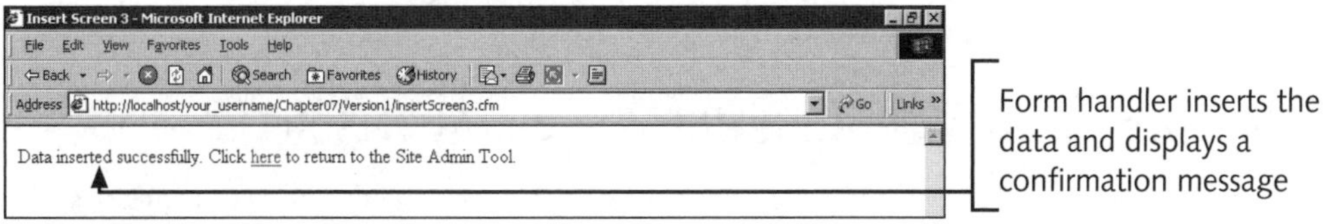

Figure 7-5   Insert Screen 3 page

12. Start Microsoft Access and open **C:\Inetpub\wwwroot\your_username\ Databases\Realtor.mdb**. If necessary, click **Tables** on the Objects bar. Double-click the **Properties** table to open it in Datasheet view. Scroll down

to the bottom and notice that a new record has been inserted and it has the data entered in the form. See Figure 7-6.

PropertyID	TypeOfHouse	YearBuilt	NumBedrooms	NumBathrooms	Area	Rooms
NIK4865	two-story home	1976	3	2	2100	eat-in kitchen,formal dinin
NIK4866	split-level home	1973	4	2.5	2800	den,eat-in kitchen,great r
NIK4867	two-story home	1970	4	2.5	3500	den,eat-in kitchen,formal
NIK4868	two-story home	1995	6	4	4800	eat-in kitchen,family roon
NIK4869	two-story home	1994	4	2	3100	eat-in kitchen,formal dinin
NIK4870	single-story ranch home	1982	3	1.5	1600	eat-in kitchen,formal dinin
NIK4871	single-story ranch home	1971	3	2.5	2200	den,laundry room,recreat
NIK4872	two-story home	1971	3	1.5	1400	family room,formal dining
NIK4873	two-story home	1993	3	2.5	2200	family room,formal dining
NIK4874	split-level home	1967	4	2	2900	den,family room,laundry
NIK4875	two-story home	1996	6	4	4900	eat-in kitchen,family roon
NIK4876	two-story home	1965	3	2	2200	den,recreation room,work
NIK4878	two-story home	1975	3	2.5	2100	master bedroom,laundry
NIK4880	two-story home	1992	4	3.5	3200	den,family room,laundry
*		0	0	0	0	

Record: 1 of 312

New record has been inserted into the Properties table in the Realtor.mdb database file

Figure 7-6   Properties table in the Realtor database

13. Close Microsoft Access.

The primary advantage of using a CFINSERT tag is its ease of use. The page that you created was easy to design and use, but it does have several potential disadvantages. First, using a text box to enter the PropertyID is cumbersome because an agent will need to examine the database to identify the next available PropertyID value in sequence. A better approach would be to generate the PropertyID automatically. Second, entering an AgentID could cause errors if an agent types the wrong ID. Using the agent's last name would be a less error-prone approach. Using these suggestions, you can design a second version of the Site Admin Tool. Appropriate PropertyID and AgentID values have to be extracted from the database by using queries. Then the INSERT statement will enter these values along with the user-entered data in the other form fields to actually insert the record. Therefore, because all the data needed to be inserted is not going to be in the HTML form, you have decided to use the CFQUERY tag and a SQL INSERT statement to insert the property information.

Inserting Data with CFQUERY and SQL INSERT

As you learned in Chapter 5, the syntax for a SQL INSERT statement is as follows:

```
INSERT INTO tablename (fieldname1, fieldname2…) VALUES
(value1, value2…)
```

When you execute the INSERT command in a database that supports SQL, the database will insert a record into the table named *tablename. Value1* would be inserted into the field named *fieldname1*; *value2* would be inserted into the field named *fieldname2*, and so on. You must enter the values *value1, value2…* based on the their data types. In Access, you must enclose strings in single quotation marks and dates in pound signs. You can enter numbers directly without any delimiters.

Similar to using the CFQUERY tag for executing a SQL SELECT statement (see Chapter 6), you can execute a SQL INSERT statement using the ColdFusion Server by enclosing it in a CFQUERY tag with the following syntax:

```
<cfquery datasource="datasource_name">
INSERT statement
</cfquery>
```

When the ColdFusion Server executes this statement, it executes the INSERT statement against the database pointed to by the ODBC connection with the *datasource_name*.

If needed, you may enclose variables in pound signs in the CFQUERY tag. When you do that, the ColdFusion Server substitutes values for variables enclosed in pound signs prior to executing the SQL statement. You will create a form handler for inserting a property using the SQL INSERT statement in the Version2 subfolder of the Chapter07 folder. Files in the Version2 folder provide functionality similar to files in the Version1 folder. In the Version1 folder, you are using CFML tags for inserting and updating data, and in the Version2 folder, you are using SQL statements for inserting and updating data with the CFQUERY tag. Obviously, you'll just need one of these approaches when you are working on a real project. By the end of this chapter, you should be able to figure out an appropriate approach depending on the situation.

To preview version 2 of the Site Admin Tool:

1. Using your Web browser, open the page **http://localhost/your_username/ Chapter07/Version2/admin.cfm**. This page is similar to the one in the Version1 folder, except this page uses a different background color, and the hyperlinks for items 3 and 4 are not activated.

2. Click the **Insert** hyperlink.

3. Using Windows Explorer or FTP software, copy the file **MVC-201E.JPG** from the Chapter07 folder to the Images folder on the server. You are doing what an agent would do for inserting a property into the database.

4. Type **MVC-201E.JPG** in the text box, and then click the **Continue** button. The Web browser opens the insertScreen2.cfm page, as shown in Figure 7-7.

7

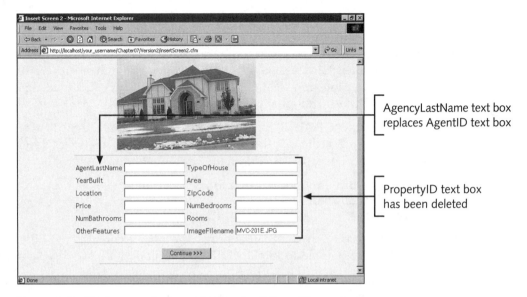

Figure 7-7   Web page displayed by Version2/insertScreen2.cfm

Similarly to the first version of this page that you used, the property's picture is displayed in the form along with text boxes for collecting data about the property. There are two primary differences between this form and the previous one. This form does not contain a text box for the PropertyID, and it includes a new text box with the label "AgentLastName" instead of the former text box with the label "AgentID." Because the CFINSERT tag only inserts form fields and you need to insert other data here, you will not be able to use a CFINSERT tag. Your task now is to create the insertScreen3.cfm file for handling the form data and inserting a record using the SQL INSERT statement. To identify the PropertyID and the AgentID to insert in a new record, you will need to query the Realtor database prior to inserting the data.

To create the new form handler and select the PropertyID:

1. Switch to ColdFusion Studio, and click the **New** button on the Standard toolbar.

2. On line 5, change the title "Untitled" to **Insert Screen 3**.

3. Your first task is to get a new PropertyID for the record. Recollect that property IDs start with the three letters NIK and are followed by four digits. The value for the next available PropertyID is one more than the highest PropertyID value in the table. You can execute a SQL SELECT statement using a CFQUERY tag to determine the highest PropertyID.

4. On line 1, in column 1, press the **Enter** key, and then press the **Up Arrow** key to go back to the new line.

5. Type **<cfquery datasource="your_username" name="getKey">**, and then press **Enter**.

6. On line 2, in column 1, type **SELECT Max(Right(PropertyID,4)) + 1 AS newPropertyID FROM Properties**, and then press **Enter**. The SQL Right function works exactly like the ColdFusion Right function. It extracts four characters from the right of the PropertyID. The Max function computes the maximum value for the number extracted by using the Right function. You are adding 1 to this maximum value to figure out the new propertyID to use.

7. On line 3, in column 1, type **</cfquery>**, and then press **Enter**.

There are two ways to access the value of the newPropertyID from this query object. One way, as seen in Chapter 6, is to use a query loop and set the value of a variable to the value of the field. A simpler way is to use the query_name.fieldname syntax for accessing the value. Similar to the query_name.recordcount variable that the ColdFusion Server creates when it executes a query, the Server also creates variables in the format query_name.fieldname having values corresponding to the values in the current record retrieved by the query. In this case, it is easier to use this syntax because you are interested in extracting only one value from the current record. You are adding 1 to the four digits to the right of the property ID extracted using the RIGHT function and will concatenate it with "NIK" to generate the new property ID.

Your second task is to extract the AgentID corresponding to the last name of the agent. You have to design a query for this task, as well. The name of the text box for the Agent's last name in the HTML form is AgentLastName. In the form handler (insertScreen3.cfm), you can access the data entered in the AgentLastName text box by using a variable named FORM.AgentLastName. If you are designing a SQL SELECT statement to look up the ID of the person with the user-entered last name, you have to be aware that lowercase and uppercase letters are different in SQL. You can use the LIKE operator to perform a case-insensitive comparison.

 Review the concepts of forms and form handlers in Chapter 4, if necessary.

To select the AgentID using the user-entered AgentLastName:

1. On line 4, in column 1, type **<cfquery datasource="your_username" name="getAgentID">**, and then press the **Enter** key.

2. On line 5, in column 1, type **SELECT AgentID FROM Agents WHERE LastName LIKE '#FORM.AgentLastName#'**, and then press **Enter**.

3. On line 6, in column 1, type **</cfquery>**, and then press **Enter**.

You have to account for the possibility that there may not be an agent in the database with the user-entered last name. To process an unknown last name, you will use a CFIF tag and test whether the number of records extracted by the SELECT statement is zero. If it is true, then you need to send a message back to the user and stop processing the template.

4. On line 7, in column 1, type **<cfif getAgentID.recordcount EQ 0>**, then press **Enter**.

5. On line 8, in column 1, type **Error: There is no agent in the database with the last name you entered**, then press **Enter**.

6. On line 9, in column 1, type **<cfabort>**, then press **Enter**. The CFABORT tag will cause the Server to stop processing the page if the user-entered last name does not exist in the database.

7. On line 10, in column 1, type **</cfif>**, then press **Enter**.

The next task is to enter the SQL INSERT statement and the CFQUERY tag.

To add the INSERT statement and CFQUERY tag to the form handler:

1. On line 11, in column 1, type the following CFQUERY statement for inserting a new property. Press **Enter** at the end of lines 1, 2, 5, and 12.

```
<cfquery datasource="your_username">
INSERT INTO Properties
(PropertyID,TypeOfHouse,YearBuilt,NumBedrooms,
NumBathrooms,Area,Rooms,OtherFeatures,Price,Location,
ZipCode,ImageFilename,AgentID)
VALUES
('NIK#INT(getKey.newPropertyID)#','#FORM.TypeOfHouse#',
#FORM.YearBuilt#,#FORM.NumBedrooms#,
#FORM.NumBathrooms#,#FORM.Area#,'#FORM.Rooms#',
'#FORM.OtherFeatures#',#FORM.Price#,'#FORM.Location#',
'#FORM.ZipCode#','#FORM.ImageFilename#',
'#getAgentID.AgentID#')
</cfquery>
```

Notice that most of the data being used in the INSERT statement is from the form. The PropertyID and the AgentID fields are populated with the data extracted from the respective queries. You are using the query_name.field-name syntax for extracting the field value from the current record for the values of PropertyID and AgentID fields.

2. Insert the cursor below the BODY tag, and type **Data inserted successfully. The PropertyID for the new property is <cfoutput>NIK#INT(getKey.newPropertyID)#</cfoutput>. Click <a href="admin.cfm">here</a> to return to the Site Admin Tool.** You are using the INT function to format the value as a number without a decimal part. (Be sure to type the code on one line.)

3. Save the file as **insertScreen3.cfm** in the Version2 subfolder in the Chapter07 folder.

4. Switch to the Web browser, and enter the following data into the form:

AgentLastName: **Petrie**
TypeOfHouse: **two-story home**
YearBuilt: **1997**
Area: **4000**
Location: **Hudson**
ZipCode: **50643**
Price: **425000.00**
NumBedrooms: **4**
NumBathrooms: **4**
Rooms: **den,family room,laundry room,master bathroom,master bedroom,workshop**
OtherFeatures: **central vacuum system,fireplace(s),hardwood floors**
ImageFilename: **MVC-201E.JPG** (this value has been entered already)

5. Click the **Continue** button. A new record is inserted into the Properties table. The PropertyID for the new property is NIK4881. The confirmation page (insertScreen3.cfm) opens in the browser, as shown in Figure 7-8. Similarly to what you did in the previous exercise, you can use Microsoft Access to verify whether a record has been inserted.

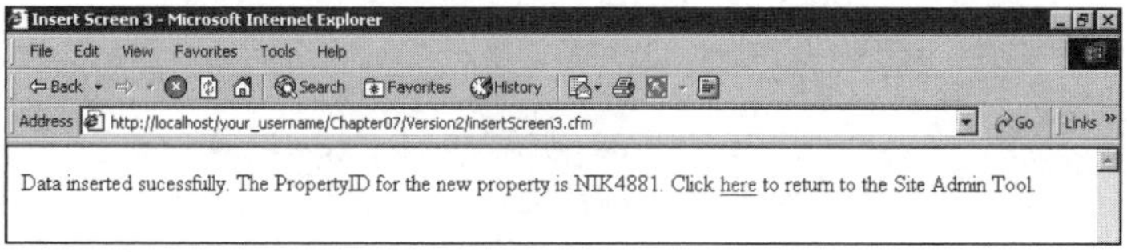

Figure 7-8   Confirmation message displayed by Version2/insertScreen3.cfm

You have successfully inserted a new property into the Realtor database using the CFQUERY tags and the SQL INSERT statement.

UPDATING DATA

In a database-driven Web site, you must provide options for changing and deleting data in addition to providing options for inserting data. In ColdFusion, you can update data in two ways. The easiest way is to use the CFUPDATE tag when there is an exact match between the fields in an HTML form and the table that needs to be updated. The second method is to use a CFQUERY tag and the SQL UPDATE statement. This method is more flexible and can be used in all situations.

Updating Data with CFUPDATE

Updating data with a CFUPDATE tag usually requires two pages. The first page contains an HTML form and the second page is a form handler containing the CFUPDATE tag.

When designing the HTML form for use with the CFUPDATE tag, you have to use names for the form fields that are identical to the field names in the table where data is to be updated. Also, you have to make sure that there is a form field corresponding to the primary key in the table that should be updated. The CFUPDATE tag updates the record with a matching value of this field. The CFUPDATE tag has the following syntax:

```
<CFUPDATE
    DATASOURCE="datasource_name"
    TABLENAME="table_name"
    FORMFIELDS="formfield1, formfield2..."
    >
```

When you are updating data, be sure that the correct record is being updated. When the ColdFusion Server executes the form handler with a CFUPDATE tag, it examines the FORMFIELDS parameter. The primary key should be a part of the FORMFIELDS parameter. The ColdFusion Server updates the record with a primary key matching the contents of the primary key form field. All the other fields' data is overwritten with the contents of the identically named form fields in the form. The Server leaves the data unchanged in any fields in that table that are not part of the FORMFIELDS parameter. For example, the following CFUPDATE tag performs the same action as the SQL statement that appears below it:

```
<cfupdate datasource="your_username" tablename="Properties
" formfields="PropertyID, Price">

UPDATE Properties SET Price = #FORM.Price# WHERE
PropertyID = '#FORM.PropertyID#'
```

Essentially, the Server constructs the WHERE clause of the SQL UPDATE statement by using the primary key field(s) and uses the other fields in the SET part.

Nikitha wants to change the Site Admin Tool so agents can change the prices of properties and other property descriptions to maintain the Web site. You will use a form that is similar to the one used for inserting data for this purpose. You will use a CFUPDATE statement in the form handler for updating the database with user-entered data from the form. You will work with the files in the Version1 subfolder for this exercise.

To preview the Change a property's description screens:

1. Switch to your Web browser, if necessary, and then open the location **http://localhost/ your_username/Chapter07/Version1/admin.cfm**.

   The second item is a hyperlink that opens a page for changing an existing property's description.

2. Click **Change**. The first page in the process for changing a property's description opens. See Figure 7-9.

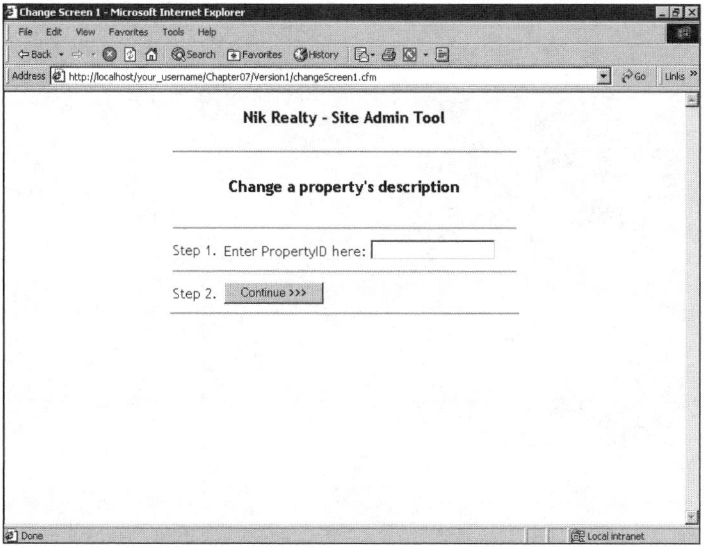

Figure 7-9   Web page displayed by Version1/changeScreen1.cfm

As shown in Figure 7-9, the first screen in the process for changing a property is an HTML form containing a text box for entering the primary key (PropertyID) value. Notice that the name of the document you are currently browsing is changeScreen1.cfm, and it is located in the Version1 folder.

3. Switch to ColdFusion Studio, close all open files, and then open the **changeScreen2.cfm** file in the Version1 folder on the server.

4. On line 3, change the value of the DATASOURCE attribute to your username.

5. Save the file.

6. Switch to your Web browser.

7. Click in the text box, type **NIK4881**, and then click the **Continue** button. See Figure 7-10.

Figure 7-10 shows the second screen in the process for changing a property. This page uses an HTML form that contains the data for the requested PropertyID from the Properties table. (You entered this record in the previous section.) Notice that the name of the document you are currently browsing is changeScreen2.cfm, and it is located in the Version1 folder.

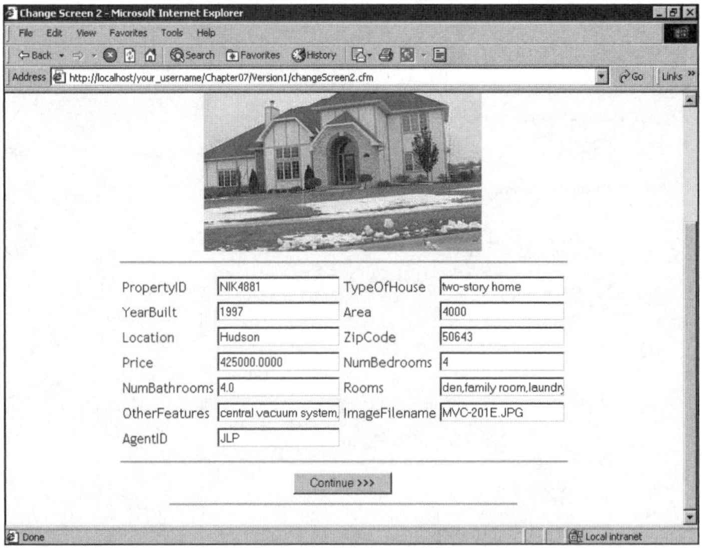

Figure 7-10   Web page displayed by Version1/changeScreen2.cfm

Examine the form handler template. The program design follows a general procedure for creating an update form. First, data from the requested record is extracted from the database using the primary key (PropertyID) and displayed in the form. If there is no matching record for the requested PropertyID, then an error message is displayed and the processing is aborted. If a matching PropertyID is found, a query loop outputs the data in the form's fields. To update the displayed data, the user would make required changes in the text boxes and then click the Continue button. Notice that the form handler is named changeScreen3.cfm—your next task is to design this form handler. This form handler will use the CFUPDATE tag and make modifications to the data. Because the change process is very similar to the form handler for the insert process (insertScreen3.cfm), you will copy the insertScreen3.cfm file in the Version1 folder and then modify it to create the form handler for the change screen.

To change data using CFUPDATE:

1. In ColdFusion Studio, open the file **insertScreen3.cfm** in the Version1 folder, and then use the Save As command on the File menu to save it as **changeScreen3.cfm** in the same folder.

2. On line 2, change cfinsert to **cfupdate**.

3. Change the title of the document from Insert Screen 3 to **Change Screen 3**.

4. On line 13, in the confirmation message, change inserted to **changed**.

5. Save the file. You have now created a form handler for updating data.

6. Switch to the Web browser, change the price of the property from 425000.00 to **399000.00**, and then click the **Continue** button. A confirmation page opens and indicates that the data was successfully changed.

7. Click the **here** hyperlink to return to the Site Admin Tool page.

8. Click **Change** to pick the second item on the menu.

9. Click in the text box, type **NIK4881**, and then click the **Continue** button. The price is 399000.00, indicating that you successfully modified the data for this PropertyID.

Similar to CFINSERT, the primary advantage of using a CFUPDATE tag is that it is easy to code. However, just like with CFINSERT, you can enhance a user's experience with the form and ensure data accuracy by making a few improvements. The first problem with the HTML form is that the PropertyID is displayed in a text box. If a user changes the PropertyID value, the user might update the wrong record. The PropertyID field should be a part of the form, so users can use it to identify the current record, but at the same time you must prevent users from being able to change the PropertyID value. You can use a hidden field to make the PropertyID a part of the form and prevent users from changing it. You can display the PropertyID as plain text so users know which property they are updating. The second problem with the HTML form is that agents must once again use AgentID numbers instead of last names, which could potentially cause errors.

In Version 2 of the admin tool you will implement these changes. If these changes are made, then you will not be able to use a CFUPDATE tag and you have to use the SQL UPDATE statement enclosed in CFQUERY tags.

Updating Data with CFQUERY and SQL UPDATE

You learned in Chapter 5 that the syntax for a SQL UPDATE statement is as follows:

```
UPDATE tablename
SET fieldname1 = value1, fieldname2 = value2 …
[WHERE condition]
```

When you execute the UPDATE command in a database system that supports SQL, it will update one or more records in the table named *tablename* where the *condition* is true. For these records, *value1* would be the new value of the field named *fieldname1*; *value2* would be the new value of the field named *fieldname2*, and so on. Just like when using the INSERT command, you must delimit the values *value1, value2…* correctly, based on their data types. You can execute a SQL UPDATE statement using the ColdFusion Server by enclosing it in a CFQUERY tag with the following syntax:

```
<cfquery datasource="datasource_name">
SQL UPDATE statement
</cfquery>
```

When the ColdFusion Server executes a CFQUERY statement, it executes the SQL UPDATE statement against the database pointed to by the ODBC connection with the *datasource_name*.

Similarly to what you did in the previous section, you can use variables in the CFQUERY tag enclosed in pound signs to substitute their values prior to executing the SQL statement. You will be working with files in the Version2 subfolder of the Chapter07 folder.

To preview the version 2 change screens:

1. Open **changeScreen2.cfm** in the Version2 subfolder in the Chapter 07 folder in ColdFusion Studio.

2. Change the value of the DATASOURCE attribute to your username on line 3.

3. Save the file.

4. Use your Web browser to open the location **http://localhost/ your_username/Chapter07/Version2/admin.cfm**.

   The second menu item is a hyperlink to the first screen in the process of updating a new property.

5. Click the **Change** hyperlink.

6. Type **NIK4585** in the text box, and then click the **Continue** button. The Web browser displays the changeScreen2.cfm document.

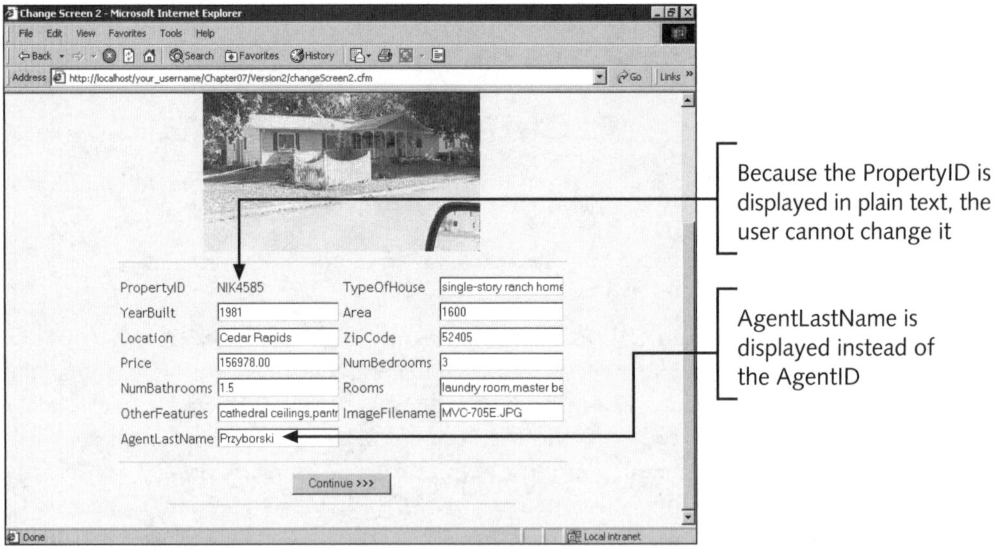

Figure 7-11   Web page displayed by Version2/changeScreen2.cfm

Similarly to the first version, a picture of the property appears with an HTML form containing the property's description. There are two primary differences between this form and the previous one. In this form, the PropertyID text box has been eliminated and only the PropertyID value appears in the form, so users cannot change it. In addition, the listing agent's last name appears in a new AgentLastName text box instead of the agent's AgentID number. Because the AgentLastName replaced the AgentID, you will not be able to use a CFUPDATE tag to change this field. You have to query the database and extract the AgentID that matches the AgentLast Name entered and then update the AgentID field to the extracted AgentID value. Because this is not a form field, you will have to use a SQL UPDATE statement with the value from the query. Your task now is to create the changeScreen3.cfm file for handling the form data and updating a record using a SQL UPDATE statement.

To update records using CFQUERY and SQL UPDATE:

1. Switch to ColdFusion Studio, and study the code in changeScreen2.cfm in the Version 2 Subfolder. You will notice that the query for extracting the data uses a join of the Properties and Agents tables based on the AgentID field. This join allows you to extract the agent's last name from the Agents table and to display it in the AgentLastName text box in the form. On line 47, #PropertyID# displays the PropertyID as plain text. On line 62, a hidden field named PropertyID posts the value of the PropertyID to the form handler for use in the update. The hidden field allows you to pass the PropertyID value to the form without giving the user an opportunity to change the primary key value.

2. Switch to your Web browser, click **View** on the menu bar, and then click **Source**. Your Web browser displays the source code for the document. If necessary, maximize the window. See Figure 7-12.

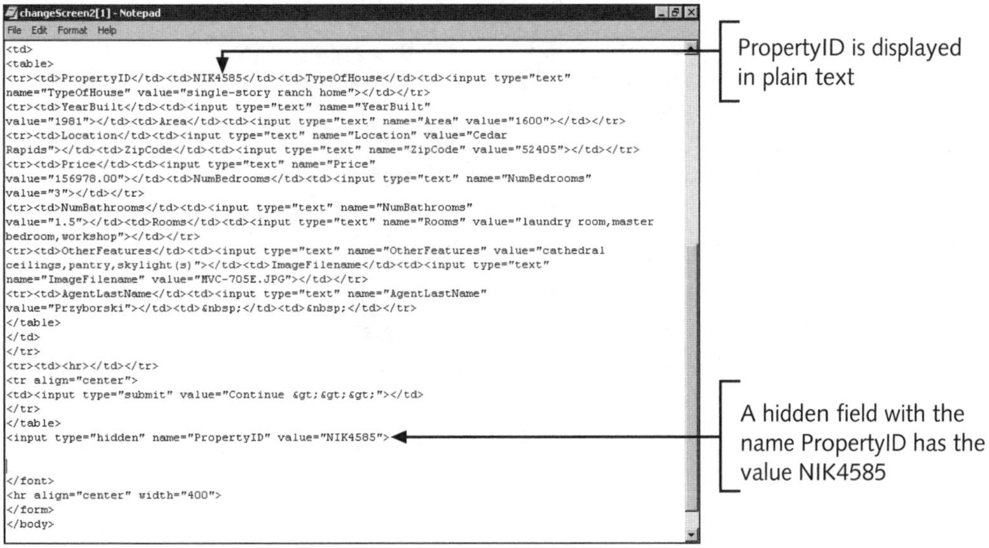

```
<td>
<table>
<tr><td>PropertyID</td><td>NIK4585</td><td>TypeOfHouse</td><td><input type="text"
name="TypeOfHouse" value="single-story ranch home"></td></tr>
<tr><td>YearBuilt</td><td><input type="text" name="YearBuilt"
value="1981"></td><td>Area</td><td><input type="text" name="Area" value="1600"></td></tr>
<tr><td>Location</td><td><input type="text" name="Location" value="Cedar
Rapids"></td><td>ZipCode</td><td><input type="text" name="ZipCode" value="52405"></td></tr>
<tr><td>Price</td><td><input type="text" name="Price"
value="156978.00"></td><td>NumBedrooms</td><td><input type="text" name="NumBedrooms"
value="3"></td></tr>
<tr><td>NumBathrooms</td><td><input type="text" name="NumBathrooms"
value="1.5"></td><td>Rooms</td><td><input type="text" name="Rooms" value="laundry room,master
bedroom,workshop"></td></tr>
<tr><td>OtherFeatures</td><td><input type="text" name="OtherFeatures" value="cathedral
ceilings,pantry,skylight(s)"></td><td>ImageFilename</td><td><input type="text"
name="ImageFilename" value="MVC-705E.JPG"></td></tr>
<tr><td>AgentLastName</td><td><input type="text" name="AgentLastName"
value="Przyborski"></td><td> </td><td> </td></tr>
</table>
</td>
</tr>
<tr><td><hr></td></tr>
<tr align="center">
<td><input type="submit" value="Continue &gt;&gt;&gt;"></td>
</tr>
</table>
<input type="hidden" name="PropertyID" value="NIK4585">


</font>
<hr align="center" width="400">
</form>
</body>
```


Figure 7-12 HTML source code for Version2/changeScreen2.cfm

Notice that there is a hidden field named PropertyID with a value of "NIK4585" in the form. Also, notice that NIK4585 is displayed as plain text in the table cell. Close Notepad.

3. Switch to ColdFusion Studio, and click the **New** button on the Standard toolbar to create a new document.

4. Save the file as **changeScreen3.cfm** in the Version2 subfolder in the Chapter07 folder.

5. On line 5, change the title of the document from "Untitled" to **Change Screen 3**.

6. Open the **insertScreen3.cfm** file in the Version2 folder on the server, select lines 4 through 10 (these lines extract the AgentID given an agent's last name), and then click the **Copy** button on the Edit toolbar.

7. Click the **changeScreen3.cfm** tab to switch to that file, click line 2, column 1, and then click the **Paste** button on the Edit toolbar. When the ColdFusion Server executes these statements, it extracts the AgentID corresponding to the agent's last name. If there is no agent in the table with the last name entered, the Server generates an error message.

8. Your next task is to code the SQL UPDATE statement. All the fields in the record for the property have to be updated to the user-entered values in the form fields. On lines 9–24, type the following:

```
<cfquery datasource="your_username">
UPDATE Properties
SET TypeOfHouse = '#FORM.TypeOfHouse#',
YearBuilt = #FORM.YearBuilt#,
NumBedrooms = #FORM.NumBedrooms#,
NumBathrooms = #FORM.NumBathrooms#,
Area = #FORM.Area#,
Rooms = '#FORM.Rooms#',
OtherFeatures = '#FORM.OtherFeatures#',
Price = #FORM.Price#,
Location = '#FORM.Location#',
ZipCode = '#FORM.ZipCode#',
ImageFilename = '#FORM.ImageFilename#',
AgentID = '#getAgentID.AgentID#'
WHERE PropertyID = '#FORM.PropertyID#'
</cfquery>
```

Notice that all the fields except the AgentID field are prefixed with the "FORM." notation. The AgentID field is extracting the data from the getAgentID query.

9. Type the following confirmation message in the body of the document: **Data changed successfully. Click <a href="admin.cfm">here</a> to return to the Site Admin Tool.**

10. Save the file, and then switch to the Web browser. Change Screen 2 is the current page.

11. Triple-click in the **OtherFeatures** text box to select all of the data in the text box, and then type **pantry**.

12. Click the **Continue** button. A confirmation page opens indicating that the update was successful.

13. Click the **here** hyperlink to return to the Site Admin Tool page, and then click the **Change** menu item.

14. Enter **NIK4585** in the text box, and then click the **Continue** button. The OtherFeatures text box displays the value "pantry," indicating you successfully changed this record in the Properties table.

7

DELETING DATA

In addition to inserting and changing records, NikRealty agents must also have a way to manage properties that are sold or in the process of being sold, so they can delete records from the database. Unlike inserting and updating data, ColdFusion does not have a specific tag for deleting data. To delete records, you must use a CFQUERY tag and the SQL DELETE statement. The safest way to delete a record involves using the record's primary key value to ensure that only the requested record is deleted. In addition, you must be careful when deleting data because this action is not reversible.

Deleting Data with CFQUERY and SQL UPDATE

You learned in Chapter 5 that the syntax for a SQL DELETE statement is as follows:

```
DELETE FROM tablename
    [WHERE condition]
```

When you execute the DELETE statement, it will delete one or more records in the table named *tablename* where the *condition* is true. You will work with files in the Version1 subfolder in the next exercise.

To preview the delete screens:

1. Switch to your Web browser, if necessary, and then open the location **http://localhost/your_username/Chapter07/Version1/admin.cfm**.

   The third menu item is a hyperlink to the first page in the process for deleting a record.

2. Click **Delete**. The first page in the process for deleting a property opens. See Figure 7-13.

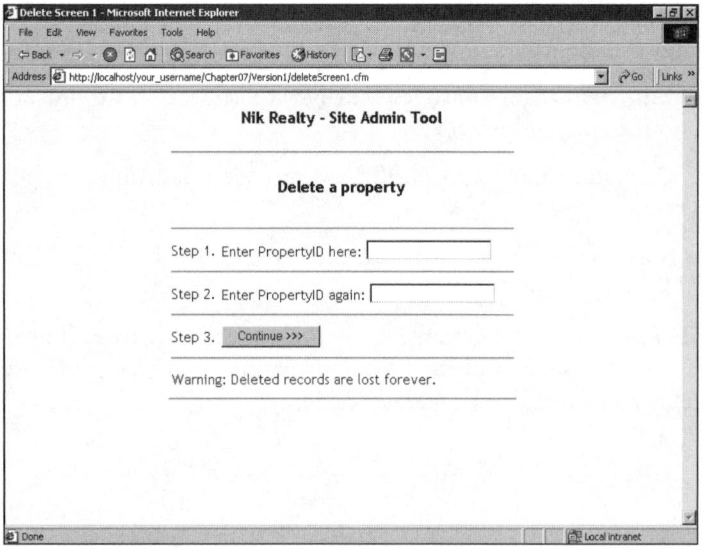

Figure 7-13 Web page displayed by Version1/deleteScreen1.cfm

Because you should ask a user to confirm any deletion from the database, the first page in the process for deleting a property consists of two text boxes named PropertyID1 and PropertyID2. The user must enter the same PropertyID in both text boxes to prevent accidental deletion of records. When the user clicks the Continue button, the form handler compares these two values. If they are equal, the record with the specified PropertyID is deleted; otherwise, the deletion is cancelled.

To delete records using a DELETE statement:

1. Switch to ColdFusion Studio, close all files, and then open **deleteScreen1.cfm** in the Version1 folder on the server. The form handler is deleteScreen2.cfm; you will create this page next.

2. Click the **New** button on the Standard toolbar.

3. Save the new file as **deleteScreen2.cfm** in the Version1 subfolder in the Chapter07 folder.

4. On line 5, change the title of the document ("Untitled") to **Delete Screen 2**.

5. On line 9, enter the following CFIF statement to compare the values entered in the PropertyID1 and PropertyID2 text boxes: **<cfif FORM.PropertyID1 NEQ FORM.PropertyID2>**.

6. Press the **Enter** key, and then type **PropertyID verification failed. Go <a href="deleteScreen1.cfm">back</a> and try again.**

7. Press **Enter**, and then type **<cfelse>**.

8. Press **Enter**, and then type **<cfquery datasource="your_username">**.

9. Press **Enter**, and then type **DELETE FROM Properties WHERE PropertyID = '#FORM.PropertyID1#'**.

10. Press **Enter**, and then type **</cfquery>** to close the query tag.

11. Press **Enter**, and then type **Data deleted successfully. Click <a href= "admin.cfm">here</a> to return to the Site Admin Tool.**

12. Press **Enter**, and then type **</cfif>** to close the CFIF tag.

13. Save your work.

When a user enters identical values in the two text boxes, the Server will delete the record with the specified PropertyID from the database.

To delete a record:

1. Switch to the Web browser, and then type **NIK4870** in the first text box and **NIK4877** in the second text box.

2. Click the **Continue** button.

3. A PropertyID verification failed message appears because the values in the two text boxes are different. See Figure 7-14.

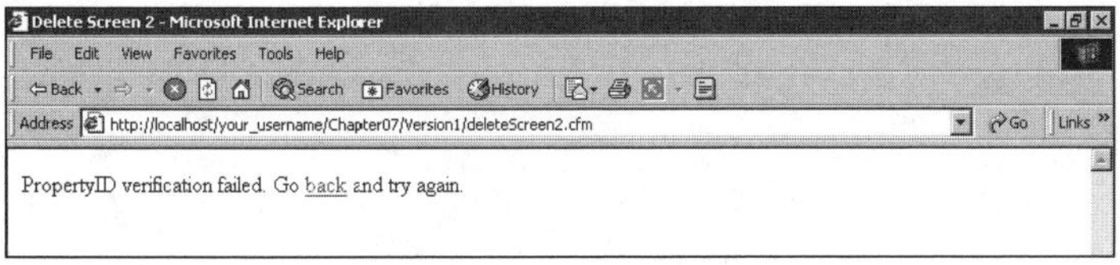

![Delete Screen 2 - Microsoft Internet Explorer window showing the address http://localhost/your_username/Chapter07/Version1/deleteScreen2.cfm and the message "PropertyID verification failed. Go back and try again."]

Figure 7-14   PropertyID verification failed message

4. Click the **back** hyperlink. Delete Screen 1 is displayed.

5. Type **NIK4870** in both text boxes.

6. Click the **Continue** button. A page opens and indicates that the record has been deleted.

You have successfully designed a form handler that deletes a record from a database using the primary key field value.

 The delete operation that you just performed deleted the requested record from the database, but it cannot delete the image file associated with that record. In a later chapter, you will learn how to delete the image file associated with a deleted property. For now, you could display a message informing the user to delete the image file associated with the deleted property. Before deleting the record, you could use a SQL SELECT statement to identify the image filename for the PropertyID that you are about to delete. Then you could display a message in the confirmation page to identify the image to delete along with a reminder to the user to actually delete the file.

CREATING TABLES USING COLDFUSION

On rare occasions, when you are working from a remote location and you do not have access to the database management system, you may have to create tables or alter the structure of tables by using ColdFusion. Creating tables with ColdFusion is easy because you can execute any valid SQL statement in CFQUERY tags.

Instead of just permanently deleting a sold property, as you just did, Nikitha has decided to create a new table named SoldProperties in the Realtor database in which to store data about sold properties. Keeping data about sold properties will provide Nikitha with a means of analyzing sales data. The structure of the new SoldProperties table is similar to the Properties table, with two additional fields: SalePrice and SaleDate. The SalePrice field is a currency field that stores the sale price of the property and the SaleDate field is a date/time field that stores the date the property was sold. The Price field will be used for storing the list price of the property. One of your project members figured out the SQL to create the SoldProperties table. Your task is to create the template for creating the SoldProperties table. Note that you will execute this template only once.

To create a database table using ColdFusion:

1. Switch to ColdFusion Studio, and close all files.

2. Click the **New** button on the Standard toolbar.

3. On line 5, change the title of the document from untitled to **Create Database Table**.

4. On line 9, column 1, below the BODY tag, type the following CFQUERY for creating the SoldProperties table:

```
<cfquery datasource="your_username">
CREATE TABLE SoldProperties(
PropertyID CHAR(7) PRIMARY KEY,
TypeOfHouse CHAR(50),
YearBuilt INTEGER,
NumBedrooms INTEGER,
NumBathrooms REAL,
Area INTEGER,
Rooms CHAR(150),
OtherFeatures CHAR(150),
Price MONEY,
Location CHAR(50),
ZipCode CHAR(10),
ImageFilename CHAR(50),
AgentID CHAR(3),
SalePrice MONEY,
SaleDate TIMESTAMP)
</cfquery>
Database table SoldProperties has been created successfully.
```

5. Save the file as **createTable.cfm** in the Chapter07 folder.

6. Switch to your Web browser, type
http://localhost/your_username/Chapter07/createTable.cfm in the
Address text box, and then press the **Enter** key.

A Web page is displayed with a message that says that the SoldProperties table
has been created successfully. See Figure 7–15.

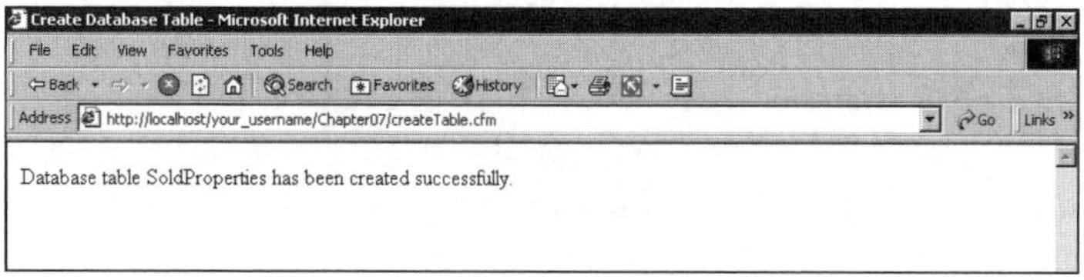

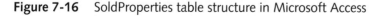

Figure 7-15   Web page displaying a table creation confirmation message

7. Start Microsoft Access, and open **Realtor.mdb** in the Databases folder on
your Data Disk.

8. Click **Tables** on the Objects bar, if necessary, right-click the **SoldProperties**
table, and then click **Design View** on the shortcut menu. If necessary, maximize the window to see all fields. See Figure 7-16. Notice that the design
corresponds to the design of the Properties table with two additional fields
for the SalePrice and SaleDate.

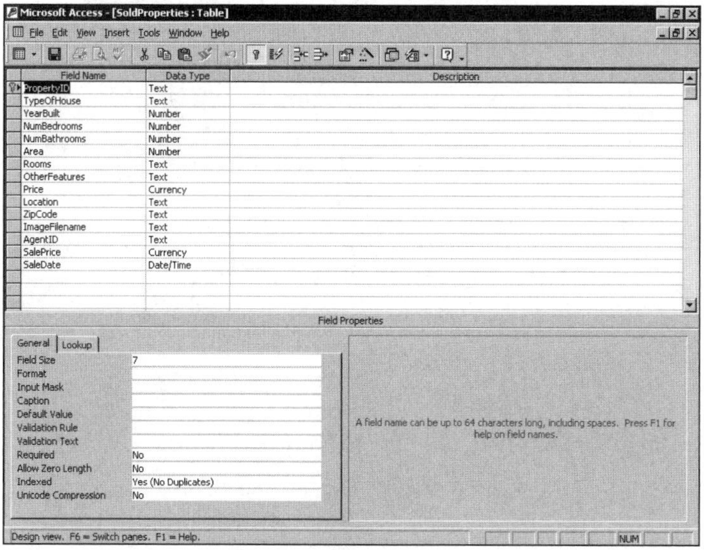

Figure 7-16   SoldProperties table structure in Microsoft Access

9. Close Microsoft Access.

In the next section, you will create templates to add data to this table.

TRANSACTION PROCESSING

In many situations, you will need to perform multiple database operations to accomplish a particular task. For example, when an e-commerce Web site sells a product, an update operation must change the product's inventory level, and a second update operation must change the customer's invoice. If either of these operations fails, but the other proceeds, then the data in the database would be in an inconsistent state—the inventory level of a product may have been reduced without billing a customer for the reduction, or a customer may have been charged for a product that was not actually received. Both these operations should be performed or neither of them should be performed to leave the database in a consistent state. These two operations are part of a database transaction. A **database transaction** is a logical set of database operations that must be entirely completed or aborted; no partial set of operations is acceptable. A transaction changes a database from one consistent state to another.

You implement database transactions in ColdFusion by enclosing all the database operations (cfqueries) in a set of CFTRANSACTION tags. All the changes will be made in the database only when all of them are successful. In case any single operation fails, none of the changes are committed to the database. The syntax for the CFTRANSACTION statement is as follows:

```
<CFTRANSACTION>
Database operations
</CFTRANSACTION>
```

When the ColdFusion Server encounters a CFTRANSACTION tag, all the database operations encountered after it are treated as a part of the transaction. When the Server encounters the closing CFTRANSACTION tag, all the changes are committed to the database. In case there is a problem prior to the processing of the closing CFTRANS-ACTION tag, all the changes are **rolled back** and the database remains in its initial state prior to encountering the opening CFTRANSACTION tag.

When a property is sold, the data with the correct PropertyID will be inserted into the SoldProperties table and then the record with the correct PropertyID will be deleted from the Properties table. Obviously, both operations have to be successful for the database to be in a consistent state, so you will treat these database operations as a transaction.

To preview the process sale screens:

1. Switch to your Web browser, and then open the location **http://localhost/ your_username/Chapter07/Version1/admin.cfm**.

   The fourth menu item is a hyperlink to the first page for processing a sale of a property.

2. Click **Process**. The first page for processing the sale of a property opens. See Figure 7-17.

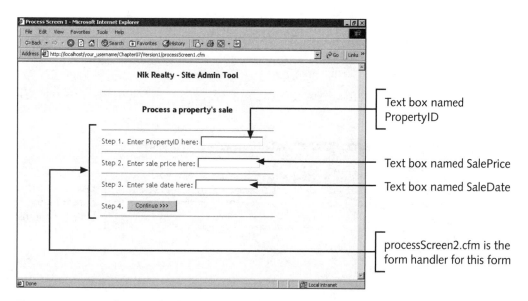

Figure 7-17 Web page displayed by Version1/processScreen1.cfm

The form that opens contains three text boxes, which collect the PropertyID, the sale price, and the sale date. When the user clicks the Continue button, the form handler must find the information for the requested property by using the PropertyID. Then the form handler has to insert the complete property's description, SalePrice, and SaleDate into the SoldProperties table. Once the data is inserted, the form handler will use the PropertyID value to delete the record from the Properties table. These two operations must be part of the same transaction.

To create the form handler:

1. Switch to ColdFusion Studio, close all files, and then open the file **processScreen1.cfm** in the Version1 folder on the server. The form handler for this form is processScreen2.cfm. The names of the form fields are PropertyID, SalePrice, and SaleDate. Your task now is to code this form handler ColdFusion template.

2. Click the **New** button on the Standard toolbar.

3. Save the file as **processScreen2.cfm** in the Version1 subfolder in the Chapter07 folder.

4. On line 5, change the title of the document to **Process Screen 2**.

5. Click line 1, column 1, and press the **Enter** key to insert a new line.

6. Click line 1, column 1, type **<cfquery datasource="your_username" name="getData">**, and then press **Enter**.

7. On line 2, type **SELECT * FROM Properties WHERE PropertyID = '#FORM.PropertyID#'**, and then press **Enter**. This statement will extract all the property data from the Properties table using the PropertyID value that the user entered.

8. Type **</cfquery>** to close this query tag, and then press **Enter**. See Figure 7-18.

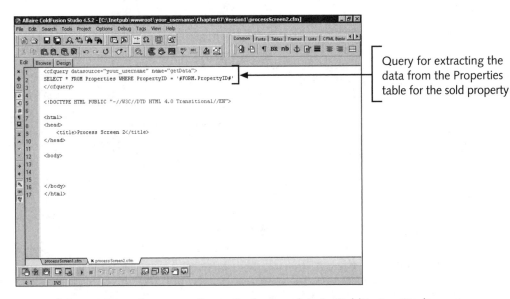

Query for extracting the data from the Properties table for the sold property

Figure 7-18   Editing the processScreen2.cfm template in ColdFusion Studio

The next two operations will insert this data into the SoldProperties table and then delete the record from the Properties table. These two operations are part of a single transaction.

To create a transaction for processing the sale of a property:

1. On line 4, type **<cftransaction>** to initiate a database transaction, and then press the **Enter** key. You need to write a query for inserting data into the SoldProperties table. You can copy the SQL INSERT code you created earlier and modify it for this purpose.

2. Open **insertScreen3.cfm** in the Version2 folder.

3. Select lines 11 through 16 to select the CFQUERY tags and the INSERT statement, and then click the **Copy** button on the Edit toolbar.

4. Click the **processScreen2.cfm** tab at the bottom of the Editor window, make sure that the insertion point is on line 5, column 1, click the **Paste** button on the Edit toolbar, and then press **Enter**.

5. On line 6, change the statement INSERT INTO Properties to **INSERT INTO SoldProperties**. See Figure 7-19.

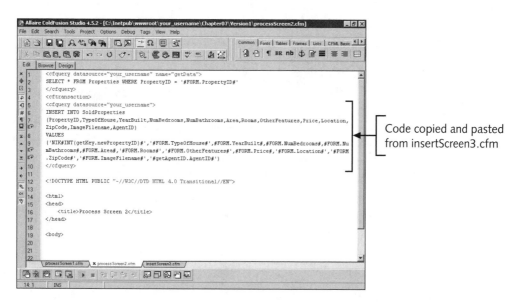

Figure 7-19 processScreen2.cfm with the newly pasted code from insertScreen3.cfm

6. On the next line and in the field list, click between AgentID and), and then type **,SalePrice,SaleDate**.

7. On line 9, change 'NIK#INT(getKey.newPropertyID)#' to **'#getData.PropertyID#'**.

8. Select the INSERT statement, click **Search** on the menu bar, and then click **Replace**. You are editing the INSERT statements as you are inserting data from the query instead of inserting data from the form.

9. Type **FORM.** in the Find what text box, press the **Tab** key, and then type **getData.** in the Replace with text box.

10. Click the **Selection** option button in the Direction box, and then click the **Replace All** button.

11. Click the **OK** button to confirm that 11 replacements were made, and then click the **Cancel** button in the Replace dialog box to close it.

12. Replace #getAgentID.AgentID# with **#getData.AgentID#** in the VALUES list.

13. Add two values to the value list immediately after the AgentID by typing **,#FORM.SalePrice#, ###FORM.SaleDate###**. Note that there are three pound signs around FORM.SaleDate. #FORM.SaleDate# substitutes

the user-entered date and the pound signs are equivalent to the pound sign delimiter in Access for date-time fields. See Figure 7-20.

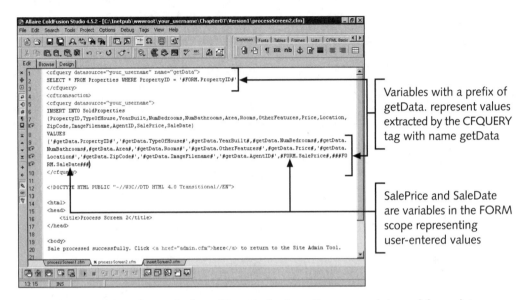

Variables with a prefix of getData. represent values extracted by the CFQUERY tag with name getData

SalePrice and SaleDate are variables in the FORM scope representing user-entered values

Figure 7-20 processScreen2.cfm with code for inserting query data and form data

14. Click at the end of line 10 (the closing CFQUERY tag), press **Enter**, and then type the following code to delete the property. (Do not press Enter after typing the equal sign.)

```
<cfquery datasource="your_username">
DELETE FROM Properties WHERE PropertyID =
'#FORM.PropertyID#'
</cfquery>
```

15. Press **Enter**, and then type **</cftransaction>** to close the transaction. Delete any additional blank lines below this tag. See Figure 7-21.

You've completed the transaction that extracts property data from the Properties table, inserts it into the SoldProperties table along with user-entered form data, and then deletes the record from the Properties table. If all of these operations are successful, the transaction will take place. Next you will enter some text in the page to let the user know that the transaction was successful.

16. Click line 23, column 1 (the first blank line in the BODY tags), and then type **Sale processed successfully. Click <a href="admin.cfm">here</a> to return to the Site Admin Tool.** Your code should correspond to Figure 7-22.

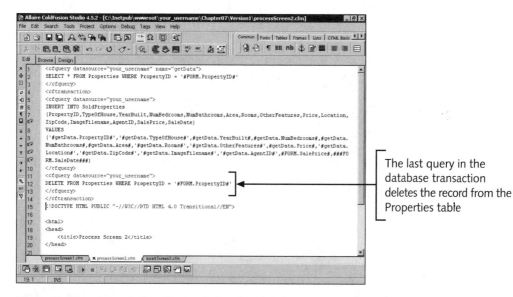

Figure 7-21   Completing the code for the database transaction

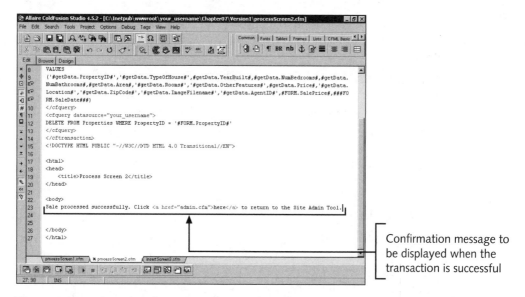

Figure 7-22   Completed processScreen2.cfm template in ColdFusion Studio

17. Save the file, switch to your Web browser, and then enter **NIK4868** in the first text box.

18. Press the **Tab** key, enter **385000** as the sale price, press the **Tab** key, and then enter **6/24/03** as the sale date.

19. Click the **Continue** button. A page opens indicating that you successfully processed the sale. See Figure 7-23.

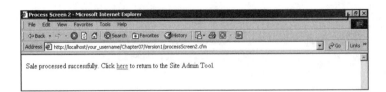

Figure 7-23   Web page with a sale processed successfully confirmation message

You have successfully designed a ColdFusion template to process a database transaction. You have extracted data from a table, inserted data into another table, and then deleted a record. You can open the database file in Microsoft Access and verify the database transaction.

To verify the database transaction:

1. Start Microsoft Access, and open **Realtor.mdb** in the Databases folder.

2. Double-click the **SoldProperties** table to open it in Datasheet view. Notice that the table contains a record with a PropertyID of NIK4868. See Figure 7-24.

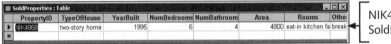

NIK4868 record in the SoldProperties table

Figure 7-24   Records in the SoldProperties table

3. Close the Datasheet window.

4. Double-click the **Properties** table to open it.

5. Scroll down to the bottom, and verify that the table does not contain a record with a PropertyID of NIK4868. See Figure 7-25.

6. Close Microsoft Access. You have verified that there is a record in the SoldProperties table and that the corresponding record in the Properties table has been deleted.

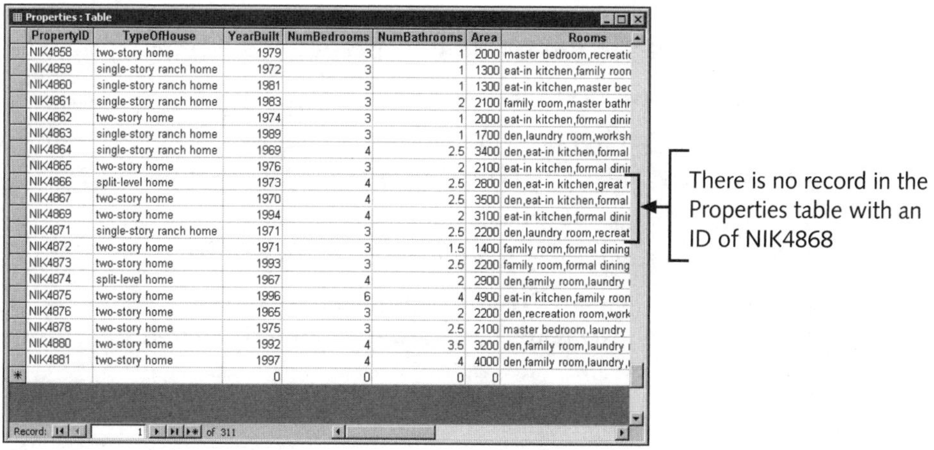

There is no record in the Properties table with an ID of NIK4868

Figure 7-25   Properties table in Microsoft Access

If you review all your activities so far, you will realize that this new capability has created a logical problem with the NikRealty site design. You just extracted data from the Properties table, inserted it into the SoldProperties table, and then deleted the data from the Properties table. Earlier in this chapter, you designed a template for inserting a new property into the Properties table by computing the value of the primary key field (PropertyID) as the maximum value of all existing PropertyID values in the Properties table, incremented by 1. Now that you are deleting existing PropertyID values from the Properties table and moving them to the SoldProperties table, the current method of adding 1 to the maximum PropertyID value in the Properties table might cause a duplicate primary key value in the SoldProperties table when the property gets sold. To ensure that all PropertyID values—in both the Properties and SoldProperties tables—are unique, you must take the PropertyID values in both tables into account when computing a PropertyID value for a new property. You task now is to change Chapter07/Version2/insertScreen3.cfm to take into account values from both tables. You will use queries to figure out the maximum PropertyID + 1 from both the tables and then use the higher of these two as the PropertyID for the new property.

To modify insertScreen3.cfm to assign unique PropertyID values:

1. In ColdFusion Studio, switch to the file **insertScreen3.cfm** in the Version2 folder on the server. Look at the title bar and verify that you are indeed editing the file in the Version2 folder.

2. Click at the end of line 3 (the closing CFQUERY tag), and then press the **Enter** key.

3. On line 4, type **<cfquery datasource="your_Username" name="getSoldKey">**, and then press **Enter**.

4. On line 5, type **SELECT Max(Right(PropertyID,4)) + 1 AS newPropertyID FROM SoldProperties**, and then press **Enter**.

5. On line 6, type **</cfquery>**.

6. On line 18 and in the VALUES list, replace getKey.newPropertyID with **Max(getKey.newPropertyID,getSoldKey.newPropertyID)**.

7. On line 28, replace getKey.newPropertyID with **Max(getKey.newPropertyID, getSoldKey.newPropertyID)**.

8. Save the file, switch to your Web browser, type **http://localhost/your_username/Chapter07/Version2/admin.cfm** in the Address text box, and then press **Enter**.

9. Click the **Insert** hyperlink.

10. Copy the file **MVC-206E.JPG** from the Chapter07 folder to the Images folder using Windows Explorer or your FTP software.

11. Switch to your Web browser, type **MVC-206E.JPG** in the image filename text box, and then click the **Continue** button. The Web browser opens the insertScreen2.cfm page.

12. Use the form to enter the following data about a new property:

    AgentLastName: **Little**
    TypeOfHouse: **two-story home**
    YearBuilt: **1988**
    Area: **2300**
    Location: **Hudson**
    ZipCode: **50643**
    Price: **215000.00**
    NumBedrooms: **3**
    NumBathrooms: **2.5**
    Rooms: **master bedroom,recreation room,workshop**
    OtherFeatures: **breakfast bar,walk-in closet(s),wet bar,whirlpool**
    ImageFilename: MVC-206E.JPG (this value has been entered already)

13. Click the **Continue** button. A new record is inserted. The PropertyID for the new property is NIK4882, which is higher than all the PropertyIDs in the Properties and SoldProperties tables.

14. Verify the above using Microsoft Access.

15. Close your browser and ColdFusion Studio.

CHAPTER SUMMARY

❑ Data maintenance operations include inserting, updating, and deleting data and processing database transactions.

❑ You insert data by using the CFINSERT tag or the SQL INSERT statement. Inserting data is usually accomplished as a series of steps. An HTML form is displayed with form fields for users to enter data. The form handlers insert data into the databases.

❑ The CFINSERT tag is simple to use, but has a restricted application when compared with inserting data by using a SQL INSERT statement enclosed in CFQUERY tags.

❑ You update data by using the CFUPDATE tag or the SQL UPDATE statement.

❑ Updating data is usually accomplished as a series of steps. An HTML form is displayed. Ideally, data is extracted and prefilled in the HTML form to ensure a good user experience. The form handler either contains a CFUPDATE tag or a CFQUERY tag with a SQL UPDATE statement for updating the data.

❑ Similar to using the CFINSERT tag, the CFUPDATE tag is simple to use but is restricted in application when compared with using a SQL UPDATE statement enclosed in CFQUERY tags.

❑ You delete data by enclosing a SQL DELETE statement in CFQUERY tags. Deleting data is a permanent action, so you must be careful to ensure that the proper data is being deleted and you should build in checks to ensure data accuracy prior to deleting records.

❑ A database transaction is a logical set of database operations that must be entirely completed or aborted; no partial set of operations is acceptable. A transaction changes a database from one consistent state to another. Database transactions are implemented by using the CFTRANSACTION tag.

REVIEW QUESTIONS

1. Why is database maintenance important for database-driven Web sites?

2. List three operations that are part of database maintenance.

3. Using sites that you visit often, list five examples of database maintenance operations that you encounter.

4. What tags are useful for inserting data using ColdFusion? What is the typical procedure for inserting data?

5. What are the advantages and disadvantages of using SQL INSERT and CFINSERT to insert data in a database?

6. What is the process for generating a value for the primary key field when using a ColdFusion template to insert data into a database table?

7. What tags are useful for updating data using ColdFusion? What is the typical procedure for updating data?

8. What is the role of the primary key when using a ColdFusion template to update database data?

9. Which attribute of the HTML text input control displays prefilled values when a form is displayed? What is the importance of this attribute with respect to the process of updating data in a database?

10. What are the advantages and disadvantages of using SQL UPDATE and CFUPDATE to update database data?

11. What tags are useful for deleting database data using a ColdFusion template? What is the typical procedure for deleting data?

12. When you are designing a delete capability in ColdFusion, what process can you use to ensure that data is not accidentally deleted?

13. What is the syntax for including form variables containing dates in SQL statements in CFQUERY tags?

14. What tags are useful for creating database tables using ColdFusion? How many times would you typically execute a template for creating tables?

15. What is a database transaction? Provide one example not mentioned in the chapter that requires you to treat multiple database operations as a transaction.

16. How do you implement transactions in ColdFusion?

17. Suggest some improvements in the design of HTML forms presented in this chapter that would improve the user experience by answering the following questions:

   a. What form control other than a text box is more appropriate to use for specifying the Agent's last name?

   b. What form controls other than text boxes are more appropriate to specify rooms and other features than a text box?

   c. Is there any other control that would simplify the input of the type of house characteristic?

HANDS-ON PROJECTS

Project 1: Design Templates for Inserting a New Agent's Information

Add item number 5 with a caption "Add a new agent" to the Site Admin Tool page in the Version1 folder. The word "Add" should be a hyperlink that opens a page (insertAgentScreen1.cfm) for adding a new agent to the Agents table in the Realtor database. See Figure 7-26. Design a template named **insertAgentScreen1.cfm** in the Version1 folder that contains a form with all the fields in the Agents table. See Figure 7-27 for an example. Design a form handler named **insertAgentScreen2.cfm** that uses a CFINSERT tag for inserting a new agent's record. Display an appropriate message when the data insertion is successful, as shown in Figure 7-28. Enter your information as a test case, and submit it to the database.

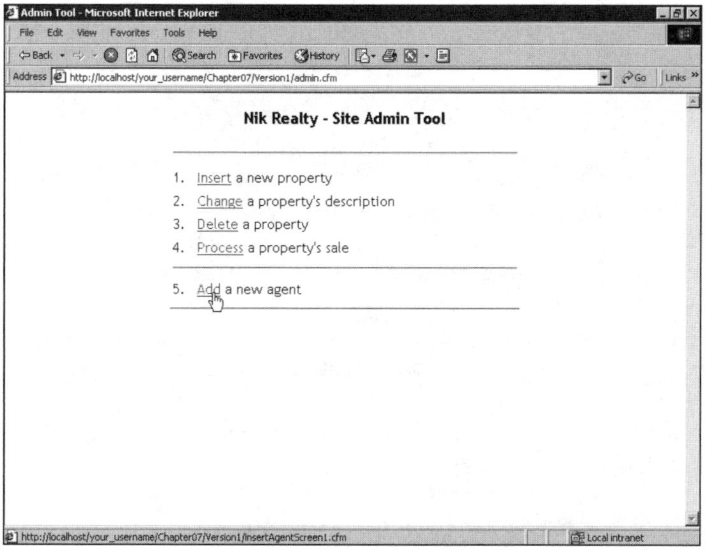

Figure 7-26

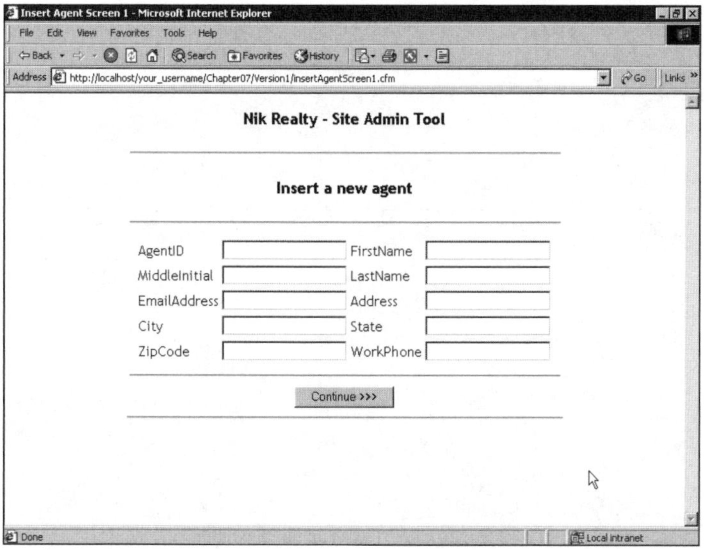

Figure 7-27

Figure 7-28

Project 2: Design Templates for Inserting a New Agent's Information by Computing the Primary Key Value

Add item number 5 with a caption "Add a new agent" to the Site Admin Tool page in the Version2 folder. The word "Add" should be a hyperlink that opens a page (insertAgentScreen1.cfm) for adding a new agent to the Agents table in the Realtor database. See Figure 7-29. Design a template named **insertAgentScreen1.cfm** that contains a form with all the fields in the Agents table except the AgentID field. See Figure 7-30 for an example. Design a form handler named **insertAgentScreen2.cfm** that computes a new primary key value by combining the first letter of the first name, middle initial, and the first letter of the last name and uses a SQL INSERT statement for inserting a new agent's record. Assume that no two agents will have the same combination of letters. Display an appropriate message along with the AgentID of the new record when the insertion is successful, as shown in Figure 7-31. Insert a friend's information as a test case, and submit it to the database.

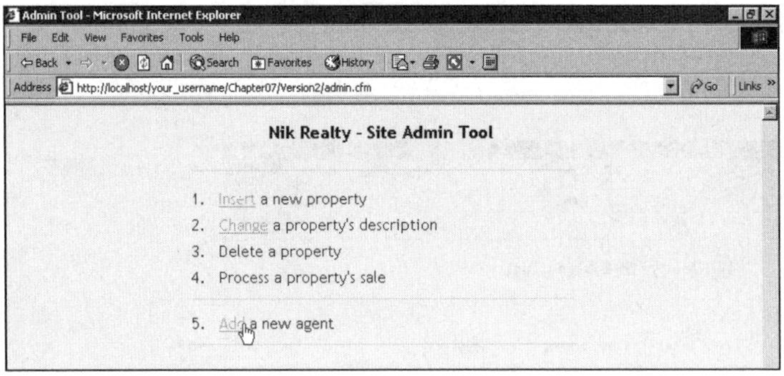

Figure 7-29

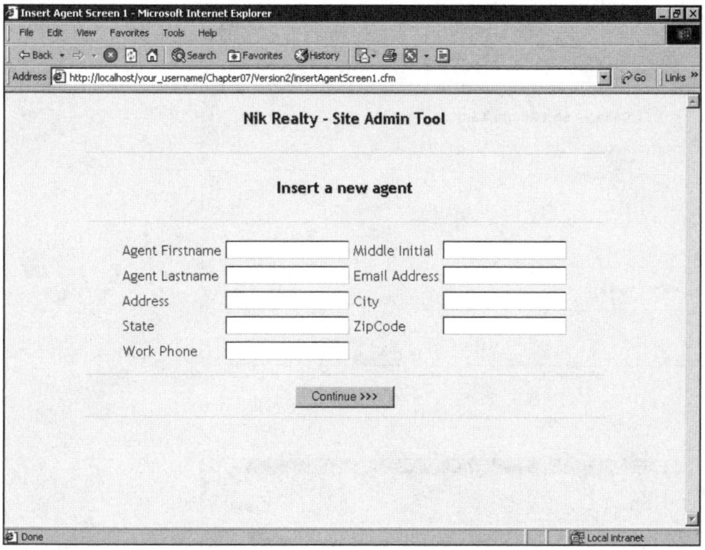

Figure 7-30

Figure 7-31

Project 3: Design Templates for Updating an Agent's Information

Add item number 6 with the caption "Change an agent's information" to the Site Admin Tool page in the Version1 folder. The word "Change" should be a hyperlink that opens the first screen (changeAgentScreen1.cfm) for changing an agent's information in the Realtor database. See Figure 7-32. Design the template named **changeAgentScreen1.cfm** that contains an HTML form with a text box where a user can enter an AgentID, as shown in Figure 7-33. Design a form handler for this form named **changeAgentScreen2.cfm** that extracts data from the Agents table that corresponds to the user-entered AgentID and displays it in an HTML form, as shown in Figure 7-34. Design a form handler for this form named **changeAgentScreen3.cfm** that updates the data using a CFUPDATE tag and displays a confirmation message. See Figure 7-35. Change your record to test the templates.

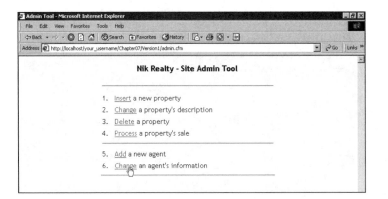

Figure 7-32

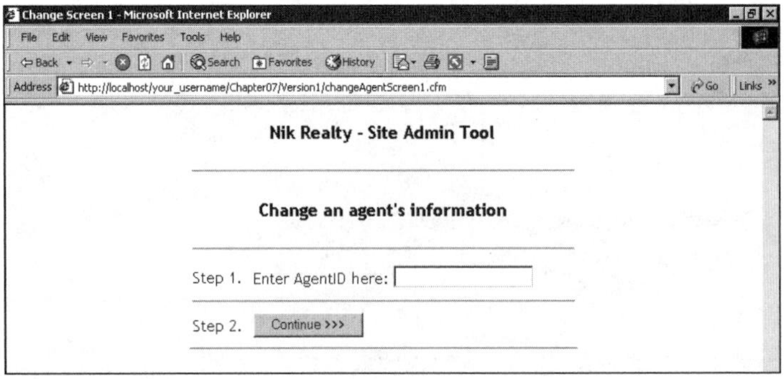

Figure 7-33

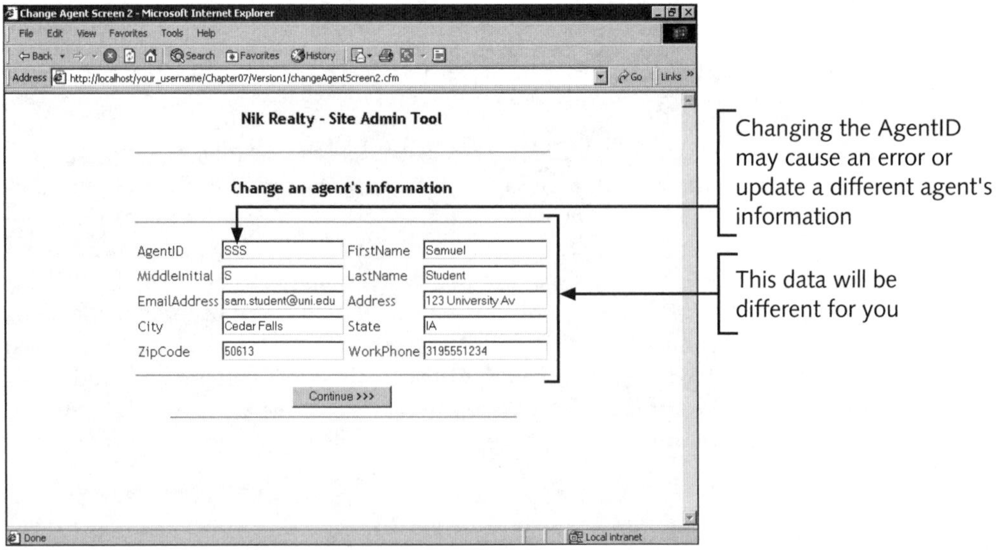

Changing the AgentID may cause an error or update a different agent's information

This data will be different for you

Figure 7-34

Figure 7-35

Project 4: Design Templates for Updating an Agent's Information Using a Hidden Field for the Primary Key

Add item number 6 with the caption "Change an agent's information" to the Site Admin Tool page in the Version2 folder. The word "Change" should be a hyperlink that opens the first screen (changeAgentScreen1.cfm) for changing an agent's information in the Realtor database. See Figure 7-36. Design a template named **changeAgentScreen1.cfm** that contains an HTML form with a text box where a user can enter an AgentID, as shown in Figure 7-37. Design a form handler for this form named **changeAgentScreen2.cfm** that extracts data from the Agents table corresponding to the user-entered AgentID and displays it in an HTML form. Display the AgentID as plain text, as shown in Figure 7-38, and use a hidden field to post this AgentID to the next screen. Design a form handler for this form named **changeAgentScreen3.cfm** that updates the data using a SQL UPDATE statement and displays a confirmation message, as shown in Figure 7-39. Change your friend's record to test the templates.

Figure 7-36

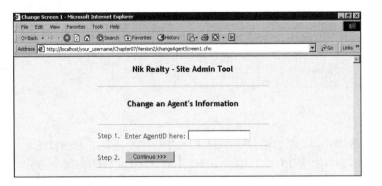

Figure 7-37

This data will be different for you

Figure 7-38

Figure 7-39

Project 5: Design Templates for Deleting an Agent

Add item number 7 with the caption "Delete an agent" to the Site Admin Tool page in the Version1 folder. The word "Delete" should be a hyperlink that opens the first screen (deleteAgentScreen1.cfm) for deleting an agent from the Realtor database. See Figure 7-40. Design the template named **deleteAgentScreen1.cfm** that displays an HTML form for deleting an agent. Use two text boxes for confirming that the user is entering the same AgentID in both text boxes. Add an additional text box that asks the user for the AgentID of the agent who is going to take over the properties that are listed with the agent being deleted. See Figure 7-41. Design a form handler for this form named **deleteAgentScreen2.cfm** that compares the AgentIDs entered in both the text boxes and then deletes the record accordingly. If there is a mismatch in terms of the AgentIDs, an error message should be displayed. Update all the properties, replacing the AgentID of the agent being deleted with the alternate AgentID entered in the form by the user. Include the deletion of the agent and the updating of the properties in a database transaction. Display a confirmation message at the end, as shown in Figure 7-42. Delete your record and your friend's record from the database. Use NKL as the AgentID for the agent who is going to take over the properties.

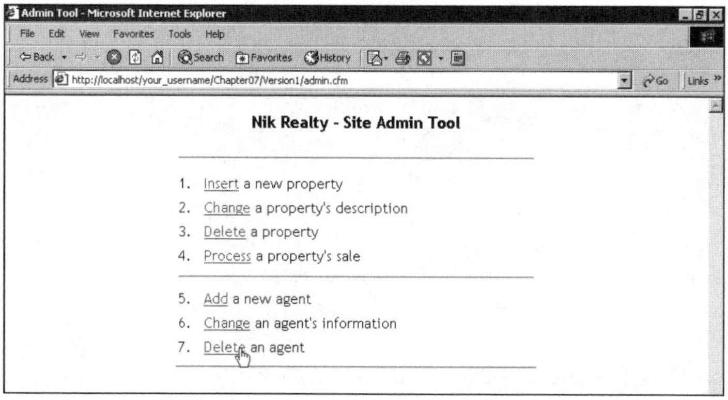

Figure 7-40

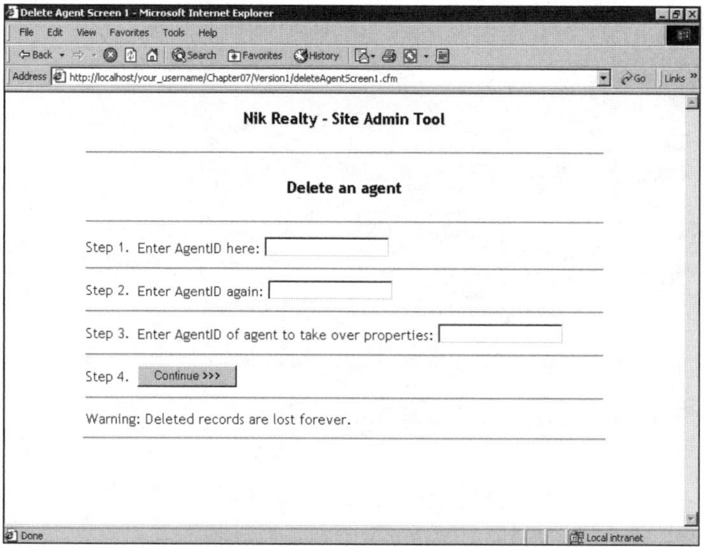

Figure 7-41

Figure 7-42

Project 6: Design Templates for Deleting a Customer Request

Add item number 8 with the caption "Delete a customer request" to the Site Admin Tool page in the Version1 folder. The word "Delete" should be a hyperlink that opens the first screen (deleteRequestScreen1.cfm) for deleting a customer request from the Realtor database. See Figure 7-43. View http://localhost/your_username/Chapter07/Version1/admin.cfm in your Web browser, and then click the Delete hyperlink in item 8. The deleteRequestScreen1.cfm opens with a list of all customer requests in the database, as shown in Figure 7-44. Open deleteRequestScreen1.cfm in ColdFusion Studio, and add a table cell to each row with a form and a submit button captioned Delete. See Figure 7-45. Use deleteRequestScreen2.cfm as the form handler for the form, and use a hidden field to capture the RequestID for the request. When the user clicks a Delete button, the corresponding request should be deleted from the database and a confirmation message should be displayed, as shown in Figure 7-46. Delete the requests for both properties listed by agent Lowell, one at a time.

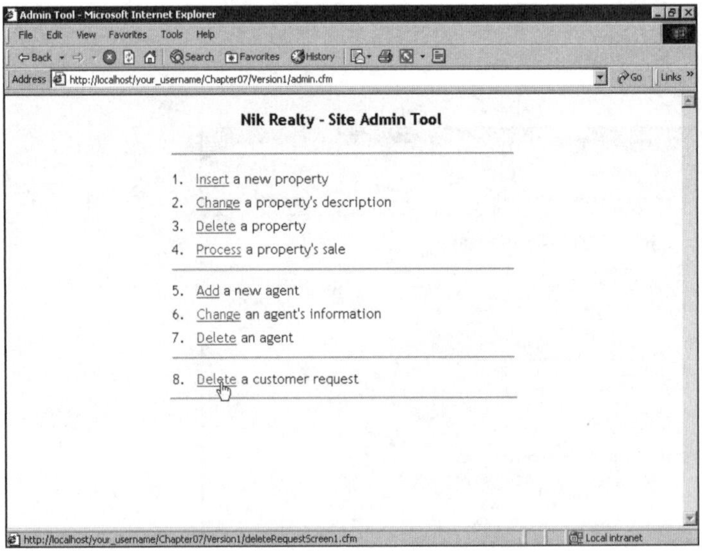

Figure 7-43

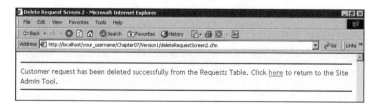

Figure 7-44

Figure 7-45

Figure 7-46

CASE PROJECTS

Case Project 1

Open and examine the HardwareStore.mdb database in the databases folder. Design an admin tool for the hardware store case. The admin tool should have a capability for data maintenance including the capabilities for inserting, updating, and deleting products available for sale.

Case Project 2

Research *Amazon.com* with a particular emphasis on their shopping cart. Design a shopping cart application for the hardware store.

Case Project 3

Copy the Schedule a Showing form and its form handler that you created in Chapter 4 to the Chapter07 folder. Modify the copied files and create additional files as needed to insert data directly into the Customers and Requests tables in the Realtor database.

8

DATA VALIDATION

In this chapter, you will:

♦ Learn about data validation and its importance

♦ Learn about client-side and server-side data validation

♦ Implement data validation techniques such as data completeness checks, data type checks, range and limit checks, picture checks, and algorithmic checks using CFML

♦ Learn about ColdFusion forms and controls including text boxes, radio buttons, checkboxes and select boxes

♦ Dynamically populate select boxes with data extracted from databases

In earlier chapters, you learned about the importance of data for organizations. You have seen how data is stored in databases and how to use ColdFusion for maintaining data using a Web browser and HTML forms. However, even if you can store and retrieve data efficiently, the data is not useful if it contains errors. Imagine the consequences of inaccurate and erroneous data: customers are unhappy, employees mistrust the system and try to outguess it, operations become inefficient, and the organization spends time and money to correct the problems. How can you ensure that the data is as accurate as possible? Can you use proper system design and programming techniques to prevent data inaccuracy problems? Can you validate data when it is entered into the system? ColdFusion provides a range of **data validation** methods to help you respond to these questions. This chapter introduces the concept of data validation and explores techniques you can use to validate data using ColdFusion.

When you are designing a system for database maintenance, similar to what you did in the previous chapter, you decide whether a user is entering valid data by comparing user-entered data with known standards for good data. The simplest of errors occurs when users forget to enter data. Validation techniques that check to see that users enter data are known as **data completeness checks**. Validation checks that verify whether the data is a proper date, time, decimal number, or an integer are known as **data type checks**. **Range and limit checks** allow you to enforce criteria on the data. For example, you can check that data fall between two numbers or have an upper or a lower limit. **Picture checks** allow you to check whether the data contains a certain number of digits and is according to a specific pattern. **Self-checking digits** are used in algorithmic checks for validating data according to mathematical formulae.

PERFORMING SERVER-SIDE AND CLIENT-SIDE DATA VALIDATION

When users submit forms, you can validate data in the form handlers prior to performing database maintenance operations. You can set up the form handlers to use CFIF tags or other selection constructs to compare user-entered values to known standards for good data. If you detect a problem, you can alert the user and provide suggestions for corrective actions. If no problems are detected, you can perform the database operations. When you use form handlers in this way, you are validating data by using the ColdFusion Server. In other words, you are performing **server-side data validation**.

Similarly to the way embedded scripting languages work on the server to implement server-side processing, you can perform some processing on the client side by using embedded languages, such as JavaScript or VBScript. ColdFusion focuses on JavaScript because it is supported by most of the Web browsers. As opposed to validating data on the server, in this case you are performing client-side processing, or **client-side data validation**. The Web browser would perform client-side data validation after the user enters data and submits the form. In case there is valid data, the Web browser would send an HTTP request to the Web server along with the data. In case there are errors, the Web browser would alert users and give them a chance to change the data.

Using JavaScript to Validate Data

JavaScript is a scripting language developed by Netscape to add interactive features to Web documents. JavaScript is event driven, which means it responds to user events such as button clicks, mouse movements, and text entry. You can use JavaScript to program a Web page so that the client computer responds to user events. For example, you can set images to change color when a user moves a mouse over them or have a dialog box appear with a message when the user clicks a button. If you are creating Web applications, you can use JavaScript to perform calculations and check forms to validate data. For example, you can check to see if a text box contains nine digits for entering Social Security numbers and then display a message box in case the number of digits is not nine.

Although Netscape originally developed it, JavaScript runs on both the Netscape Navigator and Internet Explorer browsers.

JavaScript is a complex and full-featured scripting language that can require significant time and attention to master. Fortunately, you do not need to know JavaScript to perform client-side data validation. ColdFusion has special form input control tags that automatically generate data validation programs in JavaScript for you.

DESIGNING FORMS WITH COLDFUSION

To incorporate data validation capabilities into your Web pages, you need to design your Web pages as ColdFusion templates containing ColdFusion forms. You learned how to design HTML forms in Chapter 4. As an alternative to designing forms in HTML, you can design forms by using CFML. The ColdFusion Server generates the HTML form when it processes the CFML form tags. Similar to forms in HTML, the CFFORM tag encloses the entire ColdFusion form. ColdFusion forms can contain text, other CFML tags, HTML tags, graphics, and one or more controls. Recall that a control is an object in a form that you use to collect data. For example, text boxes and radio buttons are controls. In CFML, you use the CFINPUT tag to create controls that users can use to enter data in a form. You will learn about these tags and their usage in the following sections.

Creating ColdFusion Forms

As mentioned previously, you use a set of CFFORM tags to create a ColdFusion form. A CFFORM tag has two required attributes: ACTION and NAME. The value for the ACTION attribute is the URL of the ColdFusion form handler that will process the form after it is submitted. The NAME attribute can be any word or a sequence of letters. When the ColdFusion Server processes the CFFORM tag, it creates an HTML form with the METHOD attribute set to post. The Web browser displays the Web page along with the form. A user completes the form and submits it; the Web browser sends an HTTP request to the Web server along with user-entered form data, then the Web server passes the user-entered data to the ColdFusion Server along with the name of the ColdFusion form handler specified in the ACTION attribute. The ColdFusion Server makes this data available to the form handler specified in the ACTION attribute and then executes the code in the form handler. The following example illustrates a simple ColdFusion form. This code example is provided in the Example8-1.cfm file on your data disk in the Chapter08 folder. The highlighted line shows the CFFORM tag with the ACTION and NAME attributes.

```
<html>
<head>
<title>Example 8-1</title>
</head>
<body>
```

```
<cfform action="debug_a_form.cfm" name="myForm">
<table>
<tr>
<td align="right">PropertyID</td>
<td><input type="text" name="PropertyID"></td>
</tr>
<tr>
<td align="center" colspan="2"><input type="submit" value=
"Continue"></td>
</tr>
</table>
</cfform>
</body>
</html>
```

In the following exercise, you will run Example8-1.cfm and learn about ColdFusion forms.

To learn about ColdFusion forms by using Example8-1.cfm:

1. Start your Web browser.

2. Type **http://localhost/your_username/Chapter08/Example8-1.cfm** in the Address text box of your browser, and press the **Enter** key. See Figure 8-1.

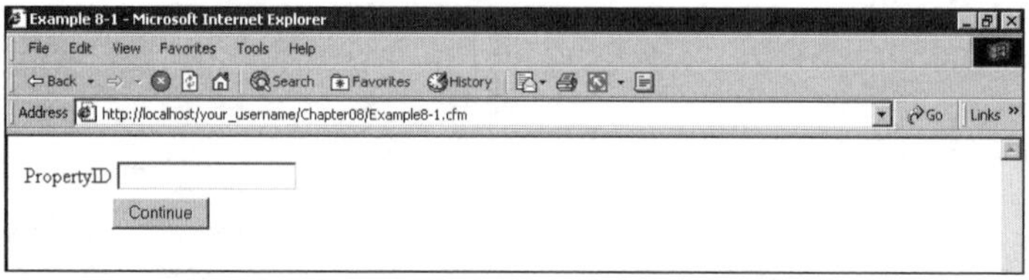

Figure 8-1   Web page displayed by Example8-1.cfm

When you request http://localhost/your_username/Chapter08/Example8-1.cfm, the Web server receives the request and then transfers control to the ColdFusion Server. When the ColdFusion Server executes Example8-1.cfm, it processes the CFFORM tags to create an HTML form. The Web page containing the HTML is sent to the browser. The Web browser displays the page.

3. Click **View** on the menu bar, and then click **Source**. If necessary, maximize Notepad. Figure 8-2 contains the HTML source code the ColdFusion Server produced for this form.

Netscape users should click View on the menu bar, and then click Page Source to view the HTML source code.

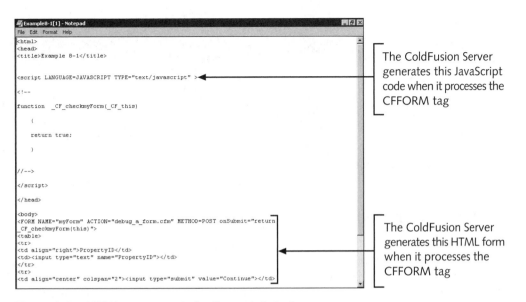

```
Example8-1[1] - Notepad
File Edit Format Help
<html>
<head>
<title>Example 8-1</title>

<script LANGUAGE=JAVASCRIPT TYPE="text/javascript" >

<!--

function _CF_checkmyForm(_CF_this)

    {

    return true;

    }


//-->

</script>

</head>

<body>
<FORM NAME="myForm" ACTION="debug_a_form.cfm" METHOD=POST onSubmit="return
_CF_checkmyForm(this)">
<table>
<tr>
<td align="right">PropertyID</td>
<td><input type="text" name="PropertyID"></td>
</tr>
<tr>
<td align="center" colspan="2"><input type="submit" value="Continue"></td>
```

The ColdFusion Server generates this JavaScript code when it processes the CFFORM tag

The ColdFusion Server generates this HTML form when it processes the CFFORM tag

Figure 8-2   HTML source code for Example8-1.cfm

Notice in Figure 8-2 that the effect of the CFFORM tag is twofold. First, an HTML form is generated when the ColdFusion Server processes the CFFORM tag. The name of the HTML form is myForm, the same name used for the CFFORM in the highlighted code in Example 8-1.cfm. The action of the HTML form—debug_a_form.cfm—is the same as the action of the CFFORM, the method is set to POST, and a JavaScript function is coded for handling the form submission. Second, at the top in the head section of the HTML document, JavaScript code is generated that will be executed when the form is submitted. Because the form contains only HTML form controls, this function is currently empty and would not process data when a Web Browser submits this form on the client side. ColdFusion will generate JavaScript code for validating data here when you use appropriate CFML tags later on in the chapter.

To take advantage of ColdFusion's ability to validate data entered in forms, you have to use ColdFusion input controls instead of using HTML input controls. As mentioned earlier, these controls include text boxes, radio buttons, and checkboxes that let users enter data and make selections. To include a control on a form, you use a particular control tag in the CFML code. Table 8-1 contains a list of ColdFusion input controls along with their partial tags. You will learn about all these controls and their attributes in the following sections.

8

Table 8-1   ColdFusion Form Controls

Input Control	ColdFusion Control Tag
Text box	<cfinput type="text" ...
Radio button	<cfinput type ="radio" ...
Checkbox	<cfinput type ="checkbox" ...
Select box	<cfselect ...

The following section explains how to create text box controls. Radio buttons, check-boxes, and select boxes are covered in the "Checking for Completeness" section.

Text Box Controls

You use a text box control to collect a limited amount of data, such as a person's name or address. You create text boxes in a form by using the CFINPUT tag with a value of "text" for the TYPE attribute. The NAME attribute is required for uniquely identifying the control and its data. Other useful attributes include SIZE, which lets you specify the text box width in characters, and the optional VALUE attribute, which lets you specify a default value in the text box when the form is loaded. Use the following syntax to create a text box control:

```
<cfinput type="text" name="text box name" size="size" value
="initial value">
```

The following example illustrates a form with a ColdFusion text box control. This code is included in the Example8-2.cfm file in the Chapter08 folder on your Data Disk. The text box control is defined in the highlighted line of code.

```
<html>
<head>
<title>Example 8-2</title>
</head>
<body>
<cfform action="debug_a_form.cfm" name="myForm">
<table>
<tr>
<td align="right">PropertyID</td>
<td><cfinput type="text" name="PropertyID"></td>
</tr>
<tr>
<td align="center" colspan="2"><input type="submit" value="
Continue"></td>
</tr>
</table>
</cfform>
</body>
</html>
```

In the following exercise, you will run Example 8-2.cfm and learn about the CFINPUT tag.

To run Example8-2.cfm:

1. Close the window with the HTML source code for the previous example.

2. Type **http://localhost/your_username/Chapter08/Example8-2.cfm** in the Address text box of your browser, and press the **Enter** key. See Figure 8-3.

Figure 8-3   Web page displayed by Example8-2.cfm

When you request http://localhost/your_username/Chapter08/Example8-2.cfm, the Web server receives the request and then transfers control to the ColdFusion Server. When the ColdFusion Server executes the Example8-2.cfm, it processes the CFFORM tags to create an HTML form. It processes the CFINPUT tag to create an HTML input control. The Web page containing the HTML is sent to the browser. The Web browser displays the page with the form.

3. Click **View** on the menu bar, and then click **Source** (or **Page Source**, if you use Netscape). If necessary, maximize Notepad. Figure 8-4 contains the HTML source code the ColdFusion Server produced for this form.

```
<html>
<head>
<title>Example 8-2</title>

<script LANGUAGE=JAVASCRIPT TYPE="text/javascript" >

<!--

function  _CF_checkmyForm(_CF_this)

    {

    return true;

    }

//-->

</script>

</head>

<body>
<FORM NAME="myForm" ACTION="debug_a_form.cfm" METHOD=POST onSubmit="return
_CF_checkmyForm(this)">
<table>
<tr>
<td align="right">PropertyID</td>
<td><INPUT TYPE="text" NAME="PropertyID"></td>
</tr>
<tr>
<td align="center" colspan="2"><input type="submit" value="Continue"></td>
```

The ColdFusion Server generates this HTML INPUT control when it processes the CFINPUT tag

Figure 8-4   HTML source code for Example8-2.cfm

The primary difference between Example 8-2 and Example 8-1 is the use of the ColdFusion text box control. Notice that the code generated for Example 8-2 is very similar to the code generated for Example 8-1. Actually, the CFINPUT tag when the attribute TYPE is set to TEXT generates an HTML INPUT tag with TYPE set to TEXT. The primary advantage of using the CFINPUT tag is that it allows for several more attributes that are useful for validating data. In the next section, you will learn about data completeness checks and how you can implement them on text boxes in ColdFusion by using the attributes of the CFINPUT tag.

CHECKING FOR DATA COMPLETENESS

The simplest of errors occurs when users forget to enter data or inadvertently skip a field. Data validation techniques designed to prevent this kind of error are known as completeness checks. You implement a completeness check in ColdFusion by using an attribute for the CFINPUT tag named REQUIRED and set its value to YES. An example of this tag is shown in the highlighted line in the following code. When the ColdFusion Server processes such a tag, it generates the JavaScript code that checks to see whether the user has entered any data in the field. If the user has entered data, the request is sent to the Web server; if the user has not entered data, a message is displayed explaining that the user must enter data in that field. The Web browser performs this client-side data validation.

The following example illustrates a form with a ColdFusion text box control with a data completeness check. This code is included in the Example8-3.cfm file in the Chapter08 folder on your Data Disk. The REQUIRED tag that specifies the completeness check is defined in the highlighted line of code.

 All text box validation techniques work with password boxes too. You can generate a password box by setting the value of the TYPE attribute of the CFINPUT tag to PASSWORD.

```
<html>
<head>
<title>Example 8-3</title>
</head>
<body>
<cfform action="debug_a_form.cfm" name="myForm">
<table>
<tr>
<td align="right">PropertyID</td>
<td><cfinput type="text" name="PropertyID" required="Yes"></td>
</tr>
<tr>
<td align="center" colspan="2"><input type="submit"
value="Continue"></td>
```

```
</tr>
</table>
</cfform>
</body>
</html>
```

To learn about data completeness checks using Example8-3.cfm:

1. Close the window with the HTML source code for the previous example.

2. Type **http://localhost/your_username/Chapter08/Example8-3.cfm** in the Address text box of your browser, and press the **Enter** key. See Figure 8-5.

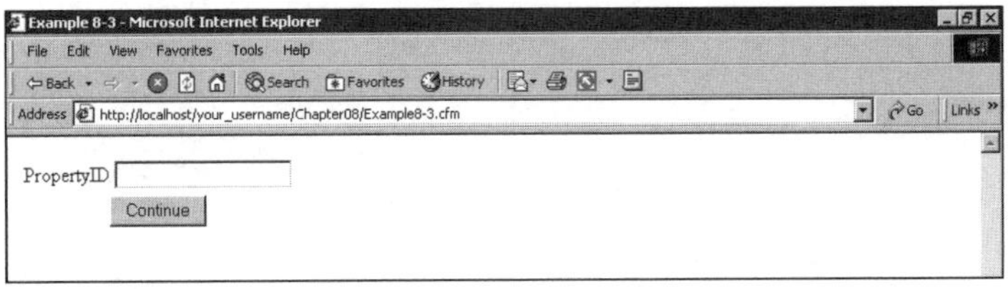

Figure 8-5   Web page displayed by Example8-3.cfm

When the ColdFusion Server executes Example8-3.cfm, it processes the CFFORM tags to create an HTML form. It processes the CFINPUT tag to create an HTML input control. It processes the REQUIRED attribute of the CFINPUT tag and creates JavaScript code to implement a data completeness check. The Web page containing the HTML and the JavaScript is sent to the browser. The Web browser displays the page with the form.

3. Click **View** on the menu bar, and then click **Source** (or **Page Source**, if you use Netscape). If necessary, maximize Notepad. Figure 8-6 contains the HTML source code the ColdFusion Server produced for this form along with the JavaScript for the data completeness checks.

4. Close the window with the source code.

5. In your Web browser, click the **Continue** button without entering any data in the text box. A message box appears with a message "Error in PropertyID text." See Figure 8-7. When you submit the form, the Web browser executes the JavaScript event handlers. The JavaScript event handlers check to see if there is any data entered in the text box. Because the JavaScript event handlers are implementing a data completeness check, if there is no data a default error message is displayed. In the next section, you will learn about customizing this error message to create a better user experience.

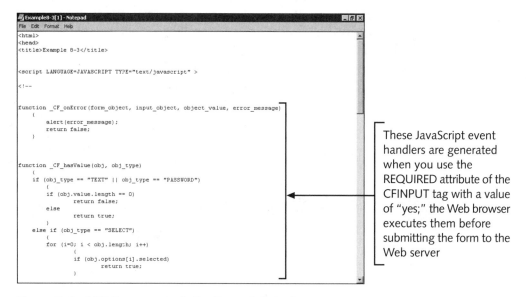

```
Example8-3[1] - Notepad
File  Edit  Format  Help
<html>
<head>
<title>Example 8-3</title>


<script LANGUAGE=JAVASCRIPT TYPE="text/javascript" >

<!--

function _CF_onError(form_object, input_object, object_value, error_message)
    {
        alert(error_message);
        return false;
    }


function _CF_hasValue(obj, obj_type)
    {
    if (obj_type == "TEXT" || obj_type == "PASSWORD")
        {
        if (obj.value.length == 0)
                return false;
        else
                return true;
        }
    else if (obj_type == "SELECT")
        {
        for (i=0; i < obj.length; i++)
            {
            if (obj.options[i].selected)
                    return true;
            }
```

These JavaScript event handlers are generated when you use the REQUIRED attribute of the CFINPUT tag with a value of "yes;" the Web browser executes them before submitting the form to the Web server

Figure 8-6   HTML source code for Example8-3.cfm

PropertyID [   ]
        [Continue]

Microsoft Internet Explorer
    ⚠ Error in PropertyID text.
            [OK]

Figure 8-7   Error message box displayed by JavaScript

6. Click **OK**. Notice that the form was not submitted.

7. Type **NIK4828** in the PropertyID text box.

8. Click the **Continue** button. The Web browser displays the form handler with user-entered data, as shown in Figure 8-8. Prior to sending the request to the

Web server, the Web browser executes the JavaScript event handlers. Similarly to what happened before, the JavaScript event handlers check to see if there is any data entered in the text box. The JavaScript event handlers find data in the text box, and the Web browser sends the request to the Web server along with user-entered data. The ColdFusion Server executes the debug_a_form.cfm ColdFusion template. This template is available on your Data Disk and it simply echoes all the data entered in the form. It provides a list of all the form fields the server receives along with the user-entered data.

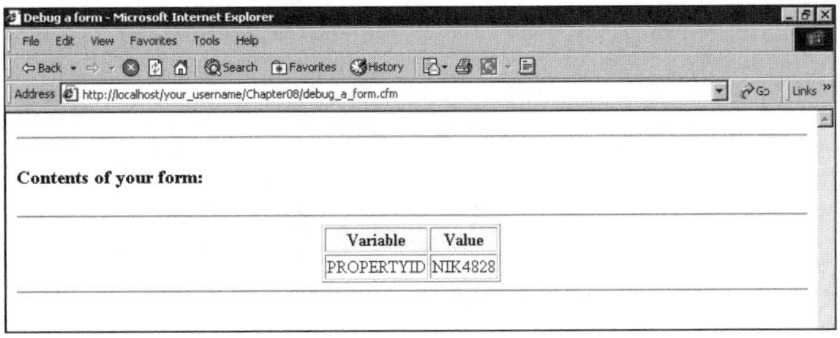

Figure 8-8   Web page displayed after submitting the form with data

The message that appeared when the validation failed was cryptic and not very helpful. This default message does not provide information regarding the cause of the error and the corrective action to be taken by the user. In the next section, you will learn about the attribute needed for generating useful error messages.

Generating Customized Error Messages

You can customize the error messages generated by the JavaScript data validation functions by using the MESSAGE attribute of the CFINPUT tag. When the completeness check fails (that is, the user does not enter any data), the value of the MESSAGE attribute is displayed. Recall from the earlier section that the default message is displayed if the MESSAGE attribute is not present. You can design user-friendly systems by using clear descriptions of what is expected from users in these messages.

The following example illustrates a form with a ColdFusion text box control with a data completeness check and a customized error message. This code is included in the Example8-4.cfm file in the Chapter08 folder on your Data Disk. The MESSAGE attribute that specifies the error message is defined in the highlighted line of code.

```
<html>
<head>
<title>Example 8-4</title>
</head>
<body>
<cfform action="debug_a_form.cfm" name="myForm">
<table>
```

```
<tr>
<td align="right">PropertyID</td>
<td><cfinput type="text" name="PropertyID" required="Yes"
message="Please enter a PropertyID to continue..."></td>
</tr>
<tr>
<td align="center" colspan="2"><input type="submit" value=
"Continue"></td>
</tr>
</table>
</cfform>
</body>
</html>
```

To learn about customized error messages using Example 8-4:

1. Type **http://localhost/your_username/Chapter08/Example8-4.cfm** in the Address text box of your Web browser, and press the **Enter** key. Notice that the Web page displayed is similar to the Web pages in the previous examples. See Figure 8-9.

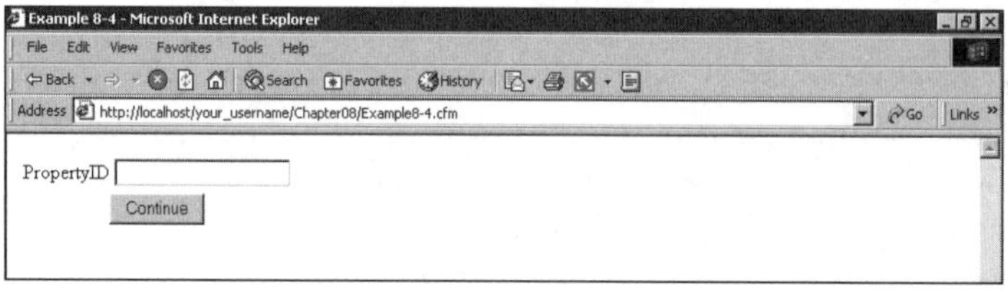

Figure 8-9   Web page displayed by Example8-4.cfm

2. Click **View** on the menu bar, and then click **Source** (or **Page Source**, if you use Netscape).

3. Maximize the window with the source code. Scroll down and look at the code. Notice that the JavaScript generated includes the customized error message. See Figure 8-10.

4. Close the source code window.

5. Click the **Continue** button without entering any text in the text box. The Web browser executes the JavaScript event handlers. Because there is no data in the text box, an alert message is displayed. Notice that this is a customized message showing the value of the MESSAGE attribute. See Figure 8-11.

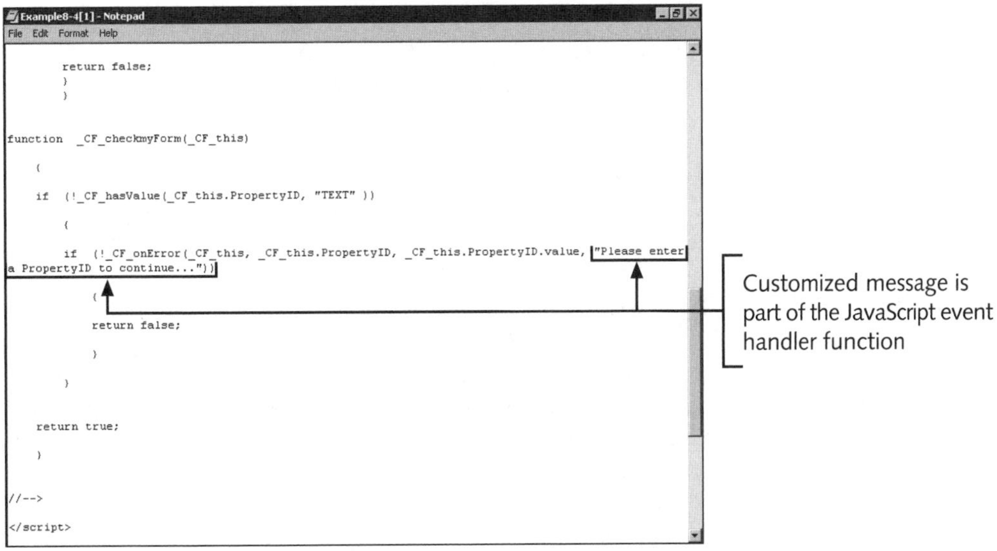

Figure 8-10   Source code for the Web page generated by Example8-4.cfm

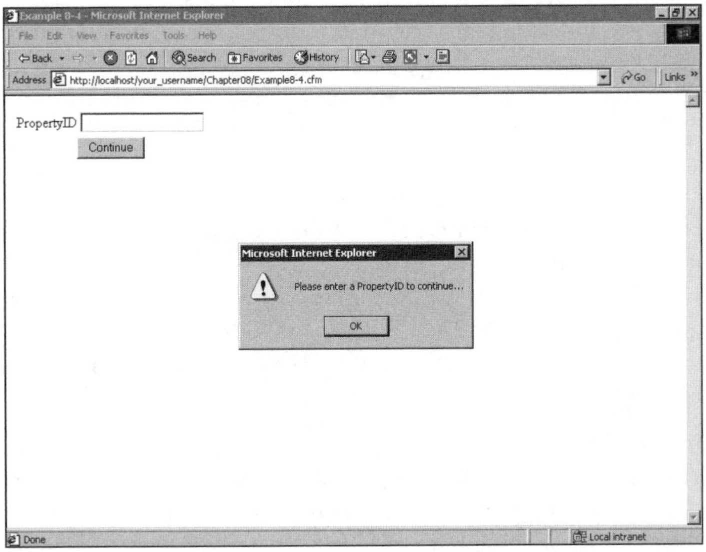

Figure 8-11   Message box with the customized error message

    6. Click **OK**.

    7. Type **NIK4829** in the PropertyID text box.

    8. Click the **Continue** button. The Web browser displays the form handler with user-entered data, as shown in Figure 8-12.

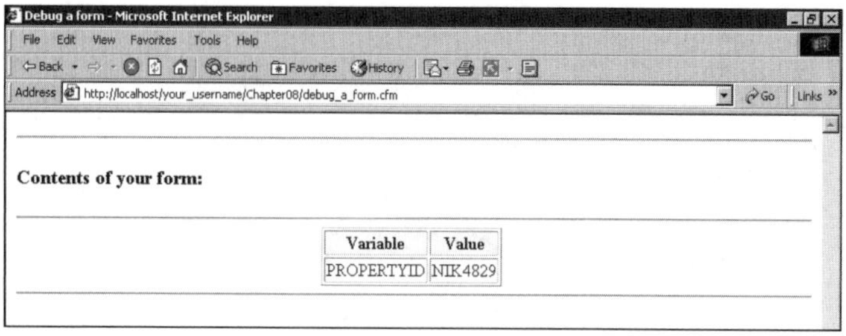

Figure 8-12   Web page displayed after submitting the form in Example 8-4 with data

As mentioned earlier, you do not need to be proficient in JavaScript to use the data validation functions provided by ColdFusion. The explanations of JavaScript are intended to help you understand how the Web browser can use the information you are coding in the CFML tags to validate data without any processing on the server side.

In addition to validating data entry in text boxes, you can use other form design techniques to ensure that users enter valid data. Forms often include groups of options where users have to select one or more of the options. Use proper design techniques when creating forms; for example, limit the number of options in a group and use appropriate controls such as radio buttons, checkboxes, and select boxes. These controls help to ensure that the user enters valid data. For example, suppose you are developing a form that helps agents add properties in the database. One field on the form asks agents to identify the region where the property is located, such as north, south, east, or west. You could use a group of radio button controls, with each control corresponding to a region. Using radio buttons ensures that agents will choose a region that corresponds to how you classify listings in your area. If you used a text box, agents could enter data they think is correct, such as "downtown" or "riverfront," but that your database considers invalid because search forms are designed to use only north, south, east, or west to describe regions. ColdFusion allows you to implement data completion checks on radio buttons, checkboxes, and select boxes.

Nikitha is very impressed with the schedule private showings form that you created in Chapter 4. However, she is concerned that some of the data on the form that her office is receiving by e-mail is incomplete and erroneous. For example, users forget to type their names and e-mail addresses. She has requested that you study the data received and build controls that would reduce incomplete and erroneous data entry. After studying the data, you decide that incomplete e-mail addresses and names are the first problems to tackle. You are planning to implement a data completeness check on the e-mail address and name text boxes.

To check for data completeness on text boxes:

1. Start ColdFusion Studio.

2. Click the **Resource Tab** button on the View toolbar to display the Resource Tab window.

3. If necessary, click the **Files** tab in the Resource Tab window.

4. Navigate to the Chapter08 folder in the folder list window.

5. In the file list window, scroll down until you see scheduleShowing.htm and increase the column width of the Name column to display entire filenames, if necessary.

6. Right-click the **scheduleShowing.htm** file, point to **File**, and then click **Rename** on the shortcut menu.

7. Type **scheduleShowing.cfm** to rename the file, and press the **Enter** key. To implement data validation using ColdFusion, you must create the form with CFML tags; the file should therefore have a .cfm extension.

8. Switch to your Web browser, and type the proper URL in the Address text box to open the scheduleShowing.cfm file. Your screen should look similar to Figure 8-13. Your task is to implement data completeness checks on the Name and E-mail address text boxes.

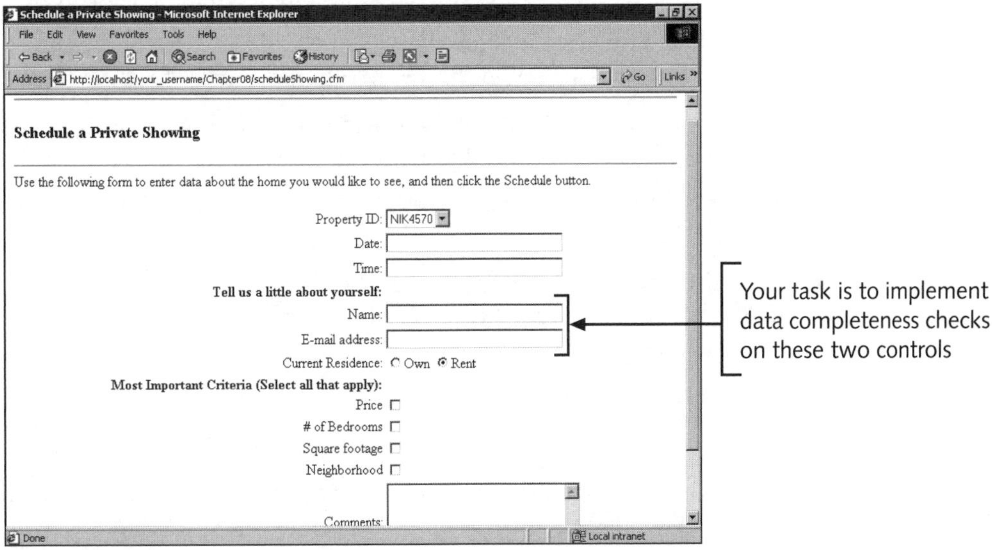

Figure 8-13   Web page displayed by scheduleShowing.cfm

The first step in setting up the data completion check is to create the CFFORM object by using CFFORM tags.

To create the form:

1. Switch to ColdFusion Studio, and click the **Resource Tab** button to close the Resource Tab window.

2. Open the file **scheduleShowing.cfm** in the Chapter08 folder.

3. Select **form** on line 13, and type **cfform** to replace it. Select and delete **method="post"** on the same line. CFFORM creates an HTML form with the METHOD attribute set to a value of POST automatically. You do not have to explicitly use the METHOD attribute.

4. Insert the cursor at the end of **cfform**, and press the **spacebar**. When the tag insight menu appears, double-click **name** on the tag insight menu, and type **sForm** as the name for the form. This creates a ColdFusion form with the name sForm (short for schedule a private showing form) so that you can use controls with data validation attributes in it.

5. Select **/form** on line 81, and type **/cfform** as the closing tag for the CFFORM object. Notice that ColdFusion Studio color-codes the tag, recognizing that it is a valid CFML tag.

After you create the form using the CFFORM tags, you are ready to set up the data completeness check on the controls. Start by making sure users complete the client name and e-mail fields by specifying that these fields are required.

To set up a data completeness check for the clientName and clientEmail fields:

1. In scheduleShowing.cfm, click between **<** and the keyword **input** on line 41, and then type **cf** to change the HTML input control to a CF input control.

2. Click between **size="30"** and **>** on the same line, and press the **spacebar**. Double-click **required** on the tag insight menu.

3. From the list of values, select **Yes**. This specifies that the user is required to complete the clientName field.

4. To set up a data completeness check on the clientEmail text box on line 45, change the input to **cfinput** and add a **required="Yes"** attribute value pair, as in Steps 1–3.

5. Save the file with the same name in the Chapter08 folder.

6. Switch to your Web browser and refresh **scheduleShowing.cfm**.

7. Submit the form without entering any data. You receive an error message that says "Error in clientName text." See Figure 8-14. Click **OK**.

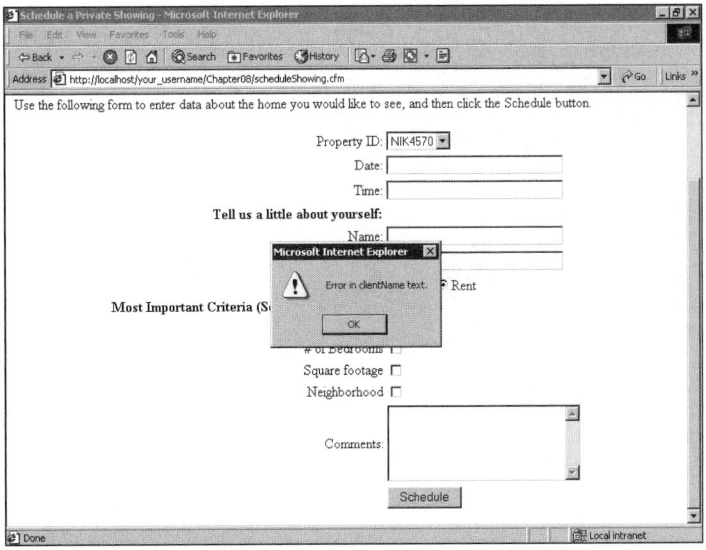

Figure 8-14 JavaScript alert with the default error message when the name check fails

This error message could be more informative—it's not clear whether the user entered incorrect data or failed to enter any text at all. A more helpful error message explains what the user should do to correctly complete the field. You can customize the error message to provide more helpful information.

To customize the error message:

1. Switch to ColdFusion Studio.

2. Add customized error messages by clicking between **required="Yes"** and **>** on line 41. Press the **spacebar** and select **message** from the tag insight menu by double-clicking it. Type **Please enter your name...** as the value for this attribute.

3. Use the same method to add the following customized error message on line 45: **Please enter your e-mail address...**

4. Save your file using the same name in the Chapter 08 folder.

5. Switch to your Web browser and refresh the file. Submit the form without entering any data, and notice the customized error message that you see, as shown in Figure 8-15.

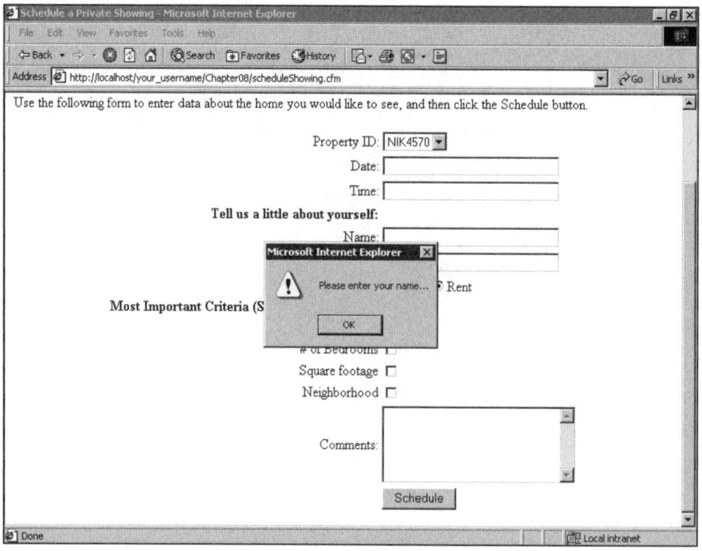

Figure 8-15   Customized error message displayed when the name check fails

6. Click **OK** to close the message.

7. Click in the **Name** text box. Type **Sandy Marshall**, and then click the **Schedule** button. The error message that you see now is because of the incomplete e-mail address text box, as shown in Figure 8-16.

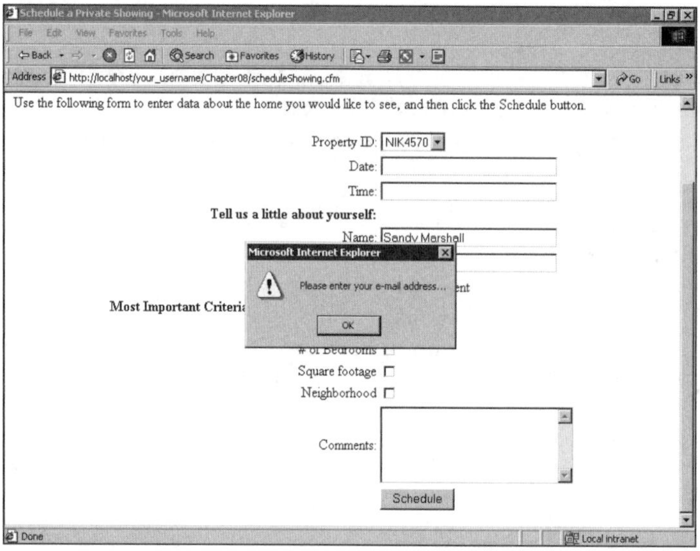

Figure 8-16   The name completeness check passes and the e-mail address check fails

8. Click **OK**.

9. Click in the **E-mail address** text box. Type **smarshall@uni.edu**, and then click the **Schedule** button. See Figure 8-17.

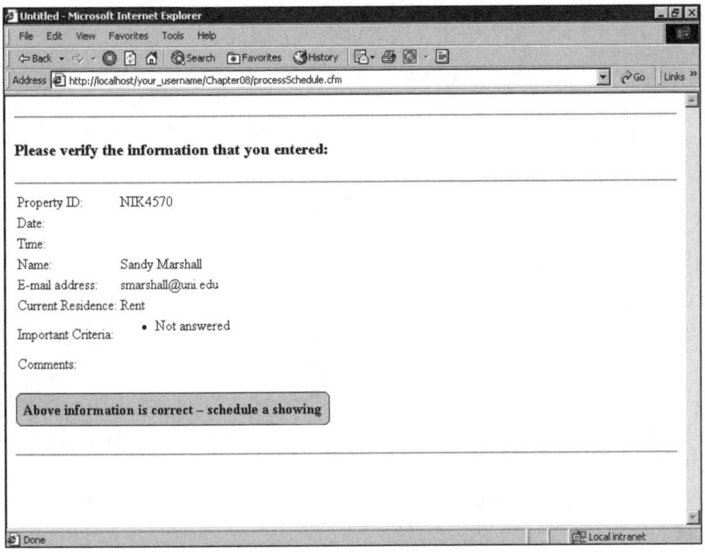

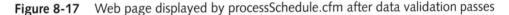

Figure 8-17   Web page displayed by processSchedule.cfm after data validation passes

Because there is data in both fields now, the form is submitted and the processSchedule.cfm form handler is executed. You have successfully implemented data completeness checks on text boxes.

In the next section, you will learn about radio buttons and how you can implement data completeness checks on them.

ColdFusion Radio Buttons and Data Completeness Checks

In situations where the data entry is restricted to one of several different options, you should use radio buttons instead of text boxes. Text boxes allow users to enter any text, creating a greater chance of minor variations in data that users enter. For example, when agents enter new properties into the NikRealty database, in the TypeOfHouse field they could enter single-story home, ranch home, ranch-style home, single-story contemporary home, and so on, all to describe a single-story ranch home. Such inconsistencies in the data will cause problems while searching through the database. If a user requests a search for all single-story homes in a certain area, the properties that were described as ranch homes will not be part of the search results. There is a good chance of losing potential sales in that situation. Your team has decided to redesign the property insertion screens using radio buttons. The following syntax creates a ColdFusion radio button:

```
<cfinput type="radio" name="radio button name" value="a
value">
```

The following syntax creates a set of radio buttons:

```
<cfinput type="radio" name="radio button name" value=
"value1">
<cfinput type="radio" name="radio button name" value=
"value2">
<cfinput type="radio" name="radio button name" value=
"value3">
```

One way of making sure that a user selects a radio button is by using the CHECKED attribute for the most commonly selected radio button. When the Web browser processes a radio button with the CHECKED attribute, it selects the radio button when the form is displayed. If necessary, the user can select any other radio button in the group. However, there is a chance that a user may inadvertently skip over the group of radio buttons and submit erroneous data. You can make sure that a user does not skip over a group of radio buttons by not using the CHECKED attribute at all. The Web browser would display the form with all radio buttons unchecked. Next, you should use the REQUIRED attribute and set its value to YES to implement a data completeness check to ensure that the user checks a radio button. If the user submits the form without clicking any of the radio buttons, the JavaScript event handlers would remind the user to select a radio button because of the data completeness check. Because you are forcing the user to select a radio button, there is a greater chance of accurate data being entered into the database.

One of your project members redesigned the TypeOfHouse input control using radio buttons in the insertScreen2.cfm file that you used in the previous chapter. Your task is to implement a data completeness check on this control.

To implement data completeness checks in the screen for inserting new properties:

1. Type **http://localhost/your_username/Chapter08/insertScreen2.cfm** in the Address text box of your Web browser, and press the **Enter** key. Your Web browser displays a page with a picture and a form, as shown in Figure 8-18. Notice that the TypeOfHouse field is now a group of radio buttons. None of the buttons are checked.

2. Switch to ColdFusion Studio.

3. Open **insertScreen2.cfm** in the Chapter08 folder on your Data Disk. See Figure 8-19. Notice that your team member has modified the template a little. There is a CFPARAM tag at the beginning of the template to specify a default image. The HTML form is now a ColdFusion form with CFFORM tags. The ACTION attribute of the form has been changed to "debug_a_form.cfm." Your first task is to change the HTML radio buttons to CFML radio buttons.

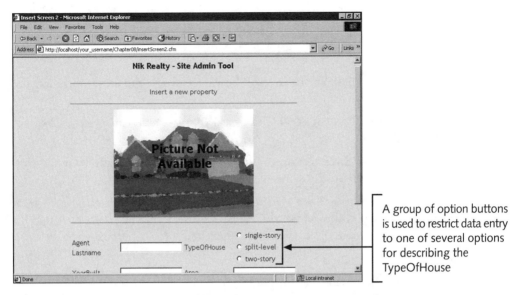

Figure 8-18   Web page displayed by Chapter08/insertScreen2.cfm

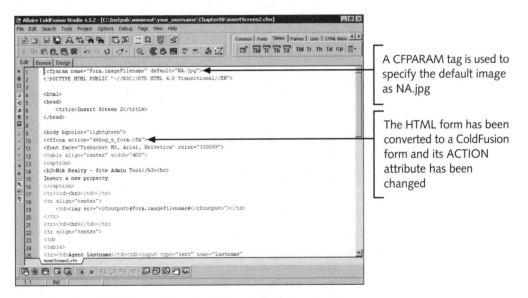

Figure 8-19   Initial insertScreen2.cfm in ColdFusion Studio

4. Select **input** on line 28, and type **cfinput**. You have converted the first HTML radio button into a ColdFusion radio button.

5. Use the same technique to convert the HTML radio buttons in lines 32 and 36 to ColdFusion radio buttons.

6. Insert the cursor to the left of the closing angle bracket (>) for the radio button on line 28 and press the **spacebar**. The tag insight menu opens.

7. Double-click **required**. ColdFusion Studio inserts the REQUIRED tag.

8. Double-click **Yes** to specify the value for this attribute, and then press the **spacebar**.

9. Double-click **message** and type **Please select the type of house to continue...**

10. Click the **Save** button on the Standard toolbar to save your file using the same name in the same location.

It is not necessary to use the REQUIRED button on all the other radio buttons in the group. Typically, you should use the REQUIRED attribute on the first radio button in a group for implementing a data completeness check. Your next task is to test the template.

To test insertScreen2.cfm:

1. Switch to your Web browser.

2. Refresh insertScreen2.cfm.

3. Click the **Continue** button without entering any data. See Figure 8-20. Notice that the data completeness check on the radio buttons fails and the Web browser displays a JavaScript alert.

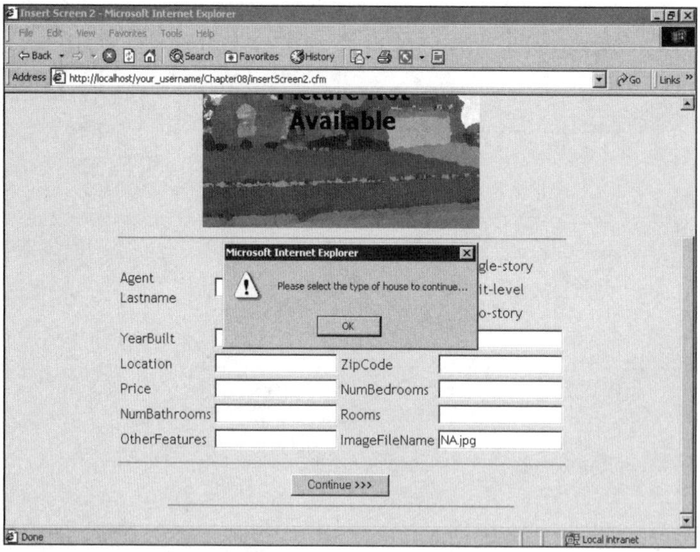

Figure 8-20   JavaScript alert displayed when the type of house data completeness check fails

4. Click **OK**.

5. Click the **two-story** radio button as the TypeOfHouse.

6. Click the **Continue** button to submit the form. The type of house data completeness check passes this time, and the Web browser displays debug_a_form.cfm with the contents of your form, as shown in Figure 8-21.

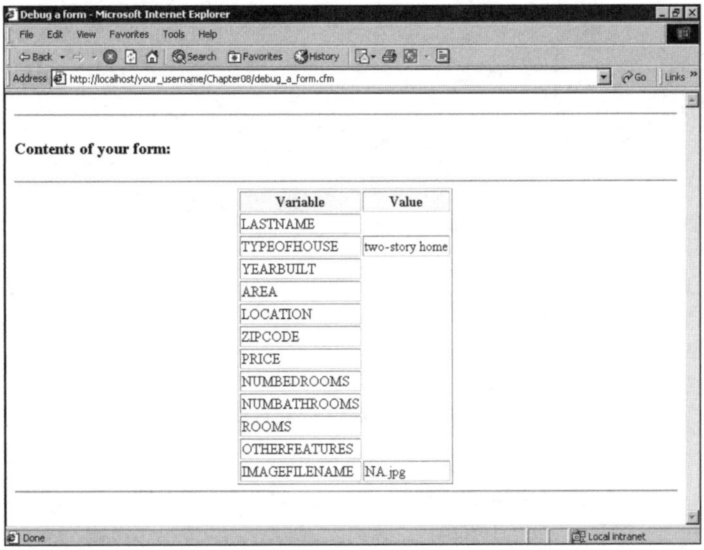

Figure 8-21   Web page displayed when the type of house data completeness check passes

You have successfully implemented data completeness checks on a radio button by using the required="Yes" attribute value pair. So far, you have seen that you can implement data completeness checks on text boxes and radio buttons. Table 8-2 contains a table of several controls and data validation checks. You can use this table as a reference throughout this chapter. The table contains a row for each control and a column for each data validation technique. To implement a particular data validation technique on a particular control, you have to use the attribute-value pairs shown in the intersection of the row for the control and column for the data validation technique.

Table 8-2   Attribute-Value Pairs for Implementing Data Validation Checks on ColdFusion Controls

Control\Check	Completeness	Data Type	Range and Limit	Picture	Algorithmic
Text Box Password	required= "yes"	validate= "date" validate= "time" validate= "float" validate= "integer"	range="min_value, max_value" (Enforces validate= "float")	validate= "social_security_number" validate= "telephone" validate= "zipcode"	validate= "creditcard" (Implements Mod10 Algorithm)
Radio Button	required="yes"	<----------	Indirectly by design		---------->
Checkbox	required="yes" (1)	<----------	Indirectly by design		---------->
Selectbox	required="yes" (2)	<----------	Indirectly by design		---------->

(1) Meaningful only when used with multiple checkboxes (implements "check at least one" logic)
(2) Meaningful only when size >1

CF Checkboxes and Data Completeness Checks

As seen in Table 8-2, you can implement data completeness checks on checkboxes as well as radio buttons and text boxes. Recall from Chapter 4 that checkboxes are useful for situations that require users to select none or one or more options from several options. For example, when agents insert new properties, you may want to use checkboxes for specifying important features of the house. Instead of having agents describe important features of the house in a text box, you may want to use checkboxes, one for each of the following features: breakfast bar, cathedral ceilings, central vacuum system, fireplace(s), hardwood floors, intercom system, pantry, skylight(s), vaulted ceilings, walk-in closet(s), wet bar, and whirlpool. Data entry would be simplified, agents are reminded what to look for when entering data, and search programs would extract the right properties.

When a data completeness check is implemented on multiple checkboxes, it essentially implements a logic of "check at least one box." In the previous example, a data completeness check would ensure that an agent checks at least one other feature for describing the house. You saw in an earlier chapter that according to HTTP/HTML specifications, checkboxes are handled in a manner a little different from other controls. A single checkbox needs a CFPARAM tag to handle the situation when the user does not check the checkbox. Therefore, a data completeness check for checkboxes is meaningful only when a form contains multiple checkboxes with the same name. The following syntax creates a ColdFusion checkbox:

```
<cfinput type="checkbox" name="checkbox name" value="a
value">
```

The following syntax creates a set of checkboxes:

```
<cfinput type="checkbox" name="checkbox name" value=
"value1">
<cfinput type="checkbox" name="checkbox name" value=
"value2">
<cfinput type="checkbox" name="checkbox name" value=
"value3">
```

You can use the REQUIRED attribute and set its value to YES to implement a data completeness check. As mentioned previously, the user has to check at least one box to pass this check. Typically, the REQUIRED attribute is used on the first checkbox.

Nikitha is pleased with an initial demonstration of the data completeness checks on the request for a private showing form. During this demonstration, she is concerned that clients are not taking time to indicate what criteria are important to them when choosing a home, such as square footage or neighborhood. She feels that understanding client needs is an important part of running the business well. She asks you to design a control that makes clients check at least one important criteria before scheduling a showing.

To set up data completeness checks on checkboxes:

1. If necessary, switch to ColdFusion Studio.

2. If necessary, click the **scheduleShowing.cfm** document tab at the bottom of the window.

3. Change input to **cfinput** on lines 57, 61, 65, and 69 to convert the HTML checkboxes to ColdFusion checkboxes.

4. Click between **value="Price"** and **>** on line 57, and then press the **spacebar**.

5. Select **required** from the tag insight menu, and select **Yes** from the list of values. Note that it is not necessary to include the required attribute on every checkbox in the set.

6. To design a customized error message, start by pressing the **spacebar**. Select **message** from the tag insight menu, and type **Please select at least one important criterion to continue...** See Figure 8-22.

7. Click **Save** on the Standard toolbar to save your file.

8. Switch to your Web browser, and type the URL to open scheduleShowing.cfm.

9. Refresh the document.

8

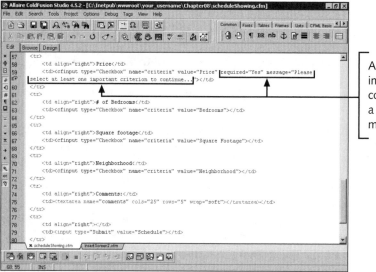

Attribute-value pairs for implementing a data completeness check with a customized error message on a checkbox

Figure 8-22   CF Studio Editor displaying scheduleShowing.cfm with data completeness checks on the checkboxes

10. Type **Sandy Marshall** in the Name text box and **smarshall@uni.edu** in the E-mail address text box, and then click the **Schedule** button. The name and e-mail address data completeness checks pass, but the important criteria check fails and an alert is displayed accordingly, as shown in Figure 8-23.

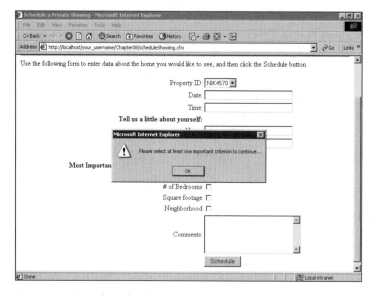

Figure 8-23   Alert displayed when the important criteria data completeness check fails

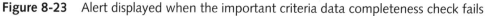

11. Click **OK**.

12. Select **Price** and **# of Bedrooms** as the important criteria, and then click the **Schedule** button. All three data completeness checks pass and the form handler displays user-entered data. See Figure 8-24.

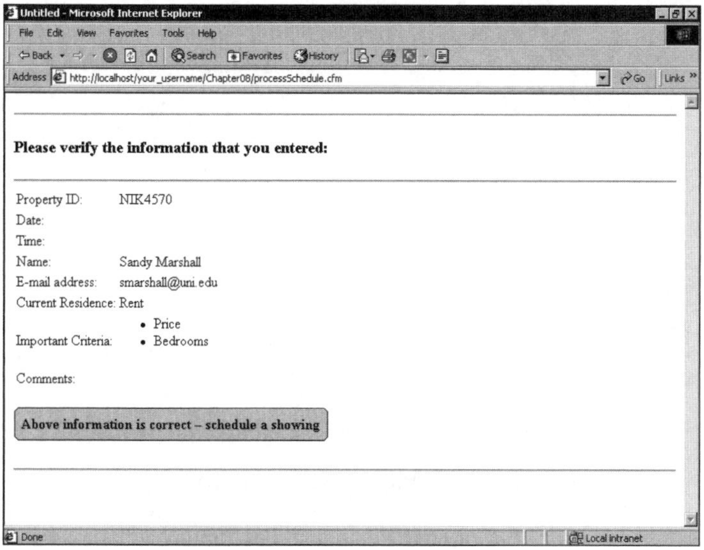

Figure 8-24   Web page displayed when the important criteria data completeness check passes

In the next section, you will learn about implementing data completeness checks on select boxes.

Cold Fusion Select Boxes and Data Completeness Checks

As seen in Table 8-2, you can implement data completeness checks on select boxes, too. Recall from Chapter 4 that select boxes work similarly to radio buttons. They can be used in situations that require users to select one option from a list of several options. Select boxes occupy less space on the screen and expand in response to a user click. When you use the MULTIPLE attribute for a SELECT tag, users can select multiple items from a select box. In that case, a select box works like a set of check boxes.

By design, if the size of the select box is 1, meaning that the list contains only one item, and only one item is displayed, it is obviously selected and you do not need a data completeness check. If the SIZE attribute of a select box is 2 or more, meaning that the list contains more than one item, and multiple options are displayed, then you should set up a data completeness check to require a user to select an option. The syntax for generating a select box in ColdFusion that allows you to implement a data completeness check is as follows:

```
<cfselect name="select box name" size= "2 or more">
<OPTION value="value1">option 1
<OPTION value="value2">option 2
<OPTION value="value3">option 3
...
</cfselect>
```

You can use the REQUIRED attribute and sets its value to YES to implement a data completeness check when the size is two or more. In the following exercise, you will implement a data completeness check on the PropertyID select box in the request for a private showing form.

To implement a data completeness check on a select box:

1. Switch to ColdFusion Studio.

2. Change **select** to **cfselect** on lines 18 and 24 to convert the HTML select box for the PropertyID to a ColdFusion select box.

3. Click to the left of **>** on line 18, and press the **spacebar**.

4. Double-click **size** on the tag insight menu, and type **4** as its value.

5. Click again to the left of **>** and press the **spacebar**.

6. Double-click **required** on the tag insight menu, and then double-click **Yes** in the list of values.

7. To design a customized error message, start by pressing the **spacebar**. Double-click **message** on the tag insight menu, and then type **Please select the property you wish to schedule a showing for...** See Figure 8-25.

8. Click **Save** on the Standard toolbar to save your file.

9. Switch to your Web browser, and type the URL in the Address text box to open scheduleShowing.cfm.

10. Refresh the document.

11. Click the **Schedule** button. The PropertyID data completeness check fails and a message is displayed, as shown in Figure 8-26. Notice in Figure 8-26 that the PropertyID select box displays four options because the SIZE attribute is set to a value of 4.

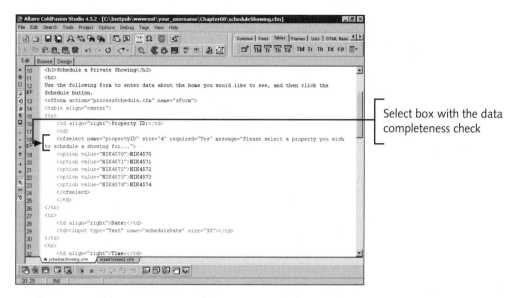

Figure 8-25   CF Studio Editor displaying scheduleShowing.cfm with data completeness check on the select box

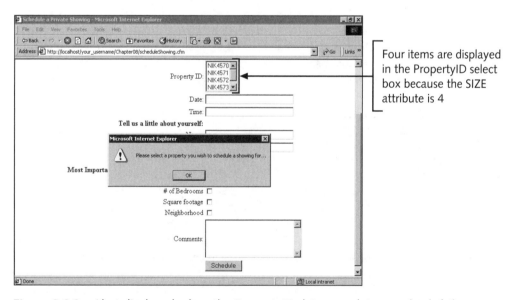

Figure 8-26   Alert displayed when the PropertyID data completeness check fails

12. Click **OK**.

13. Select **NIK4571** in the PropertyID select box.

14. Click the **Schedule** button. Notice that the PropertyID check passes and the Name check fails now, as shown in Figure 8-27.

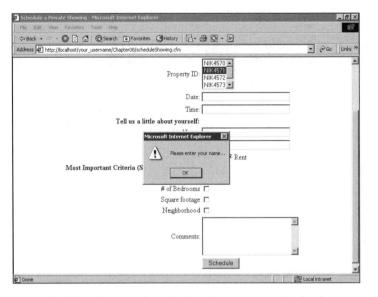

Figure 8-27   Alert displayed when the PropertyID check passes and the Name check fails

15. Click **OK**.

You have successfully implemented a data completeness check on a select box. Actually, the CFSELECT tag is very sophisticated and allows the use of other attributes that can dynamically populate the values and options. These features of the CFSELECT tag are covered later in the chapter.

DATA TYPE VALIDATION CHECKS

Checking for completeness is the simplest type of data validation you can perform on a control. The next level of sophistication in data validation is a check to determine whether the data entered is of the proper data type. For example, an agent may inadvertently type a letter in the NumBedrooms field that expects only integer numbers. Data validation techniques designed to prevent this kind of error are known as **data type validation checks**. You implement a data type validation check in ColdFusion by using an attribute for the CFINPUT tag named VALIDATE and set its value to date, time, float, or integer. When the ColdFusion Server executes this tag with a value of date, it generates JavaScript code that verifies whether the data entered is in the form mm/dd/yyyy. If it is, the form is submitted. If it is not, it generates an error message. You can generate customized error messages by using the MESSAGE attribute. If the value is time, data is verified by comparing it with hh:mm:ss. When the value is float, data is checked to see whether it is a valid decimal number. Similarly, a value of integer ensures that only integers are allowed as entries.

The following example illustrates a form with a ColdFusion text box control with a data type validation check along with a completeness check. This code is included in the Example8-5.cfm file in the Chapter08 folder on your Data Disk. The highlighted code shows how to set up the data type validation check by using a VALIDATE attribute set to a value of INTEGER. This means that users must enter an integer value in the NumYears text box to correctly complete the form.

```
<html>
<head>
<title>Example 8-5</title>
</head>
<body>
<cfform action="debug_a_form.cfm" name="myForm">
<table>
<tr>
<td align="right">How many years are you planning to live
in this house?</td>
<td><cfinput type="text" name="NumYears" required="Yes"
validate="integer" message="Please enter a number
(1,2,3,...) to continue..."></td>
</tr>
<tr>
<td align="center" colspan="2"><input type="submit" value=
"Continue"></td>
</tr>
</table>
</cfform>
</body>
</html>
```

To investigate data type validation using Example8-5.cfm:

1. Type **http://localhost/your_username/Chapter08/Example8-5.cfm** in the Address text box of your Web browser, and press the **Enter** key. The Web page shown in Figure 8-28 is displayed.

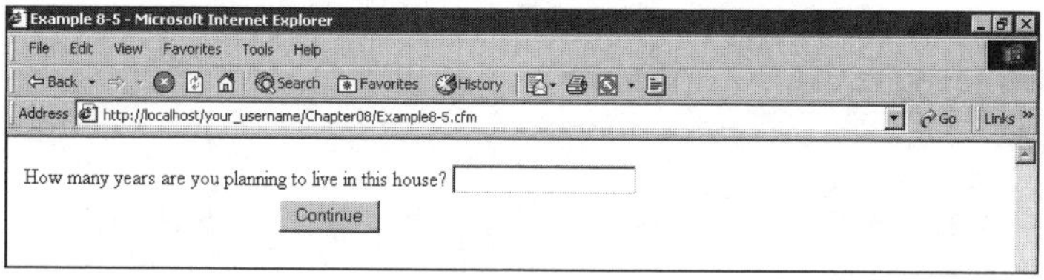

Figure 8-28   Web page displayed by Example8-5.cfm

2. Click **View** on the menu bar, and then click **Source**. The Web browser opens a window and displays the HTML source code generated when the ColdFusion Server executes Example8-5.cfm. Maximize the window and examine the code

by scrolling down. See Figure 8-29. When the ColdFusion Server processes a CFINPUT tag with the VALIDATE attribute set to INTEGER, it generates JavaScript functions in the output that would be executed just prior to the submission of the form by your Web browser. When you click the Continue button, these JavaScript functions would check the contents of the text box. If the data entered in the text box is not a valid integer (for example, s12d), a message is displayed that says that there is an error in the data entered. If the data in the text box is a valid integer (for example, 4), the form is submitted. When the form is submitted, the debug_a_form.cfm ColdFusion template is executed. This template echoes all the data entered in the form.

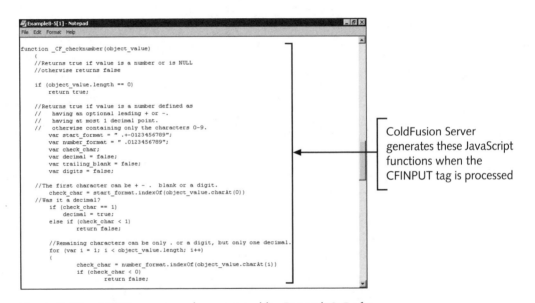

ColdFusion Server generates these JavaScript functions when the CFINPUT tag is processed

Figure 8-29   HTML source code generated by Example8-5.cfm

3. Close the window with the HTML source code.

4. Type **s12d** in the text box, and click the **Continue** button. Because s12d is not an integer, the data type validation check fails and an alert message is displayed, as shown in Figure 8-30.

5. Click **OK**.

6. Select **s12d** in the text box, and type **4** to replace the selection.

7. Click the **Continue** button. The data type validation check passes and the form is submitted. The form handler displays a page, as shown in Figure 8-31.

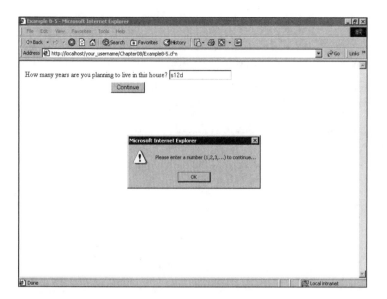

Figure 8-30 Alert message displayed when the data type validation check fails

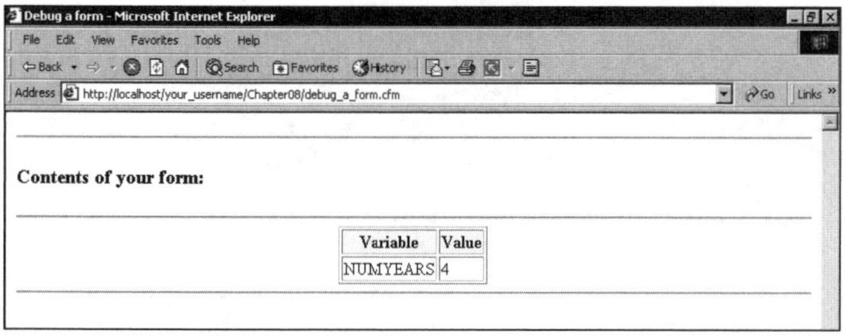

Figure 8-31 Web page displayed by the form handler when the data type validation check passes

In the previous example, you learned how to validate integer data. Similarly, you can validate data to check and see whether it is a valid date, time, or a real number (float). Some of the NikRealty agents have commented to Nikitha that the dates and times some clients entered in the scheduling form are creating problems. For example, one client from England who recently obtained a job with a local agricultural equipment manufacturing company entered a date starting with the day followed by the month, as in 13/7/03, instead of the standard U.S. format of starting with the month followed by the day, as in 7/13/03. Your task is to ensure that users are entering valid dates and times.

To set up data type checks on text boxes:

1. Switch to ColdFusion Studio, and open the **scheduleShowing.cfm** file, if necessary.

2. Change input to **cfinput** on lines 29 and 33 for the text boxes named scheduleDate and scheduleTime to convert them to ColdFusion text boxes.

3. Click between **size="30"** and **>** on line 29, and press the **spacebar**.

4. Type **validate="date" required="Yes" message="Please enter a date in the form mm/dd/yyyy..."**. See Figure 8-32.

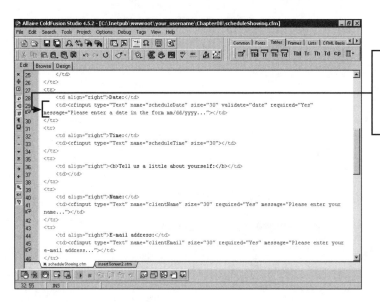

A data completeness check, a data type check, and a customized message are implemented on this control

Figure 8-32   Data type validation on the date field

When the ColdFusion server executes this tag, it generates JavaScript code that will be executed prior to the submission of the form to the server. This code will check to see whether that data entered in this box matches the specified date format. If the format matches, the form is submitted. If the format does not match, the user sees the message specified in the MESSAGE tag.

5. Click between **size="30"** and **>** on line 33, and press the **spacebar**.

6. Type **validate="time" required="Yes" message="Please enter a time entry in the form hh:mm..."**.

7. Click the **Save** button on the Standard toolbar to save your work.

Now you can test the file in your browser and verify that the data validation checks ensure that users enter complete and accurate information.

To test the modified file:

1. Switch to your Web browser, and type the URL to open scheduleShowing.cfm. Refresh the page.

2. Click **NIK4571** in the PropertyID select box.

3. Click the **Schedule** button. Notice that you are prompted to enter a date. The error message appears because you set the REQUIRED attribute to YES in Step 4.

4. Click **OK** to close the alert dialog box.

5. Type **13/7/2003** as the date, and then click **Schedule**. You see the error message again because the date is in the wrong format. See Figure 8-33.

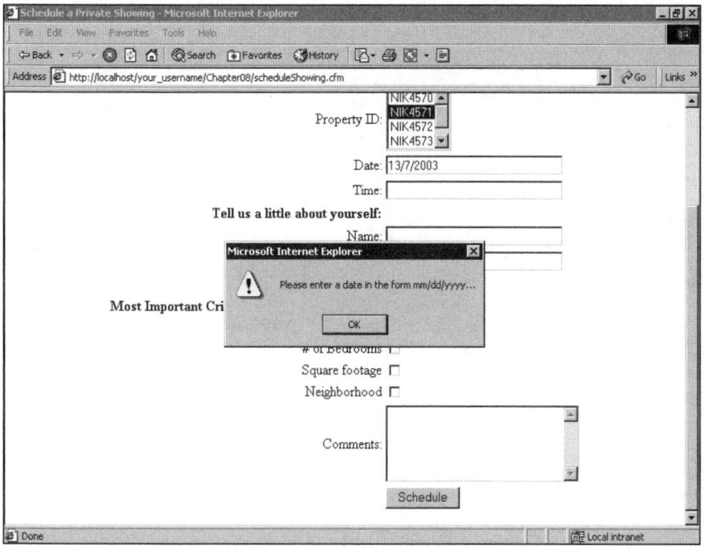

Figure 8-33   JavaScript date alert displayed when the date data type check fails

6. Click **OK** to close the error message.

7. Change the date in the date text box to **7/13/2003**.

8. Click the **Schedule** button. The date is accepted, but you see a message alerting you to enter a valid time. See Figure 8-34.

9. Click **OK** to close the error message.

10. In the Time text box, type **10:30**. Then enter a name and an e-mail address, and select **Price** as the important criterion.

11. Click the **Schedule** button. All the data passes the validation checks and the form is submitted.

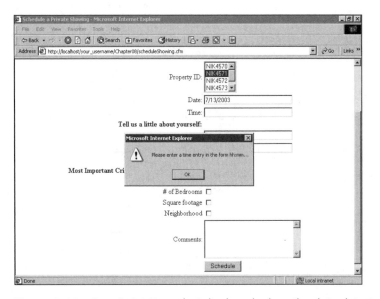

Figure 8-34   JavaScript time alert displayed when the date data type check passes and the time data type check fails

You have successfully implemented data type checks on two controls in this exercise. In the next section, you will learn about range and limit checks.

USING RANGE AND LIMIT CHECKS

For numerical data, you can design further tests to ensure that data is entered according to certain mathematical guidelines. For certain data items, you can design theoretical limits within which the data has to fall. For example, you can specify and check for the maximum and minimum possible values for an item. Checking for these values helps increase the accuracy of the data collected.

ColdFusion can generate JavaScript code that checks to see whether the data entered is between specified values. Such checks are known as **range and limit checks**. You implement a range and limit check in ColdFusion by using an attribute for the CFINPUT tag named RANGE and set its value to "*min_value, max_value*," where min_value is the theoretical minimum value that you expect and the max_value is the theoretical maximum value you expect. When the ColdFusion Server executes this tag, it generates JavaScript code that verifies first whether the data entered is a number and then whether it is between the specified min_value and max_value. If it is, the form is submitted; otherwise, an error message is generated. You can generate customized error messages by using the MESSAGE attribute.

The following example illustrates a form with a ColdFusion text box control with a range and limit check along with a completeness check and a data type check. The highlighted code shows how to design a range check by setting the RANGE attribute to "1,30." This means that users must enter text between 1 and 30 in the text box to correctly complete the form. This code is included in the Example8-6.cfm file in the Chapter08 folder on your Data Disk. You can run this example and experiment with it as you did in the previous sections.

```
<html>
<head>
<title>Example 8-6</title>
</head>
<body>
<cfform action="debug_a_form.cfm" name="myForm">
<table>
<tr>
<td align="right">How many years are you planning to live
in this house?</td>
<td><cfinput type="text" name="NumYears" required="Yes"
validate="integer" range="1,30" message="Please enter a
number (1,2,3,...,30) to continue..."></td>
</tr>
<tr>
<td align="center" colspan="2"><input type="submit" value=
"Continue"></td>
</tr>
</table>
</cfform>
</body>
</html>
```

When the ColdFusion Server processes the CFINPUT tag in this code, it generates JavaScript, including a function to validate the data in the NumYears text box. When you click the Continue button, this JavaScript function checks the contents of the text box. If the data entered is not between 1 and 30 (for example, if you enter 40 or −3), an error message is displayed. By default, the error message indicates there is an error in the data. You can customize the error message by using the MESSAGE attribute, as in previous examples. If the data in the text box is between the two limits (for example, if you enter 4), the form is submitted. When the form is submitted, the debug_a_form.cfm ColdFusion template is executed. This template echoes all the data entered in the form.

USING PICTURE CHECKS

Often, you are required to design forms that ask users to enter their telephone numbers, Social Security numbers, and zip codes. Users must enter this type of data in a certain pattern. For example, Social Security numbers follow the pattern ###-##-####, where # represents numbers separated by hyphens or spaces. If you design input controls that check to see whether data fits a specified pattern and alerts users if it does not, you are using **picture checks**.

You implement picture checks in ColdFusion by using the VALIDATE attribute for the CFINPUT and set its value to social_security_number, telephone, or zip code. When the ColdFusion Server executes this tag, it generates JavaScript code that verifies whether the data entered is a valid Social Security number, telephone number, or zip code. When the value is "telephone," ColdFusion generates JavaScript that verifies a telephone entry. Telephone data must be entered in the pattern ###-###-####. The hyphen separator (-) can be replaced with a space. The area code and exchange must begin with a digit between 1 and 9.

When the value is specified as "zipcode," the generated JavaScript routine implements a check so that the number entered is either five digits or nine digits in the form #####-####. The hyphen separator can be replaced with a blank.

When the value is "social_security_number," the Number must be entered in the pattern ###-##-####. The hyphen separator (-) can be replaced with a blank. You can generate customized error messages by using the MESSAGE attribute.

The following example illustrates a form with a ColdFusion text box control with a picture check. The highlighted code shows how to design a picture check by setting the VALIDATE attribute to a value of "telephone." This means that users must enter text that matches the ###-###-#### pattern to correctly complete the form. This code is included in the Example8-7.cfm file in the Chapter08 folder on your Data Disk. You can run this example and experiment with it as you did in the previous sections.

```
<html>
<head>
<title>Example 8-7</title>
</head>
<body>
<cfform action="debug_a_form.cfm" name="myForm">
<table>
<tr>
<td align="right">Please enter your telephone number
(999-999-9999):</td>
<td><cfinput type="text" name="Phone" validate=
"telephone"></td>
</tr>
<tr>
<td align="center" colspan="2"><input type="submit" value=
"Continue"></td>
</tr>
</table>
</cfform>
</body>
</html>
```

When the ColdFusion Server processes such a CFINPUT tag, it generates JavaScript including a function to run a picture check. When you click the Continue button, this JavaScript function checks the contents of the text box. If the data entered in the text box is not in the pattern of ###-###-#### or ### ### #### (for example, if you enter 555 1234), an error message is displayed. By default, the error message indicates there is an error in the data. You can customize the error message by using the MESSAGE attribute, as in previous examples. If the data in the text box is formatted as a telephone number (for example, if you enter 319 555 1234), the form is submitted. When the form is submitted, the debug_a_form.cfm ColdFusion template is executed. This template echoes all the data entered in the form.

The last task Nikitha asks you to perform is to include a text box for the client's phone number and implement checks to make sure the phone number is formatted correctly.

To set up a picture check:

1. Switch to ColdFusion studio, and open **scheduleShowing.cfm** if necessary.

2. Click at the beginning of line 43, and select the entire row of the table by dragging to the beginning of line 47.

3. Press **Ctrl+C** to copy the highlighted row to the Clipboard.

4. Click at the beginning of line 47, and then press **Ctrl+V** to paste the copied row.

5. On line 48, select the caption **E-mail Address**, and then type **Phone number (999-999-9999)** to replace it.

6. On line 49, select **clientEmail**, and type **clientPhone** to change the name of the text box to clientPhone.

7. On line 49, change the message to **"Please enter your phone number in the format 999-999-9999..."**.

8. Click to the left of the **>** bracket. Press the **spacebar**, and double-click **validate** on the tag insight menu.

9. Double-click **telephone** in the list of values. See Figure 8-35.

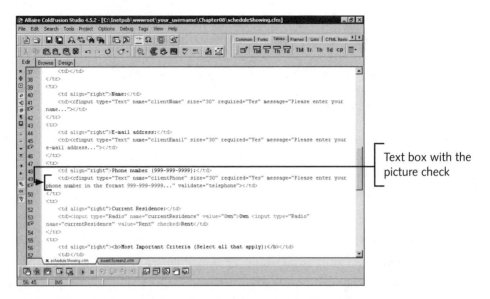

Text box with the
picture check

Figure 8-35 Picture check on the phone number field

10. Click the **Save** button on the Standard toolbar to save your work.

Now you can test the file in your browser and verify that the picture check ensures that users enter complete and accurate information.

To test the modified file:

1. Switch to your Web browser, type its URL, and open **scheduleShowing.cfm**.

2. Refresh the file.

3. Select a PropertyID.

4. Enter the date, time, a name, and an e-mail address.

5. In the Phone number text box, type **999-12345**, and then click the **Schedule** button. Notice that the picture check validation fails because the data entered is not a valid phone number. See Figure 8-36.

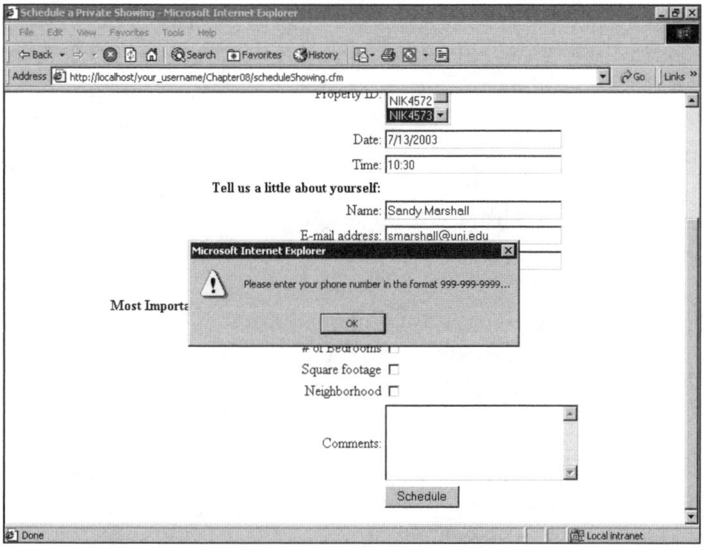

Figure 8-36   Error message displayed when the phone number picture check fails

6. Click **OK**.

7. Change the phone number to **319 555 1234**, and then click the **Schedule** button. Notice that the phone number is valid, but the important criteria validation check fails. Click **OK**.

8. Select **Price** and then click the **Schedule** button. The form passes all the checks you have set up and the form is submitted. Don't worry that the processSchedule.cfm does not display the phone number. Your focus in this exercise is on picture checks.

In the previous exercises, you implemented completeness checks, data type checks, and picture checks. In the next section, you will learn about self-checking digits or algorithmic data validation checks.

USING SELF-CHECKING DIGITS OR ALGORITHMIC CHECKS

On some forms, certain key values are designed so that one of the digits can be mathematically computed by using the other digits. For example, a certain digit in credit card numbers can be computed by using the other digits. The data entered is separated into two parts, and the digits are processed according to this mathematical algorithm. If the result matches the other digit, the data is valid; otherwise the data is not valid and an error message is generated. Such checks are known as **self-checking digits** or **algorithmic checks**.

As mentioned previously, credit card numbers are a good example of data for which you should use an algorithm check. An algorithm known as the Mod10 algorithm assigns credit card numbers. By multiplying the first 15 digits in the credit card numbers individually, each with a certain predetermined value based on its position, adding up the products, and then dividing the sum by a certain number, you should get a result that matches the last digit. If the result matches the last digit, you have a valid credit card number; otherwise not. ColdFusion allows you to implement a Mod10 algorithm on credit card numbers by using the VALIDATE attribute and setting its value to "creditcard." When the ColdFusion Server executes this tag, it generates JavaScript code that would verify whether the data entered is a valid credit card number by processing it using the Mod10 algorithm. Blanks and dashes are ignored while processing the data. You can generate customized error messages by using the MESSAGE attribute.

The following example illustrates a form with a ColdFusion text box control with an algorithmic check. The highlighted code shows how to design an algorithmic check by setting the VALIDATE attribute to a value of "creditcard." This means that users must enter text in a valid credit card format. This code is included in the Example8-8.cfm file in the Chapter08 folder on your Data Disk. You can experiment with this example as you did with the examples earlier in this chapter.

```
<html>
<head>
<title>Example 8-8</title>
</head>
<body>
<cfform action="debug_a_form.cfm" name="myForm">
<table>
<tr>
<td align="right">Please enter your credit card number:
</td>
<td><cfinput type="text" name="ccNumber" validate=
"creditcard"></td>
</tr>
<tr>
<td align="center" colspan="2"><input type="submit" value=
"Continue"></td>
</tr>
</table>
</cfform>
</body>
</html>
```

When the ColdFusion Server processes the VALIDATE tag, it generates JavaScript code including a function that checks the contents of the Credit Card text box when you click the Continue button. Spaces and dashes are removed, and the number is processed using the Mod10 algorithm. If the data entered is not valid according to the algorithm, a message is displayed that says that there is an error in the data entered. If the data in the text box is according to the algorithm, the form is submitted. When the form is submitted, the debug_a_form.cfm ColdFusion template is executed. You can customize the error message by using the MESSAGE attribute. As mentioned previously, all the text box data validation techniques can be used on password boxes too. Therefore, you can implement this algorithm on a password box, in case you want credit card numbers to be hidden when they are typed.

Dynamically Populating Select Boxes with the CFSELECT Tag

One of the best ways to ensure that data is consistent is by dynamically extracting option values and descriptions from databases and populating select boxes. The technique is especially useful for primary keys and foreign keys in relational databases. When tables have to be joined on common fields, designers have to ensure that the data in the common fields is consistent in terms of content as well as case. For example, when inserting a new property into the NikRealty database, you can use a select box for specifying the listing agent's last name. The select box should contain all the agents' last names as option descriptions, and the values should be the corresponding AgentIDs. If data is extracted from the database and then used to populate the select box, you can be sure that there will be no record in the Properties table that does not have a proper AgentID associated with it.

Dynamically populating SELECT boxes involves two steps: the first is to design and execute a query that extracts the data from the databases that is to be used in the select boxes, and the second is to actually use the CFSELECT tag to generate the select box. The CFSELECT tag works like a QUERY loop and outputs the data from the records, one option in the select box for each record in the query.

The syntax for the CFSELECT box with the parameters necessary for you to do this is:

```
<CFSELECT NAME="selName"
REQUIRED="Yes/No"
MESSAGE="text"
SIZE="integer"
MULTIPLE="Yes/No"
QUERY="query_name"
SELECTED="column_value"
VALUE="value_column"
DISPLAY="display_column">
</CFSELECT>
```

In the CFSELECT tag, *query_name* is the name of the query that is executed to extract data from the database tables. The CFSELECT tag works much like a QUERY loop created with CFLOOP. The first record is processed, and the data in the *value_column* field is the value for the first item. This value would also be displayed as the description visible to users if the DISPLAY= "*display_column*" is omitted. If this attribute value pair is not omitted, the contents of the *display_column* field are used as the description for the item. Similarly, the next record is processed, and so on, until all the records in the query are processed and there is an option for each record in the query. The ColdFusion Server generates a SELECTED attribute for the option when the value in the *value_column* matches the *column_value* specified in the SELECTED attribute.

To dynamically populate the select box for the Property IDs:

1. Switch to ColdFusion studio, and open the **scheduleShowing.cfm** file, if necessary.

2. Click at the beginning of line 1, and press the **Enter** key.

3. Press the **Up Arrow** key, type **<cfquery datasource="your_username" name="getData">**, and then press **Enter**.

4. Type **SELECT PropertyID FROM Properties**, and then press **Enter**.

5. Type **</cfquery>** to close the query tag. You have created a query to extract data from the NikRealty database.

6. In line 21, in the CFML for the select box, click to the left of the **>** character, and press the **spacebar**.

7. Double-click **query** on the tag insight menu.

8. Type **getData** as the name of the query. Press the **Right Arrow** key.

9. Press the **spacebar** and double-click **value** in the tag-insight menu.

10. Type **PropertyID** as the value column.

11. Select and delete lines **22** to **26**. See Figure 8-37.

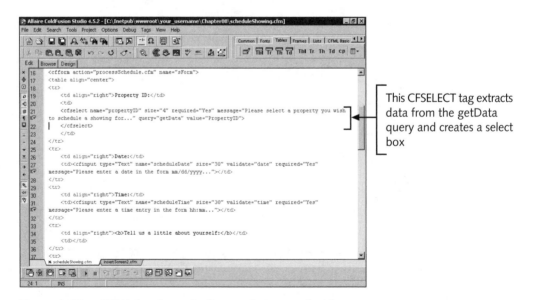

This CFSELECT tag extracts data from the getData query and creates a select box

Figure 8-37   CFML for dynamically populating a select box

12. Click the **Save** button on the Standard toolbar to save your work.

Now you can test the file in your browser and verify that you can dynamically populate the select box.

To test the modified file:

1. Switch to your Web browser, and reload the **scheduleShowing.cfm** file.

2. Scroll down the PropertyID select box and notice that every property listed in the database is displayed in the list. See Figure 8-38.

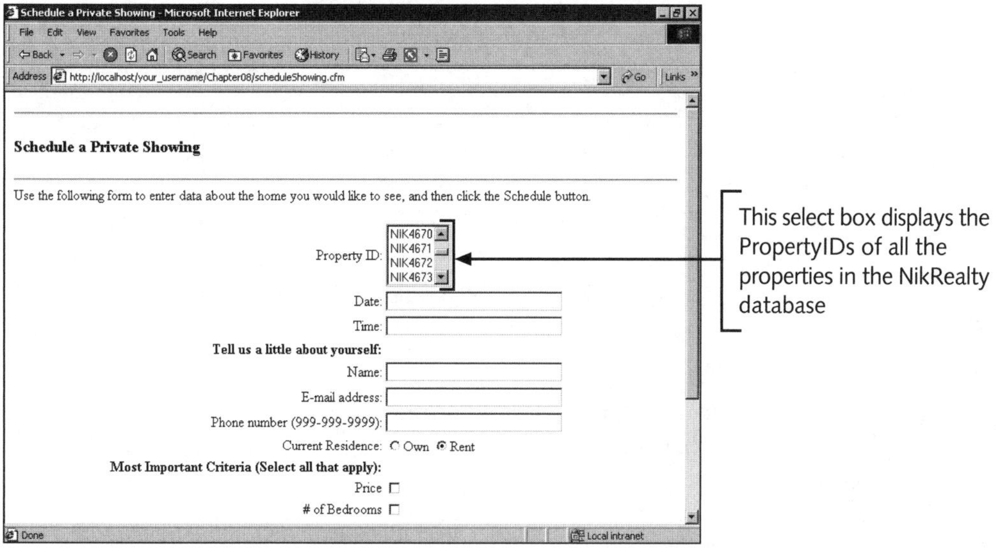

> This select box displays the PropertyIDs of all the properties in the NikRealty database

Figure 8-38   Form with the dynamically populated select box

3. View the source for the file, scroll down, and examine the code. See Figure 8-39. Notice the select box that is generated when the ColdFusion Server executes the CFSELECT tag.

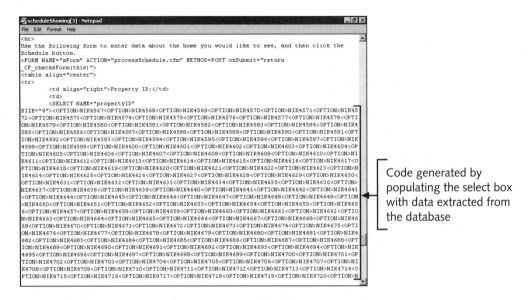

Figure 8-39   HTML source code generated by the CFSELECT tag

    4. Close all programs.

You have successfully populated a select box with data extracted from databases. Now you can be sure that users will select a PropertyID for a property that is listed for sale.

CHAPTER SUMMARY

❐ Control techniques used in system design and implementation to prevent erroneous data at the source of data entry are known as data validation techniques.

❐ You implement data validation in ColdFusion by using ColdFusion forms and controls.

❐ The CFFORM is used for creating a form, and the CFINPUT and CFSELECT tags are used for creating controls.

❐ The TYPE parameter for the CFINPUT tag can be assigned the values TEXT, PASSWORD, RADIO, and CHECKBOX to create text boxes, password boxes, radio buttons, and checkboxes, respectively.

❐ The simplest of errors occurs when users forget to enter data. Validation techniques that check to see that users enter data are known as completeness checks.

❐ The REQUIRED attribute for ColdFusion input controls can be set to either YES or NO and allows you to implement a data completeness check.

❐ Validation checks that verify whether the data is a proper date, time, decimal number or integer are known as data type checks.

- The VALIDATE attribute for ColdFusion input controls allows you to implement a data type check when its value is date, time, float, or integer.

- Range and limit checks allow you to enforce a criterion that the data must be between two numbers or have an upper or a lower bound.

- The RANGE attribute of the CFINPUT tag implements range and limit checks.

- Picture checks are implemented by using the VALIDATE attribute when the value taken is social_security_number, telephone, or zipcode.

- Self-checking digits are used in algorithmic checks to validate data such as credit card numbers.

- Extracting data from databases and publishing it in a select box is a two-part process. The CFQUERY tag is used for executing SQL SELECT statements to create query record set objects with data extracted from databases. A QUERY loop created using the CFSELECT tag is used for implementing a repetition flow-control structure to access and display data values and descriptions of items.

8

REVIEW QUESTIONS

1. What is data validation? Why is it important?
2. Distinguish between client-side and server-side data validation.
3. Which ColdFusion tag do you use to create a form? Describe its attributes.
4. Which tag do you use to create form data controls such as text boxes? What attribute-value pairs of this tag create text boxes, password boxes, radio buttons, and checkboxes?
5. What are the different kinds of data validation techniques?
6. What is a data completeness check? How do you implement it in ColdFusion? How do you customize the error message displayed when the check fails?
7. What is a data type check? How do you implement it in ColdFusion? What types of data can you check for in ColdFusion?
8. What are range and limit checks? How do you implement them in ColdFusion?
9. Describe the purpose of picture checks. How do you implement them in CFML?
10. How would you validate credit card numbers in ColdFusion? When you validate credit card numbers, what type of data validation checks are you performing?
11. Briefly describe the procedure for populating select boxes with data extracted from databases.

HANDS-ON PROJECTS

Project 1: Implement Data Validation Checks on the New Property Insertion Form

In your Web browser, open the insertScreen2.cfm template located in the Chapter08 folder on your Data Disk. See Figure 8-40.

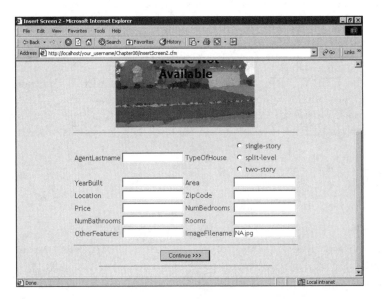

Figure 8-40

This is the form from Chapter 7 that you worked on earlier in this chapter. Your task now is to implement additional measures to prevent erroneous data from being input into the properties database when agents use this screen. Implement the following:

1. Add data completeness checks on all the fields: Agent Lastname, YearBuilt, Area, Location, ZipCode, Price, NumBedrooms, NumBathrooms, Rooms, OtherFeatures, and ImageFileName. Add appropriate error messages that would be displayed if data validation checks fail. Note that you will have to delete the CFOUTPUT tags in the CFML for the ImageFilename control when you convert to it to a ColdFusion input control.

2. Implement data type checks as shown in the following table, and modify the error messages to describe this data type requirement.

Field	Data type
YearBuilt	Integer
Area	Float
Price	Float
NumBedrooms	Integer
NumBathrooms	Float

3. Implement a range and limit check on the YearBuilt field. Assume that houses should be built after 1900 and before 2025. Modify the error messages to describe this requirement for the YearBuilt field.

4. Add a picture check on the ZipCode field. Customize the error message for this field accordingly.

5. Design a query to extract all the agent last names from the Agents table. Change the text box control for the Agent last name into a select box and dynamically populate this select box with the data extracted from the Agents table. Order the data alphabetically by last name. See Figure 8-41.

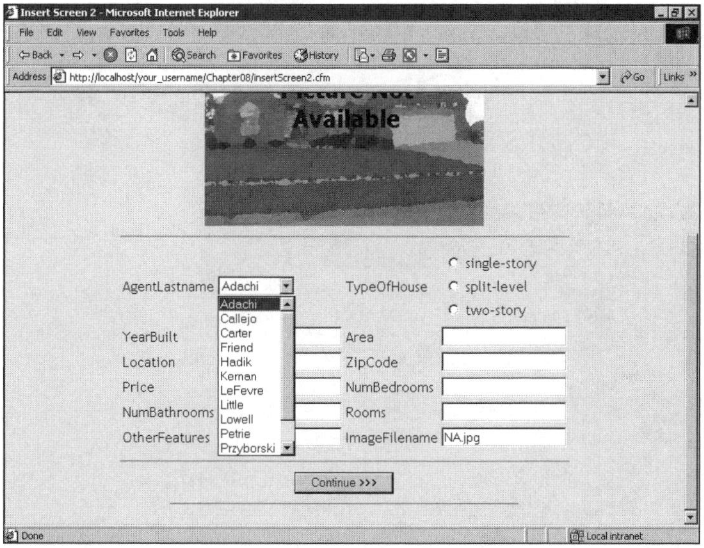

Figure 8-41

6. Change the location text box into a select box and dynamically populate it with *distinct* locations extracted from the properties table. Order the data alphabetically by location. See Figure 8-42.

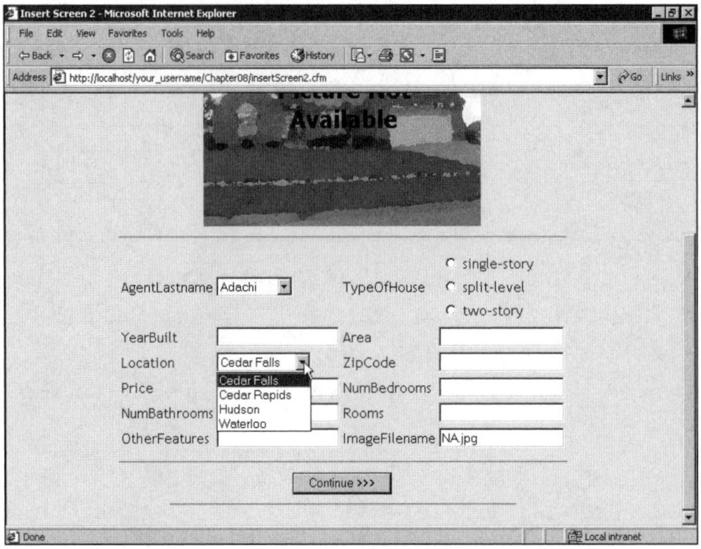

Figure 8-42

Project 2: Add Data Validation to the New Agent Insertion Screen

Open http://localhost/your_username/Chapter08/insertAgentScreen1.cfm in your Web browser and then in ColdFusion Studio. See Figure 8-43.

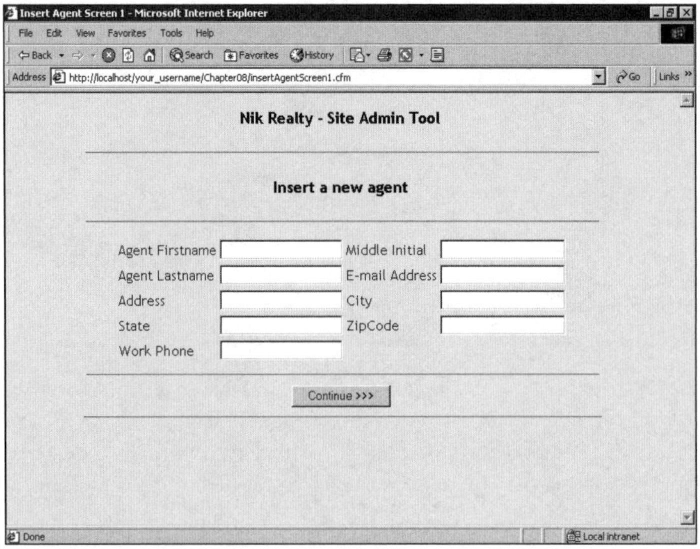

Figure 8-43

Add appropriate data validation checks to this form, as shown in the following table:

Control\Check	Completeness	Picture
Agent Firstname	X	
Middle Initial		
Agent Lastname	X	
E-mail Address	X	
Address	X	
City	X	
State	X	
ZipCode	X	X
Work Phone	X	X

Display clear and useful error messages when data validation checks fail.

Project 3: Add Data Validation Checks to an Online Exam

In your Web browser, open the exam.cfm template located in the Chapter08 folder on your Data Disk. See Figure 8-44.

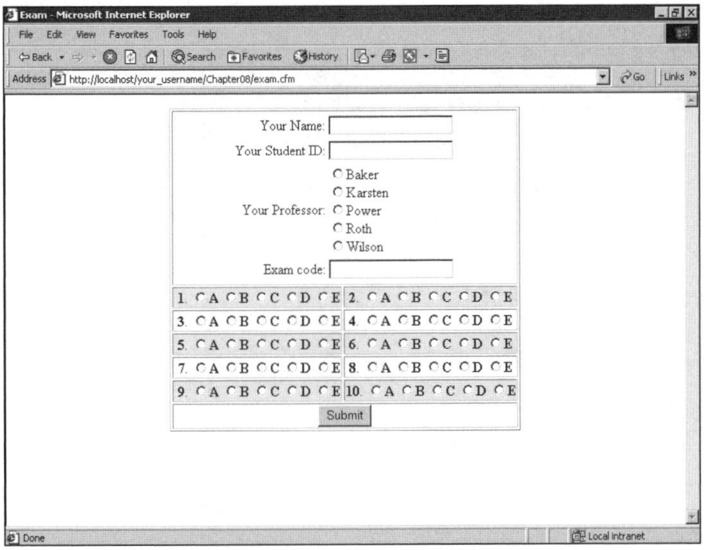

[Exam - Microsoft Internet Explorer screenshot showing a form with Your Name, Your Student ID, Your Professor radio buttons (Baker, Karsten, Power, Roth, Wilson), Exam code field, and questions 1-10 with answer choices A B C D E, and a Submit button]

Figure 8-44

This is the form that some professors designed for administering exams online. Open the file in ColdFusion Studio and carefully study the code. Your task is to prevent erroneous data from being input by the students. Implement the following:

1. Add data completeness checks on all the fields: Name, ID, Professor, and Exam Code. Add appropriate error messages that would be displayed if data validation checks fail.

2. Implement data type checks, as shown in the following table, and modify the error messages to describe this data type requirement.

Field	Data Type
Student ID	Integer
Exam Code	Integer

3. Implement a range and limit check on the Exam Code field. Exam Codes are three digits long (>=100 and <= 999). Modify the error messages to describe this requirement.

4. Carefully study the ColdFusion FOR loops and the HTML source code generated. Add data completeness checks to the answers. Create a customized error message that informs the student which question is unanswered, if any, as shown in Figure 8-45.

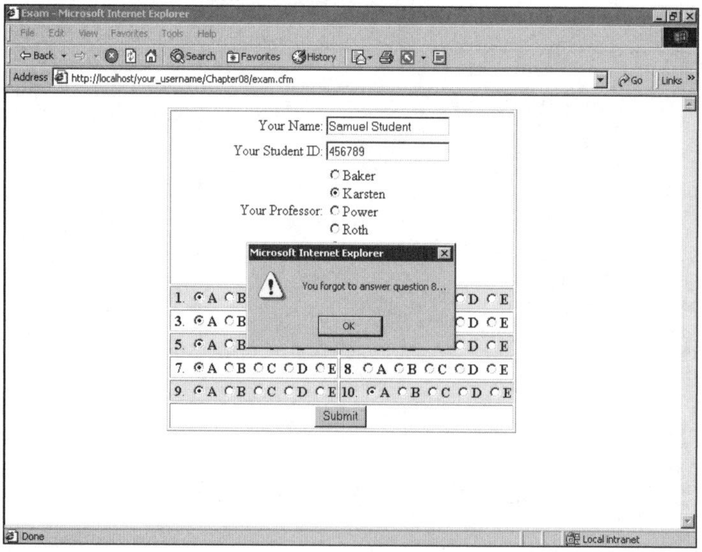

Figure 8-45

Project 4: Add Data Validation to a Pay Computation Form

Open the computePay.cfm template located in the Chapter08 folder on your Data Disk. See Figure 8-46. It is impossible to work more than 60 hours in a week. Implement data validation on the control for hours worked such that the 60-hour criterion is met. Make sure that the data entered in the pay rate field is between 10 and 30. Implement checks that ensure that users enter data in both boxes prior to the submission of the form. Add appropriate error messages in case these checks fail.

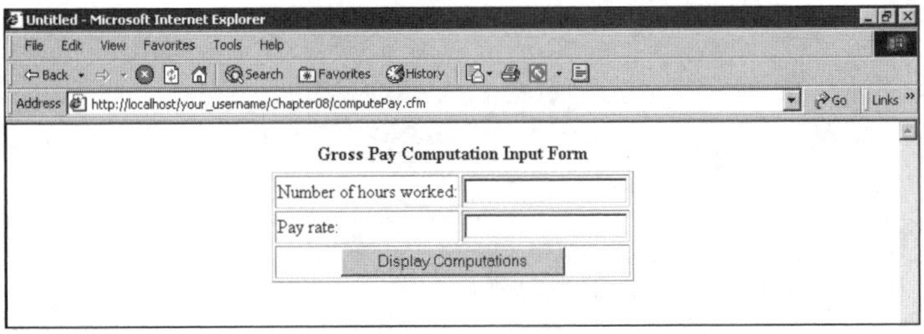

Figure 8-46

8

Project 5: Validate Data Entered in an Online Order Form

Open the subsForProgrammers.cfm template. See Figure 8-47.

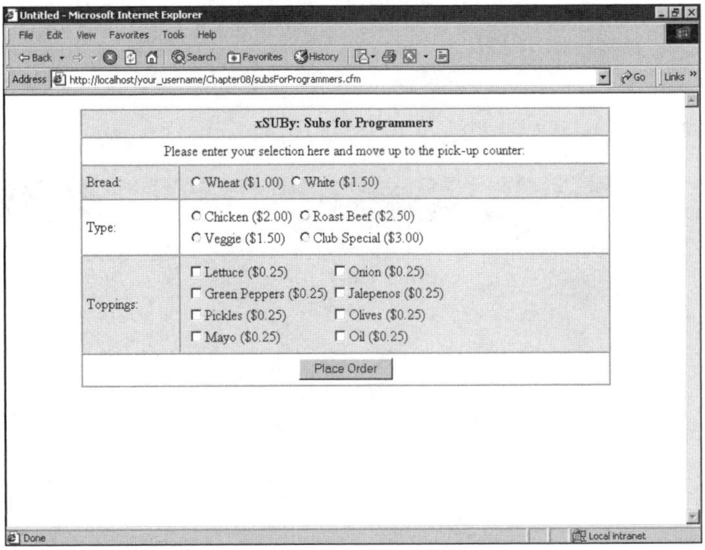

Figure 8-47

Change the HTML form to a ColdFusion form. Design input controls to ensure that the user selects the bread, the type of sub, as well as at least one topping. Display appropriate error messages when data validation checks fail.

Project 6: Validate Data Prior to Searching Matching Properties

Open the searchForm2.cfm template in the Chapter08 folder on your Data Disk. See Figure 8-48. This is the form that you used in Chapter 6 to search for properties in the NikRealty Web site.

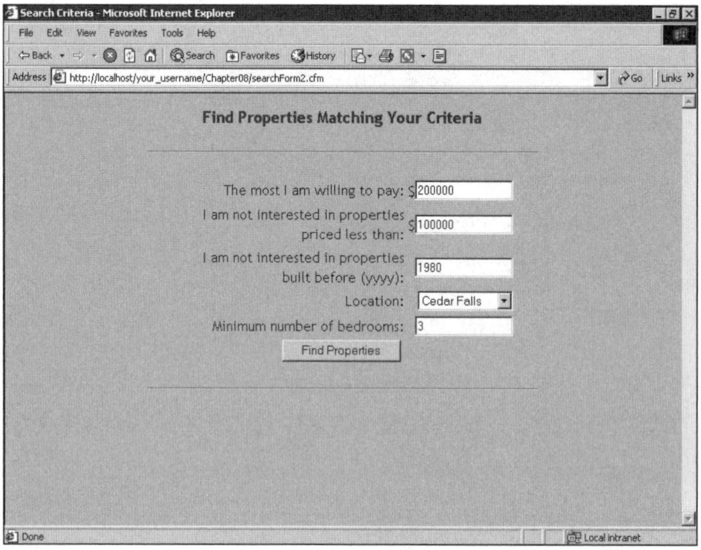

Figure 8-48

1. Add appropriate data validation checks to this form, as shown in the following table:

Control\Check	Completeness	Data Type	Range and Limit
MaxPrice	X	Suitable for amounts	
MinPrice	X	Suitable for amounts	
minYearBuilt	X	Integer	Less than or equal to the current year; four-digit number (*Hint:* Use the Now() and Year() functions to compute the current year; a number greater than or equal to 1000 is at least four digits long)
minBedrooms	X	Integer	Greater than 0; single-digit number (*Hint:* a number greater than 0 and less than or equal to 9 is a single-digit number)

2. Display clear and useful error messages when data validation checks fail.

3. Redesign the select box for the location by using CFSELECT tags.

CASE PROJECTS

1. In the previous chapter, you designed an admin tool for the hardware store case. The admin tool had a capability for data maintenance including the capabilities for inserting, updating, and deleting products available for sale. What are the appropriate data validation checks for the form controls? Sketch the data validation requirements using the following template:

Template name:_____.cfm

Control\Check	Completeness	Data Type	Range and Limt	Picture	Algorithmic
1.					
2.					
3.					
4.					

2. In the previous chapter, you designed a shopping cart application for the hardware store. Sketch the data validation requirements using the above template. Implement the data validation requirements in the shopping cart applications.

3. Visit a Web site of your choice that requires users to register. Critically examine the form that they use for registering users. Experiment by entering several values in each of the controls. What are the data validation checks that are implemented? List some additional checks that may improve the data accuracy.

8

THE COLDFUSION APPLICATION FRAMEWORK

> **In this chapter, you will:**
> ◆ Learn about the concepts of statelessness and state
> ◆ Manage state by using HTTP cookies
> ◆ Learn about the ColdFusion application framework
> ◆ Design and use the application.cfm template
> ◆ Create and use client variables
> ◆ Create and use session and application variables
> ◆ Learn about locking shared resources

The Web is a stateless system. A system is **stateless** if its output depends only on the most recent input and is not influenced by earlier inputs or earlier outputs. In other words, a stateless system has no memory. For example, a coin toss constitutes a stateless system. Your chance of tossing a heads is 50%, and your chance of tossing a tails is 50%. Even if you tossed heads three times, your chance of tossing heads again is still 50%. A Web server is a stateless server because every request from a client to a server is treated the same way. Typically, the Web server cannot track the history of a request when it processes one. Whether a request is the first one or the tenth one does not make any difference—the server retrieves HTML documents and serves them, the server transfers control to the ColdFusion server for CFML documents and passes the document back to the client, and so on.

In most situations, such a system works well: it is easy to understand because you don't have to worry about the history of the requests when developing your applications; it is easy to use because users don't have to remember what they have done prior to requesting a new action; and it is efficient and simple because the Web server does not need programming to keep track of all visitors and what they have done. In other situations, this kind of a model does not work well. For example, for security purposes you may want a user to log on to the system by using a username and password and have only these users access the ColdFusion templates. In such a case, the server must identify whether a user has logged in correctly prior to serving documents. In most e-commerce situations, when users are browsing through a list of products and want to store products in a shopping cart for check out at a later time, the server should have a capability to track who the different clients are and what is in their shopping carts. If the designers of a site want users to be able to customize the appearance and contents of the site, the Web server should incorporate programming to remember the clients and their preferences.

A system is not stateless or has **state** if the output produced by it depends on the most recent input as well as earlier inputs and earlier outputs. For example, the game of chess has state. Your next move depends upon your opponent's previous move as well as all your earlier moves and your opponent's earlier moves. Applications like those described in the previous paragraph require the system to remember clients and their prior interactions with the server. In other words, you need to build state into the system. Using ColdFusion, you can manage state with cookies, client variables, session variables, and application variables.

HTTP State Management and Cookies

Faced with a need to track the history of user requests and build sophisticated Web-based applications, the World Wide Web Consortium (W3C) developed a specification in the HTTP protocol to support state management and introduced the concept of a cookie. A **cookie** is a small piece of information sent by a Web server to be stored by the Web browser on the client computer. Once a cookie is stored the Web browser sends it to the Web server with every request it makes. The Web server uses this information to identify the client and customize its response. In addition to other pieces of information, the HTTP protocol allows the server and client to exchange two headers (pieces of information): set-cookie and cookie. Both contain a unique variable and a value that the server can track. In a Web-based application, whenever you need to establish state, such as when a user wants to add a product to a shopping cart, through appropriate programming you can make the server send a set-cookie header to the client along with its response. The Web browser processes the set-cookie header and, if the user allows it, stores a cookie on the client computer. When a user requests another document, the client sends the data contained in the cookie along with the request to the server using the cookie header. The Web server receives the cookie and tracks the history of user requests by storing the cookie value and the requests in a database or its memory, based on the CFML or other programming, and displays the data when needed. For example, a user can view the contents of their shopping cart by requesting a template that extracts appropriate data and displays it.

Using cookies allows designers to build state. For example, suppose a customer is logging on to a commerce site and the server must check whether that client has already logged on; the server can examine the client's cookie header to see if it contains the variable and value that the server sent in the set-cookie header when the user originally logged on. This process is illustrated in Figure 9-1.

WEB SERVER

CLIENT

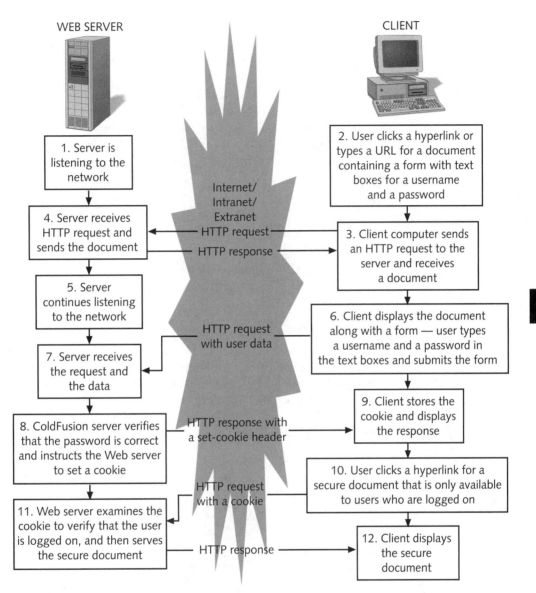

1. Server is listening to the network

2. User clicks a hyperlink or types a URL for a document containing a form with text boxes for a username and a password

Internet/ Intranet/ Extranet

4. Server receives HTTP request and sends the document

HTTP request

HTTP response

3. Client computer sends an HTTP request to the server and receives a document

5. Server continues listening to the network

9

6. Client displays the document along with a form — user types a username and a password in the text boxes and submits the form

HTTP request with user data

7. Server receives the request and the data

9. Client stores the cookie and displays the response

8. ColdFusion server verifies that the password is correct and instructs the Web server to set a cookie

HTTP response with a set-cookie header

10. User clicks a hyperlink for a secure document that is only available to users who are logged on

HTTP request with a cookie

11. Web server examines the cookie to verify that the user is logged on, and then serves the secure document

12. Client displays the secure document

HTTP response

Figure 9-1 HTTP state management with cookies

In Figure 9-1, a user requests a document containing a form with textboxes to enter a username and a password. The Web server sends the form in the HTTP response. The user enters his or her username and password and submits the form. The Web server receives the form data and the name of the form-handler in the HTTP request. The Web server transfers control to the ColdFusion Server and makes the user data available to it. The ColdFusion Server creates variables based on the user data and executes the form handler. The form handler has code to verify whether the password is correct by checking it against the data in the database. If the password is correct, the ColdFusion Server includes a set-cookie header containing the username along with its response. The Web server sends the response along with the set-cookie header to the client. The client receives the response and stores the cookie. The next time the client makes a request to the server, the client sends the cookie along with its request. If the request is for a secure ColdFusion template, the ColdFusion Server receives the cookie and verifies that the user is logged in and continues to process the request and sends an appropriate response to the user. If a user requests a secure document without logging in, the ColdFusion Server does not receive a cookie, terminates processing the request, and sends an error message back to the client.

To set a cookie, you a need a unique name for the cookie, a value, and an expiration period. You set a cookie in ColdFusion by using the CFCOOKIE tag. For example, in the form handler for logging in a user, once you verify that the username and password are correct you can set a cookie by using the CFCOOKIE tag. The syntax for the CFCOOKIE tag is as follows:

```
<CFCOOKIE NAME="cookie_name"
   VALUE="text"
   EXPIRES="period">
```

The NAME attribute is required. It identifies the cookie's name and is useful for accessing its value in further requests from the clients. You will see this later in the chapter. The VALUE attribute is optional but can be any text. The EXPIRES attribute specifies when the cookie is deleted from the client computer. It can be a date (11/01/02), number of days (10, 20), NOW, or NEVER. If the EXPIRES attribute has a value NOW, the client immediately deletes the cookie.

The following example illustrates the code for setting a cookie. This example is in the Chapter09 folder on your data disk with the filename set_cookie.cfm. Your first task is to learn about cookies from this example.

```
<cfcookie name="username" value="great_agent" expires=
"NEVER">
<!DOCTYPE HTML PUBLIC "-
//W3C//DTD HTML 4.0 Transitional//EN">
<html>
<head>
    <title>untitled</title>
</head>
<body>
A cookie has been set.
</body>
</html>
```

To learn about cookies by using set_cookie.cfm:

1. Start Windows Explorer, and navigate to the **C:\Documents and Settings***your_W2000_username***\COOKIES** folder. Use your Windows 2000 username for "your_W2000_username" in the above path. Your Windows 2000 computer system stores cookies in this folder. Examine the contents of this folder. See Figure 9-2. For a new computer system, there is only one file named index.dat in this folder. There are no cookies (other files) in the folder. Your particular system may have more files in this folder depending on how many Web sites you or others may have visited.

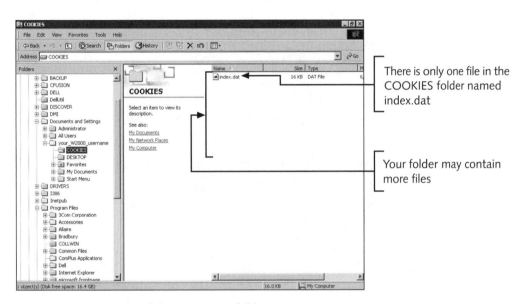

Figure 9-2   Contents of the COOKIES folder

The COOKIES folder might be on a different drive for a customized Windows 2000 installation. Also, the folder name might appear in lowercase. If you are using a different Windows operating system or a Web browser other than Internet Explorer, search for files or folders matching the *cookie*.* wildcard combination to find the folder where cookies are stored.

2. Start your Web browser, type **http://localhost/your_username/ Chapter09/set_cookie.cfm** in the Address text box, and then press the **Enter** key. Your Web browser sends a request to the Web server on your computer. The Web server invokes the ColdFusion Server, and the ColdFusion Server starts processing the set_cookie.cfm template. When the ColdFusion server executes the highlighted CFCOOKIE tag, it generates a set-cookie header in the HTTP response. The set-cookie header contains the name of the cookie (username), the value (great_agent), and an expiration period (NEVER). The rest of the document contains HTML code and is sent as is to

the Web server. The Web server sends the document along with the set-cookie header to your Web browser. When the Web browser processes the set-cookie header, it sets a cookie in your computer and displays the document, as shown in Figure 9-3.

Figure 9-3   Web page displayed by set-cookie.cfm

3. Switch to Windows Explorer.

4. Click **View** on the menu bar, and then click **Refresh**. See Figure 9-4. Notice that this folder now contains a new file named your_w2000_ username@localhost[1].txt. Your Web browser created a file for storing the information in the cookie.

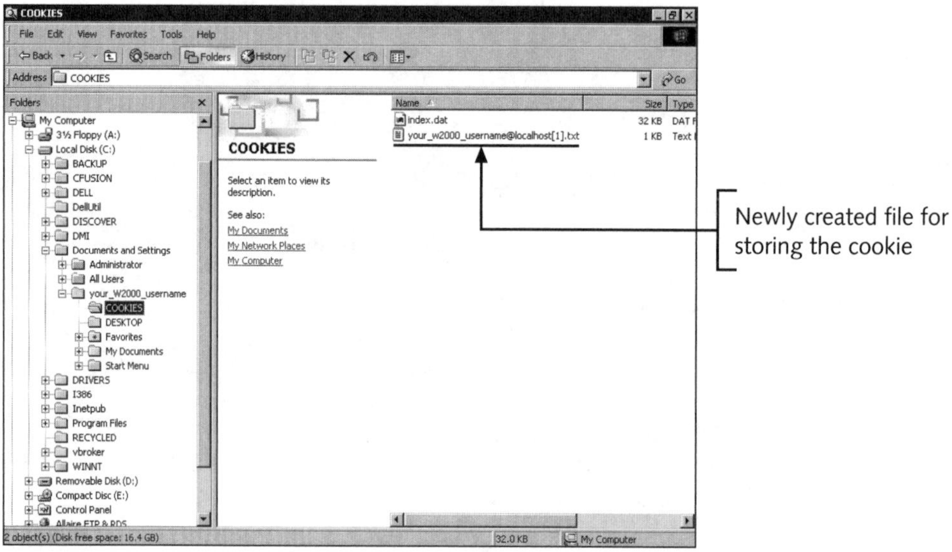

Newly created file for storing the cookie

Figure 9-4   Contents of the COOKIES folder after the Web browser has created a cookie

5. Double-click the newly created file to open it in Notepad.

6. If necessary, maximize Notepad. See Figure 9-5. Carefully examine the text and make sure that the name of the cookie (USERNAME) and its value (great_agent) are stored in it. Subsequent requests from the client computer to the Web server will include the cookie header with the variable USERNAME and its value "great_agent."

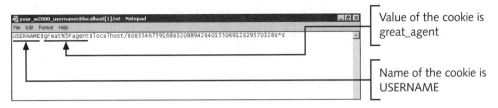

Value of the cookie is great_agent

Name of the cookie is USERNAME

Figure 9-5   Contents of the cookie file displayed by Notepad

   7. Close Notepad.

When the user makes a request to another ColdFusion template on the same server, the Web server uses the HTTP protocol, retrieves the information contained in the cookie, and passes it to the ColdFusion Server. Similarly to how the ColdFusion server creates URL and FORM variables, it creates COOKIE variables based on the information in the cookie it received. For each cookie received by the server, a COOKIE.variable is created that you can access in the ColdFusion template. For example, when the user makes a request after the cookie in the example has been set, the ColdFusion Server creates the variable COOKIE.username and assigns it the value (great_agent) retrieved from the client. You can use the variable and assign its value to other variables and use it to perform database queries or perform any other processing that is required by the application.

The following example illustrates this concept by displaying the value received in the cookie by the server. This example is stored in the Chapter09 folder on your Data Disk as examine_cookie.cfm.

```
<!DOCTYPE HTML PUBLIC "-
//W3C//DTD HTML 4.0 Transitional//EN">
<html>
<head>
     <title>Untitled</title>
</head>
<body>
Value of username cookie: <cfoutput>#cookie.username#
</cfoutput>
</body>
</html>
```

To retrieve and display the value in a cookie:

   1. Switch to your Web browser.

   2. In the Address text box of your Web browser, type
      http://localhost/your_username/Chapter09/examine_cookie.cfm,
      and press the **Enter** key. See Figure 9-6.

Figure 9-6   Web page displayed by examine_cookie.cfm

When the ColdFusion server executes the examine_cookie.cfm template, it creates a variable named cookie.username and assigns it a value "great_agent" based on the information in the cookie sent by the client computer. When the highlighted code is executed, the value of this variable is displayed at the appropriate location in the output, as seen in Figure 9-6.

Once a cookie is set, the client computer deletes it as specified by the value of the EXPIRES attribute. Recall that this value can be a date (7/7/03), number of days (10, 20), NOW, or NEVER. If the EXPIRES attribute has a value NOW, the client immediately deletes the cookie. The following example illustrates the code needed to delete a cookie. This example is stored in the Chapter09 folder on your Data Disk as delete_cookie.cfm.

```
<cfcookie name="username" expires="NOW">
<!DOCTYPE HTML PUBLIC "-
//W3C//DTD HTML 4.0 Transitional//EN">
<html>
<head>
    <title>Untitled</title>
</head>
<body>
Cookie username has been deleted.
</body>
</html>
```

To delete a cookie:

1. In the Address text box of your Web browser, type **http://localhost/your_username/Chapter09/delete_cookie.cfm**, and press the **Enter** key. See Figure 9-7. When the ColdFusion Server executes this template, it sends a set-cookie header in the HTTP response with an expiration of NOW. When the client Web browser receives this header, it sets a cookie that expires immediately, effectively deleting it. After the browser processes the headers, it displays the rest of the document by parsing the HTML appropriately and showing the message "Cookie username has been deleted."

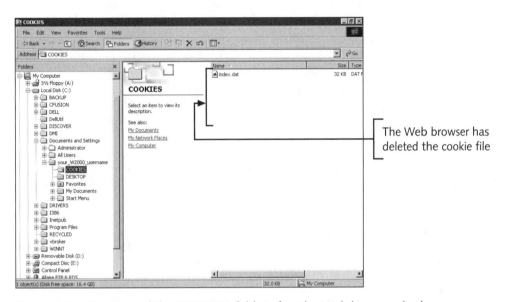

Figure 9-7   Web page displayed by delete_cookie.cfm

2. Switch to Windows Explorer. Navigate to the COOKIES folder and refresh the view, if necessary. Notice that the Web browser has deleted the cookie file. See Figure 9-8.

The Web browser has deleted the cookie file

Figure 9-8   Contents of the COOKIES folder after the Web browser displays delete_cookie.cfm

3. Switch to your Web browser, and type the URL to open the examine_cookie.cfm file. Refresh the document. Notice that this time the template generates an error, as shown in Figure 9-9, because the server does not receive any cookies. The username cookie was deleted in a previous step.

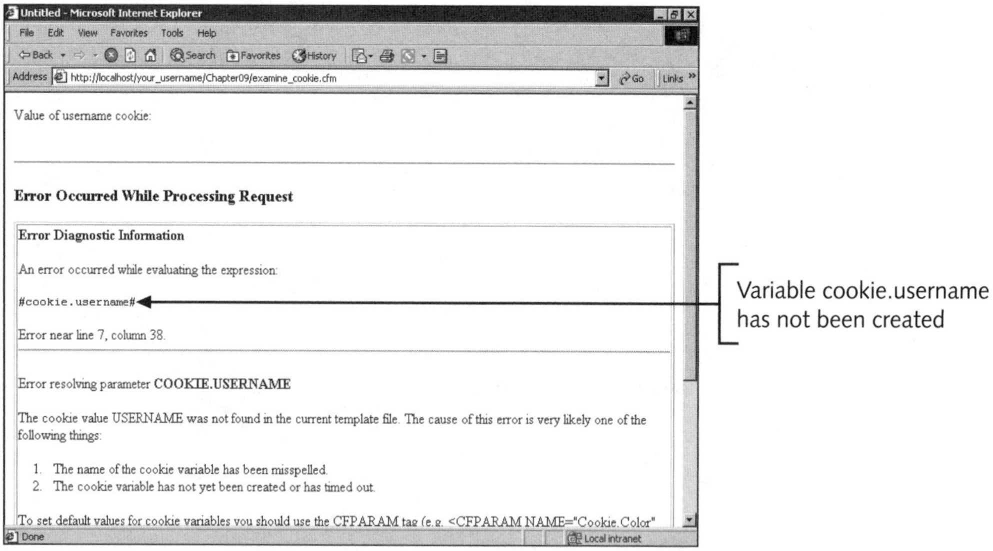

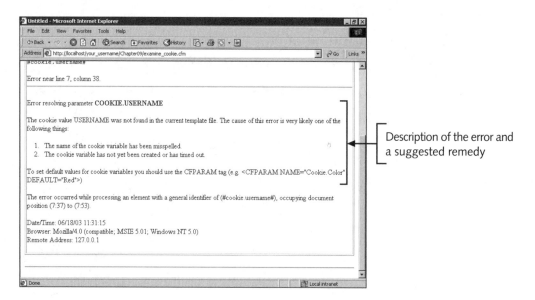

Figure 9-9 Web page with an error message displayed by examine_cookie.cfm after the cookie has been deleted

4. Scroll down to the bottom of the document, and read the complete error message. See Figure 9-10. You can set default values for cookies by using the CFPARAM tag to prevent such errors.

Figure 9-10 Web page displaying a suggested method to prevent cookie errors

Default Values for Cookie Variables

Use the CFPARAM tag to set default values for cookie variables and prevent errors when cookie values are accessed. As you learned in Chapter 4, a CFPARAM tag for handling this situation is <cfparam name="cookie.username" default="none">.

The following code is a modification of the examine_cookie.cfm file that you saw in the previous section. It is stored in the Chapter09 folder on the Data Disk as examine_cookie2.cfm.

```
<cfparam name="cookie.username" default="none">
<!DOCTYPE HTML PUBLIC "-//W3C//DTD HTML 4.0
Transitional//EN">
<html>
<head>
     <title>Untitled</title>
</head>
<body>
<cfif cookie.username EQ "none">
The server did not receive a cookie named username.
<cfelse>
Value of username cookie: <cfoutput>#cookie.username#</cfo
utput>
</cfif>
</body>
</html>
```

To run examine_cookie2.cfm:

1. Type **http://localhost/your_username/Chapter09/ examine_cookie2.cfm** in the Address text box of your Web browser, and press the **Enter** key. When the ColdFusion server executes this template, it processes the CFPARAM tag. If the ColdFusion server had received a cookie with a variable named username, it would have created a variable named cookie.username with the value received from the client. If it finds a variable cookie.username, the CFPARAM tag has no effect. Because the server did not receive any cookies and there are no variables created in the cookie scope, the CFPARAM tag creates a variable named cookie.username and assigns it the value "none." The highlighted CFIF statement is testing the value of this variable. If it is "none," that indicates that the server did not receive any cookies and the browser displays an appropriate message, as shown in Figure 9-11.

9

Figure 9-11   Web page displayed by examine_cookie2.cfm after the cookie has been deleted

2. Type the URL to display set_cookie.cfm. The Web browser sets the username cookie again.

3. Type the URL to display examine_cookie2.cfm again. Refresh the document. This time the server receives the username cookie, and the ColdFusion Server creates a variable named cookie.username. The CFPARAM tag has no effect because the variable cookie.username exists. The ColdFusion Server evaluates the CFIF condition as false and executes the statement between the CFELSE and /CFIF. The Web browser displays the value of the variable cookie.username, as shown in Figure 9-12.

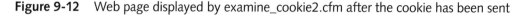

Figure 9-12   Web page displayed by examine_cookie2.cfm after the cookie has been sent

Cookie-Based Logon Security

Nikitha is concerned that the admin tool that you created for NikRealty is not secure and unauthorized users might delete or change data. She asks you to allow only her and her agents to make changes. You decide to protect data by requiring users to log on and provide a valid username and password before they can work with the NikRealty database. To keep matters simple, Nikitha suggests that you use the agent's last name as the username and the agent's ID as the password.

To design cookie-based logon security using ColdFusion:

1. Start your Web browser, if necessary.

2. In the Address text box, type **http://localhost/your_username/Chapter09/Version1/admin.cfm**, and press the **Enter** key to open admin.cfm located in the Version1 subfolder in the Chapter09 folder on your Data Disk. You see the NikRealty Site Admin Tool page, shown in Figure 9-13. This is the page that you created in Chapter 7 to maintain the NikRealty database. Now you will install logon security to prevent unauthorized access to these pages.

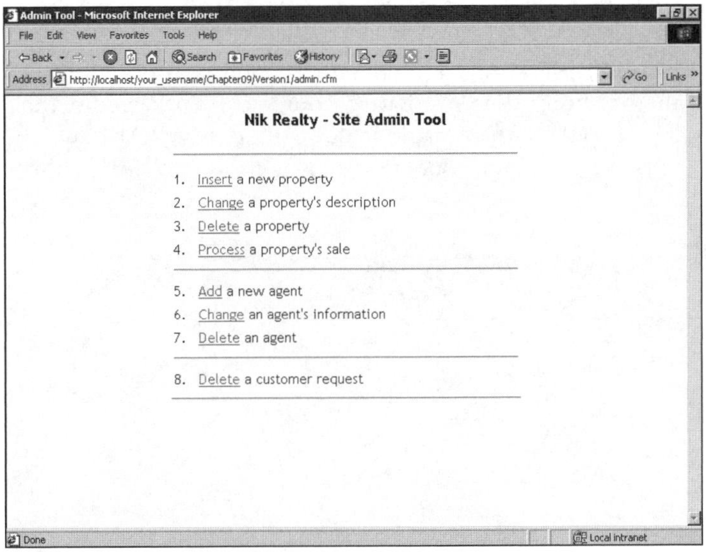

Figure 9-13   NikRealty Site Admin Tool

3. Start ColdFusion Studio, and open **admin.cfm** from the Version1 folder.

   You will check that users have logged on by using cookies and a cookie variable named loggedin. Use a CFPARAM tag and set the default to "no" in case the client does not have a cookie set, meaning that users have not logged on.

4. On line 1, column 1, type **<cfparam name="cookie.loggedin" default="no">**, and press **Enter**.

   If the user is logged on, a cookie is stored on the client computer with a variable named loggedin. The variable will have the value "yes" if the user is logged on or "no" if the user is not logged on. If the user is not logged on, you have to redirect the user to another page that contains a log on form.

5. Type **<cfif cookie.loggedin IS "no">**, and press **Enter**.

6. Press the **Tab** key, type **<cflocation url="login.cfm">**, and press **Enter**.

   Now, if the user is not logged on, the client is redirected to load login.cfm, a logon form, from the same folder. There is a file named login.cfm in the Chapter09/Version1 folder on the Data Disk. If the user is logged on, the rest of the code in admin.cfm is processed. Recall from Chapter 3 that the CFLOCATION tag issues an HTTP redirect response and the Web browser loads the document specified in the redirect response.

7. Press the **Backspace** key, and type **</cfif>** to close the if statement. Press **Enter**.

8. Click the **Save** button on the Standard toolbar to save the document after making the changes.

9. Switch to your Web browser, and refresh the **admin.cfm** document.

A logon form, The NikRealty Logon Screen, appears as shown in Figure 9-14. Because your computer does not have a cookie named loggedin, the variable cookie.loggedin receives the default value by the CFPARAM tag. The CFIF statement tests the condition that cookie.loggedin is "no" and redirects you to the login.cfm page.

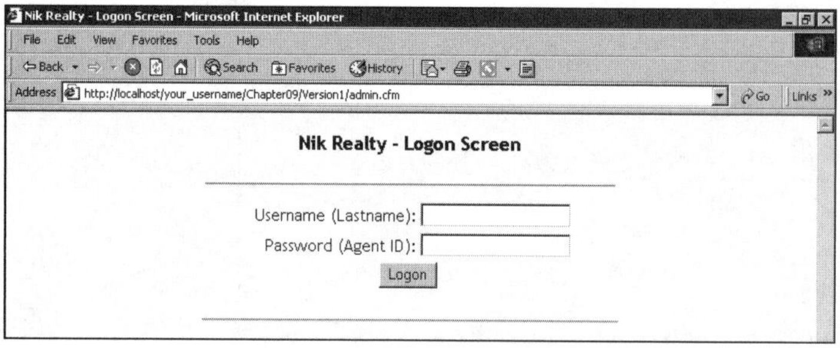

Figure 9-14   User is redirected to login.cfm

Your next task is to create the form handler for the logon form that checks to see whether the user is valid and then logs on the user (by setting a cookie) or reports a problem with the username or the password entered.

To create a form handler for logging in a user:

1. Switch to ColdFusion Studio, and open **login.cfm** in the Chapter09\Version1 folder on your Data Disk. Notice that the document contains a ColdFusion form with a form handler named processLogin.cfm. The form includes three controls: a textbox named username, a password box named password, and a submit button with the value "Logon." See Figure 9-15.

2. Click **File** on the menu bar, and then click **New Document**.

Your first task is to check to see whether the username and password match a record in the Agents table in the database. Recall the CFQUERY syntax from Chapter 6.

3. Click at the beginning of line 1, and press the **Enter** key to insert a new line.

4. Click the **Up Arrow** key to move to the newly inserted line.

5. Type **<cfquery datasource="your_username" name="checkData">**, and press **Enter**.

Your next task is to code the SQL SELECT statement for extracting data from the Agents table. You should convert the data in the username and last-name fields to uppercase in the WHERE clause. This ensures that the comparison is not case sensitive.

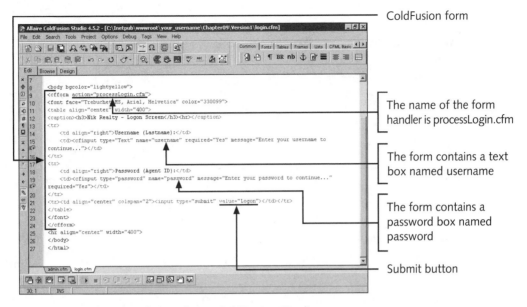

ColdFusion form

The name of the form
handler is processLogin.cfm

The form contains a text
box named username

The form contains a
password box named
password

Submit button

Figure 9-15   Viewing login.cfm in ColdFusion Studio

6. Type **SELECT * FROM Agents WHERE UCase(Lastname) = '#UCase(FORM.Username)#' AND UCase(AgentID) = '#UCase(FORM.Password)#'**, and press **Enter**. You also can use the LIKE operator to perform a case-insensitive comparison.

7. Type **</cfquery>** to close the query tag.

   If a record in the table matches the data entered, the user is a valid user and you should let the user log on by setting a cookie; otherwise display an error message.

8. Click at the beginning of line 12 below the BODY tag.

9. Type **<cfif checkData.recordCount GT 0>**, and press **Enter**.

10. Type **<cfcookie name="loggedin" value="yes">**, and press **Enter**.

11. Type **Logon successful. Go to the <a href="admin.cfm">admin tool</a>**, and press **Enter**. If the logon is successful, set a cookie and direct the user to admin.cfm.

12. Type **<cfelse>**, and press **Enter**.

13. Type **Incorrect username or password. Click the back button on the toolbar and try again.**, and press **Enter**.

14. Type **</cfif>**.

15. Save the file as **processLogin.cfm** in the Chapter09\Version1 folder on your Data Disk. See Figure 9-16.

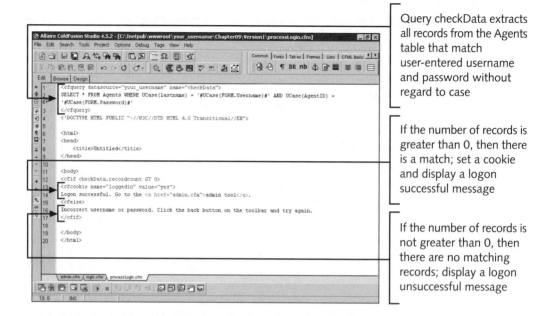

Query checkData extracts all records from the Agents table that match user-entered username and password without regard to case

If the number of records is greater than 0, then there is a match; set a cookie and display a logon successful message

If the number of records is not greater than 0, then there are no matching records; display a logon unsuccessful message

Figure 9-16   Editing the form handler in ColdFusion Studio

Once you have created the form handler, your next task is to verify that it works.

To test the logon security:

1. Switch to your Web browser, type **Little** as the username, and **10** as the password, and then click the **Logon** button.

2. Because you entered incorrect logon information, you see an error message. There are no records matching the WHERE clause in the CFQUERY tag. When the ColdFusion Server executes the query, it creates a variable named checkData.recordcount and sets its value to 0. It evaluates the CFIF condition as false because the condition 0 GT 0 is false. Next, the ColdFusion Server executes the false action between the CFELSE and the /CFIF and displays a message, as shown in Figure 9-17.

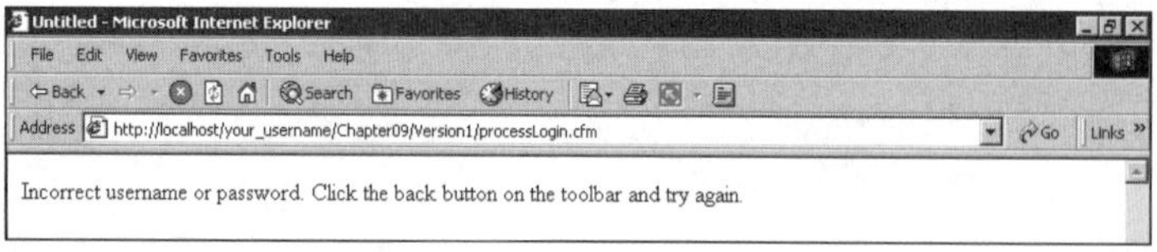

Figure 9-17   Web page displayed after entering incorrect logon information

3. Click the **Back** button on the browser toolbar.

4. Type **Little** as the username, if necessary, and **NKL** as the password, and then click the **Logon** button.

5. You see a message indicating that the logon was successful. See Figure 9-18.

Figure 9-18 Web page displayed after entering correct logon information

6. Click the **admin tool** hyperlink to go to the Admin Tool page. Because the cookie is set, you see the admin tool.

Your next task is to create a ColdFusion template that logs out users. Essentially, this logout.cfm utility will delete the cookie that has been set.

To create a logout utility:

1. Switch to ColdFusion Studio.

2. Click **File** on the menu bar, and then click **New Document**.

3. Click at the beginning of line 1.

4. Type **<cfcookie name="loggedin" expires="NOW">**, and press the **Enter** key.

5. Move to the beginning of line 10, one line below the <body> tag, and type **Logout successful**.

6. Change the title on line 6 to **Logout of the admin tool**.

7. Save the file as **logout.cfm** in the Chapter09\Version1 folder on your Data Disk. See Figure 9-19.

9

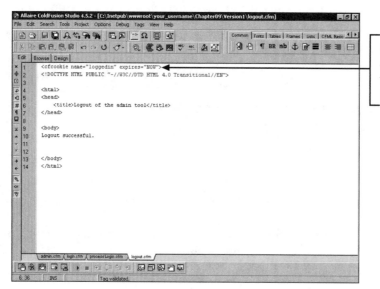

CFCOOKIE tag with an
expiration of NOW deletes
the cookie named
username

Figure 9-19   Newly created logout.cfm in ColdFusion Studio

Your next task is to provide a link to this template on the admin main page (admin.cfm). Users will click this link to log out of the admin tool once they are done with the administrative tasks.

To create a link for logging out:

1. Click the **admin.cfm** document tab to edit it in the editor. If you have closed this file earlier, reopen the document.

2. Move to the end of last /TR tag (line 53), and press the **Enter** key.

3. Type **<tr>**, and press **Enter** to insert a new row in the table.

4. Press the **Tab** key, type **<td>9.</td>**, and press **Enter**.

5. Type **<td><a href="logout.cfm">Logout</a> of the admin tool</td>**, and press **Enter** to create the next cell with a hyperlink for logging out.

6. Press the **Backspace** key, and type **</tr>**.

7. Click the **Save** button on the Standard toolbar to save the file. See Figure 9-20.

8. Switch to your Web browser, and open the **admin.cfm** file, if necessary. Refresh the document. Notice that the Web browser displays the newly created hyperlink for logging out. See Figure 9-21.

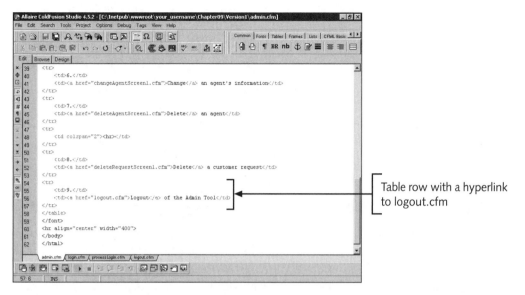

Figure 9-20   Editing the admin.cfm template in ColdFusion Studio

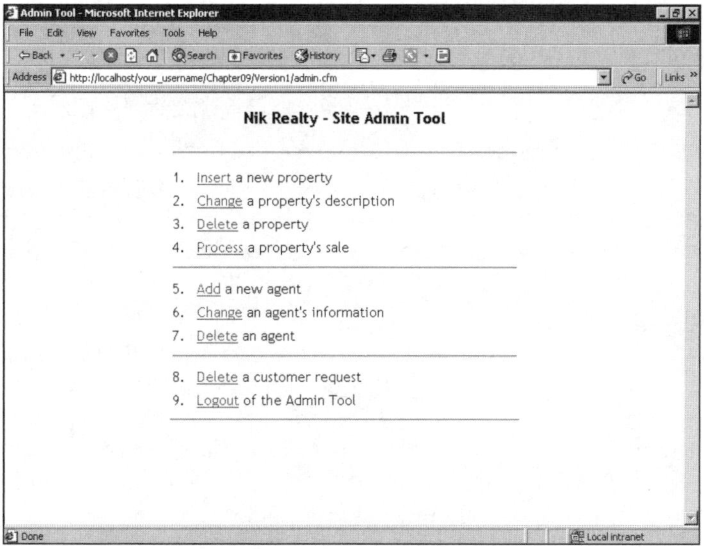

9

Figure 9-21   Site Admin Tool with a hyperlink for logging out

9. Click **Logout** to log out of the admin tool. You see a message indicating that the logout was successful.

10. Click the **Back** button, and refresh the document. Notice that now you are being asked to log on again as the cookie has been deleted by the logout.cfm template.

11. Close your Web browser and ColdFusion Studio.

You have successfully created logon security for the admin.cfm page.

In the previous exercise, even though the admin.cfm file is checking whether a user is logged on and preventing access to the menu, there is a security lapse in the logic. What would happen if a user had bookmarked the delete property screen? Any other person would be able to access the delete property screen even though the user has logged out because only the admin.cfm file has the logic built in to check whether a user is logged on. A possible solution is to tighten security by checking whether the user is logged on in every ColdFusion document in the application. To streamline this process, ColdFusion implements an application framework and uses a special file named application.cfm.

APPLICATION FRAMEWORK AND APPLICATION.CFM

A set of ColdFusion templates in a folder and its subfolders is an application. This folder is also referred to as the root folder of the application. Typically, all the ColdFusion templates in an application are logically related and part of one system. For example, all the ColdFusion documents in the Version1 folder in the previous example would be an application. The Version1 folder contains all the ColdFusion documents that are logically related and are part of a system that allows real estate agents to maintain the data in the database. The ColdFusion Application framework allows you to use two special files in the root folder named Application.cfm and OnRequestEnd.cfm. Whenever a Web browser makes a request for any ColdFusion document in an application, the ColdFusion Server executes first the Application.cfm file, then the file that has been requested, and finally the OnRequestEnd.cfm file. All the tasks that must be performed before any action is taken in a system logically belong in the Application.cfm file, and all the tasks that must be performed after any action taken in the system logically belong in the OnRequestEnd.cfm file. For example, any CFML that checks whether a user is logged on belongs to the Application.cfm file. This simplifies the system design as well as increases the security of the entire system. You may want to use the OnRequestEnd.cfm file to create a common footer for all templates. You may want to use both the Application.cfm file and the OnRequestEnd.cfm file to create your own system performance measurement statistics, for example. You do not have to store the ColdFusion template in the root folder of the application. The Application.cfm file in the root folder is executed even when the requested ColdFusion document is in a subfolder. The OnRequestEnd.cfm file should be in the same folder as the Application.cfm file.

In large applications that span multiple subfolders, you may want to customize the requirements in the Application.cfm file to subsystems in subfolders. For example, consider a site where sellers and buyers interact. Sellers post information about products that they have for sale, and buyers purchase their products. Sellers have access to some parts of the system, and buyers have access to some parts of the system. Users have to register as a seller or a buyer, and are charged different rates depending on whether they want to sell, buy, or both. For designing such a site, you want to use logic that checks whether users are sellers, and should access the sellers' subsystem, or whether users are buyers, and should access the buyers' subsystem. You can use multiple Application.cfm files in different subfolders in the system. When the ColdFusion Server receives a request for a ColdFusion document, it first checks the folder in which the requested document resides for an Application.cfm file. If it finds a file, it executes it and then processes the request. If it doesn't find an Application.cfm file in the folder, the ColdFusion server checks to see if it is in the parent folder of the folder containing the document requested. If it finds the file, it executes it and then processes the request. If the ColdFusion Server does not find the file in the parent folder, it checks its parent folder for Application.cfm and then executes it. These checks are performed up the folder hierarchy to the root folder on the Web site. Whenever the ColdFusion Server finds an Application.cfm file, it executes it, processes the request, and then executes the OnRequestEnd.cfm file (if present in the same folder as the Application.cfm file). This process is summarized in Figure 9-22.

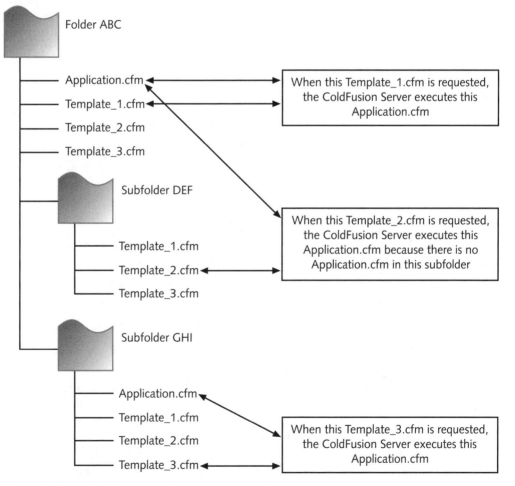

Figure 9-22   ColdFusion application framework

Because the ColdFusion Server executes the Application.cfm file whenever it receives a request for a ColdFusion document in the application, sometimes it is useful to know what template is being executed. The ColdFusion Server creates a variable named CGI.SCRIPT_NAME that contains the name of the template being executed including its path. You can use the GetFileFromPath() function to find the filename of the template being executed. To summarize, the GetFileFromPath(CGI.SCRIPT_NAME) function returns the name of the template being executed. This is useful in case you need to change the processing in the Application.cfm file depending on the template being executed.

Providing Application-Wide Logon Security

Realizing that users can bypass logon security in the admin tool by going directly to the templates in the system, Nikitha requests that you increase security in the system. You decide to implement an Application framework and transfer the logic for checking whether a user is logged on to the Application.cfm file from the admin.cfm file.

To tighten logon security with Application.cfm:

1. Start ColdFusion Studio, if necessary.

2. Open the **admin.cfm** file in the Version1 subfolder in Chapter09 folder on your Data Disk. Notice that the top four lines are implementing the logic to check whether a user is logged on. Users who are not logged on are redirected to the login.cfm template.

3. Click **File** on the menu bar, and then click **New**. The New Document dialog box opens.

4. Click to select the **Blank Document** icon, and then click **OK**. A new blank document opens in the Editor window.

5. Click the **admin.cfm** document tab at the bottom of the window to switch to admin.cfm.

6. Click at the beginning of line 1 and drag to line 5, position 1 to select the first four rows that implement logon security.

7. Press **Ctrl+X** to delete the four lines and store them on the Clipboard.

8. Click the **Untitled1** document tab at the bottom in the list of open documents.

9. Press **Ctrl+V** to paste the four lines.

10. Save this file as **Application.cfm** in the Chapter09/Version1 folder on your Data Disk.

Now the Application.cfm file would be executed prior to processing a request for any ColdFusion template in this folder. This increases the security for the entire site but poses a problem. What happens if there is a request for the login.cfm file? Even then the Application.cfm file is executed and the user is redirected again to the login.cfm file, creating an infinite loop of requests to the server. You need to implement a way to solve this problem. One way would be to check if the request is for login.cfm and then not redirect the user. Similarly, the user should not be redirected when the processLogin.cfm file is being executed.

To prevent infinite looping:

1. Click at the end of line 2 in the Application.cfm file, and press the **Enter** key. If the user is not logged in and the request is for login.cfm or processLogin.cfm, the user should not be redirected to login.cfm. You need to use the ColdFusion variable CGI.SCRIPT_NAME and the function GetFileFromPath to figure out the name of the template being executed.

2. Type **<cfif GetFileFromPath(CGI.SCRIPT_NAME) IS "login.cfm" OR GetFileFromPath(CGI.SCRIPT_NAME) IS "processLogin.cfm">**, and press **Enter**.

3. Type **<cfelse>**.

   If the template being executed is login.cfm or processLogin.cfm, there is no action to be performed in the Application.cfm file. Therefore, there are no statements between the CFIF and the CFELSE.

4. Click at the end of line 5, and press **Enter**. Press the **Backspace** key, and type **</cfif>** to close the CFIF tag. See Figure 9-23.

   The user would be redirected only if the template being executed is not login.cfm or processLogin.cfm.

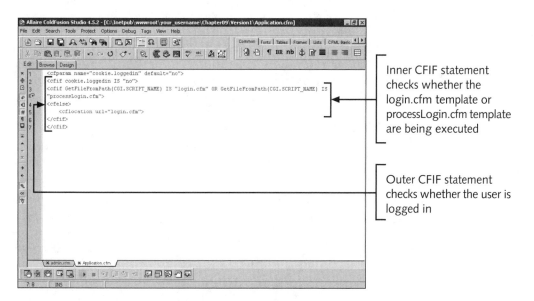

Figure 9-23   Editing the Application.cfm template in ColdFusion Studio

5. Click the **Save** button on the Standard toolbar to save the file again with the changes.

6. Click the **admin.cfm** tab at the bottom of the window, and then save the file. You have implemented logon security for the entire site by using the Application.cfm file.

7. Start your Web browser if necessary, and type the URL to open the deleteScreen1.cfm document from the Version1 folder on your Data Disk. You see the login.cfm page, as shown in Figure 9-24.

Figure 9-24 login.cfm is displayed when deleteScreen1.cfm is opened

When you click the deleteScreen1.cfm file, the Application.cfm file is executed first. The ColdFusion Server processes the CFPARAM tag and checks whether it had earlier created a cookie variable named loggedin. When it does not find a cookie, it checks to see if the template being executed is login.cfm or processLogin.cfm. Because the template being executed is deleteScreen1.cfm, the user is redirected to the login.cfm template. The Web browser receives the HTTP redirect request and sends a request for login.cfm. When the request for the login.cfm is received, the Application.cfm template is executed again. The ColdFusion Server does not find a cookie named loggedin. A default value of "no" is assigned to the variable created in the CFPARAM tag. The template being executed now is login.cfm, and the condition in the CFIF tag is true. The CFELSE part is ignored, and the ColdFusion Server executed the login.cfm document. The logon form is displayed.

8. Enter **Little** as the username and **NKL** as the password, and then click the **Logon** button. The form is submitted along with the data entered. The ColdFusion Server receives the data in the form of FORM.variable syntax and a request for processLogin.cfm template to handle the form data. The Application.cfm file is executed even in this case. The user is still not logged on. The ColdFusion Server tests the condition in the CFIF statement. The condition evaluates as true because the template being executed is processLogin.cfm file. The ColdFusion Server ignores the CFELSE part and processes the requested template. The server sends a set-cookie header to the client. The client sets a cookie and displays the hyperlink to the admin tool.

9. Click the **admin tool** hyperlink. The CF Server executes the Application.cfm file first. Because the user is logged on there is a cookie named loggedon. The condition in the first CFIF statement evaluates as false, and the server continues by processing the admin.cfm file. A menu is displayed. All functions are now available as long as the user is logged on.

10. Log out by clicking the **Logout** hyperlink.

11. Close your Web browser and ColdFusion Studio.

CLIENT STATE MANAGEMENT AND CLIENT VARIABLES

Cookies are not designed for storing lots of data, nor do browsers allow many cookies to be set from a particular site. If your application requires a lot of customization and data storage, using cookies to store the data may not be a viable option. For example, the My Excite feature at *www.excite.com* lets you tailor your page to suit your individual interests and preferences. You can personalize your page with colors, news, stock quotes, sports scores, horoscopes, and your favorite cartoons. In such situations, you need a sophisticated approach where the server stores most of the data in database tables or its memory. All you need to store in a cookie is the username or a similar primary key value that allows you to look up other customized data from database tables or the memory.

Also, there is some controversy surrounding the issue of cookies. Privacy advocates maintain that cookies can be used by organizations to track movements of consumers across the Web to discover their buying and Web-browsing habits. With this controversy in mind, most Web browsers allow users to turn off cookies. If a client computer does not accept cookies, applications such as the logon security that you created in the previous section will not work. In such situations, you need to store the data on the server again, as in the previous example, and use a primary key and its value as URL parameters on every request to look up customized data instead of using cookies. In other words, you are managing state without using cookies.

Theoretically, you could design your own CFML for keeping track of customized data. But, ColdFusion implements the concept of client state management and client variables as part of the application framework and makes the tasks of creating, storing, and retrieving such data as simple as creating regular variables, assigning values by using the CFSET statement, and retrieving values by using pound signs and functions. You create these variables by using the notation CLIENT.variable similarly to the way you used FORM.variable, URL.variable, and COOKIE.variable. Such variables created by using CLIENT.variable are named **client variables** because the server stores client-specific data in these variables. When you are managing state by using client variables, you are using **client state management**.

9

For ColdFusion to perform client state management, you have to explicitly turn on client state management by using an appropriate CFML tag. You will see this later on in this section. Once it is turned on, ColdFusion implements client state management by creating a record for each Web browser requesting a ColdFusion document that is part of an application with client state management enabled. This client record is identified by a unique token that is typically stored in an HTTP cookie in the client computer. You can create client variables of the form CLIENT.variable by using CFSET tags. Once created, these variables and their values are available to all the pages within the application for as long as the client interacts with the application. Typically, this interaction involves multiple requests. The variables are even available when the client quits the Web browser and interacts with the application later on the same day or even after a month.

You enable client state management by using the CFAPPLICATION tag. Include this tag at the top of every document that accesses client variables. The best place to use this tag is in the Application.cfm file. Because this file is executed before any other template, the client variables are available to all the templates in the application. You can create client variables or change their values in all the pages in the application.

The syntax for the CFAPPLICATION tag for enabling client state management is as follows:

```
<CFAPPLICATION NAME="Name"
  CLIENTMANAGEMENT="Yes/No"
  CLIENTSTORAGE="Storage Type"
  SETCLIENTCOOKIES="Yes/No" >
```

NAME attribute: This attribute identifies the application.

CLIENTMANAGEMENT attribute: When the value for the CLIENTMANAGEMENT attribute is YES, client state management is enabled.

CLIENTSTORAGE attribute: This attribute can take any one of three values:

- *Datasource_name*–ColdFusion stores client variables in the specified data source. To use this option, you must create a client variable storage option using the Variables page of the ColdFusion Administrator.

- *Registry*–ColdFusion stores client variables in the server's system registry. This is the default.

- *Cookie*–ColdFusion stores client variables on the client machine in a cookie. If you are convinced that users do not turn cookies off then this option is useful. A corporate intranet would be an ideal application of this.

SETCLIENTCOOKIES attribute: This attribute can take a value of YES or NO. If this value is YES, the unique token for each client is stored in an HTTP cookie on the client computer. Obviously, cookies have to be enabled for this function to work. The unique token is actually composed of two variables: CFID and CFTOKEN. If the attribute SETCLIENTCOOKIES is set to NO, then the ColdFusion server does not send set-cookie headers for storing the unique token on client computers. This option is useful if you want to design an application that has state management but does not use cookies. Then you have to design the application in such a way that each document in the application receives the values of CFID and CFTOKEN as URL parameters.

By using these values and client records stored in the system registry or the specified data source, ColdFusion implements state management without cookies—giving you a very powerful environment for designing sophisticated applications.

Creating Client Variables

Once client state management is enabled, you create client variables by using a CFSET tag as follows:

```
<cfset CLIENT.VariableName = Value>
```

You assign default values to variables by using the CFPARAM tag as follows:

```
<cfparam name= "CLIENT.VariableName" default=
"default_value">
```

When the ColdFusion server executes this tag, it checks for CLIENT.VariableName. If it does not find a variable with that name, it creates one and assigns it the default value.

Based on customer reaction, Nikitha asks you to let users bookmark pages that show their favorite houses and other properties on the NikRealty Web site. She wants users to be able to access these pages even after they turn off their computers and return to the site later. Because client variables are accessible even after the computer is turned off between interactions, you can add bookmarking ability to the NikRealty Web site by using a client variable. Your task now is to design this capability by using three subtasks:

1. Enable client state management in the Application.cfm file.

2. Design the template that receives a URL parameter and sets a client variable to the Record Number for the favorite property pages users want to bookmark.

3. Provide two hyperlinks in the template that displays properties. One link would allow users to bookmark the current property, and the second link would find their bookmarked property page and display it.

The folder Chapter09\NikRealty has the detail.cfm ColdFusion template that you created in Chapter 6 that allows users to browse property listings. Your task is to create this application in that folder.

9

To enable client state management:

1. Start ColdFusion Studio, if necessary.

2. Click the **Resource Tab** button to open the Resource Tab window.

3. If necessary, click the **Files** tab at the bottom of the window, and navigate to the **NikRealty** subfolder in the Chapter09 folder on your Data Disk.

4. Right-click in the file list window, point to **File**, and then click **Create Here**.

5. Type **application.cfm** as the name of the new file in ColdFusion Studio, and press the **Enter** key.

6. Double-click **application.cfm** to open it in the Editor window.

7. Select and delete all the code.

8. Type **<cfapplication name="NikRealty" clientmanagement="Yes">**, and press **Enter**.

9. Save the template by clicking the **Save** button on the Standard toolbar.

You have successfully created an application.cfm file that enables client state management for all the ColdFusion documents in the NikRealty folder. Your next task is to create a template that receives a URL parameter and sets a client variable to its value.

To create a client variable:

1. Start your Web browser, if necessary.

2. Open **makeFavorite.cfm** in the NikRealty subfolder in your Chapter09 folder on your Data Disk. See Figure 9-25.

Figure 9-25   Initial Web page displayed by makeFavorite.cfm

A basic HTML file is provided to speed up your task. The browser displays a message that the current property has been bookmarked as the user favorite. You task is to create a client variable in this template.

3. Switch to ColdFusion Studio, and double-click the **makeFavorite.cfm** file to open it in the Editor window. Notice that the insertion point is on line 1, position 1.

4. Type **<cfparam name="recNo">**, and press the **Enter** key. This file expects a URL parameter. You are using the CFPARAM tag to generate an error message in case this template is executed without a URL parameter.

5. Type **<cfset CLIENT.favoriteProperty = URL.recNo>**, and press **Enter**. See Figure 9-26.

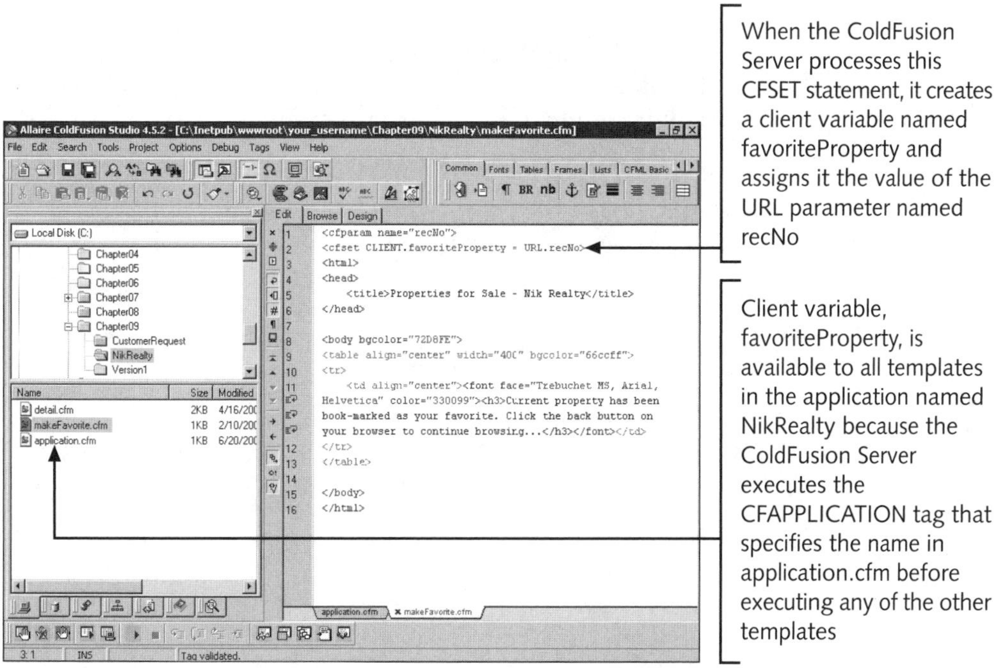

When the ColdFusion Server processes this CFSET statement, it creates a client variable named favoriteProperty and assigns it the value of the URL parameter named recNo

Client variable, favoriteProperty, is available to all templates in the application named NikRealty because the ColdFusion Server executes the CFAPPLICATION tag that specifies the name in application.cfm before executing any of the other templates

Figure 9-26   Editing makeFavorite.cfm in ColdFusion Studio

When the ColdFusion Server executes this CFSET tag, a client variable named favoriteProperty is created and assigned a value that the template receives as the URL parameter recNo.

6. Save the template by clicking the **Save** button on the Standard toolbar.

You have successfully created a template that sets a client variable and bookmarks a house or other property as a user's favorite. Your next task is to provide hyperlinks in the detail.cfm file that allow users to use this template.

To create hyperlinks for creating and displaying a favorite property:

1. Double-click **detail.cfm** to open it in the Editor window.

2. Click at the end of line 41, and press the **Enter** key.

3. Click the **Resource Tab** button to close the Resource Tab window.

4. Type **\<tr>\<td>\<font face="Trebuchet MS, Arial, Helvetica">\</font> \</td>\</tr>** to insert a new row in the table. Ignore any warning messages that you may see while typing.

5. Click between the opening and closing the FONT tags, and then click the anchor tag on the Common QuickBar. The Anchor dialog box opens.

6. Click in the HREF text box, if necessary, and type **makeFavorite.cfm?recNo= \<cfoutput>#displayRecordNumber#\</cfoutput>** as the hyperlink reference. Recall from Chapter 6 that variable displayRecordNumber stores the record number of the property being displayed.

7. Click in the description text area, and type **Bookmark as my favorite**.

8. Click **OK**. ColdFusion Studio inserts a hyperlink into the template for making the current property the favorite.

9. Click between \</a> and \</font>, and press the **spacebar**.

10. Type **– – – – –**, press the **spacebar**, and then click the **anchor tag** on the Common QuickBar.

11. Click in the HREF text box, if necessary, and type **detail.cfm?recNo=\<cfoutput>#CLIENT.favoriteProperty# \</cfoutput>** as the hyperlink reference.

12. Click in the description text area, and type **Go to my favorite property**.

13. Click **OK**. ColdFusion Studio inserts a hyperlink into the template for making the current property the favorite. See Figure 9-27.

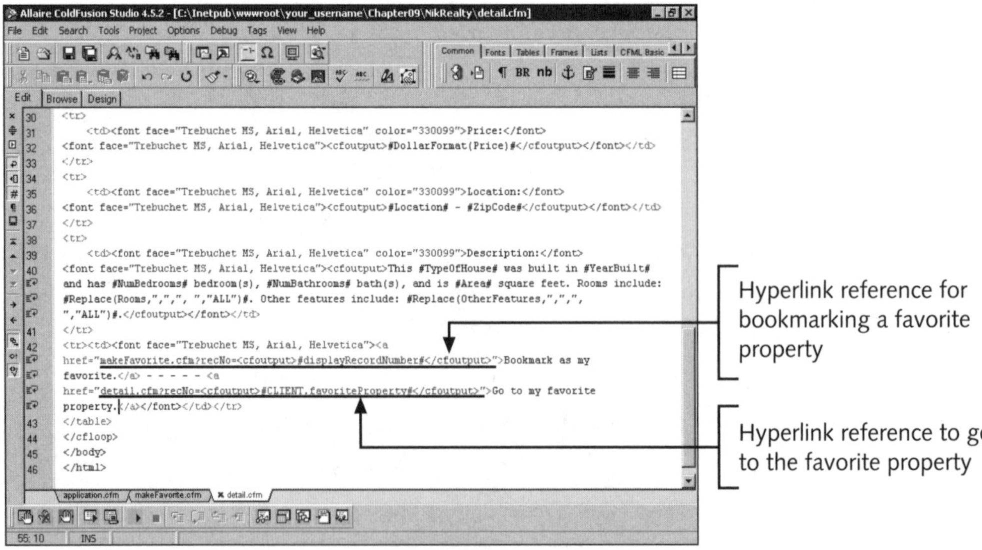

Figure 9-27 Editing the detail.cfm document in ColdFusion Studio

14. Save the file by clicking the **Save** button on the Standard toolbar.

15. Switch to your Web browser, type **http://localhost/your_username/ Chapter09/NikRealty/detail.cfm** in the Address text box, and then press **Enter**. See Figure 9-28.

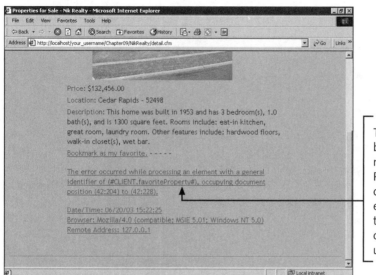

This error is produced because the variable named CLIENT.favorite Property has not yet been created. You need to execute makeFavorite.cfm to create the variable. You can prevent this error by using the CFPARAM tag

Figure 9-28   Error produced by detail.cfm

When the ColdFusion server executes this statement, it generates an error message because the user has not yet set a favorite property and there is no client variable name favoriteProperty. To deal with this you need to specify a default value for this variable.

To fix the error and complete the bookmark application:

1. Switch to ColdFusion Studio, click at the beginning of line 1 of detail.cfm, and then press the **Enter** key.

2. Press the **Up Arrow** key, type **<cfparam name="CLIENT.favoriteProperty" default="1">**, and then save the file by clicking the **Save** button on the Standard toolbar. See Figure 9-29.

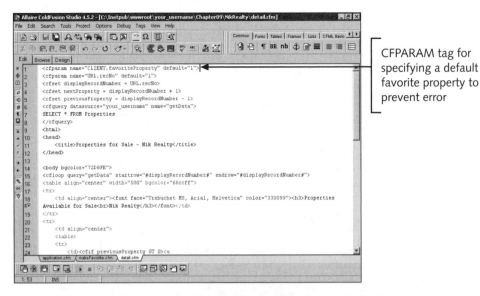

Figure 9-29 Specifying a default value for the client variable in detail.cfm

3. Switch to your Web browser, and refresh the **detail.cfm** file.

4. Browse a few properties. Navigate to the sixth property. See Figure 9–30.

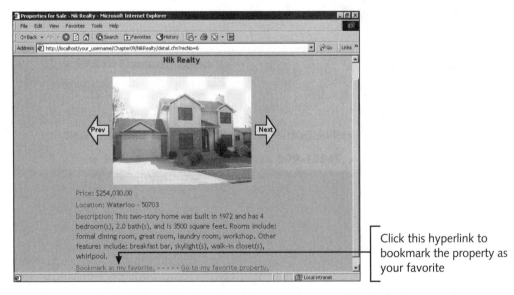

Figure 9-30 The Web browser displays the sixth property (detail.cfm?recNo=6)

5. Click the hyperlink, and bookmark the sixth property as your favorite. The makeFavorite.cfm file is executed and a client variable is set to the value of the recNo of the current record.

6. Click the **Back** button on your Web browser.

7. Browse a few more properties, and notice that the Go to my favorite property hyperlink always points to detail.cfm?recNo=6. See Figure 9-31.

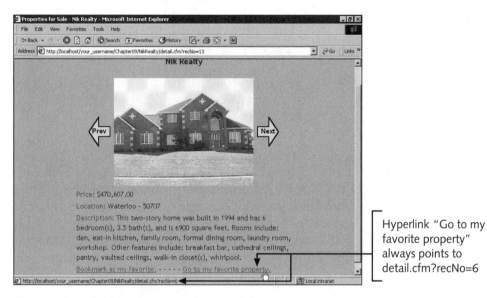

Hyperlink "Go to my favorite property" always points to detail.cfm?recNo=6

Figure 9-31   Web page displayed by detail.cfm?recNo=13 after you bookmark a favorite property

8. Click the **Go to my favorite property** hyperlink, and notice that the Web browser displays the sixth property that you bookmarked as your favorite.

9. Experiment a little with the application by making another property your favorite.

10. Close your Web browser.

11. Start your Web browser again, and navigate to the **detail.cfm** file.

12. Click the **Go to my favorite property** hyperlink, and notice what happens. Even after you have closed your browser, the server has remembered your favorite property and has returned to the same application.

13. Close your Web browser and ColdFusion Studio.

You have successfully customized the Web page by storing client preferences. The Web site displays your favorite property whenever you want. You have successfully managed state by using client variables. The biggest advantage of using client variables is that they are available even after users turn off their computers and revisit the site later. The disadvantage of using client variables is the need to store data in the system registry of the Web server or in a database. If you must maintain state for a certain amount of time (such as 30 minutes to a few hours), you can store data in the memory of the computer rather than the registry or a database. ColdFusion allows you to temporarily store data for short periods by implementing a concept of session management and session variables.

SESSIONS AND SESSION VARIABLES

A **session** is a set of interactions between a client Web browser and a Web server for a short period of time. Typically, all the interactions a user has with a site at a certain time form a session. ColdFusion allows you to implement sessions. Because you can never be sure whether a user has stopped interacting with your site or is busy for another reason, each session has a timeout limit. If the user does not return within a specific timeout period, the session is terminated.

Similarly to the concept of client state management, you enable session management by using the CFAPPLICATION tag. After you enable session management, you can create session variables of the form SESSION.variable by using CFSET tags. These variables are then available to all the pages within the application for as long as the client interacts with the application during that session. Unlike client variables that are stored in the registry or databases, these variables are stored in the computer memory and are not available after the session ends.

Similarly to usage for client state management, you should insert the CFAPPLICATION tag at the top of every document that accesses session variables. Instead of physically inserting it at the top of every document in the application, you should place this tag in the Application.cfm file. Because this file is executed prior to executing any other template, these session variables would be available to all the templates in the application. You can create session variables or change their values in all the pages in the application.

The syntax for the CFAPPLICATION tag for enabling session management is as follows:

```
<CFAPPLICATION NAME="Name"
  SESSIONMANAGEMENT="Yes/No"
  SESSIONTIMEOUT=#CreateTimeSpan(days, hours, minutes,
seconds)#>
```

NAME attribute: This attribute identifies the application.

SESSIONMANAGEMENT attribute: When the value for the SESSIONMANAGEMENT attribute is YES, the ColdFusion server enables session management.

SESSIONTIMEOUT attribute: The SESSIONTIMEOUT attribute is assigned a value returned by the CreateTimeSpan function.

Typically, the days, hours, and seconds of a SESSIONTIMEOUT are set at 0 and minutes-variable is set at 20. As soon as a client starts an interaction with the server by requesting a page in this application, a session starts. Session variables are retained in the server's memory for 20 minutes. If the client visits the server within 20 minutes, all the session variables and their values are available. As soon as a client revisits the application, the session is renewed for another 20 minutes. If the client does not visit the site for more than 20 minutes, the session is ended and all the session variables are destroyed. Similar to the concept of client variables, a session variable record is maintained for each client and is identified by the application name, the CFID, and the CFTOKEN variables. Using cookies to manage session variables is simple but optional. You can turn cookies off by setting the value of the optional SETCLIENTCOOKIES attribute to NO. If you do not use cookies, you have to ensure that the CFID and CFTOKEN variables are available as parameters to all pages in the application.

Creating Session Variables

After you set up session management, you create session variables by using a CFSET tag as follows:

```
<cfset SESSION.VariableName = Value>
```

You assign default values to variables by using the CFPARAM tag as follows:

```
<cfparam name="SESSION.VariableName" default="default_
value">
```

When the ColdFusion server executes this tag, it checks for the SESSION.VariableName. If it does not find a variable with that name, it creates one and assigns it the default value.

Locking Session Variables and Shared Resources

A user can make multiple requests and the ColdFusion Server can process them seemingly at the same time by using the multithreading feature of advanced operation systems. For example, if a document is a frameset with three frames, the ColdFusion Server is processing at least three requests. Creating and using session variables in such a scenario may cause unpredictable and unintentional results unless the process is controlled carefully. In other words, CFML that uses session variables should be locked so that only one request is executing the code at a time and the others are queued. Similarly, you should lock application variables; you will learn about application variables in the next section. Application variables are available to all users of an application and they also must be locked. Database maintenance operations such as insertion, deletion, and modification of data may be in need of locking, too. You lock code that uses shared resources by using the CFLOCK tag.

9

The syntax for the CFLOCK tag is as follows:

```
<CFLOCK
  TIMEOUT="timeout in seconds "
  SCOPE="Application" or "Server" or "Session"
  NAME="lockname">
  <!--- CFML to be locked --->
</CFLOCK>
```

You have to use only one of the attributes: SCOPE or NAME. For session variables, the SCOPE attribute has to be set to a value of "Session." This ensures that only one request per session is executing the code inside the <cflock> </cflock> tags. If the SCOPE attribute is set to application, only one request for the entire application can execute the code inside the lock at any given time. For database or file access operations, you have to use the NAME attribute. Only one request can execute the code within a lock with a particular lockname. Requests that are queued and are waiting would be terminated with an error when the TIMEOUT value in seconds passes.

Some of the agents working in NikRealty ask you to simplify the form that customers use for requesting showings. One agent has seen a Web site where a large form is split into smaller parts and each screen has only a few data entry controls. This encourages customers to complete the form because it does not seem prohibitively long. To meet their request, you can apply your knowledge of session variables and the concepts of sessions and temporary storage of variables and values in the server's memory. You think that it is a great way for storing user data and for breaking up the form into multiple pages.

You can logically break up the form that users use for scheduling showings into four pages. Your graphics department split up the original form into multiple pages, and the files are available for you in the Chapter09/CustomerRequest folder on your Data Disk. Your first task is to familiarize yourself with the files available.

To become familiar with the files available:

1. If necessary, start your Web browser.

2. Type **http://localhost/your_username/Chapter09/CustomerRequest/ scheduleShowing.cfm** in the Address text box, and press the **Enter** key. See Figure 9-32. Recall that this is the original form that you worked with in Chapter 8.

3. Type **http://localhost/your_username/Chapter09/CustomerRequest/ ShowingScreen1.cfm** in the Address text box, and press **Enter**. This is the first page of the form that has been redesigned by your graphics department. Notice that this form will ask for information regarding when customers want to a see a property, as shown in Figure 9-33.

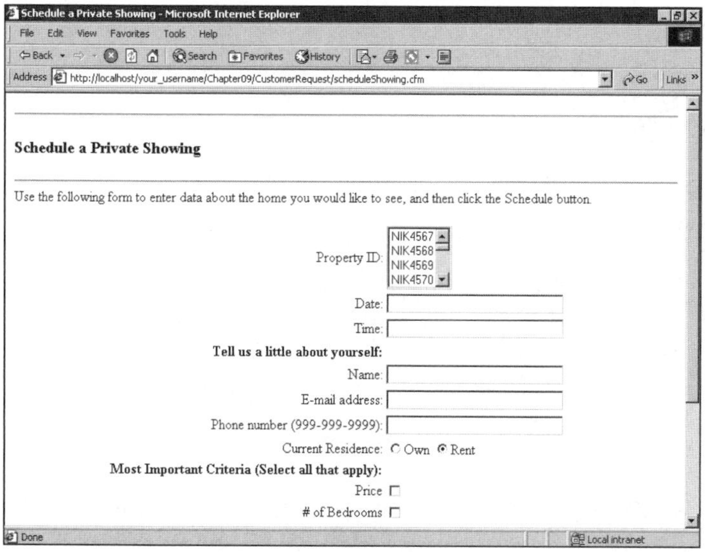

Figure 9-32 The original Schedule a Private Showing form

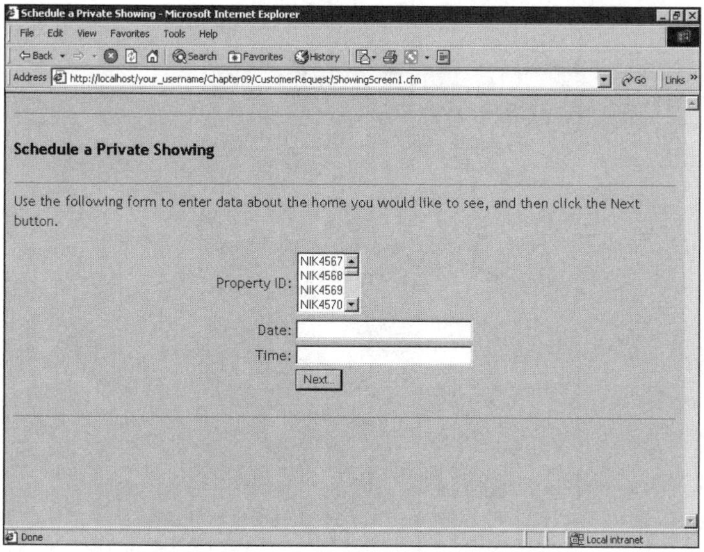

Figure 9-33 Screen 1 of the new Schedule a Private Showing form

4. Click **NIK4567**, type **7/13/2003** in the Date text box, type **10:30** in the Time text box, and then click the **Next** button. You are entering the data to clear the data validation routines. The templates currently do not process this data. The second screen is displayed as shown in Figure 9-34. Page 2 is for collecting information about customers. It is the form handler for the first page.

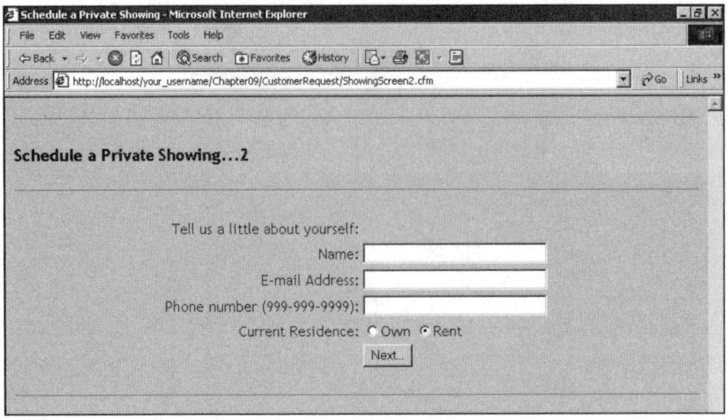

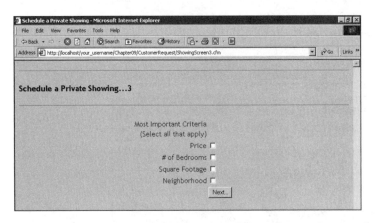

Figure 9-34　Screen 2 of the new Schedule a Private Showing form

5. Type **Sandy Marshall** in the Name text box, **smarshall@uni.edu** in the E-mail Address text box, **319 555 1234** in the Phone number text box, and then click the **Next** button. Similarly to the first case, the data is ignored by the form handler and another part of the form is displayed. Page 3 is for collecting customer preferences, as shown in Figure 9-35.

Figure 9-35　Screen 3 of the new Schedule a Private Showing form

6. Click **Price** as the most important criteria, and then click the **Next** button. The form handler displays the next page in the form. Page 4 is for user comments, as shown in Figure 9-36.

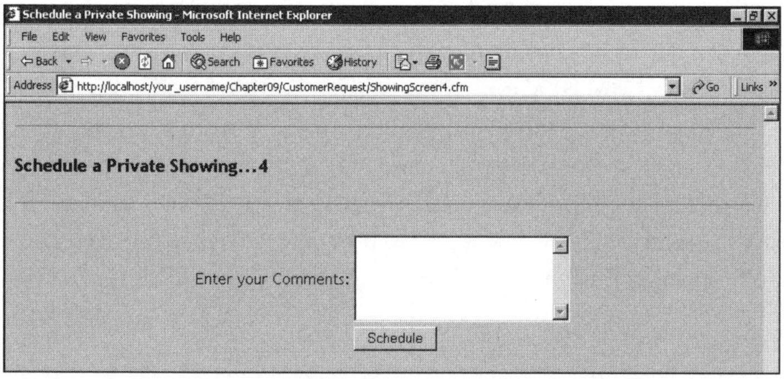

Figure 9-36   Screen 4 of the new Schedule a Private Showing form

7. Click the **Schedule** button. The processSchedule.cfm file displays an error message because it is expecting form variables for all the controls in the original form as shown in Figure 9-37. You will fix this error in subsequent exercises.

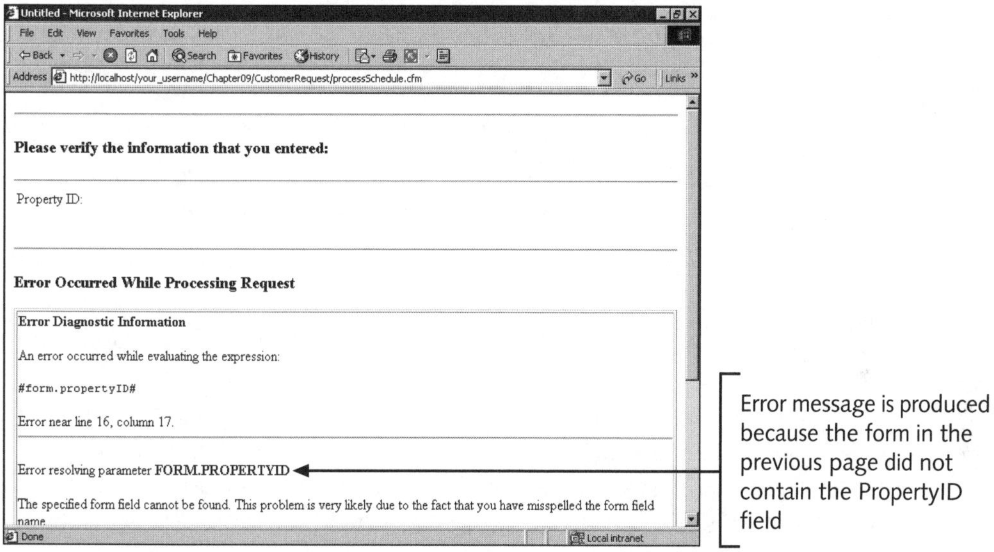

Error message is produced because the form in the previous page did not contain the PropertyID field

Figure 9-37   Error message produced by processSchedule.cfm

You may have noticed that all the controls in the smaller forms are essentially the same as those you used in the large form along with the data validation scheme that you designed in Chapter 8. The large form has been split up into the smaller parts to ease user data entry. The form handlers for each of the forms are in a sequence now. ShowingScreen1.cfm is the first part of the form. ShowingScreen2.cfm is the form handler for ShowingScreen1.cfm and so on. The form handler for the last page (ShowingScreen4.cfm) is processSchedule.cfm.

Your task is to add the code for using session variables for intermediate storage of data in the application. ShowingScreen2.cfm should handle the form data entered in showingScreen1 and store the user values in session variables and then display the second part of the form. ShowingScreen3.cfm should store the data entered in the second screen in session variables and then display page 3 and so on. Other than the use of the session variables, the rest of the code is very similar to the previous case. Before you can store data in session variables, first you need to create the Application.cfm file for enabling session management and then modify the forms for handling user data.

To enable session management:

1. Start ColdFusion Studio, and click the **Resource Tab** button to display the Resource Tab window.

2. Navigate to the **CustomerRequest** subfolder in the Chapter09 folder on your Data Disk.

3. Right-click in the file list window, point to **File**, and then click **Create Here**.

4. Type **application.cfm** as the name of the new file, and press the **Enter** key.

5. Double-click **application.cfm** to open it in the Editor window.

6. Select and delete all the code in the Editor window.

7. Type **<cfapplication name="CustomerRequest" sessionmanagement= "Yes" sessiontimeout=#CreateTimeSpan(0,0,20,0)#>**, and press **Enter**.

8. Save the application.cfm template by clicking the **Save** button on the Standard toolbar.

9. Click the **x** button on the vertical Editor toolbar in the middle of the screen to close the document.

The application.cfm file you created enables session management for all the ColdFusion documents in the CustomerRequest folder. Every page in the application can now create or manipulate session variables and their values. Your next task is to modify the form screen templates for creating and assigning values to session variables.

To create a multi-page form using session variables:

1. Start ColdFusion Studio, if necessary, and navigate to the **CustomerRequest** subfolder in the Chapter09 folder on your Data Disk.

2. Double-click **ShowingScreen1.cfm** to open it in the Editor window. This is the first page of the new multi-page form. Scroll down the document and notice that the three data entry controls are named PropertyID, ScheduleDate, and ScheduleTime. See Figure 9-38.

   Also, note that the form handler for the form is ShowingScreen2.cfm. Your task is to store user-entered data from the first form in session variables in its form handler, ShowingScreen2.cfm.

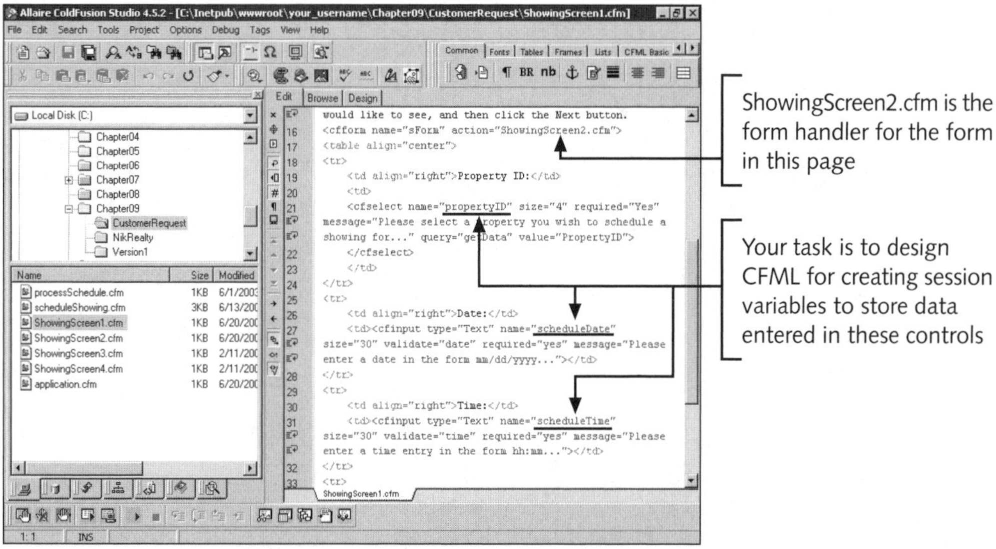

ShowingScreen2.cfm is the form handler for the form in this page

Your task is to design CFML for creating session variables to store data entered in these controls

Figure 9-38   ShowingScreen1.cfm in ColdFusion Studio

3. Double-click **ShowingScreen2.cfm** to open it in the Editor window.

4. Click at the beginning of line 1, if necessary, and press the **Enter** key.

5. Press the **Up Arrow** key to move the cursor to the first line.

Recall that it is always a good practice to lock the code that uses session variables.

6. Type **<cflock scope="SESSION" timeout="20">**, and press **Enter**. The code after this tag would be locked and multiple requests in the same session would be queued. You are anticipating that 20 seconds is enough time for the timeout. The user data should be captured in session variables so that it is available to the rest of the pages in the application.

7. Type **<cfset SESSION.PropertyID = FORM.propertyID>**, and press **Enter**. The PropertyID of the property selected in the select box is assigned to a newly created session variable named PropertyID.

8. Similarly, assign the other user data by using CFSET tags by typing **<cfset SESSION.scheduleDate = FORM.scheduleDate>** and pressing **Enter**.

9. Type **<cfset SESSION.scheduleTime = FORM.scheduleTime>**, and press **Enter**.

10. Type **</cflock>** to close the CFLOCK tag.

11. Save the file by clicking the **Save** button on the Standard toolbar. See Figure 9-39.

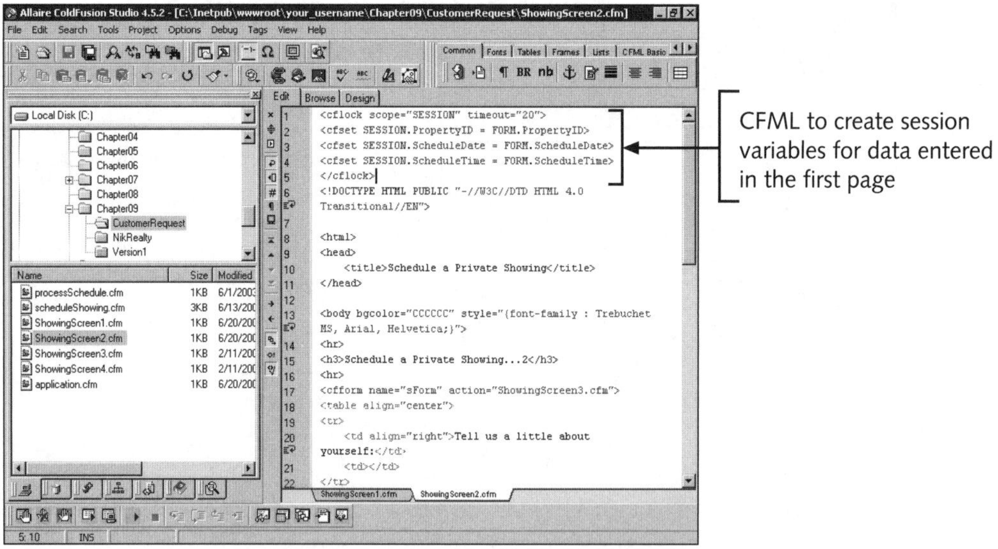

CFML to create session
variables for data entered
in the first page

Figure 9-39   Editing ShowingScreen2.cfm in ColdFusion Studio

You have designed a form handler that captures user data into newly created session variables. This form handler, in turn, displays another form. Your next task is to modify the form handlers for this page and the other pages.

To modify ShowingScreen3.cfm:

1. In ColdFusion Studio, click the **Resource Tab** button to close the Resource Tab window.

   Scroll down ShowingScreen2.cfm to see the names of the controls in the form are: clientName, clientEmail, clientPhone, and currentResidence. See Figure 9-40. Also notice that the form handler for this form is ShowingScreen3.cfm.

2. Open **ShowingScreen3.cfm** from the CustomerRequest subfolder in the Chapter09 folder on your Data Disk.

3. Click the **ShowingScreen2.cfm** document tab at the bottom.

4. Scroll up, if necessary, and select lines 1–5. The insertion point should be at the beginning of line 6.

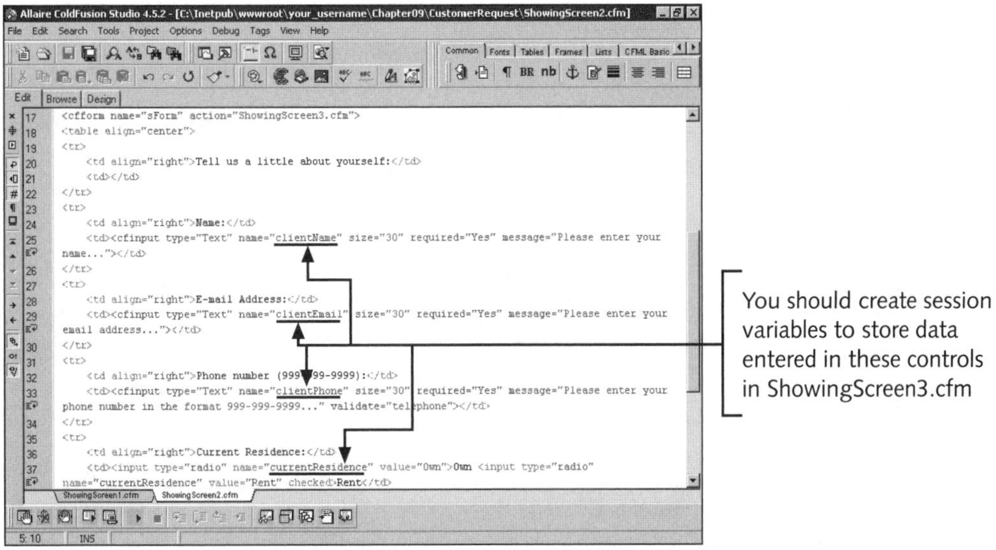

You should create session variables to store data entered in these controls in ShowingScreen3.cfm

Figure 9-40   Controls in ShowingScreen2.cfm

5. Press **Ctrl+C** to copy the code to the Clipboard.

6. Switch to **ShowingScreen3.cfm** by clicking the appropriate tab at the bottom in the open document list.

7. Click at the beginning of line 1, and press **Ctrl+V** to paste the code.

8. Select and change PropertyID on line 2 to **clientName** on both sides of the equal sign.

9. Select and change ScheduleDate on line 3 to **clientEmail** on both sides of the equal sign.

10. Similarly, select and change ScheduleTime on line 4 to **clientPhone** on both sides of the equal sign.

11. Click at the end of line 4, and press **Enter**.

12. Type <cfset **SESSION.currentResidence = FORM.currentResidence**>.

13. Save the file by clicking the **Save** button on the Standard toolbar. See Figure 9-41.

14. Scroll down and notice that the name of the control on this screen is "criteria" and the form handler is ShowingScreen4.cfm.

15. Open **ShowingScreen4.cfm** in the CustomerRequest subfolder. Notice that the insertion point is at the beginning of line 1.

16. Type **<cflock scope="SESSION" timeout="20">**, and press **Enter**.

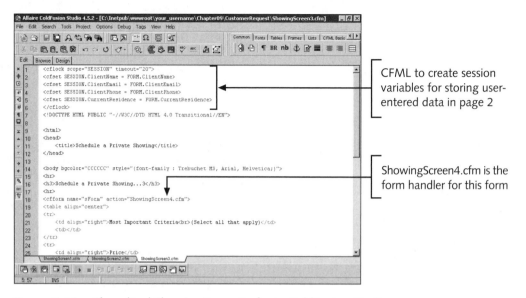

Figure 9-41 The edited ShowingScreen3.cfm in ColdFusion Studio

17. Type **<cfset SESSION.criteria = FORM.criteria>**, and press **Enter**.

18. Type **</cflock>** to close the CFLOCK tag, and press **Enter**.

19. Save this file by clicking the **Save** button on the Standard toolbar. See Figure 9-42.

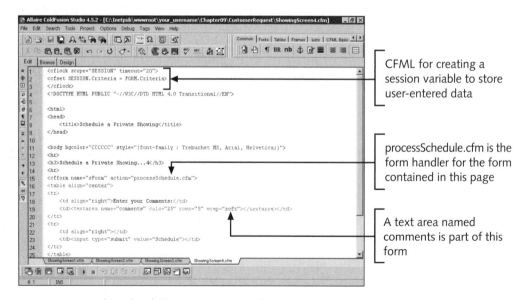

Figure 9-42 The edited ShowingScreen4.cfm in ColdFusion Studio

20. Scroll down and notice that the user data entry control is "comments" and the form handler is processSchedule.cfm, which was the original form handler for the large form.

All you need to do now is to modify the processSchedule.cfm file so that it uses the data from the session variables rather than from the original form (except for the comments field, which is the only control left in the form that invokes this form handler).

To modify the form handler to use session variables:

1. In ColdFusion Studio, select **File** on the menu bar, and then click **Close All**.

2. Open **processSchedule.cfm** from the CustomerRequest subfolder.

3. Type **<cflock scope ="SESSION" timeout="20">**, and press the **Enter** key.

4. Scroll down to the end of the code, and type **</cflock>** as the last line in the template.

5. All the form variables (except for comments) are now session variables. Click **Search** on the menu bar, and then click **Replace**. The Replace dialog box opens.

6. Type **FORM.** in the Find what text box, and press the **Tab** key.

7. Type **SESSION.** in the Replace with text box.

8. Click the **Replace All** button. ColdFusion Studio replaces all the occurrences of form. with session. until the end of the document and displays a dialog box asking you whether you want to search at the top too.

9. Click the **Yes** button.

10. A message box prompts you that 18 occurrences have been replaced. Click **OK**.

11. Click **Cancel** in the Replace dialog box.

12. Select **<cfparam name="SESSION.criteria" default="Not answered">** on line 2, and type **<cfset SESSION.comments = FORM.comments>** to replace it.

13. Save the file by clicking the **Save** button on the Standard toolbar. See Figure 9-43.

9

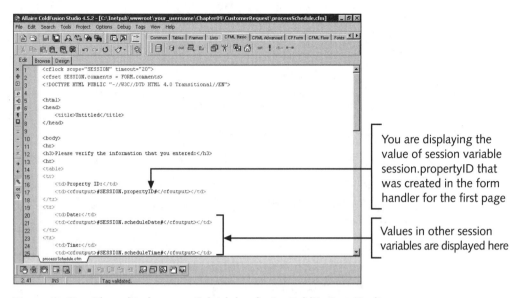

Figure 9-43 The edited processSchedule.cfm in ColdFusion Studio

Your next task is to verify the workings of the multi-page form.

To verify the workings of the multi-page form:

1. Switch to your Web browser, and open **ShowingScreen1.cfm**.

2. Enter data similar to what you entered in the previous exercise (see Figure 9-44), and click the **Next** button. Similarly, enter data in the other forms, and finally click the **Schedule** button on the last form. Notice that the processSchedule.cfm form handler is executed. It now retrieves the data from the session variables and echoes the data, as shown in Figure 9-44.

3. Close your Web browser and ColdFusion Studio. You have successfully created a multi-page form by using session variables to store intermediate data.

You have seen how useful session variables are in the previous example. Just as session variables are accessible to multiple templates requested by a particular client, you also can share data among multiple users within an application. To enable this sharing of data among multiple users, ColdFusion implements the concept of application variables.

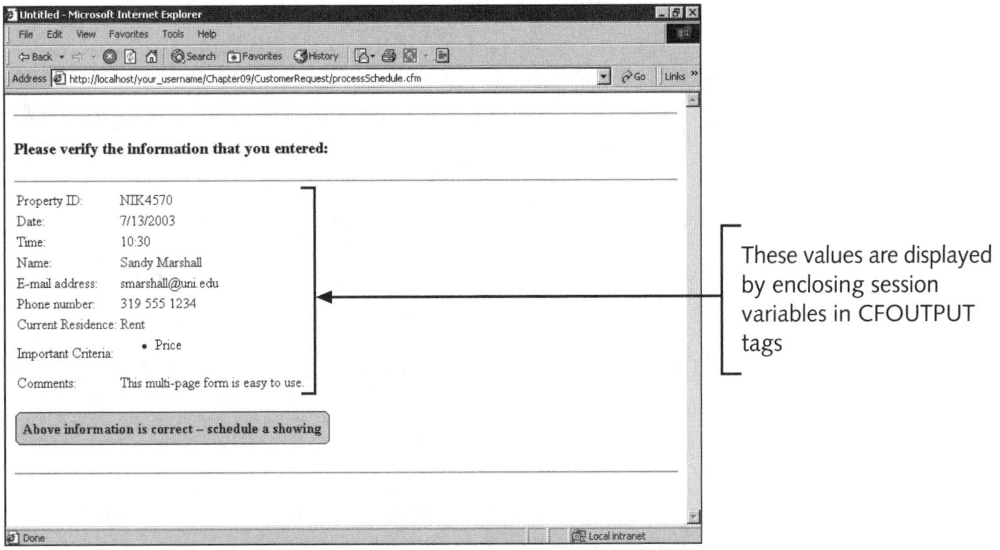

Figure 9-44   Web page displayed by processSchedule.cfm

APPLICATION VARIABLES

Application variables are available to multiple requests from multiple users within the scope of an application. Similarly to how client management is implemented by creating a unique record for each client, ColdFusion implements application variables by creating a unique record for each application. Application variables are enabled when ColdFusion executes the CFAPPLICATION tag with the NAME attribute set to the name of the application. Client information is not necessary for application variables because these are available to all clients. After you set up application variables, you create them by using CFSET tags and variables of the form APPLICATION.variablename. You must always lock the code that uses application variables to ensure data integrity and program logic. Application variables are retained for a duration specified in the ColdFusion administrator settings. Generally, the default timeout is two days. You can override the specification in the administrator settings by using the APPLICATIONTIMEOUT attribute of the CFAPPLICATION tag. You must use the CREATETIMESPAN function to initialize this attribute similarly to the way you use the SESSIONTIMEOUT attribute. Application variables are stored in the server's memory. If the server is rebooted or the ColdFusion Server is restarted, all the application variables are lost.

Based on conversations with clients and agents, Nikitha is concerned that only a few customers who open the schedule showing form are actually scheduling showings. She wants you to collect simple statistics about how many customers view the form and how many are actually scheduling a showing. You and she agree to collect these statistics by counting the number of requests for the first page and the number of requests for the last page.

You are planning to implement the logic for this requirement in two stages. First, you want to use two application variables APPLICATION.hitcountFirst and APPLICA-TION.hitcountLast for counting the number of hits on the first page and the last page, respectively. These variables would be incremented each time the first and the last pages are requested. Second, you want to create a template for reporting these statistics to Nikitha.

To collect simple daily usage statistics using Application variables:

1. Start ColdFusion Studio, if necessary, and open **ShowingScreen1.cfm**.

2. Press the **Enter** key, and use the **Up Arrow** key to return to the first line.

3. Type **<cflock scope="APPLICATION" timeout="20">**, and press **Enter**. You are creating a lock in the application scope with a timeout of 20 seconds. All requests from all clients would be queued at this point to ensure that each request is processed separately here.

4. Type **<cfparam name=" APPLICATION.hitcountFirst" default="0">**, and press **Enter**. If the server has just started and this is the first hit, this tag ensures that a variable APPLICATION.hitcountFirst is given the default value of 0.

5. Type **<cfset APPLICATION.hitcountFirst = APPLICATION.hitcountFirst + 1>**, and press **Enter**. Every request from each client increments this variable by 1. Essentially, you are counting the number of times this template is being executed, or in other words, the number of hits this page has.

6. Type **</cflock>** to end the lock.

7. Select the code you just entered, as shown in Figure 9-45, and then press **Ctrl+C** to copy the code to the Clipboard.

8. Save the file by clicking the **Save** button on the Standard toolbar, and close the file.

9. Open **processSchedule.cfm**, if necessary. Notice that the insertion point is at the beginning of line 1.

10. Press **Ctrl+V** to paste the code that you have just copied.

11. Change the application variable **hitcountFirst** to **hitcountLast** once on line 2 and twice on line 3.

12. Save the file by clicking the **Save** button on the Standard toolbar, and close the file.

13. Switch to your Web browser, and type **http://localhost/your_username/ Chapter09/CustomerRequest/ShowingScreen1.cfm** in the Address text box, and then press **Enter**. Click the **Reload** button (or the **Refresh** button) two or three times.

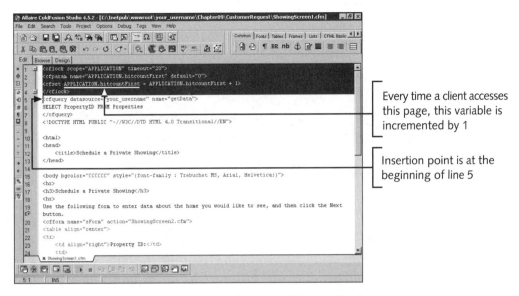

Figure 9-45   Editing ShowingScreen1.cfm in ColdFusion Studio

14. Enter some scheduling data, and click the **Next** button.

15. Repeat Step 14 until you have submitted the last form.

16. If other computers have access to your Web server, ask a few of your friends to visit your page and a few of them to enter data in the form.

You have successfully counted the number of hits on a page using application variables. But, you have not yet designed a template that allows you to view these statistics. Your next task is to implement this feature.

To create a simple Web site usage reporting tool:

1. Switch to ColdFusion Studio, and open a new document.

2. If necessary, click below the BODY tag, then type **<h3 align= "center"> Usage Statistics</h3>**, and press the **Enter** key.

3. Click the **Tables** QuickBar, and insert a 2 × 2 table using the Table Sizer (QuickTable).

4. Align the table to the center of the document. Set its border to **1**.

5. Type **First page visits** in the first cell in the first row on line 12.

6. Type **Form submissions** in the first cell in the second row on line 16.

7. Type **<cfoutput>#APPLICATION.hitcountFirst#</cfoutput>** in the second cell in the first row on line 13.

8. Type **<cfoutput>#APPLICATION.hitcountLast#</cfoutput>** in the second cell in the second row on line 17.

9. Change the title of the document to **Usage Statistics** on line 5.

10. Save the file as **reportingTool.cfm** in the Chapter09\CustomerRequest folder. See Figure 9-46.

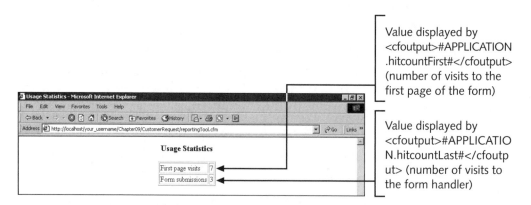

Figure 9-46　Editing reportingTool.cfm in ColdFusion Studio

11. Switch to your Web browser, and open the reportingTool.cfm file by typing its URL. See Figure 9-47. The values of the application variables are displayed in the appropriate cells. (Your values might be different.)

Value displayed by <cfoutput>#APPLICATION.hitcountFirst#</cfoutput> (number of visits to the first page of the form)

Value displayed by <cfoutput>#APPLICATION.hitcountLast#</cfoutput> (number of visits to the form handler)

Figure 9-47　Web page displayed by reportingTool.cfm

12. Open the **ShowingScreen1.cfm**, and reload it a few times.

13. Open and refresh the **reportingTool.cfm** file, and notice the statistics now. Notice that the number of first page visits goes up, as shown in Figure 9-48.

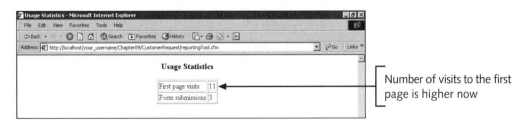

Number of visits to the first page is higher now

Figure 9-48 Web page displayed by reportingTool.cfm after loading the first page a few times more

You have successfully used application variables and created a simple usage tracking and reporting tool.

CHAPTER SUMMARY

❐ The Web is a stateless system. Each connection a client computer makes with a Web server is unique. The Web does not remember prior interactions while processing a request.

❐ You use HTTP cookies for state management. When you must build state into client–server interactions, the Web server sends a set-cookie header. The client computer sets a cookie, and on subsequent interactions with the Web server it sends the cookie back. The Web server receives the cookie and remembers prior interactions with the client.

❐ ColdFusion client variables overcome limitations of HTTP cookies. Client variables can be stored in a cookie, in the Web server's registry, or in an external database. State can be managed by using simple cookies or URL tokens. Client variables persist across sessions of interactions between clients and servers.

❐ You enable client state management by using the CFAPPLICATION tag. You create client variables by using the CFSET and variables of the form CLIENT.Variable.

❐ A set of ColdFusion templates in a folder and its subfolders is an application. The ColdFusion Application framework allows you to use two special files in the root folder named Application.cfm and OnRequestEnd.cfm. Whenever there is a request of any ColdFusion document to be executed in an application, the ColdFusion Server first executes the Application.cfm file, then the file that has been requested, and finally the OnRequestEnd.cfm file.

❐ A session is a set of interactions between a client Web browser and a Web server for a short duration of time.

❏ You enable session management by using the CFAPPLICATION tag and setting the SESSIONMANAGEMENT attribute to YES. Once session management is enabled, you can create session variables of the form SESSION.variablename by using CFSET tags. Once these variables are created, they are available to all the pages within the application for as long as the client interacts with the application during that session. These variables are stored in the computer memory and are not available after the session ends.

❏ Application variables are available to multiple requests from multiple users within the scope of an application. You can create application variables of the form APPLICATION.variablename by using CFSET tags after enabling them by using the CFAPPLICATION tag.

❏ You have to lock code that uses shared resources by using the CFLOCK tag.

REVIEW QUESTIONS

1. What does the statement "The Web is stateless" mean?
2. What are HTTP cookies? How do they work?
3. How can you make the Web remember state?
4. What are ColdFusion client variables?
5. If you can maintain state with cookies, why do you need client variables?
6. What is the ColdFusion Application framework?
7. What is the application.cfm file? Why is it important?
8. What is the name of the template that is executed after the requested template is executed?
9. What are sessions and session variables?
10. What are application variables?
11. What kinds of variables are remembered even when the computer is turned off between interactions between a browser and a server?
12. What kinds of variables are visible to all users of an application?
13. What kinds of variables are visible to all interactions between a browser and a server?
14. What kinds of variables are lost when there is no interaction between a browser and a server for a few hours?
15. What is the purpose of the CFLOCK tag?
16. What is the syntax of the CFAPPLICATION tag? Which of its attributes are important for managing sessions?
17. What attributes of the CFAPPLICATION tag are important for using application variables?
18. What attributes of the CFAPPLICATION tag are important for using client variables?

HANDS-ON PROJECTS

Project 1: Design a Note-to-Self Application

You have been asked to design a note-to-self application on a company's intranet. Your tasks are the following:

1. Create a subfolder in the Chapter09 folder named **Note2Self**.

2. Create an HTML document named **noteForm.htm** with a text area and a submit button in this folder, as shown in Figure 9-49.

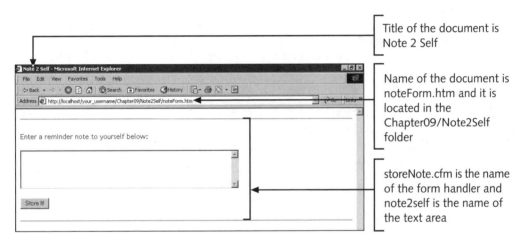

Title of the document is Note 2 Self

Name of the document is noteForm.htm and it is located in the Chapter09/Note2Self folder

storeNote.cfm is the name of the form handler and note2self is the name of the text area

Figure 9-49

3. Design a form handler for this form named **storeNote.cfm**. This template should store the note entered in the text box in an HTTP cookie named note2self on the client computer and display a message "Note to self has been stored successfully, click <u>here</u> to read the note…," as shown in Figure 9-50. Create a hyperlink so that the browser loads readNote.cfm when you click the hyperlink "here."

Hyperlink to readNote.cfm

This template stores the user-entered note in a cookie named note2self

Figure 9-50

4. Design another template named **readNote.cfm** that displays the message that is stored in the cookie, as shown in Figure 9-51. Provide a hyperlink to noteForm.htm.

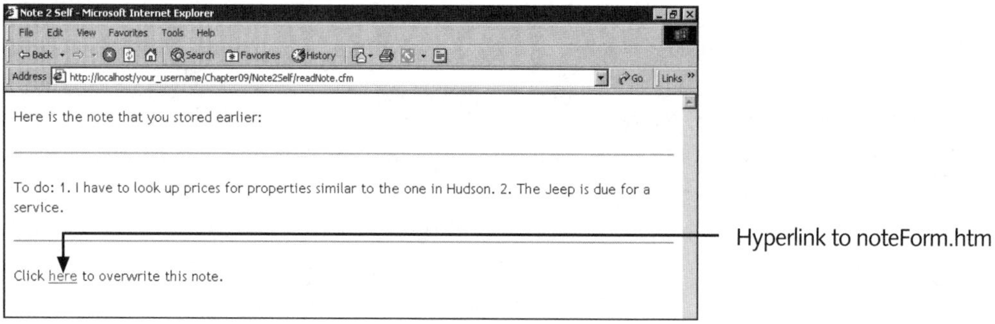

> **Note 2 Self - Microsoft Internet Explorer**
>
> File Edit View Favorites Tools Help
>
> Back • • ⊗ 🖹 🏠 ⊗Search ⌖Favorites ⊗History 🖹• ⊕ 🖹 • 🖹
>
> Address 🖹 http://localhost/your_username/Chapter09/Note2Self/readNote.cfm ▾ ⊘Go Links »
>
> Here is the note that you stored earlier:
>
> _____
>
> To do: 1. I have to look up prices for properties similar to the one in Hudson. 2. The Jeep is due for a service.
>
> _____
>
> Click here to overwrite this note.

Hyperlink to noteForm.htm

Figure 9-51

5. Enter a note to yourself in noteForm.htm and submit it. Browse readNote.cfm to read your note. Shut down and restart your computer, and open the readNote.cfm file. Does your note show up?

Project 2: Design a Customized Web Site

You have been asked to create a customized Web site for NikRealty that allows users to pick their own background colors for displaying properties. Your tasks are as follows:

1. Create an HTML document named **colorForm.htm** in the Chapter09/NikRealty folder, with a select box with a caption that says, "Select your favorite color:" and a Submit button. Use the following colors in the select box: burlywood, cyan, gainsboro, lightblue, lightsalmon, mistyrose, and any other light colors of your choice. This form is shown in Figure 9-52.

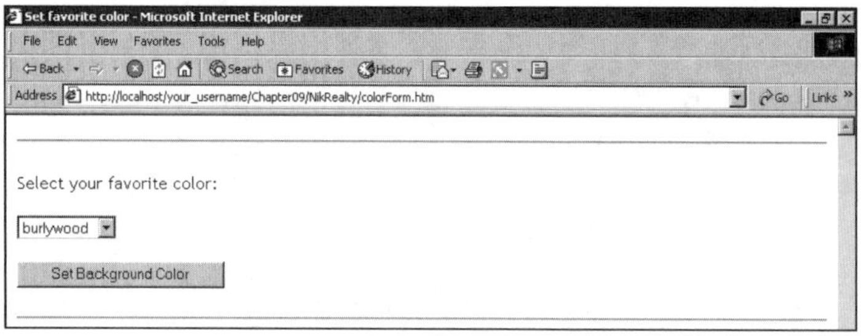

> **Set favorite color - Microsoft Internet Explorer**
>
> File Edit View Favorites Tools Help
>
> Back • • ⊗ 🖹 🏠 ⊗Search ⌖Favorites ⊗History 🖹• ⊕ 🖹 • 🖹
>
> Address 🖹 http://localhost/your_username/Chapter09/NikRealty/colorForm.htm ▾ ⊘Go Links »
>
> Select your favorite color:
>
> burlywood ▾
>
> Set Background Color

Figure 9-52

2. Design a form handler for this form named **storeColor.cfm**. This template should store the favorite color selected as a client variable named backColor and display a message "Your color choice has been stored successfully, click here to browse properties in your favorite color...," as shown in Figure 9-53. Create a hyperlink so that the browser loads detail.cfm when you click the text "here."

Figure 9-53

3. Modify the detail.cfm file so that it uses this favorite color as the background color for the document in the BODY tag as well as in the TABLE tag. Use a CFPARAM tag such that the current background color is the default if the user has not selected any favorite color. Add a hyperlink at the bottom of this page with text "Customize the background color" to colorForm.htm, as shown in Figure 9-54.

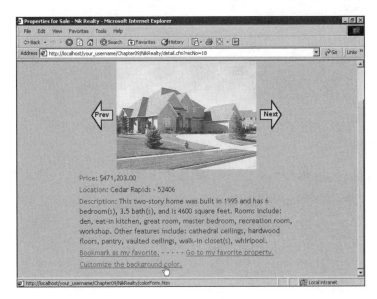

Figure 9-54

4. Experiment with several different background colors.

Project 3: Design a Multi-Page Online Order Form

Your company has been asked to redesign an existing online order form by splitting it into multiple pages. Create a new subfolder named **subsApplication**. Copy the subsForProgrammers.cfm template from the Chapter08 folder to this folder. Design a multi-page form that uses session variables by editing subsForProgrammers.cfm. Page 1 should be limited to the type of bread, as shown in Figure 9-55; page 2 should be limited to the type of sub sandwich, as shown in Figure 9-56; and page 3 should be used for specifying the toppings, as shown in Figure 9-57. The final form handler named processSub.cfm should echo the data entered, as shown in Figure 9-58.

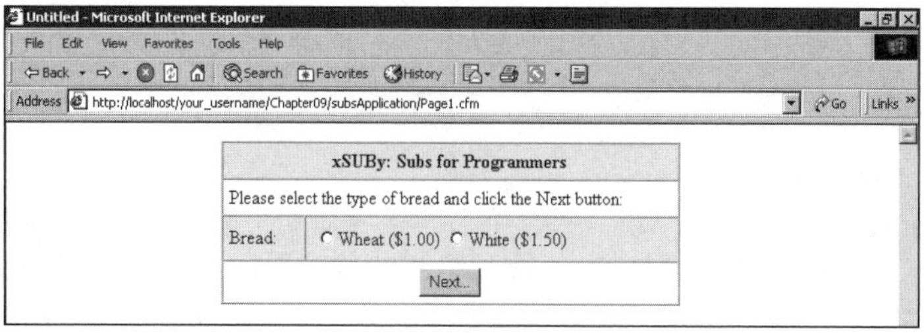

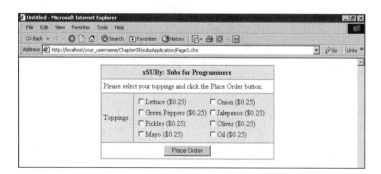

Figure 9-55

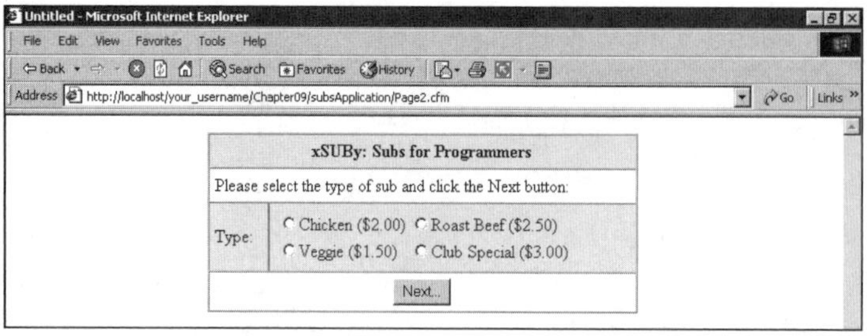

Figure 9-56

Figure 9-57

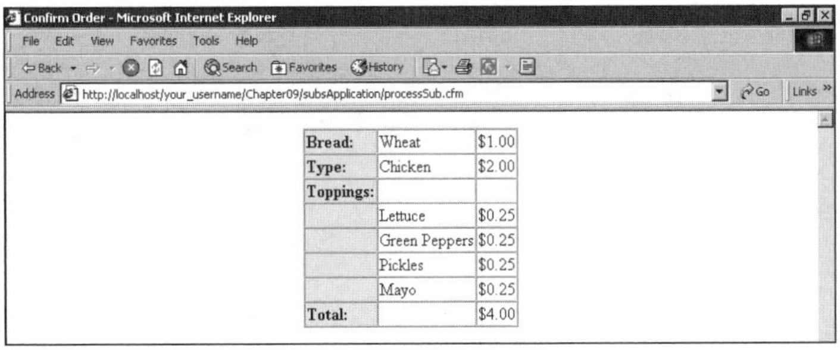

Figure 9-58

Project 4: Design a Usage Tracking and Reporting Tool

Design a usage tracking and reporting tool for the form in the previous project. Count the number of hits for the first page and the number of hits for the last page. Display the results in a neatly formatted table, as shown in Figure 9-59. Save it as **reportingTool.cfm** in the subsApplication folder.

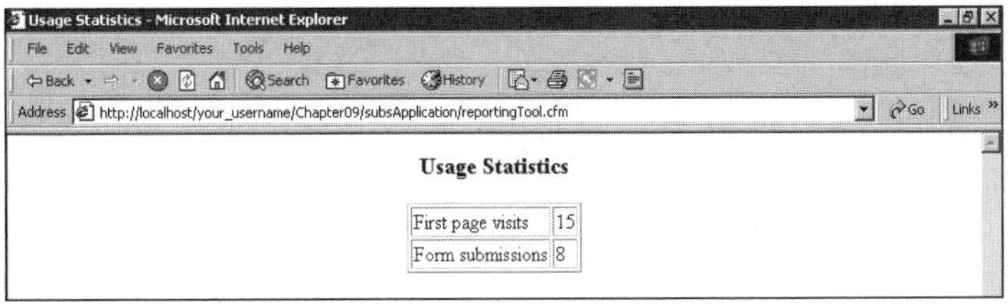

Figure 9-59

Project 5: Targeted Marketing

An e-commerce company that sells books online has hired your consulting firm for personalizing their Web site and targeted marketing. Your task is to collect users' interests and display book recommendations based on these interests. Your graphics department has designed several Web pages for this application. Your task is to examine what they have done and complete the application:

1. Using Windows Explorer or ColdFusion Studio navigate to the Chapter09\TargetMarket folder on your Data Disk and examine its contents.

2. Start your Web browser, and open location http//localhost/your_username/Chapter09/TargetMarket/interestsForm.htm. See Figure 9-60. This is a form for capturing the user's interest.

Figure 9-60

3. Select one of the interests in the select box, and click the Store It! Button. See Figure 9-61. You see a message that your interest has been stored successfully. There is no programming as yet to really store your interest. Your task is to add the programming to store user preference in a client variable.

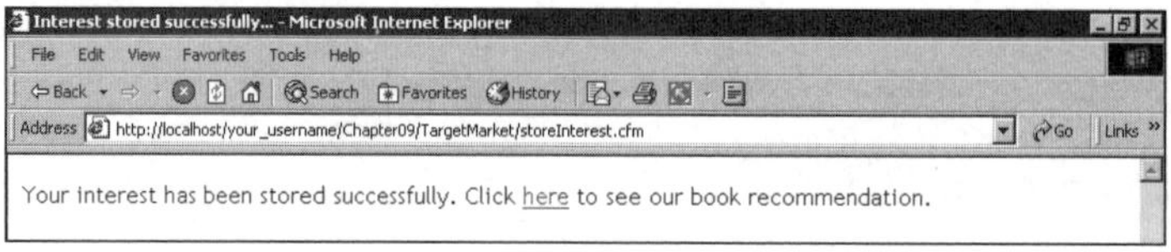

Figure 9-61

4. Click the "here" hyperlink. See Figure 9-62. A Web page displays a table with all interests and suggested books. Your task is to add programming that uses the client variable created in the previous step and displays only one row of the table that matches the user interest, as shown in Figure 9-63.

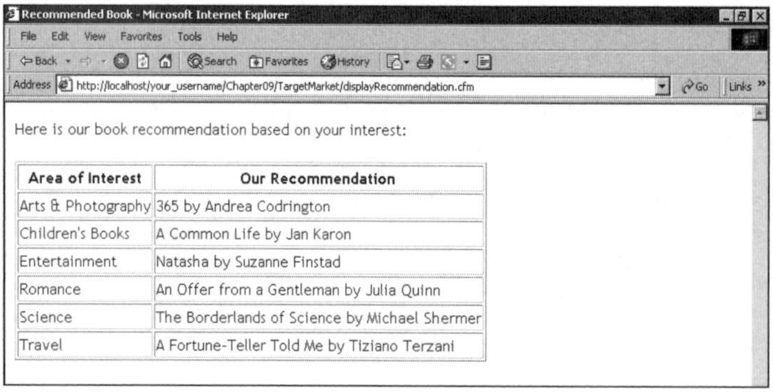

Here is our book recommendation based on your interest:

Area of Interest	Our Recommendation
Arts & Photography	365 by Andrea Codrington
Children's Books	A Common Life by Jan Karon
Entertainment	Natasha by Suzanne Finstad
Romance	An Offer from a Gentleman by Julia Quinn
Science	The Borderlands of Science by Michael Shermer
Travel	A Fortune-Teller Told Me by Tiziano Terzani

Figure 9-62

Here is our book recommendation based on your interest:

Area of Interest	Our Recommendation
Entertainment	Natasha by Suzanne Finstad

Figure 9-63

Project 6: Online Faculty Surveys

A university wants to conduct informal faculty surveys on the Internet. Even though the surveys are informal, they want to prevent faculty from filling out the survey more than once from a certain computer. A couple of pages have been designed by one of the students. Your task is to examine what they have done and complete the application:

1. Using Windows Explorer or ColdFusion Studio, navigate to the Chapter09\FacultySurvey folder on your Data Disk, and examine its contents.

2. Start your Web browser, and open location http//localhost/your_username/Chapter09/FacultySurvey/surveyForm.cfm. See Figure 9-64. Notice that there are two parts to this page. The top part is a survey and the bottom part is a message that the user has already participated in the survey. Your task is to modify this template so that the top part is displayed when a user visits this page for the first time and the bottom part is displayed when the user visits this page from the second time onward. Modify the form handler storeSurvey.cfm if needed.

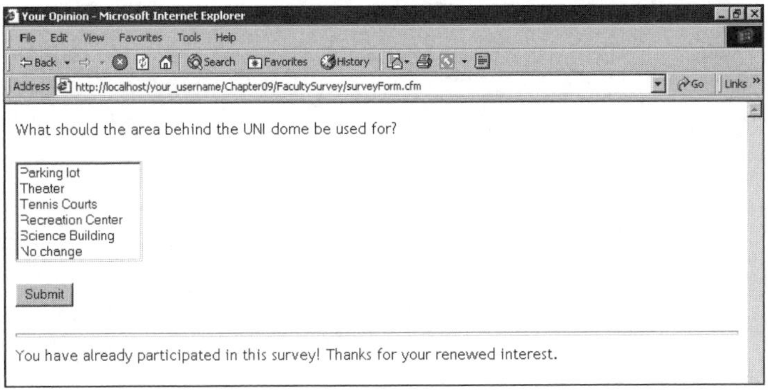

What should the area behind the UNI dome be used for?

Parking lot
Theater
Tennis Courts
Recreation Center
Science Building
No change

Submit

You have already participated in this survey! Thanks for your renewed interest.

Figure 9-64

CASE PROJECTS

1. Examine the COOKIES folder on a computer used by multiple users. Investigate the Web sites users of the computer have visited. Write a one-paragraph report speculating on the browsing habits of users of that computer.

2. In a Web site for a hardware store, build in a capability that allows shoppers to customize the look of the hardware store. Allow customers to pick the background color, the text color, the hyperlink color, and the visited link colors of the documents. The server should remember these settings.

3. Research *www.cookiecentral.com*. Write a one-page report summarizing the advantages and disadvantages of using cookies. What is being done to overcome some of the limitations of using cookies?

10

INTERACTION WITH OTHER SERVICES

In this chapter, you will:

- ◆ Learn about the capabilities of ColdFusion for interacting with other services, such as mail servers, file systems, and Web servers
- ◆ Send e-mail based on form input
- ◆ Send personalized e-mail based on database query output
- ◆ Upload, copy, rename, delete, and list files on the Web server
- ◆ Read data from and write data to text files
- ◆ Serve application files programmatically
- ◆ Design a system for rotating banner ads

Have you ever bought a book at *Amazon.com*, registered at *yahoo.com*, or completed a form at a Web site? Typically, when you buy products at e-commerce sites, register at portals, or complete forms at other Web sites, you receive e-mail confirming your actions. These e-mail messages often include information such as usernames and passwords. Have you ever wondered how these Web sites could send out personalized e-mail?

In earlier chapters, you learned about using ColdFusion for interacting with databases to create dynamic Web sites. In this chapter, you will learn about its capabilities for interacting with other services, such as e-mail servers and file systems. In particular, you will learn about sending e-mail messages based on form input into a Web browser. You will learn about uploading files and how you can manage them with ColdFusion. In the process, you will see that ColdFusion is a powerful system that makes these activities easy to perform.

USING E-MAIL

As you probably know, e-mail is the electronic transmission of messages over computer networks, especially the Internet. Most e-mail systems use a text editor for composing messages. You transmit these messages to recipients by specifying their e-mail addresses. Messages you send are transferred over the network and typically stored in the recipients' electronic mailboxes. Recipients can read their messages from their mailboxes using e-mail software. Once they read the messages, they can print, save, delete, or forward them to others. You also can send other types of files as attachments to messages.

To send an e-mail message automatically with ColdFusion, the ColdFusion Server has to interact with a mail server. The server administrator must first configure the ColdFusion Server as a client to the mail server. In this way, the ColdFusion Server is similar to the software that you use for composing e-mail messages. Once you compose your message, your e-mail software interacts with a mail server and sends the message to it. The mail server examines the e-mail address and forwards it to other mail servers on the Internet. Similarly, the ColdFusion Server composes e-mail messages and transmits them to mail servers. These mail servers then forward the e-mail to the recipient's mailbox. See Figure 10-1.

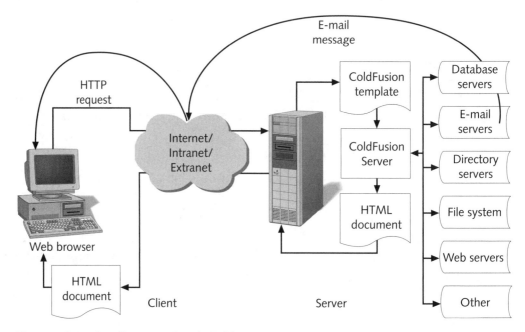

Figure 10-1   Sending e-mail with ColdFusion

To send e-mail messages with ColdFusion, you must use the ColdFusion Administrator to set up a connection to a mail server.

To set up a mail server connection:

1. Click the **Start** button on the taskbar, point to **Programs**, point to **Macromedia ColdFusion Server 5**, and then click **ColdFusion Administrator**. The ColdFusion Administrator Login page opens in a browser. See Figure 10-2.

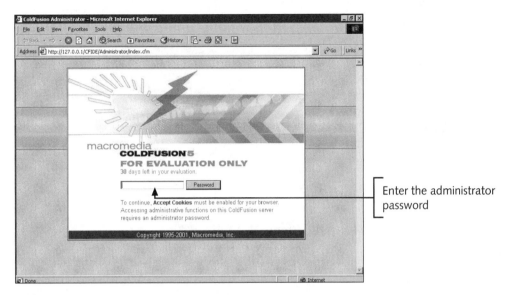

Enter the administrator password

Figure 10-2   ColdFusion Administrator Login screen

Depending on your network configuration, your instructor or network administrator may have already set up a mail server connection for you. You must have an administrator's password to complete the following steps. Check with your instructor or network administrator before completing these steps. If you cannot complete these steps at the computer, read them so you can learn how to set up and configure a mail server connection.

2. Enter the administrator password for your server, and then click the **Password** button. The ColdFusion Administrator page opens and displays the Web-based console for configuring the ColdFusion Server settings and managing its resources. See Figure 10-3.

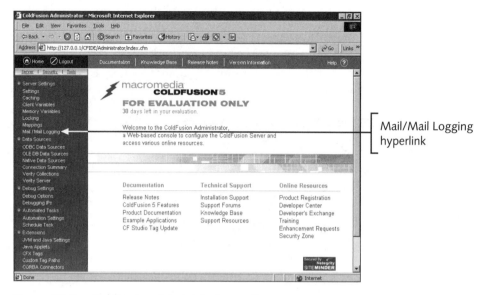

Figure 10-3 ColdFusion Administrator main screen

3. Click the **Mail/Mail Logging** link in the Server Settings section on the left side of the page. The Mail Settings page shown in Figure 10-4 opens. This page lets you select the mail server and specify other parameters that influence server performance.

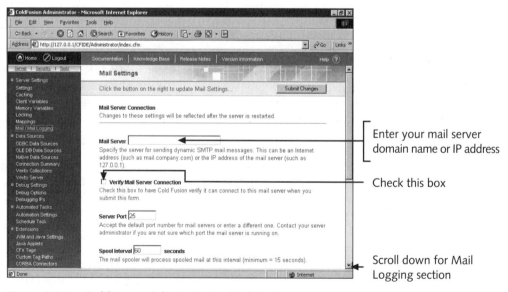

Figure 10-4 ColdFusion Administrator Mail Settings page

4. In the Mail Server text box, enter the domain name or IP address of your mail server. This can be an Internet address (such as mail.your_university.edu) or the IP address of the mail server (such as 127.0.0.1).

To prevent misuse of mail servers and junk e-mail, most systems administrators restrict access to their mail servers. If necessary, talk to your systems administrator and find out the right mail server address to use in this page. Typically, the address is the same one you use to set up your own e-mail software, such as Microsoft Outlook, Netscape Messenger, or Eudora.

5. If the Server Port, Spool Interval, and Connection Timeout numbers are similar to those shown in Figure 10-4, do not change them. The server port for mail servers is typically 25. The Spool Interval number means that every 60 seconds, the mail server sends all the mail that has not yet been sent (spooled mail). The Connection Timeout is the amount of time the ColdFusion server waits to receive a response from the mail server. Sixty seconds is typically enough time to receive a response. If the mail server is unreliable or slow, increase the Connection Timeout number.

6. Click to insert a check in the **Verify Mail Server Connection** check box.

7. Scroll down to the Mail Logging section. See Figure 10-5.

10

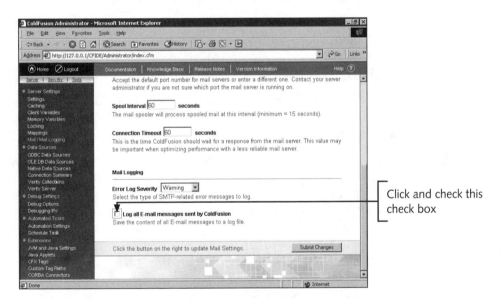

Figure 10-5   Cold Fusion Server Mail Logging section

8. Click to insert a check in the **Log all E-mail messages sent by ColdFusion** check box.

9. Click the **Submit changes** button. If you have successfully set up a connection to the mail server, you see a confirmation message, as shown in Figure 10-6.

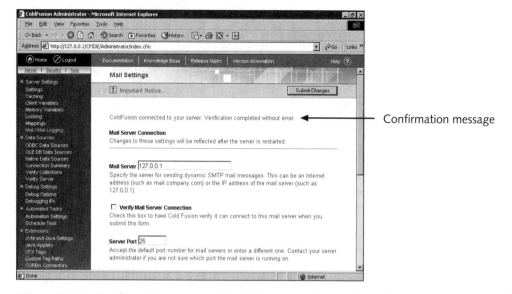
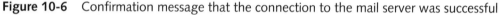

Confirmation message

Figure 10-6   Confirmation message that the connection to the mail server was successful

10. Exit the ColdFusion Administrator by closing the browser.

Now that you have established a connection between the ColdFusion server and a mail server, you can design ColdFusion templates that send e-mail.

Using the CFMAIL Tag

Similarly to the way in which you accomplish any task in ColdFusion by using appropriate tags, you can specify that the server send e-mail by using the CFMAIL tag. The syntax for the CFMAIL tag is as follows:

```
<CFMAIL to="recipient_address"
      from="sender_address"
      cc="copy_to"
      bcc="blind_copy_to"
      subject="msg_subject"
      mimeattach="path"
      server="servername"
      port="port_id"
      timeout="seconds">
Main text of the e-mail message
</CFMAIL>
```

In the CFMAIL tag, the SERVER, PORT, and TIMEOUT attributes are optional and are needed only if the ColdFusion Server has not been configured for sending e-mail as described in the previous section. Use the same values for these attributes as those described in the previous section; that is, SERVER is the domain name or IP address of your mail server, PORT is typically 25, and TIMEOUT is typically 60.

When the ColdFusion Server executes a CFMAIL tag, it sends e-mail to the recipient_address specified as the value for the TO attribute. Headers are constructed for the e-mail message based on the values for the other parameters. The value of the FROM parameter is sent as the value of the FROM header. The mail server may check the validity of this address before forwarding the e-mail.

 It is considered unethical to impersonate someone else by using their address as the value for the FROM attribute. Typically all e-mail that is sent out is logged along with the messages you send, the IP address of the client computer, the date, the time, and so on. You should use this privilege responsibly.

The CC and the BCC attributes are useful for sending carbon copies of e-mail messages as well as sending blind carbon copies. Use the SUBJECT attribute to summarize the content of the message. To send a file as an attachment to the message, specify the filename along with the complete physical path as the value for the MIMEATTACH parameter. All the text enclosed in the CFMAIL and /CFMAIL tags is sent as the body of the e-mail message. As in other tags, you can use variables enclosed in pound (#) signs as values for these attributes. The main text of the e-mail message can contain variables enclosed in pound signs too. The ColdFusion Server substitutes values for these variables prior to sending out the message.

The following example (Example10-1.cfm) illustrates a set of CFMAIL tags that NikRealty might use to send e-mail on their ColdFusion Server. It is available on the Data Disk in the Chapter10 folder. You may experiment with this example as you did in earlier chapters. Make sure that you use your username as the data source name prior to running the example.

```
<cfquery datasource="your_username" name="getAgents">
SELECT FirstName, LastName, EmailAddress FROM Agents
</cfquery>

<html>
<head>
    <title>Group Mail</title>
</head>

<body>
Here is a list of people, e-mail is being sent out to:
<ul>
<cfloop query="getAgents">
<cfmail from="nlittle@nikrealty.com" to="#Emailaddress#"
subject="Meeting...">
Dear #Firstname# #Lastname#:
```

10

```
We have an emergency meeting scheduled to address the
recent interest rate changes announced by the Federal
Reserve Board Chairman.

Please come over to the office conference room at 10:00 AM
tomorrow.

Thanks.

Nikitha Little
</cfmail>
<li><cfoutput>#Firstname# #Lastname#</cfoutput>
</cfloop>
</ul>
</body>
</html>
```

To run Example 10-1.cfm and other examples, you must first change the datasource name in the files on the Data Disk. To change the datasource name for all files in the Chapter10 folder on the Data Disk:

1. Start ColdFusion Studio.

2. Click **Search** on the menu bar, and then click **Extended Replace**.

3. Click the **In folder** option button.

4. Click the **open folder** button next to the current folder list box. The Browse for Folder dialog box opens.

5. Click to select the **Chapter10** folder on the Data Disk.

6. Click the **OK** button. The path to the Chapter10 folder is displayed in the folder list box.

7. Click in the **Find what** text box and type **your_username** exactly as shown.

8. Click in the **Replace with** text box and type *your username* (the datasource name to the NikRealty database).

9. Click to insert a check in the **Include subfolders** check box.

10. Click the **Replace** button.

11. ColdFusion Studio opens the Results window and shows that there are 10 files that have been changed.

12. Close the Results window.

You have successfully modified the data files to work with your datasource name.

When a Web browser requests this template and the ColdFusion Server executes it, the server first processes the CFQUERY tag. The names and e-mail addresses of all agents in the NikRealty database are extracted. The CFLOOP query loop processes every agent in the table one at a time. During the first loop, the first record is extracted. The server processes the CFMAIL tag and constructs a message based on the text enclosed in the CFMAIL tags. All variables enclosed in pound signs are processed, and the appropriate values are substituted. For example, "Dear #Firstname# #Lastname#" translates into "Dear Mary Carter." The rest of the text is left unchanged. Once the message is constructed, the appropriate headers are constructed. The ColdFusion Server processes the TO attribute and substitutes an appropriate e-mail address, such as mcarter@nikrealty.com, for #Emailaddress#. The other headers are constructed and the e-mail is spooled, meaning it is stored on the hard disk. The Server makes an entry in the mail log file. Based on the interval set in the ColdFusion Administrator, this spooled mail is sent to the mail server, and the mail server forwards it to the recipient. For informational purposes, the name of the agent to whom e-mail has been sent is output as a list item in the unordered list. See Figure 10-7 for the output produced by this template.

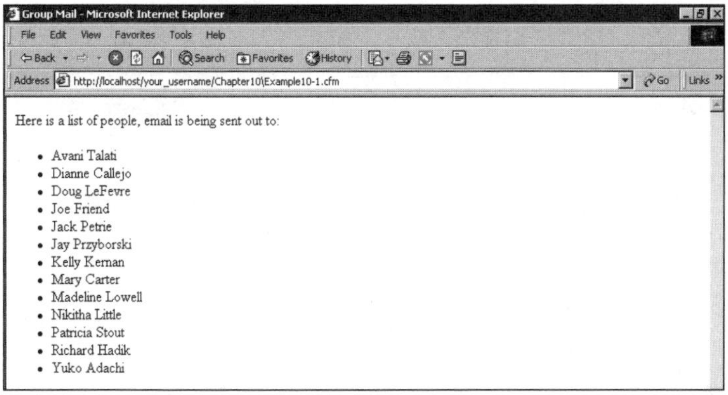

Figure 10-7   List of e-mail recipients displayed by Example10-1.cfm

Once the CFMAIL tag for the first agent is processed, the query loop is executed again, and the ColdFusion Server sends e-mail to the next agent. After the e-mail message is sent to all the recipients in the database table specified in the CFLOOP query, the ColdFusion Server creates and displays a log file, as shown in Figure 10-8. In this case, e-mail has been sent to all the agents in the database table.

```
"Information","TID=708","06/26/03","12:25:47","nlittle@nikrealty.com,atalati@nikrealty.com"
"Information","TID=708","06/26/03","12:25:47","nlittle@nikrealty.com,dcallejo@nikrealty.com"
"Information","TID=708","06/26/03","12:25:47","nlittle@nikrealty.com,dlefevre@nikrealty.com"
"Information","TID=708","06/26/03","12:25:47","nlittle@nikrealty.com,jpetrie@nikrealty.com"
"Information","TID=708","06/26/03","12:25:47","nlittle@nikrealty.com,jprzyborski@nikrealty.com"
"Information","TID=708","06/26/03","12:25:47","nlittle@nikrealty.com,kkernan@nikrealty.com"
"Information","TID=708","06/26/03","12:25:47","nlittle@nikrealty.com,mcarter@nikrealty.com"
"Information","TID=708","06/26/03","12:25:47","nlittle@nikrealty.com,mlowell@nikrealty.com"
"Information","TID=708","06/26/03","12:25:47","nlittle@nikrealty.com,nlittle@nikrealy.com"
"Information","TID=708","06/26/03","12:25:47","nlittle@nikrealty.com,pstout@nikrealty.com"
"Information","TID=708","06/26/03","12:25:47","nlittle@nikrealty.com,rhadik@nikrealty.com"
"Information","TID=708","06/26/03","12:25:47","nlittle@nikrealty.com,yadachi@nikrealty.com"
```

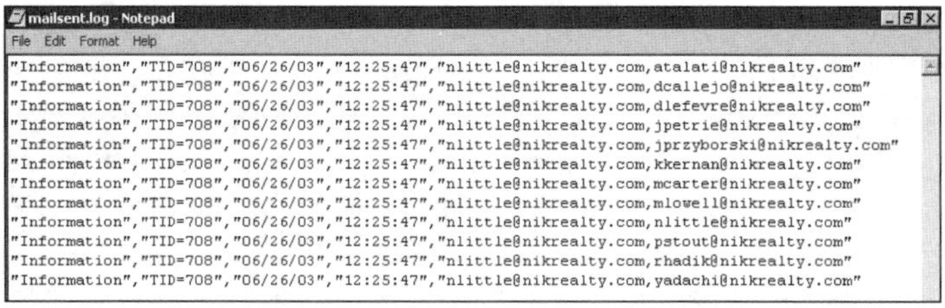

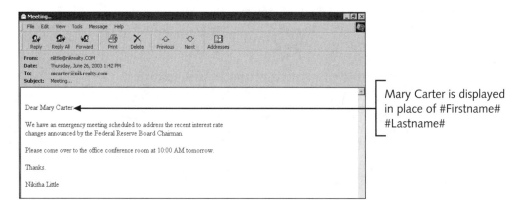

Figure 10-8 Mail log file entries

The e-mail message received is shown in Figure 10-9. Examine the CFMAIL tag and e-mail message, and note the correspondence between the attributes of the CFMAIL tags and the headers in the e-mail message.

Figure 10-9 E-mail message received by one recipient

Having learned about ColdFusion's e-mail capabilities, you mention to Nikitha that a better design for her system for scheduling property showings would be to generate server-side e-mail rather than client-side e-mail using forms. The form that you designed for scheduling showings in Chapter 9 sends e-mail using client-side e-mail. This is limited, because the client software has to be configured correctly with the appropriate parameters. Computers that are typically used by many people, such as those in a library, may not have the proper configuration. Your form will not work in such situations. Implementing server-side e-mail with CFMAIL tags would work in all situations. Nikitha is convinced about the usefulness of this approach, and she authorizes the change.

To modify the schedule showings application by implementing server-side e-mail capabilities:

1. Start your Web browser.
2. Open **ShowingScreen1.cfm** in the CustomerRequest subfolder in the Chapter10 folder on your Data Disk. This is the template that you designed in Chapter 9 for scheduling showings using multiple screens and session variables.

3. Enter an appropriate property ID, date, and time, and then click the **Next** button.

4. Continue to enter data until you reach processSchedule.cfm. Recall that this template summarizes the data you entered.

5. View the source code for this Web page by using the appropriate commands in your Web browser. The source code is shown in Figure 10-10. Recall that you used the "mailto" protocol as the action for the form in Chapter 4 for sending e-mail using the client e-mail software when the user submits the form. As mentioned earlier, the client software has to be configured properly for this feature to work. Your task is to improve the design of this system by sending e-mail on the server side to overcome this limitation.

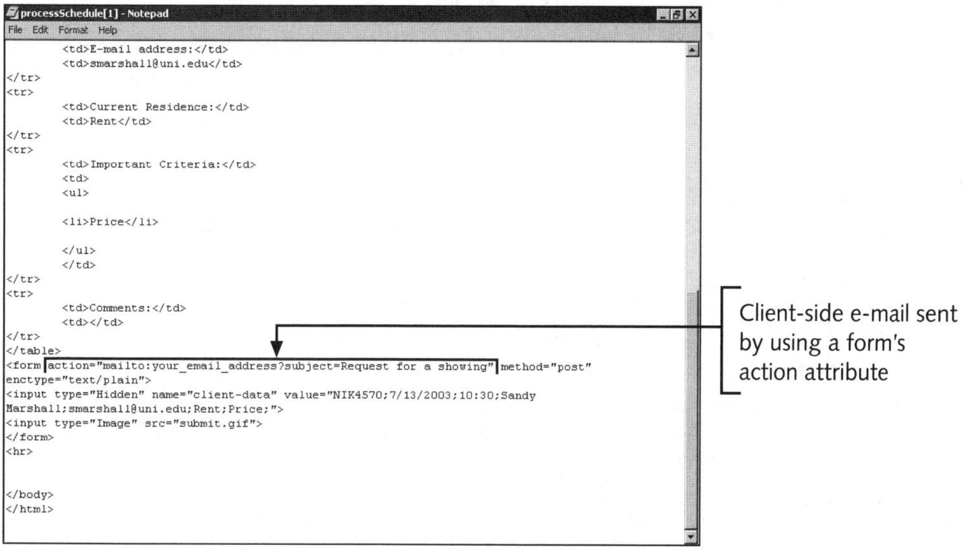

Client-side e-mail sent by using a form's action attribute

Figure 10-10   HTML source code of processSchedule.cfm

6. Close the source code window.

7. Start **ColdFusion Studio**, if necessary.

8. Open **processSchedule.cfm** in the CustomerRequest subfolder in the Chapter10 folder on your Data Disk.

9. On line 58, change the value for the ACTION attribute to **processSchedule2.cfm**, and delete the attribute value pair **enctype="text/plain"**.

   Note that the data entered by the user is part of the hidden field named client-data. You no longer need this hidden field because all the user-entered data is available as session variables.

10. Select the entire **line 59** that contains the hidden field and delete it. See Figure 10-11.

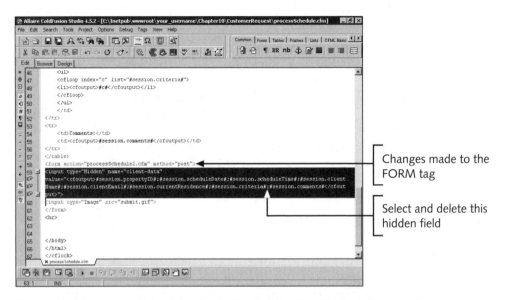

Figure 10-11   processSchedule.cfm in the ColdFusion Studio Editor window

When the user submits this form, the new form handler processSchedule2.cfm should e-mail this data to the right agent. To debug this application, you will send the e-mail to your own e-mail address. Because you are designing the e-mail application on the server side, you have greater flexibility for formatting the e-mail message so that it easy to read.

11. Click the **Save** button on the Standard toolbar to save processSchedule.cfm with your changes.

12. Click **File** on the menu bar, and then click **New Document**. ColdFusion Studio opens a new document.

13. Save this new file as **processSchedule2.cfm**. This file is the form handler for the form that echoes the client data. This form handler should send the data to a mail server and print a confirmation message for the user.

14. Click at the beginning of line 1, press the **Enter** key, and move the cursor back to the first line.

15. Type **<cflock scope ="session" timeout="20">**. Recall from Chapter 9 that you lock shared resources like session variables to coordinate the sequence of execution.

16. Click at the bottom of the template below line 14, and type **</cflock>**.

17. Click at the end of line 1, and press **Enter**.

18. Type **<cfmail to="your_e-mail_address" from="#session.clientEmail#" subject="Request for a showing - #session.propertyID#">**, and press **Enter**. When the ColdFusion Server processes this tag, it will send e-mail to you with "Request for a showing – user-selected property ID" as the subject for the message and, in a "From" field, the e-mail address that you enter in the schedule a showing form.

19. Your next task is to construct the body of the e-mail message. Type the following code in lines 3 to 11:

```
Property ID: #session.propertyID#
Date: #session.scheduleDate#
Time: #session.scheduleTime#
Name: #session.clientName#
E-mail: #session.clientEMail#
Current Residence: #session.currentResidence#
Important Criteria: #session.criteria#
Comments: #session.comments#
</cfmail>
```

20. Click below the BODY tag, and type **Your request has been sent successfully. You will be contacted by e-mail confirming your schedule.**

21. Save your file, and exit ColdFusion Studio.

To test the application you have designed:

1. Start your Web browser, if necessary.

2. Open **ShowingScreen1.cfm** in the CustomerRequest subfolder in the Chapter10 folder on your Data Disk.

3. Select **NIK4570** as the PropertyID for the property you are interested in.

4. Type **11/1/2003** as the date for your request.

5. Type **15:30** as the time for your request.

6. Click the **Next** button to open the second Schedule a Private Showing page, as shown in Figure 10-12.

10

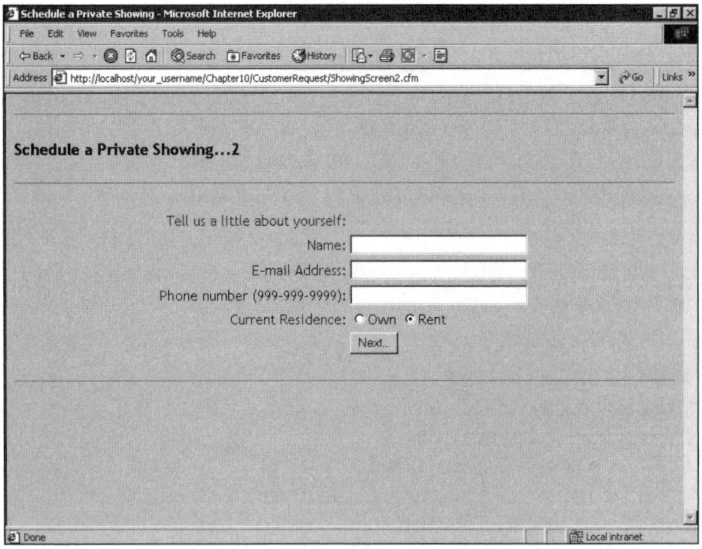

Figure 10-12   Schedule a Private Showing page 2

7. Type **Sandy Marshall** in the Name text box.

8. Type **smarshall@uni.edu** in the E-mail Address text box.

9. Type **310 555 1234** in the Phone number text box.

10. Click the **Next** button to open the third Schedule a Private Showing page, as shown in Figure 10-13.

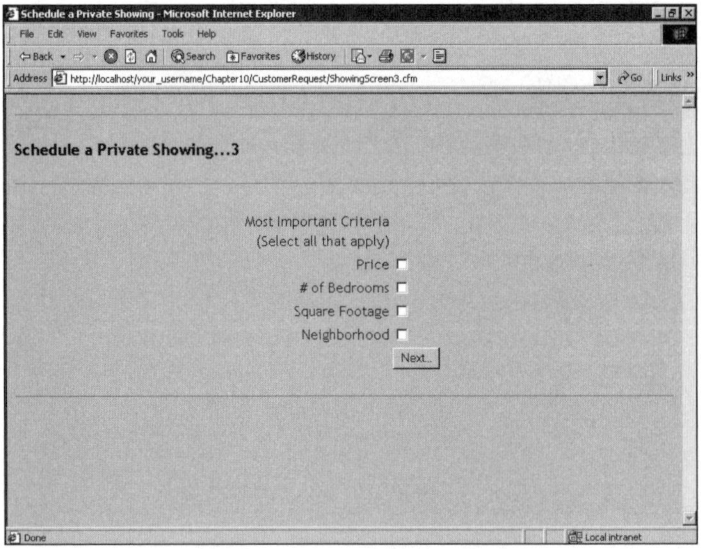

Figure 10-13   Schedule a Private Showing page 3

11. Click to select the **Price** and **# of Bedrooms** check boxes as the most important criteria, and then click the **Next** button.

12. Type **I would like some information about the schools in this location** as a comment, and then click the **Schedule** button. See Figure 10-14.

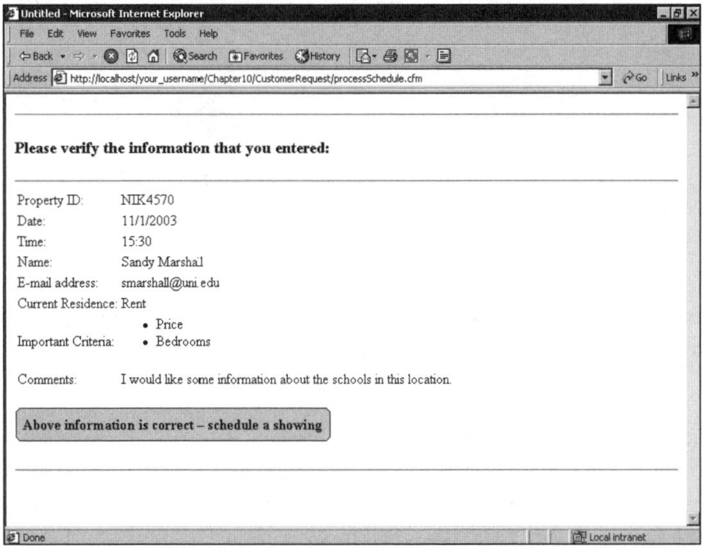

Figure 10-14   Schedule a showing verification page

13. Click the **Above information is correct – schedule a showing** image button. You receive a message that your request has been sent successfully, as shown in Figure 10-15.

Figure 10-15   Successful e-mail delivery confirmation

14. Open your e-mail software, and examine the message that you receive. Figure 10-16 shows the message in Outlook Express. The message text corresponds to the text enclosed in the CFMAIL tags. The headers correspond to the attribute-value pairs in the CFMAIL tag.

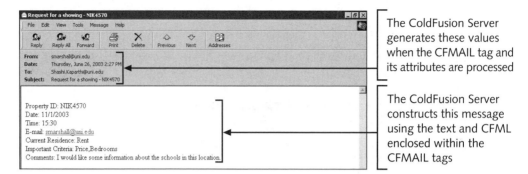

The ColdFusion Server generates these values when the CFMAIL tag and its attributes are processed

The ColdFusion Server constructs this message using the text and CFML enclosed within the CFMAIL tags

Figure 10-16   E-mail message sent by the ColdFusion Server and opened in the client e-mail software

In the next section, you will learn about using ColdFusion for interacting with the server's file system. This includes using the Web for uploading images and other files, managing files on the server, and reading and writing text files.

INTERACTING WITH THE SERVER'S FILE SYSTEM

You use ColdFusion to interact with a server's file system so that users can upload files to the server. For example, you may have used Web-based e-mail such as Hotmail or Yahoo! Mail. Whenever you attach files to messages, you first upload them to the server. Web sites such as Yahoo! Photos allow you to upload photographs, create albums, and share them with your friends. You can use ColdFusion to design systems that are capable of uploading files.

Uploading Files with ColdFusion

Similarly to designing other form-based applications, designing an application for uploading files is a two-step process: First you design the form, and then you design the form handler. In the form, you create the input control for uploading files known as the **file input control** by using the HTML INPUT tag with the TYPE attribute set to a value of "File." Further, when you design forms for uploading files, you have to set an additional attribute for the FORM tag named ENCTYPE to a value of "multipart/form-data." Files are encoded separately from the other data and transmitted to the server when the form is submitted.

The following example (Example10-2.htm) illustrates a simple form for uploading a file to the server:

```
<html>
<head>
    <title>Form for uploading files</title>
</head>

<body bgcolor="E8B175">
<form action="uploadFile.cfm" method="post"
enctype="multipart/form-data">
<table align="center">
<tr>
    <td>Select File:</td>
    <td><input type="File" name="aFile"></td>
</tr>
<tr>
    <td align="center" colspan="2"><input type="Submit"
value="Upload..."></td>
</tr>
</table>
</form>
</body>
</html>
```

This example is available on your Data Disk as Example10-2.htm. Note the ENCTYPE attribute for the FORM tag and the TYPE attribute for the INPUT tag. The ACTION attribute for the form is "uploadFile.cfm." The output produced by this template is shown in Figure 10-17.

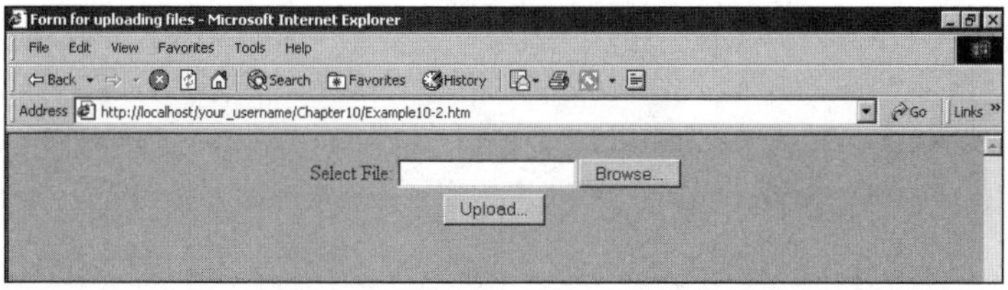

Figure 10-17   Web page with a file upload control

As shown in Figure 10-17, the browser shows a Browse button when it encounters the file input control. The user can then click the Browse button to open the Choose file dialog box shown in Figure 10-18. You use this dialog box to select the file that you want to upload from the local disk.

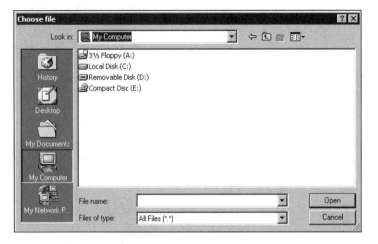

Figure 10-18   Choose file dialog box

Select a file, such as Sample.txt in the Chapter10 folder, and then click the Upload button. If a form contains other fields along with the file input control, all the data in other fields is sent along with the selected file to the server. The Web server makes all this data available to the ColdFusion Server; the ColdFusion Server creates form variables with this data and then executes the form handler. You can access the file that has been uploaded by using the CFFILE tag in the form handler.

Use the CFFILE tag to interact with the file system. The syntax for the CFFILE tag for uploading files is given below:

```
<CFFILE ACTION="Upload"
     FILEFIELD="file_input_control_name"
     DESTINATION="full_path_name"
     NAMECONFLICT="behavior">
```

Set the FILEFIELD attribute to the name of the file input control that you used in the form. Set the DESTINATION attribute to the full pathname of the destination folder on the server. For example, on a Windows system, you could set it to C:\Inetpub\wwwroot\ uploadedfiles. The NAMECONFLICT attribute specifies what the server should do if the folder already contains a file with the same name as the uploaded file. If it is set to OVERWRITE, the ColdFusion Server overwrites the existing file with the contents of the uploaded file. If it is set to MAKEUNIQUE, the ColdFusion server creates a new file with the contents of the uploaded file. Whenever a file is uploaded by using the CFFILE tag, the ColdFusion Server creates variables in the FILE scope that can be accessed to monitor the state of the file upload. If you use the MAKEUNIQUE value for the NAMECONFLICT attribute, you can access the new name for the file by using the variable FILE.ServerFile.

The following example (uploadFile.cfm) illustrates the code for the form handler needed for uploading the file for the previous example:

```
<cffile action="UPLOAD" filefield="aFile"
destination="#GetDirectoryFromPath(GetCurrentTemplatePath
())#Files" nameconflict="OVERWRITE">
<html>
<head>
    <title>File Upload Results</title>
</head>

<body>
Your file has been uploaded successfully.
</body>
</html>
```

The output produced by this template is shown in Figure 10-19.

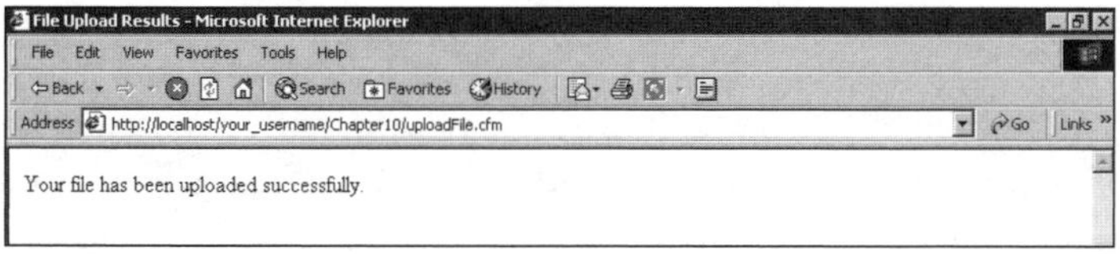

Figure 10-19　Web page displaying a file upload confirmation message

Two new functions are used in the DESTINATION attribute. The function GetCurrentTemplatePath() returns the full pathname of the current template. For example, it could return a value "C:\Inetpub\wwwroot\your_username\Chapter10\uploadFile.cfm." The function GetDirectoryFromPath(aPath) would strip the filename from the string aPath and return only the path to the folder. When the first is the argument to the second function, you get the path to the folder containing the current template. Therefore, #GetDirectoryFromPath(GetCurrentTemplatePath())# could result in a value of "C:\Inetpub\wwwroot\your_username\Chapter10\" and #GetDirectoryFromPath (GetCurrentTemplatePath())#Files would be the path to the folder name Files in the folder containing the current template, "C:\Inetpub\wwwroot\your_username\Chapter10\Files." Once the template is executed, the ColdFusion Server uploads the file to the C:\Inetpub\wwwroot\Chapter10\Files folder. Figure 10-20 displays the contents of this folder in Windows Explorer. Note that the server has uploaded the file named Sample.txt to this folder.

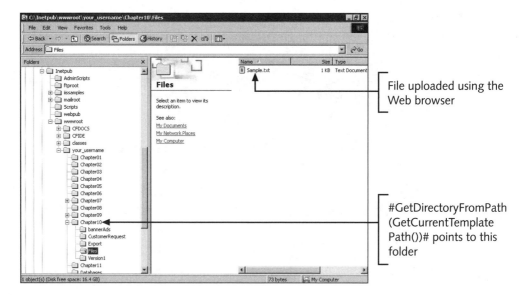

Figure 10-20   Upload file (Sample.txt) in Windows Explorer

In certain situations, especially with a multiuser system, different users can upload files that have the same names. In this case, use the MAKEUNIQUE value for the NAMECONFLICT attribute.

The following example (form: Example10-3.htm, form handler: uploadFile2.cfm) illustrates how to use the MAKEUNIQUE value for the NAMECONFLICT attribute:

```
<cffile action="UPLOAD" filefield="aFile"
destination="#GetDirectoryFromPath(GetCurrentTemplatePath
())#Files" nameconflict="MAKEUNIQUE">
<html>
<head>
    <title>File Upload Results</title>
</head>

<body>
Your file has been uploaded successfully. The name of the
file on the server is: <cfoutput>#file.serverfile#
</cfoutput>
</body>
</html>
```

When you submit the same file two times, the second time you submit the file, the server copies its contents to the disk and uses a filename that's different from the original one. Sample output resulting from this second submission is shown in Figure 10-21. When the server executes the CFFILE tag with the ACTION attribute set to UPLOAD, a variable FILE.ServerFile is created and assigned the filename that the server has used for the uploaded file. This value is being output in Figure 10-21.

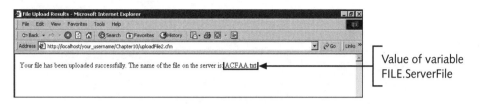

Value of variable
FILE.ServerFile

Figure 10-21   A new file is created when the NAMECONFLICT attribute is set to the value of MAKEUNIQUE (your filename may be different)

Nikitha is pleased with your work on the NikRealty Web site. She wants you to fine-tune the site to make it more convenient for her and her agents to use the system. Currently, the agents must transfer property images to the server's hard disk from a floppy disk. This means agents have to wait until they come to the office to transfer these images and set up new properties on the NikRealty Web site. She wants agents to be able to add properties and upload images by using their laptops while away from the office. She has asked you to investigate the possibility of uploading image files directly by using a Web browser.

To design file upload capabilities to the NikRealty admin tool:

1. Insert a formatted floppy disk in the A drive.

2. Copy the file **Mvc-555e.jpg** from the Version1 subfolder in the Chapter10 folder on your Data Disk to the A: drive.

3. Start your Web browser, if necessary.

4. Open **admin.cfm** in the Version1 subfolder in the Chapter10 folder. This is the administration tool that you created for NikRealty. Log on by typing **Little** as the username and **NKL** as the password.

5. Click the **admin tool** hyperlink to go to the admin tool.

6. Click **Insert** to go to the first screen for inserting a new property, shown in Figure 10-22. Notice that the current process involves copying the image to the server from a floppy, entering its filename in the text box, and then clicking the Continue button. Your task is to modify this procedure by combining Steps 1 and 2 and building in a capability for uploading image files directly from the Web browser.

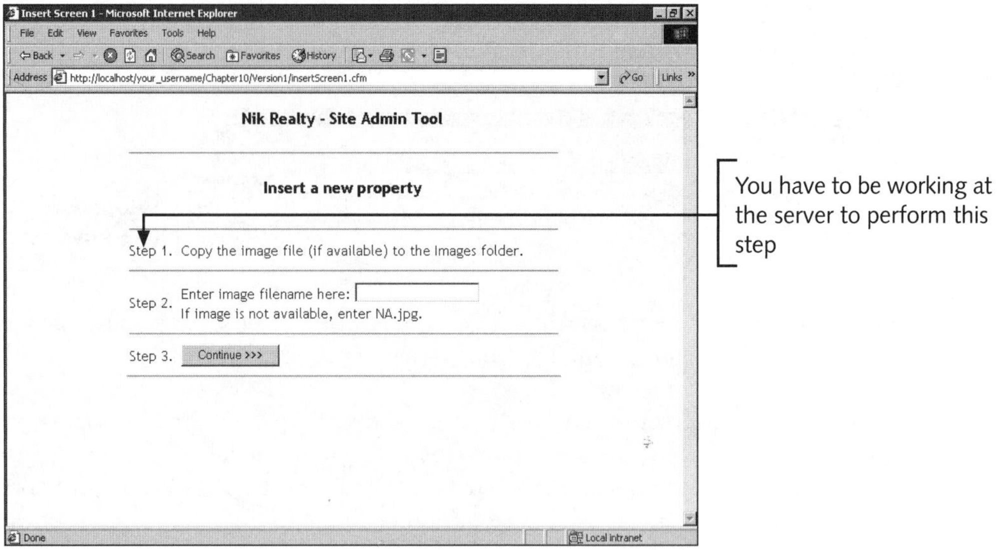

Figure 10-22   Current method for inserting a new property

7. Start **ColdFusion Studio**, if necessary.

8. Open **insertScreen1.cfm** in the Version1 subfolder in the Chapter10 folder on your Data Disk.

9. On line 19, select the text **Copy the image file (if available) to the Images folder**, and type **Insert the disk containing the image file in the floppy drive** to replace the selected text.

10. On line 24, select the text **Enter image file name here**, and type **Click browse to select image file** to replace the selected text.

11. One line 24, select the text **enter NA.jpg**, and type **select NA.jpg from the hard drive**.

12. On line 24, change the value of the TYPE attribute from text to **file**. You are changing the control from a text box to a file input control.

13. On line 9, add the ENCTYPE attribute to the FORM tag by typing **enctype="multipart/form-data"**. You are enabling the form to handle file uploads.

14. Save your file by clicking the **Save** button on the Standard toolbar.

15. Switch to the Web browser, and reload the **insertScreen1.cfm** file. See Figure 10-23. Note that the Browse button next to the text box indicates that it is a file upload control. Your next task is to modify the form handler (insertScreen2.cfm) so you can upload and display these images.

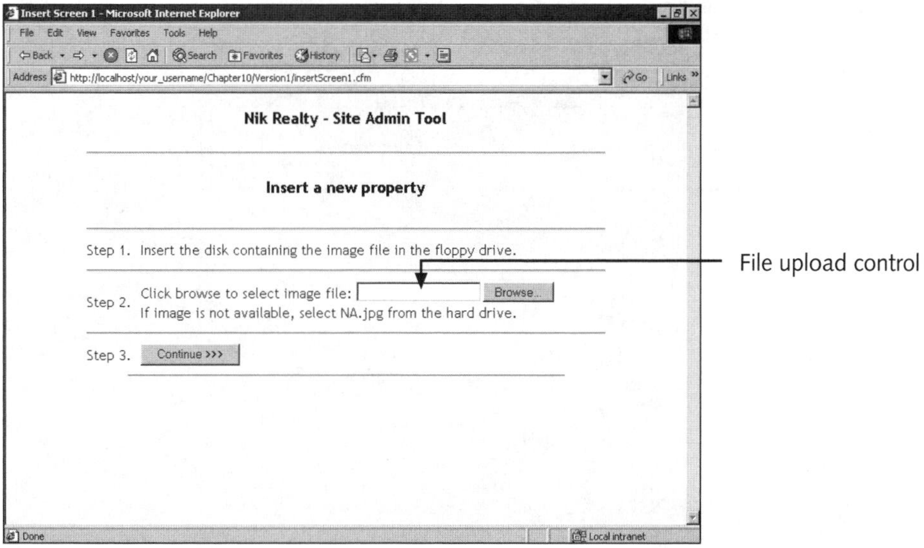

Figure 10-23   Modified screen includes a file upload control

To modify the form handler to deal with file uploads:

1. Switch to ColdFusion Studio, and open **insertScreen2.cfm**. Press the **Enter** key to add a new line at the top of the file.

2. Press the **Up Arrow** key to move to the line that you just inserted.

3. Type **<cfset thisFolder = GetDirectoryFromPath(GetCurrent TemplatePath())>**, and press Enter. When the server executes this tag, the path to the current folder is stored in the variable thisFolder.

4. Type **<cfset mainFolder = ReplaceNoCase(thisFolder,"\Chapter10\ Version1\","")>**, and press **Enter**. The server assigns your main folder on the server to the variable mainFolder.

5. On line 3, type **<cffile action="UPLOAD" filefield="imageFilename" destination="#mainFolder#\Images" nameconflict= "MAKEUNIQUE">**. When the ColdFusion Server executes this tag, the uploaded file is copied to the Images folder on the server. In case there is a file with the same name, it gives a new name to the file. Further, the ColdFusion Server assigns the name of the file to a newly created variable named FILE.ServerFile. Figure 10-24 shows this code in ColdFusion Studio.

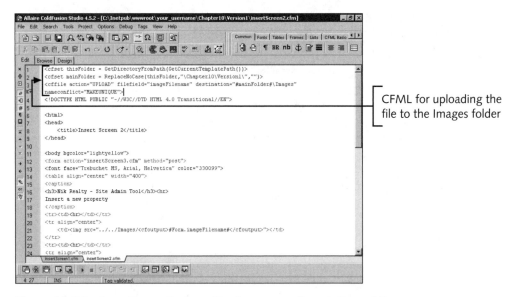

CFML for uploading the file to the Images folder

Figure 10-24   InsertScreen2.cfm with changes on lines 1, 2, and 3

6. On line 21, select **Form.imageFilename**, and type **File.ServerFile**, overwriting the selected text, to display the newly uploaded image to the user.

7. Change the value of the text box on line 32 to **File.ServerFile** from **Form.imageFilename**.

8. Save the file.

9. Switch to a Web browser, and open **insertScreen1.cfm**, if necessary.

10. Click the **Browse** button, navigate to the floppy drive, and double-click **Mvc-555e.jpg**.

11. Click the **Continue** button. See Figure 10-25. The file is sent to the Web server, which in turn sends it to the ColdFusion Server. The ColdFusion Server copies the file to the Images folder and then outputs the filename in the IMG tag. When your Web browser receives the HTML document, it processes the IMG tag and sends a request to the Web server for the newly uploaded file. The Web server sends the file and your Web browser displays it along with the rest of the input controls in the form.

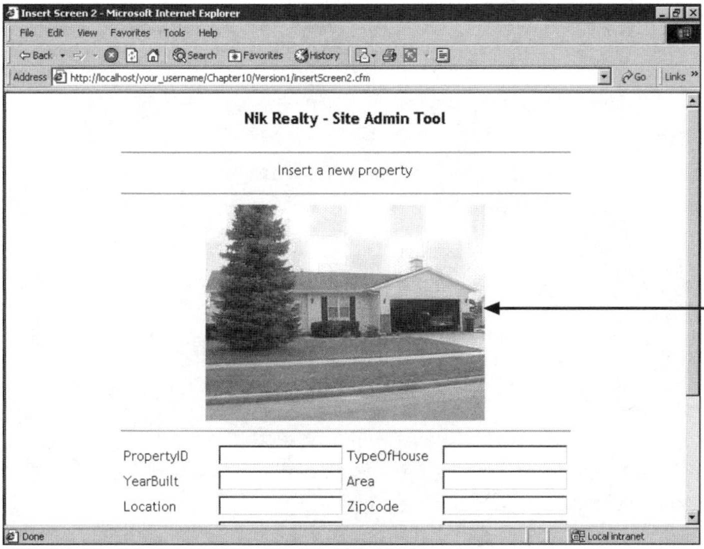

Figure 10-25   Insert screen 2 displays the newly uploaded image along with its filename

You have successfully added file upload capabilities to the NikRealty site.

In the previous case, it was easy to tell whether the file had been uploaded because it was displayed immediately after it was uploaded. The following section explains how to also display the contents of a folder.

Listing Files with the CFDIRECTORY Tag

You can list all the files in a folder by using the CFDIRECTORY tag. The syntax for the CFDIRECTORY tag is as follows:

```
<CFDIRECTORY
    DIRECTORY="full_path_name"
    NAME="query_name">
```

When the ColdFusion Server executes the CFDIRECTORY tag, it creates a query object with a record for each file or folder in the directory specified by the DIRECTORY attribute. This query object is assigned the name given in the NAME attribute. Four fields are created for each entry: Name, Size, DateLastModified, and Type. The Name field contains the name of the file or the folder, the Size field contains its size, the DateLastModified field contains the date the file or folder was last changed, and the Type field contains either the word "File" or "Dir," depending on whether the item is a file or a folder. Once the CFDIRECTORY tag is executed, you can use a query loop to output the contents of the folder.

The following example (listFiles.cfm) illustrates how to use the CFDIRECTORY tag to list the contents of the Files folder on your Data Disk that you used for uploading files in the previous two examples:

```
<cfdirectory
directory="#GetDirectoryFromPath(GetCurrentTemplatePath())
#Files" name="getFiles">

<html>
<head>
    <title>List of files and folders</title>
</head>

<body>
List of files and folders in <cfoutput>#GetDirectoryFrom
Path(GetCurrentTemplatePath())#Files</cfoutput>:
<hr align="left" width="50%">
<table border="1">
<tr bgcolor="Yellow">
    <th>Name</th>
    <th>Size</th>
    <th>Date Last Modified</th>
    <th>Type</th>
</tr>
<cfloop query="getFiles"><cfoutput>
<tr>
    <td>#Name#</td>
    <td>#Size#</td>
    <td>#DateLastModified#</td>
    <td>#Type#</td>
</tr>
</cfoutput></cfloop>
</table>
</body>
</html>
```

The output produced by the above example is shown in Figure 10-26.

When the ColdFusion Server executes the CFDIRECTORY tag, it first evaluates the function that is the value for the DIRECTORY attribute. This function is the same one that was used in the previous example and points to the Files subfolder in the Chapter10 folder on your Data Disk. A query object named getFiles is created with one record for each item in the folder. When the CFLOOP is executed, each record is processed, and the contents of the Name, Size, DateLastModified, and the Type fields are displayed in a table row.

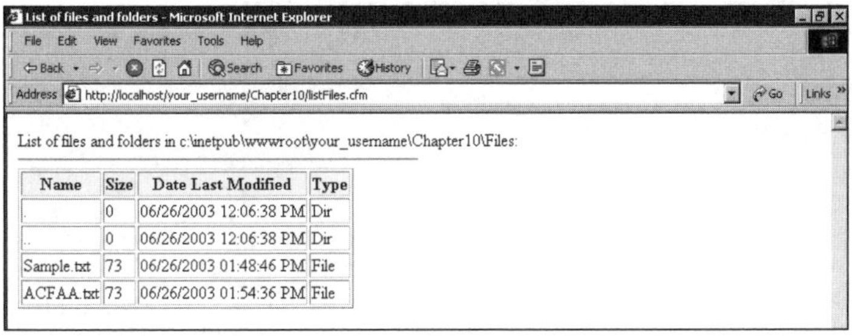

Figure 10-26   Web page displayed by listFiles.cfm

Copying, Renaming, and Deleting Files with the CFFILE Tag

You can copy files programmatically in a ColdFusion template by using the CFFILE tag with the ACTION attribute set to "copy." The syntax for the CFFILE tag with the ACTION attribute set to "copy" is as follows:

```
<CFFILE ACTION="copy"
     SOURCE="full_path_name_including_filename"
     DESTINATION="full_path_name_including_filename">
```

When the ColdFusion Server executes the previous tag, it copies the file specified as the value for the SOURCE attribute and names it the value specified by the DESTINATION attribute.

The following example (copyFile.cfm) illustrates the use of the CFFILE tag with ACTION="copy" for copying a file:

```
<cffile action="copy" source="#GetDirectoryFromPath
(GetCurrentTemplatePath())#Files\Sample.txt"
destination="#GetDirectoryFromPath(GetCurrentTemplatePath
())#Files\Sample2.txt">
<cflocation url="listFiles.cfm">
```

When the ColdFusion Server executes the previous CFFILE tag, a copy of the Sample.txt file named Sample2.txt is created in the Files subfolder on your Data Disk. Once the file is copied, the CFLOCATION tag issues an HTTP redirect response to your Web browser to the listFiles.cfm template. The listFiles.cfm template lists all the files in the Files subfolder, as shown in Figure 10-27.

10

Figure 10-27   Web page produced by copyFile.cfm

Note that there is a file named Sample2.txt in this folder now, compared to what you saw in the previous example. You might have to refresh your browser to see the new listing.

Similarly to the way you copy files, you can rename files by using the CFFILE tag with the ACTION attribute set to "rename." The syntax is as follows:

```
<CFFILE ACTION="rename"
    SOURCE="full_path_name_including_filename"
    DESTINATION="full_path_name_including_filename">
```

When the ColdFusion Server executes the previous tag, it renames the file specified as the value for the SOURCE attribute and to the value specified by the DESTINATION attribute.

You can delete a file on the server by using "delete" as the value for the ACTION attribute. The syntax for deleting a file on the server by using the CFFILE tag is given below:

```
<CFFILE ACTION="delete"
    FILE="full_path_name_including_filename"
```

When the ColdFusion Server executes the previous tag, it deletes the file specified by the FILE attribute. Make sure you specify the correct file in these tags, and make sure you use the tags correctly. You can cause serious damage to the server if these tags are misused.

Nikitha is happy with the image upload capabilities you built for the NikRealty Web site. Because the images are being uploaded directly from the Web now, you decide to automate the management of these images when properties are deleted. In other words, whenever a property is deleted, you want to automatically delete the image file associated with the property.

To automatically delete an image whenever a property is deleted:

1. Start your Web browser, if necessary, and open **admin.cfm** in the Chapter10/Version1 folder on your Data Disk. Log on if necessary by using **Little** as the username and **NKL** as the password. After logging on, navigate to the admin tool.

2. Click **Delete** to go to the first screen for deleting a property, which is shown in Figure 10-28. This screen includes two text boxes for entering the PropertyID for the property that you want to delete. Recall from Chapter 7 that the form handler for this form is named deleteScreen2.cfm. It compares these two values; if they are both equal, the property record is deleted from the properties table.

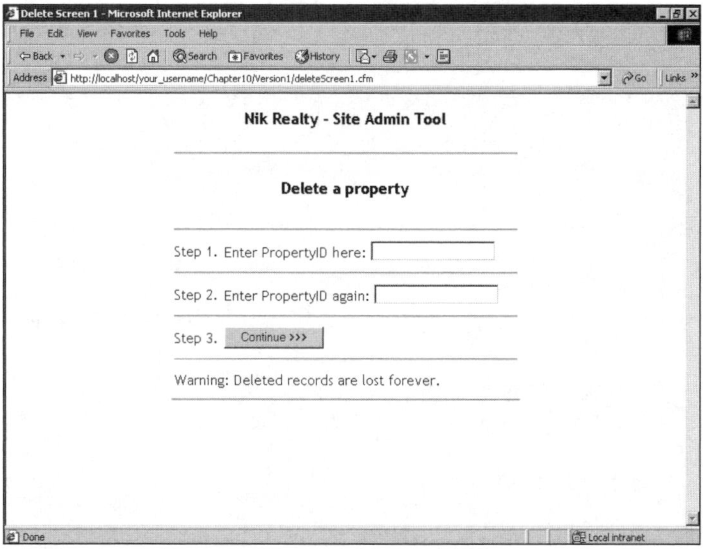

Figure 10-28   First screen for deleting a property

3. Start ColdFusion Studio, if necessary, and close all open documents.

4. Open **deleteScreen2.cfm** in the Chapter10/Version1 folder. Note that this screen includes a CFIF statement for verifying the data entered in both text boxes.

5. Click at the end of <cfelse> on line 11, and press the **Enter** key.

6. To determine the name of the image file for the specified property, type the following code, as shown in Figure 10-29:

```
<cfquery datasource="your_username" name="getImage">
SELECT ImageFilename FROM Properties WHERE PropertyID =
#form.PropertyID1#
</cfquery>
<cfif getImage.ImageFilename NEQ "NA.jpg">
<cfset thisFolder = GetDirectoryFromPath(GetCurrent
TemplatePath())>
<cfset mainFolder = ReplaceNoCase(thisFolder,"\Chapter10\
Version1\","")>
<cffile action="DELETE" file="#mainFolder#\Images\
#getImage.ImageFilename#">
```

```
<cfoutput>File #mainFolder#\Images\#getImage.ImageFilename#
has been deleted.</cfoutput>
</cfif>
```

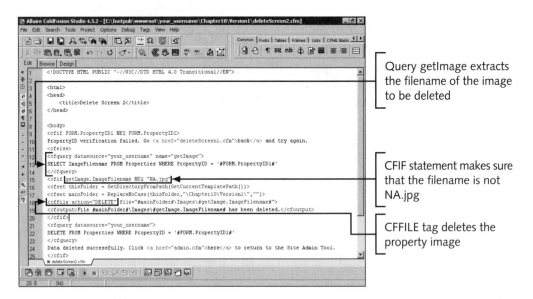

Query getImage extracts the filename of the image to be deleted

CFIF statement makes sure that the filename is not NA.jpg

CFFILE tag deletes the property image

Figure 10-29 Code for deleting an image

You use this code to query the database to find out the name of the image. Once the query is executed, the variable getImage.ImageFilename contains the name of the image. If the name of the image is not NA.jpg (which is the file that is used for properties with no images), the CFFILE tag deletes the image and then the CFQUERY tag deletes the property record from the table.

    7. Save the file.

    8. Switch to your Web browser, and delete a property by entering the PropertyID of **NIK4567** twice. Click the **Continue** button. You see a message confirming that you deleted the image file, as shown in Figure 10-30.

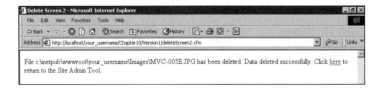

Figure 10-30 Web page with a delete confirmation message

    You have successfully automated the process of deleting image files on the server.

    9. Close all programs.

Reading and Writing Text Files

A Web application often needs to read and write text files. For example, financial institutions and stockbrokers allow clients to download their transactions in the form of text files that can be imported into other applications. Text files are ASCII files that most applications can create and read. The Notepad program is a simple text editor available in the Windows operating system. Text files are a useful bridge between existing applications and Web applications. For example, Web-based testing systems allow professors to upload exam questions contained in text files. In this section, you will learn how to read and write text files by using CFML.

You can read a text file and capture its contents into a string variable by using the CFFILE with its ACTION attribute set to "read." The syntax for using the CFFILE tag for reading text files is as follows:

```
<CFFILE ACTION="read"
        FILE="full_path_name_including_file"
        VARIABLE="var_name">
```

When the ColdFusion Server executes the previous tag, it reads the entire file given by the FILE attribute, creates a string variable named var_name, and assigns it the contents of the file it just read. This variable can be used in CFOUTPUT tags or in other computations as necessary for the logic of the application.

The following example (readFile.cfm) illustrates this capability:

```
<cffile action="read"
file="#GetDirectoryFromPath(GetCurrentTemplatePath())#Files
\Sample.txt" variable="FileContents">
<html>
<head>
    <title>File Read Example</title>
</head>

<body>
<cfoutput>
Contents of the file (#GetDirectoryFromPath(GetCurrent
TemplatePath())#Files\Sample.txt):
<hr><pre>
#FileContents#
</pre><hr>
</cfoutput>
</body>
</html>
```

10

The output produced by the previous template is shown in Figure 10-31. When the ColdFusion Server executes the CFFILE tag, the contents of the file named Sample.txt are read into a newly created variable named FileContents. This value is output later on in the body of the document.

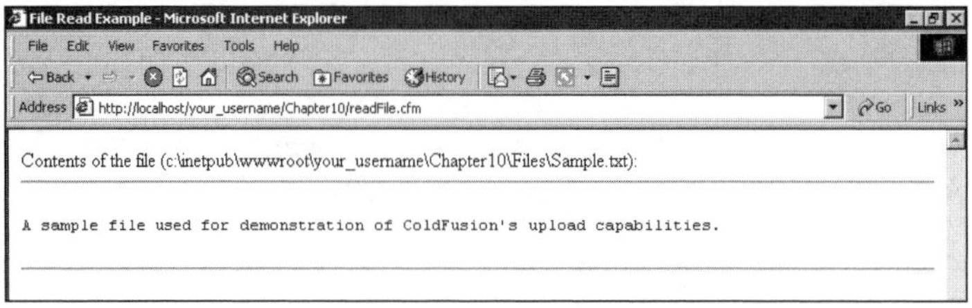

Figure 10-31   Web page produced by readFile.cfm

You can write to a text file by using the CFFILE with its ACTION attribute set to "write" or "append." The syntax for using the CFFILE tag for reading text files is as follows:

```
<CFFILE ACTION="write or append"
     FILE="full_path_name_including_file"
     OUTPUT="string">
```

When the ColdFusion Server executes this tag and the ACTION attribute is WRITE, a new file is created and the string specified by the OUTPUT attribute is written to the file. If the ACTION attribute is set to "append," the string is appended to existing files at the end. If the file is not present, a new file is created.

The following example (AppendToFile.cfm) illustrates this capability:

```
<CFFILE ACTION="Append"
file="#GetDirectoryFromPath(GetCurrentTemplatePath())
#Files\Sample.txt" output="This is a multi-line

string that is being appended to the


sample.txt file.">
<cflocation url="readFile.cfm">
```

Once the large string is appended to the file Sample.txt, the ColdFusion Server redirects the user to the readFile.cfm template that displays the newly created contents of the Sample.txt file, as shown in Figure 10-32. Notice that the string spans multiple lines and the carriage returns in the output string are written to the file, too. You may have to refresh the document to see the new contents.

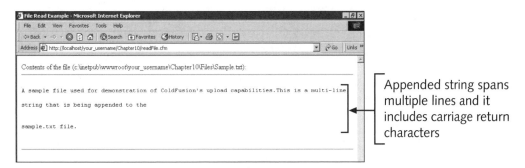

Appended string spans multiple lines and it includes carriage return characters

Figure 10-32   Web page produced after appending text to the file

Avani Talati, an agent at NikRealty, wants to produce a list of his properties that are available for sale. Assuming that the other agents are interested in such a list too, a couple of your project members have designed two templates (propertyValuesForm.cfm and propertyValuesFormHandler.cfm) located in the Export subfolder in the Chapter10 folder. Avani is also interested in a "download to Excel" utility that would allow him to download the property values data into Microsoft Excel for further analysis and planning. You know that ColdFusion can write to text files and that Microsoft Excel can read text files that have lists of values separated by commas. You want to write the records being output into a text file and make it available for download.

To examine the existing property values application:

1. Start your Web browser, and open **propertyValuesForm.cfm** in the Export subfolder in the Chapter10 folder on your Data Disk. As shown in Figure 10-33, a select box lists all the agents, pulling the agent names from a database table.

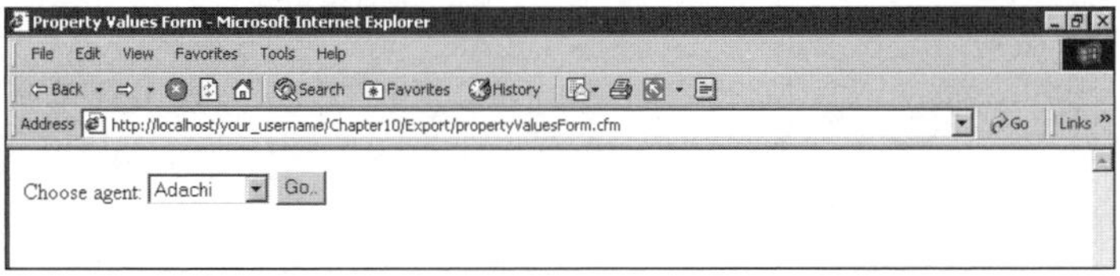

Figure 10-33   Web page produced by propertyValuesForm.cfm

2. Click the **Choose agent** list arrow, click **Talati**, and then click the **Go** button. A list of all his properties appears in the form of a table, as shown in Figure 10-34. The name of the form handler is propertyValuesFormHandler.cfm. The table includes three columns, PropertyID, Location, and Price, and sorts the data by location.

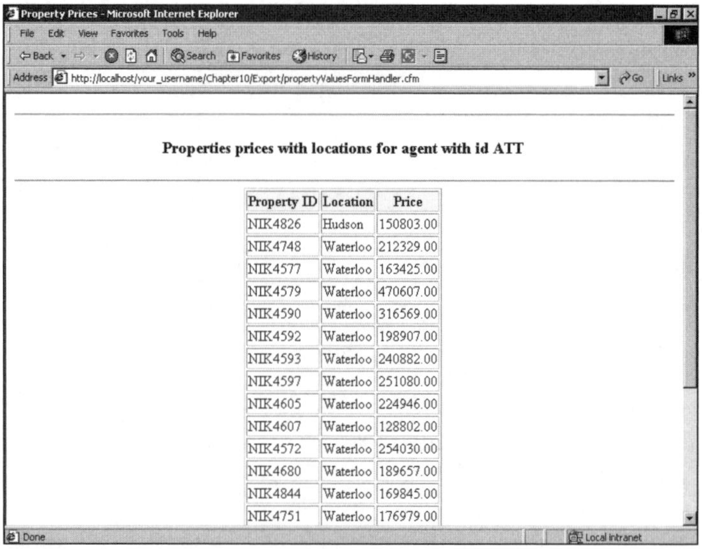

Figure 10-34   Web page produced when the form is submitted

3. Start ColdFusion Studio, and open the **propertyValuesForm.cfm** and the **propertyValuesFormHandler.cfm** files in the Chapter 10\Export folder. Note that the AgentID is used as the value for the options in the select box in the form and the form handler is querying the database table using this value in the WHERE clause.

4. You can use a CFOUTPUT tag to add a hyperlink to the second page that agents can click to download data into a comma-separated-value file that they could import into Excel. In the propertyValuesFormHandler.cfm file, click at the beginning of line 27, type **Click <a href="export.cfm?AgentID=<cfoutput>#FORM.AgentID#</cfoutput>">here</a> to download this data into Microsoft Excel.**, and press the **Enter** key.

5. Note that you are using a URL parameter to the export.cfm file named AgentID. The AgentID of the agent selected in the form is being assigned to this URL parameter. You should be able to access this value by using the variable named URL.AgentID. Save the file.

6. Click **File** on the menu bar, and then click **New Document**. A new document opens.

7. Save this new document as **export.cfm** in the Export subfolder in the Chapter10 folder.

8. Click **Edit** on the menu bar, and then click **Select All**.

9. Press the **Delete** key to delete the contents of the file.

10. On the first line type **<cflock timeout="20">**, and press **Enter**. You want to ensure that only one agent is executing this code at a given time. Recall from Chapter 9 the concept of locking shared resources. If multiple agents were executing this template, the code would be executed in the order the agents use the template.

11. Type the following code to query the database to extract all properties that are listed by this agent. Press **Enter** after each line. Remember that the AgentID is available as a URL parameter to this template:

```
<cfquery datasource="your_username" name="getData">
SELECT PropertyID, Location, Price FROM Properties WHERE
AgentID = '#URL.AgentID#' ORDER BY Location
</cfquery>
```

12. You want to ensure that the file that was created prior to this execution is deleted and the new text written over the previous text. Use the CFFILE tag with the ACTION attribute set to "write" to overwrite the previous data and output the headings for the columns. Type **<cffile action="WRITE" file="#GetDirectoryFromPath(GetCurrentTemplatePath())#Property Values.csv" output="PropertyID, Location, Price">**, and press **Enter**. This stores the data in a file named PropertyValues.csv in the same folder where this template resides. Note that the file extension is csv, indicating that it is a comma-separated-value file.

13. Design a query loop to extract the data one record at a time and append it to the above file. Type **<cfloop query="getData"><cffile action="APPEND" file="#GetDirectoryFromPath(GetCurrentTemplatePath())#PropertyVal ues.csv" output="#PropertyID#,#Location#,#NumberFormat (Price,999999999.99)#"></cfloop>**, and press **Enter**. The output string shown in Figure 10-35 contains values separated by commas. For example, during the first loop *NIK4826,Hudson, 150803.00* would be written to the file.

10

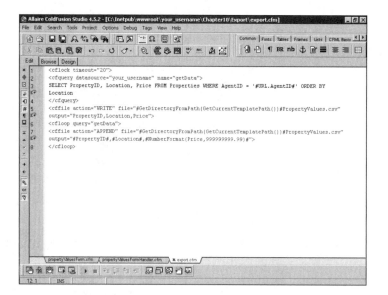

Figure 10-35 Export.cfm in the Editor window

14. Once the loop is executed, the file is ready. Redirect the user to this newly created file by using the CFLOCATION tag. Type **<cflocation url="PropertyValues.csv">** to accomplish the redirect.

15. Finally, type **</cflock>** to end the CFLOCK.

16. Save the file. See Figure 10-36.

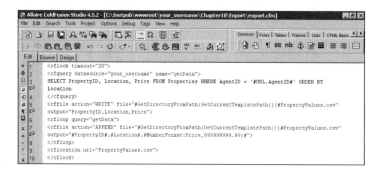

Figure 10-36 The completed Export.cfm in the Editor window

To download the CSV file and open it in Excel:

1. Switch to your Web browser, and open **propertyValuesForm.cfm** in the Chapter10/Export folder on your Data Disk.

2. Click the **Choose agent** list arrow, click **Talati**, and then click the **Go** button.

3. Scroll down and right-click the hyperlink **here**. Then point to **Save Target As**, as shown in Figure 10-37.

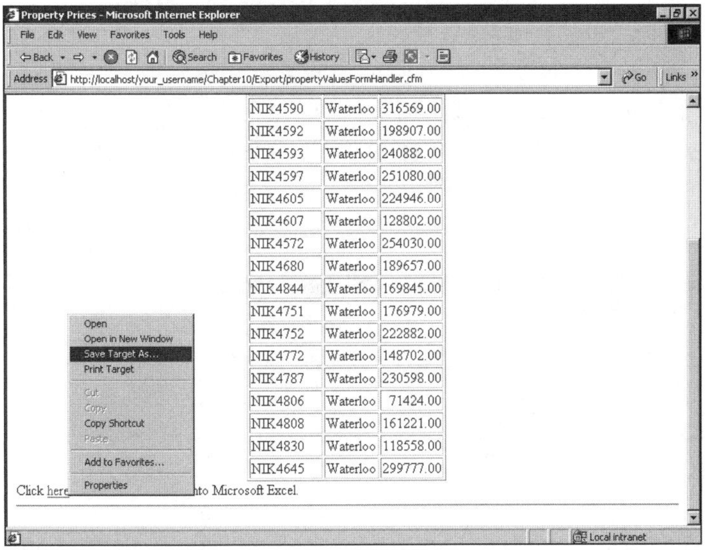

Figure 10-37   Downloading a file

4. Click **Save Target As** to download the file. The Save As dialog box opens, as in Figure 10-38. Make sure that the floppy disk is still in the floppy drive, select the 3½ Floppy drive in the Save As dialog box, and then click **Save**.

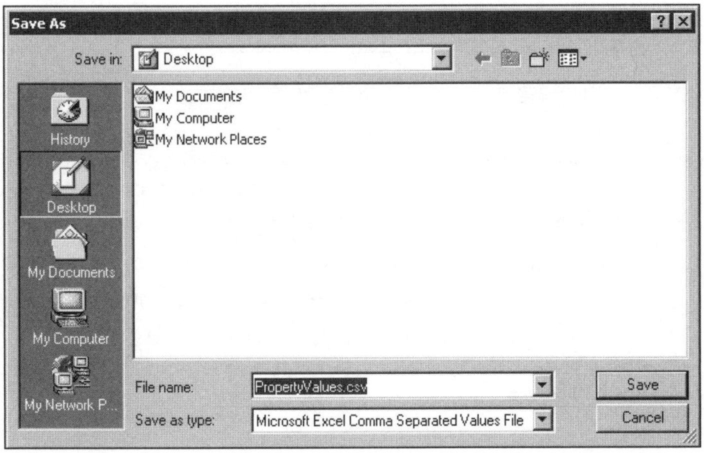

Figure 10-38   Save As dialog box

5. Click the **Close** button. Note that this process differs depending on your browser.

10

6. Start **Microsoft Excel** if available. (If Excel is not available, use another program that can open CSV files.)
7. Click **File** on the menu bar, and then click **Open**. Navigate to the location of the file that you just downloaded.
8. Click the **Files of type** list arrow, and then click **All Files (*.*)**.
9. Double-click **PropertyValues.csv** to open it in Excel. The file opens as an Excel worksheet, as shown in Figure 10-39. Note that Excel has used the commas as separators and listed the location values in Column B and the prices in Column C.

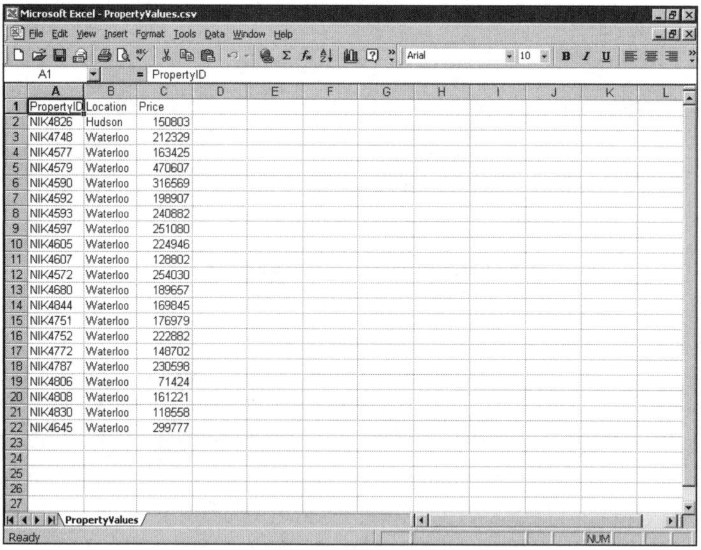

PropertyID	Location	Price
NIK4826	Hudson	150803
NIK4748	Waterloo	212329
NIK4577	Waterloo	163425
NIK4579	Waterloo	470607
NIK4590	Waterloo	316569
NIK4592	Waterloo	198907
NIK4593	Waterloo	240882
NIK4597	Waterloo	251080
NIK4605	Waterloo	224946
NIK4607	Waterloo	128802
NIK4572	Waterloo	254030
NIK4680	Waterloo	189657
NIK4844	Waterloo	169845
NIK4751	Waterloo	176979
NIK4752	Waterloo	222882
NIK4772	Waterloo	148702
NIK4787	Waterloo	230598
NIK4806	Waterloo	71424
NIK4808	Waterloo	161221
NIK4830	Waterloo	118558
NIK4645	Waterloo	299777

Figure 10-39 PropertyValues.csv opened in Microsoft Excel

10. Close all programs. You have successfully designed a ColdFusion template for extracting data from a database table and writing it into a comma-separated-value file. Further, you have successfully imported this data into Microsoft Excel.

In the steps you just completed, after writing the results of the query to the CSV file, you used the CFLOCATION tag to redirect the user to it. Recall from Chapter 4 that the CFLOCATION tag issues a response to the browser with an "object has moved to a different location" message and the browser requests the object at this location without the user realizing what has happened. This works well in most situations. In certain situations, especially when you want to send an image programmatically by using a ColdFusion template that is embedded in another document, the CFLOCATION will not work. The CFLOCATION works only when the entire document has to be served from somewhere else. In the next section, you will learn about the CFCONTENT tag and use it for serving images and other application files.

Serving Application Files by Using CFCONTENT

You can serve application files, such as images, Excel files, or Word files, by using the CFCONTENT tag. The syntax for the CFCONTENT tag is given below:

```
<CFCONTENT TYPE="file_type"
        DELETEFILE="Yes/No"
        FILE="filename">
```

When the ColdFusion Server processes the CFCONTENT tag, it serves the file specified by the FILE attribute. If the DELETEFILE attribute is set to "Yes," it deletes the file after serving it; if it is set to "No," it does not delete the file. The MIME type header of the document is set to the type specified in the TYPE attribute. **MIME** is short for **Multipurpose Internet Mail Extensions**, a specification for formatting non-ASCII files so that they can be sent over the Internet. Every document received by the Web browser has a MIME type, which identifies it to the Web browser. For example, if the MIME type is application/pdf, the Web browser opens the Adobe Acrobat reader (if installed) to process the document and display it, and if the MIME type is image/gif, it displays the file as an image in the document. You can find a comprehensive list of MIME types at *www.mime-types.com*.

The following example (serveImage.cfm) illustrates how to use the CFCONTENT object to serve an image file programmatically:

```
<cfcontent file="#GetDirectoryFromPath(GetCurrentTemplate
Path())#Mvc-201e.jpg" type="image/jpeg" deletefile="No">
```

When the ColdFusion Server executes the previous template, it finds the file Mvc-201e.jpg in the current folder and sends it as a response to the Web browser with a MIME type header defined as image/jpeg. The Web browser examines the MIME type header, handles the file sent as an image, and displays it. The output produced is shown in Figure 10-40.

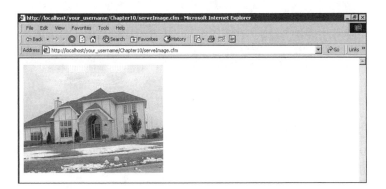

Figure 10-40   Web page produced by serveImage.cfm

This behavior may be similar to what you achieve using a CFLOCATION tag. The example below (Example10-4.htm) illustrates the usefulness of the CFCONTENT tag:

```
<html>
<head>
    <title>CFCONTENT</title>
</head>

<body>
<hr>
<h3 align="center">Here is the image returned by the
CFCONTENT tag</h3>
<hr>
<p align="center"><img src="serveImage.cfm"></p>
<hr>
</body>
</html>
```

The output produced by loading this example in your Web browser is shown in Figure 10-41.

Figure 10-41   Image displayed by the CFCONTENT tag in an HTML page

Note that this example is an HTML file. When the Web browser processes this HTML file and encounters the IMG tag, it sends a request for the resource specified by the SRC attribute. Note that this attribute has the value "serverImage.cfm." The Web server receives this request and sends it to the ColdFusion Server because it is a ColdFusion template. The ColdFusion Server executes this template and returns an image. The Web browser inserts this image in the current document and displays it. This type of processing is not possible with the CFLOCATION tag.

NikRealty has been contacted by a few companies inquiring about the possibility of placing advertisements on the Web site. Your task is to design a template that serves a banner ad every time a property is viewed. NikRealty has four banners ads named dss.gif, loans.gif, movers.gif, and yourAd.gif. Your template should randomly pick one ad from these four. The detail.cfm file from Chapter 6, which you used for browsing properties as well as the four ads are available in the subfolder named bannerAds in the Chapter 10 folder on your Data Disk. You will be using these files in this exercise.

To design an ad rotation template for the NikRealty Web site:

1. Start your Web browser, and then open the **detail.cfm** file in the bannerAds subfolder in the Chapter10 folder on your Data Disk. Click the **Next** and **Prev** arrows a few times to see some properties. See Figure 10-42. Your task is to display a banner ad in this template. Before modifying this template, design the template for serving the ad.

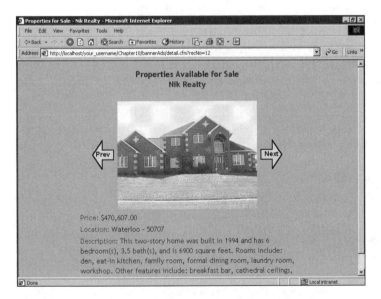

Figure 10-42 Web page displayed by detail.cfm

2. Start ColdFusion Studio.

3. Open **serveAd.cfm** from the bannerAds subfolder in the Chapter10 folder.

4. You want to randomly display one of the four ads. You can generate a random number between 1 and 4. Based on the value generated, you want to select the ad to display. A CFSWITCH statement is appropriate for this purpose. The code for this CFSWITCH statement is shown in Figure 10-43. Note that a

variable named adToDisplay is used to capture the name of the image file that should be displayed. This file is in the same folder as the current template being edited.

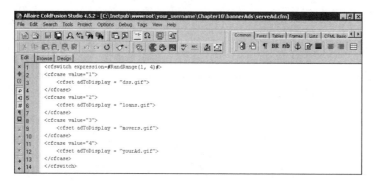

Figure 10-43   serveAd.cfm in the Editor window

5. Click at the end of line 14, and press the **Enter** key.

6. Display the ad by using the CFCONTENT tag. Type **<cfcontent file="#GetDirectoryFromPath(GetCurrentTemplatePath())##adTo Display#"**, and press the **spacebar**. Double-click **type** on the tag insight menu. Double-click **image/gif** from the list of values, and then type **>** to close the tag.

7. Save the file.

8. Switch to your Web browser, and open **serveAd.cfm**. See Figure 10-44.

Figure 10-44   Web page produced by serveAd.cfm

9. Refresh your browser several times. Each time you refresh, one of the four ads is displayed in the browser. Because the ad is displayed randomly, it could be different from the existing one or be the same one.

Your next task is to include this image in the detail.cfm template.

To include a rotation banner ad in a template:

1. Switch to **ColdFusion Studio**, and open **detail.cfm** in the bannerAds subfolder to edit it.

2. Click at the end of the body tag on line 13, and press the **Enter** key to insert a new line.

3. Type ** <img src="serveAd.cfm?time=<cfoutput> #URLEncodedFormat(Now())#</cfoutput>"> **. Notice that you are using a URL parameter named "time" in the SRC attribute of the image. The ColdFusion template serveAd.cfm does not need this parameter. Most Web browsers cache images from IMG tags to improve browser performance. Because the time generated by the Now() function keeps changing, the Web browser is tricked into thinking that this is a different image and it sends a request to retrieve it from the Web server every time a property is viewed.

4. Save your file.

5. Switch to your Web browser, and open **detail.cfm**.

6. View a few properties and note how the banner ad is changed. See Figure 10-45 for an example.

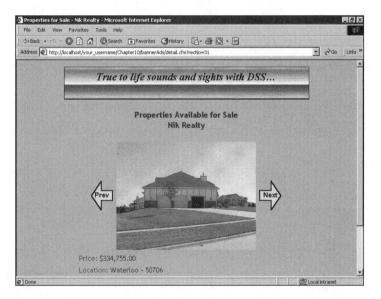

Figure 10-45   Banner ad displayed by serveAd.cfm in the Web page produced by detail.cfm

You may have noticed on most Web sites that banner ads are linked to the Web site of the company where more information is provided. If you rotate the banner ad by picking one out of four, how can you design a hyperlink that would go to the right location? A simple way to accomplish this task is to use session variables. Assign the location by using a session variable named adLocation and redirect the user to that location when the banner ad is clicked.

To complete the banner ad application by redirecting the user to the appropriate location:

1. Switch to ColdFusion Studio.

2. Click **File** on the menu bar, click **New**, and double-click **Blank Document** to open a new blank document.

3. Type **<cfapplication name="bannerAds" sessionmanagement="Yes" sessiontimeout=#CreateTimeSpan(0,0,20,0)#>**.

4. Save the file as **application.cfm** in the bannerAds subfolder.

5. Switch to **serveAd.cfm**.

6. Click at the end of the CFSET tag on line 3, and press the **Enter** key to insert a new line.

7. Type **<cfset session.adLocation = "http://www.dss.com">**. You are using a session variable to capture the location in case this ad is served.

8. Click at the end of the CFSET tag on line 7, and press **Enter** to insert a new line.

9. Type **<cfset session.adLocation = "http://www.loans.com">**.

10. Click at the end of the CFSET tag on line 11, and press **Enter** to insert a new line.

11. Type **<cfset session.adLocation = "http://www.movers.com">**.

12. Click at the end of the CFSET tag on line 15, and press **Enter** to insert a new line.

13. Type **<cfset session.adLocation = "http://www.NikRealty.com/adInfo.htm">**.

14. Because you are using session variables, you have to lock the code. Insert a new line at the top of the file.

15. In the new line, type **<cflock** and press the **spacebar**.

16. Double-click **scope** on the tag insight menu, and then click **SESSION** in the list of values.

17. Press the **spacebar**, and double-click **timeout** on the tag insight menu.

18. Type **20** as the value for this attribute, move to the end of the line, and type **>** to close the tag.

19. Click at the end of the </cfswitch> tag on line 19, and press **Enter**.

20. Type **</cflock>**.

21. Save your file.

Your next task is to design the adClick.cfm template that would redirect the user to the location specific to the ad.

To design a template for processing ad clicks:

1. Click **File** on the menu bar, and then click **New Document**.

2. Save the new document as **adClick.cfm** in the bannerAds subfolder.

3. Click **Edit** on the menu bar, and then click **Select All**. Press **Delete** to delete all the code.

4. Type **<cflocation url="#session.adLocation#">**. You are redirecting the user to the appropriate location.

5. Save your file.

6. Your next task is to link the images when the banner ads are displayed. Open **detail.cfm** in the Editor window.

7. Select the entire **IMG tag** on line 14.

8. Click the **Anchor** button on the QuickBar, and type **adClick.cfm** as the value for the HREF attribute. See Figure 10-46.

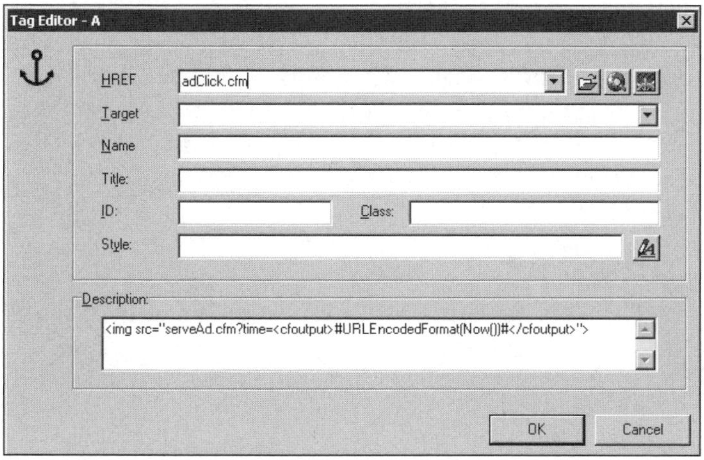

Figure 10-46   Set up a hyperlink to the banner ad

9. Click the **OK** button.

10. Save your file.

11. Switch to your Web browser, and reload the **detail.cfm** file.

12. Experiment by clicking the ads.

13. Close all programs.

You have successfully created an application that rotates banner ads.

Interacting with Other Web Servers

ColdFusion is a powerful application server that can interact with other Web servers. Similarly to how the ColdFusion Server interacts with e-mail servers, ColdFusion can request documents from other Web servers just like a Web browser requests a document. The Web server assumes that it is a request like any other request it receives, it sends the document to the ColdFusion server. The CF Server captures the document in a string variable. This variable and its contents can be processed subsequently. You can use this capability to get content from other Web servers and repackage it. This is useful when you do not have control over other servers but have a right to use their content. Obviously, you should not violate any copyright laws by using this capability. You can make ColdFusion interact with other Web servers by using the CFHTTP tag. A simple syntax of the CFHTTP tag for retrieving a document on the Web is the following:

```
<CFHTTP URL="aURL"
        METHOD="get"
        RESOLVEURL="Yes/No">
</CFHTTP>
```

When the ColdFusion Server executes the previous tag, it sends an HTTP request for the document specified by the value of the URL parameter just as a Web browser does. The Web server treats this request as any other request made by any other Web browser and serves it the document. The Web server could be located anywhere on the Internet. The ColdFusion Server receives this document and substitutes the complete URLs for image and other links in the document if the RESOLVEURL attribute is set to "Yes." It then creates a variable in the CFHTTP scope named FileContent (that is, CFHTTP.FileContent) and assigns it the source code in the document received. This variable can be processed as another variable in a ColdFusion template.

The following example (getMacromediaCode.cfm) illustrates the CFHTTP tag:

```
<cfhttp method="GET" url="http://www.macromedia.com"
resolveurl="Yes">
</cfhttp>
<html>
<head>
     <title>CFHTTP</title>
</head>

<body>
<hr>
<h3 align="center">Macromedia Home Page - Source Code</h3>
<hr>
<form>
<textarea  cols="80" rows="30">
<cfoutput>#CFHTTP.FileContent#</cfoutput>
</textarea>
```

```
</form>
<hr>
</body>
</html>
```

When you load this template in your Web browser, it would produce the output shown in Figure 10-47.

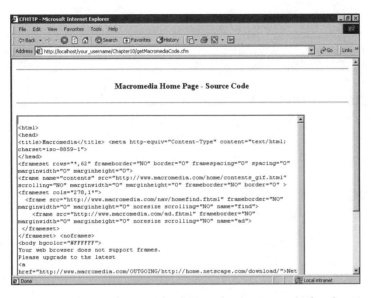

Figure 10-47   Web page displaying the source code for the Macromedia home page

When the ColdFusion Server executes this template, it first processes the CFHTTP tag. It sends a request to the Web server located at *www.macromedia.com*, which is the domain name for the Macromedia Corporation. The Web server located at Macromedia receives this request and sends the home page document back as the response. The ColdFusion Server receives the document, resolves all the anchors and images, creates a variable named CFHTTP.FileContent, and assigns it the text received. This content is then output in the text area in the previous template.

If the Web server serves a CSV file, you can use the CFHTTP tag to import this data directly into a query object and treat it as any other SELECT query executed against a database connection. This syntax for the CFHTTP tag is given below:

```
<CFHTTP URL="aURL_for_a_CSV_file"
     METHOD="get"
     NAME="query_name"
     COLUMNS="query_columns"
     TEXTQUALIFIER = "delimiter">
</CFHTTP>
```

When the ColdFusion Server processes this tag, it sends a request for the CSV file specified by the URL attribute. The remote Web server sends the CSV file, and the ColdFusion Server receives it. After receiving the file, the ColdFusion Server creates a query object with the name specified by the NAME attribute. The delimiters for text values should be specified by the TEXTQUALIFIER attribute. Use a space character when there are no delimiters. The field names for the query object are created from the list specified by the COLUMNS attribute. You can use this query object in a query loop for outputting the values.

This tag is illustrated in the following example. The Yahoo! financial site distributes financial information to users on the Web. For example, the URL *http://chart.yahoo.com/d?s=intc* displays the price history of Intel (with the ticker symbol intc), as shown in Figure 10-48.

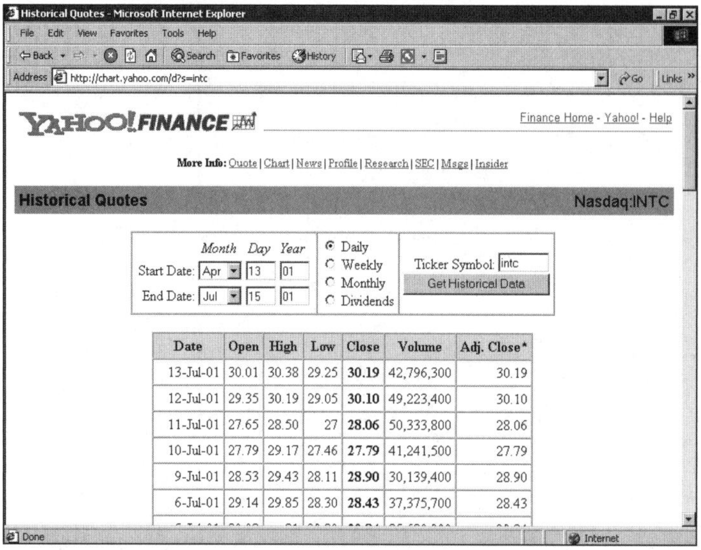

Figure 10-48   Yahoo! Web page displaying price history of Intel stock prices

Furthermore, it also makes this information available to users in a CSV format. You can download this information in a CSV format by clicking the hyperlink "Download Spreadsheet Format," as shown in Figure 10-49.

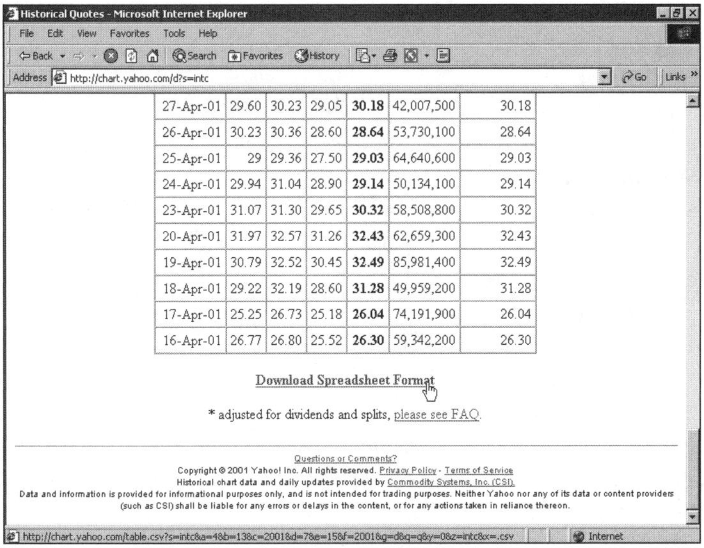

Figure 10-49   Links on Yahoo! stock page

The example (priceHistory.cfm) available on your Data Disk uses the CFHTTP tag to read this data into a query object and then outputs this data in a neatly formatted table. This example is shown below:

```
<cfset enddate = CreateDate(year(Now()), month(Now()),
day(Now()))>
<cfset startdate = enddate - 30>
<cfhttp method="GET" url="http://chart.yahoo.com/
table.csv?s=intc&a=#month(startdate)#&b=#day(startdate)
#&c=#year(startdate)#&d=#month(enddate)#&e=#day
(enddate)#&f=#year(enddate)#&g=d&q=q&y=0&z=intc&x=.csv"
name="getData" columns="Date,Open,High,Low,Close,Volume"
textqualifier=" ">
</cfhttp>
<html>
<head>
    <title>CFHTTP</title>
</head>

<body>
<hr>
<h3 align="center">One Month Price History of Intel from
Yahoo! Finance Web site</h3>
<hr>
<table align="center" border="1">
```

```
<tr>
    <th>Date</th>
    <th>Open</th>
    <th>High</th>
    <th>Low</th>
    <th>Close</th>
    <th>Volume</th>
</tr>
<cfloop query="getData">
<tr bgcolor="<cfif currentrow Mod 2 EQ 0>white<cfelse>
lightgreen</cfif>">
<cfoutput>
    <td>#Date#</td>
    <td>#Open#</td>
    <td>#High#</td>
    <td>#Low#</td>
    <td>#Close#</td>
    <td>#Volume#</td>
</cfoutput>
</tr>
</cfloop>
</table>
<hr>
</body>
</html>
```

The output produced by this example is shown in Figure 10-50.

The two CFSET tags are creating two date objects. The end date is today and the start date is one month ago. The CFHTTP tag is requesting the tables.csv resource located at the Yahoo! Finance site and supplying it the required URL parameters by processing the start and end dates. The returned document is converted into a query object with the name getData and columns Date, Open, High, Low, Close, and Volume. The query loop outputs the values in the table rows. Odd-numbered rows are colored light green and even-numbered rows are colored white by using a CFIF statement.

Adachi Yuko, one of NikRealty agents, would like to set up decision support utilities on the NikRealty Web site that would make users visit the site more often and would prob-ably result in more sales. Interest rates on mortgages are perhaps the most important fac-tor governing house sales, and your task is to design a template that would display an estimate of the current 30-year fixed mortgage interest rate. Ms. Yuko has calculated that a good approximation for this interest rate is the yield on the 10-year treasury + 1.75. You can find the yield on the Yahoo! Finance site.

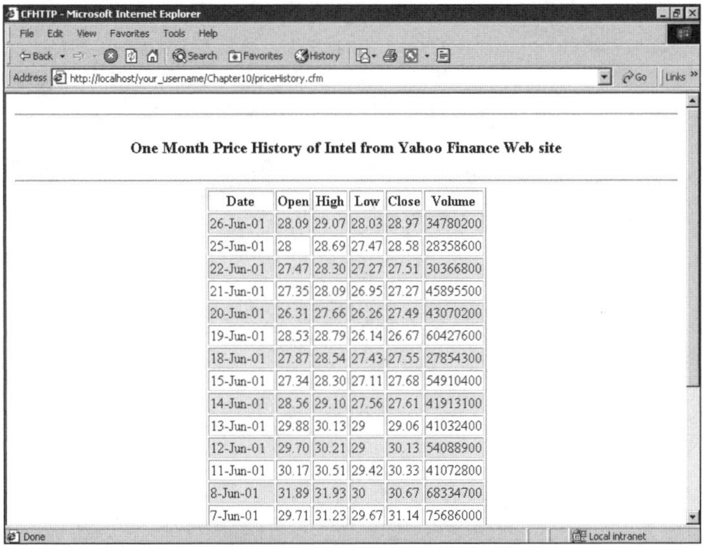

Figure 10-50   Web page displayed by priceHistory.cfm

To design a template that requests data from another Web server and uses it in a subsequent computation:

1. Start your Web browser, and open the location **http://finance.yahoo.com**. The Yahoo! Finance home page opens, and is similar to the one in Figure 10-51.

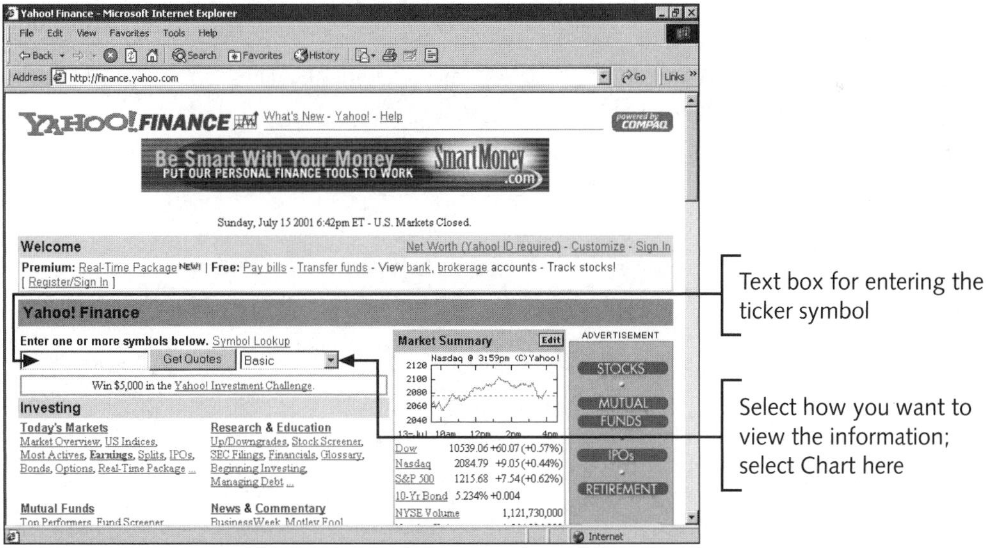

Text box for entering the ticker symbol

Select how you want to view the information; select Chart here

Figure 10-51   Yahoo! Finance home page

2. The symbol for the 10-year treasury yield is ^TNX. Type **^TNX** in the ticker symbol text box, click **Chart** in the list box, and then click the **Get Quotes** button. A Web page showing the 10-year treasury yield opens, and is similar to the one shown in Figure 10-52.

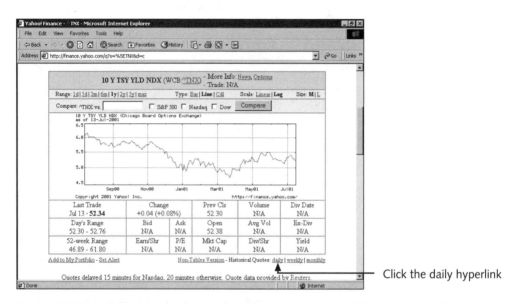

Figure 10-52   Web page displaying the 10-year treasury yield from Yahoo! Finance

3. Click the **daily** hyperlink in the Historical Quotes section at the bottom of the chart.

4. Study the table to see the current yield, and then click the **Download Spreadsheet Format** hyperlink.

5. If you are using Internet Explorer and have Excel installed, you see the dialog box shown in Figure 10-53 that asks you whether you want to open the file or download it.

6. Select the **Open this file from its current location** option button, and then click the **OK** button. The file is displayed in an Excel spreadsheet, as shown in Figure 10-54.

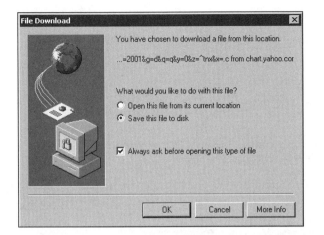

Figure 10-53   File Download dialog box displayed by Internet Explorer

	A	B	C	D	E	F	G	H	I	J	K	L
1	Date	Open	High	Low	Close							
2	13-Jul-01	5.238	5.276	5.23	5.234							
3	12-Jul-01	5.306	5.306	5.221	5.23							
4	11-Jul-01	5.251	5.289	5.225	5.285							
5	10-Jul-01	5.336	5.348	5.272	5.272							
6	9-Jul-01	5.37	5.378	5.34	5.34							
7	6-Jul-01	5.395	5.412	5.357	5.374							
8	5-Jul-01	5.361	5.425	5.348	5.412							
9	3-Jul-01	5.343	5.382	5.331	5.378							
10	2-Jul-01	5.408	5.408	5.331	5.331							
11	29-Jun-01	5.36	5.42	5.352	5.39							
12	28-Jun-01	5.203	5.326	5.203	5.326							
13	27-Jun-01	5.208	5.254	5.199	5.233							
14	26-Jun-01	5.115	5.228	4.999	5.224							
15	25-Jun-01	5.136	5.14	5.119	5.132							
16	22-Jun-01	5.165	5.165	5.124	5.124							
17	21-Jun-01	5.186	5.199	5.149	5.178							
18	20-Jun-01	5.203	5.224	5.186	5.199							
19	19-Jun-01	5.241	5.287	5.228	5.228							
20	18-Jun-01	5.215	5.249	5.215	5.241							
21	15-Jun-01	5.22	5.236	5.186	5.228							
22	14-Jun-01	5.24	5.24	5.194	5.215							
23	13-Jun-01	5.245	5.291	5.245	5.257							
24	12-Jun-01	5.291	5.291	5.24	5.24							
25	11-Jun-01	5.329	5.333	5.282	5.287							

Figure 10-54   Excel worksheet displaying the 10-year treasury yield data

The worksheet lists data in columns A, B, C, D, and E, with the latest yield in column E.

7. Start ColdFusion Studio, if necessary.

8. Click **File** on the menu bar, and then click **New Document**.

9. Save the new document as **getMortgageRate.cfm** in the Chapter10 folder.

10. Click at the beginning of line 1. Press **Enter** to add a line at the top, and use the arrow key to move back to line 1.

11. Open **priceHistory.cfm**.

12. Select lines 1 through 4, and press **Ctrl+C** to copy the lines to the Clipboard.

13. Switch to the **getMortageRate.cfm** file, and press **Ctrl+V** to paste the code.

14. Select **intc** near the end of the URL parameters list on line 3, and type **^tnx** to replace it.

15. Select **intc** near the beginning of the URL parameters list on line 3, and type **^tnx** to replace it.

16. Select **,Volume**, and delete it. The query does not include a Volume column. The code should look like the code in Figure 10-55.

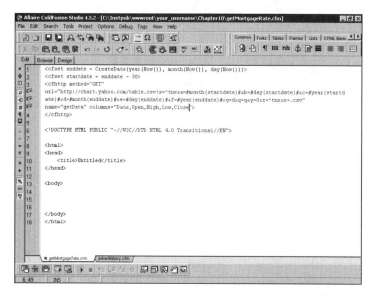

Figure 10-55   getMortageRate.cfm in ColdFusion Studio

17. Once the CFHTTP tag is executed and the query object is created, the final step is to compute the estimated value of the mortgage rate and display it. Click below the <body> tag at the beginning of line 14.

18. Type **The current interest rate for a 30-year fixed rate mortgage is estimated to be: <cfoutput>#DecimalFormat(getData.Close+1.75) #</cfoutput>%**.

19. Save your file.

20. Switch to your Web browser, and open **getMortageRate.cfm**. You see the calculated interest rate, as shown in Figure 10-56.

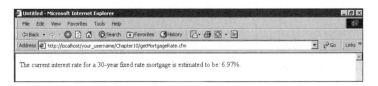

Figure 10-56   Web page produced by getMortgageRate.cfm

You have successfully created a template that queries another Web server and processes the data returned.

CHAPTER SUMMARY

❑ ColdFusion is a powerful system that interacts with e-mail servers, the server's file system, and other Web servers.

❑ Designing e-mail applications by using ColdFusion is typically a two-step process. First you design the form for users to enter data and then you design the form handler that uses this data to send e-mail.

❑ The CFMAIL tag is used for sending e-mail.

❑ You can generate customized e-mail messages by querying a database and then using the CFMAIL tag in the query loop.

❑ ColdFusion can interact with the server's file system for uploading files; for listing files; for copying, renaming, and deleting files; and for reading and writing text files.

❑ The CFFILE and the CFDIRECTORY tags are two important file management tags.

❑ The CFCONTENT tag can be used to serve application files programmatically. You can design an application for rotating banner advertisements by using this tag.

❑ The CFHTTP tag is used for interacting with other Web servers. The CFHTTP tag can be used in two different ways. It can be used to retrieve a document on another Web server into a string variable, or it can be used to retrieve a CSV document into a query object for output using a query loop.

10

REVIEW QUESTIONS

1. What is the CFML tag used for sending e-mail? Briefly describe its attributes.

2. Describe the process used for sending personalized e-mail with data extracted from databases.

3. Describe the process used for confirming form submissions via e-mail.

4. Describe the process used for designing an application that uploads files to the server.

5. What attributes of the FORM tag and their values are useful when you upload files?

6. Which functions allow you to determine the path to the folder where the current template is located?

7. Explain the difference in the action taken by the ColdFusion Server when the NAMECONFLICT attribute for the CFFILE tag used for uploading a file is set to OVERWRITE as opposed to MAKEUNIQUE. How can you figure out the name of the file after it has been uploaded?

8. Describe the syntax of the CFDIRECTORY tag.

9. What are the fields in the query object that is generated when the ColdFusion Server executes a CFDIRECTORY tag?

10. Which attribute governs what a CFFILE tag does? What are its possible values?

11. Describe the process used for reading and writing text files.

12. What is the difference between appending text to a file and writing text to a file?

13. What is a comma-separated-value file? How would you generate a CSV file using ColdFusion?

14. How would you serve application files programmatically?

15. What is the MIME type of a file? How does a Web browser use information about the MIME type of a file?

16. How is the CFCONTENT tag different from the CFLOCATION tag?

17. What is the CFML tag for requesting data from other Web servers? What are the two ways in which you can use this tag?

HANDS-ON PROJECTS

Project 1: Design an E-Mail Application

NikRealty wants you to design an application that a user can use to easily send a message to an agent. You are required to perform the following tasks:

1. Create a folder named **EZMail** in the Chapter10 folder. Save the files that you create for this application in this folder. Open the NikReallty.mdb database, and then open the Agents table. Change the e-mail address of Doug LeFevre to your e-mail address, and then close Access.

2. Create a ColdFusion template named **ezMailForm.cfm** for displaying a form, as shown in Figure 10-57. The form contains a list box of all agents' names produced by querying the NikRealty database, a text area for a message, and a Submit button to send the message.

3. Create a form handler named **sendMessage.cfm** for the form in Step 2. The form handler should send the message in the text area to the agent whose name is selected in the text box, as shown in Figure 10-58. Then it should display a confirmation message back to the user, as shown in Figure 10-59.

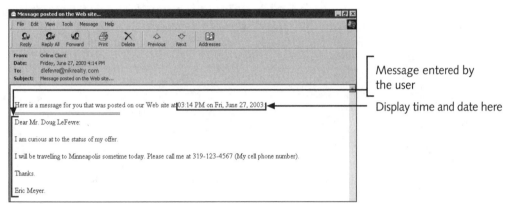

Figure 10-57

Message entered by
the user

Display time and date here

10

Figure 10-58

message sent successfully... - Microsoft Internet Explorer

File   Edit   View   Favorites   Tools   Help

Address   http://localhost/your_username/Chapter10/EZMail/sendMessage.cfm   Go   Links

Your message has been sent successfully. Please visit our Web site again.

Figure 10-59

Project 2: Design a Bulk Mail Application

Recall that the Customers table in the NikRealty database contains data about customers who make requests for showings using the Web site. Open the Customers table using Microsoft Access and familiarize yourself with its structure (See Figure 10-60).

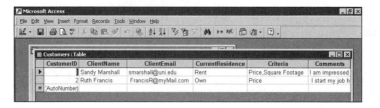

Figure 10-60

Notice that there is a field named ClientName for storing the client's name and a field named ClientEmail for storing the client's e-mail address. NikRealty wants you to design a bulk e-mail application that can be used by the agents to send occasional e-mail to customers reminding them of the services NikRealty offers. To design this application, perform the following tasks:

1. Create a folder named **BulkMail** in the Chapter10 folder. Save the files that you create for this application in this folder. Open the NikRealty.mdb database, and then open the customers table. Change the e-mail address of Ruth Francis to your e-mail address, and then close Access.

2. Create a ColdFusion template named **BulkMailForm.cfm** for displaying a form, as shown in Figure 10-61. The form contains a text area for a message, a text box for the subject of the message, and a Submit button to send the message.

3. Create a form handler named **sendMessage.cfm** for the form in Step 2. The form handler should send personalized e-mail with the message in the text area to all the customers in the Customers table, as shown in Figure 10-62. Then it should display a confirmation message back to the user displaying a list of customers to whom e-mail has been sent, as shown in Figure 10-63.

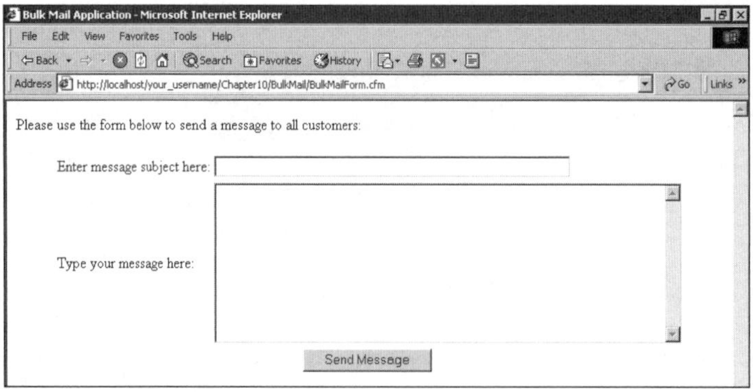

Figure 10-61

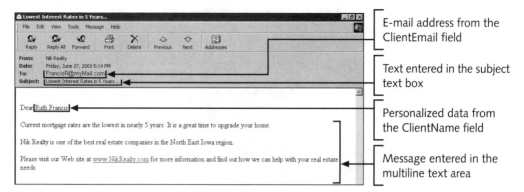

E-mail address from the
ClientEmail field

Text entered in the subject
text box

Personalized data from
the ClientName field

Message entered in the
multiline text area

Figure 10-62

Figure 10-63

Figure 10-63

Project 3: Design an Application for Uploading Resumes

An online employment agency has given you a contract for designing their Web site as
well as their Intranet. One of the design requirements is a resume upload application.
Clients should be able to upload resumes created using Microsoft Word. Perform the following tasks:

1. Create a folder named **Jobs** in the Chapter10 folder, and store all the ColdFusion
   templates that you create in this folder.

2. Create a subfolder in the newly created Jobs folder named **Resumes** for storing
   the uploaded files.

3. Design a ColdFusion template named **resumeForm.cfm** that allows users to
   upload Word documents into this folder. See Figure 10-64. The form handler name
   uploadResume.cfm should upload the submitted document to the Resumes subfolder and display a confirmation message, as shown in Figure 10-65. Make sure
   that resumes with the same name are not overwritten.

10

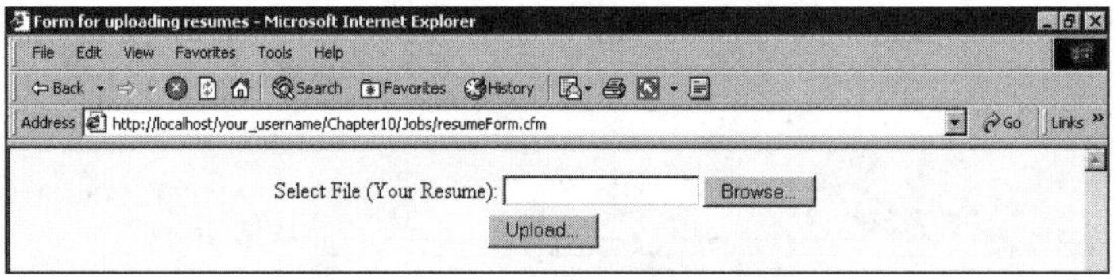

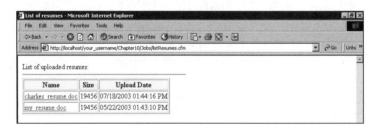

Figure 10-64

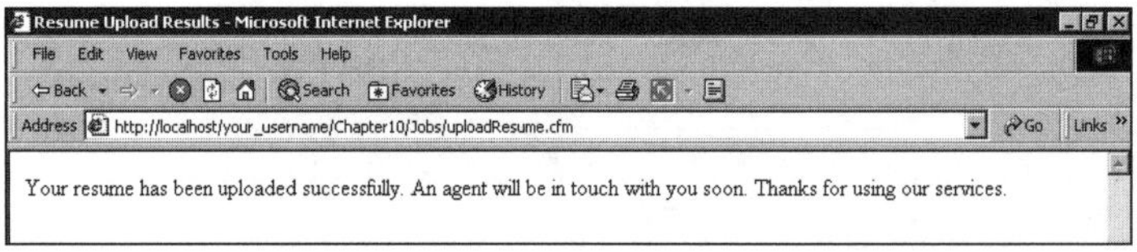

Figure 10-65

2. Design a ColdFusion template named **listResumes.cfm** that allows employees to list all files in the Resumes folder. This list should display the most recent uploads at the top. (*Hint:* The SORT attribute of the CFDIRECTORY tag should be set to a value of "datelastmodified DESC" to display the most recent uploads first). Each filename should be a hyperlink that allows you to view that document. The uploaded resumes should be displayed in a table with three columns: Name, Size, and Upload Date, as shown in Figure 10-66.

Figure 10-66

3. Add a fourth column to the table designed in Step 2 with a link that allows the employees to delete that resume. See Figure 10-67. Create a template named **deleteResume.cfm** that takes the name of the resume to delete as a URL parameter (resume) and deletes the resume. Once a resume is deleted, it should display a confirmation message, as shown in Figure 10-68.

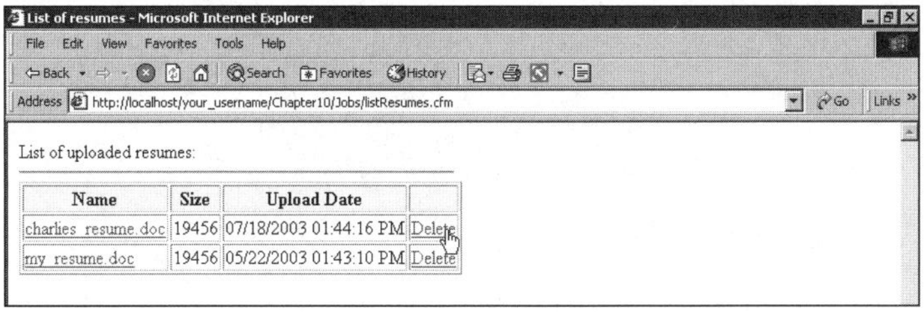

Figure 10-67

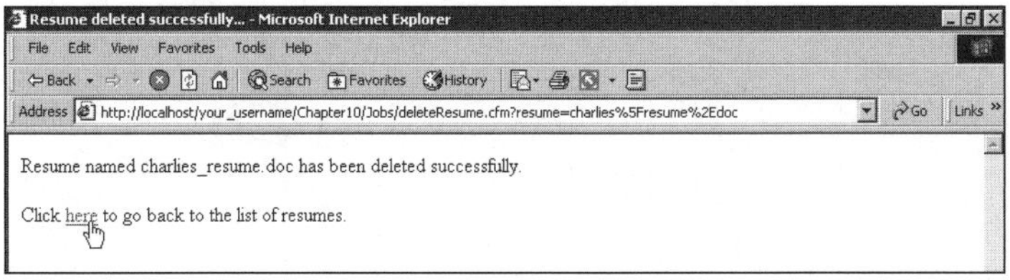

Figure 10-68

4. Add programming in the uploadResume.cfm template to log entries in a file named **resumes.csv** in the Jobs folder. Whenever a resume is submitted, add an entry in this log file with the format: Filename, Date Submitted, Time Submitted.

5. There are two files named my_resume.doc and charlies_resume.doc in the Chapter10 folder. Submit them using the application that you have designed, and open resumes.csv with Microsoft Excel. See Figure 10-69. (If Excel is not available, use another program that can open CSV files.)

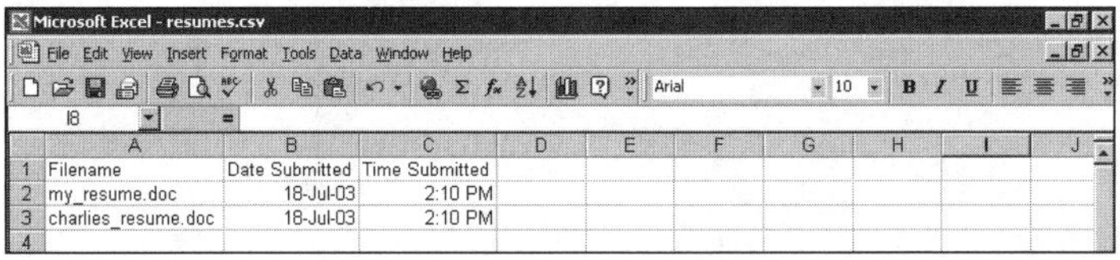

Figure 10-69

Project 4: Repackage Data from a File Located on Another Web Server

A university uses a legacy system for keeping track of faculty information. Some of the data has been exported to a comma-separated-value file. Your task is to repackage this data and display it in an attractive fashion. There is a file named faculty.csv located on the author's Web server with the URL *http://kaparthi.cba.uni.edu/ColdFusion/faculty.csv*. This file has a row for each faculty member in the Management department. The first value is the first name, the second value is the last name, and the third value is the phone number for a particular faculty member, as shown in Figure 10-70.

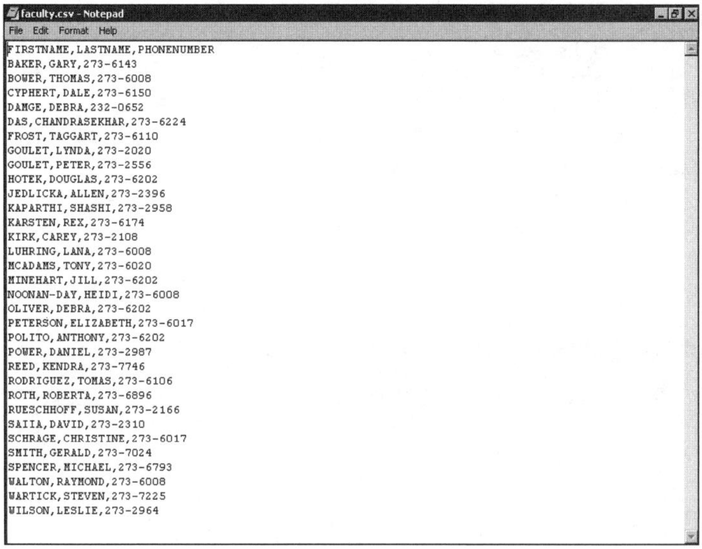


```
FIRSTNAME,LASTNAME,PHONENUMBER
BAKER,GARY,273-6143
BOWER,THOMAS,273-6008
CYPHERT,DALE,273-6150
DAMGE,DEBRA,232-0652
DAS,CHANDRASEKHAR,273-6224
FROST,TAGGART,273-6110
GOULET,LYNDA,273-2020
GOULET,PETER,273-2556
HOTEK,DOUGLAS,273-6202
JEDLICKA,ALLEN,273-2396
KAPARTHI,SHASHI,273-2958
KARSTEN,REX,273-6174
KIRK,CAREY,273-2108
LUHRING,LANA,273-6008
MCADAMS,TONY,273-6020
MINEHART,JILL,273-6202
NOONAN-DAY,HEIDI,273-6008
OLIVER,DEBRA,273-6202
PETERSON,ELIZABETH,273-6017
POLITO,ANTHONY,273-6202
POWER,DANIEL,273-2987
REED,KENDRA,273-7746
RODRIGUEZ,TOMAS,273-6106
ROTH,ROBERTA,273-6896
RUESCHHOFF,SUSAN,273-2166
SAIIA,DAVID,273-2310
SCHRAGE,CHRISTINE,273-6017
SMITH,GERALD,273-7024
SPENCER,MICHAEL,273-6793
WALTON,RAYMOND,273-6008
WARTICK,STEVEN,273-7225
WILSON,LESLIE,273-2964
```

Figure 10-70

Design a template named **listFacultyPhoneNumbers.cfm** in the Chapter10 folder that gets the data from *http://kaparthi.cba.uni.edu/ColdFusion/faculty.csv* using a CFHTTP tag and displays it in a tabular fashion, as shown in Figure 10-71.

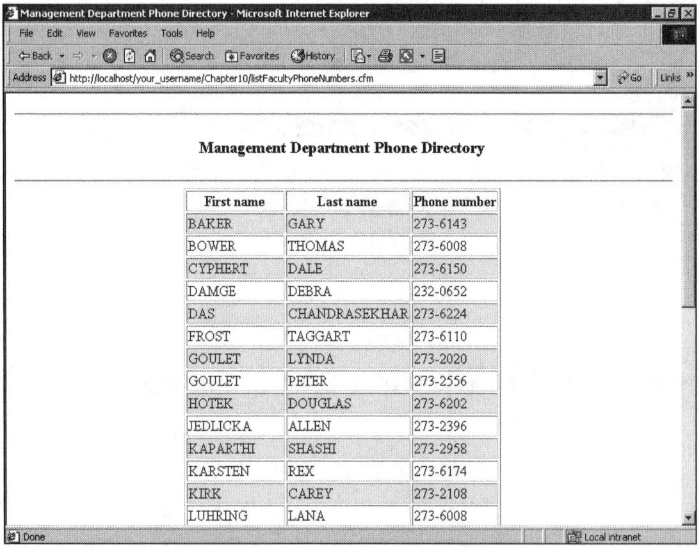

Management Department Phone Directory

First name	Last name	Phone number
BAKER	GARY	273-6143
BOWER	THOMAS	273-6008
CYPHERT	DALE	273-6150
DAMGE	DEBRA	232-0652
DAS	CHANDRASEKHAR	273-6224
FROST	TAGGART	273-6110
GOULET	LYNDA	273-2020
GOULET	PETER	273-2556
HOTEK	DOUGLAS	273-6202
JEDLICKA	ALLEN	273-2396
KAPARTHI	SHASHI	273-2958
KARSTEN	REX	273-6174
KIRK	CAREY	273-2108
LUHRING	LANA	273-6008

Figure 10-71

Project 5: Design a System for E-Mailing Favorite Properties to Friends

Based on customer feedback, NikRealty has requested that you design a system for e-mailing favorite properties to friends. Work with the files in the bannerAds folder for this project. Add a link with the description "E-mail this page to a friend" to the detail.cfm file, as shown in Figure 10-72. Note that the hyperlink points to a page named emailForm.cfm. When the user clicks this link, display a form with a text box for entering an address and another text box for the name of the user, as shown in Figure 10-73. When this form is submitted, the ColdFusion Server should execute sendEmail.cfm to e-mail the URL for the property to the user's friend and redirect the user back to the property page. The e-mail should say, "Your friend, User's name here, has requested you to look at the following page in your Web browser: http://…", as shown in Figure 10-74.

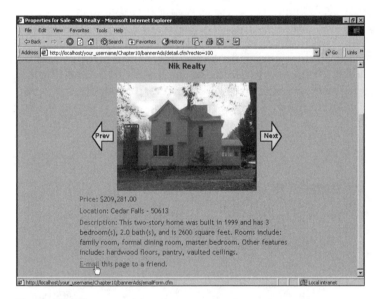

Figure 10-72

Figure 10-73

10

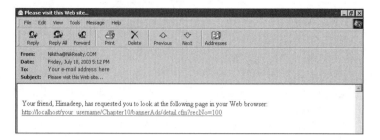

Figure 10-74

Project 6: Create a System for Analyzing Agent Statistics

Using ColdFusion Studio, open **agentStatistics.cfm** in the Chapter10 folder on your Data Disk. Edit the CFQUERY on line 1, and use an appropriate data source name. Save the file. Open *http://localhost/your_username/Chapter10/agentStatistics.cfm* in your Web browser. See Figure 10-75. It is a ColdFusion template that computes statistics for all the NikRealty agents. Your task is to create a new template named **downloadStatistics.cfm** that writes all the information in a CSV file named **agentStatistics.csv**. Do not format data using the DollarFormat function when writing to CSV files because it may insert additional commas in the data. Provide a hyperlink to this document, as shown in Figure 10-76. Click the Download hyperlink, and save the file agentStatistics.csv to your Data Disk. Open it using Microsoft Excel, and adjust column widths as necessary. You should see the spreadsheet shown in Figure 10-77. (If Excel is not available, use another program that can open CSV files.)

Agent Name	Number of properties	Total price	Average price	Maximum price	Minimum price
Avani T Talati	21	$4,402,023.00	$209,620.14	$470,607.00	$71,424.00
Dianne A Callejo	34	$6,996,541.00	$205,780.62	$415,153.00	$98,709.00
Doug C LeFevre	33	$7,068,244.00	$214,189.21	$450,871.00	$107,355.00
Joe B Friend	0	$0.00	$0.00	$0.00	$0.00
Jack L Petrie	17	$3,597,582.00	$211,622.47	$399,000.00	$118,015.00
Jay P Przyborski	46	$9,623,497.00	$209,206.46	$456,245.00	$82,467.00
Kelly O Kernan	14	$2,969,718.00	$212,122.71	$306,046.00	$110,060.00
Mary N Carter	41	$8,248,301.00	$201,178.07	$395,079.00	$92,134.00
Madeline R Lowell	19	$3,754,049.00	$197,581.53	$457,640.00	$79,576.00
Nikitha K Little	7	$1,591,059.00	$227,294.14	$315,360.00	$115,242.00
Patricia H Stout	29	$5,915,877.00	$203,995.76	$450,000.00	$93,592.00
Richard T Hadik	36	$8,069,011.00	$224,139.19	$534,388.00	$116,252.00
Yuko E Adachi	14	$2,924,239.00	$208,874.21	$332,872.00	$117,019.00

Figure 10-75

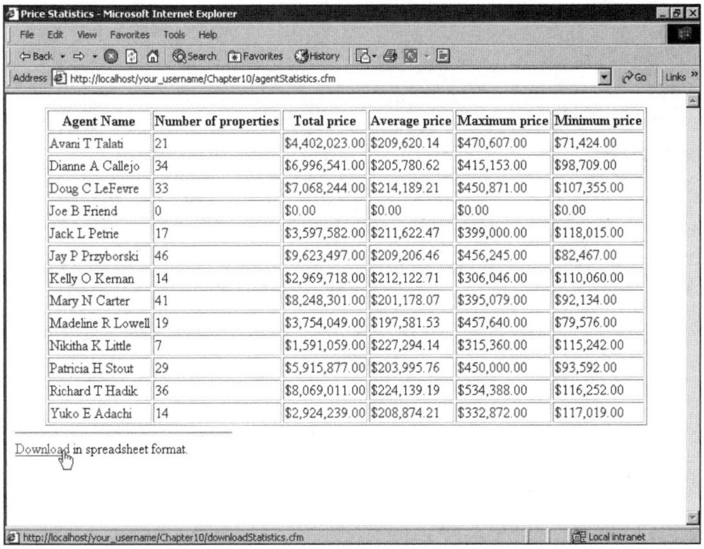

Figure 10-76

Figure 10-77

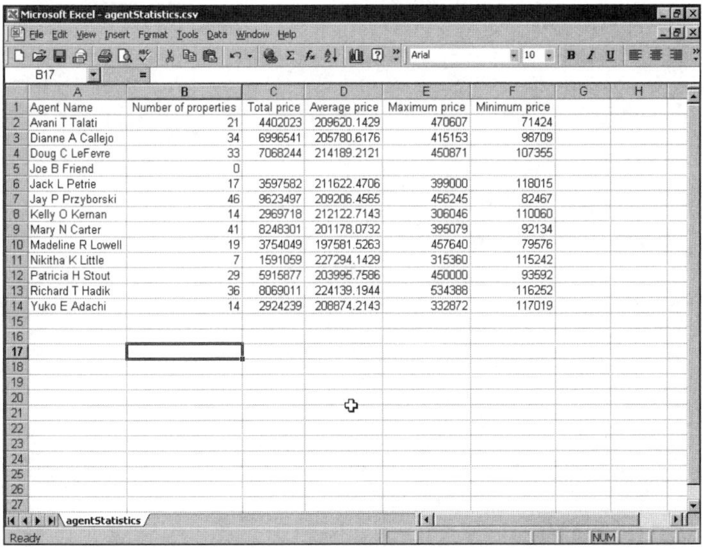

CASE PROJECTS

1. Add a feature to the hardware store application that uploads product photographs.

2. Design a checkout facility for the shopping cart application by e-mailing the order form to an authorized store representative and including a copy for the customer.

3. Design a template that takes the URL of any Web page as a URL parameter and counts and displays the number of images in it.

11

REUSING CODE AND BUILDING A COMPLETE WEB APPLICATION

In this chapter, you will:

♦ Build a complete Web application—design and implement the user interface, database, and folder structure

♦ Learn to reuse code and increase programming productivity

♦ Learn about the CFINCLUDE tag

♦ Design an administration tool for managing the web site's contents

---

In this chapter, you will build a complete Web application, pulling together everything that you have learned in the previous ten chapters. This chapter introduces a new business case—Nothebys Auction Company—and describes the type of system the business needs. After you learn what Nothebys requires, you will use ColdFusion to build a database-driven Web site for the business. In the process of building this complete application, you will learn how to increase programming productivity by reusing code.

In this chapter, you will be working on a case that is very similar to what you may encounter on the job. Because most of the concepts you will be using have been covered in the earlier chapters, the steps are more general here than what you have seen earlier. Because the steps do not contain the specific code needed, solution files are provided on the Data Disk. In case you encounter a tricky task, you may look at the solution files. You will find this chapter to be most beneficial if you work through the steps on your own without referring to the solution files unless it's necessary.

NOTHEBYS AUCTION COMPANY

Mr. Ian Nothebys founded the Nothebys Auction Company in the early 1960s, continuing a long tradition of auctioneering in the Nothebys family. Nothebys now specializes in professional auctions for industrial and construction equipment. The company is known for providing top-of-the-class service to its customers, both sellers and buyers. Although company headquarters and a permanent auction facility are located in Moline, Illinois, Nothebys conducts auctions throughout the United States. This gives two options to sellers: they can sell the products from their location or bring them to Nothebys' headquarters for sale.

Ian Nothebys believes that technology is a useful tool for increasing the effectiveness of a business organization. In the early 1980s, his company was one of the first in the Midwest to use local area networks to speed up the entire auctioning process. He has watched with interest the changes in technology and developments in the Internet and the World Wide Web. Recently, he hired your company to launch *Nothebys.com*. He wants you to design and implement the system in a series of phases. During the first phase, he wants to publish product information on the Web and make it available to customers before they attend a live auction. Currently, information about upcoming auctions and products is mailed to customers. He now wants the information presented on the Nothebys Web site so that it is appealing and easy to use. Customers should be able to find information in many ways: by auction, by product category, or by searching the database for items of interest. Information on the Web site should change quickly; when an auction is completed, all related information and products should be removed from the Web site. Nothebys staff should be able to administer the site and add and edit auctions, products, and product categories quickly and easily. Given these requirements, your team has decided to use a database-driven Web site powered by ColdFusion for *Nothebys.com*.

DESIGNING THE USER INTERFACE

After extensive interviews with the company personnel and several rounds of design and modifications, you and your development team have determined the user interface for the site. Nothebys wants a consistent look and feel for all pages on the Web site, similar to the one shown in Figure 11-1.

Because all the pages should have the same design, you might be able to use some of the same HTML and CFML code on each page. You ask one of your team members to investigate this possibility and see whether you can reuse common code.

Figure 11-1 Planned user interface for *Nothebys.com*

Reusing Code

A simple way to reuse code in ColdFusion is to create a separate file for the common code. You use the CFINCLUDE tag to include the code in this file in other templates. The syntax for the CFINCLUDE tag is as follows:

```
<cfinclude template="template_name">
```

When the ColdFusion Server executes the CFINCLUDE tag, it searches for the template given by the TEMPLATE attribute and processes the code in the template, reading the HTML and CFML in the file you specify. All the variables in the main template—the one that contains the CFINCLUDE tag—are available when processing the included code. All the variables that are created in the included code are available to the code in the main template below the CFINCLUDE tag. All modifications to variables are retained. The template treats the HTML and CFML referenced in the CFINCLUDE tag as if that code were copied and pasted into the template. The template_name could include a logical path relative to the current template in case the template to be included is located in another folder.

Reusing Code for *Nothebys.com*

Because the CFINCLUDE tag allows you to easily reuse code by including it in multiple templates, you decide to analyze the user interface requirements to identify common elements, shown in Figure 11-2.

11

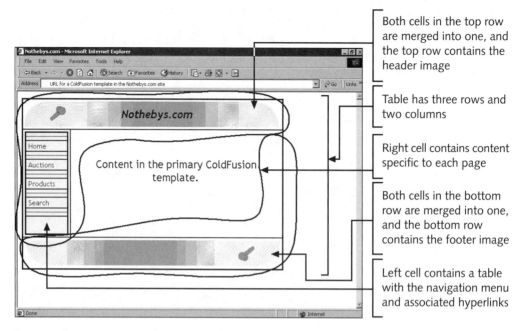

Both cells in the top row are merged into one, and the top row contains the header image

Table has three rows and two columns

Right cell contains content specific to each page

Both cells in the bottom row are merged into one, and the bottom row contains the footer image

Left cell contains a table with the navigation menu and associated hyperlinks

Figure 11-2 Common elements in the user interface

In the current Nothebys design, a page consists of a table that has three rows and two columns. The top row of the table has two cells merged into one containing the header image. Similarly, the bottom row of the table has two merged cells that contain the bottom image. The middle row has two cells. The left cell contains another table with the navigation menu and associated hyperlinks. The second cell in the middle row contains the content specific to each page. You decide to include all the code for starting the page with the document structure tags, the top row of the table along with the header image, and the navigation menu in a template named header.cfm. You will include this template in all the other templates at the top by using the CFINCLUDE tag. The code for header.cfm follows:

```
<html>
<head>
    <title>Nothebys.com</title>
</head>

<body bgcolor="LightYellow">
<table border="0" cellpadding="0" cellspacing="0"
width="589">
<tr><td colspan="2"><img src="top.gif" alt="" border="0">
</td></tr>
<tr valign="top"><td bgcolor="Yellow">
<table border="0" cellpadding="0" cellspacing="0"
width="100">
```

```
<tr><td><hr  color="Red"></td></tr>
<tr>
    <td><font face="Trebuchet MS"> Home</font></td>
</tr>
<tr><td><hr color="Red"></td></tr>
<tr>
    <td><font face="Trebuchet MS"> Auctions</font>
</td>
</tr>
<tr><td><hr color="Red"></td></tr>
<tr>
    <td><font face="Trebuchet MS"> Products</font>
</td>
</tr>
<tr><td><hr color="Red"></td></tr>
<tr>
    <td><font face="Trebuchet MS"> Search</font></td>
</tr>
<tr><td><hr color="Red"></td></tr>
<tr>
    <td><br><br></td>
</tr></table>
</td><td bgcolor="LightYellow" width="489">
```

11

The highlighted code renders the large table. The table in the first cell of the second row contains the navigation links.

You will use another template named footer.cfm for the bottom part of the page. The template will include the end tags for the second cell in the middle row, for the middle row itself, for the bottom row with the image, and for the document structure. You include this template in all the other templates by using the CFINCLUDE tag at the end of the template.

The code for footer.cfm is shown below:

```
</td>
</tr>
<tr><td colspan="2"><img src="bottom.gif" alt="" border=
"0"></td></tr>
</table>

</body>
</html>
```

The highlighted code renders the third row in the table, and the code above it ends the second row. Any content between these two blocks of code would be displayed in the second cell in the second row as the content specific to the particular template.

Considering this organization, the home page of the *Nothebys.com* site will be a set of CFINCLUDE tags with an appropriately formatted mission for the company between the tags. This template is named index.cfm, and its code is shown below:

```
<cfinclude template="header.cfm">
<font face="Trebuchet MS" size="+2"><br><br>
<p align="center">We specialize in professional auctions
for industrial and construction equipment.</p>
</font>
<cfinclude template="footer.cfm">
```

When you load the preceding template in your Web browser, you see a Web page as shown in Figure 11-3.

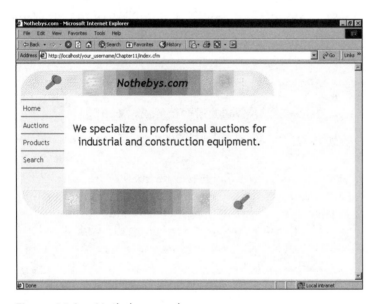

Figure 11-3   *Nothebys.com* home page

When the ColdFusion Server processes this code, it includes the code from header.cfm, the content specific to the template. Then, it includes the code from footer.cfm and creates HTML for the Web page. The HTML created is shown in Figure 11-4. Notice that the entire HTML from the three templates is strung together to create a complete Web page.

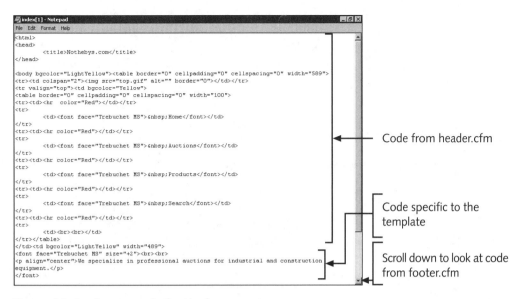

Figure 11-4   Source code for the home page

The CFINCLUDE tag is a simple and powerful tag, and the format for all templates in the Web site should be simplified to the one shown below:

```
<cfinclude template="header.cfm">
HTML and CFML specific to the template.
<cfinclude template="footer.cfm">
```

This strategy ensures that the site has a consistent user interface and increases your productivity for implementing the system. Further, if you or Nothebys want to change the site design, this strategy simplifies the recoding you'll have to do. For example, after the first phase, Nothebys may want to add rotating banner ads to the site. You simply include the rotating banner ad in the header.cfm file to display it on every Web page in the site.

DESIGNING THE DATABASE AND THE FOLDERS

After analyzing the user requirements and the existing system, you determine that the Nothebys database should have three tables. A table named Auctions will store information related to current auctions, a table named Categories will contain information related to product categories, and a table named Products will contain information about products to be auctioned.

You decide to use Microsoft Access to create the database. The Products table has a key field named ProductID, an auto number field that is incremented whenever a product record is inserted. Similarly, the Auctions table has an AuctionID autonumber field as its primary key, and the Categories table has a CategoryID autonumber field as its primary

key. The three tables are related in the following fashion: A product belongs to a particular product category and is available for sale at a particular auction. To define these relationships, the Products table has two fields named CategoryID and AuctionID. The
CategoryID defines the category for a product, and the AuctionID defines the auction
where the product is sold. A product can belong to only one category and can be auctioned off at only one auction. Figure 11-5 shows the data model for the database.

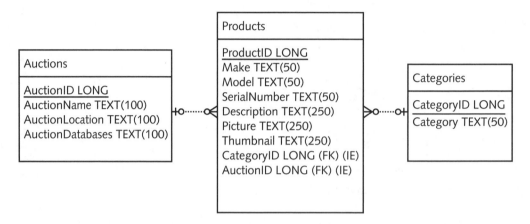

Figure 11-5   Data model for *Nothebys.com*

Table 11-1 shows the structure for all the tables in the database.

Table 11-1   Structure of Database Tables

Table: Auctions		
Field Name	*Data Type*	*Size*
AuctionID	AutoNumber (Long)	4
AuctionName	Text	100
AuctionLocation	Text	100
AuctionDates	Text	100
Table: Categories		
Field Name	*Data Type*	*Size*
CategoryID	AutoNumber (Long)	4
Category	Text	50

Table 11-1   Structure of Database Tables (continued)

Table: Products		
Field Name	*Data Type*	*Size*
ProductID	AutoNumber (Long)	4
CategoryID	number (Long)	4
Make	Text	50
Model	Text	50
SerialNumber	Text	50
Description	Text	250
Picture	Text	250
AuctionID	Number (Long)	4
Thumbnail	Text	250

Other than the primary key, the Auctions table contains the name, location, and dates for the auction. The Categories table contains the description of the category. The Products table contains the make, model, serial number, and description of the product. Further, it has a Picture field where users can enter the path and filename of the product picture and a Thumbnail field where users can enter the path and filename of a thumbnail picture of a product. The thumbnail (a small version of the product picture) will appear instead of the full-size product picture when multiple products are displayed, minimizing download time. If users want to examine a product more closely, they can click the thumbnail to see the full-size picture.

Planning the Folder Structure

After extensive discussion, your team has decided to design the folder structure for storing the templates and pictures as follows:

- The home page and all the other templates used by customers will be in the main folder or the root folder of the Web site.

- The database will be stored in a subfolder named Database.

- Product pictures will be stored in a subfolder named Pictures, and the thumbnails will be stored in a subfolder named Thumbnails.

- The templates used for administering the Web site will be in a subfolder of the root folder named Admin.

- Graphics associated with the user interface will be in their respective folders.

In addition, the Data Disk contains a subfolder in the root folder named Solutions for the templates that you would create in the root folder. There is also a subfolder in the Admin folder named Solutions for the templates that you would create for administering the Web site. As mentioned previously, look at these solutions only when you encounter a difficult task.

11

Making an ODBC Connection to the Database

When designing a data-driven Web site, you have to set up an Open Database Connectivity (ODBC) connection. If necessary, set up an ODBC connection named your_username_Nothebys to the database. The database file named Nothebys.com is in the Database subfolder of the Chapter 11 folder on your Data Disk. See Chapter 6 for more details about setting up an ODBC connection.

BROWSING PRODUCTS REQUIREMENT

When users click the Products hyperlink in the navigation menu, they should be able to browse all the product categories and then find detailed information about the products that interest them. All the product categories should be displayed in a two-column table, as shown in Figure 11-6. Only those categories that currently have products available for auction are to be displayed.

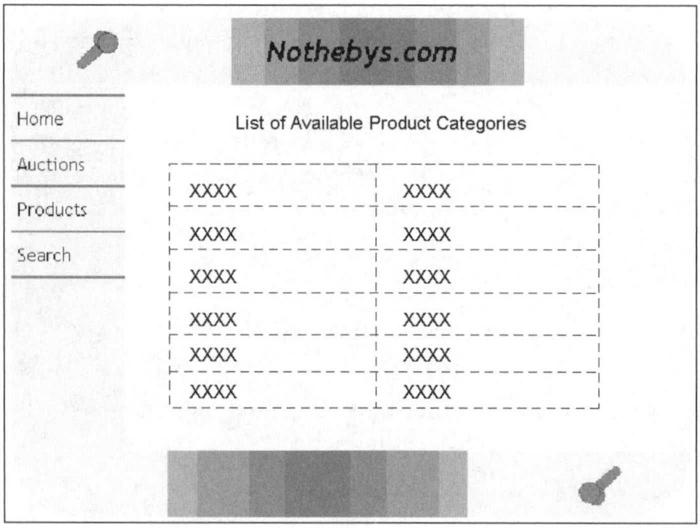

Figure 11-6   Web page design for displaying all product categories

You have decided to approach the program logic as shown in Figures 11-7 and 11-8.

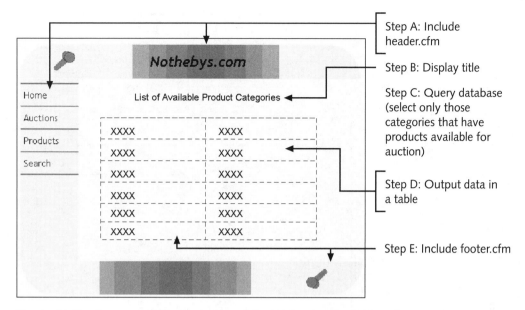

Step A: Include header.cfm

Step B: Display title

Step C: Query database (select only those categories that have products available for auction)

Step D: Output data in a table

Step E: Include footer.cfm

Figure 11-7   Program logic for design of the Web page for listing all categories

11

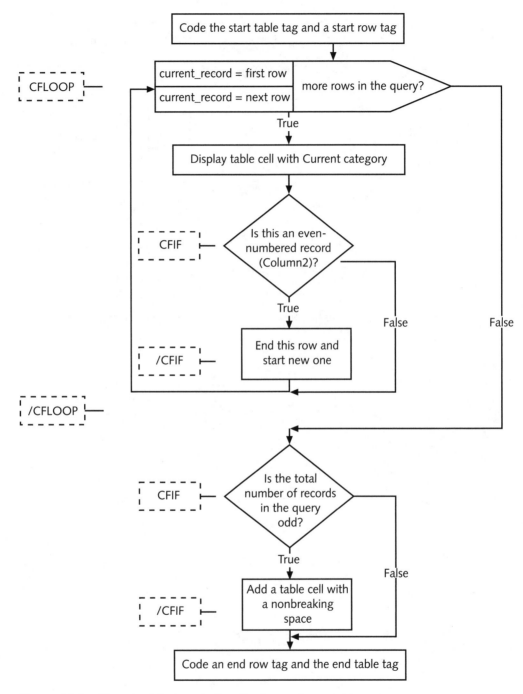

Figure 11-8   Flowchart for generating the two-column table

In the following exercise, you perform the steps described in Figures 11-7 and 11-8.

To create a Web page that displays all product categories in a two-column table:

1. Start ColdFusion Studio.

2. Click **File** on the menu bar, and then click **New**.

3. Click **Blank Document**, and then click **OK**.

4. Write the CFML to include the header.cfm template (Step A in Figure 11-7).

```
<cfinclude template="header.cfm">
```

5. Include the title for the template (Step B in Figure 11-7).

```
<font face="Trebuchet MS" size="+1">
<p align="center">List of Available Product Categories
</p>
</font>
```

   Note that Trebuchet MS is the primary font in the Nothebys Web page design.

6. Write a CFQUERY to extract all categories and their IDs from the Categories table that have products available for auction (Step C in Figure 11-7). The easiest way to do this is to join the Categories table and the Products table in the WHERE clause and select a Category from the Categories table, as in the following code:

```
<cfquery datasource="your_username_Nothebys"
name="getCategories">
SELECT DISTINCT Category, Categories.CategoryID FROM
Categories, Products
    WHERE Products.CategoryID = Categories.CategoryID
    ORDER BY Category
</cfquery>
```

7. For completing Step D in Figure 11-7, follow the flowchart in Figure 11-8.

   a. Code the start table tag and a start row tag. Set the width of the table at **489**.

   b. Create a query loop and display the category in a table cell. Use the Trebuchet MS font for the display.

   c. Use a CFIF statement to display an end row tag and start a new row after the loop loops the second time, the fourth time, and so on. For even-numbered records, expression CurrentRow MOD 2 is 0. Type the following code to achieve the above:

```
<cfif CurrentRow MOD 2 IS 0>
    </tr>
    <tr>
</cfif>
```

   d. Type the code to close the Query loop.

11

e. Once all the categories are displayed in the above manner, there are two possibilities. If the query selected an even number of categories, then the table is full; if it selected an odd number of categories, the second cell in the last row is empty. Use a CFIF statement to check whether the number of categories returned by the query is odd by evaluating the condition query_name.RecordCount MOD 2 EQ 1. If the number of categories is odd (true), add a table cell with   as its data. End the CFIF statement. Type the following code:

```
<cfif getCategories.RecordCount MOD 2 EQ 1>
    <td> </td>
</cfif>
```

f. End the row and the table.

8. Include footer.cfm (Step E in Figure 11-7) to complete the template.

```
<cfinclude template="footer.cfm">
```

9. Save your file as **listAllCategories.cfm** in the Chapter11 folder on your Data Disk.

10. Start your Web browser, and open **listAllCategories.cfm**. It should look similar to the page illustrated in Figure 11-9. If necessary, fix any errors before continuing.

Figure 11-9 Web page produced by listAllCategories.cfm

Now that you have created a template for extracting all product categories for available products and displayed the results in a two-column table, you can add a hyperlink to the navigation menu. Users can click this link to list the product categories.

To create a hyperlink to the template for listing all categories in the navigation menu:

1. Switch to ColdFusion Studio, and open **header.cfm** in the Chapter11 folder on your Data Disk.

2. Select **Products** on line 20, and create a hyperlink to listAllCategories.cfm, as shown in Figure 11-10.

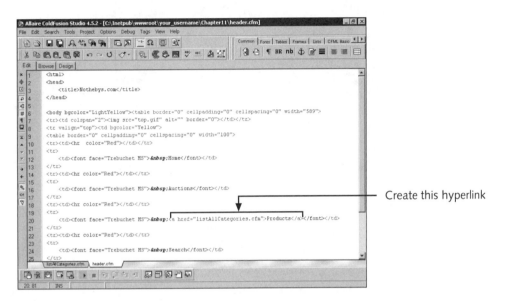

Figure 11-10   Create a hyperlink to Products in header.cfm

3. Select **Home** on line 12, and create a hyperlink to index.cfm.

4. Click the **Save** button on the Standard toolbar to save your template.

5. Switch to your Web browser, and open **index.cfm** in the Chapter 11 folder. Products and Home are now hyperlinks in the navigation menu. See Figure 11-11.

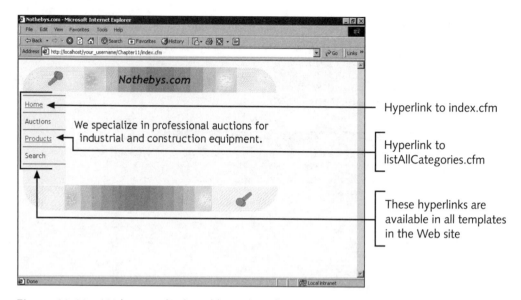

Figure 11-11   Web page displayed by index.cfm

6. Click the **Products** hyperlink to verify that it works.

7. Click the **Home** hyperlink to verify that it works.

You have successfully added hyperlinks to the navigation menu. Note that these hyperlinks are part of the header.cfm file; therefore, they would be available in all templates that are to be designed for this site. Now you have to further modify the listAllCategories.cfm template so that each of the categories is a hyperlink to a list of all products within the category.

To create category hyperlinks:

1. Switch to ColdFusion Studio.

2. Click the document tab for **listAllCategories.cfm**, if necessary.

3. Write the following code to create a hyperlink to the category description:

```
<a href="listProductsInACategory.cfm?CategoryID=#Category
ID#">#Category#</a>
```

listProductsInACategory.cfm is the name of the template that will display all the products in a category. You will design this template in the next section. Notice that this template will receive a URL parameter named CategoryID and will display all the products in that category.

4. Click the **Save** button on the Standard toolbar to save the file.

5. Switch to your Web browser, click **Products**, refresh if necessary, and compare the Web page to Figure 11-12.

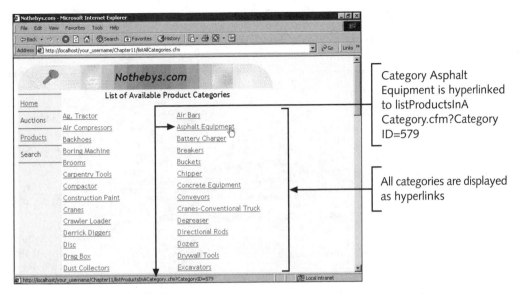

Figure 11-12   Web page produced by listAllCategories.cfm with hyperlinks

Creating a List Products Template

When a user clicks a category, the Web page should display a list of all products within that category. The planned output design for this page is shown in Figure 11-13.

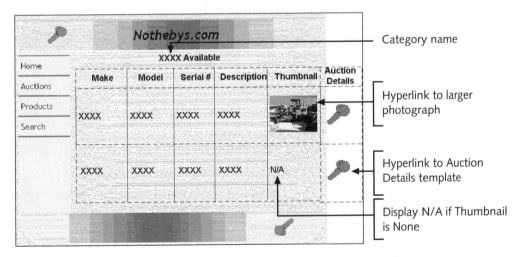

Figure 11-13   Planned layout of the Web page for listing all products in a category

You need to create a List Products template to show the information illustrated in Figure 11-13. The program logic for the List Products template is outlined in Figure 11-14.

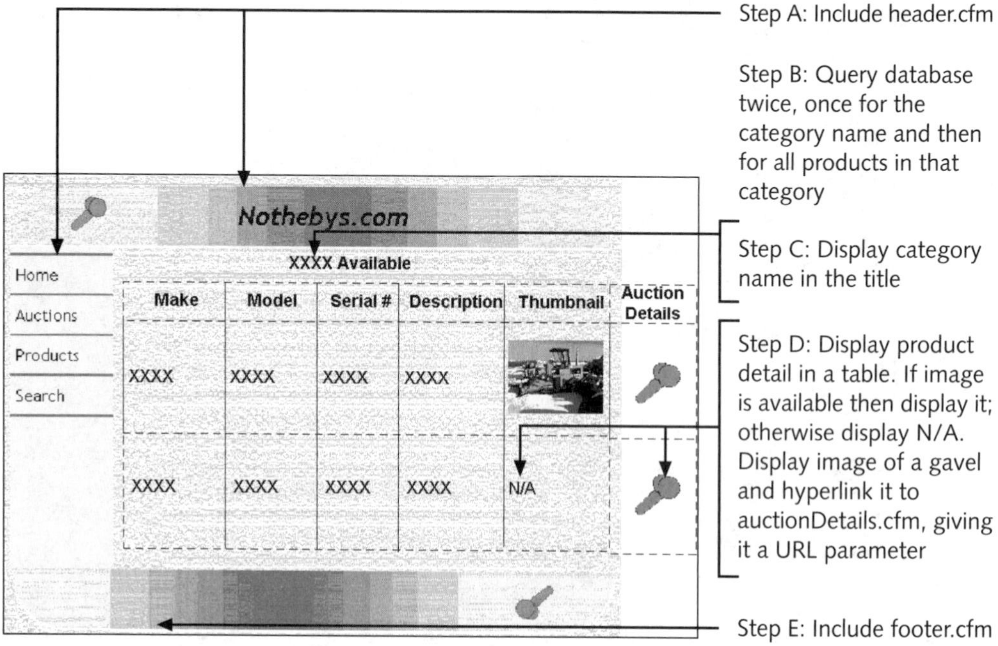

Figure 11-14   Program logic for listing all products in a category

To create a Web page that displays all products in a category with CategoryID passed as a URL parameter:

1. Switch to ColdFusion Studio.

2. Click **File** on the menu bar, and then click **New**.

3. Click **Blank Document**, and then click **OK**.

4. Follow Step A in Figure 11-14, and write the CFML for including the header.cfm template.

5. Follow Step B in Figure 11-14, and write two CFQUERIES—One named getCategory for extracting the category name, giving the CategoryID as a URL parameter, and another one named getProducts for extracting all product details where the CategoryID is the one passed as the URL parameter.

6. Follow Step C in Figure 11-14, and output the category name in the title in the same font as you used in the previous exercise. You may use the query_name.fieldname syntax because you need to output only one value.

7. Follow Step D in Figure 11-14, and display the product details in a table:

   a. Code the start table tag and the header row with its contents. Use appropriate attributes and values for the table.

   b. Code a query loop to loop over all the records selected from the Products table.

   c. Output the product details as table cells. Refer to the data model if necessary. Use a CFIF statement for the following: If the content of the Thumbnail is "None," display "N/A" as the contents in the cell; otherwise, display the image. Note that the image is in the Thumbnails subfolder in the Chapter11 folder. The image file for displaying the gavel is named gavel.gif, and it is in the Chapter11 folder. Set the border of both the images to 0.

   d. Every thumbnail image should be a hyperlink to the template that displays the larger photograph. Assume that the name of this template is largerPhoto.cfm and that it receives the name of the photograph as its argument. Hyperlink all thumbnails to largerPhoto.cfm?PhotoFile=filename. Assume that all products with thumbnails have photographs available. You have to use the URLEncodedFormat function, as described in earlier chapters, to make sure that all the characters in the filename are encoded properly.

   e. Hyperlink the gavel image to auctionDetails.cfm with a URL parameter named AuctionID. Use the AuctionID from the query output as the value for this parameter.

   f. Code the end table tag after closing the query loop.

8. Follow Step E in Figure 11-14, and include the footer.cfm template.

9. Save your file as **listProductsInACategory.cfm** in the Chapter 11 folder.

10. Switch to your Web browser, and click **Products**, if necessary.

11. Click the **Conveyors** hyperlink. See Figure 11-15. Correct any errors you receive.

11

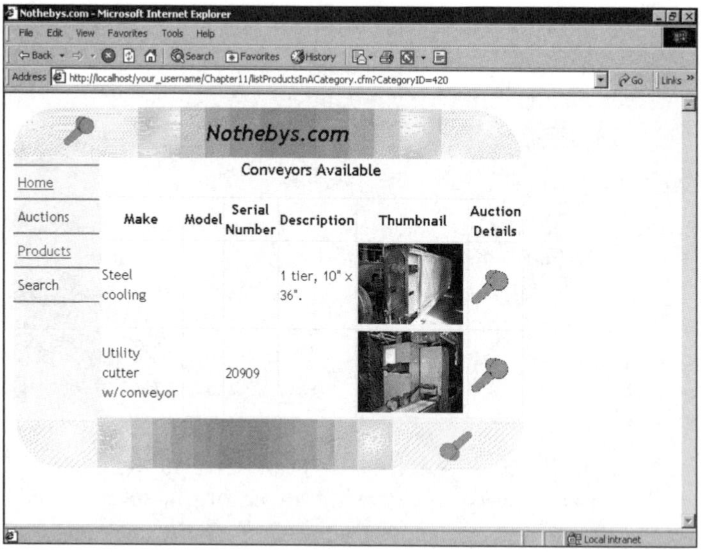

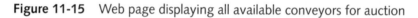

Figure 11-15   Web page displaying all available conveyors for auction

12. Click the **Back** button on the toolbar. Click any other hyperlink to test it.

To create the template for displaying the larger photograph:

1. Switch to ColdFusion Studio.

2. Click **File** on the menu bar, and then click **New**.

3. Click **Blank Document**, and click **OK**.

4. Use a CFINCLUDE tag, and include **header.cfm**.

5. Start a paragraph tag, and align its contents to the center.

6. Code an image tag, and set the value of its SRC attribute to **Pictures/<cfoutput>#URL.PhotoFile#</cfoutput>**.

7. End the paragraph tag.

8. Use a CFINCLUDE tag, and include footer.cfm.

9. Save the file as **largerPhoto.cfm** in the Chapter11 folder.

10. Switch to your Web browser, and open **index.cfm**.

11. Click **Products**.

12. Click **Air Bars**. See Figure 11-16.

13. Scroll down if necessary, and click the thumbnail for **Fuller & Johnson 7 hsp. Engine**. See Figure 11-17.

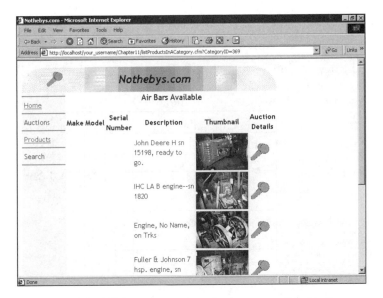

Figure 11-16   Web page produced when you click Air Bars

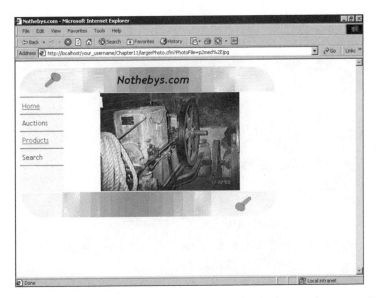

Figure 11-17   Web page showing the larger photo when you click the thumbnail

To create the template for displaying the auction details:

1. Switch to ColdFusion Studio.

2. Click **File** on the menu bar, and then click **New**.

3. Click **Blank Document**, and then click **OK**.

4. Use a CFINCLUDE tag, and include **header.cfm**.

5. Display the title as **Auction Details**.

6. Query the database, and Select all the fields from the Auctions table where the AuctionID is equal to the value of the URL parameter named AuctionID. Use getAuctionDetails as the name of the query.

7. Create a two-column by three-row table, and display the auction name, location, and the dates with appropriate labels in the first column. Right-justify the labels and left-justify the details. Set the table's width to **485** pixels, border size to **1**, border color to **Yellow**, and the cell spacing to **0**. See Figure 11-18.

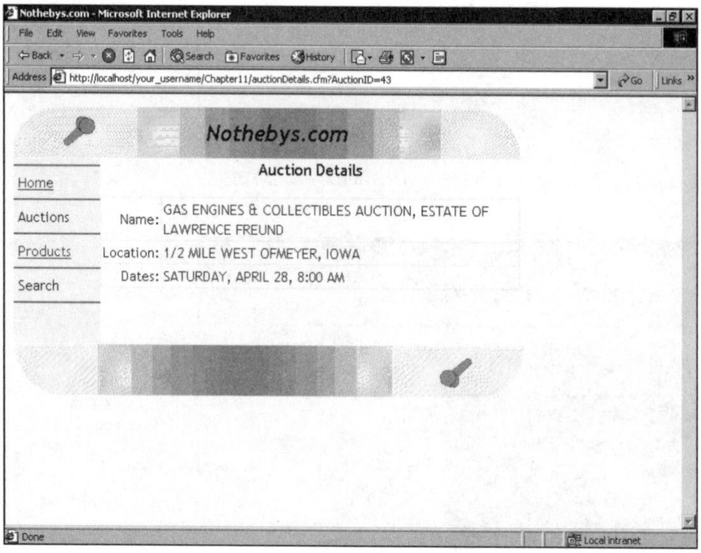

Figure 11-18   Web page with auction details

8. Use a CFINCLUDE tag, and include **footer.cfm**.

9. Save the file as **auctionDetails.cfm** in the Chapter11 folder.

10. Switch to your Web browser, and then click **Home**.

11. Click **Products**.

12. Click **Air Bars**.

13. Click the **gavel** next to Fuller & Johnson 7 hsp. Engine. The auction details should be displayed, as shown in Figure 11-18.

14. Close all open programs.

BROWSING AUCTIONS REQUIREMENT

When users click the Auctions hyperlink in the navigation menu, they should be able to browse all the current auctions and then select the product categories and products that interest them. The auctions will be displayed in a table, as shown in Figure 11-19.

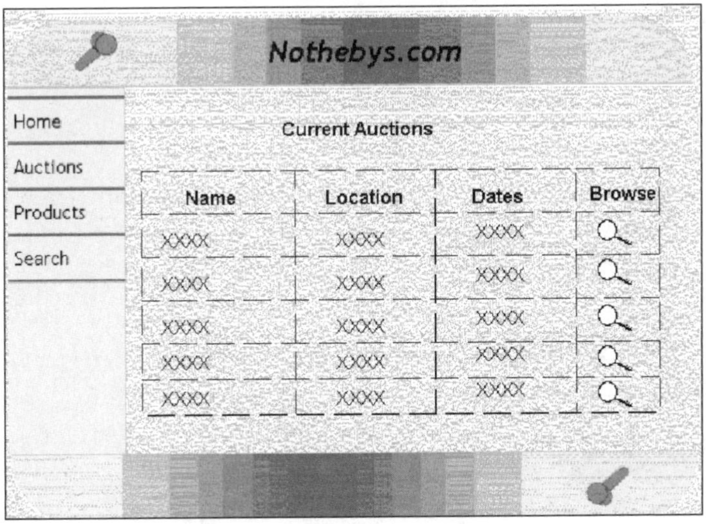

Figure 11-19   Web page design for displaying all auctions

To create a Web page that displays current auctions:

1. Start ColdFusion Studio.

2. Click **File** on the menu bar, and then click **New**.

3. Click **Blank Document**, and then click **OK**.

4. Use a CFINCLUDE tag, and include the **header.cfm** template.

5. Display the **Current Auctions** title.

6. Write a CFQUERY to select all the records from the Auctions table in the your_username_Nothebys datasource named getAuctions.

7. Design a four-column table. Set its width to **485**, its border to 1, its border color to **Yellow**, and its cell spacing to **0**.

8. Use the following names as the column headers: **Name**, **Location**, **Dates**, and **Browse**. Use an appropriate font.

9. Design a query loop to loop over all the records selected from the Auctions table.

10. Output the values from those records in a table row using an appropriate font.

11. Embed the **mGlass.gif** image in the Browse column, hyperlink it to the categoriesByAuction.cfm template, and pass in the AuctionID as a URL parameter. Set the border size of the image to **0** for aesthetic purposes.

12. Save the file as **listAuctions.cfm** in the Chapter11 folder.

13. Switch to **header.cfm** by clicking its document tab, or, if necessary, open it for editing.

14. Hyperlink the Auctions menu item to listAuctions.cfm.

15. Save the file.

16. Start your Web browser, and then click the **Home** hyperlink. Refresh if necessary. Notice that Auctions is a hyperlink now.

17. Click the **Auctions** hyperlink. See Figure 11-20.

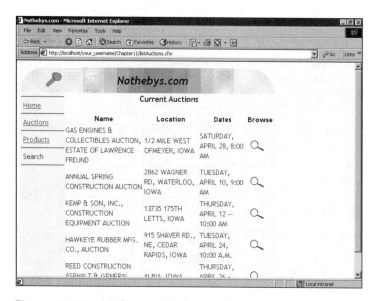

Figure 11-20   Web page displaying all current auctions

You have successfully created a Web page for displaying all current auctions and hyperlinked this template to the navigation menu. Because this hyperlink is part of the header.cfm template, it will be available in all the Web pages of this system.

When the user clicks the Browse auction image for a particular auction, all the product categories available at that auction should be displayed similarly to the Web page that displays all the product categories when the Products hyperlink is clicked. The easiest way to design this template is by modifying the listAllCategories.cfm template to restrict the data extracted to the auction specified as the URL parameter.

To design the Web page that displays categories specific to an auction:

1. Switch to ColdFusion Studio, and close all open documents.

2. Open **listAllCategories.cfm** from the Chapter11 folder.

3. Save this template as **categoriesByAuction.cfm**.

4. Modify the SQL SELECT statement, and restrict the selection by adding an additional clause:

   ```
   AND Products.AuctionID = #URL.AuctionID#
   ```

5. Save the template.

6. Switch to your Web browser, and click the **Home** link.

7. Click the **Auctions** link.

8. Click the **magnifying glass** in the ANNUAL SPRING CONSTRUCTION AUCTION row. See Figure 11-21.

Figure 11-21 Web page displaying categories specific to an auction

Notice that the hyperlink for displaying the products still points to listProductsInACategory.cfm. See Figure 11-22.

11

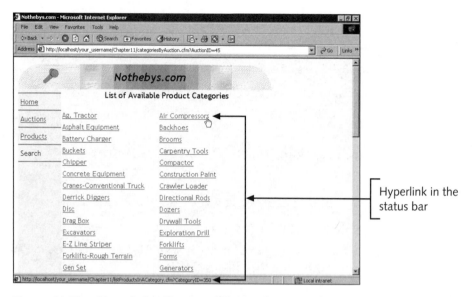

Figure 11-22   Hyperlink still points to listProductsInACategory.cfm

This template lists all products in a category whether they are being auctioned in the current auction or not. This hyperlink has to be changed so that all products that belong to a particular category and to a particular auction are displayed. This new template needs two URL parameters, CategoryID and AuctionID.

To design and hyperlink a template that displays products within a particular category and a particular auction:

1. Switch to ColdFusion Studio, and open **categoriesByAuction.cfm**, if necessary.

2. Modify the HREF attribute for the anchor tag to:

   ```
   productsByAuction.cfm?CategoryID=#CategoryID#&AuctionID=#
   URL.AuctionID#
   ```

   Note that the #CategoryID# is a variable from the query and #URL.AuctionID# is a variable from the URL.

3. Save the template.

4. The easiest way to design the productsByAuction.cfm template is by modifying the listProductsInACategory.cfm template. Open **listProductsInACategory.cfm**.

5. Save it as **productsByAuction.cfm**.

6. Add a set of CFQUERY tags to extract the name of the auction.

7. Modify the SQL SELECT statement that extracts data from the Products table, and restrict the record selected further by adding the clause:

   ```
   AND AuctionID = #URL.AuctionID#
   ```

8. Add an additional table row below the current title and display the name of the auction.

9. Delete the sixth column in the table. There is no need for an auction details hyperlink because the user knows at which auctions these products are being auctioned.

10. Save your template.

11. Switch to your Web browser, click **Auctions**, and click the **image** to browse the ANNUAL SPRING CONSTRUCTION AUCTION.

12. Click the **Excavators** hyperlink. See Figure 11-23.

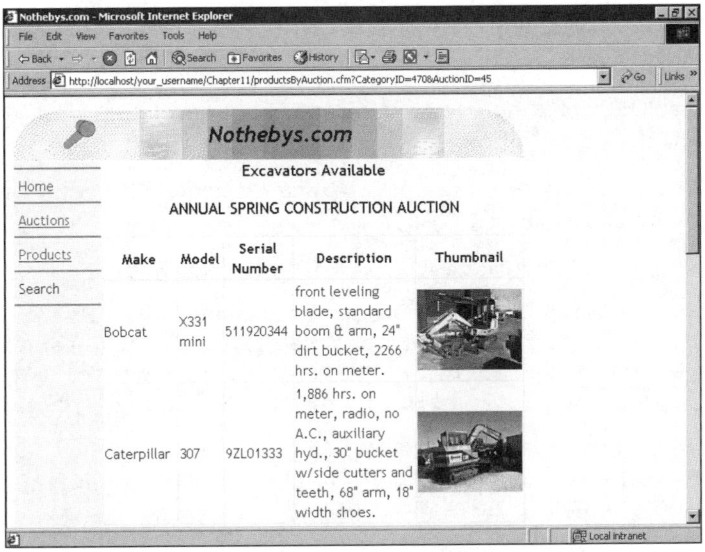

Figure 11-23 Web page displaying all excavators available at the annual spring construction auction

13. Close all open programs.

You have successfully created a Web page that displays all products that belong to a particular category and a particular auction.

SEARCHING PRODUCTS REQUIREMENT

To complete the user interface design, you must add a feature that lets users search for products. The search item in the navigation menu should be linked to a form that allows users to search the database and displays a list of products that match the search keyword they specify. You use a two-step process to implement this requirement. First, you design the search form, and then you design the form handler.

The search form is a simple form with one text box, a caption "Enter keyword:", and a Submit button with a value "Search." Use processSearch.cfm as the name for the form handler.

To design a search form:

1. Start ColdFusion Studio.

2. Click **File** on the menu bar, and then click **New**.

3. Click **Blank Document**, and click **OK**.

4. Use the CFINCLUDE tag, and include **header.cfm**.

5. Type the HTML for generating a horizontal rule, and set its COLOR attribute to the value **Yellow**.

6. Display the title **Search for products** in Trebuchet MS font in a paragraph aligned in the center. Make the title boldface.

7. Type the HTML for generating a horizontal rule, and set its COLOR attribute to the value **Yellow**.

8. Type the CFML for a ColdFusion form, and set its ACTION attribute to **processSearch.cfm** and its NAME attribute to **sForm**.

9. Type the following to create a text box and a Submit button:

```
<p align="center"><font face="Trebuchet MS">Enter
keyword: <cfinput type="Text" required="Yes" message="
Please enter a keyword..." name="searchKeyword"> 
<input type="submit" value="Search"></font></p>
```

Note that you are implementing a data completeness check on the text box so that the user enters a keyword prior to clicking the Submit button. The form is aligned horizontally in the center.

10. Close the ColdFusion form.

11. Type the HTML for generating a horizontal rule, and set its COLOR attribute to the value **Yellow**.

12. Use the CFINCLUDE tag, and include the footer.cfm template.

13. Save the file as **searchForm.cfm** in the Chapter11 folder.

14. Open **header.cfm** for editing.

15. Hyperlink the Search item in the navigation bar to the template that you just created. Save the file with the changes.

16. Switch to your Web browser, type **http://localhost/your_username/ Chapter11/index.cfm** in the Address text box, and press the **Enter** key. Notice that the Search item is now an anchor.

17. Click **Search**. See Figure 11-24.

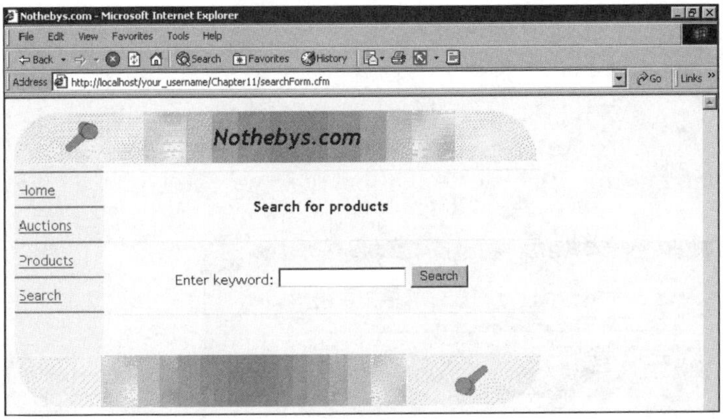

Figure 11-24   Web page displaying the search form

Your next task is to design the form handler. The results it displays should be similar to the Web page that displays the list of products. To do so, you modify the listProductsInACategory.cfm template by modifying the SQL to implement the search.

To design the search form handler by modifying the Web page for listing products:

1. Switch to ColdFusion Studio, and open **listProductsInACategory.cfm**.

2. Save the file as **processSearch.cfm**.

3. Delete the query for extracting the Category name.

4. Modify the SQL for selecting products as follows:

```
SELECT * FROM Products
    WHERE    Description LIKE '%#form.searchKeyword#%' OR
             Make LIKE '%#form.searchKeyword#%' OR
             Model LIKE '%#form.searchKeyword#%' OR
             SerialNumber LIKE '%#form.searchKeyword#%'
```

Recall that the LIKE operator allows you to search databases for similar items by using wildcards. Also it performs a case-insensitive comparison. All the products whose description, make, model, or serial number contain the search keyword will be displayed.

5. Use a CFIF statement, and check to see whether the search produces any results. If the record count of the query object is 0, then display the message "No matching results found, go back and try again…"

6. Enclose the title and the table for the results in the CFELSE part of the CFIF.

7. Modify the title to:

```
Your search for "<cfoutput>#form.searchKeyword#
</cfoutput>" produced the following results…
```

8. Close the CFIF statement.

9. Save your template.

10. Switch to your Web browser, and then click the **Search** hyperlink if necessary. Make sure the search feature responds correctly if users enter an item not included in the database. Search for **uvwxyz**. See Figure 11-25.

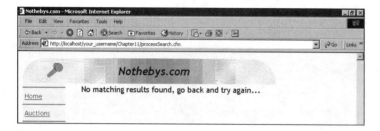

Figure 11-25   Search Web page with no matching results

11. Click **Search** and enter **deere**. See Figure 11-26.

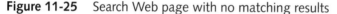

Figure 11-26   Web page displaying search results

12. Close all open programs.

You have successfully created a system for searching through a database by specifying keywords and then displaying the results.

BUILDING THE ADMINISTRATION TOOL

With any database-driven Web site, administrators of the Web site maintain the data in the database. Typically, the admin tool consists of subsystems for adding, editing, and deleting records in database tables; uploading and deleting images associated with content that changes; routines for tracking the usage of resources; decision support tools; and other maintenance activities.

For the Nothebys site, you must also develop an admin tool. Start by creating basic data-maintenance routines for all the tables in the database and managing the files associated with product pictures and thumbnails. You decide to develop this part of the application in a folder named Admin, as mentioned in an earlier section. Similarly to the structure of the main site, you want to use a header.cfm template and a footer.cfm template for inclusion in all Web pages. These templates are provided for you. The main document in this application is admin.cfm, and it is available to you on your Data Disk in the Chapter11\Admin folder. Figure 11-27 shows the admin.cfm Web page.

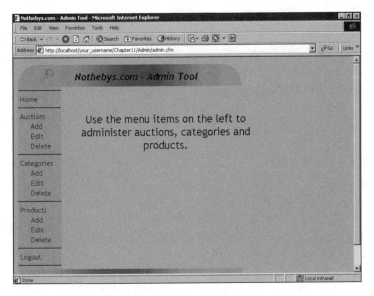

Figure 11-27   Web page produced by admin.cfm

The Web page produced by admin.cfm is implemented by including the header.cfm, a properly formatted paragraph that forms the primary content in the template, and the footer.cfm template at bottom. The navigation menu is part of the header.cfm template. Similarly to the main site, the template for any other document in the admin tool would be as shown below:

```
<cfinclude template="header.cfm">
HTML and CFML specific to the admin template.
<cfinclude template="footer.cfm">
```

Guidelines for Implementing the User Interface

The user interface, or Web page design, has to be consistent across the entire application. The figures shown in this chapter use the following guidelines:

- All tables are aligned in the center, have the border size set to 1, the cell spacing set to 0, and the border color set to 66CCFF.

- All horizontal rules have the color set to 66CCFF.

- All text is displayed in the Trebuchet MS font.

- Headings are bold and aligned in the center using a P tag.

- Forms are always designed in tables.

- Captions for form controls are aligned to the right, and the form controls are aligned to the left.

- Submit buttons are enclosed in cells that span multiple columns and are aligned in the center.

- A horizontal rule appears at the bottom.

The other requirements for the admin tool are presented in the following sections.

Adding the Auctions Administration Requirement

You use the auctions part of the navigation menu to perform basic data maintenance operations on the Auctions table in the database by using Add, Edit, and Delete menu items.

Add Auction Requirement

The add auction subsystem allows a user to add a record to the Auctions table in the database. The primary key in the Auctions table is an auto-number field. The name, location, and dates are the other attributes. When the user clicks the Add item under the Auction category in the navigation menu, the ColdFusion Server should execute the addAuctionScreen1.cfm template and display a form, as shown in Figure 11-28.

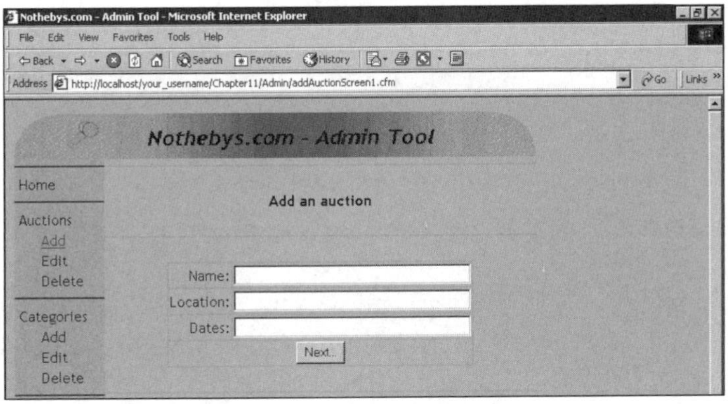

Figure 11-28   Web page displayed when a user clicks the Add item in the Auctions category

To design the addAuctionScreen1.cfm template:

1. Start ColdFusion Studio.

2. Click **File** on the menu bar, and then click **New**.

3. Click **Blank Document**, and then click **OK**.

4. Type the CFML to include the **header.cfm** template.

5. Display the title **Add an auction** according to the guidelines specified in the previous user interface requirement.

6. Design a ColdFusion form with an action set to **addAuctionScreen2.cfm**.

7. For inserting a record into the Auctions table, the data to be collected has to correspond to the table structure in the Auctions table. Note that the controls have to be placed in a table formatted according to the user interface guidelines above. Implement the controls listed in Table 11-2.

Table 11-2   Controls in the addAuctionScreen1.cfm Template

Label	Control Name	Type	Size	Value	Validation
Name:	AuctionName	Text	40		Completeness
Location:	AuctionLocation	Text	40		Completeness
Dates:	AuctionDates	Text	40		Completeness
		Submit		Next...	

8. Close the form.

9. Insert a **horizontal rule**, and include the **footer.cfm** template.

10. Save the file as **addAuctionScreen1.cfm** in the Chapter11/Admin folder.

11. Open **header.cfm**, and hyperlink the **Add** item under the Auctions category to addAuctionScreen1.cfm.

12. Save the file.

13. Start your Web browser, and then open **Chapter11\Admin\admin.cfm**.

14. Click the **Add** item in the Auction category to see the Web page displaying the form. See Figure 11-28.

The next step is to design the form handler for inserting the data entered by the users into the Auctions table. Because the form controls and the fields in the table match exactly, you can use a CFINSERT tag to insert the data into the table. The primary key (AuctionID) is an auto-number field and is automatically generated by Access. Typically, this value is the highest value of the AuctionID + 1. This template displays a confirmation message, as shown in Figure 11-29.

Figure 11-29 Web page displayed when an auction is inserted

To design the form handler (addAuctionScreen2.cfm) for inserting an auction:

1. Switch to ColdFusion Studio.

2. Click **File** on the menu bar, and then click **New**.

3. Click **Blank Document**, and then click **OK**.

4. Type the CFML to include the **header.cfm** template.

5. Type the CFINSERT tag for inserting the user-entered form data into the database table.

   ```
   <cfinsert datasource="your_username_Nothebys" formfields=
   "AuctionName, AuctionLocation, AuctionDates" tablename=
   "Auctions">
   ```

6. Copy the title and the table from the addAuctionScreen1.cfm template and paste it into the current document.

7. Modify the title, as shown in Figure 11-29.

8. Modify the contents of the table, and display the values form.AuctionName, form.AuctionLocation, and form.AuctionDates by using CFOUTPUT tags.

9. Delete the table row containing the Submit button.

10. Insert a **horizontal rule**, and include the **footer.cfm** template.

11. Save the file as **addAuctionScreen2.cfm** in the Chapter11/Admin folder.

12. Switch to your Web browser, and then click **Auctions – Add**, if necessary.

13. Type **Mid West Implement Co – Farm Equipment Auction** in the Name field.

14. Type **123 Main Street, Cedar Rapids** in the Location field.

15. Type **May 12-13, 9:00 AM** in the Dates field.

16. Click **Next**.

   The ColdFusion Server inserts this record and displays a confirmation Web page, as shown in Figure 11-29.

You have successfully designed a form handler for inserting an auction.

Edit Auction Requirement

The edit auction subsystem allows a user to edit a record in the Auctions table. First, a list of available auctions is displayed for the user to select one for editing. Once the user selects an auction, data for the auction is displayed in a form and the user is allowed to edit the data. When the form is submitted, the database is updated accordingly. This requirement has to be implemented by using three screens. The first screen displayed when the user clicks the Auctions – Edit hyperlink is shown in Figure 11-30.

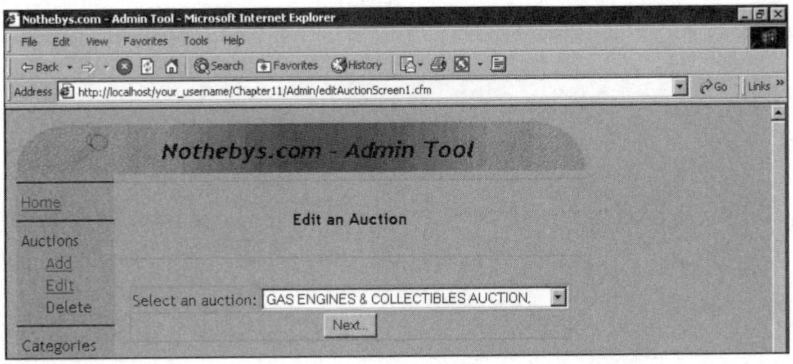

Figure 11-30 Web page produced by editAuctionScreen1.cfm

To design a screen for displaying existing auctions in a select box:

1. Switch to ColdFusion Studio.

2. Click **File** on the menu bar, and then click **New**.

3. Click **Blank Document,** and then click **OK**.

4. Type the CFML to include the **header.cfm** template.

5. Type the following code to design a CFQUERY to extracts all records from the Auctions table:

```
<cfquery datasource="your_username_Nothebys"
name="getAuctions">
SELECT * FROM Auctions
</cfquery>
```

6. Write the HTML to display the title **Edit an Auction** according to the user interface guidelines.

7. Design a CFFORM with the action attribute set to **editAuctionScreen2.cfm**.

   To allow the user to select a record for editing, all the available auctions have to be displayed in a select box using a Query loop. Even though the name for the auction is displayed, the value submitted by the control should be the AuctionID because it is the primary key for the Auctions table. Implement the controls shown in Table 11-3 in the form. Notice that the text field for the auctionName is very long and only the first 35 characters will be displayed for aesthetic reasons.

Table 11-3   Controls in the editAuctionScreen1.cfm Template

Label	Control Name	Type	Value	Display
Select an auction:	AuctionID	Select	AuctionID	Left(AuctionName,35)
		Submit	Next…	

8. Close the form.

9. Insert a **horizontal rule**, and include the **footer.cfm** template.

10. Save the file as **editAuctionScreen1.cfm** in the Chapter11/Admin folder.

11. Open **header.cfm**, and hyperlink the Edit item under the Auctions category to the above template.

12. Save the file.

13. Switch to your Web browser, and then open **admin.cfm**.

14. Click the **Edit** item in the Auction category to see the Web page displaying the form for selecting an auction.

You have successfully created a form for selecting an auction for editing.

Once an auction is selected and the form is submitted for the next step, the selected auction's record has to be extracted from the Auctions table and its data displayed for editing. Once the changes are made and the second form is submitted, the changes are committed to the database. The third template needs the AuctionID of the selected auction for the purposes of updating data. Because there is a need for passing data from the first screen to the third screen, you have to use session variables. To be able to use session variables, you must turn on session management and use the application.cfm template for implementing the application framework.

To enable session management in the admin application:

1. Switch to ColdFusion Studio.

2. Click **File** on the menu bar, and then click **New**.

3. Click **Blank Document**, and then click **OK**.

4. Type **<cfapplication name="NothebysAdmin" sessionmanagement= "Yes" sessiontimeout=#CreateTimeSpan(0,0,20,0)#>** and press the **Enter** key.

5. Save the template as **application.cfm** in the Admin subfolder, and then close the document.

You have successfully created an application.cfm file that enables session management for all the ColdFusion documents in the Admin folder.

The form for editing the auction data should be identical to the form used for adding an auction. See Figure 11-31.

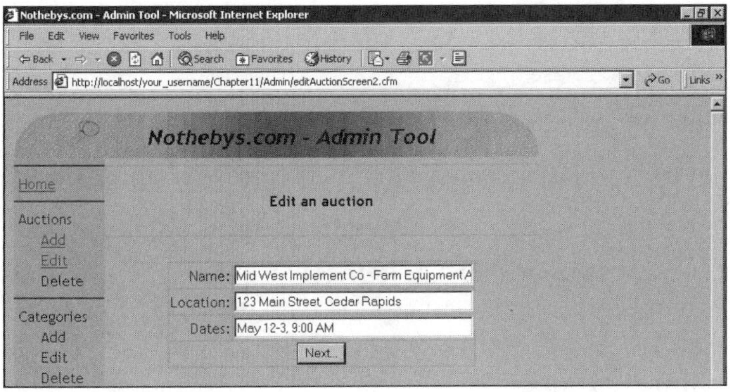

Figure 11-31 Web page design for editAuctionScreen2.cfm

You can simplify the process of creating this form by copying addAuctionScreen1.cfm and modifying it.

To create editAuctionScreen2.cfm by copying and modifying addAuctionScreen1.cfm:

1. In ColdFusion Studio, open **addAuctionScreen1.cfm**, if necessary.

2. Save it as **editAuctionScreen2.cfm**.

3. As mentioned previously, this subsystem requires three screens. Because you must pass data from the first screen to the third, you have to use a session variable to store the AuctionID of the selected auction. Remember that you have to lock code that manipulates session variables. Type the following code starting on line 1:

```
<cflock scope="SESSION" timeout="20">
<cfset session.AuctionID = form.AuctionID>
</cflock>
```

4. Type the following code to extract data for the selected auction:

```
<cfquery datasource="your_username_Nothebys"
name="getAuction">
SELECT * FROM Auctions WHERE AuctionID = #form.AuctionID#
</cfquery>
```

5. Change the title to **Edit an auction**.

6. Change the ACTION attribute for the CFFORM to **editAuctionScreen3.cfm**.

7. Display the name of the auction in the text box by adding a value attribute to the auctionName control as **value="#getAuction.AuctionName#"**.

8. Display the location of the auction in the location text box by adding a value attribute as **value="#getAuction.AuctionLocation#"**.

9. Display the dates for the auction by adding a value attribute to the auctionDates control as **value="#getAuction.AuctionDates#"**.

10. You do not need to change any of the other attributes. Save your file.

11. Switch to your Web browser, and then open **admin.cfm**.

13. Select **Mid West Implement Co – Farm Equipment Auction**, and then click **Next**. Recall that you are displaying only the first 35 characters of the name.

12. Click **Auctions – Edit**.

The ColdFusion Server extracts data for the selected auction and displays it in a form, as shown in Figure 11-31.

You have successfully created a template for extracting a record from the Auctions table and displaying the data in a form for enabling a user to edit the data.

Finally, the third screen in the edit auction process updates the appropriate records and displays a confirmation message, as shown in Figure 11-32.

Figure 11-32   Web page showing an update confirmation message

The logic for implementing the update is similar to the logic that you used for inserting the record. A quick way to design the form handler for updating an auction is by copying and modifying the form handler for inserting an auction.

To create editAuctionScreen3.cfm by copying and modifying addAuctionScreen2.cfm:

1. Switch to ColdFusion Studio, and open **addAuctionScreen2.cfm**.

2. Save it as **editAuctionScreen3.cfm**.

3. Delete the code for inserting a record.

4. Type the following code for updating a record in the place of the code for inserting a record:

```
<cflock scope="session" timeout="20">
<cfquery datasource="your_username_Nothebys">
UPDATE Auctions
SET AuctionName = '#form.AuctionName#',
AuctionLocation = '#form.AuctionLocation#',
AuctionDates = '#form.AuctionDates#'
WHERE
AuctionID = #session.AuctionID#
</cfquery>
</cflock>
```

Remember that you used a session variable to keep track of the auction that is being edited. You are using that variable in the WHERE clause of the SQL statement. This is the reason you cannot use a CFUPDATE tag here. Also, because you are using a session variable, you are locking the code in the session scope.

5. Change the title to **The following auction has been edited successfully....**

6. You do not have to make any changes to the rest of the template because it is just echoing the form input received. Save your file again.

7. Switch to your Web browser, and then open **admin.cfm**.

11

8. Click **Auctions – Edit**.

9. Select **Mid West Implement Co – Farm Equipment Auction**, and then click **Next**.

10. The ColdFusion Server should extract data for the selected auction and display it in a form, as shown in Figure 11-31.

11. Change the address of the auction to **1234 Main Street**, and then click **Next**.

    The ColdFusion Server executes **editAuctionScreen3.cfm** and produces a confirmation message after updating the data, as shown in Figure 11-32.

12. Close all programs.

You have successfully implemented a capability for editing an auction in the Nothebys admin tool.

You will create the feature for deleting an auction after you design the category delete and product delete features. Recall that the Products table is related to the Auctions and Categories tables. A product belongs to a category and is auctioned at a particular auction. Before deleting an auction, you have to make sure that all the products associated with that auction are deleted. Therefore, you should first add the feature for deleting products before adding the feature to delete auctions. And you must first design the capability for adding and editing categories and products before you can delete them.

Adding the Categories Administration Requirement

Product categories are used to simplify the organization and retrieval of products. You must create the product categories before you create the product data. Similarly to the auctions capability, your clients will perform basic data maintenance operations on the Categories table in the database by using the Add, Edit, and Delete menu items.

Add Category Requirement

The add category subsystem allows a user to add a record to the Categories table in the database. The primary key in the Categories table is an auto-number field. The Categories table also includes a Category text field where users can enter a description of the category. When the user clicks the Add item under the Categories category in the navigation menu, the ColdFusion Server should execute the addCategoryScreen1.cfm template and display a form, as shown in Figure 11-33. The capabilities of this system are similar to the one for administering the auctions. A productive way of designing it would be by copying and modifying the templates from the Auctions system.

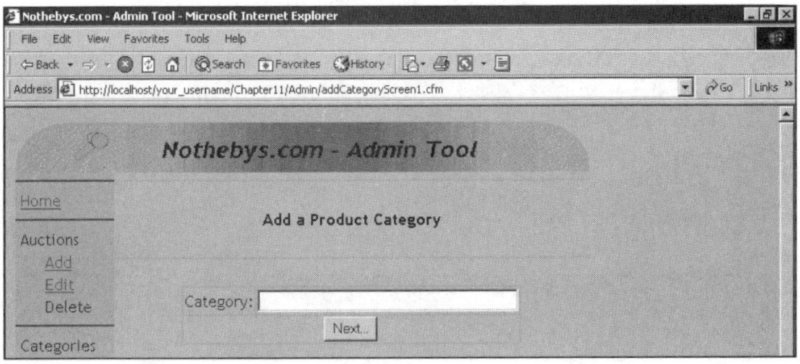

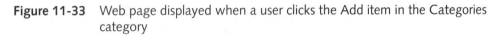

Figure 11-33   Web page displayed when a user clicks the Add item in the Categories category

To design the addCategoryScreen1.cfm template:

1. Start ColdFusion Studio, if necessary.

2. Open **addAuctionScreen1.cfm**.

3. Save it in the same folder as **addCategoryScreen1.cfm**.

4. Modify the title to **Add a Product Category**.

5. Change the ACTION attribute of the form to **addCategoryScreen2.cfm**.

6. For inserting a record into the Categories table, the data to be collected has to correspond to the table structure in the Categories table. Delete two rows in the table and implement the controls shown in Table 11-4. Modify the error message appropriately.

Table 11-4   Controls in the addCategoryScreen1.cfm Template

Label	Control Name	Type	Size	Value	Validation
Category:	Category	Text	40		Completeness
		Submit		Next...	

7. Save the file again after making the changes shown in Table 11-4.

8. Open **header.cfm**, and hyperlink the Add item under the Categories category to addCategoryScreen1.cfm.

9. Save the **header.cfm** file.

10. Start your Web browser, and then open **admin.cfm**.

11. Click the **Add** item in the Categories category to see the Web page displaying the form, as shown in Figure 11-33.

11

You have successfully created a form for adding a product category.

Your next step is to design the form handler for actually inserting the data entered by the users into the Categories table. Because the form controls and the fields in the table match exactly, you can use a CFINSERT tag to insert the data into the table. The primary key (CategoryID) is an auto-number field and is generated automatically by Access. This template displays a confirmation message, as shown in Figure 11-34.

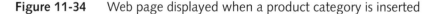

Figure 11-34 Web page displayed when a product category is inserted

To design the form handler (addCategoryScreen2.cfm) for inserting a category:

1. Switch to ColdFusion Studio.

2. Open **addAuctionScreen2.cfm**.

3. Save it as **addCategoryScreen2.cfm**.

4. Change the CFINSERT statement to **<cfinsert datasource="your_username_Nothebys" formfields="Category" tablename="Categories">** for inserting the data entered by the user in the form.

5. Modify the title, as shown in Figure 11-34.

6. Modify the contents of the table, and display the value form.Category by using CFOUTPUT tags.

7. Save the file again.

8. Start your Web browser, open **admin.cfm**, and then click **Categories – Add**, if necessary.

9. Type **Lawn Trimers** in the Category field. Note that the category is misspelled intentionally. You will correct that later in this section.

10. Click **Next**.

The ColdFusion Server inserts this record and displays a confirmation Web page, as shown in Figure 11-34.

You have successfully designed a form and a form handler for inserting a product category in the Nothebys admin tool.

Edit Category Requirement

The edit category subsystem allows a user to edit a record in the Categories table. First, a list of available categories is displayed for the user to select one for editing. Once the user selects a category, it is displayed in a form and the user is allowed to edit the data. When the form is submitted, the database is updated accordingly. Similarly to the edit auction feature, this requirement has to be implemented by using three screens. See Figures 11-35, 11-36, and 11-37.

Figure 11-35   Web page produced by editCategoryScreen1.cfm

11

Figure 11-36   Web page produced by editCategoryScreen2.cfm

Figure 11-37   Web page produced by editCategoryScreen3.cfm

Actually, most applications for editing records in a table would be structured similarly to this one and the one for editing auctions. A productive way of creating this application is to modify the three screens that you developed for editing auctions.

To design a screen for displaying existing categories in a select box by copying the one that displays auctions:

1. Switch to ColdFusion Studio.

2. Open **editAuctionScreen1.cfm**, and then save it as **editCategoryScreen1.cfm**.

3. Delete the query that extracts data from the Auctions table, and type

```
<cfquery datasource="your_username_Nothebys"
name="getCategories">
SELECT * FROM Categories ORDER BY Category
</cfquery>
```

to design a CFQUERY to extracts all records from the Categories table. Because the system can contain many product categories, order the list alphabetically.

4. Modify the title to **Edit a Product Category**.

5. Change the action attribute of the form to **editCategoryScreen2.cfm**.

6. Modify the Query loop for the Select box, and implement the controls shown in Table 11-5.

Table 11-5 Controls in the editCategoryScreen1.cfm Template

Label	Control Name	Type	Value	Display
Select a category:	CategoryID	Select	CategoryID	Category
		Submit	Next...	

7. Save the file again.

8. Open **header.cfm**, and hyperlink the Edit item under the Categories category to the editCategoryScreen1.cfm template.

9. Save the file.

10. Switch to your Web browser, and then click the **Home** link. Refresh the document.

11. Click the **Edit** item in the Categories category to see the Web page displaying the form for selecting a category.

You have successfully created a form for selecting a category for editing by copying the one for editing an auction.

As mentioned previously, you can simplify the process of creating the form for editing a category by copying editAuctionScreen2.cfm and then modifying it.

To create editCategoryScreen2.cfm by copying and modifying editAuctionScreen2.cfm:

1. Switch to ColdFusion Studio, and open **editAuctionScreen2.cfm**.

2. Save it as **editCategoryScreen2.cfm**.

3. Because you must pass data from the first screen to the third, you have to use a session variable for storing the CategoryID of the selected auction. Modify the code by substituting CategoryID for AuctionID:

   ```
   <cflock scope="SESSION" timeout="20">
   <cfset session.CategoryID = form.CategoryID>
   </cflock>
   ```

4. Change the query to the following code for extracting data for the selected category:

   ```
   <cfquery datasource="your_username_Nothebys"
   name="getCategory">
   SELECT * FROM Categories WHERE CategoryID =
   #form.CategoryID#
   </cfquery>
   ```

5. Change the title to **Edit a Product Category**.

6. Change the ACTION attribute for the CFFORM to **editCategoryScreen3.cfm**.

7. Delete two rows in the table, and display the name of the category in the text box by modifying the value attribute of the Category control as **value="#getCategory.Category#"**. Change the caption for the control to **Category**. Modify the error message appropriately.

8. Save your file.

9. Switch to your Web browser, and then open **admin.cfm**.

10. Click **Categories – Edit**.

11. Select **Lawn Trimers**, and then click **Next**. Recall that you intentionally spelled the category name incorrectly so that you can edit it later using the edit feature.

    The ColdFusion Server extracts data for the selected category and displays it in a form, as shown in Figure 11-36.

You have successfully created a template for extracting a record from the Categories table and displaying the data in a form for enabling a user to edit the data.

Finally, the third screen in the edit category process updates the appropriate records and displays a confirmation message, as shown in Figure 11-37. A quick way to design the

11

form handler for updating a category is by copying and modifying the form handler for updating an auction.

To create editCategoryScreen3.cfm by copying and modifying editAuctionScreen3.cfm:

1. Switch to ColdFusion Studio, and open **editAuctionScreen3.cfm**.

2. Save it as **editCategoryScreen3.cfm**.

3. Type the following code for updating a Categories table record in place of the code for updating an Auctions table record:

```
UPDATE Categories
SET Category = '#form.Category#'
WHERE
CategoryID = #session.CategoryID#
```

4. Change the title to **The following product category has been edited successfully....**

5. Change the Name label to **Category**.

6. Change the value displayed to **#form.Category#** from #form.auctionName#.

7. Delete the other rows in the table.

8. Save your file again.

9. Switch to your Web browser, and then click **Home**.

10. Click **Categories – Edit**.

11. Select the **Lawn Trimers**, and then click **Next**.

    The ColdFusion Server extracts data for the selected category and displays it in a form, as shown earlier in Figure 11-36.

12. Change the category description to **Lawn Trimmers**, and then click **Next**.

13. The ColdFusion Server should execute editCategoryScreen3.cfm and produce a confirmation message after updating the data, as shown in Figure 11-37.

You have successfully implemented a capability for editing a category in the Nothebys admin tool.

Once you complete the products administration system, you will revisit the categories administration to design the system for deleting a category. When a product category is deleted, you must also delete all the products in that category to maintain the integrity of the database.

Adding the Products Administration Requirement

The products part of the navigation menu lets you maintain the product information. Even though the operations to be performed are similar to the other two systems, the products administration system is more complicated for the following reasons:

- The table for the products data has to store the AuctionID of the auction where a product is being auctioned. However, users typically reference auctions by name, not ID number. The system should let users select auctions by name.

- The Products table stores product category information in the CategoryID field. However, users need to reference this information by product category name.

- The products administration system handles image files for the thumbnails and product pictures. Administrators must be able to add and delete these files when they add and delete products.

Add Product Requirement

To add a new product, you insert data into the Make, Model, SerialNumber, Description, AuctionID, CategoryID, Thumbnail, and Picture fields in the Products database table. The primary key field, ProductID, is automatically incremented when a new record is inserted. Similarly to the other two systems, you must first design the form for the user to enter the data and then design the form handler for actually processing the data. You have decided to name these two templates addProductScreen1.cfm and addProductScreen2.cfm.

To design the addProductScreen1.cfm template:

1. Switch to ColdFusion Studio, and close all open documents.

2. Click **File** on the menu bar, and then click **New**.

3. Click **Blank Document**, and then click **OK**.

4. Type the CFML to include the **header.cfm** template.

5. You need to extract data from the Auctions table and subsequently present it in a select box so that the user can specify where the product is being auctioned. This select box is similar to the one that you designed previously for the edit-auction capability. You can open **editAuctionScreen1.cfm** and copy the following code into the document being edited:

```
<cfquery datasource="your_username_Nothebys"
name="getAuctions">
SELECT * FROM Auctions
</cfquery>
```

11

6. You also need a select box for allowing a user to select the product category. Open **editCategoryScreen1.cfm**, and copy the following code into this document:

```
<cfquery datasource="your_username_Nothebys"
name="getCategories">
SELECT * FROM Categories ORDER BY Category
</cfquery>
```

7. Display the title **Add a Product** formatted according to the common user interface guidelines.

8. Design a ColdFusion form with an action set to **addProductScreen2.cfm**. Because products are associated with images, this form must be able to transmit multipart data. Set the ENCTYPE attribute of the form to **multipart/form-data**.

9. To insert a record into the Products table, the data to be collected has to correspond to the table structure in the Auctions table. Implement the controls shown in Table 11-6. Set the size attribute for all text boxes to 40. A quick way of coding the Select boxes for the auctions and the categories is to copy the code for the Query loops from editAuctionScreen1.cfm and editCategoryScreen1.cfm.

Table 11-6   Controls in the addProductScreen1.cfm Template

Label	Control Name	Type	Query	Value	Display	Validation
Select an auction:	AuctionID	Select	getAuctions	AuctionID	Left(Auction Name,35)	
Select a category:	CategoryID	Select	getCategories	CategoryID	Category	
Make:	Make	Text				
Model:	Model	Text				
Serial Number:	SerialNumber	Text				
Description:	Description	Text				Completeness
Thumbnail:	Thumbnail	File				
Picture:	Picture	File				
		Submit		Next...		

10. Close the form.

11. Insert a **horizontal rule**, and include the **footer.cfm** template.

12. Save the file as **addProductScreen1.cfm** in the Chapter11/Admin folder.

13. Open **header.cfm** and hyperlink the **Add** item under the Product category to the above template.

14. Save the file.

15. Switch to your Web browser and then open **admin.cfm**.

16. Click the **Add** item in the Products category to see the Web page displaying the form. See Figure 11-38.

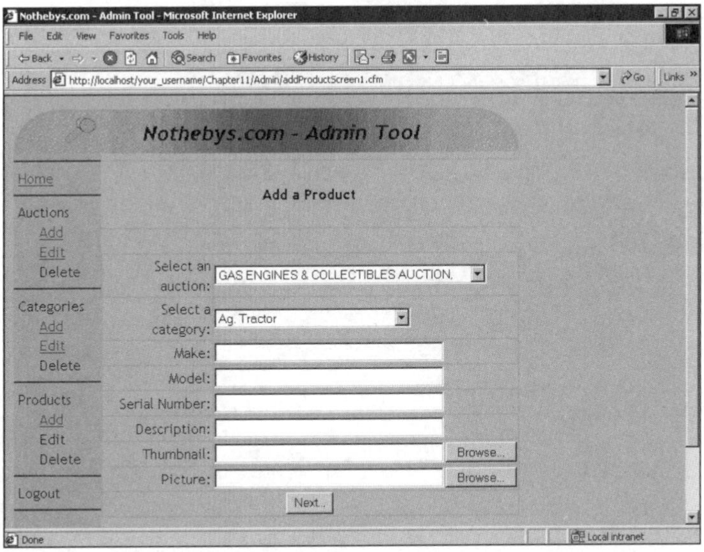

Figure 11-38 Web page displaying the Add a Product form

You have successfully created a form for adding a product.

Your next step is to design the form handler for actually inserting the data entered by the users into the Products table. Prior to the insertion of the data, the form handler has to upload the product thumbnail and the picture if available. Once the images are uploaded and the record is inserted, a confirmation message is displayed, as shown in Figure 11-39.

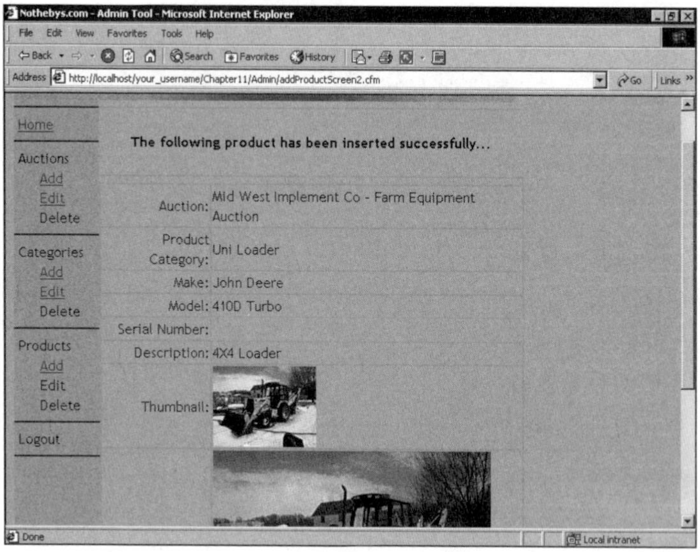

Figure 11-39   Web page displayed after a product has been inserted

To design the form handler (addProductScreen2.cfm) for inserting a product:

1. Switch to ColdFusion Studio.

2. Click **File** on the menu bar, and then click **New**.

3. Click **Blank Document**, and then click **OK**.

4. Type the CFML to include the **header.cfm** template.

5. You need to determine whether the user has uploaded a thumbnail for this product. If yes, you need to upload it to the thumbnails folder; otherwise, you need to set the thumbnail to "NONE." If necessary, review the concepts for uploading files in Chapter 10. Type the following CFIF statement:

```
<cfif form.Thumbnail EQ "">
<cfset Thumbnail = "NONE">
<cfelse>
<cfset thisFolder = GetDirectoryFromPath(GetCurrent
TemplatePath())>
<cfset mainFolder = ReplaceNoCase(thisFolder,"\
Admin","")>
<cffile action="UPLOAD" filefield="Thumbnail"
destination="#mainFolder#Thumbnails" nameconflict=
"MAKEUNIQUE">
<cfset Thumbnail = file.serverfile>
</cfif>
```

6. You also need to process the picture submission. Type the following CFIF statement:

```
<cfif form.Picture EQ "">
<cfset Picture = "NONE">
<cfelse>
<cfset thisFolder = GetDirectoryFromPath(GetCurrent
TemplatePath())>
<cfset mainFolder = ReplaceNoCase(thisFolder,"\
admin","")>
<cffile action="UPLOAD" filefield="Picture" destination=
"#mainFolder#Pictures" nameconflict="MAKEUNIQUE">
<cfset Picture = file.serverfile>
</cfif>
```

7. Finally, you need to insert the record prior to displaying the confirmation message. Type the following code:

```
<cfquery datasource="your_username_Nothebys">
INSERT INTO Products
(AuctionID, CategoryID, Make, Model, SerialNumber,
Description, Thumbnail, Picture)
VALUES (#form.AuctionID#, #form.CategoryID#, '#form.Make#
', '#form.Model#', '#form.SerialNumber#', '#form.
Description#', '#Thumbnail#', '#Picture#')
</cfquery>
```

8. You need to query the database to figure out the auction name and the product category based on the ID values supplied in the form. Type the following code:

```
<cfquery datasource="your_username_Nothebys" name="
getAuction">
SELECT * FROM Auctions WHERE AuctionID = #form.AuctionID#
</cfquery>
<cfquery datasource="your_username_Nothebys" name=
"getCategory">
SELECT * FROM Categories WHERE CategoryID = #form.
CategoryID#
</cfquery>
```

9. Design the title, as shown in Figure 11-39.

10. Copy the table from addProductScreen1.cfm. Modify the contents of the table, and display the values getAuction.AuctionName, getCategory.Category, form.Make, form.Model, form.SerialNumber, and form.Description by using CFOUTPUT tags. Delete the last row of the table.

11. Display the thumbnail if it is present by using the following code:

```
<cfif Thumbnail EQ "NONE">N/A<cfelse><img src="../
Thumbnails/ <cfoutput>#Thumbnail#</cfoutput>"></cfif>
```

12. Display the picture if it is present by using the following code:

```
<cfif Picture EQ "NONE">N/A<cfelse><img src="../Pictures/
<cfoutput>#Picture#</cfoutput>"></cfif>
```

11

13. Insert a **horizontal rule**, and include the **footer.cfm** template.

14. Save the file as **addProductScreen2.cfm** in the Chapter11/Admin folder.

15. Switch to your Web browser, open **admin.cfm**, and then click **Products – Add**, if necessary.

16. Select **Mid West Implement Co – Farm Equipment Auction** in the Auction field.

17. Select **Uni Loader** in the Category field.

18. Type **John Deere** in the Make field.

19. Type **410D Turbo** in the Model field.

20. Type **4X4 Loader** in the Description field.

21. Click **Browse** next to the Thumbnail field, and then select **410dThumbnail.jpg** from the Chapter11 folder.

22. Click **Browse** next to the picture field, and then select **410dPicture.jpg** from the Chapter11 folder.

23. Click **Next**.

    The ColdFusion Server inserts this record and displays a confirmation Web page, as shown in Figure 11-39.

You have successfully designed a form handler for inserting a product.

Edit Product Requirement

The edit product subsystem allows a user to edit a record in the Products table. Because the table can include many products, you need a simple way to find the product that you want to edit. You have decided to first list the product categories available and then list the products in that category for the user to select one for editing. This logic is very similar to the logic that you used at the beginning of the chapter for listing products. You can copy those templates and modify them for this purpose. You are planning to design this system by using four screens. The first lists the categories (Figure 11-40), the second lists the products (Figure 11-41), the third is a form that displays the text fields (Figure 11-42), and the fourth updates the data and display a confirmation message (Figure 11-43).

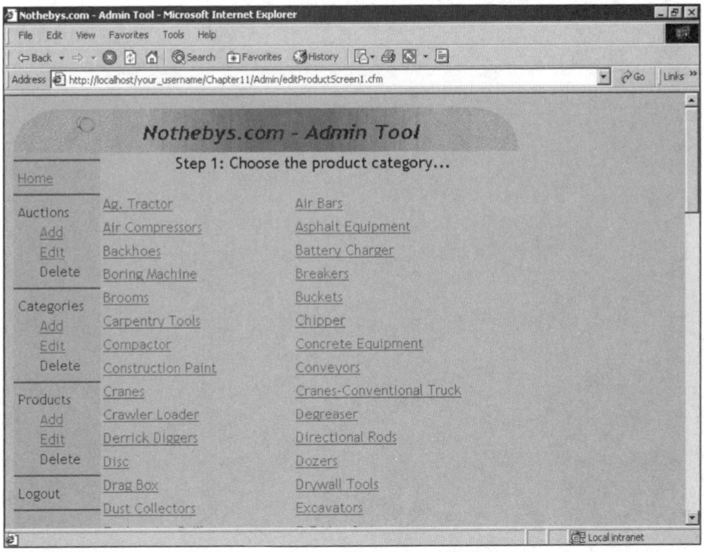

Figure 11-40   Web page displayed by editProductScreen1.cfm

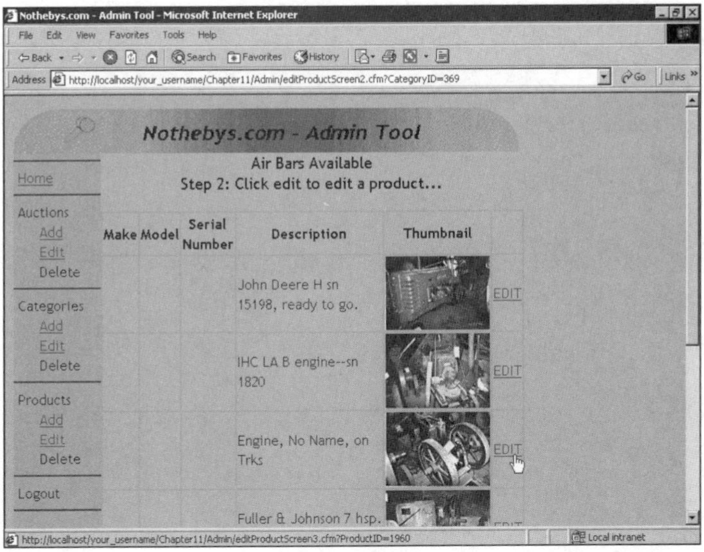

Figure 11-41   Web page displayed by editProductScreen2.cfm

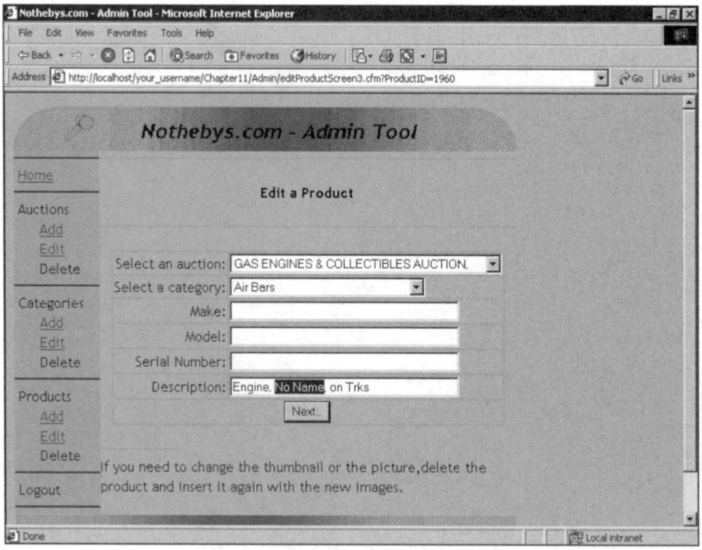

Figure 11-42   Web page displayed by editProductScreen3.cfm

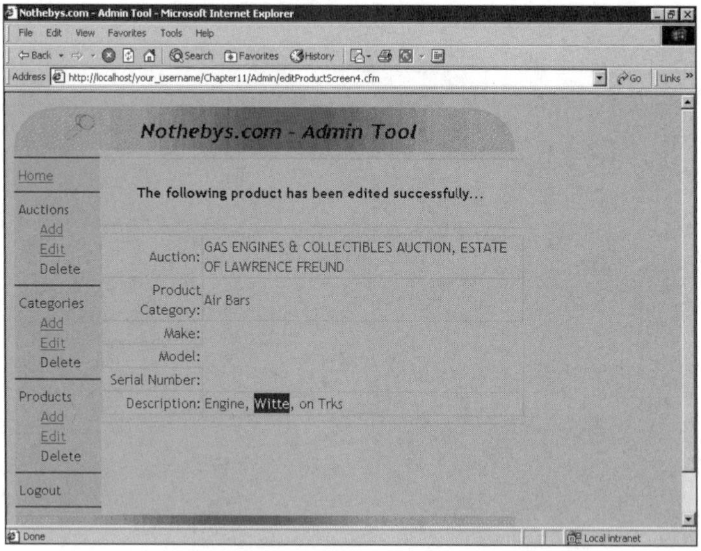

Figure 11-43   Web page displayed by editProductScreen4.cfm

To implement the Edit Product requirement:

1. Switch to ColdFusion Studio, and close all open documents.

2. Open **listAllCategories.cfm** in the Chapter11 folder.

3. Save the file as **editProductScreen1.cfm** in the Admin subfolder in the Chapter11 folder.

4. Change the title to **Step 1: Choose the Product category....**

5. Change the HREF attribute of the Anchor tag from listProductsInACategory.cfm to **editProductScreen2.cfm**.

6. Save the file again.

7. Open **header.cfm** in the Admin folder, and hyperlink the **Edit** item under products to editProductScreen1.cfm.

8. Save the **header.cfm** file.

9. Open **listProductsInACategory.cfm** in the Chapter11 folder.

10. Save it as **editProductScreen2.cfm** in the Chapter11/Admin folder.

11. Add a second line to the title as **
Step 2: Click Edit to edit a product....**

12. Change the border color of the table to **66CCFF**.

13. Replace the Auction Details header with a nonbreaking space (** **).

14. Replace the gavel.gif hyperlink with **<a href="editProductScreen3.cfm? ProductID=<cfoutput>#ProductID#</cfoutput>">EDIT</a>**.

15. Because this template is in the Admin subfolder, you need to type **../** and change the SRC attribute of the thumbnail image to **../Thumbnails/ <cfoutput>#Thumbnail#</cfoutput>**. Delete the anchor tag around it.

16. Save the file.

17. Open **addProductScreen1.cfm**, and save it as **editProductScreen3.cfm**.

18. Use a CFQUERY to extract the data for the product selected below the CFINCLUDE tag for the header.cfm. Type the following code:

```
<cfquery datasource="your_username_Nothebys" name=
"getProduct">
SELECT * FROM Products WHERE ProductID = #URL.ProductID#
</cfquery>
```

19. Change the title to **Edit a Product**.

20. Change the ACTION attribute of the form to **editProductScreen4.cfm**. Delete the **ENCTYPE** attribute. You are designing this form to allow users to change the text fields. If they want to change the product thumbnails or pictures, you ask them to delete the product and reinsert them.

21. You want the current auction to be preselected in the select box. Type the following CFIF tag in the OPTION tag to perform the selection:

```
<cfif AuctionID EQ getProduct.AuctionID>SELECTED</cfif>
```

22. Similarly, add **<cfif CategoryID EQ getProduct.CategoryID>SELECTED</cfif>** to the OPTION tag in the Category select box.

23. Add VALUE attributes to the text boxes for displaying the current make, model, serial number, and description as **value="#getProduct.Make#"**, **value="#getProduct.Model#"**, **value="#getProduct.Serial Number#"**, and **value="#getProduct.Description#**, respectively.

24. You have decided to pass the ProductID as a hidden field to the next screen. Prior to the end tag for the CFFORM, type the following code:

```
<input type="Hidden" name="ProductID" value="<cfoutput>#
URL.ProductID#</cfoutput>">
```

25. Delete the table rows containing the file input controls for the thumbnail and the picture. add a footnote prior to the CFINCLUDE for the footer.cfm as: **Resize the horizontal rule and <hr color="66CCFF" align=" left" width="20%"> <font face="Trebuchet MS">If you need to change the thumbnail or the picture, delete the product and insert it again with the new images.</font>**

26. Save the file.

27. Open **addProductScreen2.cfm**, and save it as **editProductScreen4.cfm**.

28. Delete the **CFIF statements** for the thumbnail and the picture. Delete the **CFQUERY** for the SQL INSERT, and type the CFUPDATE tag for updating the record as:

```
<cfupdate datasource="Nothebys" tablename="Products" form-
fields="ProductID, Make, Model, SerialNumber, Description,
AuctionID, CategoryID">
```

29. Change the title to **The following product has been edited successfully....**

30. Delete the **table rows** for displaying the thumbnail and the picture.

31. Save your file.

32. Switch to your Web browser, and check out the workings of this subsystem. See Figures 11-40, 11-41, 11-42, and 11-43, and correct any errors that you encounter.

You have successfully and productively designed a system for editing the product records in the Nothebys site.

Delete Product Requirement

This subsystem should allow a user to delete a product from the Products table and its associated thumbnail and picture files from the server's disk storage. You have to carefully plan the design of this system because it is useful when users delete auctions as well as categories. If a user deletes an auction, all products that are auctioned at that auction and their images should be deleted. Similarly, when a category is deleted, all products in that category should be deleted, too. As this functionality is needed in three places, you want to use a separate template that deletes a product named deleteProduct.cfm and include it by using the CFINCLUDE tag in the other three templates. Using the CFINCLUDE statement this way is different from using it for the header.cfm and the footer.cfm templates. The deleteProduct.cfm template can only delete a product if it can determine which product to delete; in other words, it needs to know the ProductID of the product to be deleted. So, you will include the deleteProduct.cfm template by using two statements. The first statement would be a CFSET statement that initializes a variable named deletePID to the value of the ProductID of the product that should be deleted, and then the CFINCLUDE statement would be used to call the deleteProduct.cfm template. The deletePID variable would be used in the deleteProduct.cfm template for specifying which product has to be deleted.

The deleteProduct.cfm template which follows is available in the Admin subfolder in the Chapter11 folder on your Data Disk.

```
<!---A variable named deletePID has to be initialized prior to includ-
ing this template --->
<!--- Query the database to extract product data  --->
<cfquery datasource="your_username_Nothebys" name="getProduct">
SELECT * FROM Products WHERE ProductID = #deletePID#
</cfquery>
<!--- If thumbnail is present, delete the file --->
<cfif getProduct.Thumbnail NEQ "NONE">
<cfset thisFolder = GetDirectoryFromPath(GetCurrentTemplatePath())>
<cfset mainFolder = ReplaceNoCase(thisFolder,"\Admin","")>
<cffile action="DELETE" file="#mainFolder#Thumbnails\#get
Product.Thumbnail#">
</cfif>
<!--- If picture is present, delete it --->
<cfif getProduct.Picture NEQ "NONE">
<cfset thisFolder = GetDirectoryFromPath(GetCurrentTemplatePath())>
<cfset mainFolder = ReplaceNoCase(thisFolder,"\Admin","")>
<cffile action="DELETE" file="#mainFolder#Pictures\#get
Product.Picture#">
</cfif>
<!--- Once the images are deleted, delete the record --->
<cfquery datasource="your_username_Nothebys">
DELETE FROM Products WHERE ProductID = #deletePID#
</cfquery>
```

11

You first extract the data from the database for the record that should be deleted. Then you delete any associated images. Finally, you delete the record from the table.

You have to integrate this template into the admin tool to let users delete products. The first two screens for selecting the product to be deleted would be similar to the first two screens that allow you to select a product for editing.

To implement the delete product requirement:

1. Close all open files. Using ColdFusion Studio, open **deleteProduct.cfm** from the Admin subfolder in the Chapter11 folder. Examine the code.

2. Select the existing data source name on line 3, and replace it with the data source name for the Nothebys database. Also replace the data source name on line 19 with the data source name for the Nothebys database.

3. Save the file with the changes.

4. Open **editProductScreen1.cfm**, and save it as **deleteProductScreen1.cfm**.

5. Change the hyperlink from editProductScreen2.cfm to **deleteProductScreen2.cfm**, and save the file again.

6. Open **header.cfm**, and hyperlink the **Delete** item in the products category to the template that you just created. Save header.cfm with this change.

7. Open **editProductScreen2.cfm**, and save it as **deleteProductScreen2.cfm**.

8. Modify the second line in the title to **Click Delete to delete a product...**.

9. Highlight the entire code in the table cell containing the EDIT hyperlink, and replace it with the following code to create a Delete button:

```
<form action="deleteProductScreen3.cfm" method="post">
<input type="button" value="Delete" onclick="
if (confirm('Are you sure?')){ this.form.submit() }
"><input type="hidden" name="ProductID" value="
<cfoutput>#ProductID#</cfoutput>"></form>
```

You are creating a separate form for each product record and using a hidden field to pass the ProductID when the user clicks the delete button for that product. A JavaScript confirmation script is used to give users a chance to cancel the deletion.

10. Save the file.

11. Create a blank document. (Click **File** on the menu bar, and then click **New**. Click **Blank Document**, and then click **OK**.)

12. Save the blank document as **deleteProductScreen3.cfm.**

13. Type the CFML to include the **header.cfm** template.

14. Type **<cfset deletePID = FORM.ProductID>** to initialize the deletePID variable.

15. Type **<cfinclude template="deleteProduct.cfm">** to include the code for the actual deletion.

16. Display a confirmation message **Product has been deleted successfully** formatted according to the user interface guidelines. Then insert a horizontal line.

17. Include the **footer.cfm** template, and then save the file.

18. Switch to your Web browser, and then click **Home**. Refresh the document.

19. Click **Delete** in the Products category.

20. Scroll down and click **Uni Loader**. Your Web browser displays a Uni Loader available and a Delete button, as shown in Figure 11-44.

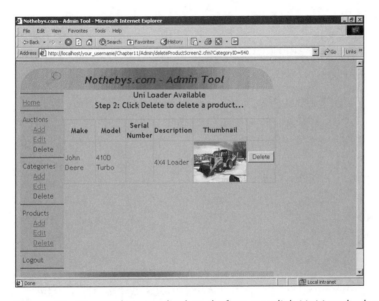

Figure 11-44   Web page displayed after you click Uni Loader by delete ProductScreen2.cfm

21. Click the **Delete** button, and then click **OK** to confirm the deletion.

The ColdFusion Server deletes the 4x4 loader that you inserted earlier in the chapter, as well as its thumbnail and product pictures, and then displays a confirmation message, as shown in Figure 11-45.

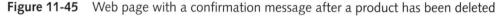

Figure 11-45   Web page with a confirmation message after a product has been deleted

You have successfully implemented the delete product capability in the Nothebys site.

Now that you have designed a method for deleting products, you can design capabilities for deleting auctions and categories.

Delete Auction Requirement

The first screen for deleting an auction is similar to the one for editing an auction. The second template queries the Products table for all the products that belong to this auction, deletes those products, and then deletes the record from the Auctions table.

To implement the delete auction requirement:

1. Switch to ColdFusion Studio, and then close all open documents.

2. Open **editAuctionScreen1.cfm**, and save it as **deleteAuctionScreen1.cfm**.

3. Change the action attribute of the FORM tag to **deleteAuctionScreen2.cfm**.

4. Open **deleteProductScreen2.cfm**, and copy the code for the Delete button, and then paste it over the Next button in the form to overwrite it.

5. Change the title to **Delete an Auction**.

6. Save the file.

7. Open **header.cfm**, and hyperlink the **Delete** item in the Auctions category to the above template. Save the **header.cfm** template.

8. Create a new, blank document.

9. Query the database to get a list of all products that were auctioned at this auction. Type the following code:

```
<cfquery datasource="your_username_Nothebys" name="get
Products">
SELECT ProductID from Products WHERE AuctionID = #FORM.
AuctionID#
</cfquery>
```

10. Use a Query loop to delete all these products and their associated images. Type the following code:

```
<cfloop query="getProducts">
<cfset deletePID = ProductID>
<cfinclude template="deleteProduct.cfm">
</cfloop>
```

11. Delete the record from the Auctions table. Type the following code:

```
<cfquery datasource="your_username_Nothebys">
DELETE FROM Auctions WHERE AuctionID = #FORM.AuctionID#
</cfquery>
```

12. Include header.cfm and footer.cfm, and display a confirmation message as follows:

```
<cfinclude template="header.cfm">
<hr color="66CCFF">
<p align="center"><font face="Trebuchet MS"><b>Auction
has been deleted successfully...</b></font></p>
<hr color="66CCFF">
<font face="Trebuchet MS"><cfoutput>#getProducts.Record
Count#</cfoutput> product record(s) and associated images
 have been deleted too.</font>
<cfinclude template="footer.cfm">
```

13. Save the file as **deleteAuctionScreen2.cfm**.

14. Switch to your Web browser, and then click **Home**. Refresh the document.

15. Click **Delete** in the Auctions category. See Figure 11-46.

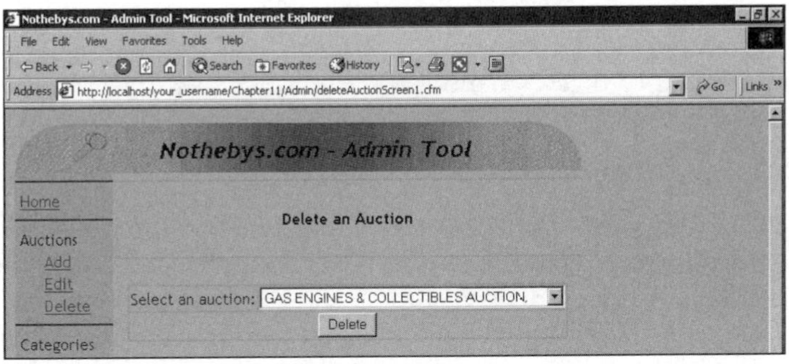

Figure 11-46   Screen 1 for deleting an auction

16. Select **Mid West Implement Co – Farm Equipment Auction**, and then click the **Delete** button. Click **OK** to confirm the deletion.

The ColdFusion Server queries the database and extracts all the products that are to be auctioned at this auction. If it finds any, it deletes them and their associated image files. Then it deletes the auction record and displays a confirmation message, as shown in Figure 11-47.

Figure 11-47   Web page with confirmation message after an auction has been deleted

You have successfully designed a method for deleting auctions in the Nothebys site.

Delete Category Requirement

The delete category requirement is very similar to the delete auctions requirement. You must first delete all the products in the category to be deleted before you can delete the category.

To implement the delete category requirement:

1. Switch to ColdFusion Studio.

2. Open **editCategoryScreen1.cfm**, and save it as **deleteCategoryScreen1.cfm**.

3. Modify the template using the same techniques you learned earlier for implementing a method to delete auctions. Be sure to change the title, the form handler, and the Submit button.

4. Modify **header.cfm**, and hyperlink the **Delete** item in the Categories category.

5. Design **deleteCategoryScreen2.cfm** by copying and modifying **deleteAuctionScreen2.cfm**. Change the query to extract all the products in the selected product category. Change the query for deleting the auction to deleting a category and change the title. Modify the error message as appropriate.

6. Test the system that you just designed by deleting the product category named Lawn Trimmers. See Figures 11-48 and 11-49.

Figure 11-48   Screen 1 for deleting a category

Figure 11-49   Web page with confirmation message after a category has been deleted

You have successfully designed a capability for deleting categories in the Nothebys site.

Specifying Default Documents

You have one final task to finish. Very often, URLs for Web sites do not include a file-name. For example, *www.intel.com* loads the home page for the Intel Corporation's Web site. When a URL does not include a filename, the Web server serves the **default document** for that folder. You set the default document to serve by using the appropriate service manager software for your Web server.

To set up default documents for the Nothebys site:

1. Refer to documentation for your Web server, and then set **index.cfm** as the default document in the Chapter11 folder.

2. Set **admin.cfm** as the default document to serve in the Admin folder.

3. Switch to your Web browser, and enter the URL
   http://localhost/your_username/Chapter11. See Figure 11-50.

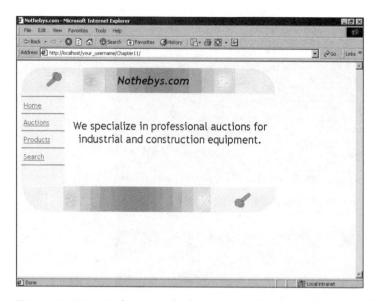

Figure 11-50   Web server displays index.cfm when there is no filename specified
in the URL

4. Open URL **http:// localhost/your_username /Chapter11/Admin**. See
Figure 11-51.

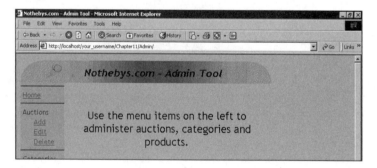

Figure 11-51   Web server displays admin.cfm when there is no filename specified
in the URL

5. Close all open programs.

You have successfully created a complete database-driven Web site for a company.

CHAPTER SUMMARY

◻ Reusing code increases programming productivity. Plan by considering the possibility of reusing code.

◻ You use the CFINCLUDE tag to include common code.

◻ A logical way of structuring a Web application is to divide each template into three parts: Part 1 would be a common header for all files, Part 2 would be the content specific to the template, and Part 3 would be a common footer for all files.

◻ Typically, database-driven Web sites have two components. The first is visible to all the users, and the second is an administration tool for changing the content and for other purposes. You can give a better experience to users if you design the part visible to all the users before designing the administration tool. Obviously, you need data in the database to be able to do this.

◻ You can build multi-level capabilities in a Web site to simplify the process of finding items of interest. Typically, the interface would be designed in multiple screens. You may have to use session variables to capture user clicks and make the information available to subsequent screens.

◻ You can use the SQL LIKE operator to build a search capability.

◻ Examine the data model critically for building the admin tool. Typically, you first want to implement add and edit capabilities for tables that do not have any foreign keys. For edit capabilities, you first have to design a system that allows users to easily select records for editing. This could be a single-page select box or a series of linked pages organized into categories and subcategories, if needed. Second, you want to implement add and edit capabilities for tables that have foreign keys. You can copy and modify the pages that you designed for allowing users to select records for editing into pages that allow users to select data for insertion into foreign key fields. Third, you want to design delete screens for tables that have foreign keys. Finally, you want to design delete screens for tables that have no foreign keys. There is a possibility of reusing code in these situations, too.

◻ You should secure administration tools using usernames and passwords for authorized administrators.

11

HANDS-ON PROJECTS

Project 1: Enhance the Search Feature

Based on customer feedback, your task is to enhance the search capability in the Nothebys Web site:

1. Design a ColdFusion template named **searchForm2.cfm** in the Chapter11 folder containing a form, as shown in Figure 11-52. Users have an option of searching for products using multiple keywords in two different ways. The first option is to search for products with contents in the Description, Make, Model, or Serial Number fields matching all the keywords entered. The second option is to search for products with contents in the Description, Make, Model, or Serial Number fields matching any one of the keywords entered.

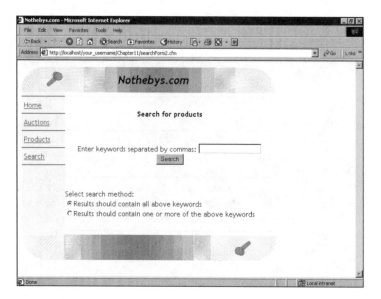

Figure 11-52

2. Create a form handler named **processSearch2.cfm** for the above form that searches through the database in a manner that depends on the option selected and displays the results as shown in Figure 11-53 and Figure 11-54. Open processSearch.cfm, and save it as **processSearch2.cfm**. Enclose the WHERE clause of the SQL statement in parentheses and repeatedly process it in a LIST loop. Use logical operators AND or OR, depending on the search method specified.

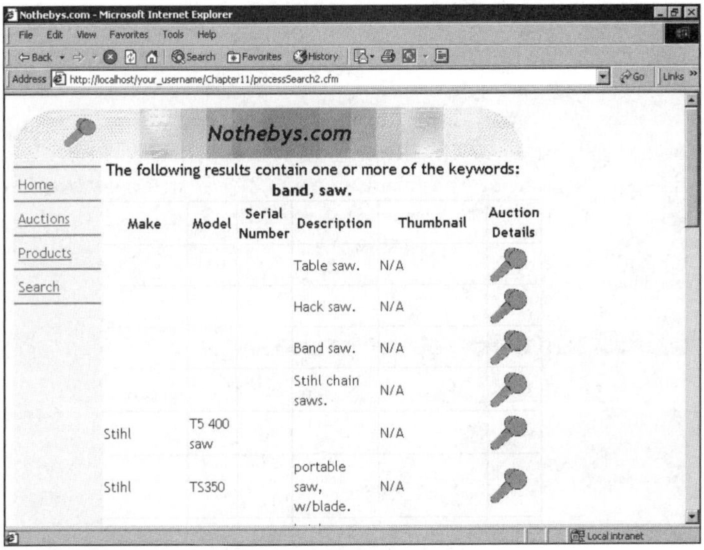

Figure 11-53

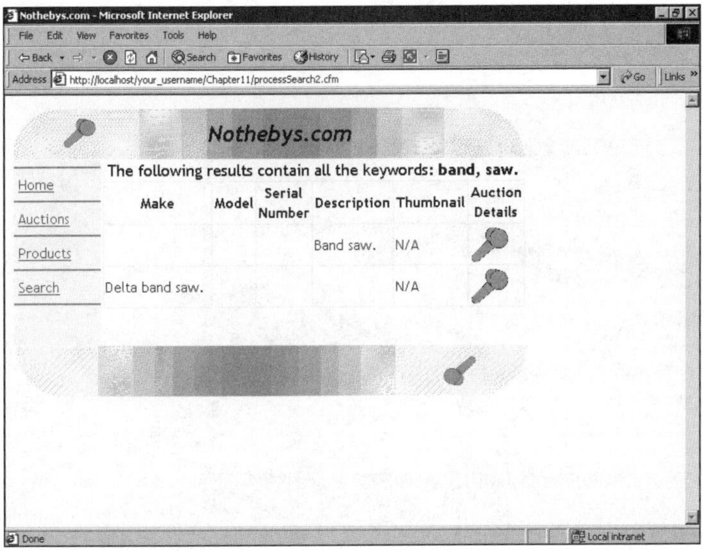

Figure 11-54

Project 2: Add Login Security

Implement login security to the admin tool using session management concepts. Allow access to only those users whose username and password match the records in the Administrators table in the Nothebys database. The user interface for the login templates should be similar to the user interface for other templates in the admin tool. See Figures 11-55, 11-56, and 11-57. Use a session variable named **session.loggedin**, a login form template named **login.cfm** with a form handler named **processLogin.cfm**, and a template named **logout.cfm** for logging out. Hyperlink the appropriate text in header.cfm to logout.cfm. When login is successful, redirect the user to admin.cfm.

Figure 11-55

Figure 11-56

Figure 11-57

Project 3: Data Validation

Mr. Nothebys is extremely happy with the Web site that you have designed. Over the course of time, he has noticed that his staff are creating similar product categories with minor variations. He has requested you to analyze the data and come up with a strategy to solve this problem. Your team has decided to enhance the system by implementing the following data validation requirement: Prior to inserting a new product category, search the database for a similar category. If there is a similar category, warn the user about it and take an action specified by the user. To implement the above requirement, perform the following tasks:

1. Open addCategoryScreen1.cfm, and save it as **addCategoryEnhancedScreen1.cfm**. See Figure 11-58.

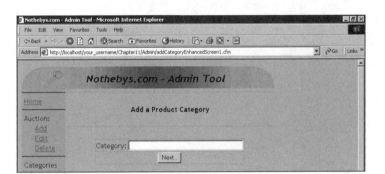

Figure 11-58

2. Open addCategoryScreen2.cfm, and save it as **addCategoryEnhancedScreen3.cfm**.

3. Modify the ACTION attribute of the forms to use the new template names. Design a template named **addCategoryEnhancedScreen2.cfm** that searches through the database for similar categories (Category LIKE '%#FORM.Category#%') and displays a list, as shown in Figure 11-59.

11

Figure 11-59

4. Implement the following logic in addCategoryEnhancedScreen3.cfm. If the user selects the "I would like to use one of the above categories, do not create a new category…." option, then redirect the user to the admin.cfm home page; otherwise, add the category, as shown in Figure 11-60.

Figure 11-60

Project 4: Enhance the Add Product Feature

Users have requested you to enhance the add product requirement. Typically, a lot of products are added for the same auction and the same category. They want the system to "remember" which auction and category the previously added product belonged to and they want these items to be selected automatically when the add product hyperlink is clicked. To implement the above requirement, perform the following tasks:

1. Open addProductScreen1.cfm, change the ACTION attribute of the form to **addProductEnhancedScree2.cfm** and save it as **addProductEnhancedScreen1.cfm**.

2. Open addProductScreen2.cfm, and save it as **addProductEnhancedScreen2.cfm**.

3. Use session variables to store the AuctionID and the CategoryID when a product is inserted.

4. Implement programming to preselect the auction and the category whenever the first screen for adding a product is invoked, as shown in Figure 11-61. Experiment by adding the product from the add product section for the REED CONSTRUCTION auction.

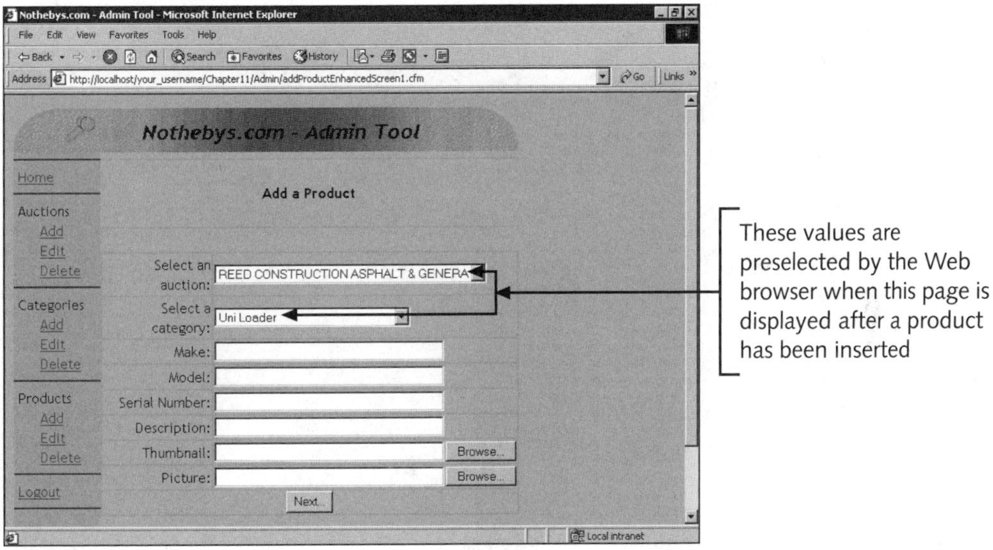

These values are preselected by the Web browser when this page is displayed after a product has been inserted

Figure 11-61

Project 5: Design New Header and Footer Files

Design a new set of **header.cfm** and **footer.cfm** files. Browse the site by using these new files. Can you think of other ways in which you can speed up the process of creating a new look for the site?

Project 6: Build an Online Bidding System

Build an online bidding system for the Nothebys site. Customers can register for the online bidding when they visit the regular auctions. There is a table named Customers that contains data collected about the customers. Examine it carefully and then design the system. To implement the above requirements, your tasks are the following:

1. You need a database table named **Bids** containing three fields: **CustomerID**, **ProductID**, and **BidAmount**. Use the CustomerID and the ProductID fields together as the primary key for the table. Choose appropriate data types for these fields. Create the table by using Access or by running a ColdFusion template.

2. Open listProductsInACategory.cfm in the Chapter11 folder using ColdFusion Studio. Add an additional column to the table. Create a hyperlink to a template named **placeBid.cfm?ProductID=<cfoutput>#ProductID#</cfoutput>** with the description **Place Bid** in each row of the table. See Figure 11-62.

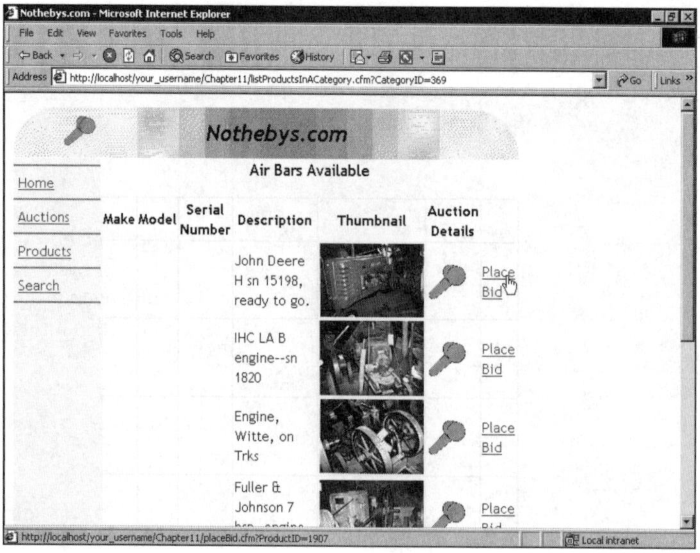

Figure 11-62

3. Design the template named **placeBid.cfm**, as shown in Figure 11-63.

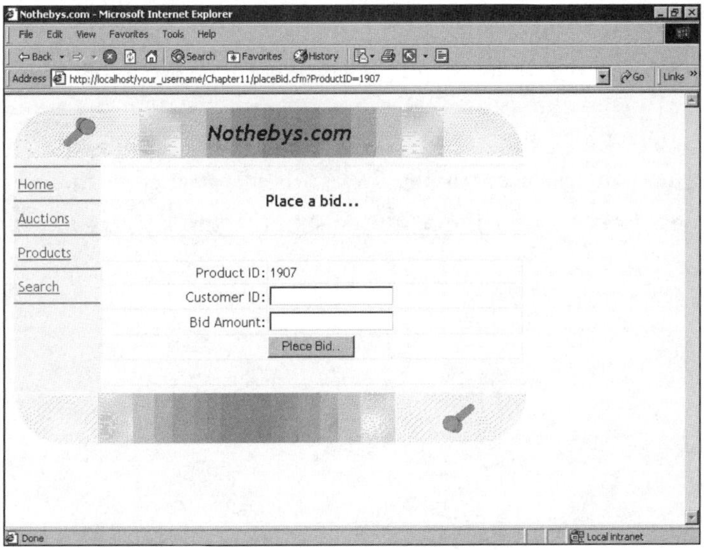

Figure 11-63

4. When the bid is submitted, execute its form handler named **processBid.cfm** that inserts the data into the database table named Bids and displays a confirmation message, as shown in Figure 11-64.

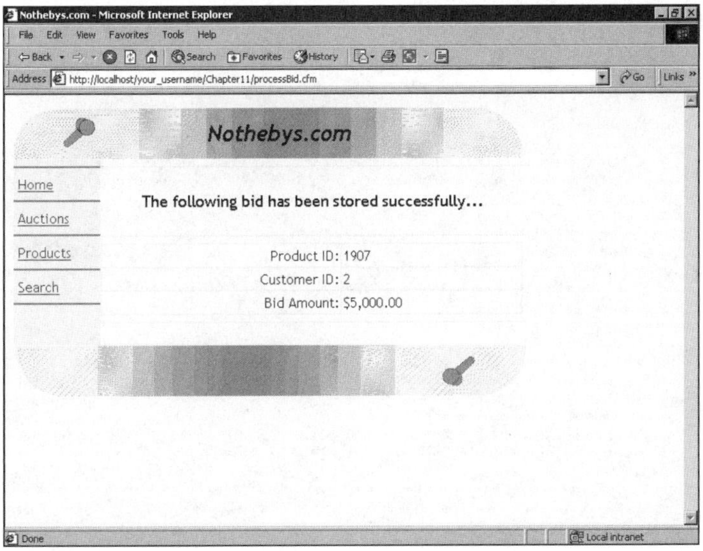

11

Figure 11-64

CASE PROJECTS

1. Design a user interface for the NikRealty site with the following items: Properties, Agents, and Search. Design a user interface for the admin tool. Reuse code appropriately.

2. Design a user interface for the hardware store. Reuse code appropriately.

3. Design an admin tool for the hardware store. Reuse code appropriately.

INDEX

& (ampersand), 56, 74–80

<> (angle brackets), 2, 30, 82, 404

* (asterisk), 74–80, 262

: (colon), 74–80

, (comma), 41, 74–80, 136

$ (dollar sign), 40, 74–80

" (double quotes), 183

= (equal sign), 56, 74–80, 183

! (exclamation point), 30, 74–80

/ (forward slash), 74–80

- (hyphen), 74–80

() (parentheses), 74–80

+ (plus sign), 75, 89

(pound sign), 33–36, 40, 83–84, 505

? (question mark), 56, 74–80

' (single quote), 74–80

[] (square brackets), 238

_ (underscore), 67, 74–80, 139

A

Abs function, 42

absolute location, 161

Access (Microsoft), 338, 343–344, 360–361, 555–556

  databases, opening, 243–246

  launching, 243

  transaction processing and, 368–370

ACTION attribute, 175–176, 178, 182–183, 215, 220, 322, 385, 402, 509, 515, 518, 526, 529–530, 533, 592, 602, 605, 609, 619

add auction requirement, 594–599

Add button, 44

add category requirement, 604–610

add product requirement, 611–616, 635

administration tools, building, 595–628

age, computing, 111, 232–233

Agents table, 244

aggregate functions, 276

algorithmic checks, 422–428

ALIGN attribute, 22, 185

Amazon.com, 5, 175, 499

ampersand (&), 56, 74–80

Anchor button, 63, 97, 303, 225, 317

anchor tags, 60–66, 76

AND operator, 134, 137

angle brackets (<>), 2, 30, 82, 404

application framework (Cold Fusion)

  application.cfm and, 458–463

  application variables and, 485–489

  basic description of, 439–498

  cookies and, 440–458

  HTTP state management and, 440–458

application programming interfaces (APIs), 4–6, 56, 177–178

application variables, 485–489

APPLICATIONTIMEOUT attribute, 485

Apply button, 284

arguments, basic description of, 41

arithmetic

  expressions, 31–33, 262–263, 277–278

  operators, 31–33, 37

ASCII (American Standard Code for Information Interchange), 2, 74–80, 529

ASP (Active Server Pages), 6

asterisk (*), 74–80, 262attribute(s).
See also attributes (listed by name)

  basic description of, 2–3

  databases and, 238–240

  -value pairs, 3

  working with, 238–240

attributes (listed by name). See also attributes

  ACTION attribute, 175–176, 178, 182–183, 215, 220, 322, 385, 402, 509, 515, 518, 526, 529–530, 533, 592, 602, 605, 609, 619

  ALIGN attribute, 22, 185

  APPLICATIONTIMEOUT attribute, 485

  BGCOLOR attribute, 124

  CHECKED attribute, 193, 196, 402

  CLIENTMANAGEMENT attribute, 464

  CLIENTSTORAGE attribute, 464

  COLOR attribute, 592

  COLS attribute, 209

  DATASOURCE attribute, 287, 351, 354

  DEFAULT attribute, 197

  DELETEFILE attribute, 537

  DESTINATION attribute, 516, 517

  ENCTYPE attribute, 612, 619

  ENDROW attribute, 291–292, 294, 296–302

  EXPIRES attribute, 442, 446

  FILE attribute, 537

  FILEFIELD attribute, 516

  FROM attribute, 141

HREF attribute, 64–65, 98, 100, 543, 619
INDEX attribute, 141, 152
MESSAGE attribute, 393–401, 412, 416, 418, 420–421, 424–425
METHOD attribute, 175–177, 216, 341, 385
MULTIPLE attribute, 206, 409
NAME attribute, 176, 178, 192, 197, 209, 287, 385, 388, 442, 474, 523, 546
NAMECONFLICT attribute, 516, 518–519
OUTPUT attribute, 530
PORT attribute, 504–505
RANGE attribute, 419
REQUIRED attribute, 404, 407, 410, 417, 490–491
ROWS attribute, 209
SCOPE attribute, 474
SELECTED attribute, 206, 207, 426
SERVER attribute, 504–505
SESSIONMANAGEMENT attribute, 472
SESSIONTIMEOUT attribute, 472–473, 485
SETCLIENTCOOKIES attribute, 465, 473
SIZE attribute, 176, 206, 409–410
SOURCE attribute, 525
SRC attribute, 220, 538
STARTROW attribute, 291–292, 294, 296–302, 306
SUBJECT attribute, 505
TEXTQUALIFIER attribute, 546
TIMEOUT attribute, 504–505
TO attribute, 141
TYPE attribute, 220, 514–515, 520, 388, 490, 537
VALUE attribute, 192–193, 196, 206, 212, 216, 388, 442
WIDTH attribute, 316
WRAP attribute, 209–210

auctions, 587–591, 596–604, 624–626, 636–637
Autobytel.com, 7, 338
AutoNumber data type, 241
AVG function, 271

B

Back button, 203
BETWEEN operator, 263–264
BGCOLOR attribute, 124
BODY tag, 15, 21, 24, 156, 487, 453, 552
Boolean values, evaluating expressions with, 102–104
BORDER property, 22
Browse button, 515
Browse for Folder dialog box, 506
Browse Server button, 284
Browse tab, 25, 44, 62, 186, 189, 295, 319, 322
button(s)
  basic description of, 176–177
  designing/handling, 192–196
  image, 220–228
  radio, 192–196

C

C (high-level language), 5
C++ (high-level language), 5
case-sensitivity, 34
Ceiling function, 42
CERN (European Laboratory for Particle Physics), 2
certificates of deposit, 49–50, 169
CF Settings button, 285
CFAPPLICATION tag, 463, 472, 485
CFCASE tag, 137–140
CFCONTENT tag, 536, 537–543
CFCOOKIE tag, 442–443
/CFDEFAULTCASE tag, 137, 140
CFDEFAULTCASE tag, 137–138, 140
CFDIRECTORY tag, 523–528

CFELSE tag, 114–120, 126–130, 152, 214, 593
CFELSEIF tag, 130–133
CFFILE tag, 333, 525–526, 528–530
CFFORM tag, 385–389, 391, 397–398, 402, 600, 602, 609
CFHTTP tag, 544–553
CFID variable, 473
/CFIF tag, 114–120, 127–130
CFIF tag, 114–130, 132–136, 152, 165–166, 347
CFILE tag, 516, 518
CFINCLUDE tag, 567–571, 584, 586–587, 592, 621
CFINPUT tag, 385, 388–391, 393–401, 412–414, 418, 420–421
CFINSERT tag, 338–349, 598, 606
CFLOCATION tag, 161–163, 451, 525, 534, 536, 538–539
CFLOCK tag, 473–474, 479, 482, 524, 534
CFLOOP tag, 140–161, 287, 291–294, 312–313, 320, 507
CFMAIL tag, 504–514, 507, 508, 513
CFML (Cold Fusion Markup Language). See also tags (listed by name)
  basic description of, 29–42
  case-sensitivity and, 34
  Language Reference, 86
  using the QuickBar to insert, 15
CFML Basic tab, 31, 67
CFML Flow tab, 312
CFOUTPUT tag, 33–36, 67–69, 81–84, 120, 139–140, 155, 179, 190, 195, 215, 287, 290–291, 294, 297–299, 319, 342, 529, 532, 599, 606, 615
CFPARAM tag, 197–198, 200, 202–203, 206, 316, 406, 448, 449–452, 462

CFQUERY tag, 287, 289, 295–297, 306, 312, 316, 322, 344–349, 353–360, 364, 369, 454, 507, 528, 577, 582, 590, 600, 608
CFSELECT tag, 412, 425–428
CFSET tag, 29–33, 55–58, 67, 69, 81, 83, 89, 95, 157, 463–464, 467, 472, 542, 621
/CFSWITCH tag, 137–140
CFSWITCH tag, 137–140, 166, 169, 539–540
CFTRANSCACTION tag, 362
CFUPDATE tag, 349–353, 375–376, 603, 620
CGI (Common Gateway Interface), 4–5
checkboxes, 196–205, 406–409
CHECKED attribute, 193, 196, 402
CLIENTMANAGEMENT attribute, 464
CLIENTSTORAGE attribute, 464
Clipboard, 99–100, 481, 486
Close All command, 155, 181
Close button, 45, 246, 250, 255, 254, 256
Cold Fusion Administrator, 9, 12–13, 284–286, 501–502, 507
Cold Fusion application framework
  application.cfm and, 458–463
  application variables and, 485–489
  basic description of, 439–498
  cookies and, 440–458
  HTTP state management and, 440–458
Cold Fusion Server
  basic description of, 9–12
  redirection and, 161–163
  settings, configuring, 284
  string variables and, 67–73
  using e-mail with, 500–514
Cold Fusion Studio
  basic description of, 9–10
  creating new Web pages with, 15–16

enhancing static documents with, 20–28
  Help system, 17–18
  previewing new Web pages with, 16–17
  string variables and, 67–68, 71
  tag completion feature, 144
  workspace, exploring, 13–17
coins, counting, 230
colon (:), 74–80
color
  background, 22, 124, 129–130
  -coding, 9
  generating, with nested LIST loops, 168
  preferences, specifying, 111
  RGB (Red-Green-Blue), 168
COLOR attribute, 592
COLS attribute, 209
columnar report generation, 294–299, 329
columns, extracting, 259
comma (,), 41, 74–80, 136
comments, 30, 32, 211
Comments text box, 211
commissions, computing, 50
Common tab, 97, 316
components, basic description of, 9–13
concatenation, 80–84, 262
conditional formatting, 124–127
conditions
  basic description of, 114
  extracting rows using, 261–262
Configuring Web Browser topic, 17
confirmation messages, 233–234
control(s)
  basic description of, 175
  checkboxes, 196–205, 406–409
  data validation and, 387–388
  HTML tags for, 175–177
  select boxes, 206–209, 236, 409–412, 425–426
  text boxes, 176, 209–212, 388–390
  variables, 141

cookies, 440–458
Copy button, 185, 202, 210
copying
  files, 525–526
  selected text, 99–100
COUNT function, 270–271
Crayola.com, 7–8, 173
Create button, 286
CREATE TABLE command, 249
CreateDate function, 91, 95
CreateDateTime function, 90–91, 95
CreateTimeSpan function, 95, 472, 485
cross-platform compatibility, 7
Currency data type, 241
customer status, displaying, 165
Customize dialog box, 313–314

D
data. See also data maintenance; data retrieval; data validation
  completeness checks, 384, 390–412
  drill-down capability, 319
  source names, 283
  types, 55, 123–124, 384, 412–418, 240–243
data maintenance
  basic description of, 337–382
  deleting data, 357–359, 378–381
  inserting data, 338–349
  transaction processing, 362–370
  updating data, 349–357, 375–378
data retrieval
  basic description of, 281–335
  CFLOOP tag and, 291–294
  columnar report generation and, 294–299, 329
  creating navigation options for, 302–309
  displaying specific records, 299–302
  group totals report generation and, 319–322, 330–331

interactive data extraction and, 322–327
QUERY loops and, 287–291
tabular report generation and, 309–319, 330, 332–333
data validation, 383–437, 633–634
client-side, 384–385
data completeness checks, 384, 390–412
data type validation checks, 384, 412–418
generating customized error messages, 393–401
performing, 384–385
picture checks, 384, 419–423
range and limit checks, 384, 418–419
self-checking digits, 384, 422–428
server-side, 384–385
database(s). *See also* tables
basic description of, 237–280
connectivity, 286–294
deleting records in, 257–258
designing, 571–574
extracting data from, 258–266
grouping data in, 272
inserting data in, 251–253
opening, 243–246
organizing data in, 238–243
relational, 269
rolling back changes to, 362
sorting data in, 266–267
summarizing data in, 270–272
transaction processing and, 362–370
updating data in, 255–257
upsizing, 273
Database tab, 17
Datasheet view, 251–253, 255–258, 338, 343–344
DATASOURCE attribute, 287, 351, 354
DateAdd function, 95–97
DateDiff function, 95
DateFormat function, 92, 95, 98
Date/Time data type, 241

date-time values, 90–102, 108–109, 241
debugging, 33
DecimalFormat function, 41
DecrementValue function, 42
DEFAULT attribute, 197
default documents, specifying, 627–628
Delete Record button, 257
DELETEFILE attribute, 537
deletePID variable, 621
deleting
auctions, 624–626
category requirements, 626–627
files, 525–526
general data, 357–359, 378–381
products, from the Products table, 620–624
DESC keyword, 266
Design button, 244, 251
Design view, 246–249, 261
DESTINATION attribute, 516, 517
development mappings, 42–43
Development Mappings button, 43
discounts, computing, 231
DISTINCT keyword, 269–270
documents
color-coding of, 9
default, specifying, 627–628
static, 4, 20–28
dollar sign ($), 40, 74–80
DollarFormat function, 40–41
dollars and cents, computing, 47
double quotes ("), 183
Drive List window, 14

E

edit auction requirement, 599–604
edit category requirement, 607–610
edit product requirement, 616–624
Edit tab, 17, 31, 87, 188, 190
Editor tab, 14
Editor window, 20
e-mail
applications, designing, 554–555

bulk mail applications, 555–556
Cold Fusion Administrator and, 12–13
sending form results via, 214–419
sending URLs via, 561–562
server connections, setting up, 501–504
using, 500–514
embedded language(s)
basic description of, 2
HTML as an, 2
ENCTYPE attribute, 612, 619
ENDROW attribute, 291–292, 294, 296–302
equal sign (=), 56, 74–80, 183
error messages, customized, 393–401
Eudora, 503
Excel (Microsoft), 531, 533–536, 550–551, 562–563
Excite.com, 463
exclamation point (!), 30, 74–80
Exp function, 42
EXPIRES attribute, 442, 446
expressions
arithmetic, 31, 262–263, 277–278
basic description of, 31
extracting rows using, 262–263
evaluating, with Boolean values, 102–104
selector, 137
string, 80–84

F

faculty surveys, 497
field(s)
basic description of, 239
data types, 240–243
designing/handling, 212–214
hidden, 212–214
names, 239
size, 240
file(s). *See also* data
copying, 525–526
deleting, 525–526

extensions, 32, 77
input control, 514–523
listing, 523–528
located on other servers, repackaging data from, 559–560
renaming, 525–526
systems, interacting with, 514–553
uploading, 514–523, 557–559
FILE attribute, 537
File menu
    Close All command, 155, 181
    New Document command, 88, 155
    Open command, 61, 67, 71
    Save As command, 77, 145
FILEFIELD attribute, 516
Files tab, 17, 57, 223
financial statements, creating, 52
Find function, 85
Find Stores button, 173, 174
FindNoCase function, 85, 97
Fix function, 42
flow control
    basic description of, 113–170
    CFIF tags and, 114–118, 124–127
    CFSWITCH statement and, 137–140
    FOR loops and, 141–152
    LIST loops and, 152–157
    logical operators and, 134–137
    performing repetitive tasks and, 140–163
    redirection and, 161–163
    relational operators and, 114, 118–124
    structures, sequence, 113
    using selection to control, 114–150
    WHILE loops and, 157–161
Folder List window, 14
folder structure, planning, 571, 573
FONT tag, 223, 468
FOR loops, 141–152
foreign keys, 248
form handlers. *See also* forms
    basic description of, 171–236
    for computing age, 232–233

for computing discounts, 231
for counting coins, 230
creating, 189–191
data maintenance and, 339–340, 363–364
handling form data with, 177–180
for student transcript course titles, 232
FORM tag, 175–177, 180, 183, 215, 514–515, 520
FORMFIELDS parameter, 339, 343, 350
forms. *See also* form handlers
    basic description of, 171–236
    checkboxes in, 196–205
    for computing age, 232–233
    for counting coins, 230
    creating, 180–189, 385–388
    data maintenance and, 337–382
    data validation and, 383–437
    designing, 230, 385–390
    fields in, 212–214
    HTML tags for, 175–177
    image buttons in, 220–228
    multi-page, 493–494
    performing calculations on data entered in, 234–235
    radio buttons in, 192–196
    results of, sending, via e-mail, 214–219
    scrolling text boxes in, 209–212
    select boxes in, 206–209
    for student transcript course titles, 232
    understanding, 172–175
    users of, sending confirmation to, 233–234
forward slash (/), 74–80
FROM attribute, 141
FTP (File Transfer Protocol), 162, 341, 345
functions. *See also* functions (listed by name)
    aggregate, 276
    basic description of, 40
    formatting numbers with, 40–42

grouping data using, 272
string, 85–90
summarizing data with, 270–272
using, 87–90
functions (listed by name)
    Abs function, 42
    AVG function, 271
    Ceiling function, 42
    COUNT function, 270–271
    CreateDate function, 91, 95
    CreateDateTime function, 90–91, 95
    CreateTimeSpan function, 95, 472, 485
    DateAdd function, 95–97
    DateDiff function, 95
    DateFormat function, 92, 95, 98
    DecimalFormat function, 41
    DecrementValue function, 42
    DollarFormat function, 40–41
    Exp function, 42
    Find function, 85
    FindNoCase function, 85, 97
    Fix function, 42
    GetCurrentTemplatePath function, 517
    IncrementValue function, 42
    Int function, 42
    IsDate function, 103
    IsDefined function, 103
    IsLeapYear function, 103
    IsNumeric function, 103
    LCase function, 85, 88
    Left function, 85
    Len function, 85, 86
    Log function, 42
    Log10 function, 42
    Max function, 42, 271
    Mid function, 85
    Min function, 42, 271
    Now function, 95, 96
    NumberFormat function, 41
    Rand function, 42
    Randomize function, 42
    RandRange function, 42
    Replace function, 85, 299

ReplaceNoCase function, 85
Reverse function, 85
Right function, 85, 347
Round function, 42
SUM function, 271
Trim function, 85
UCase function, 85, 86–87
URLEncodedFormat function, 76–80, 327

G

GetCurrentTemplatePath function, 517
Go button, 227
GROUP BY clause, 272

H

Help Resource tab, 86
Help systems, 17–18, 86
Hotmail.com, 175
HP-UX, 7
HR tag, 181–182, 190
HREF attribute, 64–65, 98, 100, 543, 619
HTML (HyperText Markup Language). *See also* tags (listed by name)
 basic description of, 2–4
 documents, saving, 32
 enhancing static documents with, 20–28
 form tags, 175–177
 server-side scripting languages and, 5–6
HTTP (HyperText Transfer Protocol), 10–12, 26, 544–553
 checkboxes and, 197
 cookies, 463
 data validation and, 384, 406
 file systems and, 525
 redirection, 161–163
 special characters and, 75
 state management, 440–441
 URL parameters and, 56
Hyperlink data type, 241
hyphen (-), 74–80

I

image buttons, 220–228
IMG tag, 316, 522, 538, 543
IN operator, 264–265
Include subfolders check box, 506
IncrementValue function, 42
INDEX attribute, 141, 152
inner conditions, 127
INPUT tag, 175–176, 180, 193, 200, 220, 390, 514–523
INSERT INTO command, 254
INSERT statement, 339, 344–349, 364–365
Int function, 42
integers, 31, 169, 241–242, 322–327. *See also* numbers
Internet Explorer browser, 25, 35, 218, 550–551
Internet Protocol (IP), 10, 25
Internet Server Application Programming Interface (ISAPI), 5
IsDate function, 103
IsDefined function, 103
IsLeapYear function, 103
IsNumeric function, 103

J

Java, 10, 20
JavaScript, 10, 20, 384–385, 387, 391–412

L

LCase function, 85, 88
Left function, 85
Len function, 85, 86
LIKE operator, 265–266, 347
limit checks, 384, 418–419
LIST loop, 140, 152–157, 167–168, 200, 204–205
Log function, 42
Log10 function, 42
logical operators, 134–137
login security, 450–457, 632–633
Lookup Wizard data type, 241
lowercase vowels, removing, 109–110

M

Macromedia.com, 545
Maintain database connections checkbox, 286
marketing, targeted, 495–497
masks, 41, 92–93
maturity values, calculating, 169
Max function, 42, 271
Memo data type, 241
MESSAGE attribute, 393–401, 412, 416, 418, 420–421, 424–425
METHOD attribute, 175–177, 216, 341, 385
Microsoft Access, 338, 343–344, 360–361, 555–556
 databases, opening, 243–246
 launching, 243
 transaction processing and, 368–370
Microsoft Active Server Pages (ASP), 6
Microsoft Excel, 531, 533–536, 550–551, 562–563
Microsoft Internet Explorer, 25, 35, 218, 550–551
Microsoft Internet Information Services, 18
Microsoft Outlook, 513, 503
Microsoft VBScript, 6, 20
Microsoft Visual Basic, 5, 338
Microsoft Windows 95/98, 7
Microsoft Windows 2000, 7, 18
Microsoft Windows NT, 7
Mid function, 85
mileage requirements, computing, 50–51
MIME (Multipurpose Internet Mail Extensions), 537
Min function, 42, 271
MOD operator, 149
Move Files option, 243
MULTIPLE attribute, 206, 409

N

NAME attribute, 176, 178, 192, 197, 209, 287, 385, 388, 442, 474, 523, 546
NAMECONFLICT attribute, 516, 518–519
name-value pairs, 56, 60
navigation options, creating, 302–309
nested
 CFIF tags, 127–133
 LIST loops, 168
Netscape Messenger, 503
Netscape Navigator, 25, 38
Netscape Server Application Programming Interface (NSAPI), 5
New button, 21, 142, 162, 181, 190
New Document command, 88, 155
New Document dialog box, 460
Next button, 304, 308
No button, 251, 255, 257
NOT IN operator, 264–265
NOT operator, 137
note-to-self applications, 491–492
Nothebys.com, 565–638
Now function, 95, 96
NumberFormat function, 41
numbers. *See also* integers
 data type for, 241–242
 formatting, with functions, 40–42
 processing, 31

O

Object Not Found error page, 342
objects, understanding, 175–176
Objects bar, 244
ODBC (Open Database Connectivity), 282–287, 290, 339, 345, 353, 574
OLE Object data type, 241
Open an existing file button, 243
Open button, 178

Open command, 61, 67, 71
Open dialog box, 61
operator(s)
 arithmetic, 31–33
 precedence, 36–38, 136–137
 relational, 114, 118–124, 261–262
OPTION tag, 206, 619–620
OR operator, 137
ORDER BY clause, 266–267
outer conditions, 127
OUTPUT attribute, 530
Output on single line check box, 313

P

parameters, processing, 56–66. *See also* URL parameters
parentheses, 74–80
passwords
 Cold Fusion Administrator and, 12–13
 cookies and, 450–457
 data validation and, 390, 425
 e-mail, 501
 generating, 167
 logon, 632
Paste button, 200, 210
picture checks, 384, 419–423
pizza, calculating the price of, 167–168
plus sign (+), 75, 89
PORT attribute, 504–505
POST method, 176, 177, 341, 385
pound sign (#), 33–36, 40, 83–84, 505
Prev button, 304, 305
Primary Key button, 248
primary keys, 248–249, 374–378
product(s)
 administration requirement, 611–627
 categories, browsing, 574–594
 information, displaying, 48–49
 requirements, searching, 591–594
 templates for listing, 581–586

program button, 34, 38
Projects tab, 17

Q

QUERY loop, 141, 145, 287–292, 295, 299, 306, 320, 322–323, 425
Query Loop tab, 312
question mark (?), 56, 74–80
QuickBar, 14–15, 98, 225

R

radio buttons, 192–196, 401–406
Rand function, 42
random integers, selecting, 168
Randomize function, 42
RandRange function, 42
range and limit checks, 384, 418–419
RANGE attribute, 419
real numbers, 31. *See also* numbers
record(s)
 basic description of, 239
 deleting, 257–258
 displaying specific, 299–302
 inserting, 253–255, 274
 processing subsets of, 291–294
 updating, 256–257
redirection, 161–163
Refresh button, 38, 72, 146, 148, 317
relational database systems, 269. *See also* databases
relational operators, 114, 118–124, 261–262
relative location, 161
Reload button. *See* Refresh button
Remote Development Settings dialog box, 43–44
repetition, performing repetitive tasks with, 140–163
Replace dialog box, 483
Replace function, 85, 299
ReplaceNoCase function, 85
report generation
 columnar, 294–299, 329
 group totals, 319–322, 330–331

tabular, 309–319, 330, 332–333
reporting tools, 495–496
REQUIRED attribute, 404, 407, 410, 417, 490–491
Reset to Defaults button, 314
Resource Tab button, 20, 57, 86, 87
Resource Tab window, 16–17, 57, 224
resumes, uploading, 557–559
retirement information, calculating, 51–52
reusing code, 575, 567–571
Reverse function, 85
Right function, 85, 347
Round function, 42
rows, extracting, 260–266
ROWS attribute, 209
Run button, 250, 254

S

salary increases, displaying, 112
Save As command, 31, 77, 145
Save As dialog box, 18–19, 24, 78, 535
Save button, 18, 31, 34, 40, 58, 89
Schedule a Private Showing page, 511–513
Schedule button, 192, 195, 202, 203, 204
scientific notation, 31
scope, 56, 474
SCOPE attribute, 474
scrolling text boxes, 209–212
search criteria, adding, 333–334
security. *See also* passwords
  application-wide, 460–463
  cookie-based, 450–457
select boxes, 206–209, 236, 409–412, 425–426
Select Folder button, 43
SELECT tag, 206, 258–271, 277, 286–287, 290, 295–297, 319, 324–327, 409, 453–354
SELECTED attribute, 206, 207, 426

selection, controlling program flow with, 113–140
selector expressions, 137
self-checking digits, 384, 422–428
Send/Receive button, 219
SERVER attribute, 504–505
session variables, 472–485
SESSIONMANAGEMENT attribute, 472
SESSIONTIMEOUT attribute, 472–473, 485
SETCLIENTCOOKIES attribute, 465, 473
Settings dialog box, 43
shopping carts, adding products to, 48
Show line numbers in gutter button, 57, 148
silver, calculating the price of, 52–53
single quote ('), 74–80
Site Admin Tool page, 339–340, 350, 372–373, 378–379
Site View tab, 17
SIZE attribute, 176, 206, 409–410
SmartMoney.com, 175
Snippets tab, 17
Solaris, 7
sorting data, 266–267
SOURCE attribute, 525
source code, viewing, 78, 143, 146, 147
Source command, 78, 143, 146, 147
special characters, in URLs, 74–80
SQL (Structured Query Language)
  basic description of, 237–280
  creating tables with, 249–251
  data maintenance and, 353–356, 359
  deleting records with, 257–258
  extracting data with, 258–266, 275
  inserting records with, 253–255, 274
  updating records with, 256–257
SQL Access Group, 283

square brackets ([]), 238
SRC attribute, 220, 538
Start button, 243, 283
STARTROW attribute, 291–292, 294, 296–302, 306
state management, 440–458, 463–472
stateless systems, 439
static documents, 4, 20–28
statistics, analyzing, 562–563
string(s)
  basic description of, 55
  concatenation of, 80–84, 262
  expressions, 80–84
  functions, 85–90
  literals, 67, 83–84, 107–108
  URL parameters, 70–74
  variables, 66–80, 107–108
student grades, determining, 166
student transcript course titles, 232
SUBJECT attribute, 505
Submit button, 176–177, 213
SUM function, 271

T

table(s). *See also* databases
  basic description of, 239
  conditionally formatting, 235
  creating, 246–251, 360–361
  deleting records in, 257–258
  extracting data from, 267–270, 275
  inserting data in, 251–253
  joining, 275–276
  report generation from data in, 309–319, 330, 332–333
  sorting data in, 266–267
  structures, defining, 240–243
  updating data in, 255–257
Table Sizer (QuickTable) button, 156, 184
TABLE tag, 22, 24, 152
tag(s). *See also* tags (listed by name)
  converting, to the desired case, 34
  completion feature, 22, 144
  validation of, 33

tags (listed by name). *See also* tags
  BODY tag, 15, 21, 24, 156, 487, 453, 552
  CFAPPLICATION tag, 463, 472, 485
  CFCASE tag, 137–140
  CFCONTENT tag, 536, 537–543
  CFCOOKIE tag, 442–443
  /CFDEFAULTCASE tag, 137, 140
  CFDEFAULTCASE tag, 137–138, 140
  CFDIRECTORY tag, 523–528
  CFELSE tag, 114–120, 126–130, 152, 214, 593
  CFELSEIF tag, 130–133
  CFFILE tag, 333, 525–526, 528–530
  CFFORM tag, 385–389, 391, 397–398, 402, 600, 602, 609
  CFHTTP tag, 544–553
  /CFIF tag, 114–120, 127–130
  CFIF tag, 114–130, 132–136, 152, 165–166, 347
  CFILE tag, 516, 518
  CFINCLUDE tag, 567–571, 584, 586–587, 592, 621
  CFINPUT tag, 385, 388–391, 393–401, 412–414, 418, 420–421
  CFINSERT tag, 338–349, 598, 606
  CFLOCATION tag, 161–163, 451, 525, 534, 536, 538–539
  CFLOCK tag, 473–474, 479, 482, 524, 534
  CFLOOP tag, 140–161, 287, 291–294, 312–313, 320, 507
  CFMAIL tag, 504–514, 507, 508, 513
  CFOUTPUT tag, 33–36, 67–69, 81–84, 120, 139–140, 155, 179, 190, 195, 215, 287, 290–291, 294, 297–299, 319, 342, 529, 532, 599, 606, 615

  CFPARAM tag, 197–198, 200, 202–203, 206, 316, 406, 448, 449–452, 462
  CFQUERY tag, 287, 289, 295–297, 306, 312, 316, 322, 344–349, 353–360, 364, 369, 454, 507, 528, 577, 582, 590, 600, 608
  CFSELECT tag, 412, 425–428
  CFSET tag, 29–33, 55–58, 67, 69, 81, 83, 89, 95, 157, 463–464, 467, 472, 542, 621
  /CFSWITCH tag, 137–140
  CFSWITCH tag, 137–140, 166, 169, 539–540
  CFTRANSCACTION tag, 362
  CFUPDATE tag, 349–353, 375–376, 603, 620
  FONT tag, 223, 468
  FORM tag, 175–177, 180, 183, 215, 514–515, 520
  HR tag, 181–182, 190
  IMG tag, 316, 522, 538, 543
  INPUT tag, 175–176, 180, 193, 200, 220, 390, 514–523
  OPTION tag, 206, 619–620
  SELECT tag, 206, 258–271, 277, 286–287, 290, 295–297, 319, 324–327, 409, 453–354
  TABLE tag, 22, 24, 152
  TD tag, 23, 124–125, 127, 156, 185
  TEXTAREA tag, 209
  TITLE tag, 21, 82, 142
  TR tag, 23
  VALIDATE tag, 412–413, 420, 424
Tag completion button, 144
Tag Inspector, 17
TD tag, 23, 124–125, 127, 156, 185
template(s)
  basic description of, 29
  browsing, using the internal browser, 42–45
  CFIF statement and, 116–117

  for computing age, 111
  for converting word case, 110
  creating, 116–117
  for deleting agents, 378–380
  for deleting customer requests, 380–381
  designing, 109–112, 372–373
  for displaying salary increases, 112
  for inserting new agent information, 372–375
  for listing products, 581–587
  pathnames for, 517
  for removing lowercase vowels, 109–110
  saving, 18–19, 24, 78
  for specifying color preferences, 111
  for updating agent information, 375–378
Text data type, 241
text boxes, 176, 209–212, 388–390
TEXTAREA tag, 209
TEXTQUALIFIER attribute, 546
time
  formatting masks, 93
  stamps, 91, 249
TIMEOUT attribute, 504–505
TITLE tag, 21, 82, 142
TO attribute, 141
TR tag, 23
transaction processing, 362–370
Trim function, 85
TYPE attribute, 220, 514–515, 520, 388, 490, 537
typeless evaluation, of expressions, 103–104

U
UCase function, 85, 86–87
underscore (_), 67, 74–80, 139
UPDATE command, 256
UPDATE statement, 353–359
updating data, 349–357, 375–378
uploading files, 514–523

URL parameters, 55–66, 70–74, 120–121. *See also* URLs (Uniform Resource Locators)
basic description of, 56
AgentIDs and, 532
CFHTTP tag and, 548
URLEncodedFormat function, 76–80, 327
URLs (Uniform Resource Locators). *See also* URL parameters
absolute, 161
the Cold Fusion application framework and, 445, 462, 465, 467, 488
data validation and, 385, 397, 416
entering, 10, 25–26
HTTP and, 10–12, 26
redirection and, 161–163
relative, 161
sending, via e-mail, 561–562
special characters in, 74–80
specifying default documents and, 627–628
usage tracking and reporting tools, 495–496
user interface(s)
designing, 566–571
implementing, guidelines for, 496

V
VALIDATE tag, 412–413, 420, 424
validation, of tags, 33. *See also* data validation
VALUE attribute, 192–193, 196, 206, 212, 216, 388, 442
value-lists, 137
variables
application, 485–489
basic description of, 29
Boolean, 102–104
CFSET tag and, 29–30
client, 463–472
cookie, 449–450
creating, 465–466
date-time, 90–102, 108–109
locking, 473–474
naming, 30
session, 472–485
string, 66–80, 107–108
working with, 107–108
VBScript (Microsoft), 6, 20
Verify Mail Server Connection check box, 503
View button, 245, 246, 250, 254, 256

W
W3C (World Wide Web Consortium), 440
welcome pages, designing, 106–107
WHERE clause, 319, 320, 324–325, 350, 452, 454, 577, 603
WHILE loop, 141, 157–161, 168
WIDTH attribute, 316
Windows 95/98 (Microsoft), 7
Windows 2000 (Microsoft), 7, 18
Windows NT (Microsoft), 7
word
case, converting, 110
games, designing, 166
wrap, 209–210, 223
Word wrap button, 223
WRAP attribute, 209–210

Visual Basic (Microsoft), 5, 338
vowels, removing lowercase, 109–110

Y
Yahoo.com, 499, 546–550
Yes button, 255
Yes/No data type, 241